P9-CQW-473

THE INSIDERS' GUIDE TO

MICHIGAN'S
Traverse
BAY REGION

by
Sally Gamble
and
Mary Bevans Gillett

Insiders' Publishing
105 Budleigh St.
P.O. Box 2057
Manteo, NC 27954
(252) 473-6100
www.insiders.com

Sales and Marketing:
Falcon Publishing, Inc.
P.O. Box 1718
Helena, MT 59624
(800) 582-2665
www.falconguide.com

•

FIRST EDITION
1st printing

•

Copyright ©1998
by Falcon Publishing, Inc.

•

Printed in the United States
of America

•

All rights reserved. No part of this book
may be reproduced in any form without
permission, in writing, from the
publisher, except by a reviewer who
wishes to quote brief passages in
connection with a review in a
magazine or newspaper.

Publications from The Insiders' Guide®
series are available at special discounts for
bulk purchases for sales promotions,
premiums or fundraisings. Special editions,
including personalized covers, can be
created in large quantities for special
needs. For more information, please write
to Karen Bachman, Insiders' Publishing,
P.O. Box 2057, Manteo, NC 27954, or call
(800) 765-2665 Ext. 241.

ISBN 1-57380-059-7

Insiders' Publishing

Publisher/Editor-in-Chief

Beth P. Storie

Advertising Director/
General Manager

Michael McOwen

Creative Services Director

Giles MacMillan

Art Director

David Haynes

Managing Editor

Dave McCarter

Regional Advertising
Sales Manager

Greg Swanson

Local Advertising
Sales Representative

Carol Preuett

Project Editor

Tammy Kennon

Project Artist

Carolyn McClees

Insiders' Publishing
An imprint of Falcon Publishing Inc.
A Landmark Communications company.

Preface

As the 21st century nears, most of us are living our lives at warp speed, sustaining increasingly complex lives. Sooner or later we need to claim time to restore balance, evaluate priorities and connect with loved ones. We guarantee there's no better place than Northwest Michigan to do just that.

Welcome to our world of shimmering water, clean air and a myriad of four-season recreational opportunities. You'll find the hospitality here is genuine and our ardor for the region infectious. Relaxation comes naturally in this unhurried north-woods environment. Our unpretentious yet sophisticated home offers great culture, notable attractions, remarkable people and uncommonly beautiful scenery.

Northwest Michigan is a four-season marvel, ever-changing, ever offering a new world of opportunities to enjoy.

Dig your toes in the sand. Let the wind blow through your hair. Allow the cry of the gulls to pierce your awareness. This is summer in Northwest Michigan.

In autumn, feast your eyes on a plethora of dazzling color. Hook a mighty salmon from a wild river. Cozy up beside a fieldstone fireplace as winter announces itself.

Race down ski slopes surrounded by a majestic panorama of pines. Zip along an open trail on your snowmobile. Skate a glassy frozen lake in moonlight. This is winter in Northwest Michigan.

When bitter winds give way to spring, experience the fragrance of cherry blossoms in the sweet May air. Stumble upon a newborn fawn in the brush. Hear a thunderous chorus of spring peepers hidden in wetlands as the north woods awaken to yet another season.

The information you need to make the most of your stay in this land of natural wonders is right at your fingertips in *The Insiders' Guide®️ to Traverse Bay Region*. This guide represents the combined knowledge, experience and insight of literally hundreds of Insiders. Within these pages you'll find these Insiders' best advice on catching the big ones from Lake Michigan, spotting rare flora and fauna, and playing the area's championship courses. You'll find out what our resorts offer, where the parks and beaches are and where to see the best sunsets.

We've attempted to provide the most comprehensive source of Northwest Michigan information available. Whether this is your maiden visit, whether you have been vacationing up north all of your life or whether you have recently settled here, we hope you will find *The Insiders' Guide®️ to The Traverse Bay Region* to be a convenient, easy-to-use reference.

We look forward to hearing your comments, suggestions and inquiries regarding our book. *The Insiders' Guide®️ to The Traverse Bay Region* is one of close to 70 tourist and newcomer guides published by Insiders' Publishing, P.O. Box 2057, Manteo, NC 27954. You can write us at the above address or visit us online at www.insiders.com, where you'll find all Insiders' titles available in their entirety.

About the Authors

Sally Gamble

A Michigan native, Sally Gamble grew up amidst the state's piney forests and sparkling lakes. While many mark their life stages by weddings, births and career moves, the significant chapters of Sally's life are defined by their connection to Michigan waters. Her important passages are colored by the clear waters of Missaukee Lake, where she spent her childhood; the moody Grand Traverse Bay, where she honeymooned; and the fish-rich waters of Berry Lake in Wexford County, where she is raising her family.

After studying fine art at a small mid-Michigan college, Sally began her work life as an illustrator, creating ink drawings for a series of music education books. In 1989 she discovered writing better suited her lifestyle and began freelancing for area publications. Since then, Sally has worked as a staff writer for *The Missaukee Sentinel* and *Grand Traverse Business Journal*. She currently serves as editor of the *Cadillac Area Business Magazine* and contributes regularly to regional publications.

Inspired by Michigan's invigorating four-season climate, Sally has spent a lifetime collecting experiences in the state's wild lands, from among the region's diverse cultural offerings and from the dynamic business environment.

While her writing has focused on the north's commercial activity, in her spare time she turns her attention to the wonders of the natural world. Sally is a volunteer participant in the Michigan Frog and Toad Survey, sponsored by the Michigan Department of Natural Resources. The survey is part of an international effort to understand the decline of the world's amphibian population.

Sally's other interests include gardening and reading. Since 1984, Sally, her three children, three cats and two dogs have lived along the shores of a small inland lake. Here, bluegill, bass and sunfish dominate the waters, and turtles and mallards roam. The family resides in a geodesic dome, tucked in a tall poplar forest, where songbirds and frogs serenade nightly during the summer, wildflowers abound and neighborhood children ice skate and cross-country ski from their back doors. Sally finds contentment flows abundantly from this wonderful northern lifestyle.

Mary Bevans Gillett

Michigan has always been home for Mary Bevans Gillett. A northern Michigan native, she grew up between the lakes of Cadillac where she took glistening water, towering trees and the crisp scent of pine for granted. Education and career inched her south through Mount Pleasant, East Lansing, Detroit and Ann Arbor before she returned to the north woods in 1985. A Traverse City resident for the past 12 years, she lives on a hill overlooking the city, the bays and panoramic northern Michigan sunrises.

Mary has worked in the professional communications field for more than 20 years with experience in public relations, advertising, marketing communications, broadcast and print. Her past lives have led her to positions with the University of Michigan, Burroughs Corporation, the Michigan State Senate and the Traverse City Area Public Schools. For the past 10 years, she has enjoyed working "both sides of the word processor" as a freelance writer and public relations consultant in the Grand Traverse region. She frequently contributes feature articles to the *Traverse City Record-Eagle* and, for several years, wrote the Sampling Northern Michigan travel articles for Michigan's Booth newspaper chain. She also covers northern Michigan as a contributing writer to *Michigan Health Care News*. Specializing in the areas of tourism, personality profiles, community features and nonprofits, Mary enjoys discovering and writing about the many facets and features that breathe life into this sparkling corner of Michigan. Her local writing has explored cherry blossoms to cherry wine, bee-keepers to harbor masters and shoreline strolls to cross-country ski marathons. She finds that each encounter adds new texture to the fabric of living up north.

Mary holds a Master of Arts degree from the University of Michigan and a Bachelor of Fine Arts degree from Central Michigan University. She lives in Traverse City with her husband, Ward Gillett, and their two daughters, Katie and Alexandra.

Photo: Kevin Poirier

Welcome to our world of shimmering waters and clean air.

Acknowledgments

Sally . . .

The woods, water and people of Northwest Michigan have nurtured my spirit and graced my existence with many joys for more than four decades. This project offered an occasion to give something back to the hardworking, caring people of the region and I thank publisher Beth Storie for the opportunity.

In essence, this book was made possible by hundreds of Insiders who gave their faith and time to our research and who shared their special knowledge during the project's development. I thank every Insider I interviewed, from Ludington to St. Ignace, for their important contributions. The outcome is their voice as much as it is mine and coauthor Mary Gillett's.

I also wish to thank the staff at chambers of commerce and visitors centers throughout the Lake Michigan shoreline communities and the Little Traverse region for providing information on a regular basis. Without fail they offered reliable data with patience and cheerfulness. Their gracious attitude made my task much easier. I would like to express appreciation to the Michigan Department of Natural Resources staff at the Cadillac and Gaylord District offices for offering personal input and excellent resource materials.

Ten years from now, when I recall working on this project, I will undoubtedly remember the long telephone conversations between my coauthor Mary and myself as we struggled through tedious chapter details and juggled our personal lives to meet demanding deadlines. I want to thank Mary for investing her high professional standards in this book, for her sense of humor when things grew tense and for her friendship.

At Insiders' offices, where the project was born and shaped, I wish to thank editor Tammy Kennon for her gentle guidance, her patience in enduring revisions and her commitment to quality work. It has been a true privilege to work with Tammy and the Insiders' Publishing staff.

Most of all, I wish to thank my family and friends who supported me through the long days and nights it took to get this book on paper. Special thanks to my children, Stephanie, Jason and April, for putting up with peanut butter sandwiches and scraps of my time for weeks on end. Thanks to my two best friends, Monica and David, for believing in me, for sharing enthusiasm, for the phone calls that broke up my work days and weekend escapes to clear my mind. To both of you, your support makes the satisfaction of completing this book all the sweeter.

Finally, I wish to offer sincere appreciation to our readers for selecting *The Insiders' Guide*® *to The Traverse Bay Region*. It is my hope that it will meet your expectations and enhance your enjoyment of our truly extraordinary Northwest Michigan communities.

Mary . . .

To the many family and friends that kept asking, "Aren't you done with that book yet?" The answer is yes . . . and I'm thrilled with the results!

What a ride it's been! When we started this project, we thought it would be wise to expand our geographic boundaries to include all of Northwest Michigan to truly give an Insider's peek at our special corner of the state. I came to appreciate just how large that corner was while writing the first three chapters. Now, 23 chapters later, I've crisscrossed the region's roadways, ridden on ferries and crossed the Mackinac Bridge in this manymiled quest to share our communities' unique personalities. Along the way, I've met many wonderful people and visited countless shops and stops. I've kept the phone lines humming and the computer busy. To everyone who has patiently answered my questions, shared insights and pointed me on my way — thank you.

The Insiders team has kept us focused and prolific. Thank you to Beth Storie, Theresa Chavez and David McCarter who brought us to Manteo, North Carolina, for a two-day immersion into "IG" style and the nuts and bolts of putting together this Insiders' Guide®. Thank you to my co-writer, Sally Gamble, who worked closely with me during the past several months and who traveled just as many miles covering Little Traverse and the Lake Michigan Shoreline as I did covering Grand Traverse and the Mackinac Straits . . . both of our cars, telephones and computers are looking forward to a break. Thank you to photo gatherer Kevin Poirer, and to Carol Preuett in Traverse City and Ryan Fry in Manteo for keeping the advertising wheels turning. And finally, a special thank you to our editor, Tammy Kennon, who I've come to know, sight unseen, via e-mail, edits and phones. You've made our words sparkle, our writing consistent and our production schedule smooth — all on deadline! For your many months of hard work, thank you!

In Traverse City and throughout the region, thank you to the many folks at visitors bureaus and chambers of commerce who have been so generous with time, materials and advice. Special thanks to Nancy Sundstrom at the Downtown Development Authority and Sally Hall from the Traverse City Convention and Visitors Bureau for reviewing copy from a local perspective; Ann Clery from the Michigan Department of Transportation, Len Tankina from the Mackinac Island Chamber of Commerce, Dee Smith at Interlochen Center for the Arts and Chuck O'Connor and Susan Wilcox Olson at the National Cherry Festival for pulling photos out of hats; to my traveling companions who have often found themselves roped into reading copy in cars and planes; and to the many friends and family members that I've continually tapped for recommendations and feedback throughout this project.

My apologies to anyone who felt that we missed you in our regional sweep. Northern Michigan continues to grow and change quickly. We've tried to stay on top of all regional happenings and stay as current as possible in our coverage. With well over 1,000 square miles to write about, we may have missed a new opening or a recent change of format. We promise to keep adding to our listings with subsequent editions.

Finally, a heartfelt thank-you to my husband Ward and daughters Katie and Alex who have patiently watched as mountains of papers and files threatened to overtake the house, while I madly kept tapping away on my computer. With each met deadline, I would resurface from the chaos of my desk to your friendly faces and warm hugs. As always, you keep me grounded and make me smile.

Table of Contents

Directory of Maps

Traverse Bay Region

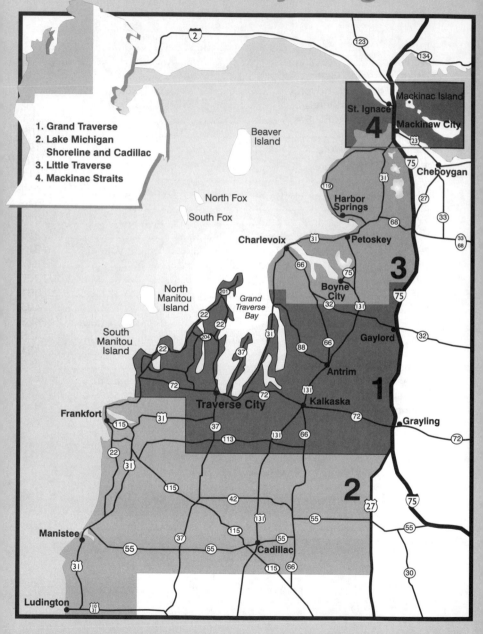

1. Grand Traverse
2. Lake Michigan
   Shoreline and Cadillac
3. Little Traverse
4. Mackinac Straits

Grand Traverse

Traverse City

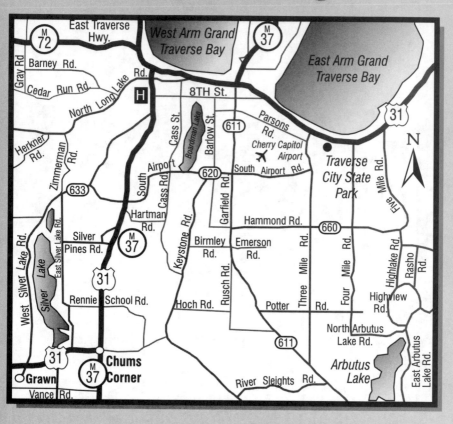

Lake Michigan Shoreline and Cadillac

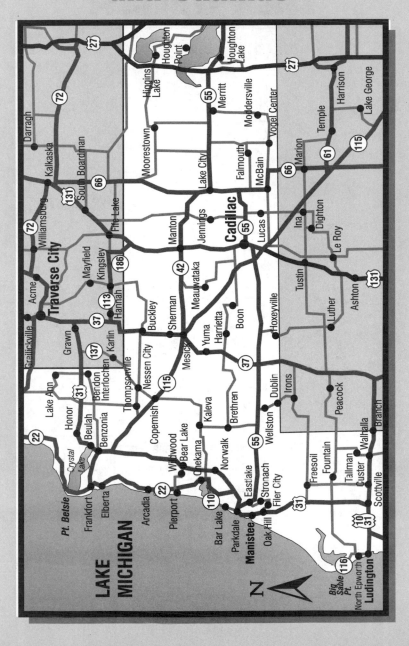

Little Traverse

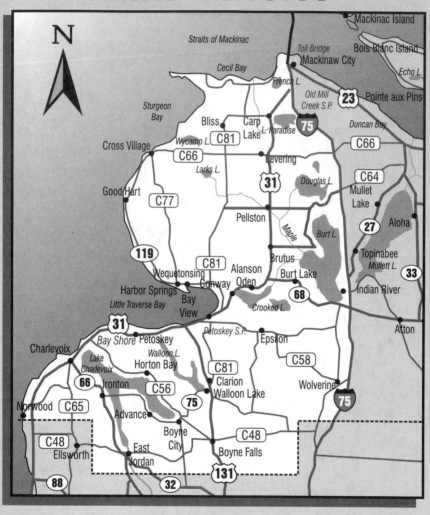

Mackinac Straits

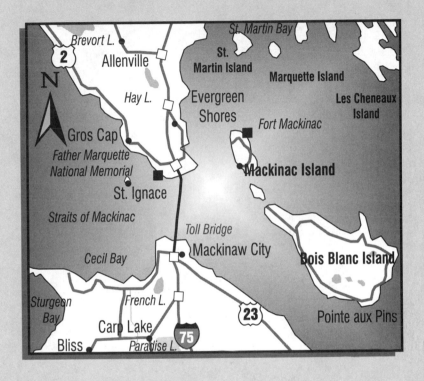

Mackinac Island

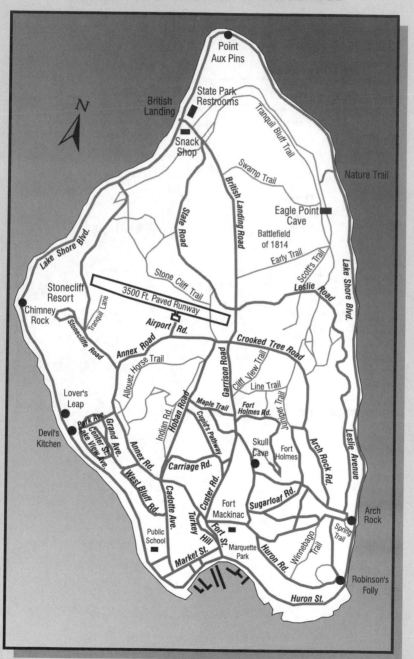

Photo: Kevin Poirier/Courtesy of the Traverse City Record-Eagle

Black squirrels are rare, except in Traverse City and the nearby area, where they are numerous in the residential parts of town.

How to Use This Book

Welcome to Northwest Michigan, land of tall pines and Great Lakes — home to skiers and sailors, summer sunsets and northern lights, vivid autumns and pristine snowfalls. To us, it's home, and we welcome you with open arms.

This Insiders' Guide will help you navigate through our beautiful north woods with maps and tips to make your journey memorable. Join us as we share our favorite haunts and native knowledge, all seasoned with a generous dose of local trivia. We love northern Michigan and are thrilled to profile the places and faces that truly make this region grand.

You'll find chapters on virtually all aspects of life and play up north. Please use them in any order that suits your needs. Looking for lodging? Peruse the chapters devoted to Camping, Bed and Breakfasts and Hotels,

Motels and Resorts. If a great meal is your top priority, turn immediately to the Restaurants chapter. The History chapter highlights our Native American, agricultural and lumbering heritage, while the Attractions, Kidstuff and various Recreation chapters list countless opportunities for vacation fun. Community life and services are highlighted in chapters on Education, Healthcare, Worship and Retirement.

A comprehensive index appears at the end of this book. Please use it when looking for a specific site or for related references in other chapters. Also, even though each chapter can be read and used independently, we hope that you will take the time to read the guide in its entirety for a multifaceted view of Northwest Michigan. Don't forget to look for the many Insiders' Tips that are tucked into the pages of each chapter.

www.insiders.com

See this and many other Insiders' Guide® destinations online — in their entirety.

Visit us today!

...la's Keys • Golf in the Card...
...xingt...
Civil
...hmond • Chesapeake Bay •
...C's Central Coast • Bermu...
... • Relocation • Boca Rato...
...olina's • NC's Mountains •
...gton • Cincinnati • Madiso...
...s • SW Utah • Salt Lake Ci...
Civil War Sites • The Poc...
...la's Keys • Golf in the Card...

Our corner of Michigan covers a significant land mass composed of 12 different counties and close to 1,000 square miles. Each chapter of this book is divided among the region's four main geographic areas: Grand Traverse, Lake Michigan Shoreline and Cadillac, Little Traverse and the Mackinac Straits.

Grand Traverse includes those areas rimming Lake Michigan's Grand Traverse Bay including Traverse City, the Leelanau Peninsula and Antrim and Kalkaska counties. The Lake Michigan Shoreline and Cadillac listings lead south from the Traverse area through the lakeshore communities of Frankfort, Manistee and Ludington and east to Cadillac and Missaukee County. The Little Traverse listings take us back north to Lake Michigan's Little Traverse Bay communities of Boyne City, Charlevoix, Harbor Springs and Petoskey. Mackinac Straits spans the tips of Michigan's upper and lower peninsulas, with listings for Mackinaw City, St. Ignace, Mackinac Island and lands adjacent to the mighty Mackinac Bridge.

The Grand Traverse section is often subdivided geographically with Traverse City, as Northwest Michigan's regional hub, leading the way.

The area code for the west side of lower Michigan is 616. The primary exceptions to the 616 rule are Mackinac Island and St. Ignace, which are part of the upper peninsula's 906 area code, and Gaylord, which lies along the dividing line between the 616 and 517 codes. To make it easier for you, we have listed the area code with each phone number. Remember, when calling between communities, you must first dial one plus the area code before the seven-digit telephone number.

We hope that you will use this book extensively during your travels north.

Relax, explore and enjoy your travels!

The region's original inhabitants arrived in Michigan 11,000 years ago, probably in search of food after the glaciers melted.

History

During the Ice Age much of the northern part of North America was engulfed in glaciers. As the climate warmed, these great ice caps advanced and receded four times, creating a complex and diverse geography in what is now the state of Michigan.

The Great Lakes were formed as the ice caps receded the fourth and final time, carving deep valleys that were then filled with water from the melting glaciers. Glaciation scooped out and filled our thousands of inland lakes and winding rivers, and pushed northern Michigan's fertile soil to the southern part of the state, leaving only an aftermath of sandy soil in the north.

Thus, Michigan current physical geography was formed before 8,000 B.C.

The Original Michiganders

The region's original inhabitants arrived in Michigan 11,000 years ago, probably in search of food after the glaciers melted. Throughout the next 10,000 years groups of Native Americans passed through the region, settling in villages for a while and then moving on. Archaeologists refer to these prehistoric settlers as the Paleo-Indians (approximately 11,000 years ago), the Old Copper People (approximately 8,000 years ago) and the Mound Builders (approximately 3,000 years ago).

About 1,000 years ago several tribes moved from North America's eastern coast westward to the Great Lakes. The Chippewa (or Ojibwa), the Ottawa (or Odawa) and the Potawatomi settled in Michigan. The three tribes lived in harmony, sharing the Algonquian language and a common culture. In fact, it was the Algonquian words "michi gami," meaning large lake, that became our state's name. The tribes considered themselves part of the same family and referred to themselves as the "Three Fires."

The Chippewa lived in the far north, through the upper peninsula and the Straits area where they survived primarily through hunting and fishing. The Potawatomi migrated to the southern part of the state where they became skilled farmers working the land's rich soil. The Ottawa settled along the Lake Michigan shoreline where they were active traders and traveled heavily through the Great Lakes region to trade with other nearby Native American groups.

The population of the many tribes in the region flourished. It is estimated that at the time the first European settlers arrived on the continent, approximately 10 percent, or 100,000, of the Native American population north of Mexico lived in the Great Lakes region.

Exploring New Worlds

In the 1600s, France, Britain and Spain established colonies throughout North America with the French claiming much of Canada. Samuel de Champlain founded New France near today's Quebec City in 1608 and, from this colony, sent explorers in search of the Northwest Passage, a direct water route to the Pacific Ocean.

These expeditions brought the first Europeans to Michigan around 1620. Led by Etienne Brulé, the explorers left Georgian Bay and paddled in canoes across Lake Huron, into the St. Mary's River and upstream until they reached a waterfall. These rapids or "sault" are today's Soo Locks in Sault Ste. Marie.

In 1634 Jean Nicolet was the first European to pass through the Straits of Mackinac. He recorded the sighting of the legendary island of "Mishi-minauk-in-ong," now known as Mackinac Island, heralded by his Native American companions as the home of the great spirits.

Many more Europeans followed in the footsteps of these explorers during the years to come: voyageurs in search of furs and missionaries in search of souls.

The most famous of the early holy men was Father Jacques Marquette who established the state's first permanent European settlement in 1668 at Sault Ste. Marie and another in 1671 at the Mackinac Straits in St. Ignace. On an expedition to the Mississippi with Louis Joliet, Marquette became ill and died on the return trip to northern Michigan. Though he was buried along the route, his remains were later reclaimed and moved to St. Ignace. (See our Worship chapter for more on Pere Marquette.)

While the missionaries traveled the frontier, the voyageurs plied the growing fur trade by transporting pelts between Great Lakes trading posts and Quebec in their birch-bark canoes. In Europe, fur was a rare luxury item exclusively for the wealthy. However, when the early explorers met the Native Americans, they saw that fur was often used in this northern wilderness for such common purposes as clothing and blankets. Since fur-producing animals such as beaver, otter, fox, mink and wolves were abundant, the fur trade flourished among the Native Americans and French voyageurs as this rich resource was traded in Europe and America's colonies. French forts became busy trading centers.

In 1715, Fort Michilimackinac, overlooking the Straits of Mackinac, was constructed by French soldiers and fur traders. It served as a commercial depot, military post and bustling community for the next 60 years. Although the fort thrived during the busy 1700s, life at Michilimackinac was not without turmoil.

War in Michigan

Although none of the French and Indian War battles were fought in northern Michigan, the effects were felt in the region. Most significant of these effects was the repeated change of command at Fort Michilimackinac.

Through acts of war and in response to war, the post would change hands six times between 1760 and 1815. Shifting allegiance began when France gave up all of its land claims in North America in the Treaty of Paris in 1763, and the British took control of the fort.

British residence at Michilimackinac was short lived, however, since the fort fell to Native Americans in a surprise attack in 1763. Approximately one year after losing control of the fort, the British returned and began leading a peaceful coexistence with the neighboring Native Americans.

War soon threatened Michilimackinac again — during the American Revolution. The British sought to secure their military hold by moving the fort across the Straits onto Mackinac Island in 1779-80. Materials, possessions and food caches were hauled across the Straits, along with dismantled homes, which were rebuilt on the island. Lumber was milled at what we call Old Mill Creek near Mackinaw City and then floated across the Straits for use in the building project. During the winter, materials were transported across the frozen Straits. The move was successful and, by summer 1780, troops were living in blockhouses while remaining fort structures and village buildings were completed. (See our Attractions chapter for more on Fort Mackinac and Old Mill Creek.)

Even though the British were ultimately defeated during the Revolutionary War, they retained control of Fort Mackinac until 1796 when troops finally relinquished it to the American army.

The British military returned to Mackinac Island one last time when it recaptured control of the fort in a surprise attack during the War of 1812. Although the British held the fort for almost three years, it was returned to the United States after both countries agreed to end all hostilities and return recaptured lands. U.S. soldiers took command of Fort Mackinac in July 1815. The American flag was flown over the fort until it was retired as a military post in 1895. (See our Attractions chapter for more on Colonial Michilimackinac.)

www.insiders.com
See this and many other Insiders' Guide® destinations online — in their entirety.
Visit us today!

Photo: Kevin Poirier

The former Perry Hannah residence in Traverse City is one of the many lumber baron mansions remaining in the region.

Blazing a Lumber Trail

Michigan's population grew as settlers pushed westward into new frontiers. The Northwest Territory, which had been mapped out in 1787, evolved into individual territories that eventually became Michigan, Ohio, Indiana, Illinois and Wisconsin. The Michigan Territory was established in 1805, followed by statehood in 1837 making Michigan the 26th state in the union.

Michigan's rich forests played a major role in the development of the state. The highly acidic sand left when the glaciers stripped the fertile soil was ideal for pine forests, which grew to towering heights by the mid-1800s.

As the pioneers flocked into the Northwest Territory lands, they needed wood to build their homes and communities. Michigan's rich forests of white and Norway pine soon became the biggest lumber source in the United States, creating great wealth for those who owned the land.

In 1852, the 15-year-old State of Michigan received official title to its 750,000 acres of land from the United States government. A significant amount of this property was promised to members of the St. Mary's Falls and

---

INSIDERS' TIP

Many of the old lumber barons' homes can still be seen today. A number have been renovated into charming bed and breakfast inns (see our Bed and Breakfasts chapter), and others stand as community resources or professional offices.

Ship Canal Company as compensation for building the Soo Locks in Sault Ste. Marie. The new owners became Michigan's lumber barons or sold their holdings to logging developers.

As lumbering land continued to change hands, its price rose from about 3¢ an acre in 1852 to almost $111 an acre by 1893. The lumber days were officially on.

The burgeoning United States had great demand for building lumber, and by 1869 Michigan produced more lumber than any other state — a record that it maintained for the next 30 years. The lumber was crafted into barns, homes and fences on the treeless Great Plains. It was used to rebuild homes following the great Chicago fire and to construct the nation's rapidly developing railways. Lumbering also spawned many related industries such as sawmills, railroad and transportation systems, and manufacturers of wooden products including furniture, dishes, pails and even railroad cars.

Between 1860 and 1900, Michigan produced more than 200 billion board feet of timber from 1 billion trees. The industry's mills and ports established Traverse City, Petoskey, Manistee and Ludington as leading lumbering towns. Lumber barons became community leaders, opened banks and stores and built mansions throughout the region.

Unfortunately, in the haste to produce lumber, few considered the consequences of clear-cutting or made any efforts toward reforestation. The stripped areas were susceptible to forest fires, which often blazed through the cutover fields. The land was rendered virtually useless.

Since the stripped land was also stripped of its value, especially to the lumber industry, several logging companies tried marketing it to new settlers as fertile farmland. Many farmers took advantage of the Homestead Act of 1862 to purchase some of this lumbered property. The poor-quality soil would not yield the crops that thrived in southern Michigan or on the East Coast. Many farmers abandoned their futile cause and left bankrupt. The State of Michigan then reclaimed this abandoned land, much of which it still holds today.

Agriculture Begins to Flourish

Even though traditional crops failed to grow in the cutover lumber fields, agriculture still played an economic role in northern Michigan, especially in those communities near the Lake Michigan shoreline. Fruit farming, in particular, was especially well-suited to the climate and sandy soil.

Farmers found that the tempering influence of lake-effect weather helped create a hospitable environment for fruit farming. This lake effect was created as westerly winds blew across Lake Michigan, causing a microclimate in which spring winds would cool the weather, thus inhibiting premature growth of fruit buds. In autumn, winds would pick up the warmer temperatures from the water and, in turn, extend the growing season until the fruit reached maturity.

Fruit farming began in earnest in the early 1900s. It was an industry born of necessity. In the Traverse City area, lumbering had dramatically declined by the early 1900s. In response, related industries, such as the town's wooden dish company, eventually closed down. The focus of the economy changed to agriculture. Potato farming had a brief heyday around the turn of the century, but by 1918, local agriculture was shifting to cherry trees, which had begun to grow prolifically in the region's sandy soil and rolling hills.

The first cherry orchard was planted, against the advice of other farmers, by Presbyterian minister Peter Dougherty on Traverse City's Old Mission peninsula in 1852. Much to everyone's surprise, the trees flourished. The

---

INSIDERS' TIP

Manistee had its share of lumber barons. During the height of the era, there were more millionaires per capita in Manistee than anywhere in Michigan. Architectural detailing from this extravagant time can still be found in many of the town's public buildings.

Photo: Mackinac Island Chamber of Commerce

Historical re-enactments entertain thousands of visitors each summer at
Fort Mackinac, Colonial Michilimackinac and Historic Mill Creek.

first commercial cherry orchard was planted in 1893 on Ridgewood farm near the original Dougherty plantings. By the early 1900s, the tart cherry industry was firmly established with production surpassing all other major crops. Success also led to related industries, such as the Traverse City Canning Company.

Many shoreline areas had similar experiences when they started growing cherries, strawberries, blueberries and other fruits. Today the Grand Traverse region is a leader in commercial cherry production, growing 75 percent of nation's tart cherries and most of the state's sweet cherries. In more recent years, farmers found that grapes also thrive in our temperate weather and sandy soil, leading to the region's emergence as a respected wine producer with nine wineries scattered between the Old Mission and Leelanau peninsulas. All are close to the 45th parallel, halfway between the equator and the North Pole, a geographic point shared with the Bordeaux region of France.

Introduction of Tourism

The effects of tourism were first felt as the railroads stretched north in the 1870s, bringing regular carloads of visitors, new settlers and goods. On the Great Lakes, steamships transported urban families up north for a summer respite. During this same era and through the turn of the century, large hotels were built around the region, including the Campbell House, which became Traverse City's Park Place Hotel, Petoskey's Perry Hotel and Mackinac Island's Victorian hotels, including the Island House, the Chippewa Hotel, the Iroquois Hotel and the famous Grand Hotel.

The Grand Hotel's opening in 1887 helped open the door for large numbers of summer visitors. The Grand was originally financed by a consortium of railroad and steamship companies who hoped to attract more passengers by providing a destination hotel on this increasingly popular island.

Mackinac Island had been in the visitor spotlight ever since President Ulysses S. Grant designated it as the second U.S. national park in 1875 (Yellowstone was the first). After the government closed Fort Mackinac, ownership of the national lands were transferred to the State of Michigan, which created Michigan's first state park in 1895. Today more than 80 percent of the island is part of Mackinac Island State Park, including 1,800 wooded acres and the fort property.

Arriving by train, steamship or carriage, Victorian visitors helped create summer colonies and cottage communities that still thrive. One of the most notable is Bay View, just northeast of Petoskey. Bay View was originally founded as a Methodist summer camp in 1875 but blossomed into a picturesque seasonal community of 435 cottages by the turn of the century. Today, Bay View is noted as a national historic landmark, with hundreds of Queen Ann cottages — many still owned by the original families — with wide porches and decked in gingerbread trim. The Bay View Association's founding goals to provide culture, education, religion and recreation are still followed with an ambitious schedule of summer lectures, concerts and classes. Similar summer colonies were established and continue to thrive, including Wequetonsing and Harbor Point in Harbor Springs, the Belvedere Club in Charlevoix and others in Northport, Leland and Antrim County.

As tourism grew, community festivals became a familiar part of the summer culture and attracted even more visitors to the region. Traverse City's National Cherry Festival dates back to 1925 when the community held its first Blessing of the Blossoms Festival, renamed the National Cherry Festival in 1933. Other favorite annual events are rooted in history like the annual Mackinac Bridge Labor Day Walk, which was first undertaken by Michigan's Governor Soapy Williams in 1957 to commemorate the bridge's opening (see our Close-up on the Mackinac Bridge in the

INSIDERS' TIP

Historians estimate that all the lumber cut during the 1800s would floor the state of Michigan with 1-inch pine boards, with enough left over to floor Rhode Island.

Getting Here and Getting Around chapter). The bridge walk has continued through four decades, attracting at least 60,000 walkers as well as Michigan's governor each year.

Tourism got an added boost from the region's recreational facilities and resorts that were added in the 1950s and 1960s. Northcountry skiing began in the 1950s by Boyne Mountain near Boyne City, at Caberfae near Cadillac and at Bud's Hill, the future Crystal Mountain, near Thompsonville. Sugar Loaf Resort, Schuss Mountain and Shanty Creek were unveiled in the 1960s. (Schuss and Shanty Creek were later combined.) Traverse City's Grand Traverse Resort in Acme signaled the latest generation of resorts when it entered the market in the mid-1980s.

Today, tourism is big business and each community in the Traverse Bay Region has a visitors bureau or similar hospitality service.

Community Highlights

As the state has grown, each of our many Northwest Michigan communities has created its unique history. Space limits our telling the heritage of each community. We tried to give a broad-brush look at the overall region in this chapter, yet each particular community deserves a closer look. We urge to you do so at the many museums and historic sites that fill our regional map. To get you started on your trip back in time, read our Attractions and Daytrips chapter for ideas.

The environment is
the essential thread
that identifies the
region and binds
us together.

Overview

Today's Northwest Michigan is a tapestry of life, work and play that reveals our heritage, values and hopes for the future. This chapter gives a brief overview of our communities and the dynamics that make them strong. The entire region is blessed with an environmental beauty that is matchless. Our scenic attributes are the legacy of the four continental glaciers that once encased the region in ice. As they receded, a new land was forged, filled by the remains of the melting glaciers that created the Great Lakes and our abundant inland waters. The departing glaciers left our soil sandy and nutrient deficient, perfect conditions for growing the great pine trees that fill our north woods. The glaciers carved the hills and valleys that give scenic character to our rolling landscape.

The environment is the essential thread that identifies the region and binds us together. It created the tourism industry that is so vital to our local economies. It hosts abundant fish and wildlife, and is home to countless recreational pursuits. The environment is, very simply, the main reason that we live and work here. You will see this theme woven through each of the geographic areas we profile here and spotlight throughout this guide.

As in the rest of this book, this overview is divided into our four main geographic areas. The numerous communities in these areas are as diverse as our vast regional landscape. Traverse City leads the lineup as the largest community, with more than 70,000 area residents, while the population in some villages is in the low hundreds. We could probably write a fascinating chapter about each community. Unfortunately, the sheer size of our regional boundaries prohibits that type of depth. Instead, we give you a native's bird's-eye view of our home along with the elements that define it as a community.

North Woods Weather

One unifying aspect of our region is the weather, and we have a lot of it! It's not unusual to experience a quick progression of sun, clouds, fog, rain, snow, wind and dramatic temperature changes — sometimes in a single day.

Though known for sun and snow, Northwest Michigan enjoys the variety of four seasons. Our summers are magnificent with sunny, blue skies and low humidity. Temperatures can fluctuate from the 90s to the 60s but generally hover around 80. Evenings can be cool, especially early and late in the season, so it's always wise to have a sweater or light jacket on hand. Summer temps will vary slightly by community with the shoreline and northernmost areas a bit cooler than our southern or more inland boundaries.

Autumn shows off the north woods' colorful glory. Our most pleasant fall days are between September and mid-October. Indian summer gives way to crisp days and cold nights with temperatures fluctuating between 35 and 65. The colder, grayer, rainy days of late autumn follow with hints of early season snow mixed with the raindrops.

It's not unusual for the first snowfalls to

INSIDERS' TIP

Welcome to the land of "lake effect" snow! Frigid winds sweeping across Lake Michigan's warmer waters bring us added precipitation in the form of snow, commonly referred to as "lake effect." It primarily affects shoreline communities during the early winter months.

come in late October or early November, but the snows rarely stick until late November or December. Winter is a heavy blanket of white snow under bright blue skies. We receive an average of 125 to 145 inches of snow each winter with December to February temperatures falling to an average of 15 to 35 degrees. Again, these will fluctuate moderately with locale.

Heavy winds combine with the temperature to create a wind chill that feels much colder than the thermometer indicates. You'll notice weather forecasters giving wind chills as part of their reports.

The key to enjoying a winter visit is to dress appropriately for the weather. Wear heavy coats, hats and mittens. You'll stay warmer if you dress in layers. And don't forget your boots! Fashion often gives way to practicality during our northern winters, when you'll see an abundance of heavy hiking or hunting-type boots on feet of all ages. Local favorites are the Canadian-made Sorel boots that sport heavy treads, replaceable felt liners and high lace-up sides. They aren't dainty, but they keep feet toasty. If you find yourself in need of north country boots, stop in any shoe shop, outfitter or department store for a good selection.

Spring can be our most unpredictable season. March temperatures fluctuate between 20 and 40 degrees while April and May temps rise to an average of 40 to 65 degrees. It's not unusual to be socked with a spring snowstorm in late March or early April, and local ski resorts are often active well into March. On the other hand, golfers could be heading to the courses and the crocuses could be popping through the ground in a display of early season optimism. Spring's true arrival is purely at the whim of Mother Nature and it varies by the year. Expect anything.

Grand Traverse

Traverse City Area

Our ancestors called Traverse City the "jewel of the north," and it's as true today as it was during the great lumbering era. Environmentally, economically and socially we are blessed to live among the riches of our region.

Marking boundaries here is like riding a winding roller coaster; there are simply no straight lines. The Traverse City area is defined along its northern edges by its physical geography, stretching more than 10 miles along the southern shores of Lake Michigan's Grand Traverse Bay.

Traverse area businesses and residential neighborhoods stretch along the shorelines from the eastern edges of East Bay, up and down the Old Mission Peninsula and to the southeastern edge of West Bay, which lies at the fringes of Leelanau County. The community extends at least 15 miles to the south, reaching toward Interlochen, Grawn, Kingsley and Buckley while weaving around our many inland lakes. Long Lake, Spider Lake, Duck Lake, Arbutus Lake, Green Lake and the Boardman River fill the local map with waterways and continue to stretch our neighborhoods around their curving, scenic shores.

The term Traverse City can be misleading to an outsider since the city limits are quite small compared to the actual business and residential area. The city boundaries encompass the north central core of the Traverse area, hosting the nucleus of community services but only one quarter of the area's population. Adjacent townships, in particular the large Garfield, East Bay and Elmwood townships, wrap around the city with ever-growing commercial and residential developments.

Several dynamics impact our local fiber. Traverse City is the regional hub, drawing employees, customers and visitors from all directions. Statistics show that more than half of the workers residing in Leelanau county are employed in Traverse City. Likewise, almost 40 percent of workers living in Antrim, Benzie and Kalkaska counties have jobs in Traverse. Specific fields such as healthcare, retail and tourism consistently draw from even broader boundaries.

The local economy is driven by tourism, healthcare, agriculture, education and light

www.insiders.com

See this and many other **Insiders' Guide®** destinations online — in their entirety.

Visit us today!

JAMES P. PREUETT, CPA

Providing Comprehensive
Financial and Tax Services
to Individuals and Small
Business in Northern
Michigan For
Over 25 Years

Publicity   Marketing
Advertising

Committed to Quality Service

**Referral service to the area's top business & personal service
providers, obtained in a lifetime of serving Northern Michigan**

1031 Lexington Drive, Traverse City, MI 49686

616.941.7878   preuett@traverse.com   **800.773.8388**

manufacturing. The single biggest employer is Munson Healthcare, with 3,500 people on staff. Other major employers include the Traverse City Area Public Schools, Northwestern Michigan College and University Center, Sara Lee Bakeries, the Grand Traverse Resort and the many hotels, restaurants, retailers and services that make up the hospitality industry.

Manufacturing accounts for one fifth of local employment, while the varied service-producing fields claim nearly three-quarters. Our unemployment statistics are consistent with state averages. Unfortunately, pay scales lag behind our downstate cousins. As the saying goes, "a view of the bay is half the pay." Salaries, whether for professionals or entry-level positions, are traditionally 10 to 15 percent lower than in other cities in the state. This is partially attributable to the higher number of workers who want to live in Traverse City and are willing to accept a lower pay scale to do so.

Our community, and its related job force, is well-educated. Approximately one quarter of the residents in Grand Traverse and Leelanau Counties have earned college degrees, far exceeding state averages.

Continual growth is an ongoing local issue. Traverse City has doubled in size in the last 30 years. Statistics show that populations are rising in both Grand Traverse and Leelanau Counties at a rate of 17 to 18 percent per decade. State projections estimate the number of Traverse area residents to grow from the current 70,000 to near 100,000 by the year 2010. As the population grows, so must the infrastructure to support it. Residents, new and old, continue to debate how to deal with overtaxed roadways, increased need for services and the threat of urban sprawl while retaining the environmental beauty and small-town charm.

Leelanau County

Leelanau County extends from Traverse City's northwestern boundaries to encompass the entire Leelanau peninsula or the "little finger" on our Michigan mitt. Like the Traverse City area, water is a defining characteristic. The peninsula is surrounded by Lake Michi-

INSIDERS' TIP

For the latest snowmobiling and downhill and cross-country skiing conditions, call (800) 72-SKI-TC between November 15 and the end of March.

Photo: Kevin Poirier/Courtesy of the Traverse City Record-Eagle

The hills surrounding the bay offer great opportunities for sledding in the winter, providing fun for young and old alike.

gan to the west and West Grand Traverse Bay to the east with 80 miles of shoreline. Lake Leelanau stretches 22 miles down into the peninsula from Leland almost all the way to the Traverse area. Big and Little Glen Lakes surround Glen Arbor and Glen Haven near the Sleeping Bear Dunes National Lakeshore in the county's southwest corner. Nearby, North and South Manitou Islands hover in Lake Michigan in the watch of Sleeping Bear. Rolling hills and orchards fill the lands in the peninsula's interior.

The peninsula is home to approximately 18,000 residents who live in dozens of small communities dotting the local map. The state estimates the population will grow to only around 19,000 by the end of the century.

The local economy relies on agriculture and tourism with some of the region's largest cherry orchards within the county's lines. More than 29 percent of Leelanau's property is farmland, ranking it 38th among Michigan counties with agricultural property. Many artists, entertainers and writers live and work here, drawing creative energy from the peninsula's peaceful beauty.

This is the home of the Grand Traverse Band of Ottawa and Chippewa Indians, whose headquarters are in Peshawbestown, north of Suttons Bay. The Band operates the Leelanau Sands Casino, Bingo Palace, Leelanau Sands Lodge and gift shop, which provide a stable economy and ongoing employment opportunities.

Leelanau communities are individual and very small. Suttons Bay is closest to Traverse City, just 15 miles north of the Traverse City limits on West Grand Traverse Bay. With more than 2,000 residents, it is the largest of the peninsula's towns and easily functions as a year-round community with scenic waterfronts and a charming downtown.

Many of the remaining villages follow the rhythms of the seasons with high activity during summer winding down into quiet winters, with many shops closing and seasonal residents heading south. All host some year-round businesses, although life definitely takes a slower pace as the temperatures drop. Northport, at the very tip of the peninsula, is flanked by the shoreline villages of Omena and Leland, while Glen Haven, Glen Arbor and Empire edge the Sleeping Bear National Lakeshore and Big and Little Glen Lakes. Inland, the village of Lake Leelanau sits at "the narrows," where Lake Leelanau's two branches meet in a skinny stream, while Maple City and Cedar hover near Sugarloaf Resort in the peninsula's rural center.

Antrim-Kalkaska

Farther along the eastern shores of Grand Traverse Bay, is the geographic area designated by our guide as Antrim-Kalkaska. This area spreads north and east to include Kalkaska, the Antrim County communities and Gaylord. Our Antrim-Kalkaska area is defined by the two counties plus the area between the eastern boundary of the counties and I-75.

Kalkaska County, due east of Traverse City, which has a countywide population of 13,000, is an extremely rural area that still operates an updated one-room schoolhouse in its most remote corner. The main town is the city of Kalkaska, which supports several small manufacturers. Much of the lifestyle is geared around outdoor recreation, hunting and fishing. Over 50 percent of the county's land, which includes 69 inland lakes, belongs to the State of Michigan. You will know that you are in Kalkaska when you pass its trademark sculpture of a trout standing on its tail in the middle of town.

Heading north, we sweep through Antrim County, which is characterized by its hilly, scenic terrain and collection of charming villages along its scenic waterways. This is the home of the Chain of Lakes, which is a series of 14 individual lakes with miles of connecting rivers and tributaries as well as some of the highest water quality in the United States. The chain, which includes Torch Lake and Elk Lake, begins just east of the city of Central Lake, threading through the communities of Alden, Bellaire and Ellsworth before emptying into Grand Traverse Bay near Elk Rapids.

Many of the Antrim towns are known as havens for visitors and seasonal residents. Each has its unique flavor while sharing a common up-north persona. Moving our way south to north, let's begin with Elk Rapids. This community is one of the county's largest with a population of approximately 1,600. It is nestled between the Grand Traverse Bay shoreline to the west and Elk Lake to the right. Since Elk Rapids is only 10 miles north from the outskirts of Traverse City, a number of year-round residents commute to work there. Continuing due north, travelers follow Michigan Highway 31 along the narrow strip of land that separates the Grand Traverse Bay shoreline from Torch Lake. Often referred to simply as Torch, this magnificent inland lake stretches at least 20 miles long, paralleling the bay shores. The

INSIDERS' TIP

What time is it? Northwest Michigan follows Eastern Standard Time between late October and early April, then switches to Eastern Daylight Time during the spring and summer months.

towns of Kewadin, Torch Lake and Eastport sit, south to north, on the land between the waters. The charming village of Alden is on the southeast edge of Torch Lake. Alden is known for its quaint shops, which wind along the main street through town. A few miles farther northeast is Bellaire, home to the large Shanty Creek resort. Shanty Creek offers extensive accommodations and convention facilities along with ski areas, golf courses and recreational facilities at properties in Bellaire and nearby Mancelona (see our Hotels, Golf and Recreation chapters). Continuing north, we pass through the town of Central Lake and near the northern shore of Torch Lake. In the county's northernmost reaches, we find the village Ellsworth, which is home to two nationally acclaimed restaurants, Tapawingo and the Rowe Inn (see our Restaurants chapter).

From Ellsworth, we shift to the east, approximately 30 miles, to Gaylord, which is included in this area's mix. Located about 75 miles northeast of Traverse City, Gaylord sits on the edge of I-75, 60 miles directly south of the Mackinac Bridge. The landscape here is marked by rolling hills, heavy trees and Otsego Lake just south of town. Gaylord is one of Northwest Michigan's golfing meccas, and is home to a number of championship courses and resorts (see our Golf chapter for more information).

Apart from tourism, the region's year-round economy relies on the oil and gas industry and light manufacturing. The Diocese of Gaylord, which oversees Catholic churches and schools throughout northern Michigan, is headquartered here as well. Gaylord's area population is close to 5,000.

Lake Michigan Shoreline and Cadillac

A shoreline county, Benzie is also bordered by Leelanau County to the north, Grand Traverse County to the east and Manistee County to the south.

You can't overstate the natural wealth of Benzie County. Rolling hills, rugged coastal dunes, 621,052 acres of state forest land, two large, gorgeous lakes, an excellent harbor and two highly renowned sport fishing rivers all grace the county's 322 square miles.

The county has one of the smallest county populations (12,200) in the region. Beulah, the county seat, is 30 miles southeast of Traverse City. In recent years Beulah and other Benzie communities, Benzonia, Frankfort, Elberta, Honor, and Lake Ann, have experienced an overflow effect from Traverse City's commercial and population explosion. During the past five years, people have discovered they can live in the serene setting of Benzie County and easily commute to work in Traverse City. Others have learned that Benzie is a pleasant retirement haven. Consequently, the No. 1 concern of Benzie County citizens is coping with rapid population growth.

It may be difficult to grasp how quickly the influence of urban life has descended upon small northern communities, but consider this: there wasn't a golden arch in sight in any of the little towns until about five years ago. Now they are almost as common as gas stations. The penetration of fast food chains heralded change in many of the north's quaint, attractive communities. Some communities fiercely fight to preserve their quiet lifestyles, yet realize progress is not to be stopped. The challenge is to accommodate development while protecting the fisheries, forests and watersheds, as well as the quality of life residents enjoy. Like other environmental organizations in Northwest Michigan, several Benzie County groups are tackling the issue, including Citizens for Positive Planning, Citizens Advisory Committee for Land Use and the Michigan Land Use Institute. Protection of resources is not simply a matter of stewardship, it's also in the best economic interest of counties depending heavily on tourist dollars, and Benzie County is no exception. The county intends to enhance its four-season tourist industry by pumping promotion of winter recreation: Nordic and Alpine skiing, snowmobiling and ice-fishing opportunities. Fruit production and food processing have long been a key part of the county's economic strength and are expected to hold a place in the county's promising future.

Manistee County is another shoreline county in the heart of beautiful Northwest Michigan. It is bordered by Benzie County to the north, Wexford County to the east and Lake and Mason counties to the south. It is a blend of natural and historic treasures and innovative social experiments. Coastline cities include Onekama, Arcadia and Bear Lake. Inland communities include Copemish, Kaleva, Brethren and Wellston. The county population totals 20,000.

The City of Manistee, with a population of 7,000, is the county seat. It is a Victorian port city that came alive during the great lumbering era. At that time, the city boasted of having more millionaires per capita than anywhere else in the nation. While numerous northern communities that built on the lumbering industry eventually became ghost towns, Manistee diversified its commercial base to survive changing times.

Manistee is a pilot region for two state experiments. In 1997, it was one of a dozen economically depressed Michigan locations designated to become Renaissance Zones that establish tax-free commercial areas to attract industrial development. One of these tax-free areas is a 200-acre industrial park 5 miles outside of the Manistee city limits. A second zone was established in the county at the Kaleva Industrial Park in Manistee County. In less than one year, the program has production rolling in one new industry with several others pending. Project Zero, another state pilot program being tested in Manistee County and 11 other Michigan sites, aims to remove all capable adults from the welfare role. The program's goal is to remove all barriers preventing welfare recipients from retaining productive work. If the project proves successful, the program will be duplicated statewide.

Mason County is bordered on the west by the stunning Lake Michigan coastline, on the north by Manistee County, on the east by Lake County and on the south by Oceana County. Mason County visitors won't soon forget the incessant cry of gulls, the rhythmic sound of lapping surf, or the sight of boaters leisurely trolling for the big catch. Covering 495 square miles, the county is known for its pristine sandy beaches, panoramic vistas, landmark lighthouses and great sport fishing along the Pere Marquette, a Nationally Designated Wild and Scenic River. Ludington, with a population of 9,000, is the county seat. Custer, Scottville, Wallhalla, Freesoil and other small communities make up a county population total of 26,000. While the county is known for its rich natural beauty and resources, it's probably most widely recognized for providing 100 years of carferry service across Lake Michigan. Today, the S.S. *Badger*, docked in the Ludington harbor, is the only remaining carferry on Lake Michigan. From mid-May until mid-October the steam-powered auto passenger ship travels between Ludington and Manitowoc, Wisconsin. (See our Getting Here, Getting Around chapter for more details.) The Ludington State Park, two gorgeous sandy Ludington city beaches, bountiful Hamlin Lake and historic White Pine Village are a few favorite sites.

Rich in maritime history and a modern boating mecca, Mason County's past, present and future lie in its water resources. This is visible in the ongoing importance of the area's sentinels of the freshwater sea, the Big Sable Point and Little Sable Point lighthouses and the North Breakwater Light. The 112-foot-tall Big Sable Point lighthouse is 8 miles north of Ludington. Little Sable Point Lighthouse, constructed in 1874, is 30 minutes south of Ludington near Silver Lake. The 107-foot red brick tower, still in use, was automated by the U.S. Coast Guard after lighthouse keepers had kept the lantern burning for 100 years. The most active sentinel is the North Breakwater Light in downtown Ludington, which has been guiding ships through the harbor since 1871. Renovated just two years ago, this beacon of marine heritage reaches 19 miles across the water, guiding today's travelers to safety.

Building on this resource to enhance its

INSIDERS' TIP

Can you find the northern lights? The aurora borealis appear without warning to paint our night skies with a magnificent light show. Our northern geography and lack of light pollution allow us to enjoy these fleeting sweeps of light and, sometimes, color. You can see the northern lights year round, but you'll most likely spot them during the summer.

Photo: Kevin Poirier

The hills outside Traverse City afford a picture-perfect view of the city.

all-important tourism base, the Ludington community plans to construct an all-new city marina and waterfront park. Still in the development stage, it represents the area's strong commitment to the tourism industry. While Mason County is an unforgettable place to visit, it's also a nice place to live. Its small towns are family-oriented, quiet and safe. County residents have the best of two worlds because the peaceful rural towns are located just a comfortable distance from metropolitan areas, their services and cultural offerings. Muskegon lies on the coastline 58 miles to the south of Ludington, and Grand Rapids, 95 miles south.

Inland, just south of Grand Traverse County and east of Manistee County, lies Wexford County, which marks the geographic center of Michigan. It is bordered on the east by Missaukee County and to the south by Lake and Osceola counties. The county population

hovers around 24,000, and like nearly all of Northwest Michigan counties, the population is mostly rural. Cadillac, with 11,000 residents, is the county's largest community as well as the county seat. Other communities include Harrietta, Manton and Mesick.

It's somewhat surprising to discover that the friendly, small town of Cadillac — surrounded by rivers, lakes and the lush Manistee National Forest — is considered the industrial center of Northern Michigan. Here, global companies cast metal; manufacture molded-rubber products, boats, vacuums, and auto and marine horns; and create precision parts for the nation's major auto makers. In recent years, tourism has become an increasingly significant component of the county's economic strength. The area approaches a new century on a healthy economic basis, but not without significant challenges.

In the year 2,000, U.S. 131, the main corridor along the western section of Michigan, is scheduled to open a Cadillac bypass. The bypass will divert traffic from downtown Cadillac, a timesaver for travelers and a blessing for commercial transportation, but a potential threat to downtown businesses. In a race against time, businesses are scrambling to compensate for the loss of traffic by working to establish Cadillac as a destination in itself. To this end, much effort has been devoted to developing the city's lakefront. The investment is paying off. In 1997, Cadillac was judged as having the best lakefront in the Midwest by a *Chicago Tribune* travel writer. The park is noted for its shoreside performing arts pavilion, dock, launch and picnic facilities that connect to a 7.5-mile paved pedestrian/bike path encircling Lake Cadillac.

As with many communities in the region, the migration of Michigan residents to the north has put a serious squeeze on Cadillac housing. Continued economic progress hinges on the community's ability to house, educate and otherwise serve an increased population.

Directly east of Wexford County you'll find Missaukee County. It is bordered to the north by Kalkaska County, to the east by Roscommon County and to the south by Clare and Osceola counties. Tourism has long been a cornerstone of the economy for this county blessed with areas of rolling hills, maple-birch and hickory-oak forests and 20 lakes. Camping, boating, snowmobiling, hunting and fishing swell the year-round population of 12,000 each summer. Lake City, with a population of 850, is the county seat. Other communities include Falmouth and McBain.

Missaukee County has a long-standing reputation as one of the nation's largest producers of Christmas trees. About one million trees are shipped from here each holiday season. It's always a reminder that Christmas is around the corner when northern residents spot the first semi-loads of bundled pines speeding down the highways to destinations in the nation's deep south.

You won't travel too far here without seeing a herd of grazing Guernseys because dairy farming is Missaukee County's second key industry. In fact, the county is home to about as many cows as people. While most farms are relatively small, maintaining herds of around 100 head, the industrious dairy producers of Missaukee County have earned a national reputation for consistently maintaining high production levels and implementing innovative production methods.

Little Traverse

For nearly 100 years, the population of the Little Traverse area remained fairly constant. However, a growth trend that began in the 1960s is projected to boom dramatically by the year 2000. Emmet County's population is predicted to grow by 21 percent to 30,000. Statewide, the average growth rate is only 3 percent.

At the tip of the mitt, Emmet County is bordered by Lake Michigan to the west, Cheboygan County to the east and Charlevoix County to the south. Rolling hills, woods and inland lakes wrap the county, which is situated in the northwest corner of the lower peninsula. Petoskey, the county seat, Harbor Springs and Boyne City are often collectively referred to as Boyne Country. The major communities are on a 30-mile stretch along the Little Traverse Bay coastline. Although Boyne City is actually a part of Charlevoix County, geography naturally links the sister cities. Other communities in Emmet County include Pellston, Conway and Cross Village.

A premier Midwest vacation center since the 1800s, Emmet County's population burst is attributed to the development of new, world-

INSIDERS' TIP

The 45th parallel cuts through Northwest Michigan, sweeping by the tip of the Old Mission Peninsula, near the middle of the Leelanau Peninsula and through the woods near Kewadin in Antrim county. Coincidentally, it also passes through the Bordeaux region of France. The 45th parallel areas on our local peninsulas are home to several fine wineries.

class resort communities, improved highway access, an increased demand for lakefront and forest property and the county's success in achieving economic diversification.

Add seasonal population surges to the population formula and you get a significant demand for development land and goods and services of all kinds, including public services and city infrastructure. To protect Emmet County's integrity and to combat sprawl, county and city officials and local citizens drafted a master plan. The plan, adopted by the Emmet County Planning Commission in July 1997, is unusual in that it encompasses 21 governmental jurisdictions, including 16 townships, two cities and three villages, 289,036 acres of land, 10,400 acres of water and 60 miles of Lake Michigan shoreline. The master plan provides a countywide vision for growth and guidelines for compact development.

The upscale ambiance, natural beauty and popularity of the region is bringing big investors to the county. Bay Harbor, a new multi-million dollar luxury resort community along 5 miles of Little Traverse Bay, features homes, condos, world-class golf facilities, a yacht club, marina and equestrian facilities with a luxury inn scheduled to open in the fall of 1998.

While new construction is everywhere, much of the charm of the area still rests with its heritage. Petoskey's downtown historic Gaslight District offers 90 distinctive specialty shops and fine-dining opportunities. Historic hotels, marinas, eclectic shops, galleries and gracious restaurants attract tourists to the county as they have for generations. But what attracts people to settle here permanently? Insiders claim it's the simple things they value about Emmet County: a strong family orientation; safe, clean streets; and an unpretentious lifestyle.

Positioned between Antrim and Emmet counties, Charlevoix County is bordered by 102 miles of Lake Michigan shoreline. Beaver Island and the Beaver Island group of isles, 32 miles offshore, are a part of this recreational paradise. The county's year-round population is about 21,000, with an estimated 10,000 additional summer residents. Key communities are Charlevoix, East Jordan, Ironton, Boyne City and Boyne Falls.

You'll find 29 Great Lakes marinas within the county and a total of 719 boat slips, 215 miles of bountiful rivers and streams, 19 lakes, 58,000 acres of recreational land, championship golf courses, top-notch ski slopes, historic inns and contemporary condos. In addition to natural attractions and fine resorts, visitors enjoy shopping, dining and an array of special events and festivals. Even the commonly known name for the county seat, Charlevoix the Beautiful, tells you this area is something special.

Situated among three lakes, the city of Charlevoix is made even more lovely each spring when citizens join efforts in Operation Petunia. Established in 1982, this annual volunteer effort has received national acclaim as an outstanding example of community pride. One day each spring — Operation Petunia day — citizens get down on their hands and knees to plant 50,000 petunias along four miles of Charlevoix's main thoroughfare. Volunteer participation is so high that the job is usually completed in one hour.

In the summer of 1995, the city initiated a program unique to northern communities by putting a city police officer on horseback. During the summer season, when Charlevoix's population swells, the mounted patrol easily maneuvers through congested streets. Observing the success of Charlevoix's mounted patrol, the Traverse City Police Department is starting a similar program.

East Jordan is in the south arm of Lake Charlevoix, with the Jordan Valley and pristine Jordan River in its backyard. Residents plan a renovation of the historic downtown. Many private historic Victorian homes are also

INSIDERS' TIP

Traverse City natives often speak of "the peninsula," meaning the Old Mission Peninsula between East and West Grand Traverse Bays. When they talk about "the bay," they mean Grand Traverse Bay making no distinction between the east and west sides.

under renovation, preserving the charm and character of the friendly city. At the same time, local government, schools and the business community share an aggressive attitude toward maximizing the community's human and natural resources. A new city charter, the development of innovative educational programs, and accelerated industrial growth have the quiet community solidly positioned to meet a new century.

Offshore, a heritage of another type is gaining recognition and growing in popularity with tourists. Beaver Island, with a year-round population of 450, is called "America's Emerald Isle" because of its Irish legacy. As life on the mainland becomes increasingly complex, greater numbers of people are seeking the solitude and simplicity found on the Beaver Island Archipelago. A specially designed Great Lakes cruise ship has attracted visitors to the quiet wilderness isles from as far away as Germany. The island's growing reputation for great outdoor adventure promises to mark Beaver Island as a key destination in the years ahead.

Mackinac Straits

The Mackinac Straits has the smallest boundaries of our four geographic areas, yet is likely the most distinctive. The Straits include Mackinaw City at the northern tip of Michigan's Lower Peninsula, St. Ignace at the southern tip of the Upper Peninsula and historic Mackinac Island just off both cities' Lake Huron coastlines. The economy and lifestyle of the entire area are dependent on tourism and the seasonal ebb and flow of activity. The year-round population for all three communities barely reaches 4,000, most living in St. Ignace.

Mackinac Island is the land that time forgot. Automobiles are banned and Victorian architecture is everywhere. The steady clip-clop of horses' hooves remind us of slower, gentler times. The island's hospitality services usually run from early May through October before its few hundred residents button up for the winter. Arnold's ferry service usually runs through the holidays but relies on Mother Nature for its timetable. After the ferries end, all transportation on and off the island is by air service.

The island is physically fascinating. It measures only 3 miles long by 2 miles wide with high shoreline cliffs, limestone formations, caves and ravines. Much of the island is owned by the State of Michigan, which maintains it as part of the Michigan State Historical Parks, which include the island lands and Fort Mackinac, Colonial Michilimackinac in Mackinaw City, and Historic Mill Creek near Cheboygan.

Mackinaw City is developing a modern era of tourism as civic leaders work to establish it as a travel destination and not just as a place to wait for the ferries. Several new shopping and hotel developments have been introduced to an enthusiastic response.

St. Ignace is the seat of Mackinac county, which includes Mackinac Island. (Mackinaw City is actually part of Petoskey's Emmet county.) St. Ignace is the local hub for shopping, recreation and services. Like the other Straits communities, many of its hotels, restaurants and shops close or restrict hours during the winter.

Michigan

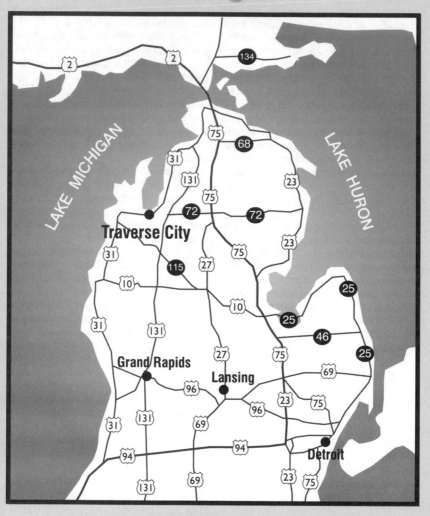

Getting Here and Getting Around

The slogan says "all roads lead north," but let's be a bit more specific. As we all learned in elementary school, Michigan's lower peninsula bears an uncanny resemblance to a child's mitten. So, let's use our left hands for reference. Our regional boundaries edge the western tip of the mitt. Interstate 75 bisects Michigan from Detroit at the base of the thumb to the top of the middle finger, also known as the Mackinac Straits area. Interstate 94, Interstate 96, U.S. Highway 131, Interstate 69, Michigan Highway 127 and Michigan Highway 23 weave north from the southern state line near the wrist. Northwest Michigan lies to the west of I-75 in the scenic hills and shores that stretch across the middle, ring and little fingers. Lake Michigan sculpts the outer edge to our mitten, enfolding the shoreline communities of Ludington, Manistee and Frankfort and then leading north to Traverse City and Grand Traverse Bay at the tip of the little finger and Petoskey and Little Traverse Bay on the ring finger. Not to be forgotten is Mackinac Island, which sits on our northern periphery, surrounded by Lake Huron near the Straits.

Now, let us show you the nuts and bolts of traveling to and through Northwest Michigan. Visitors arrive by land, air and water. We've listed the major modes of transportation and entries below divided between the Getting Here and Getting Around categories. Since Michigan is a peninsula, we know that boat services and harbors are essential for water travelers and have included them as well. Also, look for information and tips on crossing the Mackinac Bridge, shuttling to the islands and hailing the closest bus.

By Land

Major Roadways

It's easy to navigate to your favorite Michigan vacation stops by car. Remember that I-75 is the major artery that divides the northern lower peninsula in half and then extends over the Mackinac Bridge, into St. Ignace and onward to Sault Ste. Marie and the Canadian border. Numerous state and federal highways weave off from or run parallel to I-75. Mich. 55 generally marks this guide's southern boundaries with its east-west orientation from I-75 through Lake City, Cadillac and Manistee. Also stretching east-west is Mich. 72, running from I-75 at Grayling to Traverse City and continuing to Empire and Lake Michigan. Mich. 115 slices diagonally from Cadillac northwest to Benzonia and Beulah. Mich. 31 runs along the Lake Michigan shoreline from Ludington to Frankfort, through Traverse City and north through Elk Lake, Charlevoix and Petoskey before connecting to I-75 near Mackinaw City. Other scenic drives lie along Mich. 22 near Frankfort and Manistee, and loop the Leelanau peninsula. Parallel to I-75, U.S. 131 leads north-south from Cadillac through Kalkaska, Mancelona and on to Petoskey.

Sound confusing? Just remember, if you drove from Detroit, Ohio or Canada, you've probably traveled via I-75. If you're motoring from Chicago or Indiana, chances are you headed north along U.S. 131. Virtually every other major highway will intersect at least one of these during your trek north. Try to pick up a local map along the way. Most are free and are gladly distributed at visitors centers and in shopping districts. With the many rural roads, shorelines and inland lakes that weave through the region, the individual community maps zero in on local roadways (including the area's more common names for state and county highways) and highlights travel nuances and points of interest. One of our perennial favorites is the Travelers Pocket Map produced by the Candle Factory in Traverse City, which is not only graphically beautiful but also packed with tips for auto tours, day trips and fun. The Candle Factory map illustrates Benzie, Grand Traverse, Antrim and Charlevoix counties, extending from Frankfort to Little Traverse Bay. Another good bet is the Fen's Rim series of maps that have been designed around each area's unique characteristics whether that's county-wide (such as the Leelanau County map), community based (Elk Rapids) or interest (Traverse Area Trails). Fen's Rim publishes the biweekly *Lake Country Gazette* newspaper, which covers environmental issues and local happenings for much of Northwest Michigan. A final favorite is the Mackinac Island Visitor Information Locator Map. The charge for this is $1 but it is as much a souvenir as it is a guide. Colorful artists' images illustrate the Straits of Mackinac, island roads and trails, the business district and historic hot spots. A full business directory with map locators is included.

www.insiders.com

See this and many other **Insiders' Guide®** destinations online — in their entirety.

Visit us today!

Bridges

Mackinac Bridge

Once known as "the bridge that couldn't be built," the Mackinac Bridge has stood as an engineering feat since 1957. The Mighty Mac — linking Michigan's upper and lower peninsulas — still holds the world record for overall length of a suspension bridge, measuring 8,344 feet from anchor block to anchor block and spanning 5 miles over the Straits of Mackinac. Millions of cars cross the bridge each year, while pedestrians look forward to Labor Day and the annual walk from St. Ignace

over the Mighty Mac. To cross the bridge from the north or south, stay on I-75 and follow the signs. Speed is limited to 45 mph for autos and 20 mph for loaded trucks. In the case of extremely high winds, low visibility or particularly ferocious winter weather, the bridge may be closed temporarily. Weather conditions and daily bridge information can be monitored by listening to AM radio channels 1610 and 530. Tolls are $1.50 and are paid on the St. Ignace side of the bridge. (See our Close-up on the Mackinac Bridge in this chapter.)

Ice Bridge

One of the more fleeting structures to span the Straits is the annual "ice bridge" that forms each winter between Mackinac Island and St. Ignace. The opening of the ice bridge signals the time of the year that islanders are not dependent on set ferry or airline schedules. The bridge usually forms in February when the Strait waters between the island and the mainland freeze to a safe thickness for snowmobile travel. Once full passage is assured, islanders haul out their old Christmas trees to plant as route markers from island to shore. The ice bridge can last for just a few days or for up to two months, depending on each winter's temps.

Bus Service

Greyhound Bus Lines
3233 Cass Rd., Traverse City
• (616) 946-5180, (800) 231-2222
Cadillac • (616) 775-0333
Petoskey • (616) 347-4400
St. Ignace • (906) 643-9861

Commercial bus service to northern Michigan is limited. Greyhound is the only carrier and has just one route running from Cadillac north with subsequent stops in Traverse City, Petoskey, Mackinaw City and St. Ignace. The bus departs early evening from Cadillac and returns from St. Ignace early each morning. Greyhound operates ticket offices in each of the towns listed. The bus also stops in Mackinaw City in front of City Hall, but there is no ticket office; pay cash directly to the bus driver. Local hours are limited, so it's wise to call ahead.

Airports

Grand Traverse

Cherry Capital Airport
1330 Airport Access Rd., Traverse City
• **(616) 947-2250**

Cherry Capital Airport is the regional link for air travelers in northern Michigan. More than 300,000 travelers pass through Cherry Capital's gates each year as they venture northward for work and play. Year-round service is provided by American Eagle, Northwest Airlines, Northwest Airlink and United Express with several flights per day connecting through Chicago O'Hare and Detroit Metropolitan Airports. Additional flights and airlines are often added during the summer's peak tourist period. Northwestern Airlines offers the only jet service, with three flights per day. With only two gates, the Cherry Capital terminal is small by urban standards but its size offers less harried and more comfortable surroundings than its larger cousins in the metro areas. Parking lots, check-in, baggage pickup, transportation and amenities are within steps of each other. Two taxi services, T.C. Cabs and Classy Cabs, are on site as are Avis, Budget, Hertz and National rental cars and Passageways-Carlson Travel agency. Suncatchers Restaurant is open throughout the day for dining, while coffee connoisseurs can frequent the J. Fenwicks Coffee & Tea cart. Cherry Capital opens at 5:30 each morning, approximately one hour before the first flights leave, and closes around midnight, shortly after the final flights arrive.

Lake Michigan Shoreline and Cadillac

Manistee Blacker Airport
223 Airport Rd., Manistee
• **(616) 723-4351**

Manistee Blacker Airport operates 8 AM to 7 PM daily with daily flights to Chicago O'Hare Airport from United Express. Its 5,500-foot runway accommodates small- to medium-size jets. Orchard Beach Aviation also uses the Manistee Airport as the base for its charter service.

Wexford County Airport
8040 E. 34th Rd., Cadillac
• **(616) 779-9525**

The Wexford County Airport is open 7 AM to 7 PM for private and business aircraft. Its 5,000-foot runway can accommodate small- and medium-size jets.

Little Traverse

Welky Airport
East Side Dr., Beaver Island
• **(616) 448-9221**

Island Airways manages Welky Airport on tiny Beaver Island northwest of Charlevoix. Its 3,500-foot runway can accommodate single- and light-twin engine aircraft. Island Airways runs daily flights for passengers and freight between Welky and Charlevoix Municipal Airport. Daily hours are 8 AM until dark.

Charlevoix Municipal Airport
111 Airport Dr., Charlevoix
• **(616) 547-2141**

Also managed by Island Airways, the Charlevoix Municipal Airport is the base for daily charter service to and from Beaver Island. The airport is open daily from 8 AM until

---

INSIDERS' TIP

For a panoramic view of West and East Bays, the Old Mission Peninsula and the city, drive to the top of Wayne Hill in Traverse City. At night, you can see the city lights glittering and the moon shining off the bays.

Photo: Kevin Poirier

Catch a view of Traverse City from the air.

dark and operates a 4,300-foot runway suitable for small- to medium-size jets.

Mackinac Straits

Pellston Airport
Pellston • (616) 539-8441,
(616) 539-8442 fueling only 5 to 8 PM

The Pellston Airport, 15 miles south of the Mackinac Bridge, sees 60,000 travelers pass through its gates each year. Approximately six to seven commercial flights are offered daily by Northwest Airlink, Great Lakes Air and United Express. United Express flies to and from Chicago O'Hare while Northwest Airlink connects with airports in Traverse City, Escanaba, Detroit and Rhinelander, Wisconsin. Great Lakes Air will also shuttle incoming passengers on to Mackinac Island. The Pellston Airport is frequently used by private jets and charter services. The airport is open 24 hours a day with fueling services operating from 5 AM to 10:30 PM. Wolverine Taxi Service is operated on site and rental cars are available in the airport from Avis or nearby from Hertz. Dining is available inside at the Brass Rail Restaurant and Lounge, which is a favorite eatery among the locals as well as air travelers.

INSIDERS' TIP

Duck alert! While driving along the shoreline roads, be on the lookout for mother ducks and trailing ducklings who often waddle across the roadways during spring and early summer.

Mackinac County Airport
St. Ignace • (906) 943-7327

Based in St. Ignace, Mackinac County Airport is the home base for Great Lakes Air, which is the charter service for Mackinac Island shuttles. The airport is currently renovating its existing 3,400-foot runway by extending it to 3,800. Renovations are slated for completion in late 1998, but until then the original runway is in full operation. The facility is open during daylight hours, usually 8 AM to 5 PM daily.

Mackinac Island Airport
Mackinac Island • (906) 847-3561

This airport features a 3,500-foot paved runway suitable for small aircraft. Many summer visitors fly their own planes in or take advantage of the Great Lakes Air shuttle to Pellston or St. Ignace. During the snowy winter months when ferry service is closed, the air shuttle is the only mode of transportation between the island and the mainland.

Private Air Services

Island Airways
111 Airport Dr., Charlevoix
• (616) 547-2141

Island Airways is the resource for air travel to and from Beaver Island. The company manages the airports in Charlevoix and on Beaver Island, as well as its own air charter service and a fleet of four- to nine-passenger twin engine aircraft. Island Airways can be chartered to fly anywhere but the mainstay of its business is the Beaver Island-Charlevoix shuttle. There are at least four round-trip flights daily between the island and Charlevoix, but the frequency during the day increases during the busier seasons. If you're planning to travel during summer's peak, it's best to make advance reservations at least a week ahead of time. Beaver Island flights last about 15 minutes and cost $60 for adults and $30 for children.

Great Lakes Air
St. Ignace • (906) 643-7165

Flights between Mackinac Island and the mainland are the specialty at Great Lakes Air. Based at Mackinac County Airport in St. Ignace, the company also provides charter service to Cherry Capital Airport in Traverse City, the Pellston Airport or any other location in Michigan. Great Lakes Air is the only transportation link between Mackinac Island and the mainland during the winter months when there is no ferry service. The service runs daily shuttles transporting residents and delivering such essentials as groceries, mail and supplies. During the summer, sightseeing flights circling the Straits area are offered. All planes accommodate up to six passengers. Rates vary with the service and the season. Winter rates for shuttles to and from Mackinac Island are $28 per person, while the summer rate to fly between the Pellston and Mackinac Island Airports are $55.

By Water

Grand Traverse

Manitou Island Transit
Fishtown, Leland • (616) 256-9061

The North and South Manitou Islands are 15 miles off from Leelanau County's Lake Michigan shore. Visitors bound for these largely undeveloped islands use Manitou Island Transit to reach their destination. The daily South Manitou ferry leaves Leland's Fishtown docks at 10 AM and leaves the island at 4 PM for the 90-minute ride June through August. The North Manitou run operates every day except Tuesday and Thursday during July and August, departing Fishtown at 10 AM and the island at 11:10 AM. Check-in takes place 30 minutes earlier. Ferry service to both islands is available on a reduced schedule from May through October and to North Manitou for the

INSIDERS' TIP

The Mackinac Bridge is the longest suspension bridge in the world. Measuring 5 miles long, it is the only physical link between Michigan's upper and lower peninsulas.

deer hunt in November. Call for specific schedules during fall and winter as they vary with each season. Round-trip rates are $19 for adults, $13 for children younger than 12 and $50 for the North Manitou deer hunt in October and November.

Lake Michigan Shoreline and Cadillac

Lake Michigan Carferry — S.S. Badger
700 S. William St., Ludington
• **(616) 845-5555, (800) 841-4243**
Reminiscent of a slower era, the SS *Badger* transports autos and passengers across Lake Michigan between Ludington and Manitowoc, Wisconsin each summer. The ferry services, which originated in 1897 to transport railroad cars across the Great Lakes, had their heyday in the auto era of the 1950s. Today, the *Badger* stands as Lake Michigan's only remaining coal-burning ferry. It departs Manitowoc each afternoon between mid-May and mid-October for the four-hour ride to Ludington with return trips early each morning. An additional 12:30 AM "red-eye" ride from Manitowoc and early evening return from Ludington joins the schedule during the peak tourist season from mid-June to mid-August. Round-trip fares in 1997 were $57 for adults, $52 for seniors, $27 for children 5 to 15. Vehicle fares ranged from $10 for bicycles to $90 for automobiles. Additional fees are charged for RVs, campers and use of a state room.

Little Traverse

Beaver Island Boat Company
103 Bridge Park Dr., Charlevoix
• **(616) 547-2311**
Visitors ride the hulking Beaver Islander or the smaller South Shore from Charlevoix to travel to the tiny village of St. James on Beaver Island. Beaver Island, 32 miles off the coast of Charlevoix, is the most remote inhabited island in the Great Lakes. The Beaver Island Boat Company transports people, pets, vehicles and freight between April and December. Rides last 2¼ hours on the Beaver Islander and three hours on the South Shore. During the summer peak, the company runs two to four trips per day. Spring and fall schedules vary from daily service in May and September to just three runs per week in April and December. Call for the most current schedule and plan to check-in at least one hour ahead of time. Round trip rates are $30 for adults, $15 for children, $12 for bikes, $10 for pets and starting at $101 for vehicles.

Mackinac Straits

The Mackinac Island experience begins with the ferry ride from the mainland. Ferries shuttle visitors and locals between the island and docks in St. Ignace and Mackinaw City. Schedules vary with the season and the carrier but, during the summer peak, ferries generally depart every half hour or so from sunrise to long after sundown. Spring and fall schedules are usually limited to daytime runs with 60-90 minutes between departures. Check with the companies for the most up-to-date schedules and plan to arrive early during the busier seasons. Bikes and luggage are often transported with the passengers.

As frequent island visitors, we'll offer two tips — take the bikes and travel light! If you're a serious biker, you'll be much happier riding familiar wheels with a comfortable seat and multiple gears. Many of the rental bikes are older models with pedal brakes. Packing lightly can't be stressed enough. Remember that there are no cars here, so every bag must be carried to your destination. Hotel porters meet each ferry to help with luggage and dray services can be scheduled ahead for large loads. Day trippers can take advantage of short term lockers near the Star Line and Shepler docks on the west side of the island. Regardless of departure city or service, the docks are easily found with ample daily and overnight parking. Mackinaw City docks are along Huron Street (U.S. Highway 23) and can be reached from exits 37, 338 and 339 off from I-75. The St. Ignace docks stretch along State Street (Business Loop I-75) and can be reached from exits 344 or 348 from I-75. Round trip rates for all of the ferries averages $12.50 for adults, $7 for children age 5-12 and free for children younger than five. Bike fees are $5.

Arnold Mackinac Island Ferry

Huron St., Mackinac Island
• (906) 847-3351
801 Huron St., Mackinaw City
• (616) 436-5542, (800) 542-8528
303 S. State St., St. Ignace
• (906) 643-9177

The Arnold Line dates back to 1878, when their steamers first began transporting Victorian tourists to the island for the summer. Today's fleet includes two fast triple-deck, twin-engine catamarans as well as several slower traditional ferries. The large, twin-hulled "Cats" make the trip in less than 20 minutes while passengers relax in spacious, glass enclosed walk-around cabins decked with booth seats and tables that are great for families. In the warm weather, or for the very hardy, outdoor seats are perched on the roof top and half of the middle deck. We like sitting inside on the middle deck. It's fascinating to watch the ship captains in action as they pilot their crafts from behind a glass-enclosed command post. The older ferries offer a nostalgic look back at the leisurely cruises that used to transport passengers across the Straits in earlier decades. The traditional ferries run from St. Ignace between June and August with rides lasting approximately 45 minutes. Since the Arnold transports so much freight to the island, it provides the longest running ferry service from April through the New Year. Docks are in Mackinaw City and St. Ignace.

Shepler's Mackinac Island Ferry

556 E. Central St., Mackinaw City
• (616) 436-5023, (800) 828-6157
N. State St., St. Ignace • (906) 643-9440

Shepler's bills itself as the fastest fleet to the Island with 16-minute hydroplane rides across the Straits. Passengers can ride on bench seats on the windowed, indoor main deck or in the fresh air on the top deck. Service runs May through October from docks in Mackinaw City and St. Ignace. The Mackinaw City dock is directly across from the Mackinaw Crossings at the corner of Central and Huron Streets.

Star Line Mackinac Island Ferry

711 Huron St., Mackinaw City
• (616) 436-5045
587 N. State St., St. Ignace
• (906) 643-7635, (800) 638-9892

It's easy to identify the Star Line fleet by the high rising "rooster tail" of water jetting behind each craft. Star Line's Hydro-jet ferries, like the other two ferry services, makes the trip between island and mainland in less than 20 minutes. The boats feature a glass enclosed lower deck and two upper level, open air observation decks. The Star Line is headquartered in St. Ignace with two docks there and one in Mackinaw City. Service runs from early May through late October.

Major Harbors

As the Great Lakes State, Michigan is committed to boater safety and in providing the facilities that boaters need in navigating the waters surrounding our beautiful state. The Michigan Department of Natural Resources (DNR) regulates the state's 73 protective harbors and public marinas including 18 in Northwest Michigan. The DNR's goal is to maintain a network of harbors along the state shorelines so that no boater will ever be more than 15 shoreline miles away from a safe harbor. The harbors rely on VHF-FM radio communication with Channel 16 (156.8 MHz) being the primary monitoring, distress and calling channel. Channel 9 (156.45 MHz) is the working channel for general communication and navigational assistance between boaters and the harbor. Channel 22 (157.1 MHz) is the U.S. Coast Guard's working channel. Fees are

INSIDERS' TIP

It's wise to give Mackinac Island's horses a wide berth. Bicycling too close or running haphazardly nearby can frighten them and cause accidents. Ample space also helps you avoid a personal encounter with the horses' more unpleasant by-products!

based on the size of the craft but generally range from $16.75 to $70.20 per day with transient docking usually limited to seven consecutive days. Advance reservations are not allowed. The Michigan Harbors Guide, a comprehensive annual listing of the state's harbors, marina facilities and regulations is available from the Michigan Department of Natural Resources, Parks and Recreation Division, P.O. Box 30257, Lansing, MI 48909, (517) 373-9900.

Grand Traverse

Duncan L. Clinch Park Marina
Traverse City • (616) 922-4903, (616) 922-4910 off season

The Duncan L. Clinch Marina sits in the heart of downtown Traverse City, surrounded by Clinch Park Beach, Clinch Park Zoo, the Open Space and beautiful West Grand Traverse Bay. Approximately 40 of the marina's 102 slips are available for transient use. The harbor can accommodate craft up to 60 feet long, and provides facilities for laundry, restrooms, showers, fuel, electricity, holding tank pump-out and public launch. Due to its central Traverse City location, the Clinch Marina fills up quickly during the summer peak. The best days to arrive are Wednesdays and Thursdays, and remember to bring your boat because slips will only be rented if your boat is in the water and ready to be docked. A harbormaster is on site, hours are 8 AM to 6 PM mid-May through mid-October, and extended hours of 6 AM to 9 PM mid-June through Labor Day.

Elmwood Township Harbor
Greilickville • (616) 946-5463, (616) 946-0921 off season

One mile northwest of Traverse City, Elmwood Township Harbor overlooks West Grand Traverse Bay and northern Michigan's magnificent sunrises. Transient dockage is available if seasonal slips are vacant. Restrooms, showers. Holding tank pump-out and a launch ramp are on site. Elmwood Township Park and Beach share the adjacent shoreline and offer a relaxing area for families to picnic, lounge or play. Harbormaster hours are 7 AM to 9 PM from May 1 through November 1.

Leland Township Harbor
Leland • (616) 256-9132, (616) 256-9535 off season

The Leland Township Harbor overlooks Lake Michigan and the historic Fishtown area in a setting reminiscent of the century's early seafaring villages. All 40 of harbor's slips are designated for transient dockage and, since it is designated as a "harbor of refuge," no boater will be turned away. Facilities include fuel, electricity, restrooms, showers, holding tank pump-out and a launch ramp. The docks lie just behind Leland's charming downtown with restaurants and shopping just steps away. The harbormaster is on duty 7 AM to 6 PM from May 1 through mid-October, and 6:30 AM to 9:30 AM between mid-June and Labor Day.

G. Marsten Dame Marina
Northport • (616) 386-5411, (616) 386-5182 off season

G. Marsten Dame Marina sits on the tip of the Leelanau Peninsula near downtown Northport. Fifty of the marina's 100 slips are designated for transient use in addition to two breakwalls, measuring 150 and 50 yards. This is a harbor of refuge, so all boaters will be allowed to dock. In case all of the slips and the breakwalls are full, rafts are set up to tie down additional boats. On-site facilities include fuel, electricity, restrooms, showers, cable TV hookup, holding tank pump-out and a launch ramp. The Marina is within easy walking distance of the Northport shopping area and its quaint village neighborhoods. Harbormaster hours are 7 AM to 9 PM daily from mid-May through the end of October.

Suttons Bay Municipal Marina
Suttons Bay • (616) 271-6703, (616) 271-3051 off season

The Suttons Bay Municipal Marina is next to one of the peninsula's nicest public beaches and parks, adding to the scenic ambiance that Suttons Bay shares with its many boating friends. Only 25 of the marina's 150 slips are designated for transient use, so it's wise to plan to arrive early. The shallowness of this harbor limits its use to smaller boats. Deep draft sailboats are cautioned not to try docking since the 7-foot water is insufficient for their use. Facilities provide for gasoline, restrooms, showers, electricity and a launch ramp. Suttons Bay's downtown area surrounds the marina, beach and park, so restaurants, shopping and a wonderfully old-fashioned theater are just a few steps away. The harbormaster is on duty from mid-May through mid-October from 8 AM to 8 PM.

Edward C. Grace Memorial Harbor
Elk Rapids • (616) 264-8174, (800) 235-5267, (616) 264-9274 off season

Also known locally as the Elk Rapids Marina, the Edward C. Grace Memorial Harbor is 20 minutes north of Traverse City on West Grand Traverse Bay. Its 213 slips include at least 35 that are set aside for transient dockage. On-site facilities include electricity, fuel, restrooms, showers, holding tank pump-out and a launch ramp. The marina is off River Street near Elk Rapids' unique downtown and slightly away from the usual tourist trail north. The season in Elk Rapids runs from mid-May through mid-October with a harbormaster on duty from 8 AM to 6 PM all season, extending to 8 AM to 9 PM between mid-May and Labor Day.

Lake Michigan Shoreline and Cadillac

Frankfort Municipal Marina
412 Main St., Frankfort • (616) 352-9051, (616) 352-7117 off season

Four marinas welcome Lake Michigan boaters into Frankfort. Another two marinas provide docking service across the harbor in Elberta. To enter the Frankfort harbor, boats pass two piers into an easily navigable channel. A harbormaster is on duty between 6:30 AM until 9 PM from early May until mid-October. Radio channels 16 and 9 are monitored for navigational assistance.

Frankfort Municipal Marina features 40 transient slips and 29 seasonal slips. Onshore facilities include electricity, water, restrooms, showers, holding tank pump-out and a fish-cleaning station. Fuel and ice are also available. Restaurants, laundry facilities, groceries and shopping are all only a stone's throw from the docks.

Manistee Municipal Marina
480 River St., Manistee • (616) 723-1552, (616) 723-2558 off season

The Manistee River Channel provides access to a 36-slip docking facility situated along the Manistee Riverwalk in this historic port town. Additional parallel tie-ups are available along the walkway. Radio channels 16 and 9 are monitored for navigational assistance. You will find a harbormaster on duty daily between 6 AM and 10 PM from early May until early October. Fuel, water and ice, electricity, restrooms, showers and a holding tank pump-out are available. Dining, shopping and land transportation are available one block from the docks.

Ludington Municipal Marina
201 S. William St., Ludington • (616) 843-9611, (616) 845-6237 off season

As it has for decades, the 55-foot Ludington lighthouse guides boaters safely to its harbor. Radio channels 16 and 9 are monitored to provide boaters navigational information. Once in harbor, boaters can anchor at the Ludington Municipal Marina. The marina features 158 transient and seasonal slips. Fuel, water and ice, electricity, restrooms, showers, a holding tank pump-out, laundry facilities and public telephones are available. To help boaters unwind or weather storms, the marina offers cable television hookup, a day room, a picnic area and gazebo. Ludington's commercial district is one block north of the marina.

Little Traverse

Charlevoix City Marina
408 Bridge St., Charlevoix • (616) 547-3272, (616) 547-3270 off season

Coming in from Lake Michigan you must pass under the Charlevoix drawbridge at the mouth of the entrance channel. Between 6 AM and 10 PM, the bridge opens on the hour and the half hour to allow boats passage. During night hours, the draw bridge opens in response to one long and one short horn blast. Charlevoix City Marina offers 11 seasonal and 32 transient slips. Only radio channel 9 is monitored to provide navigational assistance. A harbormaster is on duty daily between 8 AM and 8 PM, May through September. Fuel, water, electricity, restrooms, showers, a pump-out, long-term parking, a launch ramp and a two-hour shopping dock are available and bike and car rentals are available nearby.

The Charlevoix harbor provides docking for both private and public entities. The U.S. Coast Guard ice cutter, *Acacia*, docks here. Tours of the Great Lakes ship are offered to the public on special occasions. At docks near the city marina, you can also catch a ferry to Beaver Island. The Beaver Island Boat Company provides ferry service from early spring through autumn. Round-trip fees are $30 for adults and $15 for children five to 12 years of age. There is no charge for children younger than five. For departure times, call the ferry company at (616) 547-2311.

Petoskey Municipal Marina
100 W. Lake St., Petoskey
• (616) 347-6691, (616) 347-2500 off season

Boaters easily identify their Petoskey Harbor destination when they come within sight of the breakwater. The Petoskey Municipal Marina harbormaster is on duty daily between 6 AM until 10 PM, from May 7 until Labor Day. Radio channels 16 and 68 are monitored for navigational assistance and communications. Half of the marina's 100 slips are dedicated for transient dockage. Fuel, water, ice, electricity, laundry and restroom facilities are available at the marina. Along Petoskey's Bay Front Park, boaters are able to enter the downtown area through a lighted tunnel accessed from the park.

Mackinac Straits

Mackinac Island Marina
Mackinac Island • (906) 847-3561, (906) 627-9011 off season

Like the island itself, the Mackinac Island Marina has one of the most picturesque and historic settings in the Midwest. It sits across from Marquette Park at the base of Fort Mackinac, adjacent to the downtown district on the west and a Victorian residential area to the east. This is one of the busiest harbors in the state, and, due to its overwhelming popularity, stays are limited to four consecutive days. The busiest times are the second and third weekends in July when almost 300 boats descend on the island for the Chicago to Mackinac and Port Huron to Mackinac races. All slips are saved for racers those weekends. With the exception of the two race weekends, there are at least 75 transient slips available in the harbor or along its breakwall. Marina officials recommend arriving early in the day. Boaters who arrive and place their names on the daily waiting list by 8 AM will almost always get a slip within a few hours. On-site facilities include electricity, showers, restrooms and holding tank pump-out. The harbormaster hours coincide with the ferry schedules, running 8 AM to 9 PM during July and August, and 8 AM to 5 PM during the rest of the time between mid-May and mid-October.

Rental Cars

To really see Northwest Michigan, you need access to a car (with the exception of Mackinac Island. The four major rental car agencies are represented at Cherry Capital Airport in Traverse City while Avis and Hertz are at the Pellston Airport. Listed below are the major agencies, their local airport telephone numbers as well as the national 800 numbers for each. Independent rentals are also available at selected gas stations, auto dealerships and small agencies throughout the region. We've listed a few examples of these below, as well, but recommend a quick check with the local yellow pages for further options.

Airport Rental Services:

Avis, (616) 946-1222 in Traverse City; (616) 539-8302 in Pellston; (800) 831-2847.

Budget, (616) 947-3883 in Traverse City; (800) 527-0700.

Hertz, (616) 946-7051 in Traverse City; (616) 539-8404 in Pellston; (800) 654-3131.

National, (616) 947-1560 in Traverse City; (800) 227-7368.

Alternate Rental Services:

Enterprise, (616) 933-7000 in Traverse City; (800) RENT A CAR.

Rent A Wreck, (616) 946-2012 in Traverse City; (800) 535-1391.

Thrifty, (616) 935-3600 in Traverse City; (800) 367-2277.

Taxis and Limos

There are a limited number of taxi and limousine services available in the larger cities of Northwest Michigan. If you will be relying only on these services, please remember that the local fleet of vehicles is much smaller than in urban centers, and that travel and response time may take a bit longer than at home and plan accordingly.

Grand Traverse

Classy Cabs
Traverse City • (616) 929-1999, (616) 929-7433

Classy Cabs promises dependable, reliable and courteous service with its 24-hour taxi service. Based at Cherry Capital Airport, Classy Cabs will drive anywhere in the state. Rates start at $2.75 for the first mile and $1.50 per mile after that.

Grand Traverse Limousine Service
Elk Rapids • (616) 946-LIMO, (616) 264-6116, (800) 350-4502

Grand Traverse Limousine Service offers limousine or sedan service for sightseeing tours, airport transportation, shopping expeditions and special occasions. The service runs 24 hours per day and offers hourly and flat rates. Major credit cards are accepted.

T.C. Cabs
Traverse City • (616) 941-TAXI, (888) 298-8294

Based at Cherry Capital Airport, T.C. Cabs provides 24-hour taxi service and airport shuttles. Rates are $2.70 for the first mile and $1.50 for each mile after. Drivers say that they will drive anywhere, and charge a variety of flat rates for transportation to out-of-state towns. T.C. Cabs will accept major credit cards.

Lake Michigan Shoreline and Cadillac

S.L. Haner Taxi and Parcel
(616) 723-7607

Haner Taxi operates 24 hours for pre-booked rides. Otherwise, hours of operation are from 8 AM until midnight. Fees within the city are a flat $4. Outside of Manistee, the rate is 90¢ per mile. Haner Taxi provides service to and from airports, including Detroit Metropolitan Airport. Commercial and residential parcel delivery service is also available.

Radio Cab
805 S. Madison St., Ludington
• (616) 843-2545

Radio Cab's three-car fleet offers 24-hour service to any destination, 365 days a year. Aiming to take good care of area tourists, drivers offer information regarding local attractions. Fares for destinations within the city of Ludington are a flat $3.50. Fares extending beyond city limits are $1.25 per mile. The company also offers a package delivery service. Credit cards are not accepted.

Little Traverse

Friendship Center Transit
453 E. Lake St., Petoskey
• (616) 347-3211

This demand-response transportation gives priority to seniors and handicapped individuals, although anyone may use the system. Busses run from 9 AM to 4:30 PM, Monday through Friday. One-way fares for seniors and handicapped persons are 75¢ within Petoskey and $1.50 for runs outside city limits. Regular fares are $1.50 within city limits and $3 beyond city borders. Transportation is

INSIDERS' TIP

Transportation and rental schedules can vary dramatically with the season. As a rule of thumb, the summer's peak runs from mid-June through late August. Other busy times include the winter ski season from Christmas until early March, and the fall color season from mid-September through October.

Snowmobiling is a popular way to get around in Northwest Michigan.

limited to sites within Emmet County. Same-day service is usually available, however, it's best if you make reservations one day in advance.

Charlevoix Taxi
306 Nettleton St., Charlevoix
• **(616) 547-6129**

Charlevoix Taxi company operates 24 hours a day and charges a flat rate of $5 for in-town destinations. Airport shuttle rates and package delivery rates vary. Credit cards are not accepted.

Petoskey Cab Service
6150 Indian Garden Rd., Petoskey
• **(616) 347-8755**

Petoskey Cab Service will take you any-where you want to go. The company operates from 7 AM until 5 PM and evenings by appointment. In addition to passenger service, Petoskey Cab offers package delivery. Rates for both services are subject to change. Credit cards are not accepted.

Sun Cab Service
3217 Heydey St., Conway
• **(616) 357-3040**

Providing service in the Petoskey area, Sun Cab operates 24 hours a day. The flat rate for in-city transportation is $3.50. Beyond city limits, rates are an additional $1 per mile. Upon special request, Sun Cab provides service to destinations anywhere within a 300-mile radius of Petoskey. Credit cards are not accepted.

INSIDERS' TIP

Where do all the horses go? Cooler weather signals a winter vacation for hundreds of Mackinac Island's working horses. Most are transported — via Arnold's ferry — off the island to spend their winter break lounging at farms in the upper peninsula.

Sunshine Enterprises Limousine
59 Knollwood Dr., Harbor Springs
- **(616) 526-3904**

Providing special transportation 24 hours a day, Sunshine Enterprises Limousine company prides itself on providing friendly service. Reservations are encouraged, but not required. The company's two vehicles are typically engaged for weddings, parties and casino trips. Rates are $65 per hour. Special rates are sometimes available for airport shuttles. Credit cards are accepted only on a limited basis.

Mackinac Straits

Wolverine Stages
Pellston • (616) 539-8635

Based at the Pellston Regional Airport, Wolverine Taxi Service frequently travels between the airport and the Mackinac City ferry docks just 15 miles away. Costs for a one-way trip to the docks are $20 for adults, $10 for children ages 6 to 11 and free for those younger than five.

Carriage Tours — Taxi Service
Market St., Mackinac Island
- **(906) 847-3323**

These taxis are powered by true horsepower! Operating 365 days per year, the taxi service arm of Mackinac Island Carriage Tours transports visitors via horse and buggy around the clock. The taxi stand is between Martha's Sweet Shop and Mighty Mac Hamburgers on the island's bustling Huron Street. Just stop by and use the mounted phone to call for service or telephone from any of the area hotels

and a driver with his four-legged friends will be on hand in minutes. The largest cab carries 12 people. Costs range from $3 to $22 per person depending on the destination.

Mass Transportation

Knowing you're far from the maddening crowd is part of the pleasure of visiting and living in Northwest Michigan. Yet, the wide countryside presents local communities with some challenges in their efforts to provide public transportation. Many of the areas solve the problem by operating demand-response transportation systems. Commonly known as dial-a-ride buses, demand-response systems exist in Antrim, Grand Traverse, Charlevoix, Manistee, Mason and Wexford counties. There's no waiting in the rain or subzero temperatures with demand-response transportation. You catch your ride by calling a local dispatch number. Like a taxi, the vehicle comes to your door and drops you off at your destination. Most county systems operate only on weekdays. All offer discount rates to seniors, students and handicapped individuals. Additional mass transportation is provided on a regional basis by:

Northwest Regional Transportation — The Ride
3233 Cass Rd., Traverse City
- **(888) 228-7743**

The Ride is a transportation collaboration between five area companies to offer broad service to a six-county region. Participating counties include Grand Traverse, Leelanau, Benzie, Antrim, Kalkaska and Charlevoix. Three commuter routes to and from Traverse City

---

INSIDERS' TIP

Welcome to Main Street, U.S.A.! Many small communities refer to their busiest street as Main Street regardless of its actual name — or the name that appears on maps. For reference, Main Street should be translated to the following: Front Street in Traverse City, Mitchell Street in Petoskey, Mitchell Street in Cadillac, Bridge Street in Charlevoix, River Street in Manistee, Ludington Avenue in Ludington, St. Joseph Avenue in Suttons Bay, State Street in St. Ignace, Huron Street in Mackinaw City, and Huron Street on Mackinac Island. In Leland and Harbor Springs it really is Main Street.

are operated on Mondays through Fridays. These include a U.S. Highway 31 N. route through Charlevoix, Horton Bay, Elk Rapids and neighboring communities; a U.S. Highway 131 route through Mancelona and Kalkaska; and, a U.S. Highway 31 S. route through Frankfort and other Benzie and Leelanau communities. Cost for the commuter service ranges between $1.50 to $3 depending on the distance traveled. Riders can call ahead or simply flag down a bus at a community stop or anywhere along the route. Maps are available at each stop, from local chambers of commerce or by calling The Ride phone number. In addition to the commuter service, five health vans provide wheelchair accessible transportation to physician offices and medical facilities throughout the same six-county area. For health van service, please call the dispatcher phone listed above by 1 PM on the day before service is needed. The health vans also operate on Mondays through Fridays. Both services run from 6:30 AM to 7 PM.

Grand Traverse

BATA
3233 Cass Rd., Traverse City
• **(616) 941-2324, (800) 443-8989, (616) 941-8705 TDD**

BATA, formerly known as the Bay Area Transportation Authority, provides shuttle bus transportation throughout Grand Traverse and Leelanau counties' 600-square-mile service area with a cadre of white minibuses sporting bright blue trim. On weekdays between 6 AM and 6 PM, you can call BATA from anywhere within Leelanau county or the northern half of Grand Traverse county and a bus will transport you from your curbside to your destination. The BATA WAVE offers curbside service within Traverse City on weekdays and Saturdays as well as a continuous shuttle between the city's major shopping areas with automatic stops at the Grand Traverse Mall, Cherryland Mall, Downtown and Meijers. If you're unsure

about directions or destinations, don't hesitate to ask. The BATA dispatchers and drivers are known for their courtesy and assistance. BATA also operates an old fashioned trolley that is brought out, periodically, for community events as well as private parties and weddings. Don't be surprised to see the BATA trolley pass through town on a sunny Saturday filled with a bevy of bridal attendants along with bride, groom and a veil flowing out the back window.

Antrim County Transportation (ACT)
4700 Scenic Hwy., Bellaire
• **(616) 533-8644 Bellaire, (616) 587-9562 Mancelona, (616) 264-5005 Traverse City, Elk Rapids**

Antrim County Transportation, also known as ACT, offers Dial-A-Ride transportation to the rural and summer communities in Antrim County including Bellaire, Elk Rapids, Alden, Eastport, Ellsworth and Mancelona. If you need a ride, call the dispatcher at least one hour ahead of time with specific details as to your pickup location, your destination and the time you must arrive. Advance reservations are encouraged and can be made the day before you need your ride. ACT is busiest during the peak times before 9:30 AM and after 2 PM. If you can plan your travels during off-peak hours, the ride is bound to be less crowded and more relaxed.

Lake Michigan Shoreline and Cadillac

Manistee County Transportation
180 Memorial Dr., Manistee
• **(616) 723-6525**

Manistee County Transportation operates demand-response buses weekdays from 7 AM until 6 PM. Regular fares for city runs are $1. For destinations outside Manistee city limits, the regular fare is $2. If you have an appoint-

INSIDERS' TIP

In the Mackinac Straits, you can watch the sun rise over one Great Lake and set over another.

ment you must meet, call the bus service two hours in advance, otherwise, 30 minutes is usually adequate. For out-county runs, call one day in advance.

Ludington Mass Transit
410 E. Dowland St., Ludington
• **(616) 845-6218**
Ludington Mass Transit operates between 6:30 AM and 5:30 PM, Monday through Friday. Saturday hours are 8 AM until 3:30 PM. Transportation is limited to destinations within the city limits and Scottville. Regular fares within the city are $1. Regular fares to Scottville are $1.50. Call for dial-a-ride service at least 30 minutes in advance for Ludington destinations. Call early in the day to check times for Scottville runs.

Cadillac Wexford Transit Authority
1202 N. Mitchell St., Cadillac
• **(616) 779-0123**
Cadillac Wexford Transit Authority (CWTA) operates between 6 AM and 6 PM Monday through Thursday and until 7 PM on Fridays. Buses provide county-wide service on demand. If you're using the system on a regular basis for one to seven days, rides can be scheduled in advance. Otherwise, try to request a ride one hour in advance of the time you need to arrive at your destination. Wheelchair lifts are available if you notify the dispatcher. City rates are $1 for anyone older than 12. For children 5 to 12 rates are 50¢. CWTA also offers package delivery within the Cadillac city limits for $2 per package. Out-county deliveries are $3 per package.

Little Traverse

Charlevoix County Transit
1050 Brockway St., Boyne City
• **(616) 582-6900**
Charlevoix County Transit is based in Boyne City. Buses traverse the county between 6 AM and 6 PM, Monday through Friday. Regular fares for within the towns of Charlevoix, Boyne City and East Jordan are 80¢. Trips between Boyne City and Charlevoix are $1.60. Regular fares for trips between East Jordan and Charlevoix are $1.20. It is suggested you

call 24 hours in advance for service. Otherwise, drivers work you into the schedule as best they can.

Mackinac Straits

Mackinac Island Carriage Tours
Huron St., Mackinac Island
• **(906) 847-3325**
When motorized vehicles are prohibited, the bus is often a horse-drawn surrey complete with fringe on the top. Mackinac Island Carriage Tours has been transporting visitors since 1948 with a fleet of 75 horse-drawn vehicles and more than 300 horses. Drivers entertain their passengers with historical highlights and local trivia as they travel by the island's many historic and natural points of interest. Services include large guided tours, taxi service and private livery tours. The outdoor ticket office is on Huron Street right next to the Chamber of Commerce. Tour fares average $12.50 to $15 per adult and $6 for children younger than 12. Credit cards are accepted.

Bicycles, Trails and Walkways

The region is filled with hike-and-bike trails weaving through communities, downtowns and parks. Most easily accommodate walkers as well as bikers or in-line skaters who use the paths as a healthy alternative to rush-hour traffic jams.

Grand Traverse

Bay Bikes
Traverse City
Don't laugh when you see a bright, cherry-red bike pass by. It's part of the fleet of Bay Bikes that are available, for free, to anyone who wants temporary two-wheeled transportation. Bay Bikes was the brainchild of several community bikers who sought to recycle rather than destroy their cadre of old ten-speeds, while also promoting city biking. The idea caught on with donors and bike shops, and soon there were dozens of Bay Bikes on the

streets. To use one, simply take it, use it and leave it in a public place for the next rider. The best places to try to find Bay Bikes are near the Open Space or the downtown alleys between Union and Park Streets. With every inch of the cycle — tires, spokes, handle bars and frame — painted cherry red, they are hard to miss!

TART Trail
Traverse City

The Traverse Area Recreation Trail, known as the TART trail, stretches from the west side of Traverse City along the West Bay shoreline, through Clinch Park and adjacent to the downtown shopping areas before continuing southeast toward Acme, the State Park and the hotel zone. Bike racks are off the trail near downtown and the beach areas along Grandview Parkway. During the peak summer months and festival weeks, it's often faster and far more fun to bypass the traffic congestion and peddle from spot to spot. Complimentary TART Trail maps are available at the Traverse City Convention and Visitors Center, local bike shops, and many hotels and stores.

Lake Michigan Shoreline and Cadillac

Keith McKellop Walkway/Lake Cadillac Bike Path
Cadillac

From dawn until dusk and sometimes beneath a starry sky, you'll find walkers, joggers and in-line skaters enjoying the day along the Keith McKellop Walkway. Lighted by Victorian lamps, the paved pathway hugs the grassy shores of Lake Cadillac. Follow the pathway and you'll cross a charming wooden walking bridge over the mouth of the Clam River. You'll

pass a playground, boat launch and the community dock. Adjacent to Cadillac's shopping district, the pathway finally leads you to the Rotary Performing Arts Pavilion at the city's lakefront park where you can catch free jazz concerts every Thursday night throughout the summer. The pathway connects to the Lake Cadillac Bike Path, enabling you to circle beautiful Lake Cadillac, a 7.5 mile jaunt for walkers, bikers, joggers and skaters.

Manistee Riverwalk
Manistee

Stretching along the picturesque banks of the Manistee River in Manistee's historic business district, the wooden pedestrian path offers 1.5 miles of scenic opportunities for walkers and joggers. It begins behind the Manistee Chamber of Commerce building at Cypress Street and follows the river to Lake Michigan, ending at the First Street Beach. Along the way, you may spot swans, ducks and an occasional beaver or otter. You'll travel adjacent to the Manistee Marina where you can admire docked vessels or watch freighters pass by. Victorian lighting makes evening use possible.

Little Traverse

Little Traverse Wheelway
Petoskey/Harbor Springs

A state-designated bike trail, this 10-mile pathway consists of a series city and county roads and 3 miles of paved bike trails. It links Petoskey, along the southern coast of Little Traverse Bay and Harbor Springs, along the bay's northern shores. The pathway begins at the bay front park in Petoskey, travels through the Bay View Association community where connecting roads link the path to Michigan Highway 119. From there, it travels to Beach Road, east of Harbor Springs. Plans are to

INSIDERS' TIP

Child safety is an important issue with Cadillac Wexford Transit Authority. Employees are members of the Michigan Community Child Watch program. Program volunteers are trained to observe, remember and record all situations that could be labeled suspicious. Any questionable incident is reported to police.

Photo: Mackinac Island Chamber of Commerce

Close to 600 horses are stabled on Mackinac Island each summer, providing the main source of transportation for freight, taxis, tours and recreation.

The Bridge That Could

They called it the bridge that could never be built. But, today the stunning Mackinac Bridge majestically spans the Straits of Mackinac linking Michigan's upper and lower peninsulas as it has for more than four decades.

Nicknamed "Mighty Mac," the bridge spans 5 miles, making it the world's longest suspension bridge. More importantly, the bridge connects what once was two separate halves of a single state.

Passage between the peninsulas had previously been accomplished via ferry boats transporting cars and passengers between Mackinaw City and St. Ignace. This created bottlenecks for travelers, who could see their destination across the Straits, but often had to wait for hours to get across. Photos from the 1940s and early 1950s show endless strings of cars waiting to board the next ferry. Lines during the autumn hunting season reportedly stretched 23 miles.

Although talk of a bridge began as early as 1884, serious consideration didn't begin in earnest until the 1930s. Initial engineering planning was undertaken while debate raged within the state over whether a bridge should, or even could, be built. The United States' entry into World War II shelved bridge plans for a decade until renewed efforts put the project permanently on track in 1950. Construction began in early 1954, and the first car crossed the completed bridge on November 1, 1957.

Completion was no small feat. Engineers had to account for the significant depth of the waters, unusual geological formations, weather conditions and the sheer breadth of the span. This was accomplished by Dr. David B. Steinman (1887-1961), who considered the Mackinac Bridge the crowning achievement of his career as a bridge designer and engineer. Steinman developed a design that stressed aerodynamic stability by incorporating wide-open spaces between the roadway and the stiffening trusses with an open space down the center and an open grid on the inner two lanes. This design allows the bridge to remain absolutely stable against oscillations, regardless of the wind's velocity and direction. The bridge may bow or swing out as much as 20 feet on windy days, while the towers may move as much as 18 feet north or south depending on the number and weight of cars along the bridge.

All piers rest on bedrock, with 33 marine foundations supporting 4 miles of uninterrupted steel superstructure. The total bridge length, including approaches, is 26,372 feet. Two huge tower foundations are anchored 200 feet below water and rise 552 feet above water. There is a 3,800 foot span between the main towers, with 8,344 feet from cable anchorage to cable anchorage. The main cable consists of more than 42,000 miles of wire, while the rest of the bridge is made from a million tons of steel and concrete and 6 million rivets and bolts.

Boats, barges and ships transporting and supporting thousands of men, materials and machinery allowed much of the structure, including the two tower foundations, to be built from the water. During construction, approximately 350 engineers and 3,500 laborers worked on the project, with an additional 7,500 working at quarries, shops and mills. The final price tag was $96 million. If the bridge were built today it would cost $400 million.

Several books and photo displays document the construction of the bridge. Our favorite, *Mighty Mac, The Official Picture History of The Mackinac Bridge*, was written by Lawrence Rubin, Executive Secretary of the Mackinac Bridge Authority from 1950 to

— continued on next page

Photo: Linda Norris

The Mackinac Bridge — nicknamed Mighty Mac — stretches 5 miles across the Straits of Mackinac, linking Michigan's upper and lower peninsulas.

1983. He was responsible for the day-to-day operation of the bridge during much of its first three decades. The book is filled with a sampling from more than 3,000 original black and white photos documenting every stage of the bridge's construction.

To learn more about this engineering wonder, visit the Mackinac Bridge Museum on the second floor of Mama Mia's Pizza in downtown Mackinaw City. This free museum was built by a former ironworker who worked on the bridge. The museum houses memorabilia, including construction tools, photos, film footage and a ceiling full of hard hats worn by the workers. (See our Attractions chapter for more information on the museum.) You can also stop by the welcome center next to the Mackinac Bridge in St. Ignace where a model of the bridge, stretching almost the entire length of one wall, is on display.

extend the Wheelway to Charlevoix, making it a 30-mile biking system.

Mackinac Straits

Mackinac Island

On Mackinac Island, bicycles are the primary mode of transportation. Paths line the 8-mile island perimeter and crisscross the island interior. Locals estimate that at least 2,500 bikes share the roads with the horses on most days during the summer's peak season. Due to the high density of two- wheeled and four-legged traffic on the island, bikers should always follow the safety rules of the road and remember to yield to pedestrians and horses. Biking maps abound on Mackinac Island. Each bicycle livery has their own version with associated sightseeing tips, as do several fudge shops and the Chamber of Commerce. An excellent signage system, maintained by the Michigan State Parks directs bikers and hikers along their way. Rentals for single-speed, multispeed and tandem bikes are available from several bicycle liveries along Huron Street, although seasoned visitors often opt to bring their own cycles with them on the ferries. Bikers with young children might want to rent attachable buggies or mini-tandems designed for one adult and one small child. Rental shops traditionally require a $20 to $30 deposit, which is used toward your hourly fees. Rates average $4 to $7 per hour depending on bike type. Reservations are only accepted for large groups of 15 or more.

Iroquois Bike Rental
Mackinac Island • (906) 847-3321
At Iroquois Bike Rental next to the Shepler Dock you can choose from 100 quality bikes.

Island Bicycle Rentals
Mackinac Island • (906) 847-6288
Island Bicycle Rentals is the self-proclaimed Schwinn rental ship. Visitors can rent single-speed, tandem, 5-speed and 12-speed bicycles and 18-speed mountain bikes by the hour, day or week.

Lakeside/Streetside Bike Rentals
Mackinac Island • (906) 847-3351
Promising the best bike seats on the island, Lakeside/Streetside Bike Rentals offers a full range of bikes for children and adults as well as child carrier seats with helmets. The Lakeside rentals can be found at the end of the Arnold dock while the Streetside rentals sit next to the Taxi Stand on Huron Street.

Orr Kids Bikes
Mackinac Island • (906) 847-3211
Orr Kids Bikes caters to families with discounts and bikes to fit all ages. Adult and children's strollers are available, and Burley carts may be rented or purchased here.

Ryba's Bicycle Rental
Mackinac Island • (906) 847-6261
Ryba's has three Huron Street rental locations with stands at the Island House Hotel, next to the Chippewa Hotel and across from the Lakeview Hotel. Electric mobility carts are available here as well as Burley carts and strollers and single, tandem, three-speed and mountain bikes.

Horse and Carriage Rental

If you opt to drive your own horse on Mackinac Island, several liveries will rent saddle horses or horse and buggies. All of the liveries are within a short walk of downtown although the "drive your own" horses are not allowed on Huron and Market streets. Charges are hourly and will vary with size of buggy. All of the horses are well behaved and very used to strangers giving them directions. Just remember that four-legged creatures usually move at their own pace, much slower than the car generation is accustomed to! If you plan to rent during the summer peak, it's wise to do so early in the day before waits develop.

Chambers Riding Stable
Market St., Mackinac Island
• (906) 847-6231
At the corner of Market Street and Grand Avenue, Chambers Riding Stables rents saddle horses by the hour. Costs are $22 for the first hour and $20 for each additional hour. Children must be at least 9 years old to ride rental horses. A small pony ride entertains little ones.

Cindy's Riding Stable
Market St., Mackinac Island
• (906) 847-3572
Cindy's rents saddle horses by the hour from its stable on Market Street directly behind the Lilac Tree Hotel. Rentals are $22 for the first your and $20 per hour for additional hours. Saddle horses are recommended for children older than 9.

Jack's Livery Stable
Mahoney St., Mackinac Island
• (906) 847-3391
Horse and buggy rental is the specialty at Jack's Livery Stable, which offers carriages in two-, four- or six- passenger styles. You'll get a quick driving lesson before you take the reigns, but don't fear, the horses are dependable and probably know all of the island routes better than most humans. A quick word of caution, rented buggies are not allowed in the busy downtown areas along Market and Huron Streets. The staff at Jack's will provide maps and point out any restrictions. Carriages rentals range from $34 for the smallest to $50 for larger carriages.

Visitors Centers and Travel Information

Tourism is one of Michigan's top businesses, so we welcome guests with open arms and information aplenty! Visitors Centers dot the state map, providing a relaxing break on a road trip or a hometown welcome when you reach your destination. Some of the notable centers within our Northwestern Michigan boundaries are listed below, as well as a listing of the many local tourists bureaus and chambers of commerce that reside here. Across the board, staffers welcome inquiries and gladly share a wealth of travel tips.

Grand Traverse

Traverse City Area Chamber of Commerce, 202 E. Grandview Parkway, Traverse City, (616) 947-5075

Traverse City Convention & Visitors Bureau, 101 W. Grandview Parkway, Traverse City, (616) 947-1120, (800) TRA-VERS

Leelanau County Chamber of Commerce, 105 Philip Street (Mich. Highway 204), Lake Leelanau, (616) 256-9895

Elk Rapids Area Chamber of Commerce, 305 U.S. Highway 31, Elk Rapids, (616) 264-8202

Kalkaska Area Chamber of Commerce, 353 S. Cedar Street, Kalkaska, (616) 258-9103

Gaylord Area Convention and Tourism Bureau, 101 W. Main Street, Gaylord, (517) 732-6333, (800) 345-8621

Michigan Shoreline & Cadillac

Benzie Chamber of Commerce, U.S. Highway 31 and Mich. Highway 115, Benzonia, (616) 882-5801

Manistee Area Chamber of Commerce, 11 Cypress Street, Manistee, (616) 723-2575, (800) 288-2286

Ludington Area Chamber of Commerce, 5827 W. U.S. Highway 10, Ludington, (616) 845-0324

Cadillac Area Chamber of Commerce, 222 N. Lake Street, Cadillac, (616) 775-9776

Cadillac Area Visitors Bureau, 222 N. Lake Street, Cadillac, (616) 775-0657, (800) 22-LAKES

Lake City Chamber of Commerce, 229 S. Main, Lake City, (616) 839-4969

Little Traverse

East Jordan Chamber of Commerce, 118 N. Lake Street, East Jordan, (616) 536-7351

Charlevoix Chamber of Commerce, 406 Bridge Street, Charlevoix, (616) 547-2101

Petoskey-Harbor Springs-Boyne Country Visitors Bureau, 401 East Mitchell Street, Petoskey, (616) 348-2755, (800) 845-2828

Mackinac Straits

Mackinac Island Chamber of Commerce, P. O. Box 451, Mackinac Island, MI 49757, (906) 847-6418, (800) 4-LILACS

Mackinac State Historic Parks Visitors Center, Across from Marquette Park, Mackinac Island, (906) 847-3328

Mackinaw Area Tourist Bureau, 708 S. Huron, Mackinaw City, (616) 436-5574, (800) 666-0160

St. Ignace Area Tourist Association, 560 N. State Street, St. Ignace, (906) 643-8717, (800) 338-6660

Sandy shorelines,
wooded hills and
magnificent vistas are
not unusual up here,
and most inns share
their best views
and beaches with
their guests.

Hotels, Motels and Resorts

Hospitality is our business in Northwest Michigan and we're happy to roll out the welcome mat. Tourism plays a major role in our regional economy. Pair this with our gorgeous natural setting and many local diversions, and it's no surprise that we can offer you plenty of lodging options.

There are hundreds of hotels, motels and resorts scattered throughout Northwest Michigan. We've listed close to 100 below. They come in all shapes, sizes and budgets — much like our many diverse communities.

Our large resorts stand proudly alongside the top facilities in the Midwest. The Grand Traverse Resort, Grand Hotel, Shanty Creek, Homestead, Sugar Loaf, Crystal Mountain, Mission Point, McGuire's and Treetops/Sylvan are just a few of the major players. Many are homes to championship golf courses, award-winning restaurants, challenging ski slopes and unique shops. All share their scenic corners of the region with a full pallet of services and comforts to make your stay memorable.

Others like the Brookside Inn, Hotel Frankfort and Bayshore Resort offer intimate stays in romantic surroundings, while history is paramount at the Park Place Hotel, Perry Hotel and most hotels on Mackinac Island. Many more are simply memorable for comfortable surroundings, wonderful dining and topnotch hospitality.

Sandy shorelines, wooded hills and magnificent vistas are not unusual up here, and most inns share their best views and beaches with their guests. Enjoy them. They are the essence of Northwest Michigan.

We'd like to share a few general tips about local lodging. Northwest Michigan is a year-round vacation destination. The most popular times to visit are at the height of the summer months, traditionally mid-June through mid-August, followed by the Christmas holidays and the winter ski season of January and February. Things can also be quite busy during the height of our fall colors, usually during mid-October. Expect rates to be at their highest and rooms to be less available during these times. This also holds true for the days surrounding community celebrations, like Traverse City's National Cherry Festival. If you'd like to visit during those times — and we'd love to have you — try to make reservations as early as possible.

The hotels, motels and resorts listed are divided into the same geographical areas that we have been using throughout this book. You will see several dollar signs along with each listing ranging from a low of $65 or less to a high of more than $160. Rates reflect the average cost for a standard room for two adults on a summer weekend. These are general budgetary guidelines only, please contact each establishment directly for the most current rates and available accommodations.

Price Code

$	Less than $65
$$	$65 to $90
$$$	$90 to $125
$$$$	$125 to $160
$$$$$	$160 or more

Many chain hotels are available in our larger or more tourist-oriented communities, especially in Traverse City, Petoskey, Gaylord, Cadillac, Mackinaw City and St. Ignace. As a rule, we haven't listed them all but, instead, selected those whose location or amenities were significant in their communities.

You can take advantage of wonderful room rates and unique lodging and entertainment packages during the shoulder seasons in spring, winter and fall. With so many wonderful golf courses, early- and late-season golf packages are popular. Romantic getaways, leaf peeper specials, casino packages and ski weekends are other possibilities. By the way, don't limit your package shopping to those resorts that feature recreation on site. Many in-town hotels will also offer great packages that include greens fees, lift tickets, casino chips and even transportation to use them.

If you're a senior citizen or a member of AAA, AARP or another group that receives discounts on lodging or travel services, always ask if you qualify for any discounts.

Many of our best friends are animals, but pets aren't always welcome vacationers. As a rule of thumb, assume that the accommodations listed do not accept pets. If furry friends are welcome, we've made a note in the listing. We've also tried to attend to Fido's needs by listing a few options for pet boarding.

All hotels, motels and resorts are required to provide handicapped and nonsmoking facilities for their guests. If you have special needs, discuss them at the time you make reservations. There are several hotels that have made a commitment to being totally nonsmoking. If this is the case, we have identified them.

Most establishments will accept major credit cards such as Visa and MasterCard. A number will also accept American Express, the Discover Card and other cards. Please assume that all hotels, motels and resorts listed below will accept major credit cards unless otherwise noted. For specific acceptance policies, contact the establishment directly.

Grand Traverse

Traverse City Area

Bayshore Resort
$$$-$$$$ • 833 E. Front St., Traverse City • (616) 935-4400, (800) 634-4401

www.insiders.com
See this and many other **Insiders' Guide®** destinations online — in their entirety.
Visit us today!

Casual elegance and breathtaking views are the common themes carried throughout the lovely Bayshore Resort in the heart of Traverse City. Just east of downtown, the Bayshore sits along the West Grand Traverse Bay shoreline with 120 waterfront rooms. Accommodations are spacious, ranging from deluxe rooms to large suites. Many include private balconies and two-person spas. For special occasions, request a corner suite, which comes complete with spa, fireplace, wet bar and refrigerator.

This is a newer hotel, and the architecture and amenities reflect its recent entrance into the local lodging scene. Victorian-style furnishings and deep woods are coupled with soft teal and mauve accents for a comfortably classy ambiance. A fireplace adds cozy warmth to the lobby and nearby seating areas, while adjacent lobby windows overlook a bright indoor pool and whirlpool decked with hanging kites and cloud-like murals. A complimentary continental breakfast is served each morning in a spacious, private breakfast room.

The facility is totally smoke-free and has been since opening several years ago. Its 300-foot sandy beach has plenty of space for relaxing, or for playing with the water sport "toys" available for rent on site. The Bayshore is steps away from the TART recreational trail, city ten-

---

INSIDERS' TIP

Planning a trip to the Grand Traverse area? The Grand Traverse Area Convention and Visitors Bureau offers a centralized reservation service for its member hotels. Just call (800) TRAVERS.

Traverse City The Way You Like It!

Nothing comes close to Bayshore Resort . . . except our exclusive sugar-sand beach and the fascinating charm of downtown Traverse City, with its diverse dining, shopping, and nightlife.

Treat yourself and experience why you simply can't beat Bayshore Resort. Especially when you consider we offer 120 guest rooms, some with in-room spa, suites available with spa and fireplace, a heated indoor pool and whirlpool, a fully equipped fitness center, a game room, and a superb complimentary continental breakfast. And be sure to ask about our fantastic golf, ski, romance, and casino packages.

Bayshore Resort . . . no other resort comes close.

 and Senior Discounts

 Bayshore Resort is a smoke-free facility

Bayshore
RESORT
833 East Front Street
Traverse City, Michigan 49686
800-634-4401 ◆ 935-4400
www.bayshore-resort.com

nis courts are next door, and several eateries including Pepper's Grill (see Restaurant chapter) are just across the street. If you arrive in Traverse City via air, a complimentary shuttle to and from Cherry Capital Airport is available.

The Beach Condominiums
$$$$-$$$$$ • 1995 U.S. Hwy. 31 N., Traverse City • (616) 938-2228

The Beach Condominiums overlook beautiful East Grand Traverse Bay and a lovely stretch of sandy beachfront. Near Four Mile Road along the U.S. 31's Miracle Mile, the facility has 30 modern, two-bedroom condominium units available for daily rental. The condos comfortably sleep four people and include full kitchens, whirlpool baths, and cable television. If the bay waters look a little chilly, a heated outdoor pool and hot tub are always inviting.

Beach Haus Resort
$$$$ • 1489 U.S. Hwy. 31 N., Traverse City • (616) 947-3560

Bright fuchsia petunias overflow countless flower boxes adorning the outside of the Beach Haus Resort. We always know that summer is just around the corner when the Beach Haus planters are full!

An Alpen theme was used in building this hotel, which stands near the State Park along the East Grand Traverse Bay shore. Its 200-foot private beach is sandy and overlooks our scenic bay waters. There are 29 guest rooms available including some with spas and king-size beds. Other amenities include private beachfront patios, refrigerators, wet bars, microwaves, toasters, VCRs and HBO. A complimentary continental breakfast is served daily. The Beach Haus is closed in the winter.

Best Western Four Seasons
$$$-$$$$ • 305 Munson Ave., Traverse City • (616) 946-8424, (800) 823-7844

This Best Western Four Seasons is within easy walking distance of the Dennos Museum Center, Northwestern Michigan College and the Grand Traverse County Civic Center (see our Attractions chapter) at the base of Traverse City's Old Mission Peninsula. Several years ago, this facility combined the original Best Western property with its former next door

neighbor, the Shadowland Motel, to create a large, five-acre complex. The grounds are beautifully landscaped with an abundance of flowers, grass and mature trees. There are 111 guest rooms available ranging from standard to deluxe. Standard rooms, which are near the outdoor pool, include two double- or queen-size beds, in-room coffee and exterior doors. Deluxe and spa hot tub rooms include a refrigerator and microwave and are in the hotel's main building. Loft hot tub rooms are two-story deluxe suites with a queen-size bed, loveseat, refrigerator and microwave on the lower level and an upper-level hot tub, television and skylight. The Best Western's main building also houses an indoor pool, hot tub and continental-breakfast area. Casino and specialty packages are available.

Budgetel Inn
$$ • 2326 U.S. Hwy. 31 S., Traverse City • (616) 933-4454, (800) 968-4454

The Budgetel is ideally located for shopping enthusiasts. It is across the street from the Grand Traverse Mall while the Grand Traverse Crossing shopping complex, Sam's Club and Horizon Outlet Center (see our Shopping chapter) are close by. This newer hotel offers 121 moderately priced rooms with coffee makers, free local telephone calls, telephone data ports, cable television, in-room movies and video games. For additional space, leisure suites with refrigerators, microwaves and whirlpools are available. Three executive conference centers equipped with speakerphones are suitable for business needs. All guests can take advantage of the hotel's indoor pool, whirlpool spa and exercise room as well as a daily continental breakfast delivered directly to the room. A complimentary shuttle service transports guests to the mall or airport.

Comfort Inn By the Bay
$$$ • 1492 U.S. Hwy. 31 N., Traverse City • (616) 929-4423, (800) 228-5150

The recently renovated Comfort Inn is near the State Park on U.S. 31 North, east of Traverse City. East Grand Traverse Bay is just across the street. There are 96 guest rooms with double rooms, king rooms, connecting rooms, nonsmoking rooms and suites available. Some include whirlpools, refrigerators

Ellis Lake Resort

Our cozy log cabins are fully furnished & equipped with kitchen facilities. The cabins have their own yard with a private fire pit & grill. Some cabins have Franklin fire stoves.

Enjoy the many amenities of Ellis Lake Resort, whether it be fishing or canoeing the Lake, cross-country skiing or hiking the trails, or simply relaxing in the private outdoor hot tub under the stars.

For that romantic getaway or escape from reality, come...relax with us.

10 minutes south of Traverse City
$54 - $104 nightly,
$435 - $545 weekly

**8440 US-31 South - PO Box 275
Interlochen, MI 49643-0275**
616-276-9502   Fax 616-276-9553

and microwaves. All offer continental breakfast, free newspapers, free local calls, data port phones, cable television and in-room movies. Small pets are allowed. A 24-hour Clock restaurant is right next door and the TART recreational trail adjoins the property.

Days Inn & Suites
$$-$$$ • 420 Munson Ave., Traverse City • (616) 941-0208, (800) 9TC-DAYS

The Days Inn has been a long-standing institution in Traverse City. Many business people who have just transferred to the area often use the suites as temporary first homes. It's also a favorite family stop for getaway weekends with the kids. There are 182 guest units available ranging from spacious standard rooms to suites with separate living rooms, bedrooms, refrigerators and wet bars. Jacuzzi

suites with two-person spas are also an option. Guests are welcome to use the indoor pool, a large enclosed spa, the fitness room and meeting rooms. Continental breakfast is complimentary. The inn is centrally located one mile east of downtown, along a main thoroughfare, and close to East Bay Beach and the Dennos Museum Center (see our Attractions chapter). Family dining is available throughout the day at the Cottage Cafe on the same property.

Driftwood Motel
$$$ • 1861 U.S. Hwy. 31 N., Traverse City • (616) 938-1600

On the sandy beach along East Grand Traverse Bay, the Driftwood Motel is a reasonably priced facility offering clean rooms and family amenities. Each of the 39 rooms have

INSIDERS' TIP

Many Traverse City hotels lie along the "Miracle Mile," several miles of sugar-sand beach rimming East Grand Traverse Bay.

HBO, refrigerators and coffee makers. Microwaves are available. Other amenities include a large indoor pool, oversize spa and game room. Waterfront rooms feature outdoor patios or balconies while poolside rooms open directly into the pool area.

Fox Haus Motor Lodge

$$-$$$ • 704 Munson Ave., Traverse City • (616) 947-4450

The Fox Haus Motor Lodge has been owned and operated by the same family for decades. Alpen architecture clads this two-story facility, which offers 80 guest rooms and suites with in-room spas. Rooms for visitors traveling with pets are available. If you're planning a longer stay, ask for the chalet suites that have small kitchenettes. You will be able to relax in the heated swimming pool, sauna, exercise room or game room. The Fox Haus is on Traverse City's east side at the intersection of Airport Access and Munson Avenue. It is conveniently near Schelde's restaurant and a small shopping center.

Grand Beach Resort Hotel

$$$$$ • 1683 U.S. Hwy. 31 N., Traverse City • (616) 938-4455, (800) 968-1992

This is a beautiful hotel with a magnificent beach. The Grand Beach Hotel is a newer facility featuring bright, open architecture, lovely amenities and a great setting on East Grand Traverse Bay. There are 95 large guest rooms in a variety of layouts. All offer private balconies, refrigerators and HBO. A complimentary continental breakfast is served each morning in a pleasant community room. Additional amenities include an indoor pool, whirlpool spa, exercise room, guest laundry and a beautiful 300-foot beach of sugar sand, the plentiful, fine, clean sand that lines many of our bay shores. Meeting rooms are available for business travelers. The Grand Beach Resort is along the Miracle Mile, and is just a brief drive to any number of restaurants or area attractions.

Hampton Inn

$$$ • 1000 U.S. Hwy. 31 N., Traverse City • (616) 946-8900, (800) HAMPTON

The Hampton architecture doesn't deviate from its counterparts throughout the country. Features include expected Hampton amenities like complimentary continental breakfasts, in-room movies, an indoor swimming pool, an exercise room and business meeting rooms with catering and audiovisual services. Airport transportation is available. The Hampton has a great location for families. It is right next door to River Country Funland, across from the Traverse City State Park Beach and near several restaurants and attractions. There are 127 guest rooms available with 75 percent designated as nonsmoking.

Heritage Inn

$$$ • 417 Munson Ave., Traverse City • (616) 947-9520, (800) 968-0105

Friendly hospitality is shared at the Heritage Inn close to town on Munson Avenue. This bright, white motel is easily identified by the black silhouette of a horse and carriage mounted around the entrance. There are 39 guest rooms available with half featuring two-person, heart-shaped hot tubs. All rooms include VCRs and in-room movies. Other amenities include complimentary continental breakfasts, a game room, weight room and suntan bed. The Cottage Cafe and Mabel's Restaurant are right across the street, and the Dennos Museum Center and Grand Traverse County Civic Center are just a brisk walk away.

Holiday Inn

$$$$$ • 615 E. Front St., Traverse City • (616) 947-3700, (800) 888-8020

The Traverse City Holiday Inn sits in an ideal location along West Grand Traverse Bay. The TART recreational trail is steps away, stretching along a beautiful waterfront walk leading to Clinch Park Beach and Zoo, the

---

INSIDERS' TIP

Try traveling during shoulder seasons for reduced prices. Hotels often try to extend seasons in late fall and spring by offering generous room discounts or creative packages.

The Charm, The History, The Service.

All at the Historic
Park Place Hotel.
You can enjoy Victorian style with Contemporary Amenities.

Right in the Middle of Downtown Traverse City and overlooking Grand Traverse Bay.
We are in the center of everywhere you want to be.
Shopping • Dining
Year Round Recreation • Spectacular Views

Call for Reservations and Information at 800-748-0133
www.Park-Place-Hotel.com

Open Space and downtown shopping. The Boardman River flows into the bay waters next to the hotel, making it a favorite fishing haunt for locals and visitors. There are 179 guest rooms available as well as ample amenities and services like indoor and outdoor pools, a sauna, whirlpool, fitness center, game room, gift shop and boat rentals. On-site restaurants include the Bayside Patio Bar and Grill and Cygnet Bar and Grill. Shimmers Lounge is a popular stop with locals and visitors for live entertainment and dancing. Complete convention facilities are available for business gatherings. Pets are welcome. Shuttle service is provided to the airport and all other transportation centers

Knights Inn on the Bay
$$$ • 1941 U.S. Hwy. 31 N., Traverse City • (616) 938-1900, (800) 843-5644
The Knights Inn is the combination of two older establishments, the former Beachcomber Resort and adjacent Capri Motel, which have joined to offer 52 guest rooms at reasonable rates. The Knights Inn is on the Miracle Mile with a sandy 330-foot beach on East Grand Traverse Bay. Rooms include small kitchenettes with refrigerators, satellite television and HBO. Summer visitors can play in the outdoor heated pool and spa, or in the bay on Waverunners, paddleboards or pedal boats. Grills are along the beach picnic area. Snowmobile and Nordic trails just a short drive away are attractive to winter sports enthusiasts.

Main Street Inns, USA
$$$ • 618 E. Front St., Traverse City • (616) 929-0410, (800) 255-7180
Pets are welcome at Main Street Inns, USA close to downtown Traverse City. The inn has 95 guest rooms including two-room suites, Jacuzzi rooms, and rooms with kitchenettes. Pepper's Restaurant is next door, West Grand Traverse Bay is steps away, and downtown and the Clinch Park beach are just a short walk.

North Shore Inn
$$$$ • 2305 U.S. Hwy. 31 N., Traverse City • (616) 938-2365, (800) 938-2365

The North Shore Inn offers 26 luxury condominiums with one or two bedrooms. Accommodations sleep up to five adults and include full-size kitchens, VCRs, HBO and laundry facilities. A 200-foot beach and outdoor, heated swimming pool are also available.

Park Place Hotel
$$$$ • 300 E. State St., Traverse City • (616) 946-5000, (800) 748-0133

The historic Park Place Hotel stands as a central beacon in downtown Traverse City. The Park Place was built in 1873 as the Campbell House Hotel. It was later sold to lumber barons Perry Hannah and A. Tracy Lay who upgraded it to a world-class hotel. Over the decades, renovations have included the addition of towers, redecoration of the restaurants and refurbishing the rooms. The Park Place anchors downtown Traverse City from its central location just one block from Front Street and two blocks from West Bay. There are 140 guest rooms available with two suite arrangements. An indoor pool, sauna, hot tub and health club are available. Minerva's restaurant is on the main floor. Comprehensive meeting facilities and services are popular with local businesses and visiting conventioneers. Dining packages (combining meals and lodging) and recreation packages (combining lodging with skiing and golf) are available.

Pine Crest Motel
$$ • 360 Munson Ave., Traverse City • (616) 947-8900, (800) 223-4433

Friendly service is a hallmark of this modern, 35-room hotel. A favorite among business travelers, the Pine Crest offers various room options ranging from two double beds, queen- or king-size beds to water beds and spa rooms. Amenities include VCRs, HBO, an outdoor pool, an indoor exercise pool, a spa and a complimentary continental breakfast. The Pine Crest Motel is a very short walk away from the Grand Traverse County Civic Center, the Dennos Museum Center, Northwestern Michigan College and several restaurants and shops.

Pinestead Reef Resort
$$$$ • 1265 U.S. Hwy. 31 N., Traverse City • (616) 947-4010, (800) 968-1302

A 700-foot beach edges the lengthy Pinestead Reef Resort along East Grand Traverse Bay across from the Traverse City State Park. The water views are magnificent from almost any point at this resort. These suites are also timeshare units. Amenities include an indoor pool, whirlpool, sauna, barbecue deck, game room, guest laundry and water sports rentals. Rooms feature kitchens, cable television, Showtime and VCRs. The excellent Bay Winds Restaurant (see our Restaurants chapter) is adjacent to the Pinestead.

Pointes North Inn
$$$$ • 2211 U.S. Hwy. 31 N., Traverse City • (616) 938-9191, (800) 968-3422

Bright fuschia canopies mark the entrance doors to the Pointes North Inn along scenic East Bay. Each of the inn's 52 luxury suites overlook the Bay and the Inn's lovely beach. Rooms are quite spacious and feature distinctive furnishings, private balconies, a Jacuzzi, king- or queen-size beds, a sleeper sofa, microwave, refrigerator and VCR. An outdoor pool overlooks the water. Restaurants are a brief drive away.

Ranch Rudolf
$$ • 6841 Brown Bridge Rd., Traverse City • (616) 947-9529

For a moment, you may think that you made a wrong turn and ended up in the old West when you visit Ranch Rudolf. The entire facility was built to resemble a Western ranch. Rustic siding, wooden walks and hanging lanterns add to the ambiance, as do the trail horses that pass through a few times each day. Ranch Rudolf is tucked into the Pere Marquette State Forest approxi-

INSIDERS' TIP

Mackinac Island hotels traditionally charge an additional 6 percent room tax on room rates.

TRAVERSE CITY

Nestled in a valley just minutes from the Bay, the Inn is surrounded by whispering pines and majestic hardwoods. In a quiet moment, you will be even closer to the North's beauty as a deer breaks through the brush.

Lots of extras, for no extra!

- Indoor pool, whirlpool spa and exercise room
- Pay per view movies & Nintendo on demand
- Some rooms with whirlpools
- Free shuttle to the airport and area malls
- 3 conference centers, speakerphone equipped
- Telephone data ports and fax
- Suites with refrigerators and microwaves
- **FREE room-delivered continental breakfast.**

2326 U.S. 31 SOUTH • TRAVERSE CITY MI 49684
1-800-968-4454 from Canada and the U.S.

MENTION AD FOR 10% DISCOUNT
Offer Not Valid With Any Other Discount

mately 12 miles southwest of Traverse City. Guests sleep in motel rooms, bunkhouses or camp. Recreation is abundant, fun and somewhat out of the ordinary with horseback riding, canoeing, rump bumping, hiking, fishing, mountain biking, cross-country skiing, snowshoeing and snowmobiling available. The main lodge houses a restaurant, bar and fireplace.

Sugar Beach Resort Hotel
$$$-$$$$$ • 1773 U.S. Hwy. 31 N., Traverse City • (616) 938-0100, (800) 509-1995

This is the sister facility to the Grand Beach Resort Hotel (see previous listing) and is almost next door. It lies along the same scenic stretch of East Bay shoreline with its own sugar sand beach. There are 95 deluxe guest units including a number of family suites or extra-large family rooms. Beachfront rooms have private balconies, some rooms have in-room spas. All feature king- or queen-size beds, refrigerators and VCRs as well as access to the indoor swimming pool, spa, exercise room, game room and guest laundry. Meeting rooms are available. A complimentary breakfast is served each morning. The Sugar Beach Resort Hotel is near restaurants and attractions.

Travelodge and Suites
$$$ • 460 Munson Ave., Traverse City • (616) 947-5436, (800) 578-7878

Traditional hospitality is the trademark of this newer motel near the easily accessible intersection of Eighth Street and Munson Avenue. Mabel's (see our Restaurants chapter) is next door, and East Bay beach is a pleasant walk away. This pastel blue and white two-story facility offers 60 guest rooms, including several deluxe suites and spa rooms. Guests will enjoy recreational fun in the indoor pool, whirlpool, game room and exercise room. Additional amenities include refrigerators, HBO, in room coffee, dataports and a continental breakfast. Several package plans are offered including ones for golf, fishing and casinos.

Traverse Bay Casino Resorts' Traverse Beach Motel Condominium
$$$ • 877 Munson Ave., Traverse City • (616) 946-5262, (800) 634-6113

Guests can choose from one of four floor plans for their stay at the Traverse Beach Motel Condominium near Three Mile Road and Munson Avenue on East Grand Traverse Bay. There are 87 guest units available ranging from a simple double guest room to three different one- or two- bedroom condominiums. All have bayfront patios or balconies. An indoor pool, fitness room and whirlpool are open to guests as well as the 700-foot beach. The complex was recently purchased by the Grand Traverse Band of Ottawa and Chippewa Indians as part of Traverse Bay Casino Resorts, which also includes Turtle Creek Casino in nearby Acme. Casino packages are available.

Traverse Bay Inn
$$-$$$ • 2300 U.S. Hwy. 31 N., Traverse City • (616) 938-2646

The Traverse Bay Inn is an all-suite facility with 24 one- or two-bedroom units. All include kitchens, cable television, HBO and Showtime. Fireplace and Jacuzzi rooms and family and executive suites are also available. Small pets can be accommodated. An outdoor pool and hot tub as well as gas grills, picnic area, play space, gift shop and video game room provide the makings for family fun. Complimentary bicycles are available to try out the nearby TART recreational trail.

Traverse Victorian Inn
$$$ • 461 Munson Ave., Traverse City • (616) 947-5525, (800) 506-5525

The Traverse Victorian Inn is one of the area's newest hotels. Clad in shades of pastel yellow, this lovely hotel sits near the corner of Eighth Street and Munson Avenue directly across the street from Mabel's Restaurant and just a short walk away from East Grand Traverse Bay and public beach. There are 68 guest rooms. All feature fireplaces, refrigerators, hair dryers, coffee makers and cable television. A pool and hot tub are indoors.

Waterfront Resort
$$$$ • 2061 N. U.S. Hwy. 31 N., Traverse City • (616) 938-1100, (800) 551-WATER

The Waterfront Resort and its neighboring convention center overlook a scenic portion of East Grand Traverse Bay. This full-service hotel offers 128 deluxe rooms and suites with refrigerators and in-room movies as well as amenities like an enclosed pool and spa, rooftop sun deck, water sports rentals and a beach-side grill. The Waterfront's top floor restaurant has been combining outstanding views with topnotch food for years. The resort recently joined forces with High Pointe to be the official home of High Pointe's Tom Doak golf course.

Grand Traverse Resort
$$$$$ • 100 Grand Traverse Village Blvd., Acme • (616) 938-2100, (800) 748-0303

The Resort operates the largest hospitality operation in the region with 660 rooms, suites and condominiums available for guest use. Extensive services and amenities are available. The Tower Gallery of Shops are off the main lobby while three restaurants, four swimming pools, indoor and outdoor tennis courts, a beach, a health and racquet club, two championship golf courses and a children's activities center round out the recreational menu.

Knollwood Motel
$$ • 5777 U.S. Hwy. 31 N., Acme • (616) 938-2040

This interesting lodge offers a range of lodging options between its 14 guest rooms. Guest can choose among four modern cottages, four motel rooms with microwaves and refrigerators, four motel rooms with kitchenettes or in a charming porch room within a Victorian home. It's actually the Victorian that you see from the road. A complimentary continental breakfast is served each morning and a campfire is held many evenings. During the rest of the day, guests can use the motel's beach, grills, picnic tables, pedal boats, paddle boats, basketball court and sun deck. Perennial gardens brighten the landscape.

Surfside Resort
$$$ • 5229 U.S. Hwy. 31 N., Acme • (616) 938-2410

Sitting along the shores of East Grand Traverse Bay, this quiet, older motel is cheerfully painted in yellow with festive green shutters. There are 17 units available with each promising a bay view. Other amenities include in-room refrigerators, coffee makers, cable

INSIDERS' TIP

The Grand Hotel is the largest summer hotel in the world.

television and queen-size beds. The shoreline hosts a swimming area, beach and sun deck. The TART recreational trail is across the street.

Ellis Lake Resort
$$ • 8440 U.S. Hwy. 31 S., Interlochen
• (616) 276-9502

Cozy, redwood-painted log cabins decorated with blooming flower boxes await guests at Ellis Lake Resort in Interlochen. There are 10 lake-side cabins surrounded by a north woods forest. All have full kitchens while some feature Franklin fireplaces. Guests can swim, fish, boat, hike or simply enjoy the outdoor hot tub or campfire. Ellis Lake Resort is very close to Interlochen Center for the Arts and approximately 10 miles south of Traverse City.

Leelanau County

Sugar Loaf Resort
$$$$-$$$$$ • 4500 Sugar Loaf Mountain Rd., Cedar • (616) 228-5461,
(800) 952-6390

Summer, winter and in-between, Sugar Loaf Resort offers guests hospitality and a myriad of recreation options. Guests can take advantage of golf and family packages or play an all-grass miniature golf course to tune up your swing. Families will also enjoy summertime chairlift rides, barbecues, kids camp, three pools, a water slide and tennis. In the winter, Sugar Loaf shifts the fun from sun to skiing. There are more than 500 guest rooms, townhouses and condominiums available at Sugar Loaf, which is near Cedar in the heart of Leelanau County.

Homestead Resort
$$$$$ • Wood Ridge Rd., Glen Arbor
• (616) 334-5000

Lake Michigan's Sleeping Bear Dunes National Lakeshore is on either side of the Homestead Resort, which was designed to complement the surrounding environment. The extensive property encompasses the shoreline, the Crystal River, high ridges with panoramic views and rolling wooded hills. Activity centers include The Village, which hosts several shops, Nonna's Ristorante Della Famiglia Italian restaurant, Whiskers casual restaurant, a

child-care center and an arcade. An additional restaurant, The Inn, features elegant dining overlooking Lake Michigan. There are 175 guest accommodations ranging from guest rooms near The Village to one- to three-bedroom condominiums in the surrounding shoreline or ridge areas. Recreational facilities are plentiful, including downhill skiing, cross-country skiing, swimming, golf, tennis, canoeing and hiking.

The Leland Lodge
$$$ • 565 Pearl St., Leland
• (616) 256-9848

The Leland Lodge is perched at the top of a hill overlooking town and the adjacent, but private, Leland Country Club. A cheerful, carved sign invites us in with the words, "Leland Lodge . . . Food, Lodging, Cheer." Rich woods and fabrics decorate the lobby and nearby Overlook Restaurant. Lovely, well-furnished guest rooms offer a variety of lodging options including standard rooms with a single queen-size bed, deluxe rooms with king-size beds, sofa sleepers and wall bunks, and courtyard and entrance view rooms with various bed configurations. There are also seven efficiency apartments, ranging from one to three bedrooms, that are available for weeklong stays. Apartments with one bedroom have fireplaces, and all include living rooms and equipped kitchens.

Leelanau Country Inn
$ • 149 E. Harbor Hwy., Maple City
• (616) 228-5060, (800) COOK-441

Only six country rooms are available in this picturesque inn, best known as a favorite local restaurant. In fact, its promotions actually bill the inn as a restaurant with rooms. The inn is similar to a bed and breakfast with unique, hand-decorated rooms, friendly common rooms and shared baths.

Northport Bay Retreat
$$$$$ • 6512 N. West Bayshore Dr., Northport • (616) 935-0111

The Northport Bay Retreat is the perfect location for reunions, business gatherings or large family holidays. North of Omena, the entire facility is available to groups for gatherings under a single roof with a common cooking area, comfortable great room, spacious recreation room and 16 deluxe lake-side guest rooms. The open kitchen is big enough for many cooks, with two of each appliance on hand. The recreation room has pool, Foosball, Ping-Pong, air hockey, game tables, big-screen television, a stereo system and a wet bar. A private 340-foot sandy beach stretches along West Grand Traverse Bay, while a twelve-person hot tub overlooks the water from a lake-side deck. Several meeting rooms and business support services are available as well. The views here are breathtaking.

Leelanau Sands Lodge
$$$ • 2579 N. West Bayshore Dr., Suttons Bay • (616) 271-6330, (800) 930-3008

Lady Luck is your partner at the Leelanau Sands Lodge 20 miles north of Traverse City in Peshawbestown. The lodge, next door to the Leelanau Sands Casino, has 51 spacious rooms. For larger groups, the Leelanau Sands Lodge offers a beautiful beachfront chalet that sleeps up to eight people.

Antrim-Kalkaska

Shanty Creek
$$$$ • One Shanty Creek Rd., Bellaire • (616) 533-8621, (800) 678-4111

Shanty Creek is home to great golf in the summer, super skiing in the winter and lovely facilities throughout the year. The setting here is beautiful with mature trees, rolling hills and scenic vistas wrapping the lodge in natural beauty. Accommodations are plentiful and varied with 600 rooms, suites and condominiums stretching across the resort's 4,000 acres. Extensive meeting space and support services aid business people. Recreational facilities feature downhill skiing for the winter and three championship golf courses for spring, summer and fall. All year guests workout in the Fitness Center and indoor and outdoor pools, and enjoy the Wellness Spa and several on-site eateries.

Holiday Inn of Gaylord
$$$ • 833 W. Main St., Gaylord • (517) 732-2431

Families love the full-service Holidome at this Holiday Inn in the heart of Gaylord. There are 140 guest rooms available along with a full-service restaurant, cocktail lounge, pool, whirlpool, sauna and game room. Small pets can be accommodated.

Marsh Ridge
$$$$ • 4815 Old 27 S., Gaylord • (517) 732-6794, (800) 968-2633

Marsh Ridge lies in the midst of the secluded, wooded grounds that host its wonderful golf courses. Accommodations range from standard rooms to spa rooms and one- and two- bedroom suites, with 59 guest rooms available overall. All rooms have movies and refrigerators, suites also have coffee makers, kitchens and microwaves. Recreational facilities include golf courses, a driving range, putting green, nature trails, a sauna, a whirlpool and a tanning booth.

Treetops Sylvan Resort
$$$$ • 3962 Wilkinson Rd., Gaylord • (517) 732-6711

If you can peel golfers off Treetops' many golf courses, you can try out the many other recreational facilities available at Treetops Sylvan Resorts. There are 233 guest rooms and suites available as well as two outdoor pools, two indoor pools with Jacuzzis, two saunas, an exercise room, two tennis courts, hiking trails and five golf courses. During the winter, add 19 ski runs, 20K of trails and a tubing run. On-site restaurants offer casual and fine dining. Child care is available.

Lake Michigan Shoreline and Cadillac

Crystal Lake Resort
$$$ • 498 N. Michigan Ave., Beulah • (616) 882-7282

Take a room with a view and enjoy the unsurpassed beauty of Crystal Lake. Crystal Lake Resort features 100 feet of private sandy beach with docking facilities within village limits. Modern guest rooms provide television and air conditioning. Cottages ranging in size from one to three bedrooms are also available. For a good value, check out the resort's ski and golf discounts.

Photo: Kevin Poirier

The Park Place, Traverse City's original hotel, provides visitors with lodging in the heart of downtown Traverse City.

Hotel Frankfort
$$$$ • 231 Main St., Frankfort
• (616) 882-7271

Leave the children at home when you plan a stay at Hotel Frankfort. Just one block from Lake Michigan, the hotel specializes in romantic getaways. Victorian decor sets an intimate mood in rooms featuring mirrored canopy water beds, large Jacuzzis, log-burning stoves, steam and sauna baths and tanning beds. You'll find rates reflect the range of individual room amenities. Hotel Frankfort's elegant dining room serves breakfast, lunch and dinner featuring a selection of 72 items. Connoisseurs will enjoy the wide choice of German wines available from the hotel's wine cellar. Rates include breakfast and dinner for two.

Crystal Mountain Resort

$$$ • 12500 Crystal Mountain Dr., Thompsonville • (616) 378-2000, (800) 968-7686

A year-round family-oriented resort, Crystal Mountain is situated on 1,500 acres of some of northern Michigan's most scenic landscape. About 15 miles from the nearest town, the secluded facility offers an array of outdoor recreation and special programming for children and infants. Michigan Legacy Art Park, a unique outdoor permanent sculpture exhibition, is tucked into the forest among ski and hiking trails. (See our Arts chapter to learn more about the park.) You'll find great skiing for beginners and experts, snowboarding, ice skating, hiking, biking, swimming and two 18-hole championship golf courses. (See our Golf and Recreation chapters for more details.) Four types of accommodations are available. Crystal's 63-room hotel is a comfortable, modern lodge. The all-new Swedish-style Inn at the Mountain features 29 luxury suites, most with in-room whirlpools. Amenities available include indoor and outdoor pools, a whirlpool and fitness center. If you prefer group accommodations, you can rent one of 22 homes surrounding the resort or one of 17 town homes. Crystal's highly rated conference facilities accommodate up to 300 people. To stretch your budget, ask about group rates, ski and golf packages.

A full-service resort, Crystal's dining facilities cater to appetites of all sizes. You'll find fine dining as well as light meals at the Wildflower Restaurant where breakfast, lunch and dinner are served daily. For soup and sandwiches, the Main Street Grill is the place to go and on holidays and weekends lighter fare is available at the Crystal Center and Cross Country Center. Everything you need to enjoy the array of outdoor facilities can be rented at the lower level of Crystal Center, including downhill and Nordic skis, snowboards, snowshoes, ice skates, bikes and golf equipment.

Portage Point Inn

$$$$ • 8513 S. Portage Point Dr., Onekama • (616) 889-4222, (800) 878-7248

Listed on the National Register of Historic Places, Portage Point Inn was built as a family resort in 1903 and remains family-oriented today. The turn-of-the-century hotel is nestled on a wooded peninsula between the dunes and beaches of Lake Michigan and Portage Lake, giving boaters access to both bodies of water. It offers 36 smoke-free hotel rooms as well as condominium units and cottages. Amenities include two beaches, boat docks, tennis, shuffleboard, ball parks, a pool and spa. Golf and ski packages, and romantic getaway packages are available as well as snowmobile, boat, bike and Sea Doo rentals. The turn-of-the-century hotel is on the American plan so lodging prices include breakfast and dinner. Noted for its Bourbon steak, the hotel's restaurant also features popular Sunday brunches.

Best Western Manistee

$$$ • 200 U.S. Hwy. 31 N., Manistee • (616) 723-9949, (888) BW MOTEL

Overlooking Manistee Lake, the motel has 69 newly renovated guest rooms, including honeymoon suites. You'll find fine dining on site at Gregory's Restaurant, noted for its Sunday brunches and Friday night fish fry. Relax with cocktails at Jonathan's Pub. Amenities include an indoor pool, whirlpool, direct-dial phones and cable television. Conference facilities are available for up to 125 people. Skiers, check out the motel's ski packages.

Cobi Pines Golf and Resort

$$$ • 4797 U.S. Hwy. 31 S., Manistee • (616) 398-0123

Oversized rooms and queen-size beds help you settle in for a comfortable stay at Cobi resort. In a wooded setting, about 3 miles from

INSIDERS' TIP

The Grand Hotel and Mackinac Island were used in the 1977 filming of the film, *Somewhere in Time* starring Christopher Reeve and Jane Seymour. Photos from the film shoot are displayed at the hotel and in local memorabilia. The Grand hosts *Somewhere in Time* weekends in the fall.

downtown Manistee, it's the newest lodging in town. Amenities at the 55-unit resort include an indoor pool and spa, free continental breakfasts, remote televisions. Some units feature in-room Jacuzzis. You can rent golf equipment and walk from your guest room to the scenic Cobi Pines 18-hole championship golf course. Golfers, be sure to check out Cobi's golf packages.

Lake Shore Motel
$$ • 101 S. Lakeshore Dr., Manistee
• (616) 723-2667

All 20 guest rooms at Lake Shore Motel offer a beautiful view of either Lake Michigan or the Manistee harbor. Manistee's only motel on Lake Michigan, it's in the historic downtown district adjacent to the city's riverwalk and docks. The motel is surrounded by sandy beach. Nearby you'll find piers, boat launches, playgrounds, tennis courts and volleyball and basketball facilities. Amenities offered include cable television, in-room coffee, direct dial phones and for anglers, fish cleaning and freezing services.

Manistee Inn and Marina
$$ • 378 River St., Manistee
• (616) 723-4000

Manistee Inn and Marina, adjacent to the Manistee Riverwalk in the city's historic downtown, is the only motel providing dock space for those who arrive via Lake Michigan. These slips accommodate boats less than 25 feet in length. The two-story waterfront inn offers 22 well-maintained rooms, covered parking spaces, coin-operated laundry facilities, cable television and spa rooms. For anglers, there are fish cleaning and freezing services. Lake Michigan beaches, the historic Ramsdell Theater, and the port town's museum are all just a short stroll away.

The Milwaukee House
$$, no credit cards • 259 River St., Manistee • (616) 723-7880

Robin Williams slept here, and so did Reba McIntire and James Earl Jones. Built in 1873, this eight-unit historic building is as much a museum as it is a hotel. You'll find the desk of publishing king William Randolph Hearst here, as well as Frank Lloyd Wright windows, Victorian paintings, light fixtures and many other treasures. Each guest room features brass beds and marble sinks along with modern bathroom facilities. The charming exterior is accented by wrought iron fencing and a three-tiered garden courtyard. Credit cards are not accepted at this nonsmoking facility, but weekend, weekly and monthly rates are available.

Riverside Motel & Marina
$$ • 520 Water St., Manistee
• (616) 723-3554

Fine dining and great sport fishing are all just a few steps from your Riverside guest room. Situated along the Manistee River, the 20-unit motel offers dock space, free riverboat tours, charter fishing expeditions, fish cleaning and freezing service. Catch salmon, steelhead, brown trout, bluegill and bass on-site, then grill and eat them at the motel picnic site. Along the Manistee Riverwalk, you're just three blocks from the historic downtown where you'll find pleasant dining, shopping and entertainment. Amenities include cable television, a pool, coffee, ice and walkout patio doors. Pets are welcome.

Country Haven
$, no credit cards • 3263 N. Lakeshore Dr., Ludington • (616) 845-5882

Country Haven is situated on the shores of Hamlin Lake, one of the most productive fisheries in the north. Here, bluegill are regularly hooked and the crappie and walleye catch is known throughout the state. To help you take advantage of great fishing opportunities, the resort provides free rowboats, dockage, canoes and ice-fishing shanties. Lake tours and Pere Marquette River guided fishing trips are also available. Newly remodeled, the resort has six one- to three-bedroom efficiency rooms featuring oak kitchens. Jet ski rentals are available for cruising the 12-mile-long, 5,000 acre Hamlin Lake and snowmobile rentals are expected to become available in the 1997-98 season. Between July and August rooms rent only on a weekly basis. Fall, winter and spring you can get some great price breaks.

Lands Inn and Convention Center
$$ • 4079 W. U.S. Hwy. 10, Ludington
• (616) 845-7311, (800) 707-7475

After enjoying dinner theater at the Lands Inn, unwind in the pool area. Soak in

Michigan's largest spa featuring a capacity of 42, or work out on fitness equipment. Take advantage of golf and ski discounts or dinner theater packages. The theater features fall and spring seasons with performances by the Lake Forest Performing Arts Company. The Landing restaurant serves breakfast, lunch and dinner and is known for their Friday night seafood buffets and Sunday brunches. With its large-screen television, ongoing sports coverage and sport decor, the Locker Lounge is a hit with major league fans. The largest convention facility in the Ludington region, Lands Inn offers corporate rates and conference facilities to accommodate 500 people. Of the 116 guest rooms, you'll find some feature in-room hot tubs. Two- and three-room suites are available, and pets are welcome. Inn amenities include cable television and in-room movies, a laundry, and horseshoe and volleyball outdoor recreational facilities. Lands Inn is situated at the city's edge, about 3 miles from downtown Ludington.

Marina Bay Motor Lodge
$$ • 604 W. Ludington Ave., Ludington
• (616) 845-5124, (800) 968-1440

Everything you might want to do in Ludington is within walking distance of Marina Bay Motor Lodge. You can catch Wednesday night summer concerts, walk to Stearns Park to swim and stroll along the Lake Michigan shoreline or wander along the pier to the Ludington lighthouse. Marina facilities, dining, carferries and shopping are just a stone's throw away. The 24-unit lodge offers luxury rooms featuring heart-shaped whirlpools, king-size beds and in-room refrigerators and coffee. All rooms feature cable television and a continental breakfast. Pets are welcome.

Stearns Motor Inn
$ • 212 E. Ludington Ave., Ludington
• (616) 843-3407, (800) 365-1904

The only hotel/motel in downtown Ludington, Stearns Inn offers a charming atmosphere and the convenience of being near carferries, parks, public beaches, shopping and a variety of restaurants. Spacious rooms are decorated in a traditional style. Amenities include a drive-up entrance, boat parking and cable television. The on-site

lounge is a lively night spot featuring music videos and a disc jockey.

Viking Arms
$$ • 930 E. Ludington Ave., Ludington
• (616) 843-3441, (800) 748-0173

Lovely landscaping, clean, spacious rooms, some with gas-log fireplaces and in-room whirlpools, make Viking Arms a relaxing place to spend the night. Amenities include in-room coffee, televisions and VCRs with remote control and on-site movie rentals, a continental breakfast and an outdoor heated pool. Just inside Ludington city limits, the 45-unit motel is within I mile of the carferry, restaurants and recreational facilities.

Best Western Bill Oliver's Resort & Conference Center
$$ • 5676 E. Mich. Hwy. 55, Cadillac
• (616) 775-2458, (800) OLIVER 5

Bill Oliver's is best at mixing business with pleasure. It offers the largest convention facilities in the greater Cadillac area. There are nine meeting and conference rooms for groups of 10 to 500. Located in Cadillac's west side, the conference center is adjacent to a 66-unit motel. For recreational pleasure, ground-level rooms allow snowmobilers and cross-country skiers to access area trails directly from their rooms. Other amenities include an indoor pool, sauna and Jacuzzi, tennis, golf, a driving range, 12 bowling lanes, two lounges and a game center. People drive for miles for buffet feasts fit for a king at Bill Oliver's King's Table Restaurant. Continental breakfasts and lunch are also available.

Lost Pines Lodge
$$ • 3846 W. 38 Mi. Rd., Harrietta
• (616) 389-2222

With 700 acres in the heart of the Manistee National Forest, this Bavarian-style lodge is a popular snowmobile resort. From its doors you can access hundreds of miles federally designated Scenic Snowmobile Trails. Snowmobile packages, safaris and rentals are available as well as sled storage and repairs. Between April and November, Lost Pines Stables is open for horseback riding adventures. Breakfast, lunch and dinner is served casual style at the Little Switzerland Restaurant. Guests gather at the

Sugar Beach

RESORT HOTEL

TRAVERSE CITY'S NEWEST BEACHFRONT HOTEL

IMAGINE THIS BEAUTIFUL RESORT HOTEL ON THIS INCREDIBLE STRETCH OF EAST BAY BEACH!

OVER 300' OF SUGAR SAND BEACH ON EAST GRAND TRAVERSE BAY

95 Deluxe Units • 25" Remote Color TVs & VCRs • Full Cable with HBO • In-Room Hairdryers • Refrigerators & Wet Bars • Family Suites • Private Balconies • In-Room Whirlpools Available • Indoor Heated Pool & Whirlpool • Continental Breakfast Room • Exercise Room • Video Arcade Room • Guest Laundry • Meeting Room

1773 U.S. 31 NORTH • TRAVERSE CITY, MICHIGAN 49686
RESERVATIONS: 616-938-0100 OR
TOLL FREE 1-800-509-1995

website: www.sugarbeach.com / email: info@sugarbeach.com

MAKE IT MACKINAW CITY!

The Town That Loves Company!
800-666-0160

Best Western

Best Western
of Mackinaw City
800-647-8286
616-436-5544
112 Old U.S. 31
Mackinaw City

DAYS INN
THE BEST REST OF THE DAY.

616-436-5557
825 SOUTH HURON
MACKINAW CITY

800-DAYS-INN

Best Western

BEST WESTERN
Dockside
Waterfront Inn of Mackinaw City
616-436-5001 ★ 800-774-1794

Hamilton Select Inn

BEACHFRONT LUXURY
300' Sandy Beach
Free $50 Fun Money Packet
Indoor Pool & Whirlpool

1-800-301-1765

Mackinaw City
Michigan's Favorite Family Fun
Vacation Destination

★ The Mackinac Bridge ★
★ Colonial Michilimackinac ★
★ Historic Mill Creek ★
★ Mackinaw Crossings & Center Stage Theatre ★
★ World Famous Mackinac Island ★
★ Fort Mackinac ★
800-666-0610

MACKINAW CITY'S
TOP RATED HOTELS

RAMADA® INN
CONVENTION CENTER
450 S. Nicolet, Mackinaw City
616-436-5535 • 616-436-5849 fax

206 Nicolet,
Mackinaw City
616-436-8961
616-436-0000 fax

Holiday Inn
EXPRESS
364 Louvingney, Mackinaw City
616-436-7100 • 616-436-7070 fax

601 N. Huron,
Mackinaw City
616-436-5252
616-436-0000 fax

If you want the Beach and the View

Quality Inn
917 S. Huron Drive
Mackinaw City, MI 49701
800-228-5151

The
Admiral's
Table
Restaurant & Lounge
*Whitefish & Trout
Caught Fresh Daily*

**502 South Huron
Mackinaw City, MI
616-436-5687**

From coast to coast we have the guidebooks you're looking for to plan your trip – whether it's a weekend excursion, a week-long jaunt or a permanent relocation. From the picturesque harbors of Cape Cod to the lush valleys and hills of California's Wine Country; from mysterious, traditional Savannah to vibrant, rapidly expanding Salt Lake City, **65 titles** cover some of the country's most exciting places.

Written by locals who love where they live, each guide accurately portrays the area's charm and allure. Whether searching for savory local cuisine, unique regional wares, amusements for the kids, a picturesque hiking spot, new environs or a room with a view, explore America and experience the joy of travel with the Insiders' Guide® books.

Call today to find out more about all of our titles, or to place an order

1-800-582-2665

Photo: Mackinac Island Chamber of Commerce

Mackinac Island's many Victorian hotels were built during the late 1800s and early 1900s.

Snow Valley Lounge bar in the evening to relax. Lodge rooms where pets are welcome, chalets sleeping eight to 10 people and condos are all available.

MacKenzie Lodge/Caberfae Peaks Ski & Golf Resort
$$ • Caberfae Rd., Cadillac
• (616) 862-3000

MacKenzie Lodge offers only two-night packages during peak ski season. Weekend rates include Saturday and Sunday lift tickets for Caberfae Peaks, the only ski area in the Midwest totally surrounded by national forest wilderness. (See our Winter Recreation chapter to learn more about skiing Caberfae Peaks.) At MacKenzie Lodge, a 26-unit slope-side lodge, guests can dine at any of five resort restaurants featuring everything from breakfasts to sandwich fare to fine dining. The Peaks golf course, a challenging new course, is

nestled among undisturbed heather and wetlands. (See our Golf chapter to learn more about the Peaks.) Caberfae's rental building is Michigan's largest ski rental facility. Nordic and downhill skis, snowboards and golf equipment are available. A variety of packages are offered throughout the year. Pets are welcome.

McGuire's Resort
$$$ • 7880 Mackinaw Tr., Cadillac
• (616) 775-9947, (800) 632-7302

Perched on a hill overlooking the Cadillac countryside, McGuire's Resort is known for its great winter package deals featuring 13 different discounts on lodging, meals, skiing, sleigh rides and more. Summer golf packages are also popular. The resort has 122 contemporary guest rooms, an indoor pool, sauna, whirlpool and game area. Outdoor recreation opportunities include 27 holes of golf, two lighted tennis courts, volleyball, shuffleboard, miniature golf, horseshoes and 10 kilometers of groomed cross-country ski trails, three lighted for night skiing. Nordic ski equipment rentals are available. Breakfast, lunch and dinner are served at the Terrace Room restaurant, which specializes in a northern menu. Curly's Up North Bar offers a lighter fare and regular live entertainment. The resort has conference facilities for 200.

South Shore Resort Motel
$ • 1246 Sunnyside Dr., Cadillac
• **(616) 775-7641, (800) 569-8651**

Adjacent to a 7.5 mile biking and pedestrian path encompassing Lake Cadillac, South Shore Resort offers many opportunities to enjoy four-season recreation. From all 16 ground-level motel rooms you can access 500 miles of groomed snowmobile and cross-country ski trails. From the motels's sandy beach with four private docks and a private launch you can boat, fish and swim. Reserved rooms receive a complimentary fruit basket.

Sun-n-Snow Motel
$ • 301 S. Lake Mitchell Rd., Cadillac
• **(616) 775-9961, (800) 477-9961**

Nestled between lakes Cadillac and Mitchell, Sun-n-Snow is a family-owned motel offering friendly, personal service. It features a Swiss chalet-style exterior and 29 ground-level rooms and suites with warm, knotty-pine interiors. Snowmobilers can park their sleds directly in front of their rooms. Amenities include cable television, telephones, a private beach and docks. Pets are welcome. William Mitchell State Park, fine and casual dining facilities and gift shops are within a snowball's throw. Note that on weekends, there is a two-night minimum stay.

NorthCrest Motel
$ • 1341 S. Lakeshore Dr., Lake City
• **(616) 839-2075**

Popular with hunters and snowmobilers, NorthCrest Motel offers clean, affordable rooms. Located across the road from Lake Missaukee, the motel has an indoor heated pool and Jacuzzi. Public beaches, boat launches, restaurants and shopping are all within a short drive.

Little Traverse

Westbrook Motel
$ • 218 Elizabeth St., East Jordan
• **(616) 536-2674**

You're welcome to dock your boat and enjoy the private beach along Lake Charlevoix when you stay at Westbrook Motel. From here, boaters travel by water to Lake Michigan for scenic views and sport fishing. The seven-unit motel offers newly remodeled, clean rooms, cable television and a continental breakfast. Snowmobile packages are offered and snowmobile rentals are available nearby. The motel is two miles from East Jordan, a short jaunt from dining, shopping and local attractions.

Edgewater Inn
$$$$$ • 100 Michigan Ave., Charlevoix
• **(616) 547-6044, (800) 748-0424**

The only condominium/hotel in Charlevoix, the Edgewater Inn is a sophisticated north country haven offering harbor and channel views from every unit. The three-story building has one and two bedroom suites, all featuring porches or patios, kitchenettes and living rooms, some with fireplaces. Amenities include an indoor and outdoor pool, fitness room, sauna, hot tub and massage therapy by appointment. Charly's restaurant serves an unique ethnic menu of French, Indian-Malaysian and Southwestern American cuisine. From your suite, the Lake Michigan beach and pier, shopping, restaurants and entertainment are just a short stroll. Golfers, you'll want to ask about the inn's golf packages.

The Lodge Motel
$$$ • 120 Michigan Ave., Charlevoix
• **(616) 547-6565**

Large rooms and a convenient downtown location distinguish this 40-unit motel. Some rooms offer balconies with a pleasant view of Charlevoix waterways. Pets are welcome. Amenities include cable television with HBO and an outdoor pool.

Pointes North Inn
$$$ • 101 Michigan Ave., Charlevoix
• **(616) 547-0055, (800) 968-5433**

Personal attention to your needs, and contemporary, comfortable suites, many overlooking the river channel and Round Lake, all promise to make your stay at Pointes North Inn pleasant. One- and two-bedroom suites feature in-room Jacuzzis, televisions and VCRs, mini or full kitchens, lofts, balconies or patios. Located in downtown Charlevoix, the 23-unit inn has an indoor and outdoor pool and serves complimentary continental breakfast. Conference facilities accommodate up to 50 people and group rates are available. Ski and golf packages are also available.

Weathervane Terrace Inn & Suites
$$$$ • 111 Pine River Ln., Charlevoix
• (616) 547-9955, (800) 552-0025

This unusual inn is situated on a bluff above Lake Michigan and looks like a stone castle set off by numerous towers. Weathervane Terrace Inn is an architectural landmark built by local Realtor Earl Young in the 1950s. It was one of 30 stone structures the Realtor built. Recently redecorated, the facility features 68 guest rooms and suites, most with a breathtaking view of either Lake Michigan, Round Lake Harbor or the Pine River Channel. Many rooms have patios or balconies and all are equipped with refrigerators and VCRs. Suites include microwaves, and some have in-room Jacuzzis and fireplaces. The central stone and glass turret houses an eight-person hot tub. Other amenities include an outdoor pool and free continental breakfasts in the Harbor Room. Conference facilities for 40 and group rates are available. Golf, dining and casino packages are also available.

Coach House Motel
$ • 2445 Charlevoix Ave., Petoskey
• (616) 347-2593

Every room offers a majestic view of Little Traverse Bay at this 15-unit motel nestled in a tranquil, wooded setting two miles from downtown Petoskey. Wildlife watchers will enjoy encounters with deer, turkey, black squirrels and raccoon. You'll find rooms are spacious and individually decorated in a Colonial style. Amenities include free coffee, cable television and an outdoor pool.

Green Roof Motor Inn
$$ • 1420 U.S. Hwy. 131 S., Petoskey
• (616) 348-3900

Overlooking Little Traverse Bay, the Green Roof Motor Inn offers clean, comfortable, affordable rooms. Many provide a view of the bay. Two suites with kitchenettes are available and microwaves and refrigerators are available upon request. The 138-unit inn is just two miles from downtown Petoskey where you will find casual or fine dining, wonderful gift shops, galleries and antiques. Pets are welcome.

Stafford's Bay View Inn
$$$$ • 2011 Woodland Ave., Petoskey
• (616) 347-2771, (800) 258-1886

An elegant, fully-restored Victorian hotel, Stafford's Bay View Inn is a popular romantic getaway. It's situated along the rocky shore of Little Traverse Bay in the historic Bay View Association community. (See our Worship chapter to learn more about Bay View.) The three-story clapboard hotel is listed on the National Register of Historic Places. Antique furnishings, period wicker and chintz enhance the country inn atmosphere, and the lake-side lawn and gardens invite you to relax. The hotel has 30 individually decorated rooms, some with canopy beds. Most suites feature fireplaces and whirlpools, some have balconies providing spectacular sunset views over the bay. With some off-season exceptions, rates include a full breakfast for two and a complimentary bottle of wine. When it comes to dining, Stafford's Sunday brunch is legendary. Served in the Roselawn Porch, brunch features regional cuisine from a family recipe collection, including dishes and condiments made from fresh local products. Inn guests are welcome to use the Bay View beach where there is docking space, supervised swimming, sailboat rentals, swim and sailing lessons.

INSIDERS' TIP

Would you like to peek at the Grand Hotel without an overnight stay? The hotel charges $5 for a visit but will deduct the fee from your lunch bill if you choose to dine at the daily Grand Buffet.

Stafford's Perry Hotel
$$$ • Bay at Lewis St., Petoskey
• (616) 347-4000, (800) 456-1917

Friendly, warm and inviting, this historic hotel, in the heart of Petoskey's Gaslight district, offers a classic old-world atmosphere. The small boutique inn has 81 individually decorated rooms, some with balconies overlooking Little Traverse Bay. The charming European ambiance is enhanced by a variety of antique furnishings. Breakfast, lunch and dinner are available in the H.O. Rose dining room where you'll find a good selection of in-season northern specialties, including fresh whitefish, one of the most popular items on the menu. For lighter fare, sandwiches or pizza, try the Noggin Room Pub. For a relaxing outdoor dining experience when the weather is fair, eat at the Rose Garden Veranda. The cafe is in the hotel's English garden where climbing roses bloom and a pineapple fountain flows. Lunch is served here daily and cocktails are available during evening hours. Golf, ski and boutique packages are available.

The Terrace Inn
$$ • 1549 Glendale, Petoskey
• (616) 347-2410, (800) 530-9898

If you're seeking a quiet retreat from the hustle and bustle of city life, The Terrace Inn may be the perfect place for you. Guest rooms have no phones or television, one reason many guests return. All rooms are smoke-free.

Built in 1911, the inn is in the historic Bay View Association community. Bay View is one of 17 registered historic sites in Michigan. (See our Worship chapter to find out more about Bay View.) A 44-room Victorian hotel, The Terrace Inn offers a great variety of packages including murder mystery packages, women-only weekends, romantic getaways, and golf and ski deals. You'll feel at home as soon as you enter the "sitting room" lobby, where rich woodwork, a fireplace and piano set a comfortable mood. In fair weather, dine on the back porch or just wile away the time in the rocking chairs. The inn's dining room serves a continental breakfast daily and dinners only during summer months. Guests are invited to enjoy the Bay View Association beach where swimming and sailing and lessons are all available.

Winter guests will want to tour Bay View from the horse-drawn sleighs. Your tour begins right from the inn's front porch. The inn accommodates banquets and conferences and group rates are available.

Birchwood Inn
$$ • 7077 Lake Shore Dr., Harbor Springs • (616) 526-2151, (800) 530-9955

Deer, possum, porcupine and quail are your neighbors at this country inn on 40 scenic acres 3 miles north of Harbor Springs. Knotty pine walls and a huge fieldstone fireplace create an easygoing up-north atmosphere. Overlooking Little Traverse Bay, the inn features 48 guest rooms. Amenities include a continental breakfast, shuffleboard facilities, tennis courts, a playground and an outdoor pool. The inn is situated along a 25-mile scenic drive known as the Tunnel of Trees. Just a stone's throw away, you'll find Thorne Swift nature preserve where you can enjoy nature hikes, wildlife watching and beachcombing. (See our Parks chapter to learn more about the preserve.) Golf and ski packages are available as well as meeting and conference facilities for 50.

Boyne Highlands
$$$$ • 600 Highlands Dr., Harbor Springs • (616) 526-3000, (800) GO-BOYNE

Boyne USA is called King of the Mountain for good reason. The resort company installed the first chairlift in the Midwest and the world's first triple and four-place chairlifts. You'll find Boyne resorts are topnotch all the way. The Highlands is upscale, yet unpretentious and relaxed. Featuring an inviting Alpine theme, the resort is amidst some of northern Michigan's most rugged, beautiful terrain. Facilities include 42 ski slopes, tennis, swimming pools and 162 holes of world-class golf. (See our Recreation and Golf chapters to learn more about Boyne's recreational opportunities.) The Highlands has accommodations for 1,200, so take your pick of lodging facilities from among its spacious rooms, suites or one- to four-bedroom condos with kitchens, fireplaces and lofts. Base facilities offer everything you could wish for and more. You'll find two game rooms, three heated outdoor pools, a steam room, giant hot tub, ice rink, shops and a physician-staffed clinic and fitness center. For mealtime, there's a full service dining room, a cafeteria and two cocktail lounges. During the summer months, enjoy dinner theater presented by The Young Americans. Kids enjoy special programming at the Highlands, built and operated to be family-friendly. Baby-sitting and day-care services are also available. Numerous value packages are offered, and — here's a deal — in April, you ski free.

Harbor Springs Cottage Inn
$$ • 145 Zoll St., Harbor Springs
• (616) 526-5431

You'll be treated like family at this comfortable mom-and-pop inn. In the morning expect homemade muffins, fresh coffee and juice. If you're planning a hunting or fishing expedition, you can count on the friendly advice and expertise of your host, who will even accompany you on request. Pets are welcome, but if you left yours at home two resident great Danes are always willing to accompany you on a stroll through picturesque Harbor Springs. This charming 21-room inn creates an up-north cottage environment with its lovely rooms decorated in wicker and brass. Two suites are available with two bedrooms each, a kitchenette and fireplace. Swimming is just a few steps away in Little Traverse Bay across the street. Shopping and dining is only four blocks down the road. Bikes and two-person sailboats are provided free of charge and an 11-foot fishing boat is available for a minimal fee. To make the most of your vacation dollars, ask about golf and ski packages.

Trout Creek Condominium Resort
$$$$ • 4749 Pleasantview Rd., Harbor Springs • (616) 526-2148, (800) 748-0245

Two stocked trout ponds on 160 acres of hills and woods along with many amenities make this resort a relaxing getaway. Contemporary condo units featuring one to three bedrooms, spas, fireplaces and kitchens are available on a two- or three-night minimum, depending on the season. The family-friendly resort offers indoor and outdoor pools, a playground, spa, sauna and fitness center, six outdoor tennis courts and lovely on-site nature trails for hiking, jogging and cross-country ski-ing. Children's programs are available in the summer months and horse-drawn sleigh rides are offered in winter. The resort is 10 minutes from downtown Harbor Springs and 2 miles or less from the area's premier ski and golf facilities. Be sure to ask about their ski and golf discounts.

Boyne Mountain
$$$ • Boyne Mountain Rd., Boyne Falls
• (616) 549-6000, (800) GO-BOYNE

Celebrating 50 years in the ski business in 1997, Boyne USA operates both Boyne Mountain and Boyne Highlands, considered two of the best ski resorts in the Midwest. You'll find they offer everything you expect a top-class vacation facility to deliver. The charming Bavarian motif at Boyne Mountain creates the feel of a small, snowy Alpine village. (See our Recreation and Golf chapters for more information.) Built to accommodate 600 guests, lodging includes spacious hotel rooms, suites and one- to four-bedroom condos. Lodge rooms are at the base of the slopes for ski-in, ski-out convenience. A wide array of lodging/recreation deals are available, including Christmas and Presidents' Weekend packages. Facilities and amenities you'll enjoy include a heated outdoor pool, giant hot tub, sauna, ice rink, exercise room, masseuse and salon. A family resort, day-care and babysitting services are available, as well as Kids & Teen Camp, mini-camps for toddlers, ski races and lessons. Beginner slopes feature fun snowcaves and cartoon characters. While dining facilities operate on a seasonal basis, you won't ever go hungry. Boyne Mountain offers a full-service dining room, a cafeteria and two cocktail lounges. The Eagle's Nest at the top of the mountain serves sandwiches and snacks. Shopping is available at Boyne Country Sports Shop where you can find the equipment you've been dreaming of and the latest outdoor wear.

Mountainside Inn
$$ • 2784 U.S. Hwy. 131, Boyne Falls
• (616) 549-3077

Mountainside Inn is the second oldest building in Charlevoix County. Originally built as a restaurant, today, the charming lodge caters to groups, accommodating as many as 30. Located just 500 yards from Boyne

Mountain, one of the Midwest's top ski resorts, it's a favorite home away from home for ski and snowmobile enthusiasts. Snowmobile rentals are available on-site and jet skis are available here in the summer months. The brick two-story inn features six comfortable rooms with kitchenettes. After a day on the slopes, you'll enjoy soaking in the hot tub. In the morning, plan to start your day with a continental breakfast.

Wolverine Dilworth Inn
$$ • 300 Water St., Boyne City
• (616) 582-7388, (800) 748-0160

In 1911, a group of area lumber barons built the Wolverine Dilworth Inn in order to have a place to entertain their out-of-town guests. They spared little expense in constructing this grand, elegant place. The three-story brick inn, wrapped by a veranda, retains some of yesteryear's grandeur. It is a registered historic hotel, and many of the individually decorated Victorian-style rooms feature brass beds and antique dressers. Dinners are served in the inn's dining room during summer and winter months and continental breakfasts are available year round. Located in the heart of Boyne City, the quaint hotel is surrounded by restaurants and shopping.

Mackinac Straits

In our Mackinac Island listing no street addresses are included because establishments don't use them. All the hotels are on Huron Street, more commonly known as Main Street, in the busy downtown district just five blocks long. The only exceptions to this is Mission Point Resort on the western edge of town along Lakeshore Drive, Stonecliffe Resort in the island's interior, and the majestic Grand Hotel, which overlooks the island from its eastern bluff-top site. Hotel porters meet all incoming ferries to assist with luggage and directions

The hotel seasons on Mackinac Island stretch from early May through late October with the high times ranging from mid-June through mid-August. During the summer peak, it's not unusual for hotels to require you to pay a deposit equivalent to at least one night's stay, which you will lose if you cancel less than 10 days before arrival. Policies vary with each establishment, so please check for current requirements when making reservations.

Most island hotels are closed during late fall, winter and early spring. Those that offer lodging during these months are noted below.

Chippewa Hotel
$$$$ • Huron St., Mackinac Island
• (906) 847-3341, (800) 241-3341

The Chippewa Hotel stands as a historic landmark overlooking the Harbor District on the east end of Huron Street. Its waterfront location across from Fort Mackinac shares sweeping views of Lake Huron and incoming ferries and boats.

Built in 1902, the Chippewa was completely renovated a few years ago and the results are a wonderful blend of past and present. There are 61 rooms available in a range of accommodations including 26 spacious harbor-view suites with a large bedroom, living room, wet bar, microwave, refrigerator and waterfront balconies. The most luxurious of the suites are the VIP and master suites, which include concierge service, stocked refrigerators, binoculars, robes and VCRs. The master suites are larger with two-person Jacuzzis and extra wide balconies. Standard and deluxe rooms overlook the historic downtown Main Street.

Guests can enjoy the waterfront while dining at the outdoor patio, strolling along the hotel's boat dock or inside the large 25-person hot tub. Indoors, the Harbor View Restaurant and Pink Pony Bar and Grill are lined with windows overlooking the action outdoors (see our Restaurants chapter). By the way, if you're trying to find the Chippewa Hotel, just look for the three-foot pink plastic pony hanging over the sidewalk in front of hotel's restaurants.

Grand Hotel
$$$$$ • Cadotte Ave., Mackinac Island
• (906) 847-3331, (800) 33-GRAND

How do we describe the Grand Hotel? Words seem inadequate to describe the grandeur of this elegant hotel. It is Mackinac Island's crown jewel beckoning us back to a bygone era of horse drawn carriages, high tea, croquet, dressing for dinner and endlessly playing chamber music. Built in 1887, it seems to have walked out of a Victorian postcard.

The Grand's 700-foot verandah is one of the first things you see as you cross the Straits to the Island. Perched high on its blufftop site, the white verandah and hotel create an imposing vision floating in a sea of green grass. Porters in tie, tails and top hats meet guests and transport them in a shiny carriage up the long hill to the Grand's entrance. Guests enjoy an elegant breakfast, afternoon tea and a five-course dinner each day, often accompanied by piano, violin or full orchestra. Men are still required to wear jackets to dinner.

The hotel is enormous. Since it was built, the Grand has been known as the largest summer hotel in the world. It houses 324 guest rooms including luxurious suites that have hosted presidents, governors and celebrities. Additional facilities include a formal dining room, a deli, a cocktail lounge, a golf course and several floors of framed memorabilia. Spacious landscaped grounds lead to the vintage, outdoor Esther Williams pool. If you would like an advance peek at the Grand Hotel, rent the movie *Somewhere in Time* starring Christopher Reeve and Jane Seymour. The movie was filmed at the Grand, which was featured prominently. Many photos taken during the filming grace the walls of the hotel. The movie's theme music is commonly requested during dinner.

Harbour View Inn
$$$$ • Huron St., Mackinac Island
• (906) 847-0101

This stately mansion, built in 1820, has been renovated into a lovely hotel. On the eastern side of Huron Street, the Harbour View Inn features 63 luxurious rooms and suites with Jacuzzi tubs, private balconies, fireplaces and magnificent views of Lake Huron and the harbor.

The ambiance is charming. Brick paths weave across the grounds while balconies surround the inn. Inside, lace curtains line the windows and rich woods trim the walls while chandeliers glow overhead. This pleasantly cozy interior has a very French feel, perhaps hearkening back to the home's original 19th-century owner, Madame La Framboise. The

Harbour View Inn is open during some of the winter months.

Iroquois Hotel
$$$$$ • Huron St., Mackinac Island
• (906) 847-3321

The Iroquois Hotel anchors the western edge of Mackinac Island's downtown district. This historic beachfront hotel overlooks the Straits of Mackinac from a wonderful location along the shoreline. There are 47 guest rooms available in a variety of classic Victorian bedrooms and suites. Many share lovely views of the Straits.

The renowned Carriage House dining room (see our Restaurants chapter) provides elegant, fine dining while informal refreshments are served indoors or on the waterside verandah. Guests can relax along the waterfront or stroll a few short steps to shop at the Loon Feather, Balsam Shop and other nearby stores. The Star Line Ferry docks are next door.

The Island House
$$$$ • Huron St., Mackinac Island
• (906) 847-3347, (800) 626-6304

White rocking chairs deck the spacious porches at The Island House just one block from Marquette Park along Huron Street. Built in 1852, it is the oldest hotel on Mackinac Island and is registered as a Michigan Historic Landmark. There are 97 guest rooms available including three two-bedroom suites that are great for families. Recent renovations updated rooms and added a new indoor swimming pool and spa. Families with young children can work off energy at the hotel's outdoor playground or spend a quiet night out with the help of a staff babysitter. Diners can enjoy fine dining in the elegant Governors Dining Room overlooking the harbor or in the casual Ice House Bar & Grill (see our Restaurants chapter).

Lake View Hotel
$$$ • Huron St., Mackinac Island
• (906) 847-3384

A four-story atrium dramatically encloses the pool, whirlpool and overlooking guest rooms in the beautifully restored and renovated Lake View Hotel. Built in 1858, the Lake View is a registered historic site across from the Starline and Shepler's ferry docks along downtown's Main Street. There are 85 rooms available including poolside suites and rooms with private whirlpools. Banquet and meeting facilities are often used for larger groups, wedding parties and family reunions. Food and spirits are found at the Pilot House restaurant and Annie's Pub (see our Restaurants chapter) while shopping along Main Street is just a step away. By the way, if you're a chocolate lover, Kilwin's Candy Kitchen is right next door.

Lilac Tree Hotel
$$$$$ • Huron St., Mackinac Island
• (906) 847-6575

When the Lilac Tree Hotel was under construction during the late 1980s, it was the first new hotel to be built on the island in 75 years. Its birth followed a tragic fire during October 1987 that destroyed several shops and upper-level apartments in the heart of downtown. Today, the Lilac Tree stands on this central site as a modern, all-suite hotel.

Each of the 39 guest suites includes a spacious bedroom with one king-size or two queen-size beds, a parlor with a sleeper sofa and a marble-trimmed bathroom. Added amenities include a wet bar, refrigerator, microwave oven, coffee maker and two televisions with cable. Interior doors offer added privacy. Balcony and master suites include a balcony overlooking Main Street and the harbor. The master suites also include two-person Jacuzzi tubs. If a great view is a priority, request harbor or master accommodations on the fourth floor. Decor reflects the French, English and American heritage of the island with bright colors, bold floral patterns and antique and reproduction furnishings in wicker, wood and iron. Elevator doors are clad in hand-painted murals of lilac trees or similar flora and fauna.

The main entrance to the Lilac Tree is off Huron Street in a small arcade that also houses The Island Bookstore, Mackinac Hobby Horse, Roses 'n Sadie, Leather Corral and La Belle Provence (see our Shopping chapter). Park benches along the arcade walls offer a welcome place to relax or simply people watch. Nearby stairs lead to the Waters Meet Restaurant under the hotel (see our Restaurants chapter).

Mission Point Resort
$$$$$ • One Lakeshore Dr., Mackinac Island • (906) 847-3312, (800) 833-7711

The Mission Point Resort is a wonderful destinations for families. This spacious resort is on the eastern edge of town on 18 acres of lake view property. This facility has had an eclectic round of careers. It was initially built and used by Moral Rearmament during the late 1950s and early 1960s, and later served for a short time as a small liberal arts college. It has functioned as a hotel for the past 25 years, but really came into its own after being completely renovated into a full-scale resort several years ago. Lovely north-woods architecture is evident throughout the facility, which features 13 fireplaces. There are 239 guest rooms, each boasting comfy feather beds and down comforters. Three restaurants are available on-site, including one that serves outdoors. Children younger than 12 eat free. An activity center provides guests with bicycle rentals, in-line skate rentals, an outdoor pool, a Jacuzzi and a hair salon as well as a modern health club.

Pontiac Lodge
$$$ • Hoban St., Mackinac Island • (906) 847-3364

Open year round, the Pontiac Lodge is a popular stop for winter visitors or those wishing to stay for a longer time. This utilitarian lodge's 10 guest rooms are efficiency units and suites with stove tops, refrigerators, sinks, dishes and utensils. It is above the hustle of downtown activity on the upper levels of the building housing the Loon Feather, Balsam Shop and The Gallery (see our Shopping chapter). The Pontiac Lodge connects with the popular Village Inn Restaurant (see our Restaurants chapter).

Stonecliffe Resort
$$$$ • Stonecliffe Rd., Mackinac Island • (906) 847-3355, (800) 447-1339

Tucked inside Mackinac Island's wooded interior, Stonecliffe stands as one of the region's finest examples of German Tudor architecture. This former mansion, on a secluded bluff on the island's southwest side, is a peaceful retreat from Mackinac's lively downtown. Originally built as a summer home in 1904, it was converted into a hotel in 1977. Fourteen guest rooms are available, all with private baths and turn-of-the-century furnishings. Larger accommodations are available through Lake Bluff Condominiums, also on the resort grounds. Condominiums range in size from one to three bedrooms with some featuring fireplaces and balconies with beautiful views of the Straits and the Mackinac Bridge. Guests at the mansion or the condos can take advantage of an outdoor swimming pool, tennis courts and the Pond House and Woods Restaurants (see our Restaurants chapter). Biking and hiking trails link Stonecliffe with the many pathways that weave through the island's interior and into town.

Bike rentals are available on site.

Windermere Hotel
**$$$$ • Huron St., Mackinac Island
• (906) 847-3301**

The Doud family has owned and operated the Windermere Hotel since 1904 when Patrick Doud converted an 1887 vintage, two-family home into a hotel. Doud was no newcomer to construction, since he had also helped build the Stonecliffe Mansion and the Governor's Island Residence. The Windermere has continued to stand tall through the decades as subsequent generations shared their hospitality with each season's wave of tourists. Today, Margaret Doud owns and manages the property. She also serves as Mackinac Island's longtime mayor, a post that she's held for more than twenty years.

The Windermere is a bright, yellow-clad Victorian inn standing across from the shoreline on the western edge of town. White wicker furniture fills the comfortable porch, offering a welcome invitation to relax and enjoy the Straits waters. Inside, 26 guest rooms are each uniquely decorated in antiques. Many share views of the water, nearby lighthouses or the Windermere gardens. A lovely continental breakfast is served daily.

Best Western Dockside Waterfront Inn
**$$$ • 505 S. Huron Ave., Mackinaw City
• (616) 436-5001, (800) 774-1794**

This is one of the newer hotels that now line the waterfront near the Mackinac Island ferry docks. The inn's brick exterior adds strength to an already impressive facility. Rooms are spacious with 90 units available. Most feature lake views. Large family suites and honeymoon suites with heart-shaped tubs are available, as are luxurious lakefront rooms with European-style balconies. Additional facilities include a 300-foot sandy beach, an indoor pool, oversize whirlpool, a game and exercise room and in-room refrigerators, coffee makers and hair dryers. The Best Western Dockside Waterfront is right next to the north Arnold Dock and just steps from the many restaurants and shops along Huron Avenue and downtown.

Best Western of Mackinaw City
$$ • 112 Old U.S. Hwy. 31, Mackinaw City • (616) 436-5544, (800) 647-8286

The Best Western of Mackinaw City houses one of the town's largest indoor pools as well as 73 spacious single, double and triple rooms. Jacuzzi suites with wet bars are also available. Guests can also take advantage of a lovely whirlpool, sundeck, on-site laundromat and in-room movies as well as a complimentary breakfast bar. The hotel offers reasonable rates with a convenient location just a few blocks from the ferry docks, shopping and Mackinaw Crossings. The Best Western of Mackinaw City is open from mid-April to late October.

Budgetel Inn of Mackinaw
$$ • 109 S. Nicolet Ave., Mackinaw City • (616) 436-7737, (800) 4-BUDGET

The Budgetel Inn of Mackinaw is neighbor to the adjacent Mackinaw Crossings shopping and entertainment center. It is also within walking distance of most city attractions, shopping and dining. The Budgetel offers 80 guest rooms, including several Jacuzzi suites. Amenities include an indoor pool, spa, exercise room, in-room movies and coffee makers.

Days Inn Lakeview
$$ • 825 S. Huron Ave., Mackinaw City • (616) 436-5703, (800) DAYS INN

Days Inn Lakeview is on Lake Huron next to the Arnold Ferry docks. This family-friendly hotel has a nice outdoor play tower along with an indoor pool and whirlpool, putting green, shuffleboard, guest laundry, gift shop and restaurant. There are 84 guest rooms available, including rooms with king or queen beds, whirlpools and lakeview balconies.

Hamilton Inn Select — Beachfront
$$$$ • 701 S. Huron Ave., Mackinaw City
• (616) 436-5493, (800) 301-1765
This beautiful hotel overlooks Mackinac Island and boasts that it offers beachfront luxury on 300 feet of Lake Huron shoreline. With 96 guest rooms, this is one of Mackinaw City's largest hotels. Rooms feature balconies and HBO. Honeymoon suites with hot tubs and spacious two-bedroom suites are available. The Hampton also houses an indoor pool, hot tub and exercise room.

Paddle boats can be rented at the beach, and shopping, restaurants and ferries are a short walk away.

Holiday Inn Express
$$$ • 364 Louvingney St., Mackinaw City
• (616) 436-7100, (800) HOLIDAY
The Holiday Inn Express is one of the closest hotels to Colonial Michilimackinac and fort-area shopping and dining. There are 71 guest rooms available, including honeymoon and Jacuzzi suites with microwaves and refrigerators. Rooms on the third floor have private balconies. Amenities include indoor pool, spa, exercise room, game room, sundeck, HBO and a free breakfast bar. Guests heading to Mackinac Island can take advantage of the Holiday Inn's free shuttle to the ferry docks.

Motel 6
$$ • 206 Nicolet Ave., Mackinaw City
• (616) 436-8961, (800) 4-MOTEL-6
The Motel 6 sits just a short stroll from Mackinaw's many attractions. The motel offers 53 recently refurbished rooms, including a hot-tub room with heart-shaped tub. Guests will also enjoy an indoor pool, spa, sundeck, HBO and free shuttle to the ferry docks.

Quality Inn Beachfront
$$ • 917 S. Huron Ave., Mackinaw City
• (616) 436-5051, (800) 228-5151
The Quality Inn Beachfront is a favorite stop for motorcoach tours through the Straits area. The hotel stands on the Lake Michigan shoreline, with a sandy, 270-foot private beach and views of Mackinac Island and the Mackinac Bridge. There are 61 guest rooms, including several two-room units and honeymoon suites with whirlpool tubs. There are also a number of lakefront rooms with private balconies or walk-out patios. Additional amenities include an indoor pool, sauna, whirlpool, playground, picnic area, in-room coffee, refrigerators and HBO. The Quality Inn is open from early May through late October.

Ramada Inn and Convention Center
$$$ • 450 Nicolet Ave., Mackinaw City
• (616) 436-5535, (800) 2 RAMADA
Freeway access couldn't be more convenient at the Ramada Inn Convention Center. The hotel is just off Exit 338 from I-75, and is a short walk from downtown shopping. This family-friendly facility has an indoor pool, spa, sauna and game room as well as 154 guest rooms. Several two-room, two-bath suites are available, as are Jacuzzi rooms with microwaves, refrigerators and heart-shaped tubs. Hungry appetites can take advantage of two on-site restaurants, a Ponderosa Steakhouse and the Mackinaw Sports Bar. Island bound visitors can hop on the free ferry dock shuttle.

Ramada Limited Waterfront
$$$$ • 723 S. Huron Ave., Mackinaw City
• (616) 436-5055, (800) 2-RAMADA
This lovely Ramada is on Lake Huron close to the ferry docks and shopping. There are 42 deluxe rooms that feature private balconies, king- and queen-size beds, refrigerators and 32-inch televisions with cable and HBO. Jacuzzi rooms, honeymoon suites and two-bedroom suites are available. Additional amenities include a rooftop sun deck, a private sandy beach, an indoor pool with two whirlpools and a complimentary continental breakfast. The Ramada Limited Waterfront is open from late April through late October.

Super 8 Motel of Mackinaw City
$$$ • 601 N. Huron Ave., Mackinaw City
• (616) 436-5252, (800) 800-8000
The Super 8 promises "super rooms at

Grand Traverse Resort is the largest year-round full-service resort in the area.

super rates." You'll find 50 guest rooms available, including accommodations with Lake Huron or Mackinac Bridge views, private balconies and Jacuzzi suites with microwaves and refrigerators. Amenities include an indoor pool, spa, sauna, game room and HBO as well as a free shuttle to the Mackinac Island ferries.

Surf Motel
$$$ • 907 S. Huron Ave., Mackinaw City
• (616) 436-8831, (800) 922-8314

Families enjoy the Surf Motel where everyone can lounge on the 200-foot private beach on Lake Huron, play on the half-acre playground and picnic area, swim in the indoor pool, master Nintendo 64 or test their personal watercraft skills on Jet Skis and paddle boats.

The Arnold Ferry dock is a one block stroll away, and shopping is just three blocks away. There are 40 guest room available including several two-bedroom suites.

Best Western Georgian House
$$$ • 1131 N. State St., St. Ignace
• (906) 643-8411, (800) 322-8411

On Lake Huron with views of Mackinac Island, the Best Western Georgian House is a large, family-oriented complex with 85 guest rooms. It houses the area's only indoor recreation center complete with a swimming pool, whirlpool and game room. A children's playground and a 19-hole miniature golf course is also available. During the winter, snowmobiles have direct access to the trails. Casino packages are available.

Boardwalk Inn
$$ • 316 State St., St. Ignace
• (906) 643-7500

The Boardwalk Inn is the oldest hotel in St. Ignace and is also the area's only smoke-free establishment. Centrally located in the heart of the historic downtown district, the inn is just steps away from the ferries, restaurants and shopping. There are 17 guest rooms, uniquely decorated with 1920s charm. Indoor bicycle storage is available. The inn is open from May 15 through October 15, and in the winter by reservation only.

Harbour Pointe Motor Inn
$$$ • 797 N. State St., St. Ignace
• (906) 643-9882, (800) 642-3318

Evening bonfires are a highlight for guests staying at the Harbour Pointe Motor Inn. Rooms have large, ample windows to watch nearby Lake Huron and Mackinac Island. This spacious facility offers 123 one- and two-bedroom units with balconies and small refrigerators. The grounds are spacious, spreading over 11 landscaped acres on the shores of Lake Huron, with a large outdoor pool, spa and playground. An indoor pool, whirlpool, game room and guest laundry are available indoors. Harbour Pointe is along State Street, within easy walking distance of the Mackinac Island ferries and nearby shops.

Kennels

If Fido is looking for a place to stay, there are a number of kennels that are more than happy to open their "hotel" doors to four-legged guests. We have listed several of them below. If you think that you may need boarding services, make sure that your pet's shots are up-to-date, and that you bring immunization verification from your veterinarian. It's also a good idea to call ahead for reservations during the busy summer and holiday seasons.

For a full list of pet-friendly resources in each community, check with the local chamber of commerce or visitors bureau for assistance.

Grand Traverse

Traverse City Area
• Bokhara Pet Care Centers, 606 W. Front Street, Traverse City, (616) 946-7333
• Classic Canine Grooming and Boarding Kennels, 931 Duell Road, Traverse City, (616) 946-3646
• Diana's Personal Touch, 2716 Hammond Road, Traverse City, (616) 946-5630
• Marty's Pet & House Sitting Service, P.O. Box 451, Traverse City, MI 49685, (616) 929-3174
• Tulamar Kennel, 6281 Barney Road, Traverse City, (616) 947-4494
• Acme Creek Kennels, 5311 Bunker Hill Road, Williamsburg, (616) 938-9518
• Goldeneye Kennels, 10351 N. 21½, Buckley, (616) 269-3133

Leelanau County
• Leelanau Boarding Kennels, 8761 E. Kovarik Road, Northport, (616) 386-7340

Antrim-Kalkaska
• Bokhara Pet Care Centers, 11535 Elk Lake Road, Elk Rapids, (616) 264-5855
• Kintor Kennels, 3455 Kiessel Road, Central Lake, (616) 544-6519

Lake Michigan Shoreline and Cadillac
• Wagging Tail Lodge, 2266 Ellis Road, Frankfort, (616) 352-4501
• Platte Lake Veterinary Clinic, 9671 Honor Highway, Honor, (616) 325-2528

INSIDERS' TIP

Charlevoix's unique stone and turret Weathervane Terrace Inn was constructed by Realtor Earl Young. Young began building houses featuring huge stone exterior walls in the 1920s and left a legacy of 30 such structures in the community. Maps for self-guided driving tours of Young's work are available at the Charlevoix Chamber of Commerce.

•A&M Kennels, 202 Hoague Road, Manistee, (616) 723-8212

•Pattengale Kennels, 2030 Dontz Road, Manistee, (616) 723-9738

•Anderson Creek Kennels, 1042 S. Meyers Road, Ludington, (616) 843-8397

•Cadillac Canine & Feline Center, 530 Bell Avenue, Cadillac, (616) 775-4104

•Kozy Kennels, 7020 S. 45 Mile Road, Cadillac, (616) 775-2903

Little Traverse

•Donto Kennels, 05133 Barnard Road, Charlevoix, (616) 547-6866

•Bay Pines Boarding and Grooming, 8769 Michigan Highway 119, Harbor Springs, (616) 347-1383

Mackinac Straits

•Nunn's Creek Kennels, 410 St. Ignace Road, St. Ignace, (906) 484-3271

Within moments, a strange inn in a small northern town becomes a comfortable home away from home.

Bed and Breakfast Inns

You're only a stranger for a moment at a bed and breakfast. Gracious hospitality is the essential ingredient in the characteristic charm of these inns. In Northwest Michigan, we like to take hospitality one step farther by adding a healthy dose of old fashioned, small-town neighborliness. Our hosts open their hearts and their doors to guests who quickly find themselves welcomed as honorary family members. Within moments, a strange inn in a small northern town becomes a comfortable home away from home.

Northwest Michigan is filled with small towns in beautiful settings. Add our magnificent shorelines, rolling hills and forests to the region's architectural heritage and traditional visitors' attractions, and you have all the ingredients for a successful bed and breakfast environment.

Almost 150 bed and breakfast homes operate in the upper half of the state, and more open each month. We've highlighted more than half of them below. They are as unique as their hosts and their communities. Many are in turn-of-the-century Victorian houses and former lumber barons' mansions. Some are renovated farmhouses overlooking scenic countryside while others are newly built shoreline cottages or north-woods retreats. Some will send you off to enjoy the day with a light continental breakfast while others plan a multi-course gourmet meal. Some host late afternoon gatherings with hors d'oeuvres or wine and cheese or tea and cookies. A few even share late night cookies and desserts. Regardless, one of these bed and breakfasts is sure to fit your tastes.

As in other chapters, our listings are subdivided by geographical area. Nightly rates vary enormously by community, location and season. A general price guidelines for each inn is noted by the dollar signs before its address and telephone number. Bed and breakfasts often have a wide span of costs among their various rooms. We've based the rating on an average guest room with a double or queen-size bed during the peak summer weeks. Many rates will drop a bit during spring, fall and winter, or might be rolled into a special theme weekend or off-season discount package. Always check with your innkeepers to verify rates and availability. Also, double check the current credit card policy. Most establishments will accept major credit cards, so we have only made note if credit cards are not accepted. However since policies and owners can change from time to time, it's wise to confirm. It's also advisable to check with your

Price Code

Bed and breakfast rates are as varied as the properties themselves. Costs and availability often fluctuate with the seasons, and you can usually count on paying top dollar during the height of summer between late June and mid-August. Our price code is based on average room cost during the summer.

$	Less than $65
$$	$65 to $80
$$$	$80 to $100
$$$$	$100 to $125
$$$$$	$125 or more

hosts — before you arrive — on their rules regarding smoking, alcohol, late arrivals and morning meals. Some homes are not appropriate for young children while others cater to family needs. If allergies are a concern, check to see if any pets are in residence.

Our hosts want to make your stay memorable and are happy to share their hometown knowledge of the community and nearby attractions. They will also help with dinner reservations, special dietary needs, unique meal requests and even picnic lunches. All you have to do is ask. After all, to paraphrase the popular Disney song, remember "you're our guest."

dows rising to the high ceilings surround the elegant great room, unveiling breathtaking, panoramic views of the peninsula and the bay while guests enjoy the beautiful dining area, massive granite fireplace, oak bar and white concert piano. Music often fills the great room as local artists share their talents. Three guest rooms are available. Two are first-floor suites with separate sitting rooms and private baths while the third is a queen-size room on the upper level featuring a canopied bed and hand-stitched quilt, pillows and wall hangings. A full breakfast is served daily. Chateau Chantal is open year round and a two-night minimum stay is required on weekends.

Grand Traverse

Traverse City Area

Bowers Harbor Bed and Breakfast
$$$$ • 13972 Peninsula Dr., Traverse City • (616) 223-7869

A wraparound stone front porch offers a welcoming entrance to Bowers Harbor Bed and Breakfast. This newly remodeled country farmhouse overlooks beautiful Bowers Harbor along the western shore of Traverse City's Old Mission Peninsula. It's nestled within easy walking distance of three wonderful restaurants — Bowers Harbor Inn, The Bowery and The Boathouse (see our Restaurants chapter) — as well as a marina, township park and the lodge's own sandy beach. A gourmet breakfast is served daily. Three rooms with private baths are available year round.

Chateau Chantal
$$$$ • 15900 Rue de Vin, Traverse City • (616) 223-4110, (800) 969-4009

Reminiscent of a French country inn, Chateau Chantal sits atop a ridge on the northern end of the Old Mission Peninsula. This unique establishment combines a bed and breakfast with a vineyard, winery and tasting room (see the Attractions chapter for more on the wine business) on a 65-acre site. Every detail of the Chateau shares its Old World ambiance. Win-

Cedar Creek B&B
$$ • 7651 E. Timberwoods Dr., Traverse City • (616) 947-5643

Rolling hills and a wooded, rustic setting greet guests at Cedar Creek B&B, 6 miles north of the Traverse City limits on the Leelanau Peninsula. This antique-filled, historic home features oak woodwork, wood floors, a hot tub and two guest rooms with queen-size beds and private baths. Perennial flower and water gardens decorate the grounds.

Cider House Bed & Breakfast
$$$, no credit cards • 5515 Barney Rd., Traverse City • (616) 947-2833

Sitting amidst the owners' 10-acre apple orchard, the Cider House Bed & Breakfast is aptly named. During the year, guests can enjoy fragrant apple blossoms in the spring, apple picking and cider pressing in the fall, and hot, spiced cider in the winter. Five antique-filled guest rooms with private baths are available, each bearing the name of a favorite apple — Cortland, Ida Red, MacIntosh, Red Delicious and Rome Beauty. Beds are draped in patchwork quilts, down comforters or lace coverlets as well as piles of feather pillows. Heated beanbags are offered on cold nights to help keep winter beds toasty. A full breakfast buffet is served each morning, and guests can eat as they wish at a common table, individually, in their rooms or on an outdoor deck.

The Grainery

$$$ • 2951 Hartman Rd., Traverse City
• (616) 946-8325

The Grainery offers a quiet retreat on a 10-acre country lot. This home dates back to 1892 and is filled with antiques reflecting its country Victorian heritage. Five guest rooms with private baths are available including two suites with Jacuzzi tubs and fireplaces. Amenities include air conditioning, an outdoor hot tub, cable television, two golf greens and a full country breakfast.

Linden Lea on Long Lake

$$$, no credit cards • 279 S. Long Lake Rd., Traverse City • (616) 943-9182

Long Lake and its wooded surroundings provide a lovely backdrop for Linden Lea. Originally built as a summer cottage at the turn of the century, the home was enlarged several times and was massively remodeled into a bed and breakfast by its current owners. Its multilevel exterior is clad in decks overlooking Long Lake and the scenic countryside. Steps lead to a sandy beach that is perfect for swimming or exploring in the owners' rowboat. Inside, windows in the two lakeside guest rooms and the main-level living room give more opportunities to see the lake, the birch trees and magnificent sunsets. Guest rooms are cozy with queen-size beds, private baths and window seats. Plan to eat a large breakfast. Developing and cooking new recipes is a specialty of owner Vicky McDonnell. Several of her specialties have won awards and have been featured in cookbooks.

Tall Ship Malabar

$$$ • 13390 S. West Bayshore Dr., Traverse City • (616) 941-2000, (800) 968-8800

Let the gentle West Bay waters lull you to sleep on the Tall Ship *Malabar*. This floating bed and breakfast is on board one of the largest traditional sailing vessels on the Great Lakes—a 105-foot, two-masted topsail schooner. Overnight guests join the *Malabar*'s daily Sunset Cruise across West Grand Traverse Bay (more on this in the Attractions chapter), then return to spend the night docked at the ship's private pier. The *Malabar* can accommodate as many as 21 guests in its eight private staterooms. Cabins are below deck, rustic and reminiscent of the ship's heritage as a mid-1800s style windjammer. Guests can sleep on built-in wooden bunks or, weather permitting, can bring a sleeping bag and pad onto the deck to sleep under the stars. Shared toilet facilities are near the cabins. In addition, modern restroom and shower facilities are available on shore. In the morning, guests enjoy the beautiful sunrise, a mug of fresh coffee and a hearty breakfast from the galley.

Twin Oaks

$$$, no credit cards • 628 Terrace Dr., Traverse City • (616) 946-6856, (800) 587-6559

Twin Oaks offers an urban retreat in the heart of Traverse City. This charming city home, nestled in a tree-filled neighborhood, is within walking distance of East Grand Traverse Bay, Northwestern Michigan College and Grand Traverse County Civic Center. Inside, antique and wicker furniture complement the home's country atmosphere. Two guest rooms are available, one with a private bath. A full breakfast with homemade breads, pastries and jams can be served in the formal dining room or in the comfort of the homey kitchen. Specially blended, gourmet coffee is served to early risers in the sitting room. Other amenities include cable television, air conditioning and an outdoor hot tub. Twin Oaks is open May to December.

Victoriana 1898

$$ • 622 Washington St., Traverse City • (616) 929-1009

True to its name, the Victoriana 1898 welcomes guests into a gracious home filled with Victorian charm. This historic home has been lovingly restored to its turn-of-the-century elegance with tiled fireplaces, an oak staircase, and countless antiques. The grounds are also filled with historical delights including a gazebo that was actually the bell tower for the city's first high school and a carriage house with a century-old cupola. Victoriana 1898 is in the historic Boardman neighborhood, just a few blocks from downtown Traverse City and West Grand Traverse Bay. Three guest rooms with private baths are available. Breakfasts are hearty, even for the most robust appetites, and

Photo: Terry W. Phipps/Mackinac Island Chamber of Commerce

Many of the region's favorite bed and breakfasts are housed
in vintage homes dating back to the late 1800s.

always feature one of the innkeeper's special home recipes.

Between the Lakes B&B
$$ • 4570 Case Blvd., Interlochen
• (616) 276-7751
Two acres filled with northern pine and hardwoods surround Between the Lakes B&B. Sixteen miles southwest of Traverse City, it's a short walk away from the internationally renowned Interlochen Center for the Arts and the scenic Interlochen State Park. International decor fills the home, reflecting the owner's lifelong career in the foreign service. The public rooms — including a library, living room, dining room, decks and a 60-foot indoor heated lap pool — are gracious and comfortable. Six guest rooms with private baths are available year round.

Interlochen Aire
$$ • 4550 State Park Hwy., Interlochen
• (616) 276-6941
Fresh-baked cookies await guests at Interlochen Aire, 16 miles from Traverse City. This country lodge is nestled in a beautifully wooded setting on Duck Lake within walking distance of Interlochen Center for the Arts and Interlochen State Park. Hand-hewn beams grace the inside, punctuated by a massive split fieldstone fireplace. There are two spacious bedrooms with a shared bath. Both feature

INSIDERS' TIP

Most bed and breakfasts do not allow smoking indoors. Check in advance on the house rules.

Ethan Allen country furnishings. Baking is a specialty here. Breakfasts are hearty and always feature homemade breads.

Sandy Shores B&B
$$ • 4487 State Park Hwy., Interlochen • (616) 276-9763

Duck Lake is the setting for Sandy Shores B&B, which draws its name from the home's private sandy beach. Three bedrooms with shared baths are tastefully furnished. Guests can enjoy the area's natural beauty on the Sandy Shores' beach, in the yard, on the deck or inside the glassed-in porch or large living room. Sandy Shores is steps away from Interlochen Center for the Arts and Interlochen State Park.

Hall Creek Bed & Breakfast
$$, no credit cards • 7450 Hall Creek Rd., Karlin • (616) 263-2560

Hall Creek is a fairly new bed and breakfast in rural Karlin. Two hundred wooded acres, a spring-fed, crystal-clear lake and meandering Hall Creek surround this peaceful retreat. The four guest rooms have private baths with whirlpools, air conditioning, televisions and queen-size beds. Enjoy a full country breakfast in the dining room overlooking Hall Creek and the woods or relax in a comfortable chair on one of the private, screened-in porches. Hall Creek Bed & Breakfast is a seven-minute drive away from Interlochen Center for the Arts and an 18-minute drive from Traverse City.

Leelanau County

Empire House Bed & Breakfast
$, no credit cards • 11015 Lacore St. S., Empire • (616) 326-5524

Empire House Bed & Breakfast is a charming 19th century farm house near the Sleeping Bear Dunes National Lakeshore. In the village of Empire, it offers guests a quiet, homey atmosphere in a peaceful, country setting. Four rooms are available, three with double beds and a shared bath and one with twin beds and a private bath. All rooms have outside entrances. Breakfast is billed as hearty continental with fresh-ground coffee. Empire House is open year round.

South Bar Manor
$$, no credit cards • 11292 S. Lacore St., Empire • (616) 326-5304

Relax in a country setting at South Bar Manor in Empire. Spacious grounds surround this two-story home that lies along the shores of South Bar Lake. Guests can take a short walk to nearby Lake Michigan and Empire Bluff or can wander to the village's unique shops and restaurants. Four guest rooms are available including deluxe accommodations with a private bath and standard rooms with shared baths. A full breakfast is served with home-baked breads and muffins straight from the oven. South Bar Manor is open througout the year.

The Sylvan Inn
$$$ • 6680 Western Ave., Glen Arbor • (616) 334-4333

A historic landmark, the Sylvan Inn was built in 1885. It has been beautifully restored and furnished to preserve its historic charm. Fourteen rooms are available, including seven with private baths. Glen Lake, Lake Michigan and the Sleeping Bear Dunes are nearby, or guests can relax in the inn's spa or sauna. The Sylvan Inn is closed in April and November.

White Gull Inn
$$ • 5926 S. West Manitou Trail, Glen Arbor • (616) 334-4486

At the White Gull Inn, guests enjoy a continental breakfast in the country kitchen of this century-old farmhouse. Country decor is featured throughout the house, including its five guest rooms and shared baths. The inn is on an especially scenic, wooded lot in Glen Arbor, near the Sleeping Bear Dunes National Lakeshore.

Centennial Inn
$$ • 7251 E. Alpers Rd., Lake Leelanau • (616) 271-6460

Take a step back in time at Centennial Inn in rural Lake Leelanau in the center of the Leelanau Peninsula. This farm was built in 1865, and several historic buildings are on the grounds. Inside, guests will enjoy homespun hospitality. A wood stove adds to the charm of the country kitchen where a full breakfast is prepared and then served in the inn's cozy dining room. Guests can relax in the parlor by watching television or reading in front of the fireplace. Three guest rooms with shared baths are furnished with four-poster beds, quilts and coverlets.

Aspen House
$$$$ • 1353 N. Manitou Tr. W., Leland • (616) 256-9724, (800) 762-7736

Old-world charm and comfort await at Aspen House just south of Leland. Reminiscent of a European bed and breakfast, this elegantly restored 1880 farmhouse stands along the narrow peninsula separating the shores of Lake Michigan and Lake Leelanau. Three guest rooms with private baths are comfortably furnished with unique antiques, handmade games and piles of down comforters for snuggling. Overstuffed chairs, a welcoming fireplace and book-filled shelves in the living rooms create a relaxing retreat. The kitchen is always bustling in preparation for scrumptious breakfasts, afternoon snacks and delicious evening desserts, all served on antique dishes. Aspen House is along the major driving routes leading to Leland, two minutes north, Suttons Bay, 10 minutes east, or Glen Arbor, 15 minutes south.

The Highlands of Leland
$$$ • 612 N. Lake St., Leland • (616) 256-7632, (313) 292-5503

The Highlands of Leland is a contemporary redwood home surrounded by tall white Michigan pines. A short walk away from downtown Leland, this peaceful retreat features comfortable furnishings and lovely decorating in its four guest rooms and common areas. Each guest room includes a private bath, kitchenette and cable television.

Manitou Manor
$$$ • 147 N. Manitou Tr. W., Leland • (616) 256-7712

Manitou Manor is 3 miles south of Leland on a spacious country estate. Six acres of cherry trees and a beautifully landscaped yard surround the house and barn, which date back to the 1860s. Six guest rooms are available, all with individual themes, king or queen beds and private baths. Families are always welcome and suites can accommodate up to four people. Guests gather in a large common room where they can play at the game table, chat in the conversation area, peruse the wall of books or simply relax in front of the fire or on the outdoor deck or glass-enclosed porch. Fresh coffee starts each day, followed by a delicious breakfast featuring Leelanau County products and specialties.

Snowbird Inn
$$$$ • 473 N. Manitou Tr. W., Leland • (616) 256-9773

The owners of the Snowbird Inn near Leland have dubbed it Leelanau's "Grand Lady." This turn-of-the-century farmhouse has been beautifully restored to its grand heritage and sits majestically surrounded by 18 acres of rolling hills and meadows. The peaceful grounds include a large garden, cherry orchard, secluded pond and hundreds of trees and flowers including several ancient black walnut trees. Bicycle paths begin just steps from the Snowbird's door. Inside, guests can browse through books in the cozy library, relax in the large living room or sit outdoors on the wraparound veranda. Flowers in the six guest rooms add to the romantic furnishings. Two rooms have private baths, others are shared. Morning is greeted with the smells of brewing coffee and baking breads, making way for the day's lavish, gourmet breakfast.

North Shore Inn
$$$$$ • 12271 N. Northport Pt. Rd., Northport • (616) 386-7111

Guests watch fabulous sunrises over Grand Traverse Bay from their waterfront rooms at the North Shore Inn in Northport. At the scenic tip of the Leelanau Peninsula, this

INSIDERS' TIP
Your hosts at bed and breakfast inns are the ultimate Insiders. Never hesitate to ask your hosts for their recommendations on dining, touring and sights. You will always get wonderful tips, usually embellished by local lore and trivia.

spacious colonial home has its own sandy beach as well as decks and a porch to enjoy the bay's shifting colors and moods. Four luxurious rooms are available, each with a fireplace and private bath. The hosts are gracious and friendly, sharing appetizers each afternoon and serving a gourmet country breakfast in the morning. The North Shore Inn is open May through October.

Omena Shores

$$$, no credit cards • 13140 Isthmus Rd., Omena • (616) 386-7313

Scenic Omena Bay and Mougey Lake lie on either side of Omena Shores Bed & Breakfast, 22 miles north of Traverse City and within walking distance of Omena's art galleries and unique shops. Open year round, this interesting inn was once a barn, built in 1852 as part of the Omena Presbyterian Church Parsonage. Visitors will find that it's been pleasantly renovated into a country-style home that still retains the integrity of the original design. The four guest rooms have private baths and are decorated with wicker and antiques. Guests enjoy meeting at the game table in the upstairs gathering room to share conversation with new-found friends. In the morning, hot coffee or tea is delivered outside each room followed by a hearty country breakfast complete with homemade cinnamon rolls or muffins. Omena Shores offers interesting packages and holiday specials throughout the year. A few intriguing possibilities are the Wine N' Dine Weekend with visits to a local winery and gourmet restaurant and Bike Leelanau Round-Abouts for bicycling enthusiasts. Check to see what's on the calendar.

Sunset Lodge

$$$, no credit cards • 12819 Tatch Rd. (County Rd. 626), Omena • (616) 386-9080

Sunset Lodge is a country Victorian home overlooking Omena Bay. Built in 1898, the lodge features a wraparound porch and second-floor balcony with breathtaking bay views. Gourmet breakfasts are highlighted by local specialties and are elegantly served in the formal dining room. A fireside living room and music room are also welcome gathering spots. Four second-floor bedrooms are available year

round. Each has a private bath, air conditioning, television, VCR and either a queen-size bed or two twin beds.

Century Farm

$$$ • 2421 Jacobson Rd., Suttons Bay • (616) 271-2421, (800) 252-8480

Thirty acres of scenic countryside provide a peaceful setting for Century Farm, 3 miles northwest of Suttons Bay. As its name implies, the farm is over 100 years old. The home and seven outbuildings are excellent examples of 19th-century wood and stone construction. Plan to bring your walking shoes and explore the farm's grounds by climbing to the top of the hill for a beautiful bay view, walking along the brook or simply meandering through the fruit trees and gardens. Relax later on the deck or in the outdoor hot tub. Inside, antique furnishings, hardwood floors, oak trim and warm colors add to the country ambiance. Each of the guest rooms has a different theme with related accessories ranging from antique walnut in the Lincoln Room, to bright green and white in the Cottage Room, rich tones and artwork in the Folk Art Room and king-size bed and antique cradle in the Manor Room. The Great Lakes Suite offers a private sitting area, deck and handicapped-accessible bath. The Lincoln and Cottage Rooms share a bath while the others are all private. Breakfasts feature fresh fruits and breads. Box lunches and kitchen privileges can be arranged.

Lee Point Inn

$$$ • 2885 Lee Point Ln., Suttons Bay • (616) 271-6770

A secluded wooded setting surrounds the Lee Point Inn in Suttons Bay. This traditional farmhouse-style home is charming and comfortable with three rooms available for guests. One room features a private bath while the other two share a bath. Flower-filled decks and waterfront rooms overlook West Grand Traverse Bay. A full breakfast is served daily.

Morning Glory Beach

$$$$ • 378 N. Stony Point Rd., Suttons Bay • (616) 271-6047

Morning Glory Beach will be your private northern escape. A single bed and breakfast room occupies the main level of a charming cedar-shingled home. Each morning, an elegant breakfast is served at your door. Morning Glory Beach's setting is on a bay within a bay. The private guest entrance is surrounded by a gardened patio while stairs lead down to the home's private beach. Plan to watch the sunset from the beachside deck.

Open Windows Bed & Breakfast
$$$ • 613 St. Mary's Ave., Suttons Bay
• (616) 271-4300, (800) 520-3722
An old-fashioned, white picket fence circles Open Windows Bed & Breakfast. Clad with green shutters, this white, century-old farmhouse is the picture of small-town hospitality. Adirondack chairs and tables handmade by the owner fill the lawn, deck and porch, and extend a warm invitation for afternoon lounging. Perennial gardens are lovely for strolling and bikes are available for exploring the village and countryside. Inside this comfortable home, three guest rooms with private and shared baths are available, complemented by a delicious homemade breakfast.

Antrim-Kalkaska

Torch Lake Bed & Breakfast
$$$ • 10601 Coy St., Alden
• (616) 331-6424
Period furniture fills this renovated 19th-century Victorian home in the charming village of Alden. Gorgeous views of beautiful Torch Lake are easily enjoyed from this hilltop home. Torch Lake Bed & Breakfast is pleasantly decorated in period furniture, European lace and stained glass. Guests will enjoy one of three guest rooms with private and shared baths. A full breakfast is included.

Bellaire Bed & Breakfast
$$ • 212 Park St., Bellaire
• (616) 533-6077, (800) 545-0780
The Bellaire Bed & Breakfast bills itself as a comfortable gathering place for friends and couples. Comfort is its common theme. This American Gothic home sits on several acres of scenic Bellaire countryside. Guests enjoy strolling around the grounds, relaxing on the large porch, browsing through the library or playing backgammon in front of the fireplace. The four guest rooms are peaceful. One fea-

tures a private second-story porch with glider while another is noted for its claw-foot bathtub (bubble bath is provided!). Two rooms share a bath. Special theme weekends or organized visits to wineries, ski resorts, theaters or other attractions can be arranged with the owners, who are also happy to provide airport transportation.

Grand Victorian Bed & Breakfast Inn
$$$$ • 402 N. Bridge St., Bellaire
• (616) 533-6111, (800) 336-3860
The Grand Victorian is one of the nicest places you will ever stay. A former lumber baron's home, it has been magnificently renovated into an elegant bed and breakfast. Turn-of-the-century decor and museum-quality antiques fill this gingerbread mansion with accents like etched glass, exquisite woodwork, three fireplaces, an old-fashioned parlor, several balconies and a wicker-filled porch. Four guest rooms are available, all with private baths. Breakfast is a culinary experience with a five-course meal elegantly served on silver. The Grand Victorian is listed in the National Historic Register and was cited in *Country Magazine* as one of the best bed and breakfasts in the United States. The reputation is well-deserved.

Bridgewalk
$$$ • 2287 S. Main St., Central Lake
• (616) 544-8122
This bed and breakfast draws its name from the charming foot bridge leading across a meandering brook to the front porch. Amidst a grove of maple trees, Bridgewalk is a spacious country Victorian home built in 1895 by lumber baron James Cameron. Architecturally, the home reflects its heritage with large, airy windows, pocket doors, high ceilings and woodwork of birds-eye maple, cherry and mahogany. Guests gather in the parlor to enjoy the fireplace, the baby grand piano and the company. There is a music room with old recordings and an antique Victrola. Five charming guest rooms are available. All have private baths and are furnished in antiques. Homemade breads, muffins and jams highlight the full breakfast, which can be served in the dining room or on the outdoor deck.

Photo: Olave Walker Russell

The Tall Ship *Malabar* is one of our region's most unique bed and breakfasts.

Coulter Creek B&B
$$ • 7900 Darmon Pl., Central Lake
• (616) 544-3931, (800) 942-6858

Panoramic views of Hanley Lake greet guests at Coulter Creek. This comfortable 1890s colonial home features a private beach, perennial gardens and outdoor hot tub. There are three tastefully decorated guest rooms, one with a private bath. The full breakfast promises to be "guest pleasing."

Torch Lake Sunrise Bed & Breakfast
$$$$ • 3644 Blasen Shores Ln., Eastport
• (616) 599-2706

The name says it all for this pleasant bed and breakfast near Eastport. The three bedrooms have sun decks overlooking beautiful Torch Lake where guests can canoe, boat, paddleboard, swim or sun at the private beach. Each guest room has antique furnishings, telephone, private bath and a lovely view. Warm, freshly baked muffins are served daily with each full breakfast.

Cairn House B&B
$$, no credit cards • 8160 Cairn Hwy., Elk Rapids • (616) 264-8994

Cairn House is a comfortable, colonial-style home near the small town of Elk Rapids, 15 minutes north of Traverse City. Three rooms with private baths are available. A delicious full breakfast is served daily.

Candlelight Inn
$$ • 310 Spruce St., Elk Rapids
• (616) 264-5630

A restored 1890s Victorian home with many charming antiques houses the Candlelight Inn. Just two blocks from Grand Traverse Bay in Elk Rapids, its peaceful setting is noted for lovely flower gardens and a relaxing wraparound porch. Each of the three tastefully decorated guest rooms has a private half bath. A full bath is shared.

Ellsworth House
$$ • 9510 Lake St., Ellsworth
• (616) 588-7001

Filled with antiques, flowers and lace, Ellsworth House is a fully restored 1876 Colonial inn. The rolling, wooded countryside in Ellsworth adds to the peaceful setting. The inn, which is open from late May through October, features three guest rooms with private baths and a second-floor balcony overlooking the gardened grounds. It is just steps away from the nationally noted Tapawingo and Rowe Inn restaurants (see our Restaurants chapter for more on these great eateries!).

Lake Michigan's Abiding Place
$$$ • 9317 Antrim Ln., Ellsworth
• (616) 599-2808

Lake Michigan's sparkling blue waters create the picturesque setting for this unique bed and breakfast. Lake Michigan's Abiding Place was built by a West Coast architect as a one-of-a-kind California-style home. Angled beams, exposed rafters, ample windows, glass doors and a cathedral ceiling create a simple, tasteful ambiance. Enjoy scenic views of the waterfront and nearby apple orchards from the upstairs balcony, veranda terrace and the path to the shoreline. Two guest rooms with a shared bath as well as a spacious suite with private bath, fireplace and terrace are available. Breakfast is continental, featuring warm breads, local preserves and gourmet coffee and teas.

Lake Michigan Shoreline and Cadillac

The Windermere Inn
$$ • 7723 Crystal Dr., Beulah
• (616) 882-9000

The Windermere Inn is a charming, turn-of-the-century farmhouse near the rural community of Beulah in scenic Benzie County. This is a nice retreat after a day spent touring or cross-country skiing. Guests can relax in front of a fire in either of the inn's two common rooms. Four guest rooms with private baths are available.

The Birch Haven Inn
$$ • 219 Leelanau Ave., Frankfort
• (616) 352-4008

Spectacular views of Lake Michigan highlight a stay at the lovely Birch Haven Inn in Frankfort. This hilltop Victorian mansion is two blocks away from downtown shops, restaurants and the beach. Antiques fill the house. The four guest rooms have private baths. Breakfast is hearty.

Frankfort Land Company
$$ • 428 Leelanau Ave., Frankfort
• (616) 352-9267

Frankfort Land Company is the oldest house in this charming lakeside town. Listed in the National Historic Register, it is an Italianate-style Victorian home that has been carefully restored to reflect its rich heritage. Period furniture and accessories are highlighted by beautifully decorated walls and ceilings. Guests gather in the parlor or sitting room, or while dining on a delicious, full breakfast. Two bedrooms with private baths are available at this bed and breakfast, which is within easy walking distance of the Lake Michigan beach and downtown shops.

E. E. Douville House
$ • 111 Pine St., Manistee
• (616) 723-8654

Vintage furnishings and collectibles fill the E. E. Douville House near Manistee's Victorian downtown. This 1879 home has been lovingly restored with much original detailing such as hand-carved woodwork, interior shutters, pocket doors, and a soaring staircase. A sitting room welcomes guests to gather and relax. Three antique-filled guest rooms with shared baths are available. A continental breakfast is served daily.

Inn Wick-A-Te-Wah
$$ • 3813 Lakeshore Dr., Manistee
• (616) 889-4396

Inn Wick-A-Te-Wah is known for its peaceful setting and delicious country gourmet breakfasts. On the shore of Portage Lake near Manistee, it's an ideal setting to enjoy quiet sunsets over nearby Lake Michigan and panoramic views of Portage Lake. Guests can swim, sail or fish from the shoreline or simply enjoy the view from the wicker-filled porch. The inn is a 1912 bungalow with bright rooms, unusual furniture and comfortable beds in each of the four guest rooms. Two of the rooms have private baths, the other two share a bath.

Lake Shore Bed & Breakfast
$$ • 3440 Lake Shore Rd., Manistee
• (616) 723-7644

Lake Michigan is right outside the door at the Lake Shore Bed & Breakfast. Three miles west of Manistee, this newer, Western-style cedar home has a private, sandy beach and waters' edge deck. This is a lovely natural area near Orchard Beach State Park and Audubon Center. Lake Shore amenities include cable television, a delicious breakfast and private decks. Two guest rooms with shared bath are available.

Manistee Country House
$ • 1130 Lake Shore Rd., Manistee
• (616) 723-2367

The Manistee Country House is a casual two-story brick home built in 1901. On 2½ acres, this early country home is decorated in casual turn-of-the-century style. Guests can relax on the large "round-the-corner" porch, and in the parlor and living room as well as the home's four guest rooms. Two of the rooms have private baths, the other two share a bath.

The Maples
$ • 435 Fifth St., Manistee
• (616) 723-2904

Manistee's Trolley Lane is right at the doorstep of The Maples in the town's historic district. This vintage home was built in 1905 and features a large porch, open staircase and oak paneling. Three guest rooms are available during the summer months including two rooms with a shared bath and a parlor suite with a fireplace and private bath.

Doll House Inn
$$$ • 709 E. Ludington Ave., Ludington
• (616) 843-2286, (800) 275-4616

Antique dolls and family heirlooms fill the Doll House Inn, a restored 1900 American four-square home. Guests can take a leisurely stroll downtown or to the beach, or use the inn's bikes to explore this pretty shoreline community. Seven guest rooms with private baths are available including a bridal suite with whirlpool tub. The health conscious will appreciate the full heart-smart breakfast. Special weekend packages are available during the quieter seasons as well as the Ludington Association's murder mystery weekends. The Doll House Inn is open April through December.

The Inn at Ludington
$$$ • 701 E. Ludington Ave., Ludington
• (616) 845-7055, (800) 845-9170

Enjoy casual elegance in an 1890 Victorian mansion when you stay at The Inn at Ludington. Family heirlooms and collectibles decorate this historic "painted lady" near downtown and the beach. Six guest rooms with private baths are available including a bridal suite and a family suite. The breakfast buffet is excellent.

The Lamplighter Bed & Breakfast
$$$$ • 602 E. Ludington Ave., Ludington
• (616) 843-9792, (800) 301-9792

The Lamplighter combines European elegance with American comfort in a graceful Victorian setting. Original artwork and beautiful antiques complement the home's centennial architecture and help create a relaxing ambiance of luxurious tranquility. Highlights include several fireplaces, restored wood floors, lead crystal chandeliers, a curved-oak staircase and lace curtains and tablecloths. Each of the five guest rooms has been individually decorated and features a private bath, queen-size bed and telephone. A hearty gourmet breakfast is elegantly served in the formal dining room or outdoors in the gazebo. The Lamplighter hosts murder-mystery weekends in the winter.

The Ludington House
$$$-$$$$ • 501 E. Ludington Ave., Ludington • (616) 845-7769, (800) 827-7869

Three blocks from downtown, The Ludington House is a historic 1878 Victorian home. Eight guest rooms with private baths are available including family suites and a bridal suite with a whirlpool tub and fireplace. A lovely gourmet breakfast is served daily. Picnic baskets for the beach or park are happily prepared upon request. The Ludington House also hosts winter murder-mystery weekends.

Schoenberger House
$$$$$ • 409 E. Ludington Ave., Ludington • (616) 843-4435

Schoenberger House is a magnificent neoclassical mansion that has served as a family home since 1903. Built by one of the lumber barons, this elegant home is graced with beautiful woodwork, crystal chandeliers, five fireplaces, a library and music room with a grand piano. Five guest rooms with private baths are available. Guests are minutes from downtown, the marina and the beach. Schoenberger House has been featured in *Historic Homes of America* and *Grand Homes of the Midwest*.

American Inn
$$$ • 312 E. Cass St., Cadillac
• (616) 779-9000

A few short blocks from downtown Cadillac, the American Inn is centrally located to neighborhoods, shopping, the city park and waterfront. The American Inn was built in 1896 and served as a private home for several families and several generations. A major renovation transformed this comfortable home into a welcoming bed and breakfast complemented by stained glass, oak carvings and antiques. Five guest rooms with private baths are available, highlighted by a master suite with private spa, spiral staircase and walk-out deck. Amenities include cable television, air conditioning, sauna, hot tub and a hearty continental breakfast.

Bed & Breakfast in the Pines
$$$, no credit cards • 1940 S. Schneider St., Lake City • (616) 839-4876

This quaint chalet is a north-woods retreat. Nestled within a grove of pine trees, it sits on the shore of Sapphire Lake near Lake City. A large fireplace adds to the rustic charm, and serves as a focal point for guests to meet and relax. Guest rooms have shared and private baths as well as their own separate doors onto a lakeside deck. Reservations should be made at least two weeks in advance.

Little Traverse

The Florence
$$$$ • 1695 Park Ave., Bay View
• (616) 348-3322, (800) 866-1346

Vacation in the ambiance of another era in Bay View, a Victorian summer colony north of Petoskey that has been designated as a National Historic Landmark. The Florence is one of the 440 Victorian cottages in Bay View. Built in 1878 and furnished with antiques, it features eight guest rooms with private baths as well as a bright sunroom and flower-filled porch. Guests start the morning with an elegant gourmet breakfast. The Florence is open from May to October.

The Gingerbread House
$$$$ • 1130 Bluff St., Bay View
• (616) 347-3538

Another charming Bay View cottage, the Gingerbread House is filled with pastel hues and white wicker furniture. Romantic floral gardens surround the home, which was built in 1881 and lovingly renovated into a bed and breakfast. Four guest rooms are available. All have private baths and views of scenic Little Traverse Bay. A deluxe, home-baked continental breakfast is served daily. The Gingerbread House is open from May to October.

The Beardsley House
$$$ • 401 Pearl St., Boyne City
• (616) 582-9619

The Beardsley House is a Victorian delight. Built in 1898, it features original woodwork, tin ceilings, a library and a parlor. Antiques and china collections highlight the charming decor. Guests can relax in the hot tub, in front of the fireplace or on the wraparound porch overlooking the Boyne River. Four guest rooms are available with shared and private baths, and include a full gourmet breakfast.

Deer Lake Bed and Breakfast
$$$ • 00631 E. Deer Lake Rd., Boyne City • (616) 582-9039

Enjoy a waterfront stay in a peaceful country setting at Deer Lake Bed and Breakfast. On Deer Lake, this contemporary home lies within the four-season recreational area surrounding Boyne country. If you're feeling creative, the hosts will often offer a personalized jewelry class to make your own gold or silver ring. Talk to the owners about the jewelry class when making your reservation. Five guest rooms with private baths and individual heat and air conditioning controls are available at

---

INSIDERS' TIP

Ask your hosts about your bed and breakfast's history. Many boast a rich heritage of faces and times long past. The Victorian-era homes saw the heyday of Northwest Michigan's lumber barons and the early days of tourism.

Deer Lake. A full breakfast is served with china, crystal and candlelight.

Duley's State Street Inn
$$ • 303 State St., Boyne City
• **(616) 582-7855, (800) 230-4359**

Duley's State Street Inn is two blocks from Lake Charlevoix and Boyne City's downtown. The town's first bed and breakfast opened in 1989 after an ambitious renovation of this Victorian home. French country accents and romantic hues complement original woodwork and brass hardware. Three guest rooms with private baths are available including a suite that accommodates families. A gourmet breakfast is served with fine china and flowers.

Aaron's Windy Hill Guest Lodge
$$$ • 202 Michigan Ave., Charlevoix
• **(616) 547-2804**

A large river-stone porch is a lovely front for Aaron's Windy Hill Guest Lodge. Just one block from downtown Charlevoix, it is steps away from the town's unique shops and scenic drawbridge and harbor. This Victorian home has seven guest rooms with private baths. Each is spacious and beautifully decorated. Several rooms can accommodate families or up to five guests. Aaron's Windy Hill is open mid-May through October with early and late-season rates available.

Bridge Street Inn
$$$$ • 113 Michigan Ave., Charlevoix
• **(616) 547-6606**

The Bridge Street Inn is a charming colonial-revival cottage built in 1895. A relaxing wraparound porch is a wonderful retreat after exploring Charlevoix's charming shops, art galleries and restaurants. The home bears an English motif with many antique furnishings. There are nine guest rooms with private and shared baths, plush beds and lake views. A bridal suite is available for special occasions.

Caine Cottage
$$$ • 219 Antrim St., Charlevoix
• **(616) 547-6781**

The Caine Cottage was built in 1892 and was transformed into a bed and breakfast home 100 years later. Guests take advantage of a wicker-filled front porch in warm weather

and a cozy living room in the colder months. Caine Cottage is a few blocks from downtown and Lake Michigan. Three guest rooms are available with private and shared baths.

Charlevoix Country Inn
$$$$ • 106 W. Dixon Ave., Charlevoix
• **(616) 547-5134**

Guests meet each afternoon for wine and cheese socials at Charlevoix Country Inn. This 1892 inn is decorated with a charming country theme throughout its common rooms, eight guest rooms and two suites. All guest rooms have private baths. Visitors can watch gorgeous Lake Michigan sunsets or the daily flurry of boating activity from the inn's balcony or porch or at the beach next door. The Charlevoix Country Inn is open between mid-May and mid-October. Ask about off-season discounts.

The Inn at Grey Gables
$$$$ • 306 Belvedere Ave., Charlevoix
• **(616) 547-2251, (800) 280-4667**

The Inn at Grey Gables is on tree-lined Belvedere Avenue in Charlevoix. The home was built in 1887. Guests relax in hammocks or on the peaceful wraparound porch when not enjoying a full breakfast or indulging in the inn's homemade desserts. Seven guest rooms with private baths are available year around with special discounts offered during the off-season.

MacDougall House B&B
$$$ • 109 Petoskey Ave., Charlevoix
• **(616) 547-5788, (800) 753-5788**

MacDougall House sits majestically along Charlevoix's petunia-lined main street. This grand Victorian home houses five beautifully furnished guest rooms with private baths. Plan to bring your appetite to breakfast. This lavish meal features Scottish and American specialties prepared fresh each morning. MacDougall House is a popular destination during the warmer months. Stays between November and May can be arranged through advanced reservation. Off-season rates are available.

Easterly Inn
$$$ • 209 Easterly St., East Jordan
• **(616) 536-3434**

Easterly Inn is a charming three-story Victorian home two blocks away from Lake Charlevoix in East Jordan. Maple trees shade a large wraparound porch filled with wicker furniture and flowers. Inside, antique furnishings complement the inn's original woodwork, leaded glass windows and hand-painted wallpaper. Four guest rooms with private baths are available between May and early January.

Kimberly Country Estate
$$$$$ • 2287 Bester Rd., Harbor Springs
• **(616) 526-7646**
A favorite of many Northwest Michigan visitors, Kimberly Country Estate is a Colonial plantation home. It's a four-minute drive from downtown Harbor Springs and a 10 minute drive from golf, skiing and sports at Boyne Highlands and Nub's Nob. This gracious home's verandas and terrace overlook its swimming pool and the historic Wequetonsing Golf Course. The interior design is lovely, and so is the breakfast. Six beautifully appointed guest rooms with private baths are available. Kimberly Country Estate is usually closed during April.

Veranda at Harbor Springs
$$$$$ • 403 E. Main St., Harbor Springs
• **(616) 526-7782**
The Veranda at Harbor Springs promises grand Southern style complemented by the special amenities of today. This Victorian style inn is near the waterfront in the heart of Harbor Springs. Four deluxe rooms with private baths are available. Breakfast is served each morning on the harborside veranda.

Windy Ridge Bed & Breakfast
$$$$$ • 6281 S. Lake Shore Dr., Harbor Springs • (616) 526-7650, (800) 409-4095
A quiet country atmosphere greets guests at Windy Ridge. Located 4½ miles northwest of Harbor Springs, this bed and breakfast is within a gracious timber-frame home accented with oak beams and a large stone fireplace. Magnificent views of Little Traverse Bay and Lake Michigan can be seen from the home or the outdoor hot tub and garden patio. Guests enjoy a delicious, gourmet breakfast after spending the night in one of the four guest rooms that feature queen-size beds and water views.

510 Elizabeth
$$$ • 510 Elizabeth St., Petoskey
• **(616) 348-3830**
510 Elizabeth is a restored 1892 Queen Anne home filled with antiques and period decor. Petoskey's charming downtown Gaslight District is three blocks away. Three guest rooms with private and shared baths are available. A continental breakfast is served each morning.

Bear River Valley Bed & Breakfast
$$ • 03636 Bear River Rd., Petoskey
• **(616) 348-2046**
Plan to use the wood-fired Finnish sauna when you stay at the Bear River Valley Bed & Breakfast. Six miles south of Petoskey, its country setting offers a relaxing and refreshing north-woods retreat. Three guest rooms with shared baths are available. Morning promises a healthy gourmet continental breakfast.

The Cozy Spot
$$ • 1145 Kalamazoo Ave., Petoskey
• **(616) 347-3869**
The Cozy Spot is a private spot with only a single guest suite available. The large two-room suite includes a queen bed, television, wood stove, deck and private bath. Breakfast, featuring an ample continental menu, is served in the privacy of the guest suite.

Montgomery Place
$$$$ • 618 E. Lake St., Petoskey
• **(616) 347-1338**
Montgomery Place is a picturesque 1878 Victorian in a residential neighborhood near the Gaslight District. Formerly known as Benson House, it features an 80-foot veranda overlooking scenic Little Traverse Bay. In addition to a full breakfast, Montgomery Place guests are invited to enjoy wine and cheese each afternoon. Four guest rooms, including a special occasion suite, are available. All have private baths.

Serenity — A Bed & Breakfast
$$$ • 504 Rush St., Petoskey
• **(616) 347-6171**
This charming turn-of-the-century Victorian inn is within walking distance of Petoskey's Gaslight District and downtown sites. Two

glass-enclosed porches are furnished in wicker, and offer pleasant spots to relax or read. The breakfasts at Serenity are delicious, as are the cookies that accompany afternoon tea. Three guest rooms with private baths are available including two with air conditioning.

Mackinac Straits

Bay View at Mackinac
$$$$ • Huron St., Mackinac Island
• **(906) 847-3295**

Sitting along the shores of Lake Huron, Bay View at Mackinac is the island's only bed and breakfast at the water's edge. Each of the 19 guest rooms in this lovely Victorian home has its own spectacular view of the Straits of Mackinac. Guests awaken at their leisure to the aromatic smells of fresh pastries and the innkeeper's specially blended and brewed coffee. Breakfast is served in the formal dining room or on the open air veranda where one can relax while watching the boats and general hubbub of activity at the marina next door. The Bay View was built in 1891. Extensive remodeling has retained the inn's charming heritage while incorporating modern amenities like private bathrooms and well-hidden televisions and telephones. Bay View at Mackinac is open from early May through mid-October.

Bogan Lane Inn
$ • Bogan Ln., Mackinac Island
• **(906) 847-3439**

Built in 1850, this small bed and breakfast sits along residential Bogan Lane. Four bright, airy rooms with two shared baths are available. The daily continental breakfast is known for its freshly baked pastries. Bogan Lane Inn is open May through November as well as during much of the off-season.

Chateau Lorraine
$$ • Bogan Ln., Mackinac Island
• **(906) 847-8888**

Authentic Victorian antiques reflect the heritage of this turn-of-the-century home. A short walk from downtown, Chateau Lorraine offers five guest rooms ranging from those featuring twin or double beds with shared baths to full- and double-bed suites with private baths. A

formal dining room, sun porches and a beautiful courtyard garden add to the Inn's historic charm. Breakfast is continental with an ample array of wonderful jams and jellies to taste.

Cloghaun
$$$$ • Market St., Mackinac Island
• **(906) 847-3885**

Thomas and Bridgett Donnelly built Cloghaun in 1884 to house their large Irish family during the height of Mackinac Island's flourishing fishing industry. Pronounced "Clahhahn," the home was named after Tom's birthplace in County Galway, Ireland, and is Gaelic for "land of little stones." It stands today as one of the oldest Victorian homes on the island, its rooms filled with fine, family antiques and vintage elegance. A large porch stretches across the front while two balconies hang overhead connecting to their adjacent upper-level rooms. Eleven guest rooms are available, each with its own diary for guests to leave a message for future patrons and to enjoy the words of their predecessors. Several rooms are connecting and can be rented as suites, and nine of the eleven have private baths. Open May through mid-November, Cloghaun is ideally located on historic Market Street, just a few steps away from downtown.

Haan's 1830 Inn
$$$$ • Huron St., Mackinac Island
• **(906) 847-6244**

Next to the St. Anne's gardens in the east residential area of Huron Street, Haan's 1830 Inn was built on the foundation of a trader cabin that was brought from the mainland during the American Revolution. During the late 1800s, it was the private residence of Col. William Preston, one of the last officers at Fort Mackinac and island mayor at the turn of the century. This Greek revival home has been beautifully restored with seven guest rooms, each uniquely furnished with period antiques. Rooms bear the names of former island notables such as John Jacob Astor, Pere Marquette and Madame LaFramboise. Colonel Preston's namesake is a four-person suite featuring a full kitchen, bed-sitting room, sleigh bed and private bath. Five of the seven rooms feature private baths with showers while the remaining two share a bath that sports an an-

Within moments you'll feel right at home in an up-north bed and breakfast.

Photo: Terry W. Phipps/Mackinac Island Chamber of Commerce

tique claw foot tub with shower. One screened and two open-air porches provide a relaxing respite from a day of island touring. A deluxe continental breakfast is served daily in the front parlors with a menu featuring fresh fruit and an array of delicious, home-baked breads, muffins and coffeecakes. Haan's 1830 Inn is open mid-May through mid-October.

LaChance Cottage
$$ • Huron St., Mackinac Island
• (906) 847-3526

With 18 rooms, LaChance is one of the larger tourist homes on Mackinac Island. Rooms are small but several are large enough for families. All share baths with two full baths on each floor. This pleasant inn is wrapped by an open-air porch and balcony, and features a large, grassy yard. Brian's Barbecue (see our Restaurants chapter) shares the lawn and wafts wonderful aromas. LaChance Cottage is on the east end of Huron Street near St. Anne's Church and Bogan Lane.

Lilac House
$$ • Market St., Mackinac Island
• (906) 847-3708

Lilac House is a cozy, five-bedroom bed and breakfast on Market Street near the downtown Harbor District. Guests share three baths with tub/shower combinations. A continental breakfast is served daily. Owner Mary Thompson is an island native. The Lilac House operates from mid-May through mid-October.

McNally Cottage
$ • Huron St., Mackinac Island
• (906) 847-3565

McNally Cottage is a charming bed and breakfast in the heart of the downtown Harbor District. The home was built in 1889 for the McNally family, whose descendants continue to share their hospitality with island guests today. Eight rooms are available ranging from a small single unit to a spacious, family suite. Four have private baths. A continental breakfast is served daily. McNally Cottage operates from May through September.

Market Street Inn
$$$ • Market St., Mackinac Island
• (906) 847-3811

The Market Street Inn is centrally located across from Marquette Park, near the Fort, harbor and historic buildings along Market and Fort streets. Furnished in antiques, this cozy inn offers seven guest rooms furnished in antiques, four-poster beds and chintz shades in burgundy and green. All rooms have private baths. Daily breakfast is continental. The Market Street Inn is open May through October.

Metivier Inn
$$$$$ • Market St., Mackinac Island
• (906) 847-6234, (616) 627-2055 winter

Originally built as the Metivier family home in 1877, the inn has been completely remodeled and stands as one of the island's premier bed and breakfasts. Reflecting its heritage, French and English influences are felt throughout the house. The 20 guest rooms, all with private baths, are beautifully decorated in brass, wicker and antique furnishings. A spacious front porch offers a welcome spot to relax and watch the comings and goings of Market Street. Centrally located steps away from downtown and the historic sites, the Metivier Inn is open May through October and features a deluxe continental breakfast each morning.

Pine Cottage
$$$ • Bogan Ln., Mackinac Island
• (906) 847-3820

Rustic Victorian decor is featured at Pine Cottage, off Bogan Lane on the east side of town. Fifteen guest rooms are available, with cable television and a combination of shared and private baths. Fresh breads and pastries are baked daily for breakfast while coffee and tea service is offered each evening. Pine Cottage is open during much of the winter as well as the regular spring, summer and fall tourist seasons.

Small Point
$ • Lake Shore Dr., Mackinac Island
• (906) 847-3758

Quiet Small Point is away from the hustle and bustle of downtown approximately three-quarters of a mile along Lake Shore Drive. Plan to take a horse-drawn taxi or, if you're using backpacks, hop on a bike and pedal the short route. Originally known as the Sheeley House, Small Point was built in 1882 as a summer home. It features six guest rooms, most with shared baths, as well as a large porch and decks with scenic views of the Straits of Mackinac. Small Point is open during the summer, beginning in early June and running through Labor Day.

Narrowing your selection from among the hundreds of camping opportunities along Lake Michigan's rugged bluffs, birch-lined streams and city attractions is a certain challenge.

Campgrounds and RV Parks

When the call of the wild beckons you, Northwest Michigan is the place to be. Campgrounds throughout the region take you to the heart of the state's lush woodlands, scenic inland lakes and freshwater coastlines where you can enjoy a variety of world-class outdoor recreational activities year round (see our Recreation chapters).

Read over our sampling of the region's campgrounds, and you will realize the camping scene is abundant and diverse — like the Northwest forest ecosystem. Choosing a campground here won't be easy. You can set up your home away from home so deep into the wilds that it can only be reached by canoe. Or, you may want to consider a site near cultural, historical and urban attractions. For those of you who don't want to leave cable TV behind, you will find dozens of clean and inviting private campgrounds to accommodate you. Narrowing your selection from among the hundreds of camping opportunities along Lake Michigan's rugged bluffs, birch-lined streams and city attractions is a certain challenge, but with a little effort — and our help — you'll discover a park to perfectly match your camping style.

For many, the campground is not a destination in itself, but a base from which to take in the area's many natural wonders. Reading our chapters on attractions, events and recreation may help you select a campsite near the destinations that interest you.

This chapter includes Michigan state parks, state and national forest campgrounds and even backcountry island campgrounds in the northern lower peninsula's 3-million acres of public land. You'll also find a generous menu of private campgrounds and RV parks.

State park campgrounds are so plentiful in Northwest Michigan that you are never more than an hour away from one. We will introduce you to 12 campgrounds from among the Michigan State Park System. The system, now including nearly 100 parks, was established in 1919 to preserve waterways, dunes, old growth forests, Great Lake shorelines and the state's cultural heritage.

Michigan State Park facilities vary in size and amenities. They consist of anywhere from 50 to 370 modern and rustic campsites. Rates reflect the amenities available at individual parks. A motor vehicle permit is required for entrance to all parks. The permits cost $4 overnight or $20 annually and are available at entrance gates or park offices. Michigan residents 65 years or older can purchase an annual permit for $5. Fido and Fluffy are welcome at state parks in Northwest Michigan, as long as they remain on a 6-foot leash. Many state parks in our listings offer barrier-free facilities to provide recreational opportunities to all, regardless of physical ability. You can obtain detailed information on an individual park's barrier-free opportunities by calling the numbers in our listings.

We strongly recommend you make reservations as soon as your vacation is scheduled. It is almost imperative to secure reservations if you want to have a campsite during holidays and summer weekends. Reservations are accepted up to 11 months in advance. Call state park reservations at (800) 44PARKS. Prime camping spots in Northwest Michigan are in the 43 state forest campgrounds throughout the Pere Marquette and Mackinaw

State Forests. The Pere Marquette alone offers campers 521 miles of canoe-ready streams and more than 500 miles of trails for off-road vehicles as well as a variety of hiking, equestrian, cross-country skiing and snowmobile trails. Generally, state forest campgrounds have fewer than 50 campsites. Most are along inland lakes and rivers. Some campgrounds provide group sites. A few sites are so remote they can only be accessed by an ambitious hike. Some sites have a special-use designation. For example, the Sand Lakes Quiet Area prohibits motor vehicles, while, in other campgrounds, dirt bikes and off-road vehicles are welcome. Many of the campgrounds provide barrier-free facilities.

Campsites at state forests are available on a first-come, first-served basis. Fees range from $4 to $8 per night, and senior citizens camp for half-price. Leashed dogs are allowed. Campgrounds operate seasonally, depending on weather conditions, so it's smart to call ahead to confirm a campground's status. For locations in the Pere Marquette Forest, call (616) 775-9727. To check on campgrounds in the Mackinaw State Forests, call (517) 732-3541.

The Manistee National Forest offers still more opportunities to experience Michigan's array of outdoor recreation and wildlife. You'll want to keep your camera at hand in case you're fortunate enough to spot a bald eagle, black bear, wild turkey, deer or osprey in their natural habitat.

Like state forest sites, campgrounds within the Manistee National Forest are primarily along waterways. Fees at the 16 campgrounds range from free to $10 per night. While rustic and without electrical hookups, many campgrounds offer barrier-free recreational opportunities and provide handicapped-accessible campsites, restrooms and cookstoves.

Unlike the state forest or state park campgrounds, national forests allow the adventurous outdoors enthusiast to set up camp anywhere on their 540,000 acres, unless otherwise posted. Primitive camping is allowed without a permit and is free of charge. The only restriction is that campsites must be 200 feet away from lakes, streams or rivers and 150 feet away from roads and trails. For more information regarding national forest campgrounds or trails, call (616) 775-2421.

Northwest Michigan's private parks offer a selection as impressive as the public parks. Like their counterparts, private campgrounds feature rustic and modern camping, while many also provide full RV hookups and resort services. Be sure to call ahead when planning a camping trip early or late in the season since weather dictates the opening and closing of the season.

As you enjoy Michigan's treasured natural resources, please remember that preserving the quality of the environment for future generations is a responsibility for all who delight in its wonders. Remember, among other things, to use earth-friendly personal-care products. At certain times of the year, especially in late spring, the threat of wild fires in the northern woodlands is a serious concern. Keep your campfires small and make sure ashes are cold when you leave your site. Leave no trace of your visit. Simply put, pack out what you pack in. Applying good conservation practices ensures the continued existence of the unique beauty and character of Northwest Michigan's wild lands.

Grand Traverse

Traverse City Area

Traverse City State Park
1132 U.S. Hwy. 31 N., Traverse City
• (616) 922-5270

An urban park featuring a quarter mile of sandy beach along Grand Traverse Bay,

---

www.insiders.com

See this and many other **Insiders' Guide®** destinations online — in their entirety.

Visit us today!

INSIDERS' TIP

If you intend to rely on a wood fire for warmth or cooking, stack a few logs in your tent to keep them dry.

Traverse City State Park offers campers the best of two worlds: Enjoy swimming, sunbathing, boating and fishing from campsites just a stone's throw away from some of Northwest Michigan's top restaurants, specialty shops and recreational facilities. To make traveling through the commercial district fun, safe and easy, the park offers direct access to the Traverse Area Recreational Trail, a hiking, biking pathway connecting campers to downtown Traverse City (see our Recreation chapter for more details). The year-round campground features modern facilities, including electricity, flush toilets, showers and a sanitation station. The 343 campsites have private fire pits and picnic tables. Because Traverse City State Park is one of the more popular campgrounds in the area, we suggest you make reservations for peak-season camping at least six months in advance.

Yogi Bear's Jellystone Park Camp Resort
4050 Hammond Rd., Traverse City
• **(616) 947-2770, (800) 909-BEAR**

For 25 years, this franchise park has provided campers with good times and good memories. A full-service resort, the park provides outdoor activities and entertainment from May 1 through October 15. The park opens on a limited basis in mid-December for cross-country skiers. Skiers enjoy the park's lighted trail and an adjacent 27K three-county trail system winding through the Pere Marquette State Forest (see our Recreation chapter for more details). Jellystone offers 226 wooded campsites with 31 full RV hookup sites. Flush toilets, hot showers and laundry facilities are on site. From Memorial Day through Labor Day, the fee for rustic camping (no electricity or water) is $22 per night, with electricity and water $34 per night. Full hookup sites, including sewer, are $39. Prices include two adults. Additional adults are charged $5 per night per person. Children younger than 21, and accompanied by adults, stay free. Off-season rates vary but are lower than summer rates. Reservations for the upcoming year are taken beginning January 2.

Campers will not lack for entertainment at Jellystone. In addition to the trail system, the park features an in-ground pool, a tots wading pool, minigolf, volleyball, horseshoe pits and a soccer field. You will also enjoy a video arcade and outdoor theater. Planned activities for children are presented daily between 10 AM until 9 PM. Special activities are organized around theme weekends when campers may find themselves hunting Easter eggs in July or trick-or-treating in August.

Grand Traverse Camping and RV Resort
9700 Mich. Hwy. 37, Buckley
• **(616) 269-3203**

It's just a 15-minute drive from Grand Traverse Camping and RV Resort to Traverse City and a short jaunt to many of the region's popular attractions (see our Attractions chapter). Situated on 20 acres, the park offers a variety of camping and recreational experiences. The private campground is open from the beginning of May through mid-October and features a total of 91 sites, including 22 full-hookup sites for RVs and five pull-through sites. Rustic camping, sites with only water and electricity, and a five-person, genuine log rental cabin are also available. Summer rates are $26 for full hookups, $21 for water/electric sites, $21 for rustic sites and $45 for the cabin. Off-season rates are $18 for full hookups, $15 for water/electric and rustic sites and $35 for the cabin.

Everyone will enjoy the camp's petting farm where you can befriend rabbits and pygmy goats. A playground and a heated swimming pool provide hours of hot-weather recreation. You won't want to leave without trying the camp's three-wheeled bikes. These banana peels and low riders are available for $2.50 per hour. And if you left anything at home, you may find it at the on-site convenience store.

Interlochen State Park
Mich. Hwy. 137, Interlochen
• **(616) 276-9511**

Established in 1919, Interlochen State Park was the first campground in Michigan's state park system. It's nestled among one of the state's few remaining stands of virgin pine. Located between two lakes, the park offers a rustic campground along Green Lake and a modern campground at Duck Lake. In addition to enjoying a natural setting and watersports and recreation, campers can attend summer concerts given by premier entertainers next door at Interlochen National Music Camp. Walking trails lead from the campground to the cultural center.

Featuring 488 campsites, the park remains open year round. Modern campsites, at the Duck Lake campground, have restrooms with flush toilets and hot showers. Electricity and a sanitation station are also available.

The sandy swimming beach along Duck Lake provides plenty of room for building sand castles. When you're ready to cool down, you can head to the park canteen for refreshments.

Duck Lake camping fees are $14 per night. Along the tree-lined shores of Green Lake, the park offers rustic camping at a rate of $6 per night.

Campsites are situated in a shady forest across the road from the main campground. In addition to swimming, boating and fishing, Interlochen State Park offers a 1-mile self-guided nature tour through the park's old growth forest. During the winter, the park hosts cross-country skiing through its tall, snow-laden pines and ice fishing opportunities over the frozen waters.

Sand Lakes Quiet Area and Guernsey Lake State Forest Campground
8 miles west of Kalkaska via Island Lake Rd. and Campground Rd., Pere Marquette State Forest • (616) 775-9727

No motor vehicles are allowed in this specially designated quiet area. Sand Lakes Quiet Area features more than 10 miles of hiking and cross-country trails across a variety of terrain (see our Recreation chapter for more details). Weaving through the Pere Marquette State Forest, the trails are especially beautiful in autumn when hardwoods display a brilliant palette of colors. Visitors can enter Sand Lakes Quiet Area from two points. To access ski trails, travel 1.5 miles east of Williamsburg on Michigan Highway 72, go south on Broomhead Road 4 miles to a parking area located on the left side of the road. Hikers will want to travel west on Island Lake Road from Kalkaska for 9 miles to Guernsey Lake State Forest Campground and access the Sand Lakes Quiet Area from there. While Sand Lakes is primarily a day-use area, rustic camping facilities are available at the adjacent Guernsey Lake State Forest Campground. The campground offers walk-in campsites, water and vault toilets are available. There's boating, swimming and some fairly good pan fishing. Fees are $6 per night.

Scheck's Place Trail Camp/ Scheck's Place
12 mi. southwest of Williamsburg
• (616) 922-5280

Scheck's Place Trail Camp is one of many horse camps situated along an east-west 224 mile shore-to-shore riding-hiking trail stretching from Lake Huron to Lake Michigan. The open campground is host to many large organized group rides. The camp is also a popular site for those who enjoy day rides through the conifer forests and picturesque countryside. To get to the sites from Kalkaska, take U.S. Highway 131 south to South Boardman village. Turn west on Supply Road and travel about 3 miles until you come to Brown Bridge Road. Take a left and signs will direct you to Scheck's Place. Camping at Scheck's is strictly rustic. Fees are $5 per night. Only hand water pumps and outhouses are available. Additional camping facilities are available at Scheck's Place, an adjacent state forest campground with 30 rustic sites. From the campground you will find canoeing and trout fishing opportunities along the Boardman River. Camping fees are $6 per night.

Leelanau County

Lake Leelanau RV Park
3101 Lake Shore Dr., Lake Leelanau
• (616) 256-7236

To guarantee a stay at this RV park, especially in July and August, secure your reservations early in the year. The park's 700-foot beachfront, many lakeside campsites, docking space for 98 boats and 181 full RV hookup sites make it a favorite summer destination. Located along the waters of Lake Leelanau, the park is open from the beginning of May through mid-October. It features 193 sites, all with electricity, water and cable access. Most sites provide full hookups. Rates range from $21 to $28 per night for four people or one family. Off-season rates range from $17 to $24.

Watersports are big at Lake Leelanau RV Park. Boat rentals available include fishing crafts and motors, canoe, pontoon, jet ski and paddleboats. A long, clean lake, Lake Leelanau provides good fishing grounds for perch, bluegill, walleye, pike and bass. Recreational programming includes hayrides and treasure hunts for the younger set. Family fun includes ice cream socials and other organized group events during summer months.

Leelanau State Park
15310 N. Lighthouse Point Rd., Northport
• (616) 386-5422

Leelanau State Park offers visitors a sampling of Great Lakes history and beachside camping all at one site. Located at the northern point of Leelanau County, the park features a working Great Lakes lighthouse. Tours of the restored Grand Traverse Lighthouse and Museum (see our Attractions chapter) are offered daily between 11 AM and 7 PM in the summer. Off-season tours are given between noon and 5 PM on weekends. Call (616) 386-9145 for current tour schedules. Admission is $1 per person.

Campers can experience for themselves why lighthouses played an important role in Lake Michigan history when the thick fog rolls in at the park. Fifty rustic campsites are available, including 10 beach sites, situated in the mysterious foggy landscape. Camping fees are $6 per night. Two mini-cabins are also available to visitors for $32 per night. Leelanau State Park campgrounds are open from early May until snow starts falling. Call ahead to make sure the park is open if you're visiting either early or late in the season. During your stay, you can enjoy the park's 8-mile trail system, which provides hiking opportunities in the summer and cross-country skiing and snowshoeing opportunities during the winter. The all-season trail weaves through cedar and maple forests, along an

Photo: Olave Walker Russell

Michigan affords a wealth of opportunities to the outdoors enthusiast.

inland lake and through the coastal dunes at Cat's Head Bay.

Sleeping Bear Dunes National Lakeshore
Visitor Center, 9922 Front St., Empire
• (616) 326-5134

Each year Sleeping Bear Dunes draws thousands of visitors on a quest to experience the park's massive, towering coastal dunes, sweeping vistas of shimmering lakes and rich varieties of wildlife, birds and vegetation. Stretching 35 miles, tip-to-tip, along the Lake Michigan coast, covering 71,000 acres in Leelanau and Benzie counties. Sleeping Bear Dunes National Lakeshore offers camping at four parks within its borders. The park provides nature lovers excellent opportunities for hunting, fishing, boating, swimming, hiking and cross-country skiing.

Expect to pay a $7 user fee per vehicle for

INSIDERS' TIP

Be cautious when climbing or descending Lake Michigan's steep lakeshore bluffs. Avalanche conditions may exist on exposed dune slopes following heavy snows or strong winds.

a 7-day park permit or $15 for an annual permit to enter this glacier-made preserve (see our Parks chapter for more details).

From May through mid-October, the adventurous camper can ferry to either North or South Manitou islands for a backcountry experience. Manitou Island Transit runs daily trips from Leland Harbor to the two islands. Departure times for the 90-minute trips vary according to season, so call ahead for schedules. You need to contact the ferry office, (616) 256-9061, during the summer, at least one day in advance of your visit to secure reservations. During the off-season, call (616) 271-4217. Round-trip ferry tickets are $19 for adults and $13 for children 12 and younger. Camping at both islands costs $5 per night plus the user fee. User fees are paid either on the mainland or upon your arrival to the island. Camping fees are collected upon arrival.

When the ferry chugs away from the island and you're left clutching your gear, you realize its just the waves, the woods and you. Whichever wilderness island you choose to visit, bring adequate provisions. Supplies are not available on either island, and you must carry your own drinking water. There is no transportation for your gear, so pack lightly. Three designated camping areas are available on South Manitou. Most sites are designed for two tents and a maximum of four campers. Some group sites are available to accommodate up to 20 campers. The island ecosystems are extremely fragile, and campers are expected to respect the rules of low impact camping, meaning, leave nothing behind but your footprints.

During your exploration of South Manitou, don't miss the old growth cedar stand tucked along the southwest corner of the island. Some of these trees are thought to predate Columbus's trip to the New World. You will also want to examine island history. Stop to study remains of old island farms, the abandoned schoolhouse and cemetery. If you're lucky, a ranger will be on hand to give you a tour of the lighthouse, which dates back to 1871. Custom and special interest tours are provided by Manitou Island Transit. The company offers guided tours of South Manitou in open-air vehicles. The two-hour tours begin at noon daily. Fees are $7 for adults and $4 for children 12 and younger.

On North Manitou, the only way to get around is by foot. Managed as wilderness, the island is about 8 miles long and 4 miles wide, providing 15,000 acres of hikable wild country. The sites to see include Lake Manitou, located in the north central portion of the island, where fishing is permitted on these quiet inland waters surrounded by rugged bluffs. The old village area where you will find ghosts of the island's past is worth exploring. Head to Village Campground along the east island shore when you're ready to settle down for the evening. It features eight campsites, two fire rings and an outhouse.

For those who enjoy a less remote location and more modern comforts, the Platte River Campground is the best choice. The campground is located at 5685 Lake Michigan Road in Honor. In contrast to the islands, the Platte River Campground offers modern facilities, paved roads, hot showers, flush toilets and electricity. The 179 shady campsites are less than 1 mile from Lake Michigan. The park also offers eight secluded, rustic, walk-in campsites. Fees are $10 per night for the rustic sites and $14 per night plus $5 per night for electrical service for other sites.

Platte River Campground features a picnic area situated along the river's shady banks. The Platte provides excellent opportunities for family canoeing and tubing. From the water access points, you can paddle your way to the Big Lake, Lake Michigan. Anglers enjoy hooking trout and a variety of planted salmon from the Platte waters.

Like the Platte River Campground, the D.H. Day Campground is open from April through November and camping is on a first-come, first-served basis. Only 2 miles west of Glen Arbor, the D.H. Day Campground offers 88 rustic campsites. Fees are $12 per night. The campground links campers to the national park's extensive trail system.

Antrim-Kalkaska Area

Honcho Rest RV-otel and Campground
8988 Cairn Hwy., Elk Rapids
• (616) 264-8548

Bass, pike, bluegill and other panfish are what anglers hook at Honcho Rest RV-otel and Campground on the grassy banks of Bass Lake. Fishing boat rentals are available at the campground. Only a 1-mile jaunt to Lake Michigan, campers can also enjoy water recreation on the Big Lake when staying at Honcho's, or cross the street to play nine-holes of golf at a public course (see our Golf chapter). The park has 50 cement pad sites with full RV hookups, cable television and patios. Open from early May through mid-October, rates for a family of four are $22 per night for shoreside campsites and $20 per night for all other sites.

Graves Crossing State Forest Campground
10 mi. north of Mancelona, Mackinaw State Forest • (517) 732-3541

Wildflowers and wildlife are abundant in the lands and waterways surrounding Graves Crossing State Forest Campground. The campground is situated along the Jordan River near the Jordan Valley Pathway, an 18-mile hiking trail meandering through the beautiful Jordan Valley. Stunning vistas of the area can be viewed from two observation stations along the trail. In addition to the extensive trails, Graves Crossing provides a point of entry for Jordan River canoeists. The waterway is favored by canoeists and some very active beaver families. Ten rustic campsites are available at the campgrounds for $6 per night. The only available facilities are outhouses and hand water pumps. Backpackers willing to really rough it can travel from Graves Crossing to hike-in campsites hidden in the Jordan wilds.

Otsego Lake State Park
7136 Old U.S. Hwy. 27 S., Gaylord
• (517) 732-5485

Quiet, shady sites and a half mile of sandy beach make this campground a family favorite. The 62-acre park is situated among stately oaks, maples and pines along Otsego Lake. Open from April 1 through the end of October, the park features 203 large campsites, including some lakeside sites. Electricity, hot showers, flush toilets and a sanitation station are available. Sites cost $14 per night. A handicapped-accessible pier provides fishing opportunities for all campers. From the pier, anglers catch a variety of fish including bass, perch, bluegill, walleye and sunfish. Out on

the water, anglers set their bait for muskies and pike. Boat rentals are available from a privately operated park concession stand.

Lake Michigan Shoreline and Cadillac

Matson's Big Manistee River Campground
2680 Bialik Rd., Manistee
• (616) 723-5705

Whether you're interested in a primitive camping experience or prefer full hookup and the comforts of your RV, you can find camping to suit your fancy at Matson's Big Manistee River Campground. Set along the wide, deep Manistee River, the campground offers 20 rustic sites, 25 sites with electricity and 30 with full hookups. The camp is open April through November. All-season rates are $12 per night for rustic sites, $14 per night for electricity and $16 per night for full hookup. Canoeists and anglers set up camp at Matson's to relax along one of the north's most beautiful, clear rivers. The easy current of the Manistee makes it an excellent waterway for beginning canoeists. Campsite service is available from nearby canoe liveries. For boat owners, Matson's features two boat launches, boat docks and a fish cleaning station. The only other thing the Matson's angler might need to hook the river's steelhead and salmon is a little luck.

Orchard Beach State Park
2064 Lakeshore Rd., Manistee
• (616) 723-7422

Situated on a bluff overlooking Lake Michigan, Orchard Beach Park is a favorite campground of those who enjoy viewing colorful Lake Michigan sunsets or the dramatic movement of storms traveling across open waters from Wisconsin to Michigan. Orchard Beach Park is open from mid-April through October and features 175 campsites with modern restroom facilities, electricity and a sanitation station. Camping is $12 per night. One mini-cabin is available for $33 per night. We suggest you reserve the cabin well in advance. Orchard Beach offers campers a 2-mile self-guided hiking trail, home to a wide range of dune vegetation. A sandy swimming beach, grassy picnic area and pavilion are also available, as well as two playgrounds, three horseshoe pits, a volleyball court and a baseball field.

Nordhouse Dunes Wilderness
Off Nurnberg Rd., Manistee County
• (616) 723-2211

Nordhouse Dunes Wilderness is the only federally designated wilderness in Michigan's lower peninsula. Covering 3,500 acres, it features 1,200 acres of open sand dunes. The 4,000 year-old freshwater dunes dramatically tower up to 140 feet above Lake Michigan. Water holes, marshes, dune grass and woody vegetation, such as juniper and jack pine, dot the vast landscape.

You can reach the wilderness area from the adjacent Lake Michigan Recreation Area to the north or by the trailhead at the end of Nurnberg Road. Free visitor parking is available at both entrances.

Use of motorized vehicles is prohibited in the wilderness. The sound of the wind and gulls is all you'll hear as you walk along the many miles of wide golden beaches, perfect for solitary shore walks and magnificent sunset viewing. The hiking trail system within the wilderness area is minimally signed, and it's easy to lose your bearing among dunes. Pack a compass and map to help keep you out of trouble. Also, remember, that you must carry in your drinking water or be prepared to purify Lake Michigan water.

Open year round, the area provides an undeniably rich variety of hiking, hunting, fishing and camping opportunities. Wilderness campers need to be aware of regulations prohibiting campsites and campfires closer than 400 feet from the Lake Michigan waterline and 200 feet from the waterline of the inland Nordhouse Lake. Camping is also limited to areas 400 feet beyond the Wilderness boundaries along Nurnberg, Green and Lake Michigan roads. There are no fees for use of this treasured natural resource.

Ludington State Park
Mich. Hwy. 116, Ludington
• (616) 843-8671

Ludington State Park offers all breeds of outdoor enthusiasts opportunities to create lasting vacation memories. Featuring 6 miles of pristine Lake Michigan shoreline, the park appeals to the romantic-natured campers — those who enjoy walks along secluded, white beaches. Wildlife watchers enjoy opportunities to catch sight of raccoons, rabbits, skunk, turtles and snakes. Canoeists enjoy paddling the Hamlin Lake canoe trail and anglers set their sights and hopes on bass, perch or salmon.

Open between April and the end of November, the park offers 347 modern campsites. Electricity, hot showers, flush toilets and a sanitation station are all available. Camping is $15 per night.

Campground amenities include a visitors center, which provides day and evening programs, a grocery store and concession stand. Between May and mid-October, canoes, rowboats and paddleboats are available from the park's concession stand for $5 per hour.

Poncho's Pond RV Park
5335 W. Wallace Rd., Ludington
• (616) 845-6655

Friendly and clean, Poncho's Park strives to provide a family atmosphere. Situated on 21 acres, the park offers organized activities and other amenities. A hook, a line and Poncho's 3-acre pond stocked with bluegill, catfish and bullhead keeps young campers happy for hours. Paddleboats are available to cruise the pond for $3 and $5 per hour, depending on the boat's passenger capacity. Two heated swimming pools and a hot tub for adults provide relaxation and water fun. At the camp clubhouse, visitors can join planned, family-oriented programs.

INSIDERS' TIP

Try a native camping style. You can rent a replica tepee for $20 per night at Interlochen State Park (see listing in this chapter). Other state parks provide single-family tents and mini-cabin rentals.

Photo: Kevin Poirier

The state flower, the Trillium, is abundant In this region, although it is on the protected list of Michigan wildflowers.

Open from the beginning of April through October, Poncho's features 158 sites, 150 with full hookups, including sewer. There are 59 pull-through sites. All sites have cable television access, picnic tables and fire rings. Rates for campsites with water and electricity are $22 per night. Full hookup rates range from $23 to $26 per night. Both rates apply to two adults and children 18 and younger. Check for discount rates early and late in the season.

William Mitchell State Park
6093 E. Mich. Hwy. 115, Cadillac
• **(616) 775-7911**

Mitchell State Park is a haven for boating enthusiasts. Campsites dot the banks of a canal linking two of the north's famed fishing lakes, Lake Cadillac and Lake Mitchell. Here, anglers go for walleye, northern pike, bluegill and bass. The wooded campground covers 334 acres and features 215 campsites with electricity, flush toilets, hot showers and a sanitation station. Rates are $15 per night.

Camping is within strolling distance of Cadillac west restaurants, shopping, minigolf and a water park. Key northern hunting grounds, canoe liveries and area attractions are an easy drive from the campground.

Open year round, the Mitchell State Park camping experience is enhanced by programming at the adjacent Carl T. Johnson Hunting and Fishing Center (see the Close-up in this chapter). The Park's visitor center and an outdoor education facility offer interactive displays showcasing Michigan wildlife and conservation history. The facility presents hands-on outdoor programs and activities throughout the year. Many campers join the center's guided moonlight hikes, partake in hunter safety courses or catch a special presentation such as Native American legends told around a group campfire.

Peterson Bridge Campground
1.5 mi. north of Gartlets Corners, Wexford County • (616) 723-2211

One of the most popular campgrounds in the Manistee National Forest, Peterson Bridge offers direct canoe access to the Pine River, a federally designated national wild and scenic river. Exceptionally clear, the fast-moving, spring-fed river offers a world-class experience for intermediate and advanced canoeists (see our Recreation chapter).

The Peterson Bridge Campground provides 20 rustic campsites, some situated along the river's banks. Paved parking spurs and walk-in sites are both available. Campsites feature fire rings, picnic tables, one community hand water pump, vault and flush toilets. Depending on weather conditions, the campground is open between the end of April and the end of September. Camping fees are $5 per adult, per night.

To reach this rustic campground located in the Manistee National Forest, follow Mich. Highway 37 south 1.5 miles from the Mich. Highway 55 and Mich. Highway 37 junction. After crossing Peterson Bridge, turn left into the park area and follow the signs.

Goose Lake State Forest Campground
Goose Lake Rd., 2.5 mi. northwest of Lake City • (616) 775-9727

You have to follow a winding dirt road to reach Goose Lake State Forest Campground. Situated deep within the Pere Marquette Forest, the rustic campground offers 50 campsites near the quiet, calm waters of Goose Lake. The small inland lake offers swimming, boating and good pan fishing. From this se-

cluded campground you can enjoy misty summer mornings or a brilliant display of fall colors. Campsites are available on a first-come, first-served basis for $6 per night.

Little Traverse

Young State Park
02280 Boyne City Rd., Boyne City
• (616) 582-7523

One of the older campgrounds in the State Park System, Young Park has provided outdoor recreation to several generations of camping families. Great boating, swimming and fishing draw these campers back, year after year.

Perched along Lake Charlevoix, the park features 240 campsites, 10 along the inland lake shoreline. Electricity is available at all campsites. Modern restroom facilities, hot showers and a dump station are also available from Memorial Day weekend until the snow flies. Fees are $15 per night.

A stocked pond provides rewarding fishing experiences to junior campers. The park launch facilities provide boating access to both Lake Charlevoix and Lake Michigan. Lucky anglers bring home salmon, lake trout, bluegill and perch. Young and old alike are invited to participate in organized camp programs. Rangers offer guided day and night hikes and wildlife study sessions around the pond.

When winter snows bring an end to camping, cross-country skiing at the park begins. Throughout the winter months, three groomed cross-country trails are open. These 4 miles of trails provide both easy and intermediate skiing opportunities. There is no fee for winter trail use, however, you need a state park motor vehicle permit to enter the park. These are available at the park office.

Crooked River RV Park
5397 Cheboygan St., Alanson
• (616) 548-5534

Small and secluded yet easy to find, this RV park offers direct access to boating in a five-lake chain. From the camp's Crooked River dock, canoes, kayaks and motor boat enthusiasts can travel a system of five lakes and canals winding through Emmet and

The Carl T. Johnson Hunting and Fishing Center — Jewel of the Michigan State Park System's Outdoor Education Program

From moonlit cross-country skiing adventures to lessons in building wildlife nest boxes to wild turkey workshops, Cadillac's Carl T. Johnson Hunting and Fishing Center offers hands-on experiences and nature encounters guaranteed to stir your sense of wonder for Michigan's great outdoors.

Next to William Mitchell State Park along Michigan Highway 115 on Cadillac's west side, the park's visitor center is the pride of the Michigan State Park system's outdoor education program. It offers year-round programming for adults, youth, families and private groups. Visitors can easily spend an entire day enjoying the center's multimedia conservation displays and exploring the adjacent Heritage Marsh Nature Trail.

The 70-acre wildlife study area is both a scenic outdoor classroom and a pleasant escape from the bustle of city life. A marsh wetlands, it offers wildlife and bird watchers some rare opportunities in all four seasons. Hiking past the hardwood stand along the well-maintained wetland trail, you may catch sight of a bald eagle soaring, a great blue heron wading on the wetland's edge or a curious masked raccoon seeking lunch. Evening nightshade, roses, spirea and button bush splash color on the landscape, while the willow and yellow birch surrounding the marsh serve as feeding grounds for muskrat and beaver.

The center offers guided day- and nighttime hikes through the marsh. You can also venture out into the wetlands on your own. Maps are available for self-guided tours along a marked trail. Easily followed, the trail features wide walking bridges and an

— continued on next page

Photo: Carl T. Johnson Hunting and Fishing Center

One of the state's prime sites for conservation education programs, the Carl T. Johnson Hunting and Fishing Center in Cadillac, presents outdoor workshops and events throughout the year.

observation platform. In the winter, the 2.5 mile trail is available for cross-country skiing and snowshoeing.

Opened to the public in May 1992, the Carl T. Johnson Hunting and Fishing Center is operated by the Michigan Department of Natural Resources Parks and Recreation Division. The center's namesake is Northwest Michigan resident Carl T. Johnson, who served on the Michigan Natural Resource Commission for 18 years and distinguished himself as a leader in the state's conservation movement.

A stop at the Carl T. Johnson Center is worthwhile if for no other reason than to see the building itself. Constructed from Michigan pine and stone, the structure offers an attractive, natural setting for the facility's interactive exhibits, classroom and nature store. A new $150,000 educational wing is expected to open sometime in 1998. The addition will allow for expanded programming and enhance opportunities for annual events such as the Deer Hunter's Open House held each November and the June Free Fishing Weekend.

Admission and most events taking place at the Carl T. Johnson Hunting and Fishing Center are free of charge. Between the beginning of May and November 1, the center is open from 10 AM until 6 PM, Tuesday through Sunday. Winter hours are from noon until 5 PM on Friday, and 10 AM until 5 PM on Saturday and Sunday. Call the center at (616) 779-1321 for a detailed activity schedule. Fishing clinics, decoy carving workshops, hunting, boating and snowmobile safety programs are offered regularly. Wildlife experts, authors and artists, share their outdoor knowledge and skills at weekend workshops year round. You'll find making time to enjoy this jewel of the Michigan State Parks and Recreation system a rewarding and memorable experience.

Cheboygan counties. The park features 17 full RV hookup sites and is open year-round. Water is unavailable from mid-November until spring, however, hot showers, sewer hookups and modern restrooms remain open. Year-round rates are $14 per night for two people.

Fisherman's Island State Park
Bells Bay Rd., Charlevoix
• **(616) 547-6641**

Rock hounds flock to this park's 6 miles of undeveloped Lake Michigan shoreline, which is a well-known hunting ground for the state's official stone, the Petoskey. It's also a park where man's best friend is welcome. While pets are required to be leashed in the campground area, a section of beach is open to dogs, so Fido can enjoy a dip in the cool Lake Michigan waves with the rest of the family. Covering more than 2,500 acres, the park offers 90 spacious, rustic sites for $6 per night. The park remains open year round, however roads are not plowed during the winter. At that time, the area is accessible only by snowmobile, cross-country skis or snowshoes.

Petoskey State Park
2475 Mich. Hwy. 119, Petoskey
• **(616) 347-2311**

Situated along 2 miles of Little Traverse Bay, Petoskey State Park is a popular spot for beachcombers who enjoy scouring the shore for the distinct and collectible Petoskey stone. In one of the bay's warmer spots, the park's sandy-bottom lake waters provide pleasant family swimming. The park, open April through November, has 170 campsites, each with electrical hookups. Modern restroom facilities, hot showers and a sanitation station are available. Rates are $15 per night. Two mini-cabins are also available at the park and rent for $32 per night.

Park recreational opportunities include offshore fishing in Little Traverse Bay. A self-guided nature trail takes campers on a 2-mile tour of the park's woodlands. Educational programs are offered by park rangers several nights each week in the summer. During the winter months, roads are plowed to the campground area to provide for cross-country skiing adventures within the park's 300 acres.

Mackinac Straits

Wilderness State Park
898 Wilderness Park Dr., 11 mi. west of Mackinaw City, Carp Lake
• **(616) 436-5381**

At 8,500 acres, Wilderness State Park is the second-largest state park in Michigan's lower peninsula. Campers flock to this secluded campground to take advantage of its 26 miles of Lake Michigan shoreline and 16 miles of hiking and biking trails. Naturalists enjoy the park's rare flora and fauna, such as the endangered piping plover shorebird, wild orchids and iris.

Open year round, the park provides electricity at each campsite, a dump station and modern restroom facilities. Hot showers are not available between November and April. The campground has 250 sites, with 40 beach sites. Fees are $15 per night. Six mini-cabins and three bunkhouses are available at a rate of $40 and $55 per night respectively. The shelters are quite popular, so you may need to make reservations one year in advance.

Both summer and winter recreational opportunities attract campers to the park. The park features one boat launch and is known as a good bass fishing site. Some anglers enjoy getting right into the thick of it, fishing the marshy waters in waders. Except for a designated safety zone, hunting is permitted within the park in accordance with Michigan State hunting laws and regulations. Groomed trails provide the "wilderness" experience to snowmobilers during the winter months.

St. Ignace/Mackinac Island KOA Kampground
1242 U.S. Hwy. 2 W., St. Ignace
• **(906) 643-9303**

Free tourist services and a convenient location draw campers to this upper peninsula park. The KOA campground offers on-demand shuttle service to campers heading to the Kewadin Casino or Mackinac Island ferries. Camp staffers even help visitors decide what to see and do in the area and will provide you with travel information packets.

Open from early May through October 25, the campground features 200 sites including 28 full RV hookup sites. Hot showers, flush toilets and laundry facilities are available. Summer rates for two people, per night, are $17 for rustic tent sites and $21 for RV sites. Electricity and sewer hookups are each an additional $2 per night. Fees for additional campers are $2 per night for adults and $1.50 per night for children older than 5. Discount rates are available during the spring and fall.

The park offers many amenities to entertain and educate its guests. You will find a heated pool, video arcade, a Native American museum and gift shop on-site. You won't have to take a hike in the woods to see Northwest Michigan wildlife because a campground exhibit features live fox, bobcat, peacock and deer. Learn the names of the five resident deer, and they will answer your call to eat from your hand making for a great photo opportunity.

Straits State Park
720 Church St., St. Ignace
• **(906) 643-8620**

Straits State Park offers campers a majestic view of the Mighty Mackinac Bridge, sometimes called the eighth wonder of the world. The bridge links the state's lower and upper peninsulas. Near Mackinac Island ferry lines, Straits State Park provides ideal accommodations for those who wish to tour historic Mackinaw and eastern upper peninsula attractions. The park features 275 campsites, 22 of which are along the water. Electricity is provided at all sites. Modern restroom facilities and a sanitation station are also available. While the park is open year round, modern restroom facilities are available only from May to mid-October. Camping fees are $14 per night.

Our many restaurants have capitalized on the region's winning recipe — our natural beauty. Windows overlook shorelines, rolling hills, majestic trees and charming downtowns.

Restaurants

To put it simply, in Northwest Michigan we love to eat. And, with our many restaurants and gourmet gurus, we have countless chances to indulge our palates. Whether your taste runs to elegant French dining or a simple Friday fish fry, you're bound to find a menu that tickles your taste buds!

In this chapter we highlight about 200 of our favorite eateries. They represent the many diverse tastes, lifestyles and communities of Northwest Michigan. You'll find casual bistros and elegant dining, resort restaurants and local hangouts, patisseries and delicatessens, coffee shops and brewpubs. As often as not, they are rooms with a view. Our many restaurants have capitalized on the region's winning recipe — our natural beauty. Windows overlook shorelines, rolling hills, majestic trees and charming downtowns.

The atmosphere in these restaurants reflects our relaxed lifestyle. When you're up north, dressing up often means, "no jeans." Casual resort wear will usually take you into any establishment in style. A sports jacket, sweater or sports shirt are common for the men. A tie is not a necessity, unless you are dining at the Grand Hotel on Mackinac Island, which requires a jacket and tie for dinner. The more casual restaurants are even more relaxed. Remember, we know that you're on vacation!

Local chefs are topnotch and have created outstanding cuisines that have attracted widespread acclaim. You will see that we often use the term "casual dining." Don't mistake casual for ordinary. We want to make your meal memorable with innovative dishes served with comfortable up-north charm.

The menus often reflect the region's bounty. You'll see whitefish, walleye and other catches from the Great Lakes. Delicious morel mushrooms make a seasonal showing on dinner plates during May and June. Cherries, dried and fresh, are showcased in desserts, entrees and appetizers. Fresh produce grown on local farms and in local gardens is often purchased by area restaurants as are the breads, desserts and cheeses that are created by hand in small community shops. Our locally produced wines and beers top many lists.

In this chapter we have divided our restaurants along our usual geographic lines. Within each geographic region are four categories: Delightful Dining, Coffeehouses, Food on the Run, and Ice Cream and Sweet Treats.

The largest category is Delightful Dining. These full-service restaurants feature a wide array of menus, styles and prices. We have not subdivided categories by ethnic specialties, menu or atmosphere because too often the lines are blurred. We northern Michiganders are an eclectic mix and our restaurants reflect that.

What you won't see listed are national restaurant chains because we have focused on the homegrown eateries that are unique to Northwest Michigan. We certainly have numerous chain restaurants and fast food franchises, especially near the malls and high traffic areas in Traverse City.

We should note that some of our favorite eateries are also saloons. You will see several spots here that are also highlighted in our Nightlife chapter. A number of pubs listed in Nightlife also serve food. We recommend you

INSIDERS' TIP

When seeking food on the run, don't forget the local grocer. Many markets offer a full deli bar with fresh meats, cheese, soups and salads.

take a look for ideas in that chapter as well, especially if you're in the mood for a burger and a beer!

The Food on the Run category showcases the huge assortment of gourmet take-outs, pizzerias and sandwich shops in our region. Food for picnics along the shoreline or for cozying up in front of the fireplace is easily obtained, thanks to these great food emporiums. While take-out is usually the specialty, many of these eateries also have dining space inside or, during the warmer weather, at outdoor tables.

The coffee craze has swept Northwest Michigan as well as the rest of the country. You'll find a host of quaint shops in our Coffeehouses section that will brew your java just the way you like it. And, we can't let you go on vacation without a few treats so we've shared the names of our favorite neighborhood ice cream stands and candymakers in the Ice Cream and Sweet Treats section.

Unfortunately, we couldn't list every eatery in the north and, due to the quickly changing nature of the hospitality industry, new places open or older ones change daily. We have tried to stay one step ahead of the market and list our recommendations along with those of our friends, families and colleagues up north. But, keep your eyes open for new favorites, and pass on your recommendations to us for future editions.

Our restaurant price code reflects the cost of a summer dinner for two with entrees, soup or salads and nonalcoholic beverages. It does not include appetizers, desserts, gratuity or alcoholic beverages. Please remember that this is only a guideline for average costs. Prices can shift with the season, the highest peaking between early July and mid-August.

Several restaurants offer early bird dinners, even in the summer, if you eat before 6 PM. Lunch menus often reflect streamlined portions of dinner specialties at lunch prices. During the cooler months, you'll find midweek specials with creative menus, ethnic nights and great prices to draw you in. Families can take advantage of children's menus in most of the restaurants listed. It's always a good idea to check local papers for upcoming specials.

As far as credit cards go, our guidelines are split between the categories. Assume that major credit cards are accepted at the restaurants listed in the Dining Delights category unless noted otherwise.

All said, if you're ready to eat, bring your appetite and let's begin!

Price Code

Our restaurant price code reflects the cost of dinner for two with two entrees, soup or salads and nonalcoholic beverages. It does not include appetizers, dessert, gratuity or a bottle of wine or other spirits.

$	Less than $20
$$	$20 to $40
$$$	$40 to $60
$$$$	$60 to $80
$$$$$	$80 or more

Dining Delights

Grand Traverse

Traverse City Area

Apache Trout Grill
$$ • 13671 S. West Bay Shore Dr., Traverse City • (616) 947-7079
The Apache Trout Grill overlooks West Grand Traverse Bay with views of water, sailboats and an occasional pair of swans. The American grill menu features fresh saltwater fish, steaks, pastas and some of the best ribs in the area. The atmosphere is casual with lunch and dinner available daily. The restaurant is named after the apache trout whose likeness graces this pleasant eatery's roadside sign and green-sided building.

Auntie Pasta's Italian Cafe and Zio's
$$ (Zio's), $$$ (Auntie Pasta's)
• 2030 S. Airport Rd., Traverse City
• (616) 941-8147
Auntie Pasta's stretches along a scenic shore of the Boardman River at Logan's Landing. Windows line the shoreside wall giving diners ample opportunity to watch the antics of the many ducks and swans. The menu fea-

tures a variety of Italian specialties. Our favorites include veal piccata, eggplant parmigiano and three-cheese manicotti. Pasta entrees always include a daily specialty or you can choose your own mix of pasta and sauce. Caesar and tossed salads are served in large "bottomless" bowls at the table, where they are sprinkled with freshly shredded Romano cheese and ground pepper to taste. The antipasti sampler, homemade minestrone soup, and cannoli are also staples. A loaf of hot homemade bread wrapped in red-and-white-checked paper arrives while you order. It's wonderful and has become so popular that loaves are sold from baskets near the entrance. To get to Auntie Pasta's, most of us walk through Zio's pizza parlor. This casual cousin eatery also features a menu of Italian favorites like lasagna, cannelloni, calzones and spaghetti and meatballs but is especially known for its great pizza and large assortment of appetizers. Ceiling-high televisions are mounted in Zio's corners, usually broadcasting the day's sporting events. Both restaurants are open for lunch and dinner daily.

Bay Winds
$$$ • 1265 U.S. Hwy. 31 N., Traverse City • (616) 929-1044

The Bay Winds dining room is rimmed with windows jutting along the edge of East Grand Traverse Bay, treating diners to a spectacular view. During the warmer months, table service stretches onto the outdoor patio just a step away from the sugar-sand shoreline. Bay Winds and Larry's Place lounge (see our Nightlife and Casinos chapter) are both on the Pinestead Reef property, which is right across from the Traverse City State Park. The eatery is open for lunch and dinner with a menu featuring whitefish, seafood, veal, prime rib and casual fare. A breakfast buffet is served every Sunday.

Blondie's Diner
$ • 933 U.S. Hwy. 31 S., Traverse City • (616) 943-8019

For more than 27 years, the same family has been serving breakfast, lunch and dinner at Blondie's. This re-created 1950s-style diner is a Traverse City institution known for its friendly staff and finger-licking-good barbecue.

THE BLUEBIRD
Restaurant & Bar

*Fresh Leland Whitefish
is our specialty.*
*Grilled Choice Steaks & Seafood
Homemade Soups, Desserts &
Famous Bluebird Cinnamon Rolls*

Super Sunday Brunch 10-2
256-9081

Open Year Round on the River in Leland

Leland's Best
Breakfast & Lunch
101 South Main Street

Open Daily
256-9656

Ribs and smoked barbecue specialties are the favorites along with tasty diner fare. You have the choice to eat here or take your order out. Spirits are served, but smoking is prohibited.

Boathouse Bluewater Bistro
$$$ • 14039 Peninsula Dr., Traverse City • (616) 223-4030

Wonderful dining and fabulous sunsets over Bowers Harbor await diners at the Boathouse. This casual beach bistro is a local favorite for its beautiful setting, cozy ambiance and outstanding menu. Don't let the comfortable atmosphere fool you. The service is topnotch and fine-dining connoisseurs will be suitably impressed. The Boathouse is the creation of the same folks that brought Exquisite Edibles (see our Food on the Run section) to Traverse City. The same originality and commitment to fresh, creative fare is demonstrated here as well. The award-winning chefs prepare an eclectic menu that includes a number of vegetarian selections and aged beef, fresh seafood and specialty pastas. A few favorites include Portobello escargot, Madeira duckbreast Caesar salad, sesame tuna, peppered pork loin and salmon, and potato lasagna. The menu offers wine suggestions for each entree, and the staff is happy to share recommendations on the extensive collection of wines available. Serving lunch and dinner daily, the Boathouse also hosts a scrumptious Sunday Jazz Brunch each week featuring chef-attended omelet stations and live jazz using the restaurant's ivory grand piano. Reservations are recommended especially on weekends and during the summer.

Boone's Long Lake Inn
$$ • 7208 Secor Rd., Traverse City • (616) 946-3991

Boone's is almost synonymous with beef. The menu is filled with steaks in various cuts from tender filets to kabobs to huge New York strips. This is the self-proclaimed home of the 18-ounce steak and 22-ounce prime rib. As you may have guessed, portions are enormous! Equally generous are Boone's other popular entrees featuring seafood, chicken, pork chops and pasta primavera. We promise you won't go home hungry. But, if the portions seem a bit overwhelming, keep in mind that doggie bags are the norm and, for a small extra charge, meals can be split. Boone's is open daily for dinner, and from afternoons and evenings on Sundays. Guests are served in a huge facility with several spacious dining areas. A large outdoor deck overlooks adjacent pine trees and offers a pleasant interlude if you're waiting for a table. Reservations are accepted only for parties of 15 or more.

Bowers Harbor Inn
$$$-$$$$ • 13512 Peninsula Dr., Traverse City • (616) 223-4222

Enjoy an elegant dinner in the historic Bowers Harbor Inn. Bowers has long been the place that locals seek out for a special anniversary or memorable night out. But you don't need a special occasion to enjoy this wonderful restaurant overlooking Bowers Harbor on the Old Mission Peninsula. Plan to have a leisurely meal so that you can savor each course, and on weekends enjoy the marvelous music of a local acoustic guitarist. Entrees range from beef and lamb to seafood and fowl, with such specialties as Steak D'Alaska, veal chops with morel cream sauce, crab-stuffed shrimp and their signature dish, fish in a bag. Save room for French-fried ice cream or the souffle of the day, then top off the meal with Bowers specialty coffees, ice cream drinks or dessert wines and spirits. If the mood strikes, cigars are also available. Bowers Harbor Inn is the flagship for the Schelde restaurants in Traverse City, which also include The Bowery, Auntie Pasta's, Schelde's and North Peak Brewery. Reservations are recommended.

The Bowery
$$ • 13512 Peninsula Dr., Traverse City • (616) 223-4333

Head to the north side of Bowers Harbor Inn, and you'll find the entrance to The Bowery, a relaxed restaurant that brings the same meticulous attention to food preparation that

www.insiders.com

See this and many other **Insiders' Guide®** destinations online — in their entirety.

Visit us today!

the Schelde restaurants are known for. The large dining room is clad in rustic wood with high ceilings and a large fieldstone fireplace with a welcoming up north ambiance. The menu is casual but delicious with hefty appetizers (try the signature smoked whitefish dip), salads, sandwiches, ribs, steaks and seafood. A few favorites are the cherry shrimp salad, the pecan walleye and the beef medallions morel. For hefty appetites, you can combine steak or ribs with cherry shrimp, perch or hickory rotisserie chicken. Desserts are excellent with French-fried ice cream and Snickers cheesecake leading the lineup.

Casa Del Norte Mexican Restaurant
$ • 810 E. Front St., Traverse City
• (616) 941-5003

Made-from-scratch Mexican fare is showcased at Casa Del Norte. Translated as "house of the north," the small restaurant resides within a small, yellow house a short walk from downtown. It's open for lunch and dinner on Mondays through Saturdays, with a menu that features several variations each of tacos, enchiladas, flautas, burritos, chimichangas, tostadas and tamales. Everything is authentic and the portions are quite generous. The Mexican spirit is enhanced by the sound of Mariachi music and walls lined with sombreros and other Mexican knickknacks.

China Fair
$$ • 1357 S. Airport Rd., Traverse City
• (616) 941-5844

China Fair has been preparing oriental specialties for Traverse area residents for many years. The restaurant is tucked into a small strip mall close to Cherryland Mall on South Airport Road. It's easy to miss it, but well worth seeking out. The menu features numerous Cantonese, Thai, Szechwan and other Oriental specialties. Regulars give high marks to the combination plates, vegetarian dishes and fried rice variations. For a nice sampling of many house dishes, try one of the restaurant's

buffets held during the week at lunch, on Sundays and at dinnertime on Friday and Saturday nights.

Cottage Cafe
$ • 420 Munson Ave., Traverse City
• (616) 947-9261

The Cottage Cafe offers relaxed family dining in a pleasant restaurant on the Days Inn hotel property. Decorated in a bright cottage-like style, the cafe serves breakfast, lunch and dinner in homey comfort. The menu features a soup and salad bar, sandwiches and an array of homemade specialties.

Dill's Olde Towne Saloon
$$ • 423 S. Union St., Traverse City
• (616) 947-7534

Dill's Olde Towne Saloon dates back to 1896 when its doors opened as Novotny's pub. Owners and menus have changed with the times, but it always continues as a Traverse City favorite. The menu features hefty burgers and sandwiches as well as casual dinner fare featuring pasta, seafood, steak and a salad bar. Perch dinners are great as appetizers. Try Dill's signature deep-fried pickles, which have led to a series of T-shirts proclaiming, "I got pickled at Dill's." Entertainment takes center stage most evenings with karaoke, local musicians and, during the summers, the musical Golden Garter Revue (see our Nightlife and Casinos chapter).

Don's Drive-In
$ • 2030 N. U.S. Hwy. 31 N.
• (616) 938-1860

Drive on down to Don's for a trip down memory lane. Remember carhops, jukeboxes, burger baskets and old fashioned, handmade milkshakes? They're alive and thriving at the '50s-inspired Don's Drive-In. Actually the restaurant wasn't inspired by the '50s; it opened then. The owners' winning formula has served them well through four decades. The menu is simple — burgers and fixings made-to-order, Coney dogs, grilled sandwiches, chili, fries and

INSIDERS' TIP

The House of Flavors Ice Cream factory in Ludington produces 15 million gallons of ice cream annually.

onion rings. Old fashioned baskets have your favorite sandwich heaped with fries and coleslaw on the side. The kiddie baskets come in a cardboard vintage car (see our Kidstuff chapter). Not to be missed are Don's milkshakes. They only come in two sizes, but are made to be shared because both are enormous. Shakes are served in their tall mixing cups with extra glasses and spoons (which are needed because the hand-dipped ice cream is so thick). Hands down, they are the best in town. An added bonus for fruit lovers — the strawberry shakes are made with fresh berries. Don's Drive-In is open daily for lunch and dinner. Dine inside the bright diner with waitresses and booths straight out of *Happy Days* or drive up (not through!) and order from old fashioned parking stalls for carhop service. There is no alcohol served at Don's, but who wants a beer when you can have one these incredible milkshakes?

Durango's
$$ • 120 Park St., Traverse City
• (616) 941-4550

Relaxed Southwest style combined with a hefty dose of up-north hospitality await at Durango's. This casual downtown eatery is owned and operated by a Traverse City native who has been pleasing diners for the past 12 years with such delicious ventures as the Grand Traverse Dinner Train (see subsequent listing), Catering by Kelly's and the former D. J. Kelly's Restaurant. Durango's showcases steaks and seafood with eight cuts of beef from which to choose. Among other entrees are Alaskan king crab, vegetarian pasta marinara, rack of lamb and double center-cut pork chops. Appetizers include Emmenthaler and Gruyere cheese fondue, a signature favorite. If you have a hearty appetite, try the Double Dudes plates where you can combine a steak with your favorite seafood. The adjoining bar is a friendly gathering spot after work.

Gordie Howe's Tavern & Eatery
$ • 851 S. Garfield Ave., Traverse City
• (616) 929-4693

You don't have to be a hockey lover to love Gordie Howe's. This casual, smoke-free restaurant's menu stands tall with a well-rounded selection of sandwiches, soups, salads, burgers and great appetizers. Pizzas are a specialty with a number of unique variations. The Reuben pizza is a personal favorite. The bar is known for its 20-ounce "super drafts" and big-screen TVs. Diners will have fun perusing the endless photos, skates, jerseys and other memorabilia featuring the legendary career of the man known to many as "Mr. Hockey." Since Gordie Howe lives right here in Traverse City, it's not unusual for him to stop in. A gift shop sells Gordie Howe shirts, pucks, gifts and signed items.

Grand Traverse Dinner Train
$$$$$ • 642 Railroad Pl. (Woodmere and Eighth Sts.), Traverse City
• (616) 933-3768

All aboard for a moving dining experience! The Grand Traverse Dinner Train hit the tracks just a few years ago with an excellent menu. The train serves lunch, dinner and high tea aboard in classic Pullman-style service. The train with its four dining cars departs from its historic depot near downtown and travels on an excursion through the Boardman River Valley and the Pere Marquette Forest. Dinner is an elegant five-course gourmet meal served at tables for four. Lunch is more casual with a family-style, hot, gourmet meal. The evening ride lasts for three hours while lunch is a two-hour excursion. High-tea rides run for 90 minutes in the afternoon with guests enjoying an exquisite Victorian tea and dessert. Several additional rides are available including a boxcar luncheon with a one-hour ride and boxed lunch, a Santa ride (in appropriate season!) for a 45-minute excursion with St. Nick, and a casino link which serves appetizers and shuttles passengers to Turtle Creek Casino with adequate time off the train to play. Special events like murder-mystery dinners, Valentine's Day dinners, New Year's Eve tours and Victorian Christmas rides are scheduled throughout the year. The fall color rides are spectacular! The dinner train runs weekend service all year long, adding midweek service between July and October. The schedule shifts with the seasons and demand. Call for the current schedule. Reservations are required and cancellations must be made at least 48 hours in advance.

Holiday Inn
$$ • 615 E. Front St., Traverse City
- **(616) 947-3700**

The Holiday Inn is home to two restaurants. The cozy Cygnet Bar and Grill overlooks scenic West Grand Traverse Bay and a flock of beautiful mute swans from its windowed perch. Its menu features a tasty selection of soups, salads, sandwiches, appetizers and full beverage service as well as some of the best pizza in town. A big-screen television adds an entertainment twist. Cygnet is open daily for lunch and dinner. The Portage Dining Room serves breakfast, lunch and dinner in casual style. American fare, beef and seafood fill the menu. A fish fry is held on Friday evenings, while a scrumptious buffet is hosted each Saturday evening. A breakfast buffet is served on Sunday morning.

La Cuisine Amical
$$ • 229 E. Front St., Traverse City
- **(616) 941-8888**

European cuisine comes to Traverse City at La Cuisine Amical. This charming restaurant has quickly been adopted as a popular eatery among locals and visitors alike. La Cuisine Amical is a combination bistro, coffeehouse and bakery in the heart of downtown. Its cozy, brick interior is lined on one side by a working kitchen fronted by display cases filled with the day's offerings. Cozy tables, a three-sided fireplace and windows overlooking the Boardman river finish off the space. Service is cafeteria style for breakfast and lunch when quiche, croissants, pochettes, rotisserie chicken, pot pies, fresh fruits and homemade soups are standard fare. A low-fat Caesar salad is excellent while the many desserts are deliciously decadent. For dinner, La Cuisine Amical converts into a full-service bistro with an ever-changing, but always excellent, gourmet menu. At times the restaurant has featured special menu weeks showcasing recipes from various cookbooks or regional cuisines. Beer, wine and Starbucks coffee complement the meal. A sheltered sidewalk cafe is popular during warm months, while the cozy fire and intimate seating offers a respite from swirling snow in winter. Regardless of the season, La Cuisine is delightful.

La Senorita
$ • 1245 S. Garfield Ave., Traverse City
- **(616) 947-8820**

$ • 2455 U.S. Hwy. 31 S., Traverse City
- **(616) 946-4545**

$ • 737 W. Main St., Gaylord
- **(517) 732-1771**

$ • 1700 S. Mitchell St., Cadillac
- **(616) 779-3636**

$ • 1285 U.S. Hwy. 31 N., Petoskey
- **(616) 347-7750**

The Kleinrichert brothers brought full-fledged Mexican fare to northern Michigan when they opened La Senorita restaurant in 1980. That original restaurant, known then as La Margarita, sported only 35 seats and was among the few ethnic restaurants in the region. Its combination of great food, great prices and great service quickly made it wildly popular. Today, the original La Senorita on South Garfield has grown to a spacious facility with over 250 seats along with a large, comfortable bar. It is joined by additional La Senoritas in Petoskey, Gaylord, Cadillac, Sault Ste. Marie, Saginaw, Mt. Pleasant, Lansing and Alpena along with its second Traverse City restaurant on U.S. 31 South. The menu features all your Mexican favorites — nachos, quesadillas, enchiladas, burritos and chimichangas — as well as several south-of-the-border salads and American specialties. Fajitas in chicken, beef, shrimp or vegetarian combinations come sizzling to the table. Combination plates are generous and the children's Little Amigos menu appeals to all (see our Kidstuff chapter). Low-fat entrees are noted on the menu with the chicken fajita burrito a personal favorite. Expect a basket of freshly made tortilla chips to arrive with your waitress. Try to save room for dessert. Two sweet specialties are the French-fried ice cream and peanut butter pie.

Mabel's
$$ • 472 Munson Ave., Traverse City
- **(616) 947-0252**

Mabel's consistently ranks among top local favorites for casual dining and friendly service. Close to several popular hotels, Mabel's is an ideal choice for families with a nice menu for breakfast, lunch and dinner. The menu has something for everyone including prime rib, pastas, deli-style sandwiches, homemade soups and vegetarian dishes. Mabel's does not serve alcohol.

Mackinaw Brewing Company

$ • 161 E. Front St., Traverse City
• (616) 933-1100

Pub fare and handcrafted beer fill the bill at Mackinaw Brewing Company. Traverse City's first brewpub, it sits on a busy downtown corner just steps from Clinch Park Beach and Front Street shopping. Situated inside a vintage building, this former Big Boy restaurant has been designed to look like the deck of a ship with tiny lights overhead resembling the night sky. A balcony at the rear of the restaurant offers limited outdoor seating. The menu features hefty sandwiches, burgers and ribs along with traditional sides of onion rings, fries and salads. Lighter fare is also available. Evening specials change each night but have included smoked prime rib, all-you-can-eat shrimp, and ribs for "a buck a bone." Every Wednesday's family night. Genuine smokehouse barbecue is a specialty. One of our favorite sandwiches is the hand-pulled barbecued pork.

Minerva's

$$$ • Park Place Hotel, 300 E. State St., Traverse City • (616) 946-5000, (616) 946-5093

The historic Park Place Hotel stands tall as the center of Traverse City's downtown district. Its signature restaurant is Minerva's. This spacious, bright main-floor restaurant is the result of a recent, massive renovation of the eatery by the Park Place's most recent owners. The result is excellent, and diners will be pleased with the menu as well as the lovely surroundings. Dishes include innovative pastas, excellent steaks and creative sandwiches. Minerva's is open for breakfast, lunch and dinner.

Mode's Bum Steer

$$ • 125 E. State St., Traverse City
• (616) 947-9832

If you're looking for a good steak, Mode's is your place. The restaurant is a common spot for locals to meet for lunch or dinner. The menu is highlighted by custom-cut charbroiled Black Angus steaks, meaty barbecued pork ribs and fresh seafood. Mode's is open for lunch, dinner and late-night dining every day except Sundays. You won't be able to miss the State Street entrance; there's a life-size cartoon steer standing on its hind legs, smiling, next to the front door.

Molly's Bye Golly

$$ • 14091 Center Rd., Traverse City
• (616) 223-7200

Molly's brings an Irish pub ambiance to the center of the Old Mission Peninsula. This pleasant eatery serves a menu of Irish, American and regional cuisine. Steaks, burgers, pizza, seafood and salads are in the lineup. Molly's Bye Golly is open for lunch and dinner daily.

North Peak Brewery

$$ • 400 W. Front St., Traverse City
• (616) 941-7325

North Peak Brewery has been wildly popular since its eagerly anticipated opening last year. Its bar has become a local hot spot (as noted in our Nightlife chapter). On the dining side, the menu features a nice variety of interesting sandwiches, salads, entrees and wood-fired pizza. Many items are made with beers brewed on the premises such as porter-marinated steak, white-cheddar ale soup, beer-steamed cherry pecan sausage, baby-back ribs glazed in cherry porter barbecue sauce and brewhouse bread made from spent grain and steelhead red ale. If you don't plan to try the handcrafted beer, why not have a swig of North Peaks' own handcrafted root beer? It's excellent! One word of warning, the restaurant can get very busy during the summer and on weekends. Since North Peak doesn't take reservations, it's usually a good idea to arrive early.

Old Mission Tavern

$$$ • 17015 Center Rd., Traverse City
• (616) 223-7280

The Old Mission Tavern feeds your soul as well as your stomach. Original art by local artists fills the walls and shelves with creative beauty. The owner, who is also a noted artist, has showcased local talent since she first opened her doors years ago with the commitment to combine fine art with fine dining. Today, the works also spill over into the Bella

Photo: Kevin Poirier

The Traverse Bay region's majestic shorelines treat you to lovely views.

Galleria, an artists' gallery adjacent to the restaurant (see our Arts chapter for more on the gallery). The Old Mission Tavern is open for lunch and dinner with specialties like pasta rufino, whitefish provencal, rack of lamb, panfried walleye, chicken breast artichoke and prime rib. Sandwiches, soups and salads are served for lunch. You'll find daily pasta and entree specials. Watch for peirogies on Thursdays and roast leg of lamb on Wednesdays and Sundays. The restaurant is tucked into the countryside about 14 miles out on the Old Mission Peninsula, but well worth the drive for a wonderful meal in a truly unique setting.

Omelette Shoppe and Bakery
$ • 1209 E. Front St., Traverse City
• (616) 946-0590
$ • 124 Cass St., Traverse City
• (616) 946-0912

The Omelette Shoppes are synonymous with great breakfasts and fresh food. Since 1975, the Dell'Acqua family has created wonderful meals that taste good and are good for you. The restaurants are geared for breakfast and lunch, and are usually closed by 3 PM. Both are smoke-free facilities. The menu includes a huge selection of omelets and frittatas, pancakes, French toast, Belgian waffles, eggs, quiche, granola and fresh fruit. Batter dishes come with pure maple syrup.

Breakfast is served all day as are many sandwiches, salads, stir fry and the pasta of the day. Gourmet baked goods come with every meal and are so good that the shop sells more to take home. We have to share a few personal favorites — the turkey sausage scramble, sourdough French toast, create-your-own omelets and oriental turkey toss salad. The Omelette Shop has two locations. The main restaurant is across from the Civic Center on East Front Street with two spacious dining areas. The downtown Cass Street location is a cozy gathering space with more limited seating. Both are always bustling. If you plan to meet for a summer Sunday brunch, it's wise to arrive early. If you do have to wait (and, yes, the food is definitely worth the wait), there are several shops to browse through in the same strip mall.

Panda North
$$ • 2038 S. Airport Rd., Traverse City
• (616) 929-9722

Panda North promises to bring Chinatown to you. It does so from its friendly restaurant on the banks of the Boardman River at Logan's Landing. The lengthy menu includes popular oriental fare with many Szechwan, Hunan, Cantonese and Mandarin dishes to choose from. Favorites include triple harvest, Mongolian beef, sesame chicken and happy family.

A well-stocked buffet is available every evening. Luncheon specials and family dinners are available, as is a speedy take-out service. Alcoholic beverages are not available.

Pepper's Tavern and Grille
$$ • 626 E. Front St., Traverse City
• (616) 947-6260

Pepper's serves a delicious menu in a relaxed family atmosphere. The restaurant is central to several West Bay hotels, downtown and Grandview Parkway. Dinner fare includes specialties with seafood, steaks, ribs and chicken, creative salads, sandwiches, pasta and Mexican recipes. Desserts are tempting! Pepper's is open daily for lunch and dinner as well as brunch on Sundays.

Poppycock's
$$ • 128 E. Front St., Traverse City
• (616) 941-7632

In-house recipes are prepared daily at Poppycock's. This unique downtown diner is a popular gathering spot for lunch, dinner and snacks. Booths line the walls and fill the black-and-white checked floor for cozy dining. Colorful chalkboards and whimsical artwork fill nooks and crannies while the friendly staff bustles among the booths and behind the counter. The inventive menu features creative pastas, salads, sandwiches and several daily specials. One of our longtime favorite dishes is the Front Street Salad featuring goat cheese, dried cherries, pecans, spicy chicken and greens tossed in a fruity vinaigrette. Save room for dessert. Poppycock's carries a large assortment of goodies that hearken back to Mom's best recipes. On any given day, you're likely to find chocolate no-bakes, lemon bars, fresh pie, cookies and brownies. The sweets are also sold near the door for a quick detours off the downtown sidewalks or for diners on the run. Poppycock's is open daily for lunch and dinner. A full bar is available, but smoking is prohibited.

Reflections Restaurant and Lounge
$$$ • Waterfront Inn, 2061 U.S. Hwy. 31 N., Traverse City • (616) 938-2321

It's hard to match the view from Reflections' dining room on the top floor of the Waterfront Inn. Spectacular sunsets and panoramic views surround this many-windowed restaurant. The dinner menu is known for whitefish and seafood specialties, prime rib, steaks, pastas and chicken dishes. A lighter selection of delicious salads, sandwiches, soups and quesadillas are available throughout the day. The white seafood chili has been a perennial winner of the "People's Choice" award at downtown's annual chili cookoff. Reflections is open daily for breakfast, lunch and dinner.

Schelde's
$$ • 714 Munson Ave., Traverse City
• (616) 946-0981

Relaxed dining, great food and friendly service await at Schelde's. The family-friendly menu has an array of excellent entrees including steaks, seafood, sandwiches, soups and salads. You'll find a nice salad bar in the center of this spacious restaurant, which shifts to a breakfast buffet on weekends and daily during the summer. If you're looking for a light meal, try the Bayou Chicken Caesar salad or the cheddar broccoli soup and salad bar. Both are excellent. Schelde's is a popular place to meet for a casual dinner or a friendly lunch. The adjacent bar and its mounted televisions often attract the after-work and after-workout crowd. Schelde's is open daily for breakfast (weekends only October to May), lunch and dinner with additional to-go menus available for meals on the run.

Scott's Harbor Grill
12719 S. West Bay Shore Dr., Traverse City • (616) 922-2114

Scott's Harbor Grill hosts casual waterfront dining with panoramic views of West Grand Traverse Bay and the adjacent Harbor West Marina. The bustle of boats and boaters is an entertaining backdrop to dinners, which features a nice selection of fresh fish and seafood as well as several creative dinner specialties. If the weather is nice, request a table on the patio. Scott's is open year round for lunch and dinner. Reservations are accepted between October and April only.

Sleder's Family Tavern
$$ • 717 Randolph St., Traverse City
• (616) 947-9213

Sleder is a landmark. It is noted as one of Michigan's oldest continuously operated taverns (they weren't shut down during Prohibition). Sitting under the 12-foot stamped ceiling in this historic building, it is a perennially popular local restaurant as well as a neighborhood pub. It is certainly a place for families, and all will have a delightful time — whether you smooch the resident moose or simply laugh with those who do. The casual menu includes hearty sandwiches, Mexican specialties, large burgers and hefty salads along with dinner entrees with ribs, whitefish, perch, smelt, shrimp, barbecued chicken, steaks and pork chops. Bring your appetite on Friday nights when fish and smelt combos are "all you can eat." To pass along a few food favorites — our family likes the chili, the mushroom burger, the chicken burrito, the royal Reuben, the taco salad and the Slabtown ribs. Sleder's is open daily for lunch and dinner. (See the listing in our Nightlife chapter.)

T. C. Hunan
$$ • 1425 S. Airport Rd., Traverse City
• (616) 947-1388

Chinese and American cuisine is served daily at T.C. Hunan. You'll find an excellent selection of familiar oriental fare along with a few American entrees for variety. Large buffets are available several times each week. Weekday buffets are geared toward working lunch hours Monday through Friday, while dinner buffets are hosted every Friday and Saturday evening. The most elaborate repast is offered during Sunday's grand buffet. Carry-out and delivery service is available. T.C. Hunan is open for lunch and dinner daily.

T. C. Traders
$$$ • 1796 S. Garfield Ave., Traverse City • (616) 929-9885

T. C. Traders specializes in American cuisine at this restaurant next to Cherryland Mall. The setting is nautical and welcoming. Dinner fare features a range of steak and seafood specialties. Full beverage service is available. T. C. Traders is open every day for lunch and dinner.

Windows
$$$ • 7677 W. Bay Shore Dr., Traverse City • (616) 941-0100

When we sit in the dining room at Windows, we remember why we live in northern Michigan. The majestic view is absolutely mesmerizing. The panoramic vista of water, shore and sky paint a vision of nature's beauty that mere words can only attempt to describe. This smoke-free restaurant juts into Grand Traverse Bay halfway between Traverse City and Suttons Bay. As the name suggests, it is clad in windows that bring the sweeping view right to your dining table. The sophisticated menu is equally outstanding. You'll find an innovative mix of French, American and Cajun cuisines. Fresh seafood is bountiful as are the enjoyable daily specialties and appetizers (try the crab cakes for a delightful taste treat). Regardless of your dinner selection, make sure you save room for dessert. The Windows desserts have earned a well-deserved reputation for being outrageously decadent and delicious. There are hand-dipped truffles, rich homemade ice cream and sinful mousses, tortes and cheesecakes. The desserts and chocolates have been so popular that the owners opened Marafil gourmet bakery (see our Food on the Run section and our Shopping chapter) as a venue for selling them, along with a great assortment of breads and baked goods, in Traverse City. Windows is open daily for dinner although hours and days of operation may be reduced during the winter months. Reservations are recommended.

Grand Traverse Resort
$$$ • 100 Grand Traverse Village Blvd., Acme • (616) 938-2100

The Trillium is one of northern Michigan's signature wildflowers whose white, three-petaled flowers blanket the region's forests each spring. The Trillium is also the showcase restaurant and lounge that top the Grand Traverse Resort. A glass elevator transports diners to the Trillium which, on the 17th floor, is noted as the highest in the region. The sweeping views from this glass-enclosed tower are breathtaking, especially if you're lucky enough to be dining during one of our vivid northern sunsets. The atmosphere is elegant and inviting. The upscale menu was recently updated to showcase Mediterranean cuisine. The service is always excellent, as are the scrumptious desserts. After dinner, stroll to the lounge area where dance bands and piano players entertain their guests.

The Sweetwater Cafe is the newest restaurant in the Grand Traverse Resort lineup. It is the result of a major renovation that combined two previous eateries into the airy, spacious Sweetwater Cafe. The restaurant offers casual dining for breakfast, lunch and dinner in an open kitchen layout. The dinner menu is highlighted by grilled beef, pasta and fresh seafood specialties. An adjacent deli serves light sandwiches, desserts, coffee and beverages.

Giovanni's
$ • 9205 U.S. Hwy. 31 S., Interlochen
• (616) 276-6244

You'll find all your favorite Italian dishes at this family-run eatery. Giovanni's is a nice place to stop when you're on your way to an Interlochen Arts Festival performance or simply driving through the countryside near Interlochen or South Long Lake. This homey restaurant is tucked along the highway not far from Interlochen Corners (the intersection between U.S. Highway 31 and Mich. Highway 37), and just a quick drive from Interlochen State Park and Interlochen Center for the Arts. Giovanni's is open daily except Mondays for lunch and dinner.

Leelanau County

La Becasse
$$$ • 9001 S. Dunns Farm Rd., Intersection of County Rds. 675 and 616, Burdickville • (616) 334-3944

Looks can be deceiving as you drive through the Leelanau countryside and by the small, house-like building that is La Becasse. But don't be fooled. This restaurant may be cozy and outwardly unassuming but the cuisine measures to grand (or should we say la grande) proportions. French country meals are prepared with meticulous attention and excellent results. Plan for a leisurely meal so that you can savor the experience. Reservations are recommended.

Four Seasons Dining Room
$$ • Sugar Loaf Resort, 4500 Sugar Loaf Mountain Rd., Cedar • (616) 228-1820, (800) 748-0117

Sugar Loaf Resort features traditional regional cuisine and longtime favorites on the menu at its Four Seasons Dining Room. Whether you choose prime rib or a local seafood specialty, make sure to save room for one of the delicious homemade desserts. Plan to try the scrumptious Sunday brunch; it's one of the best in the region.

Sugarfoot Saloon
$$ • 4997 S. Good Harbor Rd., Cedar
• (616) 228-6166

Leelanau residents swear by the Mexican fare served at the Sugarfoot Saloon. This family friendly restaurant prepares a host of Mexican and American favorites with aplomb. The wet burritos (topped with enchilada sauce) are excellent. A game room provides added fun to the meal. The Sugarfoot Saloon is open daily for lunch and dinner.

Art's Bar
$, no credit cards • 6487 W. Western Ave., Glen Arbor • (616) 334-3754

Art's Bar is a Leelanau County institution. Open all year, its menu features burgers, steaks, pizza, whitefish and Mexican specialties. Try Art's version of surf and turf: a burger and smelt. See our Nightlife and Casinos chapter for more on this popular local gathering spot.

Boone Docks
$$ • 5858 Manitou View Blvd., Glen Arbor • (616) 334-6444

A cousin to Boone's Long Lake Inn in Traverse City and Boone's Prime Time Pub in Suttons Bay, Boone Docks serves a casual menu of sandwiches, burgers, steaks and seafood in a comfortable pine-walled restaurant filled with cozy booths and bright windows. The friendly service adds to the relaxed atmosphere. Boone Docks is open daily for lunch and dinner.

The Homestead
$-$$$ • Mich. Hwy. 22, Glen Arbor
• (616) 334-5000

The Homestead offers distinct dining options in its three restaurants: The Inn, Nonna's Ristorante Della Famiglia and Whiskers. For an unforgettable, elegant dinner, The Inn ($$$) is your choice. This beautiful restaurant is housed in an historic inn, the original "Homestead," with abundant windows overlooking the Lake Michigan shoreline and Sleeping Bear Bay. Sunsets are spectacular. The setting complements the cuisine, featuring local whitefish and regional food specialties presented in a sophisticated, delicious menu. Reservations are recommended. Nonna's Ristorante Della Famiglia ($$) offers relaxed dining in cozy surroundings in the Homestead's centrally located Village area. The menu showcases classic Italian dishes. Reservations are recommended. Whiskers ($) is the spot for pizza and burgers in a casual, comfortable setting. Like Nonna's, Whiskers is in the Village. The Inn and Whiskers are open for dinner, and Nonna's serves breakfast and dinner.

Le Bear
$$ • 5707 Lake St., Glen Arbor
• **(616) 334-4640**

The legend of Sleeping Bear leads off the menu at Le Bear, which sits along the waterfront overlooking Sleeping Bear Bay and the Manitou Islands. The restaurant is open during the summer and on fall and spring weekends for breakfast, lunch and dinner. The menu ranges from a great assortment of sandwiches and salads to an array of delicious dinner entrees. Among the offerings are a Santa Fe chicken salad, cherry chicken salad melt sandwich, chicken pot pie, South Manitou trout, five-layer veggie lasagna and classic heap of perch. Regional whitefish is prepared just the way you like it — broiled, amandine, blackened or parmesan crusted. Dessert features the chef's special apple-pecan bread pudding. Sunday brunch is held each week. Le Bear is open daily between June and September, and then begins scaling back its weekday hours. The restaurant is closed January to early April.

Western Avenue Grill
$$ • 6410 Western Ave., Glen Arbor
• **(616) 334-3362**

Casual comfort and great food are the hallmarks of the Western Avenue Grill. This friendly restaurant is nestled among the many wonderful shops and galleries that fill Glen Arbor's charming streets. The menu features pastas, seafoods, ribs, steaks and whitefish. The Western Avenue Grill is open for lunch and dinner on Tuesdays through Saturdays.

Dick's Pour House
$$ • 103 Phillips St., Lake Leelanau
• **(616) 256-9912**

Homemade specialties are on tap at Dick's Pour House. Enjoy homemade soups, sandwiches and pizzas along with a hearty selection of dinner specials. Fish frys are held every Friday night while prime rib and steamed shrimp are featured on Saturday. Make sure to save room for homemade pie for dessert! Dick's Pour House serves dinner and lunch.

Key to the County
$$ • 104 Main St., Lake Leelanau
• **(616) 256-5397**

Key to the County sits near the narrows in tiny Lake Leelanau yet this fairly new up-north restaurant is family run and consistently draws diners from miles around. The menu showcases the chef's talents with an array of contemporary entrees. Look for Thai chicken, fresh fish and an assortment of grilled steaks, chops and other specialties. Every Tuesday is Live Lobster Night. Key to the County is open daily (except Sunday) for lunch and daily for dinner.

The Bluebird
$$ • 102 E. River St., Leland
• **(616) 256-9081**

The Bluebird has long been a favorite eatery with locals and our many summer visitors. Just steps from downtown and Fishtown, it sits along the river bank as the Carp River winds its way toward Lake Michigan. Inside the atmosphere is friendly and comfortable. A well-stocked salad bar stretches through the dining room. The menu reflects the region with loads of Great Lakes fish and seafood specialties. Every meal is highlighted with fabulous cinnamon rolls, a Bluebird signature item. A brunch is held on Sunday mornings. During the winter, the Bluebird hosts an ambitious schedule of ethnic dinners every Wednesday and Thursday night from late November through April. Casual meals are served in the adjoining bar. The Bluebird is open for lunch and dinner. The

Early Bird, (616) 256-9656, next door, serves breakfast and lunch.

The Cove
$$ • 111 River St., Leland
• (616) 256-9834

Fishtown is the picturesque backdrop for The Cove. Windows overlook the historic docks, weather-beaten buildings, the Carp River and the panorama of Lake Michigan. Freshwater fish and seafood dishes highlight the menu, which also includes prime rib and sandwiches. Specialties include a hearty Fishtown stew, seafood pie and variations on whitefish. The Cove is open for lunch and dinner between mid-May and mid-October.

Riverside Inn
$$ • 302 E. River St., Leland
• (616) 256-9971

The Riverside Inn is another wonderful Leland eatery nestled along the river banks. The dining room and lobby bar share a casual atmosphere that extends to the inn's upstairs guest rooms. The bistro menu is complemented by a lengthy wine list featuring a number of locally produced wines. The Riverside Inn is open for lunch and dinner during the summer season only, from mid-May to mid-October.

Leelanau Country Inn
$$ • 149 E. Harbor Hwy., Maple City
• (616) 228-5060

The Leelanau Country Inn is the personification of the picturesque country inn of our fantasies. It sits in the heart of the Leelanau county countryside, surrounded by the region's trees and gentle rolling landscape. Birdhouses are perched along the grounds, often giving diners an entertaining show by the winged guests. Inside, guests are seated at cozy tables in the inn's rooms. The owners take pride in their cuisine, and it shows. The menu is extensive, featuring a huge selection of fresh seafood flown in from Boston, along with entrees like northern whitefish, pasta, prime rib, beef Wellington, roast rack of lamb, and beef pot pie. Innovative specialty dishes include crabmeat-stuffed chicken breast, apple-bread stuffed chicken breast and Cape Cod Jonah Stone crabmeat stuffed whitefish.

The owners decided to share their food secrets a few years ago when they published the *Leelanau Country Inn Cookbook*, which continues to be a popular publication in most area bookstores. The Leelanau Country Inn is open for dinner. Reservations are recommended.

Stubb's Sweet Water Grill
$$ • 115 Waukazoo St., Northport
• (616) 386-7611

Stubb's is known for its excellent regional cuisine and promotion of local wines. Dining is hosted in the restaurant's casual dining room or, during the warmer weather, on an outdoor porch. The recently updated menu features longtime favorites such as parmesan-crusted whitefish and paella along with newly introduced Cajun, Mexican and Asian infusion dishes. Stubb's is open for casual dining and take-out for lunch and dinner.

Woody's
$$ • 116 Waukazoo St., Northport
• (616) 386-9933

At Woody's, the slogan is "Where life is serious but food is fun!" This longtime Northport restaurant is open daily for lunch and dinner with specialties like cherry-smoked chicken and ribs along with steaks, seafood, burgers and "the best nachos in the universe." Woody's is open daily for lunch and dinner.

Eagle's Ridge Fine Dining
$$ • 2511 N. West Bay Shore Dr.,
Peshawbestown • (616) 271-7166

Eagle's Ridge Fine Dining is the dining component of Traverse Bay Casino Resorts. The restaurant overlooks the Leelanau Sands Casino and West Grand Traverse Bay. The menu showcases American, regional and Native American cuisine and is served buffet style for breakfast, lunch and dinner.

Boone's Prime Time Pub
$$ • 102 St. Joseph St., Suttons Bay
• (616) 271-6688

Boone's Prime Time Pub provides a warm ambiance in its busy restaurant. Compared to Boone's Long Lake Inn, the Prime Time Pub is tiny. On the other hand, many would argue that its cozy size plays a major role in its appeal. A central fireplace adds a glow to the rustic surroundings. Seating is split between tables and booths. The menu, like Boone's Long Lake Inn and Boone Docks, features several beef entrees including steak and burgers. All are prepared to order and served with friendly, attentive service.

Hattie's
$$$$ • 111 St. Joseph St., Suttons Bay
• (616) 271-6222

Original art fills the understated walls of Hattie's with creativity and color, which is matched by the innovative cuisine and presentation of its elegant meals. This restaurant, which doubles as an art gallery, has earned a reputation as one of the region's nicest restaurants. The menu features dishes that showcase the region and celebrate new tastes. Past specialties have included Thai scallops, morel ravioli, grilled range hen with cherry barbecue sauce, and chocolate paradise with raspberries. You will usually see an ample selection of seafood along with vegetarian options. During the off-season, Hattie's often sponsors special dinners either prepared around an ethnic or topical theme or spotlighting a local culinary expert. The restaurant has also taken an innovative step in terms of decorating. The artwork on display rotates each month as several new artists use Hattie's as a venue for their work. Hattie's is open for dinner. Reservations are recommended.

Antrim-Kalkaska

Spencer Creek
$$$$ • 9166 Helena St., Alden
• (616) 331-6147

Spencer Creek is one of several outstanding restaurants sporting an address in Antrim County. This relaxed, upscale eatery is known for menus that capitalize on local produce and regional specialties. Entrees reflect a French influence and feature variations on beef tenderloin, veal, trout, lamb, duck, salmon and venison. A popular option is the "light dinner" selection, which includes a salad and two appetizers. Presentation and service are excellent, as are the desserts. Spencer Creek is open Tuesdays through Saturday. Reservations are recommended.

Ivanhoff
$$ • Shanty Creek, 1 Shanty Creek Blvd., Bellaire • (616) 533-8621, (800) 678-4111

The Ivanhoff is the signature restaurant serving Shanty Creek with a contemporary European atmosphere. Regional cuisine is showcased in this popular resort restaurant. Several Bavarian specialties have been included which complement the resort's theme. Family-style dining is featured on Sundays. The Ivanhoff serves breakfast, lunch and dinner daily.

Peterson's 31 North
$$ • 3910 U.S. Hwy. 31 N., Eastport
• (616) 599-3130

Peterson's 31 North is a family-friendly establishment in a large, spacious, open restaurant. Casual dining is the order of the day here with entrees such as pizza, pasta, ribs, steaks, seafood, sandwiches and salads. Peterson's is open for lunch and dinner.

Vasquez' Hacienda
$ • U.S. Hwy. 31 N., Elk Rapids
• (616) 264-5892

Mexican fare is the specialty at Vasquez' Hacienda. This favorite Antrim-area eatery serves a nice selection of Mexican and American dishes for lunch and dinner. Ethnic specialties include burritos, fajitas and chimichangas. Fish frys are held on Friday nights.

Rowe Inn
$$$$ • East Jordan Rd., Ellsworth
• (616) 588-7351

Ellsworth is a teensy northern town situated on wooded rolling hills at the tip of Antrim county. It is also home to two of the most wonderful restaurants in the region, if not the entire state: The Rowe Inn and Tapawingo (see subsequent description). The Rowe Inn opened in the early 1970s in a knotty pine roadhouse. The menu featured the freshest regional delicacies, such as lake perch, whitefish, trout, duck, venison, morels, spring asparagus and summer berries in seasonal offerings that were delicious and very new to northern cuisine. The success of the Rowe affected menu planning throughout the region and pioneered the way for many of our finest dining spots. The Rowe Inn still follows the same formula of employing blue-chip chefs, using the best and the freshest of our home-grown specialties and continually creating and serving innovative, sophisticated meals. A wine list reputed to be the most extensive in the state complements the cuisine. A dinner here promises to be memorable. If you plan to visit during the fall or winter, watch for the Rowe's special dinners such as the Madrigal Dinner during the holidays or wine sampling meals. A brunch is hosted on Sundays. Reservations are recommended.

Tapawingo
$$$$ • 9502 Lake St., Ellsworth
• (616) 588-7971

Innovative American cuisine is prepared in exquisite style at Tapawingo. Like the Rowe Inn (see the previous listing), Tapawingo resides in a tiny community but has achieved national attention. The restaurant and its chef, Harlan "Pete" Peterson, have received numerous accolades, including Top Table awards from *Gourmet* magazine and nomination as Best Chef in the Midwest by the James Beard Foundation. Food lovers flock here from miles around, at times planning an entire weekend up north that is specifically worked around dinner plans in Ellsworth. A meal at Tapawingo is a full evening's experience from the first appetizer to the last bite of dessert. The menu changes frequently to reflect new dishes and the season's specialties. One of the signature entrees features rack of lamb. Others may include grilled beef, roasted salmon, or creative vegetarian ensembles. All showcase Midwest-

ern ingredients. Tapawingo is open daily for dinner during the summer but scales back slightly during the fall, winter and spring. Call ahead for the current dinner hours. Reservations are recommended.

Big Buck Brewery & Steakhouse
$$ • 550 S. Wisconsin St., Gaylord
• (517) 732-5781

There are no small words to describe Big Buck. The place is huge and often crowded. The spacious dining areas are accented by massive chandeliers made from simulated antlers that hang from high ceilings and mark the path to the bar and brewing tanks. It's not unusual to have to wait for a table, but beepers give customers the mobility to wander through the Big Buck gift shop where you can choose from the local brews, your choice of logo wear and a "Mighty Bucks" hockey shirt. If you prefer to relax while you wait, the central lobby is spacious with ample seating, including a number of twig-style chairs made by a local artisan. At dinner, the menu capitalizes on the restaurant's steakhouse reputation with beef playing a predominant role in the lineup. The generous portions are well-prepared. The service is friendly and attentive. Big Buck is open daily for lunch and dinner. The brewing operation of Big Buck Brewery is highlighted in our Nightlife chapter.

Busia's Polish Kitchen
$$ • 2782 Old 27 S., Gaylord
• (517) 732-2790

Visitors traveling through northern Michigan repeatedly seek out Busia's. This delight-

---

INSIDERS' TIP

Take a bit of the north back home to savor throughout the year with one of the many books on local cuisine. Food lovers will enjoy *The Connoisseur Up North, A Food Lover's Guide to Northern Michigan* by Sherri and Graydon DeCamp; *Pride of Northern Michigan Cookbook* by Creative Characters; *La Senorita Mexican Restaurants Favorite South of the Border Recipes* by Ken, Joe and Don Kleinrichert; and, *Leelanau Country Inn Cookery* by Linda and John Sisson. Each combines recipes with chatty commentary. The Leelanau Country Inn and La Senorita publications feature their own restaurants, while the other two books profile numerous local eateries. You'll find these books in local bookstores, specialty shops and restaurants.

ful restaurant features well-loved specialties from Poland along with its traditional American fare. The menu features peirogies and homemade kielbasa as well as prime rib and steaks. Busia's is open for breakfast, lunch and dinner.

Sugar Bowl
$$ • 216 W. Main St., Gaylord
• (517) 732-5524

The Sugar Bowl has been serving downtown Gaylord since 1919. Hearty family fare is dished up for breakfast, lunch and dinner at this historic eatery. The Sugar Bowl hosts two dining rooms, a gift shop and banquet facilities within the restaurant building. Breakfast, lunch and early dinners are served in the casual, booth-lined Family Room with menus featuring sandwiches, light lunches and homemade desserts. More formal dinners are served in the Open Hearth Room, featuring entrees of whitefish and prime rib along with a gourmet salad table and Greek specialties.

Lake Michigan Shoreline and Cadillac

Brookside Inn
$$ • 115 N. Michigan Ave., Beulah
• (616) 882-9688

Make your dining experience a rare adventure. The Brookside Inn offers cook-your-own entrees. Heated stones, sliced from Switzerland's Matterhorn, are brought to your table where you prepare your choice of meat, seafood or poultry. Antiques create a casual, relaxed atmosphere. The Brookside has one of the region's most extensive wine cellars, with an array of German wines hand-selected by the owner. Cocktails are available. The inn serves breakfast, lunch and dinner 365 days a year.

The Cabbage Shed
$$ • 198 Frankfort Ave., Elberta
• (616) 352-9843

Fine dining in an informal, funky atmosphere make your experience at the Cabbage Shed something to savor. The full menu features specialties of prime rib and whitefish. There is a full-service bar with an extensive wine list and good selection of import beers. Enjoy outdoor dining overlooking Betsie Bay. Lunch and dinner are served daily during summer months, but call for off-season hours. See our Nightlife chapter to learn about The Cabbage Shed's after-dark entertainment.

The Cherry Hut
$ • 246 Michigan Ave., Beulah
• (616) 882-4074

Customers have been flocking to The Cherry Hut for fresh-baked cherry pies for 76 years. Still using the recipe they used when the family-owned restaurant opened in 1922, The Cherry Hut sells 500 fruit pies daily. Other specialties include cherry chicken salad, roasted turkey and homemade cinnamon rolls After you enjoy a casual meal, either indoors or outdoors, stop at the restaurant shop. You can purchase fresh pies, Cherry Hut jams and jellies and souvenirs. The smoke-free restaurant is open from Memorial Day to mid-October for lunch and dinner.

Hungry Tummy
$ • 226 S. Benzie Blvd., Beulah
• (616) 882-5103

For more than 25 years The Hungry Tummy has offered family dining in downtown Beulah. Cozy booths, nightly specials and great broasted chicken draw folks back again and again. Full dinners, light fare, sandwiches, pizza and a full bar are all available. The Hungry Tummy serves breakfast, lunch and dinner daily.

Sail Inn Restaurant
$$ • 1579 Michigan Ave., Benzonia
• (616) 882-4971

A great selection of good food at reasonable prices and a comfortable atmosphere are the hallmarks of this Benzonia restaurant that serves breakfast, lunch and dinner daily. Customers can't get enough of the deep fried and steamed shrimp, fresh whitefish and prime rib. Cocktails are available.

A&W Restaurant and Drive-In
$ • Corner of Mich. Hwy. 115 and Mich. Hwy. 22, Frankfort • (616) 352-9021

Cruise into Frankfort's A&W drive-in for a trip down memory lane. This is one of the few remaining eateries still offering curb service and A&W's original brand of root beer. Full service sit-down dining is also available. (See our Kidstuff chapter for more information.)

Harbor Shores Restaurant
$, no credit cards • 727 Main St., Frankfort • (616) 352-7371

You'll find casual dining and a nautical atmosphere at Harbor Shores family restaurant. Stop here for their delicious homemade soups, broasted chicken or barbecued ribs. Harbor Shores serves breakfast, lunch and dinner, daily.

Wharfside Restaurant
$$ • 300 Main St., Frankfort • (616) 882-5300

Pasta lovers, don't even think about visiting Frankfort without experiencing the Fettucini Carbonara at Wharfside. You'll enjoy your favorite dishes and cocktails in a relaxed dining atmosphere featuring a nautical theme. The specialties here are pasta dishes and whitefish. Tables overlook beautiful Betsie Bay. Open May to October, this is a smoke-free restaurant.

The Glenwood Lodge
$$ • 4604 Main St., Onekama • (616) 889-3734

Around the turn of the century the Glenwood Lodge was a destination of choice for Chicago vacationers. The historic restaurant still reflects the quiet charm of that romantic era. During winter months the fine-dining establishment provides an intimate atmosphere and caters to couples. In summer the restaurant is frequented mainly by families who enjoy the lodge's wide range of gourmet dishes including seafoods, pasta, chicken, lamb and steak. Dessert specialties include original varieties of cheesecake and luscious hot fudge brownie sundaes. A full bar is available featuring more than 30 beers. Serving dinner only, the inn is open daily.

Crystal Mountain Resort
$-$$ • 12500 Crystal Mountain Dr., Thompsonville • (616) 378-2000

Crystal Mountain Resort can accommodate the gotta-have-it-fast burger appetite as well as diners who wish to relax with a full-course meal and cocktails. The Wildflower dining room provides a contemporary fine-dining environment, cocktails and a nice array of appetizers and entrees including their specialty, barbecued ribs. On Monday, Wednesday and Friday evenings during summer months, enjoy a Mountain-style barbecue on the sun deck featuring ribs, chicken, brats, side dishes, and snacks. The Grill is in the heart of the lodge at the Pro Shop and offers pizza, snacks, beer and wine, and take-outs. The slopeside Main Street Grill offers sandwiches, chili, snacks, beverages and fresh-baked sweet treats. Come in from the cold to warm up with some chili or try the sandwiches, baked potato bar and salads at Center Slice on the main level in Crystal Center. Beer and wine are available. The Vista Lounge, overlooking the slopes, and the Weldon Room, on the upper level of the lodge, offer light menus and full bars. Crystal Mountain Resort is a nonsmoking facility.

Armedos
$ • 1569 S. U.S. Hwy. 31, Manistee • (616) 723-3561

Kids feel right at home at this friendly Manistee family restaurant. Even the pickiest member of the clan will find something appealing on the menu. Armedos offers American and Mexican dishes, pizza, Friday fish fry and Saturday prime rib and steak specials. There's both a kids and seniors menu. The lounge, decorated with World War II memorabilia, features full bar service. Armedos serves lunch and dinner daily, except for major holidays.

Dockside
$ • 445 River St., Manistee • (616) 723-3046

The lovely Manistee Riverwalk is just a short stroll from this casual, full-menu restaurant. A nautical theme sets an easy mood, and a full bar is available. Menu items include steaks, seafood, prime rib, barbecued ribs, pizza and sandwiches. The Friday-night fish frys are very popular. Dockside serves lunch and dinner Monday through Saturday.

Four Forty West
$$ • 440 River St., Manistee • (616) 723-7902

If you delight in dining with a view, you'll enjoy the riverside Four Forty West restaurant in historic downtown Manistee, where large windows afford a calming view of the lovely Manistee River waterway. The restaurant features an extensive menu. Specialties include prime rib, fresh whitefish, perch and barbecued ribs. Four Forty West serves lunch and dinner, daily.

Gregory's
$$ • 200 U.S. Hwy. 31 N., Manistee
• (616) 723-4661

Breakfast is available any time at Gregory's. House specialties include an English scramble with ham, waffles and corned beef hash. The luncheon and dinner menu features seafood, pasta dishes, poultry, pork and their house specialty, an 18-ounce New York strip steak. Enjoy cocktails from Jonathon's Pub, right next door. Or enjoy Gregory's full menu in the pub atmosphere. Both establishments are in Best Western Carriage Inn.

Old Town Restaurant
$ • 155 E. Eighth St., Manistee
• (616) 723-4581

For two years in a row locals have ranked Old Town Restaurant's home cooking as the best in Manistee. A true Insiders' favorite, this eatery is clean and comfortable. You'll love the homemade chicken dumplings, Dutch apple and coconut cream pies and fresh-baked breads. Open daily, Old Town serves breakfast and lunch Sunday through Thursday, and dinners only Friday and Saturday.

The Pepper Mill
$ • 50 Arthur St., Manistee
• (616) 398-9225

The Pepper Mill offers family dining at reasonable prices. Breakfast specials are available Monday through Saturday. Their popular breakfast buffets are served every Sunday and feature good old-fashioned American favorites including biscuits and gravy, bacon, sausage and eggs. There are nightly dinner buffets and a full Mexican menu. The Pepper Mill serves breakfast, lunch and dinner, daily.

Beamer's Restaurant
$ • 2253 W. U.S. Hwy. 10, Ludington
• (616) 757-0008

Vacationers can hardly wait to return to Ludington for Beamer's Friday night fish fry, which accommodates 300 guests on a typical summer evening. This comfortable family eatery is also known for serving the best pizza in the Ludington area. Sauces are homemade, dough is made from scratch and the pizzas are piled with your favorite toppings. Cocktails are available. Lunch and dinner are served daily, and breakfast is served on weekends only. Beamer's is closed Monday during winter months.

Gibbs Country House Restaurant
$$ • 3951 W. U.S. Hwy. 10, Ludington
• (616) 845-0311

An Insiders' favorite since 1947, Gibbs' all-you-can-eat salad bar is the ultimate in fresh-food dining, featuring a selection of more than 30 homemade dishes. Leave some room, because they save the best for last. The dessert bar is unequaled. It features homemade cherry and peach cobbler, homemade cookies, pecan, pumpkin and rhubarb pies and fresh ice cream. There's more! They are renowned for their huge sticky buns and apple dumplings. The family-oriented restaurant offers a full menu of traditional American dishes in a casual colonial setting. Open seven days, mid-February through December, seasonal menu items are based on themes, Christmas in July, Asparagus Festival and Taste of Autumn. Free shuttle service is provided from the Ludington marina and airport.

House of Flavors Restaurant
$ • 402 W. Ludington Ave., Ludington
• (616) 845-5785

House of Flavors offers some of the best breakfast deals in town. The 1950s decor is sheer fun. From the restaurant you can watch the House factory make ice cream. (See the complete listing in our Kidstuff chapter.)

Michael's on the Avenue
$ • 129 W. Ludington Ave., Ludington
• (616) 845-7411

Michael's is where Ludington's good friends gather for food and fun. The newly remodeled pub and restaurant offers prime rib by the ounce, steaks, pizza and burgers, serving lunch and dinner daily. They feature live weekend 1970s-style entertainment (see our Nightlife chapter).

Old Hamlin Restaurant
$ • 120-22 W. Ludington Ave., Ludington
• (616) 843-4251

Owned and operated by the same family since 1926, the Old Hamlin is a friendly, home-like eatery. Nobody leaves hungry. Generous portions of chicken, prime rib and Greek cuisine are served with homemade breads from the restaurant's own bakery. The pies are irresistible. Try one of their banana cream or cherry Dutch apple pies. This is definitely the place for early birds and anglers. Old Hamlin opens at 5 AM during summer months and 5:30 AM the rest of the year, offering great, reasonably priced, breakfast buffets. Lunch and dinner are served daily, and cocktails are available.

P.M. Steamers Restaurant
$$ • 502 W. Loomis St., Ludington
• (616) 843-9555

Named for the once-famous Steamers carferry and rail line, this waterfront establishment offers excellent traditional American cuisine. The restaurant is known for gracious service, Sunday brunches and unforgettable desserts created from locally grown fruit products. Steamers' nutty walleye, chicken Caesar salad, pastas and prime rib are customer favorites. Appetizers and cocktails are served on the deck overlooking the Ludington marina. Steamers is open daily April through December.

Scotty's Restaurant
$$ • 5910 E. Ludington Ave., Ludington
• (616) 843-4033

Whether you're on a tight schedule or you're looking forward to a long, romantic dinner for two, Scotty's is the place. Relaxed, casual dining, shrimp served just the way you like it, and a great chicken Cordon Bleu distinguish this year-round restaurant. In addition to serving a full menu daily, Scotty's offers lunch specials, soup and sandwich specials and a kid's menu. Cocktails are available.

Burke's Waterfront
$ • 2403 Sunnyside Dr., Cadillac
• (616) 775-7555

Enjoy Burke's American or Mexican cuisine and great outdoor dining, featuring a fantastic view of boating activities on Lake Cadillac. Daily breakfast buffets, dinner buffets and their Friday night seafood buffet will satisfy even those teenagers known as bottomless pits. Cocktails and take-outs are available. Burke's serves breakfast, lunch and dinner daily.

The Chef's Deli
$ • 212 N. Mitchell St., Cadillac
• (616) 775-2101

A local favorite for snacks or light meals, Master Chef Hermann Suhs never disappoints his customers. You'll always find delicious salads and sandwiches to linger over in a charming European atmosphere. Beer and wine are available. Breakfast, lunch and dinner are served Monday through Saturday.

Hermann's European Cafe
$$ • 214 N. Mitchell St., Cadillac
• (616) 775-9563

Hermann's European Cafe is a Northwest Michigan destination. Master Chef Hermann Suhs opened the bistro-style cafe in 1985. Since then, his reputation for serving authentic international gourmet cuisine has drawn recognition throughout the Midwest. Swedish-style wild boar, Wiener schnitzel and Italian chicken breast piccata are standard menu items. On special occasions throughout the year, the Chef prepares ethnic buffets, including Austrian, Greek, Italian, German and Michigan game. Suhs is also a pastry chef and offers an array of tantalizing desserts to top your meal. Cocktails are available. Lunch and dinner are served Monday through Saturday.

Hillcrest Family Restaurant
$ • 1250 S. Mitchell St., Cadillac
• (616) 775-4191

The Hillcrest was known as the hottest drive-in in town during the 1960s, but time has transformed it into a comfortable casual restaurant known for outstanding buffets and a menu featuring traditional family favorites. Breakfast, lunch and dinner are served daily.

King's Table Restaurant
$$ • 5676 W. Mich. Hwy. 55, Cadillac
• (616) 775-2458

King's Table Restaurant offers customers

a feast fit for royalty every Saturday night. More than 120 items are featured in their famous weekend smorgasbord. You'll find Alaskan snowcrab legs, imported oysters, five hot entrees, a carving table and mouthwatering desserts. Their complete menu includes cut-to-order New York strip steak, Lake Superior whitefish and shrimp scampi. Sporting a new lodge look, the atmosphere is refreshing and relaxing. A full bar is adjacent to the dining room. Lunch and dinner is served seven days, year round. Full breakfasts are available during summer months only.

Lakeside Charlie's
$$ • 301 S. Lake Mitchell Dr., Cadillac • (616) 775-5332

Whether you arrive by boat, snowmobile or car, you'll enjoy fine, casual dining at Lakeside Charlie's along Lake Mitchell. Order your meal indoors or outdoors to take in the great lake view. The restaurant offers a full menu, including steak, seafood and poultry, their legendary barbecued ribs and Sunday brunch. Lakeside Charlie's serves lunch and dinner daily.

Crabby Charlie's lounge offers light meals, a good selection of imports and features a 10-foot TV for viewing popular sporting events.

Maggie's Tavern
$$ • 523 N. Mitchell St., Cadillac • (616) 775-1810

For good dining values in a relaxed turn-of-the-century atmosphere, stop at Maggie's Tavern. An Insiders' favorite haunt, Maggie herself dishes out plenty of hospitality along with a full bar, great Mexican food, good Reuben sandwiches and unbeatable buffalo wings. It's a family eatery and features a kids menu. Maggie's serves lunch and dinner Monday through Saturday.

Marina Ristorante
$$ • Mich. Hwy. 115 and Mich. Hwy. 55 Cadillac • (616) 775-9322

You won't find better Italian cuisine anywhere in Michigan. Marina Ristorante has been family owned and operated since 1959. Their traditional handmade pastas and rolls are complemented by sauces, also made from fresh ingredients on the premises. The restaurant features a full bar with a nice wine list and a good selection of imported beer. Outdoor seating provides a lovely view of Lake Cadillac and docking is available. Dinner only is served Wednesday through Monday.

Terrace Room
Curly's Bar and Grill
$$ • McGuire's Resort, 7880 S. Mackinaw Tr., Cadillac • (616) 775-9947

Enjoy regional and northern Michigan cuisine in the casual elegance of the Terrace Room. The spacious dining room offers a calming vista from the resort's hilltop perch overlooking the Cadillac countryside. You'll find an original menu featuring a delicious grapefruit whitefish and brown trout. Other favorite entrees include New York strip steak and a ginger shrimp stir-fry. For light, quick lunches try the deli bar. On weekends, enjoy the Saturday night buffet or Sunday brunch. Cocktails are available. For more relaxed dining, try Curly's Bar and Grill, sporting a new up-north look and atmosphere. You can order burgers, sandwiches and appetizers. The bar offers more than 30 imported beers and microbrews.

Thursday through Saturday night Curly's presents live entertainment (see our Nightlife chapter). Both Curly's and the Terrace Room are open daily.

Little Traverse

Ansted's by the Lake
$ • 115 Main St., East Jordan • (616) 536-2511

The view from this casual restaurant and bar is almost as delicious as the food. An outdoor deck and a glass-enclosed all-season room both overlook beautiful Lake Charlevoix. Burgers and a full menu are available, but it's the Friday fish fry and excellent frog legs that draw the hungry crowds from throughout the region. Lunch and dinner are served daily.

Boyne Mountain Beach House Restaurant
$$$ • Deer Lake Rd., Boyne Falls • (616) 549-6085

The Beach House Restaurant, on the shore of Deer Lake, offers fine dining in a relaxed atmosphere. Featuring creative American cuisine, the menu includes steaks, seafood and chicken. You can enjoy outdoor dining or cocktails on the patio. A full bar offers an extensive wine list and a good selection of imported beer. Breakfast, lunch and dinner is served daily from early May to October.

Eriksen's Restaurant
$$ • 1 Boyne Mountain Rd., Boyne Falls
• (616) 549-6059

This Boyne Mountain Resort slopeside restaurant offers light fare in a lodge setting. It caters to the most hearty appetites with homestyle traditional dishes, a Saturday night prime rib special and daily fresh fish specials. A full-service bar is available. Breakfast, lunch and dinner are served daily year round.

Boyne River Brewing Co.
$ • 419 E. Main St., Boyne City
• (616) 582-5588

Lake Trout Stout and Log Jam are two of Boyne River Brewing Co.'s signature microbrews. Enjoy reasonably priced soups, sandwiches and vegetarian fare with your ales, and dine indoors or out. This smoke-free establishment is open daily. See our Nightlife chapter for more information.

Pippins
$$ • 5 W. Main St., Boyne City
• (616) 582-3311

Pippins serves traditional American cuisine made with the freshest ingredients and desserts no one can turn down, including melt-in-your-mouth cream puffs and lemon meringue pies. The full menu includes perch, pork chops, charbroiled steaks and whitefish. Overlooking Lake Charlevoix, the restaurant offers casual dining in a friendly up-north atmosphere. Cocktails are available. Pippins serves breakfast, lunch and dinner daily, except in the winter when it is closed Tuesday and Wednesday. Be sure to call ahead for off-season hours.

Red Mesa Grill
$ • 117 Water St., Boyne City
• (616) 582-0049

While Red Mesa Grill serves wonderful authentic Latin American dishes, their claim to fame is their secret Margarita recipe. As with

their cuisine, they use only fresh ingredients in these legendary drinks. Menu Items and drinks from the full bar are served in a casual atmosphere with a Central American decor. For dessert, experience the homemade coconut ice cream topped with flaming caramel sauce and plantains. The restaurant serves lunch and dinner daily.

Stafford's One Water Street
$$ • 1 Water St., Boyne City
• (616) 582-3434

If you're seeking a fine dining experience and charming atmosphere you won't find a place that meets the bill better than Stafford's One Water Street. Set on a historic depot site, the restaurant is decorated to appear like a Victorian street. The heartland menu features game dishes including venison, whitefish and bison. Cocktails are available from the bar, which features its own casual menu. Lunch and dinner are served daily.

Walloon Lake Inn
$$ • 4178 W. Walloon Lake Rd., Walloon Lake Village • (616) 535-2999

Discover French country cooking in an intimate dining room at this classic Michigan lakeside inn. Enjoy cocktails on the deck overlooking the serene waters of Walloon Lake, a nice menu selection and fine wines. The inn serves dinner only, seven days a week, year round.

The Acorn Cafe
$ • 103 Park Ave., Charlevoix
• (616) 547-1835

Enjoy hearty American staples in a casual, homelike atmosphere at The Acorn Cafe. The eatery offers a breakfast and lunch menu featuring omelets, pancakes, French toast, homemade soups, great salads and sandwiches. Try the grilled pecan pork salad for a deliciously different taste. The cafe is smoke-free, has outdoor tables and is open daily during summer months and Wednesday through Monday the rest of the year.

Charly's
$$ • 100 Michigan Ave., Charlevoix
• (616) 547-1700

Let Charly's work its magic for you. It's

Photo: Kevin Poirier/Courtesy of the Traverse City Record-Eagle

Get a taste of yesterday on the Grand Traverse Dinner Train.

the only place in town to offer custom-packed, elegant picnic boxes complete with fine wine. The service is offered summers only, and you must place your order 24 hours in advance. On site the international menu includes American, French, Italian and Asian cuisine. The sauteed duck and whitefish are customer favorites. While enjoying fine dining at Charly's, watch boats meander down the Pine River to Round Lake. The restaurant is highly regarded for its selection of fine wines. Smoke-free, Charly's is open daily during summer months, and Wednesday through Sunday in winter.

Grey Gables Inn
$$ • 308 Belvedere Ave., Charlevoix
• (616) 547-9261

The Victorian Grey Gables Inn is the old-, est and one of the most charming restaurants in Charlevoix. All four dining rooms within the 1875 inn feature crystal chandeliers and vintage art. Their menu has American cuisine including fresh local perch, walleye, steaks, prime rib, vegetarian entrees, Maine lobster, homemade breads and scones. Owners shower guests with personal attention. Dinners only are served, daily during peak season and Tuesday through Saturday in winter. The inn's piano lounge is

known as a hot night spot (see our Nightlife chapter).

Juilleret's Restaurant of Charlevoix
$ • 1418 Bridge St., Charlevoix
• (616) 547-9212

Juilleret's is the place Charlevoix's early birds gather. It's open from 5:30 AM to 3 PM daily and serves great breakfasts throughout the day. The specialty here, cinnamon French toast, is made from homemade breads. Enjoy fresh-squeezed orange juice with your meal and unlimited coffee refills. The all à la carte menu features broiled whitefish, turkey and chicken sandwiches, and soups. Juilleret's is a smoke-free eatery with outdoor dining available. It is open on a seasonal basis, so call ahead.

Nanny's Restaurant and Lounge
$$ • 219 Ferry Ave., Charlevoix
• (616) 547-2960

This is the place to go for great all-you-can-eat surf and turf, but menu items include everything from sandwiches to seafood, Mexican dishes to children's meals. Cocktails are available. An enclosed deck that overlooks Lake Charlevoix is perfect for diners who enjoy a view. Nanny's serves breakfast, lunch and dinner daily.

Stafford's Weathervane Restaurant
$$$ • 106 Pine River Ln., Charlevoix
• (616) 547-4311

The Weathervane has been an architectural landmark for more than three decades. One of the remarkable Earl Young stone buildings, it overlooks the Pine River Channel in Charlevoix and Round Lake. (See our Attractions chapter to learn more about Young's structures.) Enjoy regional classic American cuisine in this intriguing environment. Cocktails are available. Lunch and dinner are served.

Andante
$$$$ • 321 Bay St., Petoskey
• (616) 348-3321

Discover eclectic gourmet cuisine and an enchanting view of the bay while dining at Andante. It is one of the most elegant dining establishments in the greater Petoskey area, but casual attire is perfectly acceptable. An award-winning restaurant, Andante features nouveau cuisine with a northern Michigan flair. Popular specialties include whitefish in a shredded potato crust and dark chocolate pudding cake. Andante offers an excellent wine list and full-service bar. The restaurant is smoke-free and serves dinner daily in summer and Tuesday through Saturday, October through June.

Bear River Brewing Co.
$ • 317 E. Lake St., Petoskey
• (616) 348-8467

Bring the kids to Bear River Brewing Co. to enjoy real brewed root beer. For the older set, the Gaslight District microbrewery has six ales on tap and offers two daily specials. A casual up-north atmosphere makes the entire family feel at home. The establishment features a light lunch and dinner menu. From the main level you can observe the brewery in action. The upper level offers billiards, darts and TV viewing. It's open seven days in summer, and Monday through Saturday in winter.

The Bistro
$ • 423 Michigan St., Petoskey
• (616) 347-5583

The Bistro is a cozy little cafe, just right for a friendly rendezvous or casual meal. The menu is loaded with homemade soups, salads, fresh fruit desserts, home-baked breads and daily specials. The smoke-free eatery serves breakfast and lunch, Monday through Saturday.

City Park Grill
$ • 432 E. Lake St., Petoskey
• (616) 347-0101

This is what you call atmosphere. Situated in the historic Petoskey Gaslight Shopping District, this restaurant is housed in a turn-of-the-century building featuring original tin ceilings, a cozy fireplace and an 1890s mahogany and cherry wood bar. The menu ranges from sandwiches to filet mignon and offers a variety of other familiar American dishes prepared with an innovative twist. The grill serves lunch and dinner daily and presents some hot entertainment on weekends (see our Nightlife chapter).

Papa Joe's
$, no credit cards • 307 Petoskey St., Petoskey • (616) 347-6347

This 1950s-style diner knows how to make kids feel at ease. First, place your order for Coney dogs, chicken or whitefish sandwiches, then let the kids scribble their John Hancocks on the name wall. Outdoor dining is available. Papa Joe's serves lunch and dinner daily.

Stafford's Bay View Inn
$$ • 2011 Woodland Ave., Petoskey
• (616) 347-2771

Delight yourself with the charms of another era at Stafford's Bay View 19th-century inn. The dining room menu features a wide array of entrees including creative pasta dishes and Great Lakes whitefish, but it's best known for a superior Sunday brunch, which is regularly served from Memorial Day through mid-October. The brunch offers carved ham and turkey and an impressive selection of fresh fruit toppings to smother the unbeatable homemade waffles. Breakfast, lunch and dinner are served, and cocktails are available.

Stafford's Perry Hotel
$-$$ • Bay at Lewis St., Petoskey
• (616) 347-4000

Built in 1899, Stafford's Perry Hotel in Petoskey's Gaslight District is the city's only surviving downtown hotel from the Edwardian era. Like the rest of the establishment, the gracious H.O. Rose Dining Room, Rose Garden Verandah and Noggin Room Pub recreate the hospitality and grace of that period. The H.O. Rose Dining Room offers fine dining, featuring northern Michigan specialties and Classic Old World and Mediterranean dishes as well as an extensive wine list. Full menu service is available for breakfast, lunch and dinner daily. The Rose Garden Verandah is dedicated to elegant outdoor dining in an English conservatory setting. The Noggin Room Pub in the hotel's lower level offers casual cuisine and beer selections from around the world. On weekends, it's one of the hottest night spots in Petoskey (see our Nightlife chapter).

Schelde's
$ • 1315 U.S. Hwy. 31 N., Petoskey
• (616) 347-7747

Schelde's is a hometown restaurant priding itself on great customer service. It features traditional American cuisine and Is known for tender St. Louis-cut ribs covered with homemade barbecue sauce. The casual atmosphere and full bar make for a relaxing dining experience. Schelde's serves lunch and dinner daily.

Terrace Inn
$$ • 1549 Glendale Ave., Petoskey
• (616) 347-2410

The Victorian Terrace Inn is nestled in the heart of the historic Bay View community. The charming establishment offers classic country inn cuisine served in its indoor dining room or on the lovely porch. Serving dinners only, their specialties include planked whitefish (actually served on a wood plank), fresh-baked breads and homemade desserts. No alcoholic beverages are served.

Arboretum
$$ • 7075 S. Lake Shore Dr., Harbor Springs • (616) 526-6291

Classic and eclectic cuisine are the hallmark of this fine-dining establishment on a bluff overlooking Little Traverse Bay. With twinkling white lights, fountains and different dining levels, the interior garden sets a sophisticated mood. While best known for marinated rack of lamb and fresh planked whitefish, Arboretum offers nightly specials and has a full bar and an award-winning wine list. It's open year round for dinner only, and shuttle service is available from the Harbor Springs airport and yacht basin.

Blue Corn Grill
$$ • 2983 S. State Rd., Harbor Springs • (616) 526-8000

Blue Corn Grill serves an eclectic gourmet blend of authentic Mexican and contemporary Southwestern cuisine. It boasts of having more than 30 tequilas, the state's largest selection. Customers are invited to design their own Margaritas. Blue Corn Grill also features a nice selection of champagne and wines. In mild weather you may chose to enjoy cocktails on the patio overlooking a lovely wildflower field. Menu items are seasonal depending on availability of fresh ingredients. Entrees may include pork tenderloin, grilled free-range chicken, duck breast or corn-crusted salmon. Original murals enhance the restaurant's Southwestern ambiance. Blue Corn Grill is smoke-free. Serving dinners only, it is open daily May through Thanksgiving. Hours are seasonal so call ahead.

Juilleret's
$, no credit cards • 130 State St., Harbor Springs • (616) 526-2821

Juilleret's has been family owned and operated for more than 100 years, and their experience pleasing customers is reflected in the comfortable, casual atmosphere they maintain. In addition to light meals, you can order homemade ice cream and beverage specialties from the old fashioned soda fountain. The smoke-free eatery is open daily mid-May through September for breakfast, lunch and dinner. Hours are reduced in shoulder seasons, so call ahead.

The New York Restaurant
$$$ • 101 State St., Harbor Springs • (616) 526-1904

The New York Restaurant, housed in a turn-of-the-century building, overlooks the Harbor Springs waterfront. The scenic view provides an easygoing setting for some great dining. The eclectic breakfast, dinner and lunch menu features classic and modern culinary delights from around the world, enhanced by a selection of more than 200 wines and a wide array of beers and spirits. It is open daily, and reservations are recommended.

The Pier
$-$$ • 102 Bay St., Harbor Springs
• (616) 526-6201

Unwind with excellent cuisine, fine wines and a great view of the Harbor Springs yacht basin at The Pier. A waterfront restaurant with a contemporary flair, it features two dining rooms plus a lounge. Specialties include seafood and steak. Lunch and dinner are served daily.

Legs Inn
$$ • 6425 Lake Shore Dr., Cross Village
• (616) 526-2281

Here's a restaurant that dishes out beauty, peace and history along with wonderful authentic Polish and American cuisine. Enjoy spectacular views at this one-of-a-kind landmark restaurant situated on a bluff overlooking Lake Michigan. The stone and timber building reflects a unique blend of Old World European and Native-American cultures. Dining rooms, the bar and other rooms are filled with a collection of handcarved furniture and creations made from twisted limbs, tree stumps, roots and driftwood. Garden seating, family fun, live entertainment and a complete selection of alcoholic beverages, including more than 100 varieties of beer, make Legs Inn one of the north's most popular attractions. The restaurant is open daily mid-May through mid-October.

Mackinac Straits

Carriage House Dining Room
$$$$ • Iroquois Hotel, Huron St., Mackinac Island • (906) 847-3321

The Carriage House Dining Room stands adjacent to the Iroquois Hotel with an elegant setting and lovely views. This fine dining room is heralded for its excellent food and stellar service. After the Grand Hotel, the Carriage House is the most formal restaurant on the island. A cocktail lounge and outdoor verandah are also popular. The Carriage House

serves lunch and dinner. Reservations are recommended.

Chippewa Hotel
$$$ • Huron St., Mackinac Island
• (906) 847-3341, (800) 241-3341

The historic Chippewa Hotel houses the Harbor View Restaurant and connecting Pink Pony Bar and Grill. The Harbor View's bright, windowed dining room overlooks the harbor so diners can watch the comings and goings of the Arnold ferries. The Pink Pony's wooded lounge is connected by an archway to the Harbor View. During the evening, music drifts from the Pony stage between the two eateries. An outdoor patio is lined with yellow-umbrella-topped tables. The menu features hefty appetizers along with prime rib, steaks, southern style ribs, marinated pork chops, king crab, whitefish and several pasta dishes. The Harbor View is open for breakfast, lunch and dinner.

French Outpost
$ • Cadotte Ave., Mackinac Island
• (906) 847-3772

Casual dining with festive music is found at the French Outpost. Several frequent visitors swear that this is the place to come for some of the best burgers on the island. Judge for yourself with one of the signature Trapper Burgers. Nightly entertainment keeps toes tapping inside this friendly restaurant and at its outdoor patio. You'll find the French Outpost near the corner of Cadotte and Mahoney avenues, across the street from the Little Stone Church on the hill leading to the Grand Hotel. It's open for lunch, dinner and late-night entertainment.

Governor's Dining Room
$$$ • The Island House, Huron St., Mackinac Island • (906) 847-3347, (800) 626-6304

The Governor's Dining Room hosts fine dining at the oldest hotel on Mackinac Island, the Island House. The glass-enclosed formal dining room overlooks the harbor, with sweeping views of the straits. The menu features such signature dishes as prime rib, Lake Superior whitefish, breast of chicken Mackinac, and veal Cyril. Music is performed each evening. The Governor's Dining Room serves breakfast, lunch and dinner daily. Reservations are recommended.

Grand Hotel
**$$$$$ • Cadotte Ave., Mackinac Island
• (906) 847-3331, (800) 33GRAND**

This magnificent hotel extends its hospitality in its equally magnificent dining room. The physical space is enormous and reminiscent of Victorian splendor. Its stretch of windows and immaculately set tables seem endless as you are escorted to your seat. Musicians, dressed in dinner jackets, are strategically stationed near a small dance floor. Dinner at the Grand is a formal affair. Men are required to wear jackets and ties after 6 PM, and ladies dress for dinner. The reward for this finery is an exquisite five-course meal that is presented with impeccable service. Breakfast (also served here in high style) and dinner are included in the price of your stay at the Grand. If you are staying elsewhere but would like to attend dinner, call for reservations. Another dining option that is available to the public is the Grand Buffet luncheon served daily. Make sure to bring your appetite as this buffet is presented with grand style and portions. With your buffet ticket, you are also allowed to tour the Grand Hotel, and its grounds, which are normally off limits to visitors.

The Pilot House
**$$ • Lake View Hotel, Huron St.,
Mackinac Island • (906) 847-3384**

The Lake View Hotel hosts The Pilot House restaurant overlooking the Island's busy main street. Patrons enjoy casual meals in the hotel's relaxed dining room and adjacent open-air porch. We recommend the breakfast buffet, which is served daily. It's well stocked with early morning favorites and aromatic, fresh baked goods. The prices are moderate and the buffet offers families a stress-free start to the day. The Pilot House serves breakfast, lunch and dinner.

Waters Meet
**$$ • Huron St., Mackinac Island
• (906) 847-3806**

This is one of the newest restaurants to open shop on Mackinac Island, with a bustling business that takes place below the energy and antics of main street. Waters Meet sits underneath the Lilac Tree Hotel with stairs leading to the lower-level restaurant at the front of the Lilac Tree Mall. Casual fare for lunch and dinner is the order of the day. Look for a menu featuring burgers, chicken, ribs and family favorites.

The Admiral's Table
**$$ • 502 S. Huron Ave., Mackinaw City
• (616) 436-5687**

The coffee's always on at The Admiral's Table. This friendly family eatery is open daily for breakfast, lunch and dinner at its convenient location near the ferry docks. The Admiral's Table is known for fresh-broiled whitefish and prime rib. In the summer, you can start the morning off with a delicious breakfast buffet. The restaurant is open from early May though mid-October.

Audie's
**$ • 314 N. Nicolet St., Mackinaw City
• (616) 436-5744**

Audie's is one of our favorite meal stops before crossing the Mackinac Bridge into the upper peninsula. And, with the bridge entrance just three blocks straight ahead, it's a quick detour off the route north. This pleasant, family-owned restaurant is open daily for breakfast, lunch and dinner throughout the year. You're sure to find a homestyle favorite on the menu. Specialties include fresh baked goods and fresh water whitefish. Meals are served in the spacious Family Room known for its fast, friendly service and casual atmosphere while the Chippewa Room offers a more leisurely, relaxed dining experience. Vintage photos of the bridge construction adorn the walls.

Darrow's Family Restaurant
**$ • 303 Louvingney St., Mackinaw City
• (616) 436-5514**

Darrow's Family Restaurant promises old-fashioned home cooking. This friendly restaurant is tucked near the corner of Louvigney and Jamet Street, just a two-block stroll south of Colonial Michilimackinac. It may be a bit off the beaten path, but you'll be happy that you sought it out. The menu showcases excellent homemade soups, fresh baked bread, northern whitefish and great burgers. Save room for dessert. Homemade pies are baked fresh daily. Darrow's is open daily for breakfast, lunch and dinner. Take-out service is also available if you're planning a picnic in the park.

The Fort Restaurant
$ • 400 Louvingney St., Mackinaw City
• (616) 436-5453

There's something for everybody at The Fort Restaurant's busy smorgasbord. Breakfast buffets feature pancakes, scrambled eggs, muffins, cereal and other early morning favorites. The lunch buffet will find a soup and salad bar along with spaghetti, sloppy Joes, burgers, chicken tenders and other family favorites. Dinner includes fresh whitefish, roast turkey and other home-cooked specialties. The buffets change daily, so stop by to see what's cooking. Remember to bring your appetites, it's all you can eat!

Pancake Chef
$ • 327 E. Central Ave., Mackinaw City
• (616) 436-5578

It's always time for breakfast at the Pancake Chef. You'll find your favorite morning fare all day as well as a full lineup of traditional lunch and dinner meals on the menu. Breakfast and dinner buffets and a salad bar are also available. This comfortable restaurant is a short walk away from the Shepler's Ferry Dock. The Pancake Chef is open daily.

Scalawags
$, no credit cards • 226 E. Central Ave., Mackinaw City • (616) 436-7777

If you've got a taste for fish, Scalawags is your stop. Great lakes whitefish and chips are the specialty at this casual, nautical eatery. You'll find whitefish baskets in varying sizes along with chicken fingers baskets and an array of sandwiches (including whitefish!). Try Scalawag's homemade chowder for a delicious treat. The restaurant, which is nestled behind Kilwin's on Central Avenue's village square, is open daily from mid-May to mid-October.

Bentley's Cafe
$ • 62 N. State St., St. Ignace
• (906) 643-9031

Bentley's has been serving great homemade meals for almost 60 years. This friendly, family-owned eatery conveniently stands in the center of downtown, across from the St. Ignace Marina and Mackinac Island ferry docks. Bentley's is known for its homemade soups, pasties and great French fries. If you're looking for a sweet treat, try the belly-buster ice cream sundae. Bentley's is open daily for lunch and dinner.

Driftwood Sports Bar and Grill
$ • 590 N. State St., St. Ignace
• (906) 643-9133

The Driftwood serves meals in both its lively sports bar and adjacent relaxed dining room. The menus are the same, with sandwiches and casual fare featured. For hefty appetites, try the Knute Rockney Burger, which is two big hamburger patties topped with bacon and cheese. Televisions keep you in touch with the game of the day while football, hockey and baseball memorabilia line the walls. The Driftwood is open for lunch and dinner daily.

Galley Restaurant and Lounge
$$ • 241 N. State St., St. Ignace
• (906) 643-7960

Lake Huron's scenic waters are your dining backdrop at the Galley Restaurant and Lounge. This casual, family-owned, downtown eatery overlooks Mackinac Island and the Straits. The menu showcases Great Lakes whitefish, trout and perch as well as its signature dish, whitefish livers. You'll also find prime rib, steaks, burgers, spaghetti, pasties and homemade soups. The Galley is open daily for breakfast, lunch and dinner.

Little Bob's New Frontier Restaurant
$$ • 3021 Mackinac Tr., St. Ignace
• (906) 643-3512

Little Bob's New Frontier brings the old west up north. Standing across the street from the Kewadin Shores Casino, this down-home restaurant serves country cooking with a full menu of thick sandwiches, hefty burgers, barbecued ribs and classic steaks. Local whitefish is available in sandwiches and full dinners. Dessert highlights include homemade pie á la mode and fresh strawberry shortcake. A breakfast menu includes oat-bran pancakes, cinnamon French toast and familiar morning favorites. Little Bob's New Frontier Restaurant is open daily for breakfast, lunch and dinner.

State Street Bar and Grill
$$ • 250 S. State St., St. Ignace
• (906) 643-9511

Look for the big green awning, and you've found the State Street Bay and Grill. This friendly downtown restaurant is a great spot for family fare. The menu features rotisserie-roasted chicken and ribs as well as Great Lakes whitefish and perch, steaks, burgers and homemade pizza. If you have the late-night munchies, stop here. The kitchen stays open until 1 AM. The State Street Bar and Grill is open daily for lunch and dinner.

Coffeehouses

The coffee craze has swept through the Traverse Bay Region much as it has across the country. Whether your tastes run to an espresso, cappuccino, latte, mocha, Italian soda or a simple, old-fashioned cup of coffee, you'll have many choices to quench your thirst. We give you several ideas below. Generally coffeehouses are open daily, although some will restrict or eliminate Sunday hours during the winter. In seasonal communities, some may close between late October and early May. In the listings below, assume that all are open daily year round unless stated otherwise. As in the rest of this chapter, we note along with our price code when an establishment does not accept cards.

Grand Traverse

Traverse City Area

Cafe Espresso at Borders Books and Music
$ • 2612 Crossings Cir., Traverse City
• (616) 933-0412

Borders added a new dimension to local coffeehouses when it opened its doors in 1996. Its Cafe Espresso coffee bar sits in the shop's southeast corner with ample seating and a showcase filled with fresh baked goods. The cafe is a hub for book discussion groups, per-forming musicians and relaxing patrons. Enjoy the ambiance while relaxing with a hot cappuccino. Daily specials include soups, salads and sandwiches, along with the baked goods and great coffee, teas and cocoa.

Good Harbor Coffee and Bakery
$, no credit cards • 111 W. Front St., Traverse City • (616) 935-4166

Tucked into a busy downtown corner, Good Harbor is one of our favorite spots for coffee on the run. The friendly staff chats and jokes while filling countless cups. You'll find a selection of fresh scones (our favorites are coffee cake and cherry-pecan), muffins, cinnamon and pecan rolls, biscotti and breakfast cookies. Several types of sandwiches, wraps, salads and soups are available for lunch or snacks. You can eat at one of the counters, at an outdoor table or, like most of us, on the run.

Horizon Books
$ • 243 E. Front St., Traverse City • (616) 946-7290

Combine your favorite coffee concoction with your favorite read at Horizon Book's street-level coffee bar. When the sun is shining, friends gather for coffee and conversation at the shop's outdoor tables. The coffee bar joins Horizon's lower-level Shine Cafe (see the Food on the Run section of this chapter) in serving hospitality and relaxed gathering spots at this popular downtown bookstore.

Java Central
$, no credit cards • 1060 E. Front St., Traverse City • (616) 935-4213
Java West
$, no credit cards • Oryana Natural Food Cooperative, 10th and Lake Sts., Traverse City • (616) 947-0191 Oryana

Java Central gives you gourmet coffee on the run with its unique drive-through service. This quick stop cafe occupies a former drive-through bank that has been converted to serve cappuccinos, lattes, espressos and coffee along with fresh baked goods and other go-alongs. It sounds strange, but it works well as evidenced by the steady stream of vehicles waiting at the order window. Interestingly, the back portion of the drive-through is set up for one-hour photo developing, so it is possible to drop off your film and pick up your coffee in one quick stop. Java Central's success has led to a new sibling, Java West, which just opened inside Oryana Natural Food Cooperative. You can't drive up to the counter at Java West, but you'll find the same high quality coffee and baked goods.

Ray's Coffee House
$, no credit cards • 129 E. Front St., Traverse City • (616) 929-1006

Ray's was Traverse City's first coffeehouse and continues to draw a loyal following with its relaxed, comfortable ambiance. You can sit at the long bar that stretches through much of the shop, at the cozy tables scattered throughout or, weather permitting, at picnic tables outdoors. Enjoy specialty coffees, Italian sodas, herbal teas and hot chocolate along with a daily selection of fresh baked goods.

Leelanau County

Leelanau Coffee Roasting Company
$, no credit cards • 6443 Western Ave., Glen Arbor • (616) 334-3365

Have a cup of fresh roasted coffee with the folks who are roasting it for restaurants and coffeehouses throughout the Grand Traverse area. The beans are ground and brewed fresh from the roaster. Baked goods top off a great break.

Kejara's Bridge
$, no credit cards • 302 N. Main St., Lake Leelanau • (616) 256-7720

Kejara's Bridge enters the lineup as one of the newest Grand Traverse area coffeehouses. It has quickly become a hit among Leelanau residents who enjoy the array of coffee drinks and an ample selection of fresh-baked goods and vegetarian fare.

Stone House Bread
$, no credit cards • 407 S. Main St., Leland • (616) 256-2577

The smell of freshly baking bread permeates this coffee stop, which shares space with the workings for Stone House Bread's commercial enterprise. Stop by for a cup of French roast and a whiff of that bread.

Bacchus and Brie
$ • 220 St. Joseph St., Suttons Bay • (616) 271-2626

The coffee bar at Bacchus and Brie brews your favorite coffees, cappuccino, espresso, latte and hot chocolate while you stroll through this gourmet food shop. Tables and chairs sit outside when the weather is smiling.

Antrim-Kalkaska

Apron Strings
$ • 113 N. Bridge St., Bellaire • (616) 533-5540

A full coffee bar serving espresso, cappuccino, latte and specialty coffees shares space with this charming gourmet food and kitchen shop. Apron Strings is open Monday through Saturday.

Lake Michigan Shoreline and Cadillac

Java Shoppe
$ • 123 W. Ludington Ave., Ludington • (616) 843-1995

The Java Shoppe is not just another coffeehouse serving great espressos, cappuccinos and mochas. Surrounding the coffee station is an eclectic store offering books, cards, world music, incense, candles and imported clothing. The Java Shoppe is open daily in the summer, and Monday through Saturday the rest of the year. See our Shopping chapter to learn more.

Kodiak's Internet Coffeehouse & Deli
$, no credit cards • 112 N. Mitchell St., Cadillac • (616) 775-5282

At Kodiak's you can get your favorite coffee and your e-mail too. Cappuccino, espressos, mochas and 58 flavorings are served in a comfortable family atmosphere. Kodiak's also offers a wide selection of sandwiches and vegetarian fare. The coffeehouse is open Monday through Saturday. See our Kidstuff chapter to learn more.

World Perk Internet Cafe
$, no credit cards • 5936 E. Mich. Hwy. 55, Cadillac • (616) 775-4677

World Perk uses the finest beans and syrups available in its gourmet coffees, mochas, cappuccinos and espressos. On steamy summer days you may want to try the iced and frozen mochas. Bagels, cookies and other treats are sold fresh. Browse the Internet while you enjoy your beverages. Service charges are calculated by the hour and half-hour. World Perk is open daily, but hours vary so call ahead.

Little Traverse

Sweet Sam's Java Joint
$ • 405 Bridge St., Charlevoix • (616) 547-3993

Sweet Sam's uses 100 percent Arabica coffee beans, roasted on site for the freshest gourmet coffees around. For the diet conscious, the cappuccino/espresso bar offers low-fat frozen cappuccinos, mochas and lattes, but you'll find the scones, muffins, bagels, pies and brownies are too tempting to pass up. Sweet Sam's is open daily. See our Shopping chapter to learn more about the gourmet foods available.

Leelanau Coffee Roasting Co.
$ • 205 W. Mitchell St., Petoskey • (616) 439-0400

This cozy coffeehouse offers more than 40 blends aimed to please the most discriminating connoisseur. Leelanau Coffee uses only the finest Arabica beans in its brews. Almost 70 percent of the company's business is wholesale. Based in Glen Arbor, the Leelanau Coffee Roasting Co. is able to serve the freshest brews you'll find anywhere in the region. Along with your espressos, cappuccinos and mochas, you can enjoy a view of the beautiful Little Traverse Bay. It is open daily in the summer, and closed Sunday the rest of the year.

Roast and Toast
$ • 309 E. Lake St., Petoskey • (616) 347-7767
$ • 103 S. Lake St., Boyne City • (616) 582-5020

You'll find a comfortable atmosphere and freshly brewed gourmet coffees at both Roast and Toast shops. The Petoskey location offers a full dinner menu in addition to light fare, snacks and live jazz and folk music every Sunday evening. Entertainment is offered Friday nights at the Boyne City coffeehouse, which serves dinner only in the summer. Both shops are open daily.

Island Bean Coffee Company
$, no credit cards • 110 W. Main St., Harbor Springs • (616) 526-9998

Island Bean Coffee Company is a tiny jewel of a shop found adjacent to Hollywood Gas Station in downtown Harbor Springs. You'll find quality Caravali coffee, espresso, fresh-baked goods and friendly smiles daily. It's clearly an Insiders' pick among Little Traverse coffee stops.

Mackinac Straits

J. L. Beanery
$, no credit cards • Huron St., Mackinac Island • (906) 847-6518

Enjoy a cup of your favorite brew along with a magnificent view of the Straits. This charming coffeehouse is wrapped in windows and a marina-side patio that's perfect for relaxing with your morning coffee or after-dinner cappuccino. You can choose from more than 30 coffees, teas, cappuccinos, espressos and other drinks as well as a great selection of fresh-baked goods.

Mocha Joe's Place
$, no credit cards • Huron St., Mackinac Island • (906) 847-0260

You'll find Mocha Joe's nestled in with the shops at the Horse Corral Mall along Main Street. The menu features flavored coffees, fruit drinks, cookies and other delicious treats.

Growly Bear Coffee Company
$, no credit cards • 220 S. Huron St., Mackinaw City • (616) 436-5597

Robust coffee is served on the deck at Animal Tracks Golf by Growly Bear Coffee Company. Enjoy a cappuccino, espresso or latte overlooking the Straits of Mackinac.

The Supreme Bean Coffee House

$, no credit cards • Mackinaw Crossings, 284 S. Huron Ave., Mackinaw City
• (616) 436-8608

The Supreme Bean serves specialty coffees, teas and hot chocolate from its central spot in the Food Court at Mackinaw Crossings.

Food on the Run

Grand Traverse

Traverse City Area

Broadway Bagels

$, no credit cards • 1219 E. Front St., Traverse City • (616) 922-5924

Fresh New York-style bagels and creative cream cheeses are found at Broadway Bagels. At least a dozen types of gourmet bagels are made fresh daily along with a selection of flavored cream cheeses (our favorite is pineapple). You can find fresh lox here along with breakfast bagels, bagelwiches and soups. An espresso bar serves fresh coffee drinks. Tables fill the storefront and often attract students from nearby Northwestern Michigan College and Traverse City Central High School, who stop for lunch or an after-school snack.

Cathie's Tote & Dine

$, no credit cards • 3186 LaFranier Rd. (off South Airport Road), Traverse City
• (616) 947-0300
$, no credit cards • 104 Cass St., Traverse City • (616) 929-4771

According to Cathie's, they don't serve fast food, but rather "quality homemade cuisine quick." This family-run eatery operates two locations, a large, cheerful dining room in South Airport Road's 42nd Street Plaza and a downtown sidewalk cafe at the corner of Cass and East Front streets. Bright green picnic tables illuminated by hanging lamps made out of inverted picnic baskets fill the South Airport cafeteria-style restaurant. The downtown shop is purely take-out, although the tables outdoors are always filled when the sun is shining. The menu is filled with a great assortment of submarine sandwiches, fresh salads, hamburgers and homemade soups. Vegetarians will find a number of tasty options. Desserts always include homemade cookies and cheesecake. Cathie's is open for lunch and dinner daily except Sundays.

Chef's In

$, no credit cards • 519 W. Front St., Traverse City • (616) 941-1144

Chef's In specializes in cuisine to go, and a large lunchtime clientele has made this one of the most popular stops for food on the run. Customers choose from 23 hot sandwiches or create their own cold sandwiches. A few of our favorites are the hot vegetarian sandwich and the turkey reuben. All are made before your eyes in minutes by the friendly owners. A salad bar is well-stocked for greens and toppings to go, and several kinds of cold salads and hot soups are always available. If you're planning a group meeting or are looking for great finger foods, call the day ahead and order a platter of finger sandwiches, which are actually assorted cold sandwiches cut into quarters. The Chef's In is open Monday through Saturday for lunch, and is usually closed by 4 PM.

Cousin Jenny's Cornish Pasties

$, no credit cards • 129 S. Union St., Traverse City • (616) 941-7821

Cousin Jenny's introduced pasties, the upper peninsula specialty, to Traverse City over a decade ago. Ever since, the restaurant has enjoyed a loyal following of patrons who feast on the meat-and-potato-filled pastry. The restaurant has a bright, cheerful cafeteria-style dining room. Seven pastie variations are available, such as beef, beef and cheddar, chicken, German and vegetarian. They are made fresh each morning, although some are only available on alternating days. You can eat them there, take them home hot and fully cooked, or take them partially cooked to finish baking later. Pasties can be ordered in bulk with a few days notice, or frozen and packed for shipping. We put a case in the freezer each winter to use for cozy Sunday suppers after an afternoon of skiing. A nice assortment of fresh salads, homemade soups and cheesecake also line the showcases.

Exquisite Edibles

$ • 223 W. Grandview Pkwy., Traverse City • (616) 941-4529
$ • 6037 U.S. Hwy. 31 N., Acme
• (616) 938-5884

The folks who created Exquisite Edibles have redefined our concept of fast food as fast, healthy food. A steady stream of customers go to the markets near downtown and in Acme for creative sandwiches, salads, soups, burritos and pizzas with the freshest ingredients in healthy, innovative combinations. One of Exquisite's signature specials is its big burrito made while you watch with an extra large flour tortilla wrapped around veggies, beef or chicken and dressed with their special recipe salsa, black beans, rice, cheddar cheese and sour cream. These burritos are delicious and huge, easily enough for two people. The restaurant is also known for its home-style meals in individual or family-size servings. Different dinners are served each day of the week but have included sun-dried tomato-mushroom meat loaf with mashed potatoes and gravy, spinach lasagna with garlic bread, roast turkey with stuffing and mashed potatoes, Swiss steak with mashed potatoes and tomato-mushroom gravy, and baked chicken with caramelized onions and red potatoes. Gourmet and specialty pizzas are made to order with a large assortment of familiar and unusual toppings.

Folgarelli's Import Food Market

$ • 424 W. Front St., Traverse City
• (616) 941-7651

We talk about Folgarelli's in our shopping chapter so we won't repeat all of the great gourmet reasons (and there are many) to shop here. Instead, let's focus on Folgarelli's deli counter, which prepares an incredible selection of wonderful sandwiches every day. Choose from more than 40 variations with ingredients like prosciutto, turkey, roast beef, Genoa salami, smoked salmon, corned beef, roasted peppers, sun-dried tomatoes, guacamole, Portobello mushrooms, marinated vegetables and endless types of cheese and bread. At the counter, you can also order fresh deli meats, cheeses and salads or take home some baklava or other showcased desserts. One of the newest additions to the deli area is fresh sushi, which had been a fairly unattainable commodity for us Northern Michiganders until now. A sushi bar is in the works to

expand on this already popular new treat. Folgarelli's opens in time for early lunch and remains open until early evening. You can eat at the small window-front counter or, during the warmer weather, at outdoor tables. Party trays, boxed lunches and gift baskets filled with dinner fixings are available if you order ahead.

Grand Traverse Pie Company

$ • 525 W. Front St., Traverse City
• (616) 922-7437

If you stop at Grand Traverse Pie Company early in the afternoon, you will probably walk home with pie still warm from the oven. There are always several flavors to choose from although the lineup shifts with each season's harvest. Favorites include lakeshore berry, peach, apple-cherry crumble and strawberry rhubarb. These desserts are simply delicious. Stop by and sample a piece right there or take an entire pie home for later.

Heavenly Ham

$ • 815 S. Garfield St., Traverse City
• (616) 935-4267

You'll find box lunches and sandwiches at Heavenly Ham along with the eatery's signature honey and spice glazed hams, smoked turkeys and barbecued ribs. Party platters let your group build their own sandwiches. The restaurant is open daily for lunch and dinner.

J&S Hamburg

$, no credit cards • 302 W. Front St., Traverse City • (616) 947-6409

J&S Hamburg South Airport

$, no credit cards • 1083 S. Airport Rd., Traverse City • (616) 941-8844

Longtime Traverse City residents swear that J&S makes some of the best burgers and shakes in town. These diners certainly boast a loyal following. The South Airport location has fish fries Thursday through Saturday. Both diners are open for breakfast, lunch and dinner.

Left Bank Cafe

$ • 439 E. Front St., Traverse City
• (616) 929-9060

If you're walking quickly, it's easy to miss the Left Bank Cafe. Please don't! This tiny cafe is packed with great tastes and friendly people. It draws its name from its teeny storefront perch

You'll find ample opportunity for fine dining in Northwest Michigan.

overlooking the southern bank of the Boardman River (it's the left bank if you're facing west!). The daily menu showcases creative, healthy salads, soups and sandwiches along with some wonderful desserts to leave you feeling sweet all day. Everything is made fresh each day and ready for the lunch fans that keep Left Bank bustling. Dinners are served Wednesday, Thursday and Friday evenings with entrees like roasted pork tenderloin and brie fettucine verde. The cafe is geared for take-out, but several tables are available inside for dining or drinking coffee as you peruse the morning paper.

Marifil Bakery
$ • 537 W. 14th St., Traverse City • (616) 933-0099

The owners of the popular Windows restaurant (see our listing in this chapter) opened Marafil as a retail outlet for the restaurant's highly popular hand-dipped truffles, homemade ice creams and deluxe desserts. The bakery came by its name by combining the owners' first names, Marilyn and Phil. It earned its reputation for great food by selling the freshest baked breads, pastries and sweets. Marafil often supplies goods to area stores. It's not surprising to find a tissue-wrapped loaf of fresh bread sitting on a market's shelf. Stop by for a cup of coffee and a treat at the storefront counter, or take a box of chocolates or an elegant dessert home for later.

Mary's Kitchen Port
$ • 539 W. Front St., Traverse City
• (616) 941-0525

No matter what's on the menu, if it's made at Mary's, we promise it will be delicious. This longtime Traverse City gourmet connection is a major kitchen shop (see our Shopping chapter), but it is also one of the top local spots for lunches on the run. Each morning the showcases overflow with stacks of sandwich creations and at least a half-dozen salads waiting to be consumed. By mid-afternoon, the last remaining items start to look a little lonely. It's all a testament to the long-running popularity of the shop, the outgoing owners and the wonderful staff who put it all together. An erasable board lists the daily offerings, which always include Tuba, a smoked turkey-basil pasta salad, and Mary's signature sandwich, The Gobbler, a stacked turkey with shredded lettuce, cheese, tomatoes and dressing on a croissant or focaccia. At least four other sandwiches are available at the start of the day, including one vegetarian combination and one wrap. The ingredients draw from nature's seasonal bounty and the creative whim of the chef. They might include roasted sweet potatoes, a chicken Caesar mix, black beans, roasted vegetables or classic deli meats. The combinations are always delightful. The salads are unusual but always use the freshest greens, fruits and vegetables in palate-pleasing pairings. At least two hot soups are usually simmering. Adjacent to the lunch counter is a showcase filled with cheeses and pâté. Top off your meal with a huge homemade cookie, honeybear brownie or homemade caramel that lie ready for the taking next to the cash register.

Mr. Goodcents Subs & Pastas
$, no credit cards • 822 E. Front St., Traverse City • (616) 933-1111

Subs and pasta made to order are the order of the day at Mr. Goodcents. This family-run eatery creates large submarine sandwiches with your choice of fixings on fresh-baked buns. There are 17 sub choices with endless variations of cheeses, dressings and other condiments. Pastas include lasagna, spaghetti, mostaccioli and rigatoni with your choice of sauce and sides. A variety of salads, chips and giant chocolate chip and peanut butter cookies are always available as go alongs.

The Muffin Tin
$ • 115 Wellington St., Traverse City
• (616) 929-7915
Helena St., Alden • (616) 331-6808

Bring your appetite with you when you come to the Muffin Tin. This friendly shop serves giant gourmet muffins and scones every morning. Some of the most popular muffins — or at least our favorites — are chocolate cheesecake, oat-nut topping, banana nut and peanut butter, but there is always a generous selection to choose from. The scones are also generous and equally creative. As the day goes on, the staff serves homemade soup, sandwiches, cookies and pie. The Muffin Tin operates year round from its shop in Traverse City and from early May to mid-October in Alden.

Paesano's Pizza
$ • 447 E. Front St., Traverse City
• (616) 941-5740

If you like Chicago-style pizza, head to Paesano's for the Chicago special. It's our personal favorite and often appears on our dining room tables on Sunday night. Paesano's has a well-deserved reputation for great pizza, subs and salads. All types of pizza are available — traditional, deep dish and Chicago style — along with Paesano's original sauce and ample topping options. Subs come in six varieties and two sizes. Paesano's is open for lunch and dinner for dining in, carrying out or delivery. Lunch features pizza by the slice.

Schlotzsky's Deli
$, no credit cards • 110 Munson Ave., Traverse City • (616) 929-7790

You'll find 15 sandwich specialties awaiting your choice at Schlotzsky's Deli. The bread is made from scratch each day in sourdough, wheat, rye and jalapeno cheese varieties. Pizza, soups and salads are also on the menu.

Shine Cafe
$ • 243 E. Front St., Traverse City
• (616) 946-7290

The Shine Cafe is the newest addition to the downtown Horizon Books, which has been progressively expanding its friendly bookstore into a three-floor operation. When the shop first opened at this address, it opened a coffee bar on the shop's main (and at that time, only) floor. It was so popular that when the lower level was being renovated, a larger cafe with plenty of seating was added. The original coffee-based menu has now been broadened to serve an eclectic selection of sandwiches, salads and soups. The cafe regularly hosts musicians and entertainers. By the way, the coffee bar on the main floor is still going strong.

Stage-Milliken Tea Room
$ • 204 E. Front St., Traverse City
• (616) 947-5140

The Tea Room has been serving lunch from its perch on the mezzanine of Stage-Milliken for decades. This cozy restaurant stretches around the perimeter of the department store, giving diners a bird's-eye view of the shopping bustle below. The menu has light sandwiches, salads, homemade desserts and daily specials.

Underground Cheesecake Company
$ • 406 S. Union St., Traverse City
• (616) 929-4418

Indulge your sweet tooth at the Underground Cheesecake Company. We talk about this favorite spot in our Shopping chapter. Take home a decadent dessert of cheesecake, carrot cake or gourmet brownies. Or simply sit and relax at one of the shop's little tables with a cup of fresh-ground coffee.

Leelanau County

Hose House Deli
$ • 303 St. Joseph St., Suttons Bay
• (616) 271-6303

The Hose House Deli serves Greek and American cuisine from its distinctive location inside a historic fire house. You'll find standard deli fare along with a few surprises like Greek pizza, moussaka and lamb stew. Hose House is geared for take-out, but there are several tables for dining in. The restaurant is open daily for breakfast, lunch and dinner during the summer but scales back hours and days with the seasons. Lunch and dinner are usually served Tuesday through Saturday during the cooler months but call ahead to verify the schedule. The Hose House Deli serves beer, wine and spirits but prohibits smoking.

Antrim-Kalkaska

Chef Charles
$ • 147 River St., Elk Rapids
• (616) 264-8901

Chef Charles promises pizza with pizzazz, and fans will agree that he delivers on his claims! You'll find excellent pizza, sandwiches and salads here. Pizzas are created to your whim with a huge array of toppings, cheeses and crusts. Gyro meat, calamata olives, artichoke hearts, Cajun sausage and charbroiled meatballs join the line up along with your more traditional tops. Crusts come regular, thin or Sicilian in any of combination of three flavors. If you'd rather let Chef Charles be creative, choose one of the 12 specialty pizzas, which come in such flavors as chicken fajita, bayou baby, Danish cheeseburger and vegetarian deluxe. Sandwiches made with batard loaves are piled high with meat, veggies and dressings in six combinations, while salads are available as Mediterranean, antipasto, cheese tortellini or tossed. By the way, if you'd like to try your hand at pizza creating, Chef Charles' pesto, tomato sauce and dough is sold for future use at home.

Lake Michigan Shoreline and Cadillac

Big Al's Pizza
$, no credit cards • 221 Parkdale Ave., Manistee • (616) 723-6239

Big Al's serves Chicago-style deep-dish pizza made for the cheese lover. Stromboli pizza is also a customer favorite. You'll always find fresh subs and a good, but limited Mexican menu. Lunch and dinner are served daily and delivery is available.

Chuckwagon Pizza

$ • 971 N. Lakeshore Dr., Ludington
• (616) 843-2852

There's only one word for this pizza: awesome. Chuckwagon's pizzas were named by locals as the best in Mason County for two years running. All the doughs and sauces are handmade and toppings are piled high. Subs, salads, beer and wine are available. The pizzeria is open daily, and you can request delivery.

Jean's Cookie Jar

$ • 1923 N. Mitchell St., Cadillac
• (616) 779-3000

Jean is a specialist in comfort foods. She serves more than 20 varieties of cookies made from scratch, homemade cinnamon bread, pumpkin and banana bread, muffins and gourmet candies. Homemade soups and, sandwiches, goulash and sloppy joes are available for take-out. The shop is open Monday through Saturday.

Kelly's Deli

$ • 210 N. Mitchell St., Cadillac
• (616) 775-2033

An Insiders' favorite lunch spot, Kelly's Deli is housed in Cadillac's historic City Hall building. The eatery serves soups, sandwiches, salads with house dressings and specialty breads in New York deli style. The down-home eatery is open for breakfast and lunch, Monday through Saturday, year round, and provides free deliveries.

Pizza Plus

$, no credit cards • 302 N. Mitchell St., Cadillac • (616) 775-7727

Pizza Plus is probably the most experienced pizza maker in town. They've been tossing the dough for 40 years. Pizzas are handmade from original recipes. Subs, salads, burritos and spaghetti are also available for take-out or dine-in meals. Pizza Plus serves lunch and dinner daily.

Little Traverse

J&J Bakery, Deli & Catering

$, no credit cards • 126 Main St., East Jordan • (616) 536-2022

Known for their great soups and chili, J&J

Deli also offers meats, sandwiches and salads. Their bakery features breads, doughnuts, pastries and cakes. Dine in, take out or request delivery to your place of business. J&J serves breakfast, lunch and dinner daily.

B.C. Pizza

$, no credit cards • 06535 Mich. Hwy. 66, Charlevoix • (616) 547-9999
$, no credit cards • 112 E. Main St., Boyne City • (616) 582-2288

A northern Michigan franchise, B.C. Pizza uses only the finest quality meats, cheeses and vegetables and still produces affordable pizzas. Enjoy pizzas, subs and salads dining in, on the go or delivered free. The Charlevoix shop has a big-screen TV featuring continuous sports coverage. Both locations are open daily.

Chee Peng

$ • 1129 N. U.S. Hwy. 31, Petoskey
• (616) 347-2542

For classic oriental take-out try Chee Peng. The specialty is Cantonese and Mandarin cooking. They offer daily lunch and dinner specials for take-out or dine-in customers and serve a Sunday buffet. Chee Peng is open daily.

Cormack's Deli

$ • 2569 Charlevoix Ave., Petoskey
• (616) 347-7570

Cormack's serves six delicious varieties of its homemade breads. Dine in or take out at this soup and sandwich bar known for great grilled Reubens and mouth-watering brownies, cookies and pies. The deli is open Monday through Saturday for breakfast, lunch and dinner.

Flatiron Deli

$, no credit cards • 313 Howard St., Petoskey • (616) 347-5190

Flatiron Deli offers a comfortable, cheerful atmosphere for dine-in customers, but the best seats go to the take-out crowd. Many customers take their muffins, rolls, sandwiches and soups to the adjacent Pennsylvania Park in Petoskey's Gaslight District. Flatiron serves breakfast and lunch daily during peak season and Monday through Saturday during winter months.

Grain Train Natural Food Cooperative

$ • 421 Howard St., Petoskey
• (616) 347-2381

The Grain Train is the place to go for organic, whole-grain and vegetarian sandwiches and light fare. In the deli bakery you'll find a good selection of scones, muffins, cookies and sourdoughs. Grain Train also serves organic coffee, Chai (a flavorful East Indian spiced tea) and other specialty teas. Bulk foods, produce, organic and regular dairy products, supplements and cruelty-free personal care products are all sold. It is open weekdays.

Symons General Store

$ • 401 E. Lake St., Petoskey
• (616) 347-2438

Have your meal on the run in true gourmet fashion. Grab some fresh caviar, specialty croissants or fresh-baked artichoke and mozzarella bread from Symons' incredible selection of international foods and beverages, including 107 varieties of cheese. Stop at the wine cellar and choose a fine wine from their extensive selection or order fresh-brewed Starbucks coffee, espresso or cappuccino. Whenever the whim for gourmet-on-the-go strikes, think Symons. The store is open daily.

Harbor Springs Gourmet

$ • 127 State St., Harbor Springs
• (616) 526-9607

Forget the idea that food on the go has to be boring. Harbor Springs Gourmet offers great take-out entrees including free-range Amish chicken and baby-back ribs as well as a tempting selection of fresh-baked goods, imported items and fine wines to complete your meal. Harbor Springs is open daily year round. See our Shopping chapter to learn more of what's available.

Turkey's Cafe & Pizzeria

$, no credit cards • 250 E. Main St., Harbor Springs • (616) 526-6041

Smell the bacon cooking. Turkey's Cafe serves a satisfying variety of American breakfast favorites including blueberry waffles and French toast. Dining in or on the go, enjoy their lunch and dinner sandwiches or one of their fresh pizzas. Pizza dough is made from scratch, and you'll be pleased with the variety of toppings available. The cafe is open daily and offers outdoor dining.

Mackinac Straits

Brian's BBQ

$, no credit cards • Huron St., Mackinac Island • (906) 847-3526

Ride your bike along the main road circling the island and the aroma of barbecuing chicken will encircle you as you pass Brian's BBQ. Next to the Harbor View Inn, just past the Fort and harbor area, Brian's BBQ sets up shop right on the front lawn that it shares with LaChance Bed and Breakfast. A cook in a white shirt and hat mans the grills and chats with customers as mouthwatering smells fill the air. The handwritten menu of barbecued chicken, bratwurst, hot dogs and coleslaw is posted nearby.

Doud's Mercantile

$ • Huron St., Mackinac Island
• (906) 847-3551

You'll find a little of everything at Doud's Mercantile. The store has been serving islanders for four generations with groceries, produce, meat, spirits, movie rentals and lottery tickets. Get the fixings for your own picnic here, or pick up one of the deli sandwiches or containers of hot soup and coffee that are also sold here.

Feedbag

$, no credit cards • Surrey Hills Sq., Mackinac Island • (906) 847-3593

Fresh donuts are made daily at this popular stop at Surrey Hills Square along Mackinac Island's carriage tour route. You can also chow down on the dog of your delight — hot dogs, bratwurst, Cajun dogs — along with popcorn and ice cream. Pick your seat, indoors or outdoors, and enjoy.

Mighty Mac Hamburger

$, no credit cards • Huron St., Mackinac Island • (906) 847-6384

You won't find any golden arches with this Mac, but you will enjoy a great burger at family-friendly prices. Mighty Mac has been flipping burgers and fast food fare for decades. Orders can be taken out or eaten inside. The restaurant's back dining room overlooks the harbor.

Mustang Lounge
$ • Astor St., Mackinac Island
• (906) 847-9916
The Mustang Lounge promises the best burger in town. Open year round, it is an island gathering spot in season and out. You will also see it listed as a favorite pub in our Nightlife and Casinos chapter.

Three Brothers Sarducci Pizza Co.
$, no credit cards • Huron St., Mackinac Island • (906) 847-3880
The owners promise only the best at Three Brothers Sarducci. The menu features pizza by the slice or pan, spaghetti, calzones, antipasto, submarines, specialty sandwiches and breadsticks. A chalkboard near the entrance highlights the menu and daily specials. Service is self-serve although you can call in orders for delivery by "pony express." You can eat here or take your order over to nearby Marquette Park for a picnic on the lawn.

Surrey Sandwich Shop
$, no credit cards • Huron St., Mackinac Island • (906) 847-3743
Stop here for a bowl of chili, a deli sub, or your favorite sandwich. The Surrey Sandwich shop is open until 2 AM, so it's also a great spot to appease the midnight munchies. Whether you're here for lunch or a snack, top it off with frozen yogurt.

Zach's Deli
$, no credit cards • Huron St., Mackinac Island • (906) 847-6041
Zach's Deli is a great spot to find delicious specialty sandwiches, fragrant rotisserie chicken, pizza, ice cream and fudge. Plan to stop for a bite before the ferry ride home. Zach's sits right next to the Sheplers dock.

Mackinaw Pastie & Cookie Co.
$, no credit cards • 514 S. Huron St., Mackinaw City • (616) 436-5113
Enjoy Cornish pasties at the shop that's been serving them for almost 35 years. The menu includes beef, chicken and two vegetable pasties. Special toppings — stroganoff, Mexican and Italian — create unique dinners. Pizza and ravioli are also available for the "pastie challenged."

Mama Mia's Pizza
$, no credit cards • 231 Central Ave., Mackinaw City • (616) 436-5534
Homemade pizza tops the menu at Mama Mia's Pizza. Diners can also choose from lasagna, spaghetti, tacos, sandwiches and salads. This family-friendly eatery is open daily for breakfast, lunch and dinner. Mama Mia's is also home to the Mackinac Bridge Museum (see our Attractions chapter). The restaurant owner, a former ironworker who worked on the bridge construction, built the museum on the restaurant's upper level to commemorate completion of the "bridge that couldn't be built" and salute the men who made it happen.

Madd Chadder's Deli
$ • 1143 N. State St., St. Ignace
• (906) 643-6755
Madd Chadder's offers an extensive menu for taking out or eating in from its shop in the Victorian Village. Sandwiches come in 11 varieties, or you can build your own from an ample selection of deli meats and cheeses. You can also choose from several stuffed baked potatoes, bakery sweets, appetizers and specialty salads, such as calypso chicken salad and chicken oriental salad. Summer dinners add whitefish, pastas and pizza to the lineup. Madd Chadder's is open daily for lunch and dinner from mid-June through September, and lunch and late afternoon snacks from April through mid-June and October through December. The restaurant is closed January to March.

Ice Cream and Sweet Treats

Grand Traverse

Traverse City Area

Bardon's Wonder Freeze
$, no credit cards • 1100 E. Front St.
• (616) 941-4326
Bardon's close proximity to the Civic Cen-

ter and Bryant Park make it a popular destination for nearby ball players, picnickers and swimmers as well as the many neighborhood families that regularly frequent this longtime ice cream stand. Picnic tables edge the parking lot. Bardon's often runs hot dog lovers' specials and has sold special kiddie beach buckets complete with hot dog, chips and a sand pail to take back to the beach. Bardon's is usually open between May and September.

Dairy Lodge
$, no credit cards • 405 N. Division St., Traverse City • (616) 941-4374

In our west side Traverse City neighborhood, the kids start a springtime watch to monitor the imminent opening of the Dairy Lodge. We know that winter is over and summer is definitely on the way when the Dairy Lodge opens its service windows. It has been selling soft-serve ice cream to all of us kids for years, and it has amassed a loyal following that enjoys the friendly family of owners as much as their cones and shakes. Relax with your treats at the stand's bright red picnic tables or take a stroll by the bay. West End Beach and the TART trail are just a block or so away. The Dairy Lodge is usually open May through October, although weather might extend or reduce the season.

Wares Brothers Frosty Treats
$, no credit cards • 424 W. 14th St., Traverse City • (616) 946-2313
$, no credit cards • 1409 S. Airport Rd., Traverse City • (616) 941-4277
$, no credit cards • 1300 W. Bay Shore Dr., Traverse City • (616) 946-0051

Wares Brothers is another longtime, family-run ice cream institution in Traverse City. Today, there are three locations scattered around Traverse City with indoor and outdoor seating and a menu of ice cream favorites, sandwiches, hot dogs and chips. Wares is known as the "Home of the Turtle Sundae," an ice cream specialty overflowing with caramel, chocolate, pecans and whipped topping. Other soft-serve sundaes, cones and shakes are equally tempting. Wares is also a great spot to grab a quick bite on the way to the beach or on the run. Watch for their Coney Island specials. They are a great deal, and great to eat! The Wares on

West Bay Shore Drive is usually open May to October. The other two locations are open year round, with drive-through service available at South Airport Road.

Antrim-Kalkaska

Alpine Chocolat Haus & Gifts
$ • 208 W. Main St., Gaylord
• (517) 732-1077

Stop here for a wonderful treat! Relax over a hand-dipped sundae or other frozen specialties at the Alpine Chocolat Haus's old fashioned ice cream parlor. You'll also find an indulgent array of tempting hand-dipped chocolates.

Lake Michigan Shoreline and Cadillac

House of Flavors
$ • 284 River St., Manistee
• (616) 723-2233
$ • 402 W. Ludington Ave., Ludington
• (616) 845-5785

Lick your ice cream cones in leisure while you watch boat traffic along the scenic Manistee River from the deck at Manistee's House of Flavors Restaurant. More than 32 flavors of ice cream are available, including the company's original recipe Blue Moon, a brightly hued ice cream concoction. You can also get sundaes, shakes and a good selection of frozen yogurt, fat-free and sugar-free ice cream. Open daily, House of Flavors has a full breakfast, lunch and dinner menu. At the Ludington House of Flavors not only do you get the same sweet treats, but you can watch the House of Flavors ice cream factory in action. See our Kidstuff chapter for details.

Little Traverse

Murdick's Homemade Ice Cream
$ • 307 Bridge St., Charlevoix
• (616) 547-6426

Using Murdick's own famous candies, original-recipe ice creams are made fresh on site. Feast your eyes on three cases of creamy frozen treats, including fat-free and sugar-free varieties. The shop is open daily from mid-May through mid-October.

Kilwin's

$ • 316 Howard St., Petoskey
• **(616) 347-2645**
$ • 101 Main St., Harbor Springs
• **(616) 526-2902**
$ • 330 Bridge St., Charlevoix
• **(616) 547-5013**
$ • Huron St., Mackinac Island
• **(906) 847-6500**
$ • 413 Main St., Frankfort
• **(616) 352-6107**
$ • 486 River St., Manistee
• **(616) 723-3933**
$ • 118 W. Ludington Ave., Ludington
• **(616) 845-5858**
$ • 129 E. Front St., Traverse City
• **(616) 946-2403**

Kilwin's is best known as a candymaker, but their franchise shops are scattered throughout the north and all are wonderful places to stop for original-recipe ice cream. See our Shopping chapter for the Kilwin's story.

Mary Ellen's Place

$ • 145 E. Main St., Harbor Springs
• **(616) 526-5591**

Mary Ellen's Place has been scooping ice cream in downtown Harbor Springs since 1928. Mary Ellen's serves shakes, malts, sodas, sundaes and cones at an old-fashioned soda fountain. A light breakfast and lunch menu is also served daily.

Mackinac Straits

May's Candy Shop

$ • Market and Huron Sts., Mackinac Island • **(906) 847-3832**

Master fudgemaker Marvin May brings decades of tradition in making candy, fudge,

brittle and other sweets. May's has three Island shops including two on Huron Street and one at the corner of Market and Astor Streets.

Jo Ann's Fudge

$ • Huron St., Mackinac Island
• **(906) 847-3707**
$ • 303 Central Ave., Mackinaw City
• **(616) 436-5611**

Jo Ann's promises fresh cream and butter in every batch of fudge made daily in two shops along the main street on Mackinac Island and one in Mackinaw City. The shops also feature hand-dipped candy, peanut brittle, English toffee and sugar-free treats.

Murdick's Fudge Kitchen

$ • Huron St. and Surrey Hill Sq., Mackinac Island • **(906) 847-3530**

Murdick's has been making and serving Mackinac Island fudge since 1887. Look for fudge and brittle made daily at Murdick's Surrey Hill Square and two Huron Street locations.

Ryba's Fudge Shops

$ • Huron St., Mackinac Island
• **(906) 847-3347**

You can identify Ryba's by its pink candy boxes. Today's fudgemaking Rybas represent the family's third generation. Ryba's is noted for its kettle-cooked fudge, caramel corn, hand-dipped chocolates, taffy and ice cream.

Sweet Surrender Soda Fountain

$ • 514 S. Huron St., Mackinaw City
• **(616) 436-5661**

Come on in for an old-fashioned ice cream soda, sundae, milkshake, banana split or hand-dipped cone. Sweet Surrender Soda Fountain promises old fashioned goodness at old-fashioned prices in this Victorian-inspired shop. Fresh muffins, cookies and baked goods are also available.

Remember that we live in a family-friendly region and children are often welcome in public establishments.

Nightlife and Casinos

Time to party!

Actually, nightlife isn't the first thing that comes to mind when you think of Northwest Michigan. In fact as we compiled this chapter, we were surprised at the growing list of dance clubs, pubs and casinos in our region. As we added the various entertainment venues that showcase our many local artists, along with several new brewpubs we had close to 100 listings before we knew it.

We've divided this chapter into categories describing Casinos, Dancing, Entertainment, Movies and Pubs and Brewpubs. Within those categories we've included subcategories for our Insiders' geographic regions.

The Casinos section highlights the three major casinos in the area, all operated by local Native American tribes. These casinos have become popular attractions for both residents and visitors. The Dancing section highlights nightclubs and lounges with live bands or disc jockeys that bring the clubs to life.

The Entertainment section is our most eclectic category with listings for live music series at bookstore cafes, the local comedy club, dinner performances and regular performers at local eateries and taverns. You'll probably notice that karaoke is a popular pastime up north.

In the Movies section, we give a list of local theaters and profile a few unique venues in our region.

The final category, Pubs and Brewpubs, includes a hefty sampling of our region's many bars, taverns, pubs and saloons. Many of these pubs are also favorite family restaurants. We urge you to read the Restaurants chapter for additional ideas and a more complete look at our local night scene.

Assume that credit cards are accepted unless otherwise noted. We have included general cover charges where appropriate. These prices are based on the most recent admission charges and should be used as guidelines only since they are subject to change. Cover charges may be in place periodically at venues featuring live entertainment. These costs can fluctuate with the season, the day of the week, the time of the day and, especially, with the headlining band. If a specific cover charge policy is consistently in place, we have noted it.

Remember that we live in a family-friendly region and children are often welcome in public establishments. This is especially true in the pubs that serve meals. Call ahead if you are unsure.

Finally, a word of caution. The legal drinking age for purchase and consumption of alcohol in Michigan is 21, and that the law is strictly enforced. There are also strict laws regarding driving under the influence of alcohol (.10 is the legal limit in Michigan). We value your visit and want you to return home safely. If there is any question about your ability to drive, please pass your car keys to a friend, or call a taxi.

INSIDERS' TIP

Michigan law prohibits the sale of liquor before noon on Sundays.

Casinos

Grand Traverse

Turtle Creek Casino
7741 Mich. Hwy. 72, Williamsburg
• **(616) 267-9574, (888) 777-8946**

Turtle Creek is the newest casino owned and operated by the Grand Traverse Band of Ottawa and Chippewa Indians under the umbrella of Traverse Bay Casino Resorts. Its easily accessible site along Mich. Highway 72 and is just a quick ride from its close neighbor, the Grand Traverse Resort. Turtle Creek has been wildly popular since opening its doors in 1996, with approximately 8,000 people visiting annually. The casino recently doubled its space to 29,000 square feet and now houses over 600 slot machines with progressives in nickel, quarter, 50¢ and $1 machines along with gaming tables for blackjack, Caribbean stud poker, roulette and Let It Ride. Turtle Creek is open seven days a week with slots running from 8 AM to 2 AM Monday through Thursday, 8 AM to 3 AM on Friday and Saturday, and 9 AM to 2 AM on Sunday. Table games begin at 11 AM on Monday through Saturday, and at noon on Sunday.

Leelanau Sands Casino and The Palace Bingo Hall
2521 N. West Bay Shore Dr., Suttons Bay
• **(616) 271-4104, (800) 922-2946**

The Leelanau Sands Casino was the Grand Traverse region's first casino when the Grand Traverse Band of Ottawa and Chippewa Indians opened it at their Peshawbestown reservation north of Suttons Bay in 1984. Since then, it has grown into the Traverse Bay Casino Resorts, which has become a vital part of the Band's and Leelanau county's economy. Close to 10,000 people flock to the Leelanau Sands and its adjacent bingo hall each year to try their chances with Lady Luck. Eagle's Ridge Fine Dining and the Leelanau Sands Casino Lodge are also on site for full hospitality and resort services.

Inside the 32,000-square-foot casino, you'll find a seemingly endless supply of slot machines and gaming tables. There are over 650 machines including video slots for KENO, blackjack and poker filling the halls along with myriad gaming tables for blackjack, roulette, craps, Casino War, Let It Ride, two-deck pitch blackjack and Money Wheel. Caribbean stud poker features progressive jackpots for huge cash prizes. Slot machines play in nickel, quarter, $1 and $5 denominations. Day or night, the place is filled with lights, energy, fun and excitement. Live entertainment adds to the energy on weekends and Wednesdays.

If you don't know all of the games, stop in on Thursday nights between 7 and 10 PM when you can learn to play Caribbean stud poker, Craps and Let It Ride. Casino hours begin when the slot machines open at 8 AM Monday through Saturday, and at 9 AM on Sunday. Tables games start at 11 AM Monday through Saturday, and at noon on Sunday. The playing continues until closing at 2 AM on Sundays through Thursdays and 3 AM on Fridays and Saturdays.

Bingo is the game of the day at The Palace, which operates in a 400-seat hall just north of the casino. The Palace opens daily at 8 AM and runs to midnight Sunday through Thursdays, and 2 AM on Friday and Saturday.

Mackinac Straits

Kewadin Shores Casino
3039 Mackinac Tr., St. Ignace
• **(906) 643-7071, (800) KEWADIN**

The Kewadin Shores Casino promises a Vegas experience just 3 miles north of St. Ignace. It's part of the Kewadin Casinos family which includes upper peninsula gaming, hotel and convention centers in Sault Ste. Marie (see Daytrips chapter), Christmas, Manistique and Hessel as well as St. Ignace. You can't miss the purple Kewadin signs where singing star Kenny Rogers personifies "The Gambler" as his image smiles from billboards leading north. The Kewadin Shores facility offers ex-

www.insiders.com

See this and many other **Insiders' Guide®** destinations online — in their entirety.

Visit us today!

tensive gaming in a huge, domed facility. Players will have countless games to choose from with over 1,100 slot machines as well as live KENO, roulette, craps, blackjack and other gaming favorites. Kewadin Shores is open 24 hours each day.

Dancing

Grand Traverse

The Hayloft
5100 W. Mich. Hwy. 72, Traverse City
• (616) 941-0832

Country music lovers will love The Hayloft. This popular stop opens at 10 AM with music playing until 10 PM. Live bands perform on Friday and Saturday nights, often local favorites like the Cow Puppies or North Country. Insiders love the casual country setting along with the Hayloft's menu of Mexican and American fare.

JR's Warehouse
205 Lake Ave., Traverse City
• (616) 941-4422

JR's Warehouse is the place to rock 'n' roll as disc jockeys and bands play contemporary dance hits. This popular night spot is appropriately named as it is situated within a former warehouse near downtown. Live performers are scheduled at various times throughout the year, especially during the holidays and summer. A large sign next to the building's Union Street sign lists the latest lineup. Jazz night is Tuesday, college night is Thursday, and ladies' night is on Saturday. Eighteen-year-olds are welcome most nights with appropriate photo IDs.

Northern Lites
273 U.S. Hwy. 31 S., Traverse City
• (616) 943-8555

Music and dancing light up Northern Lites. Disc jockeys play easy-listening favorites on Wednesdays while everybody shares the microphone for karaoke on Thursday nights. Live bands take center stage Friday and Saturday starting at 9:30 PM. Cover charge for live music is usually $3.

Shimmer's Nightclub
Holiday Inn, 615 E. Front St., Traverse City • (616) 947-3700

Dance the night away all week long at Shimmer's Nightclub. This popular nightclub in the Holiday Inn is centrally located next to the West Bay and downtown Traverse City. You'll enjoy top-40 dance music performed daily by live bands on Tuesday through Saturday. Disc jockeys fill in with similar tunes during breaks. Cover charges average $3. Ladies get in free on Thursday.

Trillium Restaurant and Lounge
Grand Traverse Resort, 100 Grand Traverse Village Blvd., Acme
• (616) 938-2100

The bays and the region's scenic vistas are your backdrop at the Trillium Restaurant and Lounge. Live bands perform at the top of the tower at the Grand Traverse Resort on Friday and Saturday evenings between 9 PM and 1 AM. Easy-listening favorites are performed on the Trillium's grand piano on Tuesday, Wednesday and Thursday between 8 PM and midnight. The Trillium's design connects the 17th-floor lounge with the 16th-floor restaurant so that you can enjoy the entertainment along with dinner, drinks or both. See our Restaurants chapter for more on Trillium dining.

Knickers Lounge
Holiday Inn, 833 W. Main St., Gaylord
• (517) 732-2431

Live entertainment and dancing are on tap at Knickers Lounge inside the Holiday Inn in Gaylord. A variety of bands take to the stage to play easy-listening favorites Tuesday through Saturday. Appetizers and a light dining menu are available if the munchies hit.

Lake Michigan Shoreline and Cadillac

Tiki Lounge and Nightclub at Stearns Motor Inn
212 E. Ludington Ave., Ludington
• (616) 843-3407

Get a big fix of your favorite music videos

on the Tiki's 10-foot video screens. DJs appear nightly with the latest top 40, and dancing is the name of the game. The Tiki appeals primarily to college students and young adults. During school breaks, the lounge frequently presents alcohol-free teen nights. The Tiki is a two-level bar with pool and game tables and quiet seating on the upper level while the heavy action goes on below. Things get rolling here about 10 PM.

Little Traverse

Victories
1966 U.S. Hwy. 131 S., Petoskey
• **(616) 347-4927**
Victories' claim to fame is its dance floor, the largest floor in all the north. Friday and Saturday nights Victories presents live rock, appealing to a wide audience. Look for a country band to appear monthly. Things get moving about 9:30 PM, and you can expect a $3 cover charge. A good menu selection is offered until 10 PM. It includes prime rib and a Friday fish fry. A full entertainment complex, Victories features a restaurant, bar, three big-screen TVs for sport fans, a video game room, three pool tables and a 24-lane bowling alley.

Mackinac Straits

Horn's Gaslight Bar
Huron St., Mackinac Island
• **(906) 847-6154**
This is the hot spot for music and dancing, island style. An impressive bar lines the wall while musicians perch near the front window. During the day, a piano player carries the melodies, turning over the microphone to an evening dance band. Nachos, burritos,

burgers and sandwiches are served for lunch, dinner and late-night snacks

Entertainment

Grand Traverse

Traverse City Area

Borders Books and Music
2612 Crossing Cir., Traverse City
• **(616) 933-0412**
Live music wafts around the bookshelves at Borders as local musicians perform in the bookstore cafe several times each week. The entertainment is eclectic, reflecting the rich and diverse talents of the region's many musicians and performers. The lineup changes weekly and is listed, along with the shop's frequent special events and activities, in a monthly newsletter. You can usually count on entertainment on Friday and Saturday nights as well as one or two evenings during the week. There is no cover charge.

Bower's Harbor Inn
13512 Peninsula Dr., Traverse City
• **(616) 223-4222**
Bower's Harbor Inn presents an outstanding dinner menu throughout the year (see our Restaurants chapter for more). Weekend meals are complemented by the intricate melodies of acoustic guitar. Renowned local classical guitarist John Wunsch entertains diners between 6:30 and 10 PM on Friday and Saturday nights.

Chateau Chantal
15900 Rue de Vin, Traverse City
• **(616) 223-4110, (800) 969-4009**
Chateau Chantal is a wonderful winery and

INSIDERS' TIP

Like to play games? Borders Books and Music in Traverse City hosts Chess Night on Wednesday from 6 to 11 PM in its cafe. You can also play chess on Tuesday from 6 to 11 PM at Elias Brothers Big Boy (U.S. Highway 31 S.), and at Javasite cybercafe on Wednesdays from 10 AM to 2 PM. Scrabble is the game of choice at Horizon Books when Scrabble for Singles is held at least one weekday each month in the lower-level cafe.

bed and breakfast (see our Attractions and Bed and Breakfasts chapters) nestled in the scenic hills of the Old Mission Peninsula. It's also the site for Jazz at Sunset, a delightful gathering of talented musicians who perform in the windowed Great Room for several hours once a week as the early evening skies erupt into vivid colors. The performers are led by local jazz pianist Jeff Hass, who has been a leader in bringing outstanding musicians to northern Michigan and establishing the Grand Traverse region as a venue for their art. Jazz at Sunset is held Thursday evenings between mid-June and August, and on Fridays during September and October.

Chumley's
1057 Memorial Hwy., Traverse City
• **(616) 943-8089**

It's Saturday night so get your vocal chords tuned up and head to the intersection of Mich. Highway 37 and U.S. Highway 31, known locally as Chum's Corners, for karaoke night at Chumley's. Whether enjoying the music or the company, try the burgers, sandwiches and homecooked specialties. Chumley's does not accept credit cards.

Dill's Olde Towne Saloon
423 S. Union St., Traverse City
• **(616) 947-7534**

Every night of the week, you will find plenty of up-north fun waiting for you at Dill's. Originally built in 1886 as Novotny's pub, it is Traverse City's oldest restaurant and a longtime local favorite (see our Restaurants chapter). The entertainment schedule changes by the day and the season. In the summer months, the Golden Garter Revue takes center stage with a delightful musical revue performed by a talented ensemble of college students. Two dinner shows and one late-night cocktail show are presented six nights each week. Karaoke is on deck weekends throughout the year with "Princess Laura," an energetic entertainer who has to be one of the liveliest hosts on this side of the Great Lakes. On Tuesdays, Laura leads trivia night. On Wednesday, Dill's Family Band features several of the Dill's staff who trade aprons for instruments. On the first Friday of each month the Back Room Gang, a much loved Traverse City group, plays Dixieland jazz.

Ron Getz, local jazzman, livens up the nightlife of Traverse City with the sound of his guitar.

Photo: Kevin Poirier/Courtesy of the Traverse City Record-Eagle

Horizon Books
243 E. Front St., Traverse City
• **(616) 946-7290**

Horizon Books' newest coffee bar, the Shine Cafe, is the venue for an endless array of local entertainers who perform as part of the On the Horizon . . . Live! series. You can expect to hear, for free, at least one talented performer or ensemble on Friday and Saturday evenings, and at several additional times during the week, often on Mondays and Thursdays. Open mike nights are also becoming popular. On busy weekends, seating is sometimes limited to ticket holders. Tickets cost $3 and can be partially applied as a cafe voucher. Frequent-listener passes are also available at a reduced price. Midweek, seating is usually free.

The Other Place Comedy Club
738 S. Garfield St., Traverse City
• **(616) 941-0988**

Bring your sense of humor to The Other Place Comedy Club for a night of fun and laughs. Stand-up comedy is on tap on Fridays and Saturdays with shows at 8 and 10:30 PM. Admission is $6. The club serves alcoholic beverages but no food.

Ranch Rudolf
6841 Brown Bridge Rd., Traverse City
• **(616) 947-9529**

Ranch Rudolf looks like a scene out of an old TV western, but that rustic ranch atmosphere adds to its appeal. We talk about Ranch Rudolf in our Kidstuff and Recreation chapters, so check there for more on the many activities that take place year round. During summer, holidays and most weekends, country-western entertainment sets toes tapping. You can eat while you listen. The menu includes huge burgers, barbecued beef, ribs, steaks and pizza.

Sloppy Joe's
704 E. Front St., Traverse City
• **(616) 946-1470**

You can't miss the huge, laughing cartoon face that signals the front of Sloppy Joe's. This is a pleasant Traverse City gathering spot. Grab a sandwich along with your favorite beverage then kick back and enjoy karaoke on Thursday, Friday and Saturday. Easy-listening hits are played by a disc jockey.

Tall Ship Malabar
13390 W. Bay Shore Dr., Traverse City
• **(616) 941-2000, (800) 968-8800**

With a northern Michigan sunset and beautiful Grand Traverse Bay in the background, the *Malabar* needs little beyond Mother Nature to entertain its passengers. This tall ship sailing experience is enhanced, however, by local talent during two of its midweek sunset cruises. On Tuesday, the Beach Bards share stories and songs of the sea in the oral tradition. Song of the Lakes brings its regionally known maritime folk music to the decks of the *Malabar* every Wednesday. These special summer sunset sails leave the *Malabar*'s West Bay docks at 7 PM and return by 9:30 PM between early June and late August. Recent fares were $43 for adults and $26.50 for children. Read our Summer Recreation chapter for more on the *Malabar*'s full sailing schedule, which includes up to three sails each day from spring through fall.

Union Street Station
117 S. Union St., Traverse City
• **(616) 941-1930**

This casual bar features live performances several nights each week and is repeatedly voted the best live entertainment venue in local polls. The music is predominantly rock with various local and national acts playing Thursday, Friday and Saturday. Union Street Station is a cozy pub sitting in the heart of Traverse City's downtown. Sandwiches, burgers, subs and nachos are on the menu.

Leelanau County

Cedar Tavern
9039 Kasson Rd., Cedar
• **(616) 228-7445**

In the heart of the Leelanau Peninsula, the Cedar Tavern hosts live entertainment on Saturday nights, karaoke on Friday, and open

---

INSIDERS' TIP

Check out the most up-to-date entertainment schedules by reading our local publications. *Traverse, Northern Michigan's Magazine* publishes a monthly events calendar. The *Traverse City Record-Eagle*'s arts and entertainment section is published on Friday with weekly "Things to Do" and "Nightlife" calendars. The *Northern Express*, published each Wednesday, always includes extensive entertainment coverage along with its "Night Life" and "Hot Dates" calendars. All of these publications cover the same geographic area as our *Insiders' Guide*. Noverr Publishing's *Entertainment Guide*, distributed in Traverse City hotels and restaurants, highlights Grand Traverse area happenings. See our Media chapter for more about these publications.

mike on Tuesday. This is one of the longest-running open mike nights in the area. It's been going strong for more than 11 years and often attracts high-caliber performers to the stage. If you'd like to join patrons for lunch or dinner, sandwiches lead the menu.

Antrim-Kalkaska

Shanty Creek
1 Shanty Creek Rd., Bellaire
• **(800) 678-4111**

Join the crowd at Shanty Creek for live entertainment every evening from 9 PM to closing. During the summer, diners are treated to tunes by the Schussy Cats, an ensemble of extremely talented college students who kick up their heels and belt out the best for a marvelous, musical meal in the Ivanhoff restaurant.

Treetops Sylvan Resort
Mich. Hwy. 32 East, Gaylord
• **(517) 732-6711**

Lively entertainment has toes tapping on Friday and Saturday evenings at Fairway's Grille at Treetops Sylvan Resort with the music playing from 8 PM to midnight. The resort's Horizon Room hosts a mellow piano lounge from 7 to 11 PM. If you prefer a different style of entertainment, the Top of the Hill Sports Bar sports several pool tables, television sets, a putting game, a dartboard and more than 500 brands of imported and domestic beer.

Lake Michigan Shoreline and Cadillac

The Cabbage Shed
198 Frankfort Ave., Elberta
• **(616) 352-9843**

Best known for bringing a great jazz sound north, this informal, funky restaurant/club appeals to anyone who appreciates good music. On weekends, jazz and classic rock resonate from the Shed, which Is housed in a 100-year-old warehouse along Betsie Bay. A fine-dining menu features prime rib and whitefish (see our Restaurants chapter). The full-service bar offers a variety of imports and an exten-

sive wine list. You can't beat this place for northern atmosphere.

Sleepy Bear Lounge
10919 Main St., Honor • **(616) 325-2262**

It's rock. It's blues. It's good times all the way. Sleepy Bear Lounge brings some of the best talent in Western Michigan north every Friday and Saturday night. The laid-back atmosphere makes you feel immediately at home. Pool tables and dartboards invite friendly competition, perhaps with some new friends. Sleepy Bear Lounge offers a full-service bar and a good menu, featuring homemade pizza and Mexican dishes, served until midnight. You must be older than 21 to be admitted after 9 PM.

The Sand Bar Nightclub
6319 E. Mich. Hwy. 115, Cadillac
• **(616) 775-2407**

The Sand Bar Nightclub at the Sands Resort in Cadillac offers live entertainment every Friday and Saturday night throughout the year. It's classic rock all the way, sometimes rowdy and sometimes low-key, but always hot. The club opens at 8 PM but things don't really get rolling until after 9:30 PM. The Sand Bar caters to the younger-than-30 crowd, offering a full-service bar and appetizers. Expect a nominal cover charge.

Curly's Bar and Grill at McGuire's Resort
7880 S. Mackinaw Tr., Cadillac
• **(616) 775-9947, (800) 632-7302**

The weekend begins about 8 PM Thursday night at Curly's Bar and Grill as live entertainment sets the mood for creating good times. Low-key and relaxed, Thursday is devoted to guitar and vocal performances. Curly's Friday fish fry is one of the best in the area and is followed by karaoke from 9 PM to 1 AM. Local bands take over Saturday night playing a mix of folk, country, oldies and rock. Curly's offers a full bar featuring a great selection of imported beers and microbrews.

The Pines Nightclub
5592 E. Mich. Hwy. 55, Cadillac
• **(616) 775-7752**

Saturday night is comedy night at The

Pines Nightclub in Cadillac West. Beginning at 8:30 PM Wednesday and Friday, there is dancing to DJ sounds. The club's high-energy entertainment appeals mostly to young adults A full-service bar, pizza and subs are available. The Pines is part of a full entertainment complex featuring a 12-lane bowling alley and two lighted softball fields for tournament and league play.

Lost Knights Lounge
Bill Oliver's Best Western, 5676 W. Mich. Hwy. 55, Cadillac • (616) 775-2458

This is the place for sport addicts. Four TVs run events continuously while a full bar offers a good selection of imports. Beginning about 9:30 on Friday and Saturday nights the scene livens with karaoke. A full menu from the King's Table kitchen is served in the lounge until 9 PM on weeknights and 10 PM on weekends.

Players Sports Bar and Grill
134 S. Vandermeulen Rd., Lake City • (616) 839-3200

The site, under new management, has long been one of the state's favorite hosts for summer softball tournaments. The facility features two lighted diamonds, two volleyball courts and horseshoe pits. Pool, darts and game tables offer opportunities for friendly indoor competition. There's a full bar and full menu with a good selection of Mexican fare. Country line dancing is on tap every Wednesday night, karaoke tops the bill Thursday night, and on Friday and Saturday night DJs present the top 40. Things liven up here about 10 PM, and while it's a bit off the beaten track, customers don't seem to mind the drive.

Michael's on the Avenue
129 W. Ludington Ave., Ludington • (616) 845-7411

This is where Ludington Insiders meet their friends for good food and good times. Newly remodeled, the pub atmosphere provides a relaxing backdrop to enjoy live weekend entertainment featuring 1970s hits and classic rock. Michael's is open daily offering casual dining, steaks, prime rib and light fare, pizza and burgers. (See our Restaurants chapter for more information.)

Scandals Near the Lakeshore
320 S. James St., Ludington • (616) 845-7263

One of the hottest night spots in Ludington, Scandals offers an array of live entertainment. There's blues and rock, comedy, karaoke, plenty of top 40 and great dancing. Scandals' daily happy hour is from 3 to 6 PM. Enjoy tropical drink specials on the deck. For late-night diners, Scandals serves a full menu until 2 AM. The 30- and 40-something crowd prefers Scandals during the dinner hour while the young adult set takes over after 9 PM.

Little Traverse

Villager Pub
427 Bridge St., Charlevoix • (616) 547-6925

Dust off those blue-suede shoes. The Villager Pub's 1950s theme will definitely put you in the mood for good times. On summer weekends the Pub presents first class, live entertainment. Playing oldies and classic rock, bands typically draw the young adult crowd. Expect a nominal cover charge. At other times of the year the energy is more low-key. You'll find the pub serves a full lunch, and the dinner menu includes their specialties, whitefish and broasted chicken. Food is served until 11 PM weekends, and 10 PM weeknights.

Stafford's One Water Street
1 Water St., Boyne City • (616) 582-3434

There's always something contemporary

INSIDERS' TIP

For a full lineup of entertainment, specials and other happenings at the Leelanau Sands Casino, Turtle Creek Casino or The Palace, look for the Traverse Bay Casino Resorts' quarterly Casino Calendar of Events, available at visitors centers or by calling (800) 922-2846.

and fun going on at the One Water Street lounge. Live entertainment is presented Saturday and some Friday nights throughout the year. Performances appeal to a wide audience and range from light piano fare to fiery vocals and steel drums. Call for a current entertainment schedule.

The Tannery Saloon
220 S. Lake St., Boyne City
• (616) 582-2272

On weeknights, the 30-something crowd gathers at The Tannery Saloon in Boyne City for easy-listening folk, country and rock sounds. But come the weekend, young adults make the scene for high-spirited, top-40 sounds presented by DJs and live bands. The full lunch and dinner menu features chicken, beef and seafood, and the full-service bar offers all of your favorite drinks.

Reunion Bar/Holiday Inn
1444 U.S. Hwy. 131 S., Petoskey
• (616) 347-6041

The Reunion Bar at Petoskey's Holiday Inn features a cocktail lounge with live entertainment every weekend. On Friday, talent from across the country is brought in for Comedy Night. It's good entertainment fare appealing to an older-than-30 crowd. On Saturday night DJs bring in the top 40. Things usually get hopping around 8 PM. A good selection of light fare, including pizza and sandwiches, is served until 10 PM.

Stafford's Bay View Inn
2011 Woodland Ave., Petoskey
• (616) 347-2771

Stafford's Bay View, a premier country inn, offers entertainment on special occasions throughout the year. Their annual January weekend jazz package is extremely popular. Schedules and lineups vary but you can always look forward to hearing some good jazz sounds in the dining room at least one night per week throughout the summer. Call for their current entertainment schedule.

The Pier
102 Bay St., Harbor Springs
• (616) 526-6201

Take the weekend nice and easy at The

Pier on the waterfront in Harbor Springs. The Wheelhouse Lounge offers a classic piano bar atmosphere every Friday night from 4 to 6 PM during happy hour. But the Pier is legendary for great special events featuring good local talent. Give them a call for an entertainment schedule. (To learn more about dining at The Pier, see our Restaurants chapter.)

Noggin Room Pub
Staffords Perry Hotel Bay at Lewis Sts., Petoskey • (616) 347-4000

Drink your way around the world at the Noggin Room Pub. You'll find the pub in the lower level of Stafford's Perry Hotel, a charming, restored treasure dating back to 1899. There's plenty of food, fun and foam here. After you have tried all 30 of the pub's international beers, your name is added to the honorary "Wall of Foam." Entertainment varies, but you can always count on a good time. Irish balladeer Sean Ryan is an Insiders' favorite who appears regularly throughout the year. Thursday is generally devoted to unplugged blues and jazz, and Friday is folk night. Good times begin to roll about 8 PM at the Noggin Room. A casual menu offering pizza and sandwiches is available.

Grey Gables Inn
308 Belvedere Ave., Charlevoix
• (616) 547-9261

Grey Gables Inn is a Victorian classic. Amidst its elegant crystal chandeliers, antique art and intimate dining room, you'll find a lounge renowned for old fashioned good times. Join the fun piano-bar setting Friday and Saturday night throughout the year. Music and dancing begin about 9 PM. (See our Restaurants chapter to learn more about the inn's fine cuisine.)

Young Americans Dinner Theater
Boyne Highlands, 600 Highlands Dr., Harbor Springs • (616) 526-3000

Enjoy lively, entertaining dinner theater at one of the Midwest's premier resorts. The Young Americans are at Boyne for their 21st consecutive season. It's great family entertainment and you'll love the food, which might be roast tenderloin or breast of chicken poulet. Their musical and theatrical performances fo-

Photo: Kevin Poirier

The Traverse Bay Region provides numerous social opportunities for the night owl.

cus on Americana. Expect to pay $34 for adults, and $18 for children young than 12. Doors open at 6:30 PM, and dinner is served at 7:30 PM.

City Park Grill
432 E. Lake St., Petoskey
• (616) 347-0101

In Petoskey's historic Gaslight District you'll discover some of the highest-energy entertainment. Come 10 PM Friday and Saturday night; things get hot as local jazz and blues artists plug in. The sound appeals to a wide audience. City Park Grill's kitchen closes at 10 PM, but appetizers are available until closing time. Expect a minimal cover charge. (See our Restaurants chapter to learn more.)

Flying Dutchman
1601 Mich. Hwy. 119, Petoskey
• (616) 348-3525

This is a great bar to hit after a day on the slopes or an outing at the dunes. You'll find two fireplaces and some hot sounds to warm you. There's entertainment nightly during sum-

mer months and weekends-only during the rest of the year. Look to catch a variety of live bands, karaoke, and DJs spinning top-40 tunes. You'll also find plenty of your favorite dishes on the Flying Dutchman's full menu, including prime rib, broiled whitefish steaks and shrimp, as well as lighter fare, pizza and appetizers. The action begins about 9:30 PM.

Legs Inn
6425 Lake Shore Dr., Cross Village
• (616) 526-2281

We don't know who has more fun, the bands who play Legs Inn or the guests. This is a place you have to see to believe. Its one-of-a-kind stone architecture and interior decor created from twisted limbs and tree stumps sets an unconventional, easy mood for after-dark fun. Appealing to a wide audience, Legs Inn lounge presents live entertainment for listening and dancing pleasure. The bar features more than 100 imported beers, a good wine list and all your favorite cocktails. (See our Restaurants chapter to learn about the inn's great cuisine.)

Mackinac Straits

The French Outpost
Cadotte Ave., Mackinac Island
• (906) 847-3772

The French Outpost sits halfway up the rise leading to the Grand Hotel. Nightly entertainment surrounds the restaurant and outdoor patio with the festive sounds of summer on Mackinac. From early June to late August, musicians playing to a rock beat take center stage.

Pink Pony Bar and Grill
Huron St., Mackinac St., Mackinac Island
• (906) 847-3341

It's not hard to find the Pink Pony. The bar's signature pink plastic pony hangs in the awning over the sidewalk leading inside. This pub has been an island landmark since the 1940s. It's not uncommon to hear the phrase, "Meet me at the Pony," as new generations of boaters and visitors plan to gather in this vintage bar overlooking the harbor and Straits of Mackinac. Performers, often guitar-playing singers, entertain the casual crowd.

Round Island Bar
Mission Point Resort, 1 Lakeshore Dr., Mackinac Island • (906) 847-3312

Live entertainment is on the nightly menu at the Round Island Bar inside Mission Point Resort. Enjoy the pub's spectacular view of the Mackinac Straits and Round Island along with easy-listening music and a light dining menu featuring nachos, sandwiches and salads.

Waters Meet
Huron St., Mackinac Island
• (906) 847-3806

Music rises from the alcove stairs leading to the lower-level Waters Meet restaurant under the Lilac Tree Hotel. Live entertainment every evening adds to the ambiance of this friendly family restaurant (see our Restaurants chapter for more). Nightly happy hours feature eight beers on tap, and a late-night menu is available until 2 AM.

Mackinaw Crossings
248 S. Huron Ave., Mackinaw City
• (616) 436-5030, (888) 436-5030

You can spend hours exploring the many shops, restaurants and attractions that make up the Mackinaw Crossings (see our Shopping chapter for more). Entertainment weaves through the day to add yet more fun to the mix. The outdoor amphitheater in the Performance Court hosts a revolving cast of street players and musicians who entertain visitors at the top of every hour. Past performers have included magicians, minstrels, comics and more. Plan to be at the Crossings at dusk to watch a spectacular laser and music show. An 800-seat theater will open during the 1998 season which promises to add even more entertaining possibilities. Mackinaw Crossings are open from May to November. Hours are 10 AM to 6 PM Monday through Thursday, and 9 AM to 9 PM on Friday and Saturday during most months. Summer hours expand to 9 AM to 9 PM daily between mid-June and Labor Day.

Voyageur's Jubilé Dinner Theater
Nicolet St., Mackinaw City
• (616) 436-4177, (800) 230-7469

The Voyageur's Jubilé Dinner Theater promises "a memory for the price of a meal." Guests enjoy a hearty, four-course homestyle dinner while professional entertainers sing and dance the night away. The show features rousing medleys from Broadway, rock 'n' roll's golden era and country music charts before concluding with a patriotic salute to America. This family-oriented show is entertaining with a fair dose of audience participation and special effects. The Voyageur's Jubilé begins each evening at 7 PM. Dress is casual but reservations are requested. Expect to pay about $16 for adults and teens, and $11 for children 5 through 12. Kids younger than 5 are admitted free. The price includes a meal.

Movies

The Traverse Bay Region has plenty of screens showing the latest films. We'll give you a list of the more typical venues, but first we'll tell you about a few out-of-the-ordinary cinemas.

Bay Theatre
216 N. St. Joseph St., Suttons Bay
• (616) 271-3772

Film buffs will love the Bay Theatre in

Suttons Bay. Located in a vintage Victorian Theater, "The Bay" is known for bringing film classics, foreign films and critical favorites as well as the day's most popular films to its unique, old-fashioned movie house. It also promises incredible audio, thanks to its high-tech, high-performance digital sound system, which is the only one of its kind in Michigan. Stage productions, musical performances and readings are presented periodically. Neighboring restaurant, Hattie's (see our Restaurants chapter), offers a reasonably priced dinner/theater package and periodically creates complimentary menus and hosts pre- and post-theater gatherings.

Cherry Bowl Drive-In
9812 Honor Hwy., Beulah
• (616) 325-3413
Remember Mom and Dad piling the family into the station wagon and taking everyone to the outdoor theater? Well, pile the kids in the mini-van and enjoy some big-screen nostalgia. The Cherry Bowl Drive-In is one of the last of its breed remaining. Like in the old days, you pay per vehicle, movies begin at dusk, and each car gets its own window speaker. Movies here are generally family oriented.

Petoskey Film Theatre
461 E. Mitchell St., Petoskey
• (616) 347-4337
The Petoskey Film Theatre, in cooperation with Crooked Tree Arts Council and North Central Michigan College, presents three series of international and classic films each year, fall through spring. All films are shown at the McCune Art Center's Ross Stoakes Theatre at 8 PM Friday and Saturday nights, and 2 PM Sunday. Admission is $5 for adults and $3 for students. Check the *Petoskey News Review* Friday edition for what's currently playing or call the McCune Art Center at the above number.

Jack Loeks Theatre
Mission Point Resort, Mackinac Island
• (906) 847-6448, (800) 4-LILACS
First-run films are flown to the island each week in the summer for Monday night at the movies on Mackinac Island. The movies are shown at 9 PM. Admission is $5 for adults and $3 for children younger than 12.

Grand Traverse
Elk Rapids Cinema, 205 River Street, Elk Rapids, (616) 264-8601

Grand Traverse Cinema, Grand Traverse Mall, South Airport Road and Division Street, Traverse City, (616) 941-0820

Horizon Cinemas, Horizon Outlet Center, Division Street, Traverse City, (616) 933-6394

Lake Michigan Shoreline and Cadillac
Cinema 5, 202 S. Mitchell Street, Cadillac, (616) 775-4357

Lyric Cinema, 208 S. James Street, Ludington. (616) 843-8811

Vogue Theater, 383 River Street, Manistee, (616) 723-5555

Little Traverse
Boyne Cinema, 216 S. Lake Street, Boyne City, (616) 582-3212

Cinema III, 107 Antrim Street, Charlevoix, (616) 547-4353

Gaslight Cinema, 302 Petoskey Street, Petoskey, (616) 347-3480

Mackinac Straits
Mackinaw Crossings Cinema, 248 S. Huron Avenue, Mackinaw City, (888) 436-5030

Pubs and Brewpubs

Grand Traverse

Traverse City Area

The Beacon Lounge
Park Place Hotel, 300 E. State St.,
Traverse City • (616) 946-5000
Once you visit The Beacon Lounge at the top of the Park Place Hotel, you may never want to come down again! Wrapped in windows, this lounge boasts magnificent, panoramic views of Grand Traverse Bay, the city lights and the rolling landscape. A light menu of appetizers and sandwiches complements the full beverage service.

Brady's Bar
401 S. Union St., Traverse City
- **(616) 946-8153**

You'll find Brady's by its signature window, a leaded glass shamrock. A great Irish pub, Brady's is a Traverse City institution. If you're in town on St. Patrick's Day, schedule a stop here to join the celebration. Sandwiches, burgers and homemade specials are available daily for lunch or dinner.

Dillinger's Pub
121 S. Union St., Traverse City
- **(616) 941-2276**

A distinctive 1930s-like decor helps create the ambiance at this friendly Old Town pub. A jukebox and big-screen television add to the sights and sounds. If you're hungry, Dillinger's serves a menu featuring sandwiches, burgers and soups for lunch or dinner.

Lil Bo's Bar and Grill
540 W. Front St., Traverse City
- **(616) 946-6925**

Lil Bo's sits in the "food corner" along West Front Street with neighboring Mary's Kitchen Port, Wine Country Market, Chef's In, Burritt's and Folgarelli's. Bo Beer Party Store is right next door. Stop in and quench your thirst, or try one of the "Bo Burgers." Big Bo's weigh in at a half-pound while Lil' Bo's are quarter-pounders. The pub is closed on Sundays and holidays. Credit cards are not accepted.

Mackinaw Brewing Company
161 E. Front St., Traverse City
- **(616) 933-1100**

The Mackinaw Brewing Company was the first microbrewery to set up shop in Traverse City when it converted a former Big Boy restaurant into a thriving brewpub in 1997. Guests have the chance to try any of the brewing company's five signature beers, or try a bite to eat (see our Restaurants chapter). Centrally located in the heart of downtown Traverse City, the Mackinaw Brewing Company is a small pub with an interior that gives you the illusion you're sitting on a ship at sea. Stop in during "Prime Time," from 4 to 6 PM Monday through Friday, for free appetizers and discounts on 9-ounce and 18-ounce mugs of beer. Live en-

tertainment is usually offered on Thursday nights, while every Wednesday is Family Night.

North Peak Brewery
400 W. Front St., Traverse City
- **(616) 941-7325**

North Peak is quickly becoming one of Traverse City's favorite meeting spots. After work and on the weekends, the open bar area is always bustling with activity. Sample the five handcrafted brews and pick your favorite. Or, if you can't decide, try them all with the beer sampler, which comes with five tall, slim glasses mounted in a wooden rack. North Peak also makes its own root beer. The huge vats and beer-making paraphernalia are behind the glass wall near the front entrances. North Peak is a welcome addition to the local restaurant lineup (see our Restaurants chapter).

Sleder's Family Tavern
717 Randolph St., Traverse City
- **(616) 947-9213**

Sleder's has long been one of Traverse City's favorite family taverns and, dating its opening back to 1882, claims the distinction of being the city's oldest continuously operated saloon. It is nestled in the west-side "Slabtown" neighborhood in a vintage building lined with wooden booths, century-old oak tables and ice-cream-parlor chairs. Photos from the town's past are scattered along the walls with such eclectic decorations as stuffed deer, moose heads and antler racks. The original 21-foot mahogany bar stretches the length of the central room, and an adjoining dining area is warmed by a fireplace. Signs and T-shirts implore you to "smooch the moose," a centrally located stuffed head which has accepted thousands of smooches over the years. If you feel the urge, a stepladder is available to reach the moose and, upon contact, bartenders ring a cowbell to commemorate the event. A full menu is available for dining (see our Restaurants chapter), and musicians periodically entertain from the saloon's back room.

TC Athletic Club
428 E. Front St., Traverse City
- **(616) 929-7247**

You can relax at the TC Athletic Club over a game of pool or darts, or simply watch sports on the big-screen television screen. The pub menu includes sandwiches, burgers, nachos and chicken baskets.

U & I Lounge
214 E. Front St., Traverse City
• (616) 946-8932
The U & I is one of Traverse City's favorite pubs. It's a popular meeting spot after work and after sporting events. The U & I is also known for serving Greek specialties such as gyros and Greek salads along with pizza. Sandwiched between storefronts along East Front Street, the U & I offers a pleasant detour from window shopping and sunbathing.

Leelanau County

Art's Bar
6487 Western Ave., Glen Arbor
• (616) 334-3754
Art's Bar is a Leelanau County institution. It has served as a central gathering spot for locals and summer folk for many years with a quiet friendliness that makes you feel at home. In addition to beverage service, Art's also serves complete breakfasts, burgers, Mexican fare, chicken, whitefish, smelt and steaks. It's open daily. Credit cards are not accepted.

Woody's Settling Inn
116 Waukazoo St., Northport
• (616) 386-9933
In Northport, head to Woody's for relaxing drink or a comfortable meal among friends. The pub, open daily, is a favorite gathering spot among locals throughout the year.

Antrim-Kalkaska

Big Buck Brewery and Steakhouse
550 S. Wisconsin St., Gaylord
• (517) 732-5781
The vats, tanks and kettles that brew Big Buck's handmade beers provide a gleaming backdrop to the brewery's large bar and steakhouse. We talk about the eating end of the business in our Restaurants chapter. Here, we'll tell you about Big Buck's handmade beers ranging from light ale to dark stout that are always on tap in this spacious, friendly pub. The signature beer is golden Big Buck Brew which, along with

its sibling brews, is sold at the table or in the adjacent gift shop. Special brews are created seasonally such as cherry beer or Oktoberfest beer. The bar area has big-screen televisions and, at various times during the year, live entertainment. Tours of the brewery can be arranged.

Lake Michigan Shoreline and Cadillac

Mayfair Tavern
515 Frankfort Ave., Elberta
• (616) 352-9136
Frequented by tourists in the summer months, Mayfair Tavern is an off-season hangout for locals. Good food and reasonable prices set this tavern apart. The menu includes some popular Mexican dishes, burgers, sandwiches and appetizers. Oriental and Italian dishes are often available. Meals are served until 9 PM Sunday through Thursday, and until 10 PM Friday and Saturday.

First Street Tavern
303 First St., Manistee • (616) 723-1031
First Street Tavern is where you want to be in Manistee on St. Patrick's Day. A favorite local hangout year round, they offer a full bar featuring a good selection of imports. You can play pool, darts and pinball or watch sports on a big-screen TV.

Jonathon's Pub/Best Western Carriage Inn
200 U.S. Hwy. 31 N., Manistee
• (616) 723-4661
Adjacent to the inn dining room, Jonathon's Pub is a convenient spot to enjoy your favorite cocktail. Happy hour runs from 4 to 7 PM Monday through Saturday, when appetizers are free and all drinks are discounted 50¢. One of the nicest features of the pub is that you can enjoy the restaurant's full fine-dining menu in Jonathon's relaxed atmosphere (see our Restaurants chapter).

Sportsman Restaurant and Bar
110 W. Ludington Ave., Ludington
• (616) 843-2138
If the golf bug strikes but there's snow on

the ground, you'll want to reserve a tee time at Sportsman Restaurant and Bar. Sportsman's Irish Hills indoor golf center offers interactive video play using actual photography of some of the nation's top courses, including Pebble Beach and Pinehurst. Bring your own clubs or use theirs. The center is open daily from 10 AM to 10 PM from November through April. Hourly rates range from $4 to $6 per person. Downstairs in the restaurant and bar area, you'll enjoy good pub fare including pizza, steaks and soups and all your favorite drinks. A big-screen TV provides continuous sports action.

Roaring 20's Saloon
210 S. Mitchell St., Cadillac
• **(616) 775-8411**
The good times get rolling early at Roaring 20's Saloon in downtown Cadillac. The scene comes alive between 7 and 8 PM. A traditional full-service bar, the saloon offers nightly dancing, and karaoke each Thursday and Saturday night. Pool and darts are available for friendly competition. The bar offers an extensive menu but is best known for its Roaring 20's Burger, a quarter-pounder piled high with all the fixings.

Little Traverse

Boyne River Brewing Company
419 E. Main St., Boyne City
• **(616) 582-5588**
Want to experience some unique local color while on vacation? Try original area brews like Boyne River Brewing Company's Lake Trout Stout and Log Jam ale. View the brewing process, select from six varieties on tap or enjoy a light meal in the dining area or outdoor beer garden (see our Restaurants chapter).

Bear River Brewing Co.
317 E. Lake St., Petoskey
• **(616) 348-8467**
If you're among the ranks of microbrew devotees, you'll want to try Bear River Brewing Company's pride and joy, Gaslight Gold, a light, pleasing ale, or Zach's Red Wagon, a more complex, dry brew. The family-friendly establishment serves lunch and dinner daily throughout the summer and features a game room. See our Restaurants chapter for the complete listing.

Sidedoor Saloon
1200 N. U.S. Hwy. 31, Petoskey
• **(616) 347-9291**
Sidedoor Saloon is Petoskey's neighborhood bar where town professionals and blue-collar workers unite with one purpose in mind: relaxation. Sidedoor Saloon's full-service bar offers domestic and import beers and features a good wine list. There's also a full menu featuring steaks and whitefish and tasty wrap-style sandwiches.

Mackinac Straits

Ice House Bar and Grill
Behind the Island House, Huron St., Mackinac Island • (906) 847-3347
The Ice House Bar and Grill is off the beaten path, but simply ask directions in the Island House lobby or walk along the path around the side of the building and pool. You'll quickly be at the front door. This pleasant pub carries an informal light daily dining menu along with a full beverage bar.

Mustang Lounge
Astor St., Mackinac Island
• **(906) 847-9916**
The Mustang Lounge serves brews and burgers throughout the year. This island gathering spot has long been a favorite local hangout. Billing itself as a family tavern and eatery, it also claims to make the best burger in town.

Whether you're looking for the latest fashion, a tasty treat or the perfect gift to take to friends back home, we'll help you find it.

Shopping

Ready to shop 'til you drop? Great! We're on our way! Whether you're looking for the latest fashion, a tasty treat or the perfect gift to take to friends back home, we'll help you find it. Unique shops line our downtown streets, and much shopping is centered in the Traverse City and Petoskey areas. But, don't overlook our many small towns and villages. We didn't. Each harbors its share of charming storefronts and warm hospitality. All have wonderful downtowns that are perfect for strolling and browsing.

Traverse City's downtown is a hub for community activity as well as shopping. Petoskey's downtown hosts the Gaslight District on a hill overlooking Little Traverse Bay. In Manistee, the town's Victorian heritage is showcased in its shops' vintage architecture while Gaylord's downtown is garbed in Alpen attire. Many downtowns — Charlevoix, Harbor Springs, Mackinac Island, Ludington, Boyne City and Cadillac — sit near the sparkling waters that flow around their communities. The villages throughout Leelanau, Benzie and Antrim counties combine the charm of old-fashioned, small-town storefronts with their areas' natural beauty. All reflect the personalities of their communities.

In this chapter, we'll take you on a shopping tour through Northwest Michigan. We'll lead you to the malls, tell you about our major

shopping districts and share a sampling of local favorites. Unfortunately — as much as we would like to — we couldn't list every single store in the region. We identified well over 200 stops but, with our large geographic area, we could have easily written an entire book just on this topic.

Shopping hours and the seasons vary. In general, expect weekday and Saturday hours to hover between 10 AM and 6 PM plus at least one evening and a few hours on Sunday afternoons. Mall hours average 10 AM to 9 PM weekdays and Saturday, and noon to 6 PM on Sunday. The largest communities, Traverse City, Petoskey, Gaylord, Cadillac, Manistee and St. Ignace, will have fairly consistent hours throughout the year. Traverse City, in particular, is a year-round regional shopping hub. The more seasonal communities like Mackinac Island, Mackinaw City, Alden, Elk Rapids, Leland, Northport and Charlevoix will often have shops that reduce their schedules or close during the off-seasons.

What are the off-seasons in our northern shopping world? Again, they vary. Summer is the high season everywhere, although the actual peak dates may stretch from Memorial Day to Labor Day or mid-June to mid-August. Summer in the seasonal communities usually means longer hours. Things start to wind down after Labor Day but continue to be busy through

INSIDERS' TIP

Read all about it! Northwest Michigan is home to a wealth of authors including novelist Jim Harrison, children's author Gloria Whelan, romance novelist Terry Lawrence and poet Gwen Frostic. Even Ernest Hemingway had summer roots on Walloon Lake. For a flavor of the region from the pens of its residents try reading: *Letters from the Leelanau and Lake Country* by Kathy Stocking of Lake Leelanau; *Once on this Island* or *Where the Blueberries Grow* by Gloria Whelan; *Winona's Web* and *The Spider Game* by Priscilla Cogan; the Nick Adams stories by Ernest Hemingway; and the many novels by Jim Harrison.

October for the color season. This is when Friday and weekend hours are still strong but the weekday hour might get cut back. By late October, some of the seasonal shops will have closed but might reopen on weekends during the holidays. Many will continue through New Year's. Winter is busy near the ski areas but quiet in the summer communities. If an establishment is going to close, it will probably be between January and March. By spring, things gear up again as shopkeepers welcome early season visitors and prepare for summer.

Unless otherwise noted you can assume the shops are open year round.

Ready to shop? Let's get started.

Shopping Districts

Grand Traverse

Traverse City Area

Cherryland Mall
1148 S. Airport Rd., Traverse City
• (616) 946-1500

Cherryland Mall was Northwest Michigan's first mall when it opened its doors in 1976. It continued as the region's only for the next 15 years until the Grand Traverse Mall set up shop. Cherryland is a smaller mall by today's mega-standards but its more intimate layout makes for comfortable walking among the stores. Design accents reflect elements of the north woods. The mall is anchored by Sears, Younkers and Kmart with a bevy of lesser-known but unique shops connecting along the way. You'll find specialty gift shops like Blue Moon Gallery, Korner Gem, Memory Makers, Ravissant, Rose Petal, Paper Caper Gift Shoppe and Candles, and Creams and Dreams, along with local shops for Waldenbooks, Winkleman's clothing, Camelot Music, GNC Nutrition Centers, Footlocker, Kids Carousel resale shop, CPI Photo and Paging and Cellular Express.

Downtown Traverse City
Front and Union Sts., Traverse City
• (616) 922-2050

Small-town charm is the heartbeat of downtown Traverse City. Cozy tree-lined streets, bricked walkways, unique storefronts and friendly shopkeepers create a wonderful ambiance. Parallel to West Grand Traverse Bay one block away, downtown stretches from the 100 block of West Front Street through the 300 block of East Front Street along with the side streets of Park, Cass and Union. Union Street, whose storefronts stretch to the 500 block, is also referred to as Old Town, which hearkens back to its late 1800s roots.

Many of the shops are special and several have been noted individually in the full shopping listings that follow. Merchants in the district have worked ambitiously the past several years to establish downtown as a distinctive shopping destination and an alternative to mall shopping. Their efforts have resulted in a refurbished streetscape, more uniform and expanded shopping hours, coordinated special events and the introduction of several new shops and eateries. Events are held throughout the year to draw shoppers to downtown. Among the favorites are summer's Friday Night Live, holiday festivities between Thanksgiving and New Year's, the Vasa ski sprints in February and the Cherry Festival parades in July (see our Annual Events chapter).

Grand Traverse Mall
U.S. Hwy. 31 and South Airport Rd.,
Traverse City • (616) 922-0077

Grand Traverse Mall entered Traverse City with a splash in 1991 as the "new mall" in town, introducing several major chains to Northwest Michigan. The mall is anchored by Hudson's, JCPenney, Target and T. J. Maxx, with more than 65 other shops and services. For clothing, you'll find recognizable names such as American Eagle Outfitters, Casual Corner, Victoria's Secret, Lerner New York, Express, Structure, Lane Bryant and Petite Sophisticate as well as local apparel shops J. Phillips, Northern Reflections and Traverse Bay

www.insiders.com

See this and many other **Insiders' Guide®** destinations online — in their entirety.

Visit us today!

Satisfying customers since 1966

- Beautiful gift baskets & assortments
- Hand-made fine chocolates
- Cherry treasures & other area gifts
- Major credit cards accepted
- Free catalog

Legendary Cherry Products Shipped For All Occasions
800-438-9444

Marge & Cal Little,
Proprietors
E-mail: clittle@freeway.net

Retail Store @ Campus Plaza
1215 E Front St. (Near Garfield)
Traverse City, MI 49686

Open M-F 9:30-5:30; Sat 9:30-5; Sun 9:30-2

Woolen. Electronics range from Disc Jockey for music, Suncoast Motion Picture Company for videos and Software, Etc., and Radio Shack for computer items. Specialty shops include Kountry Kids and Collectibles, the Disney Store, Outback Earthwoman, and Nature of Things. You'll also find a number of shops for jewelry, fashion accessories, books, shoes, skin care, pets and various services. A large food court hosts at least 12 eateries with shared seating. The focal point of the food court is a full-size reproduction of an antique carousel, which delights little ones with rides. Older children prefer Pocket Change, video arcade tucked into a nearby corner. At one end of the mall, GKC Theaters operates an eight-screen movie theatre.

Grand Traverse Crossing
Airport Rd. east of U.S. Hwy. 31,
Traverse City • (616) 933-0412

Grand Traverse Crossing is Traverse City's newest shopping area. It lies directly across the street from the Grand Traverse Mall in an area that is quickly developing into a major shopping hub. The layout is complemented by tasteful landscaping and a signature tower at the entrance. There are only a few stores at Grand Traverse Crossing, but they are huge. All are major national companies like Borders Books and Music, Toys 'R' Us, Staples, Wal-Mart, Eastern Mountain Sports, PetsMart and Home Depot. Two restaurants, Chili's and Fazoli's, are also on site.

Horizon Outlet Center
3639 Market Place Cir. off U.S. Hwy. 31,
Traverse City • (616) 941-9211,
(800) 866-5900

The Horizon Outlet Center brings discount shopping to the Grand Traverse area. An array of national brands are sold at manufacturers' direct prices at such outlet shops at Dansk, Corning Revere Factory Store, Sunglass Hut, Kitchen Collection, Bass Outlet, Levi's Outlet By Design, Book Warehouse, Paper Factory, Carter's Childrenswear and Russell. An added highlight is the GKC Horizon Cinemas, with 10 movie screens, that anchors the center's south end.

Grand Traverse Resort Tower Gallery of Shops
100 Grand Traverse Village Blvd., Acme
• (616) 938-2100

The Grand Traverse Resort provides an elegant setting for the Tower Gallery of Shops. The merchants offer a unique selection of high-quality shopping. You'll find American Spoon Foods, Ragamuffin and Bartling's (see subsequent individual listings) as well as Bartling's sister store, J. Rogers, Ltd., which also spe-

Photo: Kevin Poirier

Farmers markets are a great way to get a taste of the region.

"Your one STOP cherry store"

Bring Home the Taste of Traverse City or let us send it to you!

- Frozen & Dried Cherries
- Fresh Cherries in Season
- Cherry Butter & Jams
- Pleva Meat Products
- Dried Fruit Munch Mixes
- The Cookbook Nook
- Fruit Syrups • The Teapot Spot
- Michigan Made Products
- Chocolate Cherries
- Fresh Roasted Coffee • Cherry Juice
- Convenient Front Door Parking

Premium Fruit Products & Gifts
Home of Orchards' Harvest
Full Service Mail Order

426 W. Front Street • Traverse City, MI 49684
3 blocks west of Union St. next to Folgarelli's
(616) 929-3990
Out of area mail order or catalog: **(800) 286-7209**
e-mail: foodie@aol.com • www.wdweb.com/orchardsharvest

cializes in women's apparel. Other shops include The Art Company for unique home elements, Merry Crystal for elegant Christmas and crystal collectibles, Orvis Streamside Shop for the outdoors enthusiast, Diverzions for games and books, Photeos for photos and supplies, Soaps and Scents for items for the bath, and Relish for wine, cheese, gourmet snacks, rich chocolates or a hot cappuccino to go.

Leelanau County

Fishtown
River St. between Main St. and Lake Michigan, Leland

Leland's Fishtown looks similar to photos and paintings of it from the 1930s on display in local museums. Registered as a Michigan Historical Site, Fishtown consists of a clustered line of weathered buildings and shanties lining the edge of the Carp River (also known as the Leland River). It has served as a commercial fishing district for local residents for over a century. Other buildings were re-

worked during the 1970s into charming gift shops appealing to the constant stream of summer visitors. Carlson's Fisheries sells its signature whitefish pâté and fresh whitefish against a backdrop of vintage photos showing previous generations of Carlsons at work on their fishing boats. You'll also find shops with wine and cheese, shoes, cards, novelties and gifts. If you plan to visit one of the Manitou Islands, Fishtown is your stop to purchase boat tickets.

Antrim-Kalkaska

Downtown Alden

Tiny Alden's "downtown" stretches along the curving East Torch Lake Drive (County Road 593) that winds through the center of this charming village nestled near the southern shores of Torch Lake. The shops are small, quaint and definitely one of a kind with names like The Red Eye Gallery, Nature Connection, Handiworks, Ltd., Carter Candles, Jean Antiques and the Lonesome Loon. Most of the stores are open daily between mid-May and mid-October. The village hosts its summer evening strolls with minstrels and lively street entertainment on Thursday during July and August when shopping hours extend to 9 PM. Several stores are also open during the holidays while Higgins Store, Alden State Bank, Rainbow Realty, Kountry Kitchen and The Alden Bar are open all year.

Gaylord's Alpine Village
Main St., Downtown Gaylord

Gaylord's entire downtown has adopted an Alpen theme with storefronts punctuated with spires and shake shingles. Shops are local ranging from the Alphorn Sport Shop, Glenda's Gifts, Sue's Shops and the Apollo-Schulz bookstore.

Lake Michigan Shoreline and Cadillac

Downtown Manistee
Along River St. between Hancock and Cedar Sts.

Manistee's Victorian downtown business district is on the National Register of Historic Places. The great lumber barons left a legacy of opulent architecture in the riverside commercial district that today houses shops like Cornerstone Antiques & Collectibles, Hollyhock, The Sandpiper and Surroundings. A mile-long riverwalk connects the vintage downtown with the Lake Michigan waterfront. It's a great combination for strolling, browsing and taking in some history all at the same time.

Little Traverse

Downtown Charlevoix
Along Bridge St. and Mich. Hwy. 66

Charlevoix the Beautiful has it all: sparkling water, balmy breezes, great restaurants and charming shops where browsing is an art form. Downtown Charlevoix is one of the most pleasant shopping areas you'll ever come across. When you've had your fill of specialty shops and galleries, take a leisurely stroll down to the marina.

Petoskey's Gaslight Shopping District
Between U.S. Hwy. 31 and Division St., Petoskey

Petoskey's Gaslight Shopping District has earned a national reputation for its distinctive downtown. A destination in its own right, the eclectic collection of exclusive Gaslight shops is within view of beautiful Little Traverse Bay. You'll find dozens of galleries, gift and specialty shops, boutiques, antique dealers and charming bistros and cafes to enjoy a meal or snack. Some of the places you won't want to miss are Grandpa Shorter's Gifts, Hank's Dad, Christmas in the Country and the Rocking Horse Toy Company, Arktos Gallery and the Whistling Moose Studio.

Mackinac Straits

Mackinaw Crossings
248 S. Huron Ave., Mackinaw City
• (616) 436-5030

Mackinaw Crossings has brought a brand new wave of retail and entertainment to the Straits Area. Complementing the existing stretch of gift shops along Central Street, the Mackinaw Crossings is a colorful cluster of shops around six courts where street artists and performers entertain visitors every hour. A free laser-light show illuminates the sky every evening at dusk in the Performance Court. The Food Court and nearby Restaurant Court currently host eight eateries or confectioneries. Outdoor seating areas are ample and spacious for dining or simply resting. Shops are geared toward the tourist crowd but offer something for all tastes. You'll find Harbor Wear, Classic Video and Teysen's Gallery and Gift Shop in the Central Court; the Wings of Mackinaw butterfly garden, The Shirt Company, The Artist's Corner and a five screen cinema in the Theatre Court; The Michigan Peddler, Mackinac Trails and Third Rock in the Performance Court; and Mackinaw Wheels, The Mango Tree and The Lighthouse Grog & Tobacco Shoppe in the Huron Court. A large live entertainment theater is under construction and slated to open in 1998. Mackinaw Crossings is seasonal. Recent hours have been 10 AM to 6 PM Sunday through Thursday, and 9 AM to 9 PM on Friday and Saturday from May 1 to June 20 and September 2 to November 1. Between June 21 and Labor Day it is open 9 AM to 9 PM daily.

Antiques

Many Northwest Michigan antique dealers, especially those in our Grand Traverse and Shoreline geographic areas, are included in a regional "Map of Antique Shops — The Northwestern Michigan Region." This publication is compiled by local dealers and includes a highlighted map, shop listings, hours, seasonal restrictions and directions as well as major antique shows. Maps are available at area Visitors Bureaus, Chambers of Commerce and travel information stands. Several major antique shows are held each year. Our favorites are: Traverse Area Antique Club Show and Sale usually held over an early April weekend inside Howe Arena in Traverse City; the National Cherry Festival Antiques Show and Sale, usually held in mid-July during the festival's second weekend on the Civic Center grounds in Traverse City; and, the Petoskey Summer Antiques Festival, usually held during the first weekends in July and August at the Emmet County Fairgrounds in Petoskey (see our Annual Events chapter).

Grand Traverse

Traverse City Area

Antique Company East Bay
4386 U.S. Hwy. 31 N., Traverse City
• (616) 938-3000

The Antique Company East Bay is tucked into a corner building between the Troutsman and Traverse Bay Woolen Company, across from the curving East Grand Traverse Bay shoreline. It's easy to miss but well worth the effort to find. The Antique Company actually houses 25 selective dealers who promise to find whatever you're seeking. Open daily between May and December, it's open on Friday and weekends only between January and April.

NORTH COUNTRY GARDENS

Distinctive Gifts for Everyone and Every Occasion

Truely an unique shopping experience!

Don't miss

North Country Gardens
NORTHPORT
1-800-551-5031

109 Nagonaba St. • 386-5031

STORE HOURS:
Monday–Saturday 10–5, Sunday 12–4

www.northcountrygardens.com

Antique Emporium
565 W. Blue Star Dr., Traverse City
• **(616) 943-3658**

An excellent collection of antiques from toys to Tiffany await visitors to the Antiques Emporium, just off U.S. 31 South. You'll find fine art, lamps and furniture and other general items.

Bay West Antiques
221 W. Grandview Pkwy., Traverse City
• **(616) 947-3211**

You'll spot Bay West Antiques with its large glass storefront and ever-changing, whimsical messages out front. Inside you'll find a large array of antiques, collectibles and selected crafts.

Chum's Corner Antique Mall
4200 U.S. Hwy. 31 S., Traverse City
• **(616) 943-4200**

The Chum's Corner Antique Mall is virtually a furniture gallery. You'll find Victorian, primitive, revival and wicker pieces as well as linens, glass, china, sports collectibles, postcards, kitchen items, toys and dolls offered by a number of dealers.

Walt's Antiques
2513 Nelson Rd., Traverse City
• **(616) 223-4123, (616) 223-7386**

Walt's Antiques is known for its vintage gas pumps, globes and advertising displayed near the entrance to this Old Mission peninsula shop. Also featured are fine china glassware, vintage clothing, buttons and jewelry as well as a general line of antiques. Though it's open most of the year, call ahead for winter hours.

Wilson Antiques
123 S. Union St., Traverse City
• **(616) 946-4177**

Centrally located in the heart of downtown, Wilson's Antiques features the wares of more than 50 quality dealers. Fine antiques and collectibles are shown on four floors in a building that had previously been a longtime furniture store.

Leelanau County

The Old Library
103 E. River St., Leland • (616) 256-7428, (616) 256-9119

The Old Library is an appropriate name for this 1920s-era historic building. Today, this former library houses quality antiques along with a lovely selection of contemporary gifts. The shop is open daily during the summer and on a reduced schedule during the remainder of the year. Call ahead for off-season hours.

Bird-In-Hand
123 Nagonaba St., Northport
• **(616) 386-7104**

This is the spot to shop for vintage clothing, accessories and, especially, hats from the 1800s to the 1920s. You'll also find linens, petit point accessories, glassware and furniture. This shop is filled with Victorian charm. Hours vary, so call ahead.

Grandma's Trunk
102 Mill St., Northport • (616) 386-5351

Grandma's Trunk carries a general line of antiques with an added emphasis on antique paper, trade cards, postcards and local crafts. You can buy dried flowers in bulk or choose from the many ready-made arrangements often in antique containers that are on display. Grandma's Trunk is open from May to December.

Applegate Collection
405 N. St. Joseph St., Suttons Bay
• **(616) 271-5252**

Applegate Collection is the antique wicker

INSIDERS' TIP

Join the downtown community celebrations that fill the region's summer calendars. In Traverse City, Friday Night Live combines shopping with a huge block party on summer Fridays. Alden hosts its Evening Strolls with buskers and minstrels on summer Thursdays. Many towns share music and summer sunsets at local park concerts.

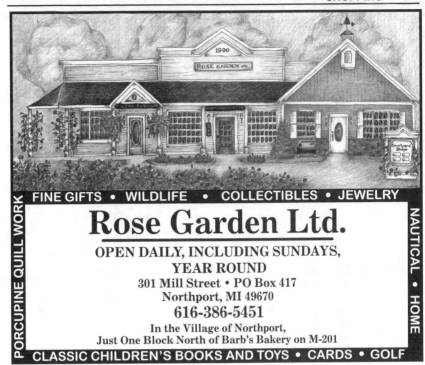

PORCUPINE QUILL WORK

FINE GIFTS • WILDLIFE • COLLECTIBLES • JEWELRY

Rose Garden Ltd.

**OPEN DAILY, INCLUDING SUNDAYS,
YEAR ROUND**
301 Mill Street • PO Box 417
Northport, MI 49670
616-386-5451
In the Village of Northport,
Just One Block North of Barb's Bakery on M-201

NAUTICAL • HOME

CLASSIC CHILDREN'S BOOKS AND TOYS • CARDS • GOLF

connection for the region. The shop also carries antique and new accessories. The wicker has been cited by *House Beautiful* magazine for its quality.

Danbury Antiques
305 St. Joseph St., Suttons Bay
• (616) 271-3211

Danbury Antiques specializes in quality English smalls for the discriminating collector. Items include brasses, boxes, ceramics ranging from ink wells to candlesticks to coal scuttles. These miniatures were selected for the shop during frequent buying trips throughout England.

Leelanau Architectural Antiques
301 St. Joseph St., Suttons Bay
• (616) 271-6821

Leelanau Architectural Antiques carries a unique selection of quality American antiques, stained and beveled glass windows, doors, fireplace mantles and furniture crafted in oak,

cherry and walnut. This shop is open from May to November and by appointment.

Up North Antiques
311 N. St. Joseph St., Suttons Bay
• (616) 271-5400

Up North Antiques evokes memories of the region's cool summers and frosty winters with its thoughtful and amusing collection of antiques. The selection is eclectic. Look for primitives to sterling silver and etchings to arts and crafts furniture.

Antrim-Kalkaska

Kalkaska Antiques
324 S. Cedar St., Kalkaska
• (616) 258-5500

General lines of quality antiques are shown at Kalkaska Antiques. The large multi-dealer showroom features more than 5,000 square feet of display space. The shop is at the crosswalk in the heart of downtown Kalkaska.

Antrim Antiques
9053 E. Torch Lake Dr. (Cty. Rd. 593), Alden • (616) 331-6468, (616) 331-6562

Antrim Antiques has one of the largest selections of vintage quilts in Michigan. The shop also carries painted furniture, fishing and sports collectibles and a line of general antiques. Antrim Antiques is centrally located in the tiny village of Alden's charming downtown. It is open from Memorial Day to mid-October.

Talponia Books, Limited
10545 Coy St., Alden • (616) 331-6324

Book lovers will love to visit Talponia Books nestled with the charming shops in downtown Alden. The shop specializes in antique, rare and limited editions. The owners will also assist with book searches and appraisals.

Sentimental Journey
7208 Cherry Ave., Kewadin
• (616) 264-6955, (616) 264-9869

The selection is always changing at Sentimental Journey. You'll find antique furniture, primitives, collectibles, folk art, fine china, glassware, linens, kitchen items, books and many unique treasures. The shop is open from May through October.

Lake Michigan Shoreline and Cadillac

The Granary Antique Market
7300 Crystal Ave., Beulah
• (616) 882-4299

Antiques, art and fine wines, the Granary has it all. This market features 10,000 square feet of antiques and art packed into a historic grain mill. After looking over the antiques, enjoy tasting Leelanau wines and browse through the shop's selection of gourmet foods.

Cornerstone Antiques & Collectibles
Corner of River and Maple Sts., Manistee
• (616) 398-9089

A general dealer, Cornerstone carries dishes, linens, toys, a nice selection of farm tools, glassware and more. Located in one of Manistee's historic downtown buildings, the best part of visiting the shop is a trip to the "dungeon" room where you'll find brick cellar walls lined with collectibles.

Cole's Antiques Villa
322 W. Ludington Ave., Ludington
• (616) 845-7414

Cole's offers quality antiques for the discriminating collector. Their selection includes furniture, country decoratives, primitives, pottery, glassware, advertising and tools. Cole's is open daily May through December, and Friday through Monday January through April.

Sunset Bay Antiques
404 S. James St., Ludington
• (616) 843-1559

Enjoy antiquing in Sunset Bay's newly restored 1890s building. They offer 8,000 square feet of antiques, art, collectibles and decorative accessories. Take a few moments to relax at their espresso bar. January through May, the store is open only on the weekends.

Royer's Antique Mall
211 Bell Ave., Cadillac • (616) 779-2434

Specializing in fishing items, pottery and depression glass, Royer's offers 4,000 square feet of treasures. Roomy aisles make it a pleasant place to browse.

Sue's Treasure Trove
433 S. Lakeshore Dr., Lake City
• (616) 839-2145

Located in a building adjacent to Sue's charming home across the street from Lake Missaukee, you'll find a good collection of general antiques including furniture, books and glassware. A longtime collector, Sue is full of knowledgeable advice. Call for hours or an appointment.

Little Traverse

Kelly's Antiques and Restoration
100 Overlook Dr., Charlevoix
• (616) 547-9409

Kelly's is the only place in the area to offer wicker repair. Restoration services include caning, repairs, stripping and refinishing. They also sell refinishing products and will even show

THE WOODEN GALLERY

FEATURING

"THE WOODEN GALLERY PROCESS"™

WITH THIS PROCESS, EXQUISITE PRINTS ARE
SATURATED AND MOUNTED WITH A SPECIFICALLY
DESIGNED ACRYLIC EMULSION WHICH ENHANCES
THE INKS AND RESULTS IN A WARM RICH LOOK WITHOUT
GLASS. THE FINAL COATS OF EMULSION ARE HAND-TEXTURED
AND INCLUDE UV PROTECTION. NEITHER HUMIDITY NOR
EXTREME CHANGES IN ROOM TEMPERATURE WILL AFFECT
THE PRODUCT. DISCOVER THIS EXCLUSIVE, LIMITED
PRODUCTION PRESENTATION DEVELOPED
BY THE WOODEN GALLERY IN
DOWNTOWN TRAVERSE CITY.

116 East Front Street • Traverse City • (616) 941-0823

you how to do it yourself. Call for hours or an appointment.

Stonehenge Gardens
02195 Mich. Hwy. 66, Charlevoix
• (616) 547-4818

Situated on an old farmstead between Charlevoix and East Jordan, this shop and its famous perennial garden is something both antique lovers and gardeners appreciate. Although it's on the highway, local ordinances restrict signing, so it's easy to drive past. To find Stonehenge, watch for a yellow hilltop house. The shop is set here, amidst a half-acre English garden graced by fences and stonework, an old grain building and two barns. It features a general line of antiques, including depression glass, porcelain, china and primitives, and specializes in Fiesta ware. Stonehenge opens Memorial Day and closes in mid-October.

Joie de Vie Antiques
1901 Mich. Hwy. 119, Petoskey
• (616) 347-1400
152 E. Main St., Harbor Springs
• (616) 526-7700

Joie de Vie offers the area's largest selection of European furniture at affordable prices. It features armoires, farm tables, nightstands and buffets. You'll also find accessories and gift items, French linens, dishes and soaps. The Harbor Springs shop closes after Christmas for the winter.

INSIDERS' TIP

Most Mackinac Island fudge purchases don't last as long as the boat ride back across the Straits. If you can resist the temptation of these wonderful sweets, you can keep your fudge fresh by freezing it.

Joseph's World
2680 U.S. Hwy. 31 S., Petoskey
• (616) 347-0121

Joseph's World specializes in art nouveau and art deco from the 19th and 20th centuries. You'll find only the rare and unusual here. The collection includes Tiffany glass, original art and even historical treasures from King Tut's tomb. Antique art appraisal service is available.

From The Four Corners
257 E. Main St., Harbor Springs
• (616) 526-9255

You don't have to travel to the four corners of the earth to uncover exotic treasures. You'll find an array of interesting antiques, jewelry, artifacts and clothing from Greece, Turkey, India, Nepal, Burma, Laos, Thailand and Indonesia at this Harbor Springs shop. Call for off-season hours.

L'Esprit
195 W. Main St., Harbor Springs
• (616) 526-9888
220 State St., Harbor Springs
• (616) 526-9644

L'Esprit offers French Country antique furniture from the regions of Burgundy and Provence. At both L'Esprit locations you'll find whimsical garden and architectural accouterments and elegant tabletop accessories. Professional interior design services are available.

Pooter Olooms Antiques
294 E. Third St., Harbor Springs
• (616) 526-6101
339 State St., Harbor Springs
• (616) 526-6101

Pooter Olooms brings you a sophisticated blend of northern European antiques and elegant and outrageous accessories. Pieces date from the 17th century to 1950. They feature quality scrubbed pine, gorgeous fruitwood, original paint, investment-quality quilts and folk art. National delivery is available. The store is open between April and January.

Mackinac Straits

Maeve's Arts and Antiques
Huron St., Mackinac Island
• (616) 847-3755

Maeve's Arts and Antiques carries a wide selection of art, artifacts, jewelry and clothing. Items are from Michigan and around the world.

Anchor In Antiques
2122 W. U.S. Hwy. 2, St. Ignace
• (906) 643-8112, (906) 643-9917

Anchor In Antiques showcases Great Lakes nautical items as well as a general line of antiques and collectibles. The shop is large, with 1200 feet of show space, and is open from early May to mid-October.

The Emporium
110 N. State St., St. Ignace
• (906) 643-6565

A fine collection of restored antique furniture and light fixtures are found at The Emporium, right across from the Arnold Ferry dock in downtown St. Ignace. You will also find original artwork by Michigan artists and the largest supply of decorator fabrics in the upper peninsula.

Bookstores

Grand Traverse

Traverse City Area

B. Dalton Booksellers
Grand Traverse Mall, U.S. Hwy. 31 & S. Airport Rd., Traverse City
• (616) 929-0775

B. Dalton has been a staple at the Grand

INSIDERS' TIP

Gaylord's Alpen theme comes to life when the Alpine Village Glockenspiel plays atop Glen's Market grocery store. The glockenspiel plays every 15 minutes between 8 AM and 10 PM, accompanied by two dancing childlike dolls, Andre and Andrea.

Gourmet To Go

A KITCHEN SHOP AND FOOD EMPORIUM

Mary's
Kitchen
Port

539 W. Front Street • Traverse City • 941-0525

Traverse Mall since its opening. Its spacious quarters house a large children's area with ample space for regional authors and interests, bestsellers, periodicals and reading material for all interests.

Borders Books and Music
2612 Crossings Cir., Traverse City
• (616) 933-0412

Borders opened its Traverse City store in November 1996 amidst much community anticipation and excitement. Two years later, the enthusiasm is still high for Borders, books and browsing. The store is at Grand Traverse Crossing and includes the usual mix of seemingly endless books, thousands of music and video titles and an aromatic coffee bar. The periodical selection is huge, including daily newspapers from most urban centers. The children's area is large with a great spot for storytelling or simply curling up with a new book. Borders often showcases local entertainers, hosts book signings

and sponsors several book discussion groups. The shop's monthly newsletter highlights its happenings with an almost daily listing of slated events.

Horizon Books
243 E. Front St., Traverse City
• (616) 946-7290, (800) 587-2147

A Traverse City original, Horizon Books has been Northwest Michigan's bookseller for years. It is headquartered in downtown Traverse City and easily serves as one of the city's favorite anchor stores. This independent bookseller hosts an array of weekly events including a writers support group, children's stories, musical entertainment, book signings and book discussion groups. There are three floors of books including a nice children's area and an extensive periodical collection. There is a coffee bar on the main floor with windows overlooking main street, while the new Shine Cafe just opened on the lower level to serve fresh soups, salads and sandwiches. The lower level also hosts several cyberstations for patrons to surf the Web or check their e-mail. See our listings for Horizon stores in Cadillac and Petoskey.

Rainbow Bookstore
1253 S. Airport Rd., Traverse City
• **(616) 946-8800, (800) 678-1346**

The region's largest Christian bookstore, Rainbow Bookstore carries an extensive collection of books, Bibles, cards, music, videos, wedding supplies, gifts and supplies for Sunday schools and churches.

Waldenbooks
Cherryland Mall, Garfield Rd. and S. Airport Rd. W., Traverse City
• **(616) 947-1340**

Waldenbooks was the first chain bookstore to enter Northwest Michigan when it was one of the original shops that opened Cherryland Mall in the mid-'70s. Waldenbooks carries a nice general line of books and periodicals as well as children's books and local interest publications.

Leelanau County

The Cottage Book Shop
5970 S. Lake St., Glen Arbor
• **(616) 334-4223**

Tucked into the Arbor Lights Building along Glen Arbor's downtown Lake Street, The Cottage Book Shop is a cozy shop that welcomes browsing among its shelves. Titles include general fiction and nonfiction as well as children's books and regional, Great Lakes and Native American publications. Watercolor and pastel art supplies are also sold here.

Leelanau Books
109 N. Main St., Leland • (616) 256-7111

Along Leland's charming Main Street, Leelanau Books combines the relaxed ambiance of cottage life with an impressive selection of reading material. Bright white shelves line the walls, nooks and crannies of this small shop that features a well-stocked children's area and a large Michigan section as well as all of the latest reads. The friendly staff shares local tips along with assistance.

Known Books
101 Dame St., Suttons Bay
• **(616) 271-6483**

Stop by Known Books for a browse through the shop's full line of new and used books.

Suttons Bay Bookstore
100 A Cedar St., Suttons Bay
• **(616) 271-3923, (800) 850-2945**

Suttons Bay Bookstore carries a nice line of general interest new and used books as well as Michigan books, locally authored books and Native American books. You will also find greeting cards, posters, puzzles and original art.

Antrim-Kalkaska

Village Books
102 E. Cayuga St., Bellaire
• **(616) 533-6692**

Village Books is a pleasurable stop for new and used books in tiny Bellaire. It's also a great place to relax with a cup of fresh coffee, a pot of hot tea and the warmth of friendly company.

Apollo Schultz
201 E. Main St., Gaylord
• **(517) 732-3836**

This unique bookstore operates inside a vintage house on the edge of Gaylord's downtown. The house has been renovated for retail sales with ample space for adult and children's books, books on tape, and CDs as well as many corners to sit and read. The shop often hosts guest authors and guests for book signings and special events.

INSIDERS' TIP

Inventory changes daily at resale stores. If you don't find what you're looking for today, check tomorrow.

AMERICAN SPOON

*Sample from our
tasting tables:*

PETOSKEY
East Lake Street

CHARLEVOIX
Bridge Street

HARBOR SPRINGS
East Main Street

TRAVERSE CITY
E. Front Street & Grand Traverse Resort

On line Shopping
www.spoon.com

FREE CATALOG
800-222-5886

Edible treasures from the orchards, fields & forests of Northern Michigan.

Lake Michigan Shoreline and Cadillac

Bookstore LTD
330 Main St., Frankfort • (616) 352-9720

You'll be pleasantly surprised by the nice selection of books found at this small shop. They seem to have something for every reader's taste and gift items including puzzles, greeting cards and kites.

Read Mor Bookstore
348 River St., Manistee
• **(616) 723-3351**
201 S. Rath Ave., Ludington
• **(616) 843-2537**

Meet the Cat in the Hat or the Berenstain Bears in person at Read Mor stores. During the summer, costumed children's book characters appear monthly at these child-friendly shops. Call for dates. Adults will also find plenty to interest them. Both stores offer the largest selection of magazines, newspapers and books in their areas.

Cadillac Newscenter
102 S. Mitchell St., Cadillac
• **(616) 775-3000**

The Newscenter carries a good selection of new releases, classics, children's titles and the largest magazine section in town. In addition, they sell collector sport cards and feature an espresso bar with plenty of window seating.

Horizon Books
2140 N. Mitchell St., Cadillac
• **(616) 775-9979**

Horizon has one of the best selections of children's fiction and nonfiction around, a good Michigan section, magazines you won't find elsewhere, beautiful blank books and nice gift books. (See the previous Grand Traverse listing for more information.)

Little Traverse

Bridge Street Book Shop
407 Bridge St., Charlevoix
• (616) 547-READ
 Pick up the latest bestseller, sporting books and books for the kids here. There's room to browse and the coffee's always perking. They also carry books on tape, stationery and fine imported cigars.

Boyne Country Books
125 Water St., Boyne City
• (616) 582-3180
 If you're an insatiable reader you'll appreciate Boyne Country Books. Open seven days a week, they offer a good selection of bestsellers, classics and periodicals. In addition, they stock thousands of used books so you can satisfy your reading appetite without emptying your pockets. You'll also find lake charts, comics and some gift items.

Horizon Books
319 E. Mitchell St., Petoskey
• (616) 347-2590
 Like the other two Horizon stores in the area, this one has a large selection of children's books. They specialize in Michigan titles with a special emphasis on local interests and authors. The newly expanded 5,000-square-foot store has a friendly atmosphere, wide aisles and large alcoves. There's a coffee bar and comfortable seating near the warmth of a fireplace.

McLean & Eakin Booksellers
307 E. Lake St., Petoskey
• (616) 347-1180, (800) 968-1910
 McLean & Eakin's carries everything the astute reader could desire and more. You'll find an extensive travel section, a large map section, offbeat greeting cards and gifts — all in a relaxed setting. Don't miss the special section devoted to author Ernest Hemingway, who spent his youthful summers in the region.

Between the Covers
152 E. Main St., Harbor Springs
• (616) 526-6658
 An old tin ceiling and stone fireplace make this bookstore a comfortable place to browse. A full-service shop, they offer new titles, hardcovers and paperbacks. You'll find a substantial children's section and a good regional section.

Mackinac Straits

Island Bookstore
Main Street Centre, Mackinac Island
• (906) 847-6202
215 E. Central Ave., Mackinaw City
• (616) 436-BOOK
 The Island Bookstore on Mackinac Island is tucked into a cozy corner storefront underneath the Lilac Tree Hotel. The shop is filled with a wonderful selection of reading material, especially titles featuring Mackinac Island, the Straits area, the State of Michigan and regional history. The Mackinaw City shop, owned by the same family, emphasizes nature and regional books along with general lines. It also carries nature and science toys and gifts.

Clothing — Children's

Grand Traverse

Traverse City Area

Dandelion Clothing and Gifts for Kids
130 E. Front St., Traverse City
• (616) 933-4340
 Comfort and style meet the younger set at Dandelion in downtown Traverse City. This is the place to find natural-fiber clothing, unique gifts and furniture for children. The fashions are fun as well as functional. Parents, as well as their children, will have a great time perusing the racks for the perfect find.

Peek a Boo Kids & Babies
236 E. Front St., Traverse City
• (616) 933-4991
 Peek a Boo showcases fashion and furnishings for children and babies with a lovely

Photo: Courtesy of Grand Traverse Mall

A shopping outing can be fun for everyone.

selection of contemporary styles, colorful gifts, layette items and room accessories. The shop has continued growing in popularity since it opened and recently moved into much larger quarters along downtown's East Front Street.

Ragamuffin
Grand Traverse Resort, 100 Grand Traverse Village Blvd., Acme
• **(616) 938-5357**

High-quality children's fashions share space with unique toys, books and games in this colorful shop located within the Grand Traverse Resort. The Ragamuffin shops are owned by a former educator who always displays a wonderful selection of books and related toys featuring such favorite characters as Curious George, Madeline, Arthur, Linnea and the American Girls. Toys are on hand to keep little hands busy while parents browse through the beautiful selection of clothing. Ragamuffin shops are also located in Leland and Grand Rapids.

Leelanau County

Ragamuffin
110 Lake St., Leland • (616) 256-5675

Located in the shops near Fishtown, this is the Leland location for the popular Ragamuffin shop for quality children's apparel, toys,

books and gifts. See the previous Traverse City listing for more information.

Antrim-Kalkaska

Alpine Kids Stuff
147 W. Main St., Gaylord
• **(517) 732-0535**

Classic apparel for boys and girls, infants to teens, is featured at Alpine Kids Stuff in downtown Gaylord. You'll find OshKosh and Heartstrings, traditional styles, dressy outfits and high-quality playwear and outerwear. There's a lovely selection of layette items, baby toys, infantwear and gifts.

Lake Michigan Shoreline and Cadillac

ABC Kidz
123 E. Ludington Ave., Ludington
• **(616) 843-3734**

All your favorite brands in kids wear are here including Baby Guess, Guess Kids, Calvin Klein and OshKosh B'Gosh. For special-occasion wear, check out their handmade clothing in sizes 2 to 10. If you really want to stretch your budget, shop ABC's consignment section where you'll find infant and children's clothing and accessories.

Little Traverse

Circus Shop Children's Apparel
323 E. Mitchell St., Petoskey
- (616) 347-3433

You'll find what's sizzling hot in kids fashions here, including Zoodles, Flap Doodles and Tomkid wear. They offer boys and girls casual and dress clothes in sizes newborn to girls size 14 and boys size 20. You'll find a beautiful selection of Beatrix Potter items to delight your baby or to give as gifts. If you can't find the perfect crib bedding for your baby, they'll special order for you.

Richard Hanten for Children
286 E. Third St., Harbor Springs
- (616) 526-7466

Parents, get your checkbooks ready, you'll want to buy the whole store. Richard Hanten features exclusive designs for boys and girls from newborn to size 14. You'll find beautiful handknit sweaters and smocked items, appliqued sweats, brother/sister and mother/daughter matching outfits. The store opens from mid-June through mid-September.

Clothing — Men's and Women's

Grand Traverse

Traverse City Area

Bartling's
225 E. Front St., Traverse City
- (616) 946-8002
100 Grand Traverse Village Blvd., Acme
- (616) 938-5298
110 N. Lake St., Leland • (616) 256-9670
5820 Shanty Creek Rd., Bellaire
- (616) 533-6203

Bartling's has been a leader in bringing top-quality women's fashions to Northwest Michigan for decades. This family-owned shop is based in downtown Traverse City with additional storefronts at the Grand Traverse Resort, Shanty Creek and in Leland. Styles range from upscale resort-wear to stylish professional attire, and from glittering evening clothes to innovative outerwear. Accessories are unique with a wonderful selection of innovative jewelry.

Cali's Cottons
242 E. Front St., Traverse City
- (616) 947-0633

Cali's is the place to find great natural-fiber women's clothing in functional, comfortable, creative styles. This longtime downtown shop also carries imaginative accessories appropriate for teens as well as adults. Items for the home are featured on the shop's upper level.

Captain's Quarters
151 E. Front St., Traverse City
- (616) 946-7066
101 Bridge St., Bellaire • (616) 533-8139

Family-owned Captain's Quarters combines friendly, small-town service with a nice selection of men's fine clothing, formal wear and sportswear. Whether you're looking for a business suit or a swimsuit, owners Maurie Allen and son Jason are usually on hand to make sure you find the styles that fit. Captain's Quarters also operates a seasonal shop in Bellaire and Tuxedo World at the Grand Traverse Mall, (616) 935-1733.

J.J. Skivvies Clothing
212 E. Front St., Traverse City
- (616) 946-9663

Boxers and pajamas brought J.J. Skivvies its reputation as a fun shop for comfortable attire. Clothing is Michigan-made with a promise of homestyle comfort. Look for colorful flannel pants and boxer shorts as well as fleece sweats and knits for lounging away a Sunday afternoon.

Pratt's
215 E. Front St., Traverse City
- (616) 946-2020

Traditional men's clothing and sportswear have been the staples on which Pratt's has built its high-quality reputation. Look for classic styles by Polo, Nautica and Tommy Bahama. Pratt's also features a beautiful selection of Waterford crystal.

Photo: Courtesy of Grand Traverse Mall

Our shopping areas offer many amenities.

Raven's Child
101 W. Front St., Traverse City
• **(616) 941-8552**

Raven's Child is advertised as a grown-up boutique for the young at heart. This downtown shop has an avid following across the ages. Its comfortable, free-flowing styles are distinctive, fun and reasonably priced.

Stage-Milliken
204 E. Front St., Traverse City
• **(616) 947-5140**

Stage-Milliken's heritage dates back to the late 1800s when the Milliken family first opened the shop in the center of this lumbering town. Until the late 1970s, the department store was owned and operated by the same, longtime Traverse City family that produced generations of community leaders including Michigan's governor from 1969-1982, William G. Milliken. Today, it is part of a Midwest chain of department stores but continues to serve as a downtown anchor store specializing in fashions and accessories for men, women and children. The mezzanine-level tea room has been a favorite meeting place for lunch or coffee for generations. Stage-Milliken has also maintained downtown stores in Manistee and Cadillac for decades.

Tootsies
118 S. Union St., Traverse City
• **(616) 947-9930**

You'll find unique and whimsical footwear for the young and young at heart at Tootsies.

INSIDERS' TIP

If you just have to have that 3-foot handcarved bear, or some other unwieldy souvenir, ask your sales clerk about shipping. Many area shops will ship gift and specialty items anywhere in the nation.

Locals affectionately call tourists "fudgies," because the visitors are so fond of the region's fudge.

Shoes are funky and modern, which makes this shop quite popular among teens and recent teens. In addition to shoes, you'll also find sunglasses, necklaces and a palette of memorable accessories.

Traverse Bay Woolen Company
4290 U.S. Hwy. 31 N., Traverse City
• **(616) 938-1250**
4833 U.S. Hwy. 10 W., Ludington
• **(616) 843-3540**
312 E. Lake St., Petoskey
• **(616) 347-7882**
312 S. Huron St., Mackinaw City
• **(616) 436-5402**

Traverse Bay Woolen Company has represented the spirit of the north since opening its first shop in 1947. The stores, which look like enormous cedar log cabins, are filled with the natural essence of the north. Look for ant-ler chandeliers, stone fireplaces, rustic seating and pine boughs and birch branches. The shops, located in Traverse City, Ludington, Petoskey and Mackinaw City, carry an outstanding collection of natural-fiber sweaters, durable outerwear, Hudson Bay blankets, rustic furniture and accessories, gifts and keepsakes. Look for brands like Woolrich, Timberland and Hudson Bay in styles for all ages. This is a north-woods "must stop" shop.

Leelanau County

Sandi's of Glen Arbor
6544 W. Western Ave., Glen Arbor
• **(616) 334-4044**

Sandi's of Glen Arbor carries a nice selection of classic ladies apparel and accessories. Lines feature David Brooks, Robert Scott, Susan Bristol and Geiger of Austria. The shop carries beautiful sweaters and complementing accessories.

Molly's
105 Main St., Leland • (616) 256-7540

Molly's carries a great selection of colorful, contemporary sweaters and lovely lines of women's clothing in comfortable, stylish designs. Like so much of Leland, the shop is cozy and charming with friendly, personal service.

Bahle's
210 St. Joseph St., Suttons Bay
• (616) 271-3841

Bahle's has been outfitting this corner of northern Michigan since 1876. This spacious, family-owned business anchors downtown Suttons Bay with a great selection of classic, casual and outdoor clothing for men and women. Several members of the recent generations of Bahles can be found managing the store and helping customers daily. The shop is a Michigan Centennial business and a registered historic site.

BG's Saddlery & Boutique
326 St. Joseph St., Suttons Bay
• (616) 271-3334

BG's is the place for pedestrian or equestrian fashions. The shop features apparel, footwear, gifts and jewelry for horse lovers and those loving the Western spirit. You'll find the Australian Outback collection, unique boutique items, books and custom horse apparel.

Antrim-Kalkaska

Alpine Apparel Co.
133 W. Main St., Gaylord
• (517) 732-7560

The Alpine Apparel Co. carries a broad selection of high-quality men's and women's apparel as well as specialty gifts. Located in the heart of downtown, it is one of Gaylord's largest department stores and has been a long-time favorite among locals and visitors.

Annie B's
232 W. Main St., Gaylord
• (517) 732-4811

Annie B's is known for its great selection of women's clothing and northern Michigan

apparel. This is a great place to come for handknit sweaters and a wonderful selection of accessories.

Lake Michigan Shoreline and Cadillac

Fernand Footwear
7 Milliron Ln., Benzonia • (616) 882-9622

In a time-honored tradition, Fernand Footwear custom-makes shoes and sandals in comfortable, easy-to-wear styles. Each sole is cut to fit the customer and shoes are constructed by hand from beginning to end. Orders take about three weeks to fill. If you prefer not to wait that long, you can take home a selection from their inventory. Custom sandals and shoes run between $44 and $160, depending on style.

Field Crafts
1058 Michigan Ave., Benzonia
• (616) 882-5885

You can find great bargains in resort wear at Field Crafts in Benzonia. Field Crafts has artistic screened and embroidered apparel featuring designs by some of northern Michigan's best-known wildlife artists. In the store's upper level you'll find their best quality T-shirts, sweats and fashion tops in men's, women's and children's sizes. The lower level is where you'll find the best deals. It features an outlet for overruns and seconds.

Stage-Milliken
400 River St., Manistee • (616) 723-3541
115 S. Mitchell St., Cadillac
• (616) 775-9757

Stage-Milliken department stores offer contemporary fashions for the entire family. You'll also find casual and dress shoes, cosmetics, accessories and gifts. See the previous Grand Traverse listing for the Milliken story.

Raven's Mens Wear
111 E. Ludington Ave., Ludington
• (616) 843-4560

From suiting to blue jeans, this shop will outfit you for the way you want to live. They carry many popular brands including Levi's, Joe Boxer, Hager, Union Bay, Woolrich, Girbaud and more.

Traverse Bay Woolen Company
4833 W. U.S. Hwy. 10, Ludington
• **(616) 843-3540**

Traverse Bay Woolen Company has adult clothing selected to celebrate the spirit of the north. Located in a historic log structure, you'll love their selection of outerwear, sheepskin slippers, blankets and accessories. See the previous Grand Traverse listing for more information on the company's northern Michigan stores.

R.J. Grants
109 N. Mitchell St., Cadillac
• **(616) 775-5641**

Personal, friendly service and a distinctive line of dress and casual wear makes R.J. Grants an easy place to shop. In downtown Cadillac, they carry leading names in both men and women's wear.

Little Traverse

Chicos
205 Howard St., Petoskey
• **(616) 347-2999**

Chicos features women's casual, easy-to-wear clothing in natural cottons, twills and rayons. Their line of slacks, shirts and tops are sophisticated, but washable and easy to care for too. You'll also find all the accessories you need for these comfortable styles, including jewelry, belts and purses.

Clothes Post
326 E. Mitchell St., Petoskey
• **(616) 347-4562**

The only strictly men's clothing shop in the area, the Clothes Post offers updated tra-ditional and contemporary wear from top designers and companies such as Corbin, Palm Beach, Cole-Hann, Gant and Woolrich. They carry everything from socks to topcoats, so you'll find what you need whether you're dressing for sailing, an important business meeting or a formal dinner.

Mettlers
400 Bay St., Petoskey • **(616) 347-1208**
211 Bridge St., Charlevoix
• **(616) 547-4035**
106 E. Main St., Harbor Springs
• **(616) 526-2197**

Based in Florida, Mettlers operates three clothing stores in the Little Traverse area. They carry updated traditional clothing for men, women, infants and toddlers and designer fashions for all occasions. The Petoskey location is open daily year round. The Harbor Springs store is open May through October, and the Charlevoix location has limited winter hours, so call ahead.

Pappagallo
402 E. Lake St., Petoskey
• **(616) 347-5830**

A name known across the country, Pappagallo's has the updated classic look in women's business and casual wear. It's one of the best places in the area to shop for business suits. They feature styles from Robert Scott, David Brooks, Corbin and Austin Reed. You'll also find a tantalizing selection of Pappagallo shoes, jewelry, hats and scarves

Traverse Bay Woolen
312 E. Lake St., Petoskey
• **(616) 347-7782**

For a relaxed northern look, check out the stylish flannels and woolens for men and women. For a complete listing, see the previous Grand Traverse section.

INSIDERS' TIP

The Boon Store, on a designated snowmobile trail in rural Wexford County, keeps a bonfire going from Friday afternoon until Sunday evening during the winter months. It's a popular pit stop for hearty snow machine drivers who have an open invitation to warm and refresh themselves.

Frivolous Sal's
210 E. Main St., Harbor Springs
- **(616) 526-6006**

Sal's boutique features original fashions, in all sizes, for women who like to dress with flair. To complete your look, visit Frivolous Soles at 236 E. Main Street, (616) 526-8890, also in Harbor Springs. Here, you'll find a good selection of resort shoes and accessories, just for the ladies.

Hilda of Harbor
107 W. Main St., Harbor Springs
- **(616) 526-6914**

This contemporary and upscale shop is packed with wonderful and hard-to-find designer apparel for men, women and children. You'll find men's clothing from Axis and Haupt, Barbour outerwear and shoes from Mephisto and Cole-Hann. In women's wear, you'll find styles from Lilly Pulitzer, handknit sweaters and designer coats. The infant, boys and girls clothing line features Sammi outerwear.

Mackinac Straits

Winkelman's Clothing and Shoe Store
40 N. State St., St. Ignace
- **(906) 643-7631**

Winkelman's is Mackinac County's largest department store. Serving the entire Straits area, it carries a full array of men's, women's and children's clothing and footwear. You'll find good quality and plenty of favorite brand names.

Nadia's Fashion Shop
Fort St., Mackinac Island
- **(906) 847-3709**

Nadia's specializes in casual and active footwear and apparel for men and women with brands like David Brooks, St. Croix, Cutter & Buck, City Girl, Guess, Calvin Klein, Columbia, Rockport, Reebok, Fila and Simple Shoes. The shop carries the area's largest selection of Tundra and Coogi sweaters.

Nephew's of Mackinac
Huron St., Mackinac Island
- **(906) 847-3462**

Women on the left, men on the right! Dis-play racks down the center of this pleasant shop literally divide it in half, separating each respective gender's clothing lines. Nephew's caters to many tastes with a broad selection of men's and women's outerwear, swimwear, casual sportswear, dressier evening clothes and shoes. Looking over the brands, you'll find such old favorites as Liz Claiborne, Polo and Nautica.

Farmers Markets

Grand Traverse

Amon Orchards
7404 U.S. Hwy. 31 N., Acme
- **(616) 938-1644, (800) 937-1644**

A visit to Amon Orchards is part shopping, part education and part family fun. This commercial orchard hosts Grandma Amon's farm market filled with its unique cherry products, home-baked goods and endless taste samples. Added activities include orchard tours, u-pick fruit, seasonal events and a weekend petting zoo. (See our Kidstuff chapter for more information about activities.)

Gallagher Farm Market
7237 Mich. Hwy. 72 W., Traverse City
- **(616) 947-1689**

This large roadside market features cherries, apples, peaches, apricots, plums and a variety of seasonal vegetables.

Selkirk's
302 E. Front St., Traverse City
- **(616) 946-0366**

Carts of seasonal flowers, fruits and vegetables overflow from Selkirk's corner spot in downtown Traverse City. The market's shop is a charmingly converted former 1920s gas station that also features a full line of locally produced jams, jellies and canned products.

Traverse City Farmer's Market
Grandview Pkwy. between Cass and Union Sts., Traverse City

Every week area farmers gather under bright blue canopies to sell their wares along the Boardman River in downtown Traverse City. Along with the freshest produce, you'll find baked

Photo: Kevin Poirier

Shoppers walk the streets of downtown Traverse City on a nice spring afternoon.

goods, bedding plants, fresh honey, homemade preserves, handcrafted items and a contagious air of energy. Bring along some bread crusts or buy a Dixie cup filled with corn to feed the ducks that nonchalantly stroll the river banks behind the farmers' stands. The Farmers Market, held in the city parking lot between Clinch Park Zoo and the 100 block of East Front Street, is open 8 AM to noon on Saturdays from Mother's Day weekend through October, and Wednesday and Saturdays between mid-July and Labor Day.

Manitou Farm Market and Bakery
40 N. Manitou Tr., Lake Leelanau
• **(616) 256-9165**
The Manitou Market and Bakery shares the fruits of the season along with a delicious array of baked goods. Stop here for the latest harvest of cherries, apples, apricots, peaches and plums.

Kilcherman's Christmas Cove Farm
11573 N. Kilcherman Rd., Northport
• **(616) 386-5637**
John and Phyllis Kilcherman moved into their new home over the Christmas holidays several decades ago and appropriately dubbed their new household, Christmas Cove Farm. Today, the farm has apples, peaches and pears, and is known for its huge assortment of antique apples. Antiques are grown from seeds that have been passed down for generations. The Kilchermans have researched many of these older varieties and happily share their knowledge with visitors at their roadside stand in front of their home while the fruit is in season, September through November. They also sell gift boxes of 12 or 18 different antiques, which are packaged along with little stories about the background of each apple.

Lake Michigan Shoreline and Cadillac

Worden's Maple Syrup Farm
1830 Marshall Rd., Beulah
• **(616) 325-3837**
Worden's is one of the largest maple syrup operations in northern Michigan. They tap 2,600 trees, supplying maple syrup to retail-

ers around the state. You can purchase fresh syrup by the pint or gallon at their shop, open daily all year. Hours are seasonal so call ahead. For a real treat, plan to visit the last Saturday in March when Worden's hosts an annual open house. Visitors at this time can experience the maple-syrup process from the tree to the sugar house to the table.

Farmer Brown's Yellow House
18455 13 Mile Rd., Copemish
• **(616) 378-2327**
Each year the Browns plant a patch of pumpkins just for area school children to pick. The popular local farmers grow a variety of fruits and vegetables, available fresh from their fields. It's always a fun experience to visit the gardens at the yellow house.

Brown's Orchards
10944 Milarch Rd., Bear Lake
• **(616) 889-4883**
All your favorite varieties of apples are available at Brown's roadside market. You'll find those sweet, red delicious and crispy Macs and great pie-baking apples. It's open year round, but you'll find fresh-picked fruits and veggies throughout the harvest period. Stop here particularly for vine-ripened strawberries, sweet cherries, apricots, peaches and pears.

Cadillac Farmers Market
At Cass St. along Lake Cadillac
You'll find the sweetest fruits and freshest vegetables here, as well as a fantastic selection of gorgeous cultivated flowers, honey, pumpkins and landscape plants. The market operates Tuesday and Friday, July through October.

Ludington Farmers Market
James St. city gazebo, Ludington
Throughout the harvest season, you'll find the best pickin's of area crops on Tuesday and Thursday at the Ludington area farmers market.

Little Traverse

Friske Orchards
County Rd. 48, Charlevoix
• **(616) 588-6185**
Open year round, Friske Orchards is an

Insiders' favorite for finding fresh, quality fruit. They sell delicious vine-ripened strawberries, sweet cherries, tart cherries, peaches and many varieties of apples. Some u-pick crops are available. Other products they stock include dried apples, cider, maple syrup, homemade fruit preserves, jams, honey, cherry burgers and sausages.

Bill's Farm Market
4450 Mitchell Rd., Petoskey
• **(616) 347-6735**

Grown on a Michigan Centennial Farm, Bill's peas, sweet corn, tomatoes are fresh, sweet and tasty. Bill's also has a good selection of in-season Michigan fruits including cherries, melons and peaches and other farm products such as honey, flowers and herbs.

Florists and Garden Shops

Grand Traverse

Traverse City Area

Garden Goods
3510 N. U.S. Hwy. 31 S., Traverse City
• **(616) 933-4769**

Set back from the highway, Garden Goods is surrounded by the many large plants, garden benches, bedding plants and hanging flowers it sells. Billing itself as a home and garden showplace, it is a nice place to come for ideas and the fixings to make them work when planning the season's new plantings or adding new garden seating or decorations. The staff is very friendly and helpful.

Hibbard's Plantasia
312 S. Union St., Traverse City
• **(616) 946-6460**

Call Hibbard's to send a birthday arrangement or to brighten up the day with flowers. The shop creates lovely bouquets for all occasions and also carries an array of seasonal plants, dried arrangements and accessories.

Saundra's Gardens
5363 N. Long Lake Rd., Traverse City
• **(616) 929-9791**

Saundra's Gardens grow just beyond her North Long Lake home. Come here for unique floral arrangements, herbs and bedding plants. The owner periodically conducts classes on varying gardening topics.

Wildflowers
332 E. Front St., Traverse City
• **(616) 935-1516**
6127 S. Glen Lake Rd., Glen Arbor
• **(616) 334-3232**

Wildflowers can quickly transform your home or any room into a work of art with its endless supply of dried arrangements, unique gifts and home accessories. The shops are filled with their artisans' handiwork, giving patrons a glimpse at any number of creative possibilities in decorating accents.

Leelanau County

Bellwether Herbs & Flowers
10203 E. Shady Ln., Suttons Bay
• **(616) 271-3004**

Tucked into a valley in the rural center of the Leelanau peninsula, Bellwether Herbs & Flowers is a treat for the senses. Owners Gail and Bart Ingraham have nurtured a beautiful herb and flower farm near their country home. You'll also find a lovely perennial nursery and garden boutique. Bellwether is open Tuesday through Sunday between May and August, and on a reduced schedule from September through December.

Busha's Brae Herb Farm
2540 N. Setterbo Rd., Suttons Bay
• **(616) 271-6284**

Here's a unique stop for fresh herbs, seasonings, herbal products and gardens nestled into the center of the Leelanau peninsula's interior. Located on an old farm, Busha's Brae hosts a number of display gardens. The owner often presents group workshops, lectures and teas on preserving and using herbs.

Plant Masters of Suttons Bay
2650 S. West Bayshore Dr., Suttons Bay
- **(616) 271-4769**

Plant Masters is enormous. The central shop is surrounded by huge greenhouses brimming with bedding plants, potted flowers, hanging plants, vegetable plants and herbs as well as garden benches, pots, bulbs, seeds and gardening accessories. If you're here over the winter holidays, get a poinsettia from Plant Masters. The shop grows its own plants, which are often sold through Grand Traverse area fund-raisers and are always festive and healthy.

Antrim-Kalkaska

Alden Floral
E. Torch Lake Dr., Alden
- **(616) 331-6164**

The charming village of Alden is the backdrop for Alden Floral. The shop specializes in fresh flower arrangements as well as unique gifts with Victorian and country tones. Unlike many local shops, Alden Floral is open throughout the year.

Thru the Grapevine
10437 S. Bayshore Dr., Elk Rapids
- **(800) 864-7273**

Thru the Grapevine brings you unique gifts from the garden at this picturesque cottage-style shop on the outskirts of Elk Rapids. The owners create beautiful, unique arrangements from hand-harvested blooms and plants. The resulting pieces capture the splendor of our region with distinctive, free-form designs. The shop also carries lovely gifts, greeting cards, candles, soaps, garden decorations, fresh flowers and herbs.

Twigs 'N Blooms
4469 Old U.S. Hwy. 27 S., Gaylord
- **(517) 732-4493**

The name summarizes this unique shop featuring bent willow and cedar furniture along with a full array of plants and flowers. At Twigs 'N Blooms, you'll spend time browsing through an extensive selection of perennials, herbs and moss baskets filled with flowering stems as well as creative birdhouses, garden benches and rustic outdoor furniture. The shop's Christ-

mas Haus highlights seasonal specialties all year long. Twig 'N Blooms, just south of Gaylord, is open daily year round.

Lake Michigan Shoreline and Cadillac

Crystal Gardens
1299 Pilgrim Hwy., Frankfort
- **(616) 352-9321**

This is the place to go in Benzie County even if you don't have a green thumb. Crystal Gardens carries everything you need to turn your yard and garden into a place of beauty. Open from April through October, they carry nursery stock, annuals, unusual and traditional perennials, flowering baskets, wreaths. They also offer full landscape services.

Yesterday's Garden
1477 Lakeshore Rd., Manistee
- **(616) 723-7487**

Situated on 5 acres, this is no ordinary garden center. Wander the lush display garden and see for yourself the possibilities for your own yard. They specialize in older and traditional varieties of annuals and perennials, such as scented geraniums and pink and blue lavender. A bulk room offers all the materials do-it-yourselfers need for crafting natural wreaths and dried flower arrangements. Friendly advice, garden gifts, potted herbs and children's nature books are also available. Yesterday's Garden is closed in January and February.

The Giving Tree Gift Baskets & Garden Center
323 W. Ludington Ave., Ludington
- **(616) 843-4087**

Open April through July, the Giving Tree offers a good selection of flowering shrubs, ornamental trees and your favorite annuals and perennials. To set off your plants, you'll find a selection of Italian pottery and Chinese planters, lots and lots of clay items and cement statuary. Custom baskets made with Michigan-grown produce are available by special order during the Christmas holidays.

Little Traverse

Gourmet Specialties

Grand Traverse

Traverse City Area

Wintergreen Herbs and Potpourri
10970 Burnett Rd., Charlevoix
• (616) 347-7399

Situated on 10 acres, Wintergreen features 32 theme gardens for you to explore. See the Shakespearean and Biblical gardens, culinary, ornamental, butterfly, medicinal, and fragrance gardens and more. Open May through December, they offer a selection of unusual herbs, ornamental plants, annual and perennial flowers in the spring. All their wreaths, soaps, medicinal and herbal products are made from homegrown plants. Landscaping service is available.

Back to Nature
207 Howard St., Petoskey
• (616) 439-9135

For fresh flowers and truly imaginative natural centerpieces, baskets, birdhouses and home accessories, visit Back to Nature in Petoskey's Gaslight District. Their great Christmas treasures, potpourri and cottage furniture bring the essence of nature into your home. Check out their handcrafted, mail-order twig chairs and barnwood theme birdhouses.

Landscape Depot
1860 U.S. Hwy. 31 N., Petoskey
• (616) 347-5757

There's nothing quite like Landscape Depot for enhancing your outdoor living. They offer a good selection of shrubs, perennials, annuals, tropical plants, designers trees, fountains, benches, planters and tables. They give friendly advice and provide residential and commercial landscape design service. Landscape Depot is open April through December.

American Spoon Foods
230 E. Front St., Traverse City
• (616) 935-4480
Grand Traverse Resort, Acme
• (616) 938-5358

Headquartered in Petoskey, American Spoon Foods carries a wonderful selection of products rooted in the produce and spirit of Northern Michigan. See American Spoon Food's main listing under the subsequent Little Traverse section in this chapter.

Benjamin Twigg's
1215 E. Front St., Traverse City
• (616) 947-2188

Benjamin Twigg's overflows with cherry products and regional gifts. This is a delightful shop with scads of wonderful treats. You'll find preserves, jams, jellies, maple syrup, sweets, fudge and a seemingly endless assortment of novelties. The shop carries all sorts of gift baskets and boxes to send to friends back home as well as an ample assortment of tasty treats to sample immediately. There is one of the best selections of cherry mementos to be found, featuring Traverse City's favorite fruit on gifts and souvenirs. Whether shopping for yourself or for gifts, the friendly staff is happy to help you find the perfect taste of Traverse City.

Burritt's Meat Market
509 W. Front St., Traverse City
• (616) 946-3300

Burritt's carries all the gourmet fixings you'll

INSIDERS' TIP

Most northern Michigan downtowns were built in the late 1800s at the height of the lumbering boom. While you're window shopping, take a moment to admire the vintage architectural detail of those windows as well as the walls, roofs and storefronts that line our streets. For a closer look, ask the shopkeepers about their building's background. Many are eager to share stories about their store's heritage.

need for a summer supper or a cozy winter meal in front of the fire. You'll find a modern meat market with old-fashioned service in this family-owned shop. Burritt's always has several entrees that are already marinated, rolled, sauced, smoked or otherwise ready for speedy preparation. For a special treat, pick up the barbecued ribs featuring Burritt's original sauce.

Carlson's Fish Market
511 W. Front St., Traverse City
• **(616) 941-9392**
  Carlson's shares the same shopping center with Burritt's (see previous listing). This is always a sure bet for finding the freshest local seafood. The Carlson family began in the commercial Great Lakes fishing industry generations ago from its Fishtown docks in Leland. The Traverse City shop sells an excellent selection of fresh fish and shellfish prepared to order as well as frozen shellfish, smoked local fish and their original recipe spreads and sauces. Try the smoked whitefish pâté. It's one of our favorites!

The Cherry STOP
426 W. Front St., Traverse City
• **(616) 929-3990, (800) 286-7209**
  You can't visit the cherry capital without taking home a few of its most memorable products. The Cherry STOP is the retail outlet for Orchards Harvest, which operates a bustling mail-order business selling premium dried fruits, jams, canned goods, sauces, syrups, coffee, cookbooks and frozen foods. You'll find the shop right next to Folgarelli's in the cluster of gourmet food shops that stretch along the 400 and 500 block of West Front Street. Inside, you can choose from dried blueberries, cranberries, sweet cherry and the over-popular red tart cherries. You'll also find the Orchards Harvest dried blends, such as cherry and apple, that are frequently served on airlines. Chocolate-covered fruits, jams and fruit syrups appeal to the sweet tooth. An array of

tins, baskets, trays and boxes are available for gift giving.

Doug Murdick's Fudge
116 E. Front St., Traverse City
• **(616) 947-4841**
4500 U.S. Hwy. 31 N., Traverse City
• **(616) 938-2330**
110 W. River St., Leland • (616) 256-7241
  Doug Murdick's is Traverse City's local fudge connection. All shops feature the same wonderful varieties of fresh fudge as well as a delicious sampling of other homemade confections. You can't miss Murdick's U.S. 31 North location. It's the small white building topped by an enormous piece of chocolate nut fudge sticking out of a Doug Murdick's box. This piece of local outdoor art, which is easily the size of the shop's rooftop, has been greeting westbound visitors to Traverse City for decades.

Folgarelli's Import Food Market
424 W. Front St., Traverse City
• **(616) 941-7651**
  Folgarelli's introduced Traverse City to Italian specialties and creative food products when it opened in the 1970s. Today, this well-stocked European deli features meats, cheeses, olives, oils, wines, beer and sandwiches along with great fresh breads and frozen homemade pasta specialties. If you're planning to prepare an ethnic meal of any variety, you'll probably be able to find the rarer ingredients here. Besides the promise of excellent food, you'll enjoy stopping at Folgarelli's for the ambiance. Bins of coffee and shelves of spices await your scoop. Barrels of fresh olives edge the front of the deli case, which is always filled with interesting cheeses and traditional deli fare. Shelves are filled with pastas, sauces and cans while baskets and breads line the walls. The vintage shop's slightly uneven floors just add to its charm while the current generation of Folgarelli's extend their hospitality with personal flair.

INSIDERS' TIP

If you need a meeting spot, use the Martinek's clock on Traverse City's East Front Street. This vintage timepiece has been a downtown landmark since 1924.

Grand Traverse Pie Company
525 W. Front St., Traverse City
• (616) 922-7437

Fresh gourmet pies of the most delicious varieties are found at the Grand Traverse Pie Company. The selection changes a bit each day and as the latest local fruits are harvested. Favorite pies are blueberry, apple, peach, cherry as well as fruitful combinations like strawberry rhubarb and Lakeshore Berry, which combines several berries in a delicious recipe. The owners have now started selling their own preserves based on their pie fillings. You can purchase an entire pie or just a piece. If you can't resist, you can eat your pie immediately topped off by fresh ice cream at one of the little parlor tables inside. Stop by in early afternoon and you might walk out with a pie that is still warm from the oven. Grand Traverse Pies are also sold at Prevo's Grocery stores and at the Traverse City Farmers' Market.

Kilwin's Chocolate Shoppe
129 E. Front St., Traverse City
• (616) 946-2403

Kilwin's is a name synonymous with sweet treats. Based in Petoskey, Kilwin's has locations sprinkled throughout our Insiders' region. The Traverse City shop was just taken over by new owners, who have renovated the longtime downtown storefront but are continuing Kilwin's candymaking traditions. (See the subsequent Little Traverse listing for more details.)

Marifil Bakery
537 W. 14th St., Traverse City
• (616) 933-0099

Marafil's creates wonderful European breads, desserts and other baked goods from this tiny shop. It is also the retail outlet where you can get the hand-dipped truffles, homemade ice cream and deluxe desserts served at Traverse City's popular Windows restaurant (see our Restaurants chapter). Whatever you choose, you won't be disappointed.

Mary's Kitchen Port
539 W. Front St., Traverse City
• (616) 941-0525

Mary's has been bringing gourmet goodies to Traverse City for years. If you love to cook, you'll love the great selection of unique ingredients, cookbooks, knives, quality cookware and indispensably fun gadgets. If you love to eat, you'll be treated to a mouthwatering selection of unique daily soups, salads and sandwiches. Large homemade cookies and the shop's special honey-bear brownies sit, temptingly, next to the checkout counter. Daily sandwiches selections always include Mary's signature "Gobbler" sandwich, a stacked turkey with shredded lettuce, cheese, tomatoes and dressing on a croissant or focaccia.

Maxbauer Market
407 S. Union St., Traverse City
• (616) 947-7698

Maxbauer's is a Traverse City institution. A longtime neighborhood grocery store as well as a specialty meat and seafood market, everybody is greeted at Maxbauer's as though they were old friends. The meat selection is excellent as is the poultry and seafood. You can usually find several grill or oven-ready entrees along with the market's many weekly specials. Maxbauer's also carries a nice selection of local wines and regional products. If you don't see something that fits your fancy, just ask. The staff's friendly, personal service is a hallmark.

Peppercorn
226 E. Front St., Traverse City
• (616) 941-4146

This pleasant kitchen shop is filled with countless items to delight the cook in all of us. Unique cookware and dinnerware, specialty gadgets, interesting cookbooks and gifts with a northern flair fill the shelves. You can also sample the local wines from Chateau Grand Traverse, which hosts a tasting area in the back of the shop.

Underground Cheesecake Company
406 S. Union St., Traverse City
• (616) 929-4418

Prepare to find the most decadent desserts. The Underground Cheesecake Company tempts patrons with a seemingly endless menu of cheesecake specialties as well as sinfully rich but wildly delicious gourmet brownies in assorted chocolate combinations. Obviously, we love this place and we think you will, too.

Take home a whole dessert or simply share a brownie with a friend and a cup of coffee at the shop's tables. In case you were wondering how the company got its name, it was started by several women in a home basement. Their quick success soon drove them out of the basement and into sunlit storefronts where they continue to enjoy accolades.

Village Wine Shoppe
875 E. Front St., Traverse City
• **(616) 941-9463**

The Village Wine Shop is filled with an ongoing list of domestic and imported wines, beers and specialty products. The staff is knowledgeable and helpful and will gladly guide you in your selections. They are also happy to discuss the merits of our many locally produced wines, prepare a case of wine to take back home or help you choose the perfect port for a special gift.

Wine Country Market
541 W. Front St., Traverse City
• **(616) 935-1776**

Traverse City's newest wine shop is next to Mary's Kitchen Port in an area increasingly filled with gourmet food shops including nearby Folgarelli's, Burritt's Meat Market, Carlson's Fish Market, the Grand Traverse Pie Company and other West Front Market shops. The shop is pleasant and spacious with selections available for all tastes and budgets. In nice weather, you can sit at one of the shop's outdoor tables and enjoy a cappuccino.

Leelanau County

Pleva's Meats
8974 S. Kasson St., Cedar
• **(616) 228-5000**

Ray Pleva has been making sausage for decades at his family's specialty meat market in tiny Cedar. When his daughter was the 1987 National Cherry Queen, she encouraged him to incorporate cherries into his products. The result was cherry-pecan sausage, Italian cherry sausage, turkey-cherry brats and 25 other cherry-enhanced meats as well as the immensely popular Plevalean, which combines cherries with lean beef, oat bran and spices for a healthy alternative to traditional ground

beef. Plevalean has received national attention since it was introduced with mentions on *Home Improvement, Oprah, Extra!,* CNN and *Home & Family.* By the way, if you're here during Cherry Festival, watch for Pleva's float to be a favorite in the Heritage Parade. It's notable because Ray and his crew usually have their sausage machine going as they make their specialty to the tunes of a live Polka band.

Cherry Republic Inc.
6026 Lake St., Glen Arbor
• **(616) 334-3150, (800) 206-6949**

Welcome to the Cherry Republic headquarters, which sells an array of locally grown and produced cherry products. Look for Cherry Republic's signature clothing, featuring a large cherry tree in full fruit, on local backs.

Leelanau Coffee Roasting Company
6443 Western Ave., Glen Arbor
• **(616) 334-3365, (800) 424-JAVA**

The Leelanau Coffee Roasting Company promises to keep the world safe from bad coffee by roasting beans daily in its shop. The company roasts coffee for a number of regional restaurants, and also sells their beans through mail order and at various specialty grocers scattered throughout Traverse City, Leelanau County and surrounding areas.

Stone House Bread
407 S. Main St., Leland • **(616) 256-2577**

Stone House Bread has become one of the Grand Traverse area's most popular suppliers of fresh baked bread. You can find their distinctive, loaf-filled, brown paper bags lined up in area grocers, specialty markets and wineries. We're thrilled because this crusty, Old World-style bread is wonderful. The bakers specialize in sourdough and sweet French baguettes, sourdough rounds, cracked wheat and the unique North Country bread, which combines several kinds of flour into a tasty loaf. If you're in Leland, stop by the shop. If you miss the shop, at least pick up a loaf of bread. Enjoy!

Leelanau Cheese
5019 N. West Bay Shore Dr., Omena
• **(616) 386-7731**

Pair up that Stone House bread with locally made Leelanau cheese. The owners studied French cheesemaking in Europe before settling in Omena and beginning the business of making rounds of raclette and tubs of fluffy fromage blanc that are often spiced with herbs. Leelanau Cheese can be found in several gourmet markets and specialty shops in the region as well as from their storefront along the Mich. Highway 22 curve in Omena. The shop includes a viewing area where visitors are welcome to watch the cheesemaking process. The only items sold here are the cheeses and a few accompaniments like bread and pickles.

Bacchus & Brie
220 St. Joseph St., Suttons Bay
• **(616) 271-2626**
This is a darling shop where you can find many of the different sauces, preserves and products created in the region as well as local wines and microbrews. There are also lines of nationally known gourmet products and a great selection of premium wines and beers. A coffee bar brews up fresh cappuccino and hot chocolate.

Antrim-Kalkaska

Alpine Chocolat Haus and Gifts
208 W. Main St., Gaylord
• **(517) 732-1077**
Candy lovers and candy makers flock to the Alpine Chocolat Haus and Gifts. The shop features a wonderful selection of hand-dipped sweets and all the supplies you'll need for your own candy making. An added treat is the shop's old-fashioned ice cream parlor. When in Gaylord, this is your top stop for a sweet treat.

Lake Michigan Shoreline and Cadillac

Randall's Big River Smokehouse
17356 Mich. Hwy. 55, Wellston
• **(616) 848-4555**
Old-timers say smoking meat is an art. At Randall's Big River Smokehouse you'll find some of the area's very best smoked fish, jerky, sausages, ham and turkey. They'll even custom smoke your fish or game. Or, you can take home fresh-frozen fish. Gifts items, custom baskets and catering services are also available. Randall's is closed on Tuesdays, and from Christmas through March.

The Granary
123 W. Ludington Ave., Ludington
• **(616) 843-1995**
Head to The Granary for unprocessed, preservative-free and natural foods. They stock grains, nuts and trail mixes and offer a good selection of vitamins and herbs.

Sweet Apple Sue's/Kilwin's
118 W. Ludington Ave., Ludington
• **(616) 845-5858**
Two of Ludington's favorite gourmet shops have merged to bring you the most delectable candies, ice cream and fudge around, along with gourmet foods, specialty wines, imported beer and country collectibles. Watch fudge being made in the old-fashioned paddle method. Creative custom baskets are available for shipping anywhere in the world.

Hermann's Chef's Deli
214 N. Mitchell St., Cadillac
• **(616) 775-2101**
Austrian Master Chef Hermann Suhs lends his European flair to this Old World-style deli. Like everything the Chef does, the deli case is a work of art. You'll find fresh seafoods, imported meats and cheeses, salads and sandwiches. There are more than 200 wines to select from, wonderful European chocolates, flavored coffees, petit fours and other sweet treats.

The Boon Store
562 S. Haskins Ave., Boon
• **(616) 775-7988**
Famous for their 22-pound wheels of aged Wisconsin cheese, The Boon Store sells 5,000 pounds of it annually. As in the old days, the cheese is sliced on the counter, wrapped in white paper and tied in string. The country store also sells handmade pickle bologna.

Photo: Terry W. Phipps/Mackinac Island Chamber of Commerce

Fort Mackinac looms over the hustle and bustle of
Mackinac Island's busy downtown shops.

Little Traverse

Sweet Sam's Java Joint
405 Bridge St., Charlevoix
• **(616) 547-3993**

Both locations offer whole-bean coffee and
espresso, roasted on site. For custom roasting and flavoring, there are more than 10,000
flavor combinations from which to choose.
Sweet Sam's also carries Michigan products
and more than 200 gourmet items including
salsas, pastas and cooking oils. Gift baskets
and certificates are available.

American Spoon Foods
411 Lake St., Petoskey • (616) 347-1739
245 E. Main St., Harbor Springs
• **(616) 526-8628**
315 Bridge St., Charlevoix
• **(616) 547-5222**

Head straight to the tasting table, and
help yourself to crackers and spoon on a
taste of this company's fruity preserves or
condiments. American Spoon Foods offers
a selection of the finest foods from the orchards, fields and forests of the Great Lakes
area. Indulge yourself. Made in small
batches, rich in fruit, the preserves, spoon
fruits and specialty foods are one of life's

simple pleasures. American Spoon Foods,
including the Grand Traverse store, offer
custom packages featuring attractive folk art
boxes or birch baskets. Mail order service is
available. The Petoskey store is open daily
year round, but the Harbor Springs and
Charlevoix shops operate limited winter
hours, so call ahead.

Breadworks
2286 Mich. Hwy. 119, Petoskey
• **(616) 347-9574**

If you have a weakness for fresh-baked
breads, take time to visit Breadworks. They
create sourdough from organic grains and
bake the fragrant loaves in a German stone-
hearth oven for Old World appeal. They'll also
tempt you with an irresistible selection of muffins, scones and sweetbreads.

Kilwin's Chocolate Shoppe
316 Howard St., Petoskey
• **(616) 347-2645**
101 W. Main St., Harbor Springs
• **(616) 526-2802**
330 Bridge St., Charlevoix
• **(616) 547-5013**
Huron St., Mackinac Island
• **(906) 847-6500**

Since 1947, when Don and Kathy Kilwin created their first recipes for handmade chocolates, their confections have developed a national reputation with chocolate lovers. Their original Petoskey location has sprouted 31 franchise stores around the country. While independently owned, all Kilwin's shops sell the same famous delectable chocolates, fudge and ice cream.

Symons General Store
401 E. Lake St., Petoskey
• **(616) 347-2438**

You'll definitely want to linger here amidst the tall shelves packed with gourmet treats and fragrant goodies. Symons features fresh baked sourdough, whole-grain breads, croissants and cookies, 250 cheeses, and an awesome selection of teas, coffees, condiments and imported candies. On their lower level, you'll find a cozy bistro with one of the best wine selections in the north.

Harbor Springs Gourmet
127 State St., Harbor Springs
• **(616) 526-9607**

Start your picnic, party or special dinner right here. Harbor Springs Gourmet offers delicacies from around the world. You'll find imported cheese, pâté, caviar, fine wines and imported beers. They also carry Seattle's Best Coffee. While famous for their carrot cake, they also offer fresh-baked breads, muffins and cookies. For meals to go, select from a menu including free-range Amish chicken, baby-back ribs or oriental cuisine. Catering is available.

Mackinac Straits

Mackinac Island's top souvenir export is likely its locally made fudge and related sweets. There are four main fudge businesses on the island. All have multiple shops along the main street, each with huge windows and open viewing areas to watch the fudge being made on marble slabs. The process is fascinating, from the first hot spread of liquid fudge to the constant folding and flipping of the cooling sweet with wood paddles to the final forming and cutting into the Island's distinctive slices. We've listed each of the major candy producers below except for an Island location for Kilwin's Chocolates, previously listed with Little Traverse shops.

Jo Ann's Fudge
Huron St., Mackinac Island
• **(906) 847-3707**
303 Central Ave., Mackinaw City
• **(616) 436-5611**

Jo Ann's promises fresh cream and butter in every batch of fudge made daily in two shops along the main street on Mackinac Island and one in Mackinaw City. The shops also feature hand-dipped candy, peanut brittle, English toffee and sugar-free treats.

May's Candy Shop
Market and Huron Sts., Mackinac Island
• **(906) 847-3832**

Master fudgemaker Marvin May brings decades of tradition to making candy, fudge, brittle and other sweets. May's has three Island shops, including two on Huron Street and one at the corner of Market and Astor Streets.

Murdick's Fudge Kitchen
Huron St. and Surrey Hill Sq., Mackinac Island • **(906) 847-3530**
204 N. State St., St. Ignace
• **(906) 643-9616**

Murdick's has been making and serving Mackinac Island fudge since 1887. Look for fudge and brittle made daily at Murdick's Surrey Hill Square and two Huron Street locations, and in St. Ignace.

Ryba's Fudge Shops
Huron St., Mackinac Island
• **(906) 847-3347**

You can identify Ryba's by its pink candy boxes. Today's fudgemaking Rybas represent the family's third generation. Ryba's is noted for its kettle-cooked fudge, caramel corn, hand-dipped chocolates, taffy and ice cream.

Jewelry Stores

Grand Traverse

Federico's
156 E. Front St., Traverse City
• **(616) 946-4252**

Federico's has made a name for itself in

bringing unique, beautiful designs to Traverse City. Stop by this friendly store for a peek at its newest pieces or watch the artisan who is often at work at a table facing the Front Street windows.

Martinek's Jewelers
217 E. Front St., Traverse City
• **(616) 946-4664**
Downtown Traverse City is known for the vintage clock standing along the sidewalk in front of Martinek's Jewelers. It has been ticking since the first generation of Martineks opened doors for business in 1878. Today, the shop continues to carry classic jewelry, clocks and watches. Jewelry repair is available.

Miners North
222 E. Front St., Traverse City
• **(616) 946-8528**
Expect top quality and unique designs at Miner's North Jewelers. Distinctive pieces are available in a nice range of designs and prices. You'll find magnificent diamonds and colored stones, 14K gold engagement rings and sterling silver bracelets.

Becky Thatcher Designs
5795 Lake St., Glen Arbor
• **(616) 334-3826**
110 N. Lake St., Leland • **(616) 256-2229**
The beautiful work of Leelanau artist Becky Thatcher is showcased in her shops in Leland and Glen Arbor. The influence of local traditions and northern scenery are captured in carved beachstones, gemstones and beads set in distinctive necklaces, bracelets and earrings. Rare gemstones set in gold or silver are a specialty.

Little Traverse

Baker Metal Works
221 Howard St., Petoskey
• **(616) 348-7034**
In this small shop, a bit off the beaten path, you'll find an artisan carefully at work creating handcrafted gold and sterling jewelry. They offer custom jewelry pieces, bronze fountains, lamps and sculpture.

Whistling Moose Studios
209 Howard St., Petoskey
• **(616) 347-5281**
This is a shop that proves good things come in big AND small packages. At the in-store studio artisans produce colorful, distinctive jewelry while the Whistling Moose wood shop produces custom canoes and dinghies that will inspire even a diehard landlubber to take to the water. The shop also carries distinctive decorative and functional pottery and a wide selection of wildlife carvings, prints and originals.

Music Stores

Grand Traverse

Traverse City Area

ABCD's
157 E. Front St., Traverse City
• **(616) 946-2112**
This well-stocked music shop hails itself as "a better compact disc store," hence ABCD's. Friendly service by a knowledgeable staff keeps its following loyal. So does the chance to try out a compact disc before you purchase it.

New Moon Records
240 E. Front St., Traverse City
• **(616) 941-1035**
New Moon Records has sold recorded music from its shop in downtown Traverse City for years. At one time, the storefront was known as Full Moon Records but changed names with new ownership. New Moon sells new and used compact discs as well as vintage LPs, cassettes, imports, collectibles and rarities.

Leelanau County

Otter Creek Music
301 St. Joseph St., Suttons Bay
• **(616) 271-7664, (800) 385-1346**
Otter Creek Music features a fine selection of unique recordings on compact disc and cassette. The shop, formerly known as Hansen's Music Gallery, features the recordings of many local and regional musicians as well as popular favorites. A gallery set-

ting is the perfect backdrop for listening to music.

Lake Michigan Shoreline and Cadillac

The Instrumental Music Store
107 S. James St., Ludington
• (616) 843-4411

Whether you make music or just enjoy listening to it, you'll want to check out the Instrumental Music Store. They sell a variety of instruments including guitars and digital pianos and also carry a good selection of instructional material and popular sheet music. In the CD department, you'll find jazz, rock, blues, soul, classical and contemporary Christian music. They also operate a repair service for guitars, electronics and band instruments.

Rising Star Guitar
117 N. Mitchell St., Cadillac
• (616) 779-1988

Cadillac's downtown music center, Rising Star carries music and instructional books, electric and acoustic guitars, amps, new and used band instruments and a variety of music accessories.

Little Traverse

Ray's Guitar & Music Supply
113 Water St., Boyne City
• (616) 582-3599

Ray's is the place to shop in Northern Michigan for string instruments. They are the only dealer around carrying mandolins, all sizes of violins and electric violins. They carry Gibson and Tacoma guitars, Casio keyboards and have a wonderful selection of harmonicas. You'll also find amps, sound equipment, tuning machines, music books and videos, special effect equipment and more.

Record World
430 E. Mitchell St., Petoskey
• (616) 347-1721

Record World carries a good selection of CDs and tapes ranging from Bach to Zappa. Classical, Celtic, New Age, folk, rock, country and kids music, it's all here. They also feature a line of T-shirts and rock wear, posters and accessories.

Resale & Thrift Shops

Grand Traverse

Traverse City

Peddler's Corner
119 S. Union St., Traverse City
• (616) 947-1198

Peddler's Corner was a leader in bringing resale shopping to Traverse City when it opened its doors more than 17 years ago. The standards are high for the consignment items that are accepted resulting in an excellent selection of name-brand clothing, accessories and treasures for the entire family.

Play It Again Sports
1425 S. Airport Rd., Traverse City
• (616) 929-1870

Play It Again is the stop to make for sports equipment that is used but not used up. The stock reflects the season with hockey, snowboarding, skiing, sledding and skating filling the walls in the winter, replaced by water skis, golf clubs, waveboards, tennis rackets, soccer shoes and baseball equipment in the summer. The shop also sells new sporting equipment.

The Silk Shop
312 S. Union St., Traverse City
• (616) 922-9282

This unique resale shop shares space with Hibbard's Plantasia florist with a selection of rarely used classic women's clothing.

Twice as Nice Consignments
318 Vine St., Traverse City
• (616) 947-2507

Twice as Nice is tucked behind Sleders Tavern in a charming blue cottage filled with women's sportswear, career fashions and designer labels that have all been gently used. Visitors will also find an array of collectibles and garden gifts for sale as well.

Lake Michigan Shoreline and Cadillac

Kids on the Grow
380 River St., Manistee • (616) 398-9180
More than a quality consignment shop for children's clothes, you can find good deals on juvenile furniture and equipment. You can also rent cribs, high chairs, car seats and strollers, by the day or by the week.

Goodwill Store
222 N. Mitchell St., Cadillac
• **(616) 779-1311**
T-shirts, formals, kids wear, you name it, you'll find it at Cadillac's Goodwill shop. The shop offers used clothing to bargain hunters while providing meaningful job opportunities for the disadvantaged workers who staff the operation.

The Salvation Army Red Shield Store
924 S. Mitchell St., Cadillac
• **(616) 775-6077**
Proceeds from The Salvation Army Store help this Christian organization provide assistance to area needy. The store is always well-stocked with used clothing and shoes for men, women and children.

Little Traverse

My Sisters Closet
1207 Bridge St., Charlevoix
• **(616) 547-7350**
Shop here to look like a million bucks on a limited budget. This upscale resale shop carries an ever-changing selection of women's and children's clothing, shoes and accessories. You can find topnotch designer styles at a fraction of their original cost. Items are kept on the racks for only 30 days, so there are always new bargains to discover.

A Penny Saved
446 E. Mitchell St., Petoskey
• **(616) 347-8303**
This clothing resale shop is very selective about items taken on consignment. You'll find good quality women's and children's apparel at great prices. In addition to offering used items they have new sales samples. Check monthly specials for even greater savings.

Those Bloomin' Kids
432 E. Mitchell St., Petoskey
• **(616) 347-4333**
A quality consignment store, Those Bloomin' Kids offers clothing for the entire family, including maternity wear. In addition, they carry used toys, books, baby furniture and baby accessories. To make your shopping easier, they provide a video area/play room for youngsters. For really super deals, check out Brenda's Bloomin' Bargain Basement, where items are reduced up to 70 percent.

Specialty Shops

Grand Traverse

Traverse City Area

Americana Collection
224 E. Front St., Traverse City
• **(616) 933-0297**
104 River St., Leland • (616) 256-9350
Collectibles and creations from artisans around the country can be found at the Americana Collection shops. You'll find a wide assortment of treasures awaiting discovery, including folk art, bronze miniatures, baskets, ceramics, cast sculptures, cotton throws, holiday ornaments and much more. The Leland shop is open daily from May through the end of October, while Traverse City's shop in the heart of downtown is open all year.

Annie's
247 E. Front St., Traverse City
• **(616) 946-6201**
Annie's is bright, colorful fun wrapped into a charming gift shop filled with greeting cards,

novelty gifts, balloons, gags, gourmet coffees and candies. If you need a balloon bouquet or a unique gift for friends back home, head to Annie's yellow-and-white canopied entrance.

Belstone
321 E. Front St., Traverse City
• (616) 946-0610

Belstone gallery's windows overlook the Boardman River and nearby greenery, providing a serene setting for this wonderful, intimate art gallery and shop. Local artists in a variety of genres are displayed with a wide array of works and price ranges. Local watercolorist Charles Murphy often has many of his latest works hanging on the walls. You will also find beautiful glasswork, memorable jewelry and unique sculptures. While at the gallery, spend a few minutes sitting on the outdoor patio amidst the beauty of Mother Nature's artistry.

The Candle Factory and Home Elements
301 W. Grandview Pkwy., Traverse City
• (616) 946-2280 Candle Factory,
(616) 946-2850 Home Elements

The Candle Factory is a mainstay in Traverse City. This unique shop is housed in an old brick building that likely housed and early era manufacturer. A candle maker creates his wares from a work area on site while much of the expansive showroom space is devoted to displaying the hundreds of candles, holders and accents that fill the shelves. Sharing the building but separated is the Candle Factory's Home Elements shop with a selection of accents and accessories for the home including a large selection of tablecloths and runners, and unique paper products for entertaining.

Cap Soleil
445 E. Front St., Traverse City
• (616) 933-9833

French provincial prints are the specialty at Cap Soleil, which brings the essence of Cote d'Azur to downtown Traverse City. This charming shop has exclusive rights in Michigan to sell duvets by Clos d'Aguzon. It also features table and kitchen linens by Marnik.

Cedar Creek Interiors
415 S. Union St., Traverse City
• (616) 933-4321

Cedar Creek showcases distinctive "made in northern Michigan" furniture in a charming shop filled with birch bark desks, bentwood chairs, unusual lampshades, handcarved bed posts and cedar log furniture. Artisans that show their work here hail from all corners of Northwest Michigan.

Celebrations
126 Lake Ave., Traverse City
• (616) 941-4554

It's always party time at Celebrations. This unique shop is the stop for all of the fixings to make any event a celebration. You'll find helium balloons, pinatas, trinkets, favors, noisemakers, hats, signs, glittery decorations and a seemingly endless supply of paper plates, napkins and supplies in a rainbow of colors and designs. It's all packed into a converted house off Union Street. You can't miss it; it's painted a startling shade of hot pink.

Country Christmas
9005 W. Mich. Hwy. 72, Traverse City
• (616) 946-6294

Country Christmas has been celebrating the holiday spirit for more than 15 years. Handcrafted ornaments, unique Santas, miniature trees, ceramic angels and whimsical snowmen fill the shop with festive flair. Many items are created by Michigan artisans.

Firehouse Fair
118 Cass St., Traverse City
• (616) 935-4442

This distinctive shop showcases a selective line of upscale gifts and home elements. Housed in the old Traverse City firehouse, the shop features works by local artisans as well as an array of hard-to-find gifts and novelties. You never know for sure what you might find at the Firehouse Fair, but it's sure to be unique.

Leaping Lizard
207 E. Front St., Traverse City
• (616) 935-4470

Eclectic is the best description for the wild assortment of fascinating items displayed at Leaping Lizard. You'll find casual clothing, small lamps and home accessories, silver jewelry, candles, dream catchers, and even Beanie Babies. You'll find a number of items reflecting Native American and South American influences. This is a fun store. Stop by for a quick browse and see how many unique gifts you can discover.

Lost Art Yarn Shoppe
123 E. Front St., Traverse City
- (616) 941-1263

Lost Art is tucked into a tiny downtown shop filled with endless skeins of yarn in colorful fibers. This shop is a favorite among needlecrafters and knitters. You'll find needles, patterns, supplies and anything you need to create your own handknit masterpiece. Or, if you need ideas, tips or lessons to get going, the staff gladly lends a helping hand.

My Favorite Things
143 E. Front St., Traverse City
- (616) 929-9665

This charming shop features an eclectic selection of decorative items, unique jewelry, Godiva chocolates, cozy throws, framed prints, silk flowers, cards, lotions, books and picture frames. Stop by to find your own "favorite things."

Nutcracker
205 E. Front St., Traverse City
- (616) 947-3126

This is the shop to find extensive collections of Department 56 ceramic houses like Snow Village and Dickens' Christmas Village. An enormous Snow Village display fills the shop's storefront and fascinates children and passersby with its detail. You'll also find a large selection of Beyer carolers, Snow Babies figurines, unique Santas and beautiful nativities as well as the shop's signature gifts, the nutcrackers. Hundreds of ornaments line one wall, displayed from green wooden pegs.

Riecker's Outdoor Gallery
134 E. Front St., Traverse City
- (616) 946-0414

Wildlife artists are featured at this unique gallery appealing to outdoors enthusiasts. Sculptures, paintings and assorted gifts are showcased in a beautifully renovated, vintage shop.

Stewart-Zacks
118 E. Front St., Traverse City
- (616) 947-2322

Quality fabrics, notions and unique home elements are the specialty at Stewart-Zacks. The shop carries a large array of decorator materials, casual throw rugs, pillows, baskets and accessories as well as fashion fabrics, patterns and embellishments.

Watermelon Sugar Gallery and Gifts
153 E. Front St., Traverse City
- (616) 929-7426

You never know what "treasure" you may find inside Watermelon Sugar Gallery and Gifts. The shop specializes in the contemporary artwork of local and state artisans and crafters.

Wooden Gallery
116 E. Front St., Traverse City
- (616) 941-0823

Take home the images of northern Michigan with one of the beautiful works carried at the Wooden Gallery. The shop features lovely framed art, which is showcased without using glass thanks to the unique, trademarked Wooden Gallery Process. Each piece uses a high-quality print, which is saturated, mounted and hand-textured for enhanced color, protection and distinctive styling. This process was developed in Traverse City by the Wooden Gallery owner and is now patented and sold around the country. You can find the Wooden Gallery's showroom by following the covered walkway leading off downtown's East Front Street in the center of the 100 block storefronts. As you pass along the brick-walled walk, you'll see a number of the Wooden Gallery's striking pieces on display.

Cranberry Christmas and Country Store
8997 E. Mich. Hwy. 72, Acme
- (616) 938-5944

Cranberry Christmas is housed inside a former Baptist church decked in a mellow red exterior. Inside, the shelves are filled with unique crafts and collectibles along with creative clothing, painted furniture and decorative antiques. Charming Santas and snowmen come in all shapes, sizes and personalities. You'll also find cherry-inspired items and quilted wall hangings.

Stained Glass Cabinet Company
4160 E. Mich. Hwy. 72, Acme
• **(616) 938-2007**

Housed in a large rustic, cedar log building, the Stained Glass Cabinet Company showcases the works and workings of its resident artisans in this combination showroom and studio. You'll find beautiful stained-glass lamps, gifts and furniture. The designs are original and elegant, often incorporating hand-engraved bevels or pressed flowers in beveled glass. Items range from small sun catchers to large chandeliers, jewelry boxes to tables and cabinets. You can watch the craftsmanship involved in creating these pieces as artisans work at benches at the rear of the building.

Leelanau County

The Front Porch
207 St. Joseph St., Suttons Bay
• **(616) 271-6895**

The Front Porch bills itself as an emporium of fine gifts and accessories for home and kitchen. This friendly shop is fun to visit with an array of unique glassware, serving dishes, table linens, kitchen gadgets, cards and gourmet coffees and specialty foods.

Lima Bean
St. Joseph St., Suttons Bay
• **(616) 271-LIMA**

You can't help but smile when you enter Lima Bean. This whimsical boutique is filled with a wild assortment of gifts, accessories and apparel. You'll find aromatherapy candles, colorful T-shirts, jewelry, greeting cards, picture frames, hats and a great selection of natural-fiber women's clothing.

The Painted Bird
216 St. Joseph Ave., Suttons Bay
• **(616) 271-3050**

The Painted Bird features fine art and contemporary crafts by over 80 regional artists. The quality is wonderful and the selection de-

lightful. You'll find handcrafted clothing, jewelry, decorative and functional art, furniture and custom rug weaving.

Sew Central
117 Broadway St., Suttons Bay
• **(616) 271-6331**

In an era of huge fabric stores filled with run-of-the-mill materials, Sew Central is a breath of fresh air. This small shop sits in a vintage building on a side street off St. Joseph Street. The front is filled with a wonderful assortment of high-quality, hard-to-find fabrics and notions while the back is set up as a sewing classroom for the many specialty classes offered here each month. Bernina sewing machines, sergers and related equipment are also sold here. Sew Central is owned and operated by two women whose love of fabric arts is contagious. They happily share their expertise in classes and with their customers and casual browsers.

North Country Gardens
109 Nagonaba St., Northport
• **(616) 386-5031, (800) 551-5031**

North Country Gardens occupies a storefront that had once housed the village food market in this charming town. Inside, the ample space is filled with distinctive home accessories, creative dishes and glassware, stationery and cards, holiday ornaments and children's gifts. The china patterns are bright and distinctive, with several styles displaying cherries in whimsical patterns. One area of the shop is set aside year round for holiday items, with trees festively decorated with intricate ornaments. Children and the young at heart will have fun with the shop's collection of puzzles, toys and games as well as collector miniatures. This is a lovely shop to browse in with many wonderful gifts for remembering northern Michigan.

Rose Garden Limited
301 Mill St., Northport • (616) 386-5451

You'll find a small treasury of museum-quality gifts at the Rose Garden. This charming store is nestled with The Courtyard Shops in a uniquely remodeled former gas station, just north of Northport. Sharing space with the Rose Garden is Northport Shirt Company, which specializes in high-quality, original t-shirts and the adjacent Northport Properties Ltd., which handles northern Leelanau real estate. All are owned by the same family. The Rose Garden's decor reflects a friendly, homey style, with handcrafted and wicker furniture showcased along with fine gifts, cards, jewelry, home accessories and collectibles. A large assortment of classic, quality children's books are featured as are the works of numerous local artists.

Tamarack Craftsmen Gallery
5039 N. West Bay Shore Dr., Omena
• **(616) 331-6324**

The Tamarack Gallery has been bringing outstanding artwork to the Grand Traverse region for more than 26 years. The shop is filled with fine art and contemporary crafts by over 100 American artists, many who live in the region. Tamarack features folk art, handblown glass, paintings, ceramics, graphics, metalwork, jewelry, fiber work, sculpture and furniture. If you love art, make time for a trip to Omena and the Tamarack Gallery.

Antrim-Kalkaska

The Framery
303 W. Main St., Gaylord
• **(517) 732-7093**

The Framery promises to supply the creative element with custom creative framing, fine prints and a lovely selection of handcrafted gifts. Look here for unique jewelry, candles, pottery, baskets, weavings and holiday items. The Framery is located in the heart of Gaylord's Alpen downtown.

Sue's Shops
132 W. Main St., Gaylord
• **(517) 732-1400**

Sue's Shops are actually six related shops together on Main Street featuring an eclectic mix of gifts, lighting and furniture. Look here for lovely handcrafted items, dried flower arrangements and craft supplies as well as an array of Michigan souvenirs and gifts.

Lake Michigan Shoreline and Cadillac

The Hitching Post
84 Cypress St., Manistee
• **(616) 723-8335**

It's Christmas all year at the Hitching Post, where you'll find one of Michigan's finest collections of Christmas ornaments and decor including plenty of items to create the northwoods lodge look. Two separate, but adjacent stores, showcase a premier collection of decorated trees. It's fun to browse through these shops in any season.

Hollyhock
431 River St., Manistee • **(616) 723-2051**

Hollyhock offers two floors of fine gifts and home accessories. See the children's closet where you'll find shelves loaded with trinkets, treasures and books for the younger set.

Sandpiper
393 River St., Manistee • **(616) 723-2889**
809 W. Ludington Ave., Ludington
• **(616) 843-3008**

Sandpiper stores offer a wide variety of quality gifts, bath products, home accessories, T-shirts, Michigan product gift baskets, local mementos and keepsakes. You'll also find lighthouse items, stuff for kids and Christmas collectibles.

Surroundings
423 River St., Manistee • **(616) 723-0637**

The humidor at Surroundings is well-stocked with aged, hand-rolled cigars, one of the finest selections of imported smokes in the area. They also offer a selection of beautiful and unusual decorator candles. On the shop's lower level, you'll find wonderful handcarved teak tables, benches and armoires and more home-decorating accessories including clocks and lamps.

Badger Boatique
700 William St., Ludington
• **(616) 843-3955**

The Badger Boatique celebrates one of Ludington's most famous landmarks, the SS

Badger carferry. For shiploads of SS *Badger* clothing, nautical decorator items, gifts, jewelry toys and more, visit this fun store. It's located dockside in the historic fish market and is open mid-May to mid-October.

Candelier of Ludington
109 S. James St., Ludington
• **(616) 845-9953**
See candles made or make your own. Candelier has 2,000 square feet of candles made in a variety of original designs including celestials, animal figures and ribbon candles. They also carry floaters, oil scents, sand and tabletop candles, floral arrangements and candle accessories.

The Java Shoppe
123 W. Ludington Ave., Ludington
• **(616) 843-1995**
Delight your five senses with pure incense, scented oils and aromatherapy gift items and much more from this alternative shop. They have imported natural clothing, personal growth books, bulk soaps and candles. Treat your taste buds; take home some whole-bean or fresh-ground bulk coffee or grab an espresso or cappuccino while you browse.

The Apple Tree
122 N. Mitchell St., Cadillac
• **(616) 775-6461**
The Apple Tree has one of the best rubber stamp departments in the north. It includes a great collection of stamps, papers and accessories. Like an old-fashioned general store, you'll find a wide variety of treats, gifts, collectibles, candles, cards and country pleasures.

Bonnie's Hallmark
108 N. Mitchell St., Cadillac
• **(616) 775-4282**
Much more than a Hallmark store, Bonnie's shop carries Disney, Precious Moments and other fine collectibles, educational toys for children, bath products, candy, gifts for the sport enthusiast, music and pet lover, great wedding, shower and baby presents. Free gift wrapping is available.

The Thistle Patch
811 Sunnyside Dr., Cadillac
• **(616) 775-3500**
There's always something unique and lovely to discover here. You'll find oversized baskets, bold and bright jewelry and accessories to turn your house into a home. The Thistle Patch also carries a good selection of artist supplies and keeps a Christmas room stocked throughout the year.

Little Traverse

Appletree
224 Bridge St., Charlevoix
• **(616) 547-2962**
The Appletree, in business for 24 years, features more than 1,000 gallery-quality, American handcrafted items. The collection is gathered from artisans across the country and includes handblown glass, sculpture, pottery and wood items.

Bullfrog Light Co. and Candle Factory Outlet
05995 Mich. Hwy. 66, Charlevoix
• **(616) 547-4407**
What Bill Stewart began as a hobby in 1981, is today a thriving Charlevoix landmark business. At the outlet shop, just south of town, you'll find the complete line of handcrafted Bullfrog candles. In addition to first-quality candles, you may find one-of-a-kind experiments and seconds at significantly reduced prices. Be sure to look for Bullfrog's great holiday and seasonal candles. The outlet also sells candles produced by other manufacturers and candle accessories.

Horton Bay General Store
05115 Boyne City Rd., Boyne City
• **(616) 582-7827**
This country store looks much the same as it did when writer Ernest Hemingway frequented the area in the early 1900s. The Horton Bay General Store is as much a shrine to the famous author as a modern convenience stop. Hemingway was married in Horton Bay and you'll find lots of memorabilia scattered around the shop. It's a must stop for Hemingway devotees.

Applewoods
325 E. Lake St., Petoskey
• **(616) 348-5086**

Pamper yourself with imported personal-care products from Applewoods, the only distributor in the nation for these natural products from Devon, England. The shop features massage oils, creams and lotions, exotic fruit shampoos, conditioners, bath gels, oils, body oils and soaps. Custom gift baskets are available for holidays, shower gifts and birthdays. The Applewood mother/baby baskets make a special gift for the new mom.

Bailey's Place
2017 U.S. Hwy. 31 N., Petoskey
• **(616) 347-8043**

If your beachcombing attempts have failed to turn up Petoskey stones, the fossil officially designated as Michigan's state stone, make a stop at Bailey's Place. They offer a selection of handcrafted Petoskey stone jewelry, paperweights, clocks, carvings, thimbles and many other gift items. They also sell polishing supplies and provide polishing services.

Barrel Craft
305 E. Mitchell St., Petoskey
• **(616) 347-3322**

If wine and beer making are your forte, visit Barrel Craft. They have the vintner and brewer supplies you need. They also carry gifts and accessories and for the cigar smoker; they offer Petoskey's most extensively stocked humidor. Call for off-season hours.

The Bristly Thistle
215½ Howard St., Petoskey
• **(616) 347-5460**

Truly the finest needlepoint shop in the north, this is a stitcher's dream. It features handpainted and custom canvases specializing in scenes of the Petoskey, Charlevoix and Harbor Springs area. Many different stitching fibers are available in an impressive multitude of colors.

Christmas in the Country
314 E. Lake St., Petoskey
• **(616) 348-1225**

You'll feel the glow and warmth of the holidays all year round at this Christmas shop. Start crossing off names on your Christmas list because you'll find ornaments to match everyone's personality, profession or hobby, whether simple or glitzy, fanciful or religious. Michigan pottery and other gift items are also sold.

Grandpa Shorter's Gifts and Trapper's Cabin
301 Lake St., Petoskey • (616) 347-2603

Visiting this shop is like visiting Grandpa's attic. Wonderful treasures are tucked into every nook and cranny. In business for more than 40 years, Grandpa Shorter's offers a delightful selection of home accessories, antiques, quilts, moccasins, quill boxes and ship models. They feature one of Michigan's largest Santa collections and one the finest selections of Petoskey stones in the nation.

Hank's Dad
14 Shoppers Ln., Petoskey
• **(616) 348-5588**

If you like whimsical folk art, this shop will make your heart sing. A small homegrown business, craftsmen produce one-of-a-kind, hand-constructed, carved and painted wood creations. The shop has interior and exterior items including birdhouses, frames, clocks, lamps, trellises and fun and functional furniture. Their popular work was featured in the fall 1997 issue of *Mary Engelbreit's Home Companion* magazine and is available in national catalogs.

The Quiet Moose
2666 Charlevoix Ave., Petoskey
• **(616) 348-5353**

Bring the north country home. Situated on 5 acres of gardens overlooking Little Traverse Bay, The Quiet Moose will captivate your nesting instinct with its more than 10,000 square feet of mountain, rustic, lodge and western home furnishings and accessories. There are 14 showrooms displaying an eclectic combination of antique and modern home-decor items.

The Tin Soldier
217 Howard St., Petoskey
• **(616) 348-5400**
157 State St., Harbor Springs
• **(616) 526-6841**

The Tin Soldier offers distinctive gifts and accessories for your home or cottage from two locations. Both shops feature items for the collector from nationally known artisans and companies including M.A. Hadley, Reed and Barton, Marilynn Tynan, Arthur Court and Wilton Armetale. You'll also find colorful hand-hooked rugs and authentic quill boxes.

Toad Hall
215 Howard St., Petoskey
• **(616) 347-5322**

For distinctive, one-of-a-kind gifts, visit Toad Hall in Petoskey's Gaslight District. They feature Bradford Williams sculpture and Jeff Flemming carvings along with authentic quill boxes, fine enamel art, Herend porcelain, Village pottery, Swarovski and 5th Avenue crystal, a Christmas selection and jewelry.

Cedar Creek Interiors
262 E. Main St., Harbor Springs
• **(616) 526-9026**

Cedar Creek brings together a unique selection of rustic home furnishings and accessories from across the country and offers custom design. To create your own north lodge look, check out their mission, wicker, twig, log, stone and incredible antler pieces. Call ahead for winter hours.

Walstrom Marine Inc.
105 Bay St., Harbor Springs
• **(616) 526-2141**

Located along the harbor, Walstrom Marine carries an outstanding selection of nautical clothing for men and women. The port store also has a nice selection of nautical books, boat supplies, and home decorating items.

Mackinac Straits

Island Scrimshander
Huron St., Mackinac Island
• **(906) 847-3792**

The Island Scrimshander spotlights the intricate artistry of Mackinac Island's Gary Kiracofe. Visitors are fascinated by these one-of-a-kind scrimshaw creations sold in the lobby of the Chippewa Hotel.

Loon Feather
Huron St., Mackinac Island
• **(906) 847-3592**

Native American art is featured at Loon Feather. You'll find an array of handcrafted works including porcupine-quill boxes, black-ash baskets, tamarack decoys, soapstone carvings, beadwork and turquoise and silver jewelry. The shop also carries Hudson Bay woolens, quality knives and island souvenirs. The Loon Feather is open May through October and by appointment during other times of the year.

Michigan Peddler
Huron St., Mackinac Island
• **(906) 847-6506, (800) 729-3180**
136 S. Huron Ave., Mackinaw City
• **(616) 436-5604, (800) 729-3180**

Stop at the Michigan Peddler for a true taste of the state. The shops specialize in Michigan-made foods, wines and handcrafted items as well as island and state logo gifts. You'll find the perfect memento of your travels north. You'll find storefronts next to the Lilac Tree Hotel on Mackinac Island and in the Courtyards of Mackinaw in Mackinaw City. Both are open between May and October.

Sandpiper Alley
113 N. Huron St., Mackinaw City
• **(616) 436-5309**

Sandpiper Alley features a nice selection of distinctive Michigan gifts including pottery, baskets, quill work, photography, watercolors, weavings, jewelry, gourmet foods, greeting cards, books and Straits-area souvenirs. Many items are created by regional artists. The shop is open from early May through October.

Sign of the Loon
311 Central Ave., Mackinaw City
• **(616) 436-5155**

This unique shop bills itself as a wildlife gallery in a wilderness setting. It's walls are filled with unique handcrafted gifts with a rustic theme. Our favorites are the handpainted, ceramic outlet and light-switch plates that bear an array of colorful designs. In-house artists create designs and artwork on shirts and glass. Visitors can watch T-shirts and sweatshirts being hand silkscreened.

Victorian Village Marketplace
1143 N. State St., St. Ignace
• **(906) 643-8175, (906) 643-6755**

This charming marketplace houses four gift shops: Back to Nature, Cinnamon Stick Floral, Amy Jane's Boutique, and Sugar-n-Spice Everything Nice. Madd Chadders deli is here as well. You'll find a lovely selection of novelties, home accessories, rubber stamps and gifts.

Sports Shops

Grand Traverse

Traverse City Area

Backcountry Outfitters
227 E. Front St., Traverse City
• **(616) 946-1339**

This is one of Traverse City's major outdoor retailers. You can order a tent, compare sleeping bags, buy a canoe, and clothe yourself against all of the elements with a single stop. The owners are outdoors enthusiasts, and the entire staff shares that enthusiasm. Armchair hikers also enjoy shopping here for clothes, books, watches and interesting gadgets. Look for clothing brands like Columbia, Woolrich and Patagonia.

Bavarian Village Ski & Golf
107 E. Front St., Traverse City
• **(616) 941-1999**
Sugar Loaf Resort, Cedar
• **(616) 228-6700**

Winter, summer, spring or fall, Bavarian Village is your stop for recreational equipment and apparel for golf, downhill skiing, cross-country skiing and snowboarding. The large downtown Traverse City shop is packed with all you'll need for slopes, trails and links. While the storefront is easily visible along Front Street, the entrance is behind the building, facing West Grand Traverse.

Bilmar Sports
211 E. Front St., Traverse City
• **(616) 947-8005**

This spacious downtown sports shop is truly a family business because father, mother and twin brothers are often at work on the floor or behind the counter. A local favorite for tennis equipment, Bilmar is well-stocked in the full gamut of sporting supplies.

Brick Wheels
736 E. Eighth St., Traverse City
• **(616) 947-4274**

Brick Wheels is a favorite location to find sports equipment and active wear for such pursuits as mountain biking, in-line skating, downhill and cross-country skiing, snowshoeing, snowboarding, hiking and city biking. The showroom is huge and the staff is very knowledgeable and extremely helpful. Brick Wheels also operates large rental and repair services.

MC Sports
3480 S. Airport Rd., Traverse City
• **(616) 933-6158**

This national chain of sports stores recently became the largest sporting goods store in Northwest Michigan when it purchased the former, locally owned outfitter Traverse Bay Tackle and merged it with its original Traverse City MC Sports store. The new store is enormous and carries equipment, apparel and supplies for all sports and recreational pursuits. Advertising heralds MC Sports as the largest sports center between here and the North Pole. Considering its new size, we would agree.

McClain Cycle and Fitness
2786 Garfield Rd. N., Traverse City
• **(616) 941-8855**

Cycle on in to McClain for the latest in high-tech bikes and in-line skates, accessories and service. The shop carries a full line of bicycles designed for all uses and skill levels. Major brands include Trek, Schwinn, Klein, Bontrager and Litespeed. You'll find wheels for the elementary school crowd and Burley buggies to haul toddlers and a range of mountain bikes, road bikes and combinations for the rest of us. In-line skates fit feet young and old along with the appropriate pads and helmets to cushion the falls. Biking attire and technical accessories line the walls, while the staff dispenses friendly advice and repair services.

The Troutsman
4386 U.S. Hwy. 31 N., Traverse City
• **(616) 938-3474**

Fishing aficionados will love the Troutsman with all the fixings to make an angling adventure memorable. In addition, look for great outerwear by Columbia and Patagonia

Varsity Golf & Tennis Centre
6450 Secor Rd., Traverse City
• **(616) 947-1185**

Traverse City's only indoor practice facility for golfers is also a great place to find your golf and tennis equipment, apparel and supplies. An added benefit is the chance to try out a club or racket in the indoor area to get a feel for its swing before you buy. Varsity Golf & Tennis sells custom golf clubs and offers racket stringing and repair services.

Alphorn Sport Shop
137 W. Main St., Gaylord
• **(517) 732-5616**

The family-owned and -operated Alphorn Sport Shop has been a Gaylord institution for decades. This is the place to come for apparel and equipment for active outdoors sports especially, fly-fishing, backpacking and bicycling. Bicycle service is also available.

Lake Michigan Shoreline and Cadillac

KP's Ski Gear and KP's Gear
12500 Crystal Mountain Dr., Thompsonville • (616) 378-4510

At Crystal Mountain Resort, KP's winter inventory includes downhill ski equipment, snowboards by Burton and Santa Cruz, Spider and Columbia ski wear for men, women and children. In the summer months, they stock what you need in golf equipment and accessories.

Manistee Cyclery & Fitness
475 Water St., Manistee • (616) 723-3100

This cycle specialist carries the top names in the bike industry including Cannondale, Gary Fisher, Schwinn and Specialized. They have all the accessories you need for the sport and also

offer repair service. Other products you'll find here are skateboards, snowboards, weight machines, exercise bikes and treadmills.

Northwind Sports
400 Parkdale Ave., Manistee
• **(616) 723-2255**

Northwind offers some of the best deals on ski packages in the north. A complete ski shop, they sell downhill and cross-country skis and offer cross-country and snowshoe rentals. They also carry a good selection of Columbia and Boulder Gear ski wear for men, women and children, Sorel boots, snowshoes and ice fishing gear. See the listing in our Fishing and Hunting chapter for more information.

Mclain Cycle and Fitness
311 N. Mitchell St., Cadillac
• **(616) 775-6161**

You'll find bikes for the entire family at Mclain's. They offer a good selection of both mountain and road bikes by Trek and Schwinn and all the gear, including helmets, gloves and jerseys. In the winter, it's the place to go in Cadillac to buy or rent snowshoes. They also carry fitness equipment and offer bike and fitness equipment repairs.

Sun 'n Snow Ski Shop
6240 E. Mich. Hwy. 115, Cadillac
• **(616) 775-2401**

Sun 'n Snow carries everything you need to enjoy a weekend on the slopes. You'll find downhill and cross-country skis, accessories, snowboards, snowshoes and ski clothing for men, women and children, all by leading manufacturers. They offer competitive prices and provide tune-up and repair service.

Little Traverse

Adventure Sports
2286 Mich. Hwy. 119, Petoskey
• **(616) 347-3041, (800) 438-6754**

One of the best backpacking outfitters in the area, Adventure Sports also sells family camping equipment, bikes, snowboards, snowshoes, cross-country skis. They offer ski and bike rentals and operate a complete bike service department.

Bahnhof Sports
1300 Bayview Rd., Petoskey
• **(616) 347-2112**
207 Bridge St., Charlevoix
• **(616) 547-4044**
Bahnhof Sports in Petoskey has one of the best repair and service centers in the area for skis, snowboards and bikes. You'll find a wide price range and good selection of Alpine and cross-country ski equipment, snowboards and in-line skates. They feature major brand names in ski apparel for men, women and children including Patagonia and Columbia. Summer wear includes general outdoor clothing, swimsuits and cycle wear. The Charlevoix location is open in spring, summer and fall and offers primarily women's sport clothing but carries some men's and children's wear, sunglasses and jewelry.

Boyne Country Sports
1200 Bayview Rd., Petoskey
• **(616) 439-4906**
This shop sells ski, golf and camping equipment, snowboards and bikes. They offer bike repair and maintenance and will even custom build a bike for you. They have adult and youth outdoor wear. If your size is not in stock, they can usually get an item for you from one of their other stores before the day is over.

Whippoorwill
305 E. Lake St., Petoskey
• **(616) 348-7061**
An Orvis fly fishing dealer, Whippoorwill carries good quality men's and women's outdoor wear. See the full listing in our Hunting and Fishing chapter.

The Outfitter
153 E. Main St., Harbor Springs
• **(616) 526-2621**
For technical outdoor clothing, including kayak wear, visit The Outfitter. They carry specialty outdoor apparel, accessories and casual summer clothing for adults and children. You'll also find a selection of cross-country and downhill skis, snowboards, snowshoes and kayaks. Equipment and kayak rentals are available as well as equipment repair services.

Mackinac Straits

Mackinac Outfitter and Marine Supply
Huron St., Mackinac Island
• **(906) 847-6100**
Boaters will find a broad selection of marine supplies along with top-quality sportswear and accessories. Look for such familiar brands as Patagonia, North Face, Revo and Columbia. Mackinac Outfitters also rents in-line skates, and serves as a U.S. and Canadian chart agent.

Tun-dra Tours & Outfitters
221 E. Central Ave., Mackinaw City
• **(616) 436-5243**
Visit this unique shop to find the best in dogsledding equipment, outdoor clothing and related wilderness equipment. The shop also specializes in small group wilderness tours in Northern Michigan, the upper peninsula, Canada and Alaska. Tun-dra helps organize the Mackinaw Mush and Wilderness Run dogsled races each winter. (See Annual Events and Winter Recreation for more on dogsledding.)

Toys & Games

Grand Traverse

Traverse City Area

Diverzions
100 Grand Traverse Village Blvd., Acme
• **(616) 938-5336**
Unique board games, complex puzzles, brain teasers and an eclectic assortment of books can be found in Diverzions. This is a fascinating shop with all sorts of memorable games and diversions for all ages.

Grand Bay Kite Company
121 E. Front St., Traverse City
• **(616) 929-0607**
Colorful windsocks sway in the breeze from this downtown storefront. Inside, patrons can choose from large stunt kits, children's toy kites, elaborate windsocks and an array of colorful toys.

Marty's Models and Hobbies
1025 E. Eighth St., Traverse City
- (616) 947-4469

Marty's Models and Hobbies helps you create the model of your dreams with supplies, kits and accessories. The shop also carries a good supply of materials for miniatures and trains.

Toy Harbor
221 E. Front St., Traverse City
- (616) 946-1131

Toy Harbor has been delighting local children and visitors for more than 15 years. Boxes of Lego sets, Brio trains and Playmobil figures line the walls along with Breyer horses and Madame Alexander and Corolle dolls. You'll find wonderful selection of arts and crafts, books, puzzles, toddler toys and science and nature items. A mounted Brio village and train set entertains little ones while parents and older siblings browse.

Trains and Things Hobbies
106 E. Front St., Traverse City
- (616) 947-1353

Model enthusiasts head to Trains and Things for kits, supplies and accessories. Train sets and individual cars ranging from the small N gauge to the popular H-O gauge and large G gauge are available along with the necessary track and materials needed to create elaborate railroad routes. You'll also find all of the makings for dollhouses and other miniatures as well a great selection of model car kits and supplies.

Leelanau County

Leland Toy Company
201 N. Main St., Leland • (616) 256-7575

The Leland Toy Company brings you classic wooden toys and popular educational favorites from its cozy shop on the edge of downtown Leland.

Enerdyne
212 St. Joseph St., Suttons Bay
- (616) 271-6033

Enerdyne offers an eclectic mix of nature, science, toys and treasures. There is something here to fascinate everyone. Adults will love the many telescopes and stargazing guides lining the back walls as well as the unique bird feeders and gardening accessories. Children can shop to their hearts' content among puzzles, toys, games and books. You'll also find science experiments, craft projects and audio tapes of the outdoors.

Antrim-Kalkaska

Little Treasures Toy Shop
115 River St., Elk Rapids
- (616) 264-6885

The tiny stone building housing Little Treasures looks like it belongs to the seven dwarves. Roof height is lower than average and the interior seems proportionately smaller than its full-size downtown neighbors. The selection stands tall with a large array of high-quality games, puzzles, science and nature toys, construction sets, models and supplies, dolls and accessories, books and arts and crafts.

Little Traverse

Rocking Horse Toy Co.
125 E. Bay St., Harbor Springs
- (616) 526-7236

Rocking Horse is loaded with toys, games and gifts for all ages. See the complete listing in our Kidstuff chapter.

Mackinac Straits

Mackinac Hobby Horse Co.
Main Street Centre, Mackinac Island
- (906) 847-6118

This tiny shop is tucked into a corner under the Lilac Tree Hotel right next door to Island Book Store. Its size is deceiving. Inside, you will find an array of educational toys and activities. Look for puzzles, travel games, arts and crafts, unique wooden toys and classic favorites.

Mackinaw Kite Company
Astor St., Mackinac Island
- (906) 847-3302
105 N. Huron Ave., Mackinaw City
- (616) 436-8051

Let's go fly a kite! At the colorful Mackinaw Kite Company, the selection is tremendous, ranging from simple toys to professional stunt kites that loop through the sky gleefully. You'll also find the assorted accessories needed to send your kite soaring as well as a great selection of windsocks, wind-powered toys and books on kite flying and kite making.

T-Shirts and Souvenirs

Grand Traverse

Traverse City

Harbor Wear
125 E. Front St., Traverse City
• (616) 935-4688

This is one of our favorite souvenir shirt shops in Traverse City, The quality is high, the selection is good and the prices are fair. Out-of-state friends always ask to return to Harbor Wear for more shirts to take home. You'll be able to find long- and short-sleeve T-shirts, sweatshirts and various shirting in sizes and designs for all ages. Check the phone book for additional locations in the Little Traverse Area and Elk Rapids.

Traverse City Shirt Company
223 E. Front St., Traverse City
• (616) 929-3352

You'll find a great selection of up north clothing for the whole family at Traverse City Shirt Company. The shop specializes in quality T-shirts, sweatshirts and resort-wear with embroidered or silkscreened names and images of the region.

Lake Michigan Shoreline and Cadillac

Seasons on the Shore
110 W. Ludington Ave., Ludington
• (616) 843-8200

For Ludington keepsakes and quality souvenirs, check out this shop. They carry lighthouse items such as mugs, magnets, ornaments and a specially designed Ludington afghan. You'll find T-shirts for kids and adults, and local gourmet products including Pentwater preserves and Brownwood salsas.

Third Coast
304 River St., Manistee • (616) 723-9890

For souvenir wear for men, women and children, stop by Third Coast in downtown Manistee. They have silkscreened and embroidered Manistee designs on shirts, sweats and hats.

Little Traverse

Harbor Wear
319 E. Lake St., Petoskey
• (616) 347-2664
161 State St., Harbor Springs
• (616) 526-6922
109 Water St., Boyne City
• (616) 582-3703
329 Bridge St., Charlevoix
• (616) 547-4359

You'll find top-quality resort wear at all four Harbor Wear shops in the Little Traverse region. They feature a good selection of name brands and many items carry town logos. Some stores close or operate on limited hours during the winter months, so call ahead.

Mackinac Straits

Mackinac Moccasins
Huron St., Mackinac Island
• (616) 847-3297

This is your stop for Indian moccasins, accessories and Mackinac Island souvenirs as well as leather jackets, gloves and purses. Mackinac Moccasins is in the Horse Corral Mall just east of the Sheplers Dock.

INSIDERS' TIP

Several shopping districts like Downtown Traverse City and the Grand Traverse mall offer gift certificates good for a variety of participating merchants.

An opera house, haunted house, butterfly house and lighthouse, wineries and wild animals, tall ships and taxidermy, you'll find something appealing to every age group and every interest in our region.

Attractions

In this chapter we offer the best of the sights and delights of Northwest Michigan. Many of these attractions are traditions that have pleased visitors for generations. Others are newcomers to the scene, but all aim to provide you with recreational, educational, natural or cultural pleasure.

History lovers will enjoy the wide selection of distinctive museums and tours of our historic communities. Nature and science lovers will enjoy our unique discovery centers (see our Kidstuff chapter for more ideas) or a thrilling coastal dune ride. Art lovers will find some of the area's finest artistic attractions, but don't miss our Arts and Culture chapter for the complete listing of our premier galleries and art organizations. An opera house, haunted house, butterfly house and lighthouse, wineries and wild animals, tall ships and taxidermy, you'll find something appealing to every age group and every interest in our region.

Keep in mind that many of our attractions operate on a seasonal basis. To avoid disappointment, it is always best to call ahead during shoulder seasons and winter months. Also, we have tried to be as current as possible with admission prices, but they are subject to change. Those of you who appreciate a bit of elbow room will find that most attractions are less crowded early in the day.

Cruise these pages for what strikes your fancy. Then set your sights on having a northern adventure you'll long remember.

Grand Traverse

Traverse City Area

City Opera House
112½ E. Front St., Traverse City
• (616) 922-2070

This 1891 Victorian landmark will give you a firsthand view of a 19th-century opera house like those that stood in so many communities. Today, only 18 such opera houses remain in Michigan. Traverse City's is being lovingly refurbished to its former splendor with gilded box seats, a colorful curtain and ceiling panels bearing the names of Sarah Bernhardt and other great stage stars of the day. The City Opera House hosts various community events throughout the year, but it is usually open during the week for visitors to peek at the work in progress. The Downtown Traverse City offices are also housed here. Donations are welcome and are used for further restoration work.

Con Foster Historical Museum
Clinch Park, Cass St. and Grandview Pkwy., Traverse City • (616) 922-4905

Since opening in 1935, Con Foster has chronicled Traverse City's history. Displays focus on the region's Native American and pioneer heritage. Galleries illustrate a general store, Victorian bedroom, blacksmith shop, livery stable, fire station and patient's room from the State Asylum. Theme displays appear on a revolving basis throughout the year. The Con

---

INSIDERS' TIP

The depot home of the Little Traverse History Museum was built in 1892 by the Chicago and West Michigan Railroad to accommodate passengers and freight traffic from western Michigan. Two other train companies ran the depot until passenger service stopped in the 1960s. The depot was restored by the local historical society and opened as a museum in 1970.

Foster collection includes 1,100 stone tools and artifacts from the area's early Native American culture. Several hands-on exhibits invite interaction. This small museum stands on the same grounds as Clinch Park Zoo and Train. It's open from 10 AM to 5 PM daily between June and August, and from 10 AM to 4 PM on Friday and Saturday the remainder of the year. Admission is $1 for adults and teens, 50¢ for children 5 through 12, and free for children younger than 5. Summer fun passes, available between June and August, include admission to the museum, zoo and train ride for $3.50 for adults and teens, $2.50 for children 5 through 12, and free for children younger than 5.

www.insiders.com

See this and many other Insiders' Guide® destinations online — in their entirety.

Visit us today!

Clinch Park Zoo and Train
Cass St. and Grandview Pkwy., Traverse City • (616) 922-4904

This longtime downtown Traverse City attraction and the surrounding Clinch Park highlights are worth checking out. The zoo is home to an array of native Michigan animals, including a pair of playful otters, a talking crow and two local buffalo. A miniature train, complete with steam engine, circles the property with loads of delighted youngsters. Check our Kidstuff chapter for more details including zoo hours.

Dennos Museum Center
1701 E. Front St., Traverse City
• (616) 922-1055, (800) 748-0566

Its slogan is "Come Alive Inside," and this community arts center is alive with activity. Don't miss the chance to visit this wonderful building nestled on the campus of Northwestern Michigan College. Inside, you'll find three art galleries with rotating exhibits, a central sculpture court, a permanent Inuit art exhibit and children's Discovery Room (see our Kidstuff chapter), a beautiful performance auditorium and a busy gift shop, community room and lecture hall. The Dennos Museum Center is fully profiled in our Arts and Entertainment chapter. Hours are 10 AM to 5 PM Monday through Saturday, and 1 to 5 PM on Sunday. Admission is $2 for adults and teens, and $1 for children 12 and younger.

Maritime Heritage Alliance
232 E. Front St., Traverse City
• (616) 946-2647

Officially known as the Maritime Heritage Alliance of Northern Lake Michigan at Traverse City, this organization is committed to preserving our Great Lakes history through exhibits, seminars and activities. The results of their efforts can be enjoyed by the public throughout the year at the Marine Library, at a restoration in progress and at the schooner *Madeline*. The *Madeline* is a 92-foot, twin-masted replica of an 1840s commercial vessel, which also served as Traverse City's first school while it was anchored in Bowers Harbor during the winter of 1850-51. Between spring and fall it tours Great Lakes ports but spends much of its time docked at Clinch Park Marina where it is open to the public. Just a few blocks farther east along West Bay, you can visit a restoration project in progress at the Maritime Academy pier. Volunteers are restoring the *Welcome*, a 55-foot sloop originally built during the 1970s for the 1976 bicentennial festivities at Fort Mackinac and Colonial Michilimackinac. It is a reproduction of the original *Welcome* built by fur trader John Askin in 1774. The original vessel was purchased by the British Navy in 1779 and converted to an armed sloop. Admission is free, donations are welcome.

Northwestern Michigan College (NMC) Joseph Rogers Observatory
Birmley Rd. between Keystone and Garfield Rds., Traverse City
• (616) 946-1787

The local community college operates this observatory just south of Traverse City. It is also the home base for the Grand Traverse Astronomical Society, which meets here on the first Friday of each month at 8 PM. The meetings are open to the public and feature discussions ranging from current sky happenings to the latest discoveries and theories. The Astronomical Society also hosts public viewing nights at least once each month where you can study the planets, the Orion Nebula,

Photo: Kevin Poirier/Courtesy of the Traverse City Record-Eagle

With its abundance of water, the Traverse Bay Region is a favorite for canoeists.

the Milky Way and other sky objects through the observatory's two high-powered telescopes. There is no admission charge. Viewings are usually held on a Saturday night in the middle of the month from 8 to 10 PM between October and April, and twice a month on Friday or Saturday from 9 to 11 PM between May and September. In addition, special community talks and viewing times will be held if an eclipse, meteor shower or comet is expected to be visible. Please call the observatory for a current schedule of public activities. Northwestern Michigan College, (616) 922-1260, offers several academic classes at the observatory each spring semester.

The Music House
7377 U.S. Hwy. 31 N., Acme
• (616) 938-9300

Take a delightful journey down melody lane at The Music House. Often referred to as a "performing museum," it is filled with beautifully restored antique musical instruments. Turn-of-the-century decor complements the wonderful sounds of yesteryear. Exhibits feature a huge Regina Corona Music Box, nickelodeons at the Hurry Back Saloon, a Reproduco Organ and Violano-virtuoso at the Lyric Theater and a Weber Duoart Grand Reproducing Piano that plays the sounds of historical keyboard artists in con-

cert. Radio and phonograph galleries trace the history of sound reproduction. A favorite is the handcarved Mortier Dance Organ, which was built in 1922 in Antwerp for the Victoria Palace Ballroom. Every visitor is treated to a guided tour in which each of the major instruments are explained and played. Plan to spend at least 90 minutes to two hours at this wonderful museum. Hours are 10 AM to 4 PM Monday through Saturday, and noon to 4 PM on Sunday between May and October. The Music House opens weekends only between Thanksgiving and New Years with the same hours. Admission is $6.50 for adults, $2 for children between the ages of 6 and 16, and free for children younger than 6.

Amon Orchards
8066 U.S. Hwy. 31 N., Williamsburg
• (616) 938-9160, (800) 937-1164

Visit Amon Orchards for a hands-on experience with the fruit that made Traverse City famous. A portion of this commercial orchard has been set aside for u-pick fruit, orchard tours and seasonal activities. Horse-drawn trolleys transport visitors through the cherry orchards as the driver gives an intro to horticulture. The friendly owners, who represent the farm's second generation, educate visitors with charm and good humor during the tours or while chatting over pie and coffee in the farm market. The market carries an extensive line of Amon food products including innovative — but delicious — concoctions such as cherry barbecue sauce, hot cherry pepper jelly and cherry mustard along with a huge assortment of sweets, preserves and baked goods made right there in the market kitchen. Our favorite is the chocolate "fudgie" sauce, which combines rich, thick chocolate with dried cherries to create a wonderful ice cream topping. Taste testing is encouraged, and samples are strategically placed throughout the shop. Kids love it here, so we talk about Amon Orchard at length in our Kidstuff chapter. It is open daily between mid-June and October, and on weekends the rest of the year.

The Ole Farm Museum
11459 Pavlis Rd., Buckley
• (616) 269-3672

Make a visit to a working farm at The Ole Farm Museum, 4 miles northwest of Buckley in rural Grand Traverse county. You'll find a collection of more than 3,000 antiques on display while guided tours discuss and demonstrate the workings of general-purpose livestock farming. Call ahead for reservations and directions. Admission is free, but donations are gladly accepted.

Leelanau County

Empire Area Museum
LaCore St., Empire • (616) 326-5568,
(616) 326-5181

This small local museum looks at Leelanau life with displays that feature a blacksmith shop, a turn-of-the-century saloon, a parlor, a one-room schoolhouse and an audiovisual center. The Museum is open weekends from 1 to 4 PM between Memorial Day and late October. Hours expand to 10 AM to 4 PM daily, except Wednesday, and 1 to 4 PM on Sunday between July 1 and Labor Day. Admission is free, but donations are accepted.

Grand Traverse Lighthouse
Leelanau State Park, 15390 N.
Lighthouse Pt. Rd., Northport
• (616) 386-9145

The Grand Traverse Lighthouse long served as a beacon guiding ships through the infamous Manitou Passage. Today you can learn more about the heritage of the inland seas and the importance of seafaring to this region at the turn of the century with a visit to the Grand Traverse Lighthouse, at the very tip of the Leelanau Peninsula. You can spend a delightful afternoon taking a scenic drive through Leelanau County to get there, followed by a tour of the restored lighthouse decked in period furnishings and nautical memorabilia. Then, relax, stroll the grounds, and enjoy a picnic surrounded by Lake Michigan's lapping waters and the tall trees of the Leelanau State Park. Read more about the lighthouse, the grounds and the tour in our Kidstuff chapter. A Michigan State Park motor vehicle permit is required for admission to the grounds. Fees are $4 a day or $20 a year, payable at any state park entrance. The lighthouse museum is open mid-May through October weekends from noon to 5 PM. Between mid-June and Labor Day, hours are extended to 11 AM to 7 PM daily. Admission is $1.

Leelanau Historical Museum
203 E. Cedar St., Leland
• (616) 256-7475

The Leelanau Historical Museum is a charming facility tucked into a pocket of woods off Cedar Street, just a short two-block stroll from the busier downtown area. It shares the grounds with the Leland Township Public Library. The property is tranquil, edged by the Leland River and surrounded by bright flowers lovingly planted by local volunteers. Inside, museum exhibits tell the story of the settlement of the Leelanau Peninsula through innovative displays. Permanent exhibits illustrate development from the time the first lighthouse was built in this northern "wilderness." Every summer, the museum stages a themed exhibit that focuses on a different facet of the county's past. A recent exhibit was titled, "Celebrate a Sense of Place — Leelanau, Artist's Words and Pictures." Another exhibit, "Postcards from Leelanau," utilized oversize postcards bearing the reminiscences of past museum-goers and Leelanau lovers. Traditional art, photographs and maritime history artifacts also are on display, along with a depiction of a one-room school. Historical archives are available to researchers by appointment. A gift shop

Photo: Mackinac Island Chamber of Commerce

Thousands of visitors enjoy a peek into history at Fort Mackinac.

sells items that are unique to Leelanau or created by local artists. The Leelanau Historical Museum is open 10 AM to 4 PM Tuesday through Saturday, and 1 to 4 PM Sunday from mid-June to Labor Day. From early May to mid-June and from Labor Day to late October it is open 1 to 4 PM on Friday and Saturday, or by appointment. Admission is $1 for adults and 50¢ for children.

Antrim-Kalkaska

The Alden Depot
Torch Lake, Alden • (616) 331-4274

Sitting along the shores of scenic Torch Lake in Alden, this historic depot dates back to 1908 when trains used to transport city dwellers who summered up north. Today it serves as the village's historical museum with photos and artifacts that chronicle Alden's past, beginning with 1849 and the lumbering era. One highlight is a model train mounted in a miniature turn-of-the-century village layout. The museum is open June through August on Thursday from 9 AM to 4 PM and 6 to 9 PM, and on Sunday from 1 to 4 PM. Admission is by donation.

Bellaire Historical Museum
202 N. Bridge St., Bellaire
• (616) 533-8631

The Bellaire Historical Museum chronicles the heritage of rural Bellaire with exhibits of vintage clothing, antique tools, general store artifacts and Civil War records. You'll find an extensive newspaper collection as well as Bellaire area pictures and maps from between 1865 and 1965. There is no admission fee to visit. The museum is open early June through September weekdays from 11 AM to 3 PM.

Central Lake History Museum
Mich. Hwy. 88, Central Lake
• (616) 544-6687, (616) 544-3322

This small historical museum is in a 100-year-old log cabin. Displays illustrate the history of this rural community and include several interesting children's exhibits. The Central Lake History Museum is open on Monday, and Wednesday through Saturday between Memorial Day weekend and Labor Day. There is no admission charge.

Elk Rapids Historical Museum
401 River St., Elk Rapids
• **(616) 264-9333**

Elk Rapids-area history is documented at this museum in displays spanning the early lumbering days through contemporary northern life. Photos and memorabilia chronicle village history beginning in 1852. There is no admission charge to this museum, which is open from 2 to 4 PM on Tuesday and Thursday during the summer, and on weekends all year.

Guntzviller's Spirit of the Woods Museum
11060 S. U.S. Hwy. 31, Elk Rapids
• **(616) 264-5597**

Beavers, otters, deer, bison, bears, mink and other North American animals and fish are displayed in dioramas simulating their natural environment at the Spirit of the Woods Museum. You'll also see exhibits of Native American arrowheads, pipes, ceremonial items, weapons, moccasins and hunting and fishing gear. The museum is open all year Monday through Saturday between 9 AM and 5 PM. Between June and August, hours extend to 6 PM Monday through Saturday, and noon to 6 PM on Sunday. Admission is $3 for adults, $2 for senior citizens and students, $1 for children 5 through 12, and free for children younger than 5.

The Bottle Cap Museum and Gift Shop
4977 Sparr Rd., Gaylord • (517) 732-1931

Just about any question you have about Coca-Cola could probably be answered with a visit to the Bottle Cap Museum. Guided tours take you through Coca-Cola history with ample displays of this favorite beverage's memorabilia. You'll see hundreds of novelty items, trays, signs, posters, clocks, bottles, dispensers and coolers dating back to 1930. With more than 3,000 items on display, this is truly a walk down memory lane. A gift shop sells more Coke collectibles, along with an assortment of souvenirs, antiques and miniature dolls. The Bottle Cap Museum is open 11 AM to 5 PM Wednesday through Saturday. Admission, which includes a free Coke, is $2.50 for adults and teens, $2 for senior citizens, $1.50 for children 6 through 12, and free for children 5 and younger.

Call of the Wild
850 S. Wisconsin Ave., Gaylord
• **(517) 732-4336, (800) 835-4347**

Visit this unique museum for a wilderness adventure wandering through at least 60 displays of North American animals. A large gift shop is on-site, and, during the summer months, you can enjoy Bavarian Falls adventure park. See our complete listing, including hours and admission prices, in the Kidstuff chapter.

Stone Circle
end of Stone Circle Dr., off U.S. Hwy. 31, Kewadin • (616) 264-9467

There is something almost mystical in the air at Stone Circle, an informal weekly bonfire where poets, storytellers, folk singers and listeners gather each summer Saturday evening to share their talents. The oral tradition is practiced in word and song under a cloak of summer sunsets and starry nights. Stone Circle, 10 miles north of Elk Rapids near the rural village of Kewadin, draws its name from the triple ring of boulders (88 in all) that surround the campfire and often function as chairs, back rests or stepstools. People of all ages are welcome to bring a blanket or lawn chair and join the gatherings, which begin at sunset and con-

---

INSIDERS' TIP

Odawa Chief Andrew J. Blackbird recorded the customs of his people in a book published in 1887. His efforts to preserve the tribe's culture led to the founding of the highly regarded Andrew J. Blackbird Museum in Harbor Springs.

tinue until the stories are done. If you have the urge, feel free to share your own story, poem or song. The only rule, in deference to the oral tradition, prohibits the use of paper; all words are spoken from the heart. Stone Circle was the brainchild of local poet Terry Wooten, who built the fire circle on the family farm. He leads each night's session with selections from his vast oral repertoire. Stone Circle gatherings start at 9 PM beginning mid-June and continue every Saturday evening through Labor Day. Admission is free, but donations of $3 for adults and $1 for children are encouraged. The money is used for upkeep and operation of Stone Circle.

Cedar Bend Farm
1021 Doerr Rd., Mancelona
• (616) 587-8126

Learn more about this rural region's agricultural heritage at Cedar Bend Farm. Tour the 120-acre farm, enjoy displays about home industries of the past, or take a class in weaving, woodworking or blacksmithing. Cedar Bend Farm is open Wednesday through Saturday all year. There is no fee for admission. Call the farm for more information about class offerings and the daily schedule.

Lake Michigan Shoreline and Cadillac

Benzie Historical Museum
6941 River Rd., Benzonia
• (616) 882-5539

Cross the threshold of this country museum, and step into north country history. The Benzie County Historical Museum, housed in an 1887 church building, features local history with a focus on the timber industry and a more romantic era, when train and carferries traveled the big lake between Frankfort, Michigan, and Wisconsin. A special exhibit is dedicated to the internationally known Civil War historian and county native Bruce Catton. Grandpa's Cellar gift shop offers a nice selection of historical books, old-time toys and candy, and local crafts. The museum operates an extensive educational program geared for all ages and is open from 10 AM to 4 PM Tuesday through Saturday, as well as Mondays during the summer. Admission is $2 for adults, 50¢ for children older than 5, and $5 for family groups.

Gwen Frostic Prints/ Presscraft Papers
5140 River Rd., Benzonia
• (616) 882-5505

Gwen Frostic is one of Michigan's most highly regarded artists and citizens. Frostic, born in 1906 in Sandusky, Michigan, has been recognized by dozens of private and governmental organizations for her lifelong contributions to conservation education. From a 250-acre personal wildlife sanctuary on the Betsie River, Frostic creates original block prints celebrating the wonders of the natural world. Framed prints, books, cards and gifts are produced on site in a truly unique building constructed from native stone. You'll discover original bird carvings by some of America's greatest wildlife carvers tucked among the displays of Frostic's works. Presscraft Papers also features one of the most complete nature libraries in Michigan, and visitors are welcome to browse through the volumes and relax in the streamside reading room. You'll enjoy the opportunity to observe the shop's 15 printing presses, which hum from 9 AM to 4:30 PM Monday through Friday. Open year round, Presscraft Papers's summer hours are 9 AM to 5:30 PM daily; May to November, it's open 9 AM to 4:30 PM Monday through Saturday. There is no admission fee.

INSIDERS' TIP

Save our lighthouses! The fate of many of these maritime treasures is in public hands. To learn how you can get involved in preservation efforts, contact the Great Lakes Lighthouse Keepers Association, P.O. Box 580, Allen Park, MI 48101.

Babcock House Museum
420 Third St., Manistee • (616) 723-9803

Unusual architectural features and a fine antique collection make the Victorian Babcock House Museum a treat for history buffs. The Manistee landmark home was built in 1882 by Simeon Babcock, a cabin designer for Great Lakes ships. The museum holds a wide variety of period furniture, glassware, Oriental rugs and a rare collection of automated musical instruments. Tours are conducted between 1 and 4 PM Wednesdays and Saturdays. Admission is $4 per person.

Manistee County Historical Museum
425 River St., Manistee • (616) 723-5531

The Manistee County Historical Museum features one of the largest collections of Victorian artifacts in Michigan. Unlike in most museums, the antiques are displayed openly, giving visitors a more realistic historical experience. The 1883 downtown Manistee building houses a general store, log cabin and eight period rooms including offices, a parlor, dining room, bedroom and kitchen. Research facilities are available. The museum is open 10 AM and 5 PM Tuesday through Saturday, and also on Monday throughout the summer. Admission is $1 for adults and 50¢ for children.

Manistee's Walk Through History
City of Manistee • (800) 288-2286

Glance into history with a self-guided residential walking tour of Manistee's vintage homes. The tour features about 25 spectacular Victorian homes with designs ranging from Colonial Revival to Italianate to Queen Anne and Victorian Gothic. A 15-stop commercial walking tour includes the Ramsdell Building, Manistee County Historical Museum and Ramsdell Theater, the only theater in Michigan using its original painted backdrops. For guide maps, visit the Manistee Area Chamber of Commerce, 11 Cypress Street, Manistee.

Water Bug Tours
(616) 889-3378

Enjoy a relaxing, narrated tour of the scenic Manistee River aboard the vessel *Water Bug*. You'll see some of Manistee's great historic and natural sites including Victorian architecture, wetlands and the port city's lighthouse. Tours are offered Wednesday through Sunday from Memorial to Labor Day.

Jacques Marquette Memorial
along S. Lakeshore Dr., Ludington

French Missionary Jacques Marquette established the first permanent settlement in Michigan and is known for his explorations, which opened the Great Lakes basin for development. Marquette died in 1675 near Ludington while returning north from a mission trip in Wisconsin. His last hours were spent at what today is known as Butterfield Peninsula. A memorial stands on the peninsula in honor of the great missionary's lasting legacy to the people of the state.

White Pine Village
1687 S. Lakeshore Dr., Ludington
• (616) 843-4808

White Pine Village is a slice of northern Michigan small-town life during the late 1800s. The Village, on a bluff overlooking Lake Michigan, features 20 historic buildings. A variety of old-time concerts and events are held on the grounds each year. White Pine Village is open from mid-April through mid-October. Spring and fall hours are 11 AM to 4 PM Tuesday through Saturday. Hours are extended to 4:30 PM in the summer. Peak-season admission is $4 for adults, $3 for students younger than 18 and $12 for families. See our Kidstuff chapter to learn more about this family-oriented attraction.

S.S. Badger Carferry
700 S. William St., Ludington
• (616) 845-5555

Experience living history along the Ludington docks. Enjoy this 100-year-old form

INSIDERS' TIP

Don't pass by those visitors centers or display stands filled with local brochures and advertising. You will often find money-saving coupons for attractions and meals.

Northwest Michigan's Silent Sentinels

Lighthouses are among the most captivating attractions along the Lake Michigan coastline. They are a reminder of both the romance of the sea and our perennial struggle against it.

More than 1,100 lighthouses once stood guard along the nation's shores. Today, fewer than 400 federally maintained stations remain. While some stand in various stages of decay, others continue to provide faithful watch. There are 23 of the legendary beacons in Northwest Michigan waiting for your visit. We highlight several of the region's most intriguing lighthouses, some of which are open for public tours. If they are available for touring, we let you know where to obtain current schedule information. Others can be viewed throughout the year from surrounding beaches, piers or from boats and are open sporadically for touring.

These lighthouses, in a variety of pleasing architectural forms, date back to the mid-1800s and stand guard on remote islands, the ends of piers and in soft dune sands.

The Great Lakes form one of the world's busiest shipping arteries and are host to a booming recreational boating industry. Despite common use of sophisticated navigational equipment by modern mariners, lighthouses are still considered significant aids in navigating the dangerous inland seas. They serve as easily recognizable landmarks, readily distinguished by radar. The U.S. Coast Guard is responsible for maintaining automated light systems within the structures, but many of the structures themselves are maintained through the efforts of local historical societies.

Each of these maritime landmarks possesses a unique character and rich individual history. The fascinating attractions line the region's coast from Ludington to the Mackinac Straits. We've listed the lighthouses, from Ludington to the Mackinac Straits, in geographical order so you can plan to visit one or more in a single day. Most are within an hour's drive of each other.

Our lighthouse trail begins in Ludington, home to two sentries, the North Breakwater Light in downtown Ludington and the Big Sable Point Light. The Big Sable Point Light is the last Michigan beacon seen by mariners heading south to Chicago. It's nestled in shifting sands, just 1.5 miles from Ludington State Park and is a favorite area attraction. Tour schedules are available from the Ludington Chamber of Commerce, (616) 845-0324.

The North Pierhead Light in Manistee features one of the last four remaining catwalks in West Michigan and is listed in the State Register of Historic Sites. An hour's drive north of Manistee, you'll find Frankfort's North Breakwater Light, a two-story square, white steel-sided tower. Ten miles north of Frankfort is Point Betsie

— continued on next page

Photo: Sally Gamble

The two-story Frankfort North Breakwater Light stands sentry.

Photo: Sally Gamble

Point Betsie Lighthouse in Benzie County is one of the most attractive in the state.

Lighthouse, the most visited and photographed lighthouse in Michigan. The pristine white lightkeeper's cottage and attached three-story tower pose a charming picture against the backdrop of cresting waves. It was the last attended lighthouse on mainland Michigan. Point Betsie marks for mariners the precarious and narrow Manitou passage.

The Sleeping Bear Dunes National Lakeshore has three lighthouses within its borders and operates a Maritime Museum. The Robert H. Manning Memorial Light, a relatively new addition, was built along the Empire coastline in 1991 as a tribute to local fishing buff Robert Manning. Located in the heart of the Sleeping Bear Dunes National Lakeshore, this sentinel is just a short drive from the Lakeshore park-operated Maritime Museum. (See our Parks chapter for more information about the Maritime Museum.) The South Manitou Island Lighthouse and the North Island Shoal Light mark the Manitou Passage. A slender spire, the South Manitou Island Lighthouse dominates the shoreline south of the harbor on the island's east side. Small elegant touches of glass and cast iron make it one of the most appealing and beautiful sentries in the region.

At the tip of the Leelanau Peninsula, at Leelanau State Park, sits the Grand Traverse Lighthouse, also known as Cat's Head. It serves as a lasting monument to the seafaring life. Built in 1851, it is today a quaint museum open for tours mid-May to October. (See our Kidstuff chapter for a complete listing.) In Grand Traverse Bay, at the tip of Old Mission Peninsula, is Old Mission Point Lighthouse. Tucked into a shoreline forest, the small wooden house resembles an old-time schoolhouse with a graceful lens parapet.

Heading toward Boyne County, you'll come to Charlevoix South Pierhead Light, a small square tower perched on a concrete pier 100 feet from shore. It guards the Round Lake Channel in downtown Charlevoix. Little Traverse Lighthouse can be viewed from Little Traverse Bay at Harbor Point, but it is privately owned and not accessible to visitors.

A series of lighthouses accentuate island landscapes from Little Traverse Bay to Mackinac. The South Fox Island Lighthouse, no longer in use, stands in the middle of a small peninsula and is accessible only by plane or boat. The Beaver Island Harbor

— continued on next page

Light and Beaver Head lighthouses, both feature brick towers. The Beaver Head Lighthouse is open to the public during summer months. Contact the Beaver Island Chamber of Commerce, (616) 448-2505 for Beaver Head Lighthouse details. Squaw Island, the northernmost island in the Beaver archipelago, is home to an elegantly constructed, brick lightkeeper's house and the Squaw Island Lighthouse. Nine miles north of Beaver Island, the Lansing Shoal Light, vintage 1928, still stands.

Traveling towards the tip of the mitt, Ile Aux Galets Light stands on a narrow strip of land northwest of Cross Village. These days this white brick tower capped in black cast iron is frequented only by crying gulls. White Shoal tower, 20 miles west of the Straits, was built in 1910 and is distinguished by its red and white candy-cane striped paint job. The dangerous waters near the Straits are also marked by the Waugoshance Shoal Light. Although in a state of sad decay, it clings tenaciously to its 100-year-old tradition of protecting the mariners on these inland seas. Old Mackinac Point Lighthouse and the surrounding grounds in Mackinaw City is maintained today as a public park. Reminiscent of a English castle, the lighthouse is a charming backdrop for a summer picnic. The last in the series of Straits lighthouses is the St. Helen Island Light. The restored brick tower and lightkeeper's cottage is a mile from the upper peninsula at the Straits. Its restoration, like that of many other lighthouses, was the result of the dedicated efforts of local civic organizations.

Lighthouses are interesting to explore any time of year. While the brilliant skies of summer illuminate the towers dramatically, the snow and ice of winter can create another kind of magic, equally impressive. In stormy seas, these landmarks stir thoughts of their noble lifesaving role. Visited on a calm, peaceful morning, the beauty of the strong, solitary structures will give you the sense of safety and rest it once provided thousands of mariners. Take your own crew on an expedition to experience these great legacies of a bygone era on Michigan's Great Lakes.

---

of transportation or a pleasant mini-cruise. The S.S. *Badger*, launched in 1952, is the only form of cross-lake service on the Great Lakes. Operated by Lake Michigan Carferry, it runs a daily four-hour trip between Ludington and Manitowoc, Wisconsin. See our Getting Here, Getting Around chapter for more information. Enjoy browsing and get S.S. *Badger* souvenirs at the unusual Boatique shop. See our Shopping chapter to learn more.

Mac Wood's Dune Rides
629 N. 18th Ave., Mears • (616) 873-2817
Bring your camera and sunglasses, and be prepared for a vacation highlight. Custom-built sand mobiles take the entire family for a scenic ride through 1,800 acres of open dune country along the Lake Michigan coastline. See our Kidstuff chapter for more information.

Wexford County Historical Museum
127 Beech St., Cadillac • (616) 775-1717
The museum is housed in a former An-

drew Carnegie Library (c. 1906). Perched on a hill overlooking Cadillac, the library was one of more than 2,000 libraries the wealthy Carnegie helped fund at the turn of the century. Today, the two-story building hosts a variety of displays and events. Key artifacts in the collection include items from the great lumbering era, Victorian clothing and numerous period display rooms. Admission is $2 for adults and $1 for children. Hours vary according to season, so call ahead.

Carl T. Johnson Hunting and Fishing Center
6087 E. Mich. Hwy. 115, Cadillac • (616) 779-1321
The Johnson Center focuses on the important role hunting and fishing have played in the development of the State of Michigan. Multimedia displays take a historical look at the conservation movements. A wildlife trail provides nature education, hiking and winter recreation activities. Ongoing programming

involves youth and adults. The center gift shop is a great resource for field and nature guides pertinent to the region. Call for a current program schedule. Admission is free. (See our Close-up on the center in the Fishing and Hunting chapter.)

Little Traverse

Portside Art and Historical Museum Society
Mich. Hwy. 66 at Elm Pointe, East Jordan
• **(616) 536-2393**

A 13-star American flag is the prized artifact in this East Jordan history museum's collection. It is one of only two such flags still in existence. The collection also features a variety of farm tools tracing local agricultural history, a military exhibit and vintage clothing. The adjacent Portside Gallery features 40 works, each selected from the East Jordan annual Portside Art Fair. The museum is open 1 to 4 PM Thursday to Sunday from June to October. Admission is free.

Wagbo Peace Center
5745 N. Mich. Hwy. 66, East Jordan
• **(616) 536-0333**

The Wagbo Peace Center was established in 1994 to provide an experiential educational environment on issues such as peace, justice, nonviolent conflict resolution and sustainable lifestyles. Situated on 212 acres, the center operates several demonstration projects. Models include a greenhouse heated with a combination of solar power and warmth generated from an attached chicken coop. Center practices include organic gardening, rotational grazing, pastured poultry, maple syrup production and sustainable forestry stewardship methods. Programming at the nonprofit facility is geared for children and adults and includes retreats, workshops and conferences. Visitors are welcome but are asked to call ahead for an appointment.

Earl Young Homes
Charlevoix Area Chamber of Commerce, 408 Bridge St., Charlevoix
• **(616) 547-2101**

Charlevoix resident Earl Young was one of a kind and left an equally individual legacy to the community. Young, a Realtor, built homes from huge boulders found in the region. Over a period of 30 years he constructed about 30 homes along Park Avenue, Boulder Park and Round Lake. His commercial projects include the Weathervane Restaurant, the Weathervane Terrace and The Lodge Motel. Pick up a map from the Charlevoix Area Chamber of Commerce for a self-guided driving tour.

Harsha House Museum
103 State St., Charlevoix
• **(616) 547-0373**

In 1891 Horace Harsha built a stately mansion capturing the true Victorian elegance and charm of the period. Today it's a Registered State Historic Site. The home housed the Charlevoix Historical Society in 1979. Tour this wonderful example of the period architecture from 1 to 4 PM Tuesday through Saturday, mid-June through Labor Day. Call for winter hours.

John Cross Fisheries
209 Belvedere Ave., Charlevoix
• **(616) 547-2532**

Want to send home an unique souvenir from the Great Lakes? Send a salmon. The John Cross Fisheries market will pack your salmon (or any other fresh fish) purchase for domestic flights or a long drive downstate. On Round Lake shores, the fishery is known as a Charlevoix landmark. It operates a retail shop and wholesales fresh Great Lakes fish to major metropolitan areas in the Midwest. In business for 60 years, it's one of a handful of fisheries selling freshwater catches. Whitefish, lake trout, perch, walleye and smoked fish are supplied to the family-owned market by Native American commercial fishermen, the only individuals allowed to harvest Great Lakes fish for commercial purposes. The market offers fish smoked with time-honored methods to achieve a truly old-fashioned, full, distinctive taste. Bring in your own fresh catch, and take it home smoked the John Cross way. While most customers get to the market by car, there are docking facilities for boat travelers. A few devoted customers even come by seaplane.

U.S. Coast Guard Cutter Acacia
Charlevoix Municipal Harbor

Charlevoix has served as a port for a succession of U.S. Coast Guard cutters. An ice breaker and buoy tender, the *Acacia* is responsible for navigational aids in northern lakes Michigan and Huron. The working Great Lakes ship is occasionally open for public viewing. Call the Charlevoix Chamber of Commerce, (616) 547-2101, to check tour schedules.

Bay View Walking Tours
Terrace Inn, 1549 Glendale Ave., Petoskey • (616) 526-9097, (616) 347-2410

Stroll back in time with tour guide John Higgins. Higgins, a fourth-generation Bay View cottager, gives an entertaining look at the historic Bay View community. The community is one of the earliest tourist destinations in the North. It features 440 cottages and is listed on the National Register of Historic Places. Wearing period clothing, Higgins dramatizes the old days, telling of the community's illustrious guests, including poet Carl Sandburg, Helen Keller and author Ernest Hemingway. Tours depart from the Terrace Inn Sundays at 1:30 PM during July and August and last about one hour. Rates are $4 for adults and teens, $2.50 for children 7 through 12; children 6 and younger get in free. Private walking tours and cross-country ski tours can be arranged in the off-season. To obtain a Bay View concert and lecture schedule, call the Bay View Association at (616) 347-4210.

Little Traverse History Museum
100 Depot Ct., Petoskey • (616) 347-2620

Operated by the Little Traverse Historical Society, the waterfront museum features Native American artifacts and collections from the area's pioneer, lumber and Victorian eras. A special exhibit features mementoes from the life of author Ernest Hemingway. (Hemingway was a frequent visitor to the area and used his experiences in the region as background for many of his famous works.) The museum is open 10 AM to 4 PM Monday through Saturday, May to November. Admission is $1 for adults. Children are admitted free.

Petoskey Walking Tour
Boyne Country Convention and Visitors Bureau, 401 E. Mitchell St., Petoskey • (800) 845-2828

Take a stroll through Petoskey's colorful past. Pick up a map for a self-guided walking tour from the Petoskey Chamber of Commerce or the Boyne Country Convention and Visitors Bureau. The 45-minute tour highlights the city's Victorian-style architecture dating from the 1870s to 1930s. You'll travel through the Gaslight District and see a former souvenir shop operated by the son of Chief Pe-to-se-ga, the town's namesake. Other sites include Symons General Store, Penn Plaza and the St. Francis Solanus Indian Mission.

Andrew J. Blackbird Museum
368 Main St., Harbor Springs • (616) 526-7731

The Andrew J. Blackbird Museum is managed by the Little Traverse Band of Odawa Indians and is the only Indian-operated museum in Michigan. The museum focuses on preserving the rich heritage of Odawa customs, arts, crafts, music and language. It is open 10 AM to 5 PM Monday through Saturday, and noon to 4 PM Sunday throughout the summer months, and weekends from September through mid-October. Admission is by donation.

Boyne City Historical Museum
319 N. Lake St., Boyne City • (616) 582-2839

Not only is the Boyne Historical Museum is adjacent to the city building, it's funded and operated by the city. You'll find a good collection of exhibits showcasing local history. The collection includes spinning wheels, a pump organ, dental office equipment and a wonderful array of photos. The museum is open 8 AM to 5 PM Monday through Friday, and from noon to 4 PM Saturday and Sunday mid-May through October. Admission is free.

Raven Hill Discovery Center
04503 Fuller Rd., East Jordan • (616) 536-3369

At Raven Hill Discovery Center, science, technology, art and history come alive with a variety of hands-on activities the entire family will enjoy. Exotic animals, interactive displays and antiques

A child gets a taste of cherries at the National Cherry Festival.

Photo: Kevin Poirier/Courtesy of Traverse City Record-Eagle

provide for a fun mix of educational experiences. See our Kidstuff chapter for more information.

Mackinac Straits

The Cross in the Woods
7078 Mich. Hwy. 68 (Exit 310 from I-75), Indian River • (616) 238-8973 shrine offices, (616) 238-8722 shrine gift shop
The Cross in the Woods has been a sym-bol of inspiration to millions of visitors of all faiths since it was erected in 1954. It is made from a 55-foot redwood tree and holds the 7-ton bronze image of the crucified Jesus Christ. It towers over hundreds of acres of serenely beautiful property. The cross is the focal point for this outdoor sanctuary that also has sculp-tures of St. Francis of Assisi, Kateri Tekakwitha, St. Peregrine, the Madonna and the Stations of the Cross. A doll museum displays 525 dolls dressed in the traditional garb of the country's

many religious orders. A gift store is on-site. The Cross in the Woods is staffed by the Franciscan Friars of the Sacred Heart. Worship services are held outdoors, weather permitting, at noon Monday through Friday, 4:30 and 6 PM on Saturday, and 8:30 and 10:30 AM on Sunday, from the last weekend of June through Labor Day. Additional indoor services are held daily at 8:30 AM all year long, and 4:30 PM on Saturday, and 9 and 10:30 AM on Sunday between Labor Day and the third week of June. Admission is free; donations are welcome.

Butterfly House of Mackinac Island
Mission Hill, behind Ste. Anne's Church, Mackinac Island • (906) 847-3972

The Butterfly House is a beautiful conservatory that showcases butterflies from around the world through educational displays and the fluttering activity of the 400 resident winged beauties. Tropical plants in full bloom add an exotic facet to the visit. See our Kidstuff chapter for a full description of this unique attraction. Admission is $3 for adults and teens, and $2 for children 12 and younger.

Fort Mackinac
Mackinac Island • (906) 847-3328

Fort Mackinac is perched high on a limestone bluff overlooking the scenic Straits of Mackinac and bustling harbor and downtown areas. Part of the Mackinac Historic Parks, it has been restored to its 1880 condition with 14 original buildings open to visitors. Costumed interpreters present historic re-enactments, musical displays and demonstrations several times each day to illustrate 19th-century fort life. Children will enjoy hands-on exhibits and games, while all will enjoy the museum store in the soldiers' barracks that's filled with fascinating books and gifts. Several nearby historical buildings provide added insight into island and fort heritage. Visits to the Indian Dormitory, Beaumont Memorial, Biddle House, McGulpin House and Benjamin Blacksmith Shop are all included with fort admission passes. Fort buildings are open from mid-May to mid-October. Hours are 10 AM to 4 PM daily, extending from 9 AM to 6 PM between mid-June and Labor Day. Admission is $6.75 for adults and teens, $4 for children 6 through 12, free for children age 5 and younger, and

$20 for families. Combination passes for unlimited seasonal admission to Fort Mackinac, Colonial Michilimackinac and Historic Mill Creek cost $13 for adults and teens, $7.50 for children 6 through 12, and $38 for families.

Haunted Theater
Huron St., Mackinac Island
• (906) 847-6545

Take a quick detour from downtown island shopping for some frightful fun. The Haunted Theater is a longtime island favorite with its spooky wax displays and haunted house effects. Standing in the center of downtown, the theater offers a fun break that promises to send shivers down your spine. (This teen favorite is profiled in greater detail in our Kidstuff chapter.)

Colonial Michilimackinac
Exit 339 from I-75, at southern end of Mackinac Bridge, Mackinaw City
• (616) 436-5563

Colonial Michilimackinac, in the western shadows of the looming Mackinac Bridge, is a reconstructed French fur-trading village and military outpost. It was founded in 1715 and served as a hub for the French and British fur trade that was thriving on the Great Lakes at that time. Following war and Indian attacks, it was dismantled during the late 1700s, moved across the Straits and rebuilt as Fort Mackinac on Mackinac Island. Today, more than a dozen wooden structures bear testament to life in the 1770s. Surrounded by an 18-foot stockade, the fort hosts a storehouse, blacksmith shop, powder magazine, barracks, the commanding officer's house, a chapel (with audio of a French wedding) and many interpretive exhibits. Every day you can watch colonial craft demonstrations, costumed re-enactments, cannon firings and the continuing progress of the nation's longest ongoing archaeological dig. Colonial Michilimackinac is open from mid-May to mid-October. Hours are 10 AM to 4 PM daily, extending to 9 AM to 6 PM between mid-June and Labor Day. Special evening and off-season events are held at various times throughout the year. Admission is $6.75 for adults and teens, $4 for children 6 through 12, free for children 5 and younger, and $20 for families. Combination passes for unlimited seasonal admission to Fort Mackinac, Colonial Michilimackinac and Historic Mill Creek are available for $13 for adults and teens, $7.50 for children 6 through 12, and $38 for families.

Historic Mill Creek
Exit 337 off I-75 to U.S. Hwy. 23 E., Mackinac City • (616) 436-7301

Historic Mill Creek is the newest of the Mackinac State Historic Parks. In a 625-acre scenic park about 3 miles south of Mackinaw City, Mill Creek is a reconstructed 18th-century sawmill and one of Michigan's earliest industrial centers. The water-powered sawmill was built in 1790, harnessing the creek's energy to produce finished lumber and grain. Much of the earliest lumber was transported to Mackinac Island to build Fort Mackinac. Visitors can watch hourly demonstrations of the huge wooden waterwheel. Several nature trails loop through the property, affording pleasant hikes near the creek headwaters, scenic overlooks and forested bluffs. Mill Creek is open from mid-May to mid-October. Hours are 10 AM to 4 PM daily, extending from 9 AM to 6 PM between mid-June and Labor Day. Admission is $5 for adults and teens, $3 for children 6 through 12, free for children 5 and younger, and $14 for families. Combination passes for unlimited seasonal admission to Fort Mackinac, Colonial Michilimackinac and Historic Mill Creek are available for $13 for adults and teens, $7.50 for children 6 through 12, and $38 for families.

Mackinac Bridge Museum
231 E. Central St., Mackinaw City • (616) 436-5534

This museum, not far from the Mackinac Bridge, commemorates the men who built it. The Mackinac Bridge Museum was created by one of the bridge's original ironworkers who housed it above his restaurant, Mama Mia's Pizza. Displays document the bridge's heritage from early planning through completion with many fascinating photos and memorabilia from the construction in the mid-1950s. Workers' hard hats line the ceiling while original tools, diving suits and cable spinning wheels fill glass display cases. A 30-minute movie and 30-minute slide show run continuously, showing actual footage of the bridge's construction and what, at that time, had been the monumental feat of connecting the state's two peninsulas. The museum is open 8 AM to midnight from May 1 through October 30. Admission is free, but donations are gladly accepted. To find the entrance, go through Mama Mia's and follow the stairs at the back. Granny's Attic Gift Shop is also inside, featuring books and souvenirs.

Sea Shell City
Mackinaw City • (616) 627-2066

Sea Shell City is the quintessential tourist stop for baby boomers' memories of travels north. You can't miss the billboards along I-75 alerting you to the nearness of giant clams and millions of seashells. What you actually find is a vintage white wooden building chockfull of rubber tomahawks, T-shirts, dolls, bangles, trinkets and an endless assortment of souvenir items emblazoned with the Mackinac Bridge or Sea Shell City. Highlighting these treasures is the "man-killing" 500-pound clam on display along with countless colorful shells. Admission is free.

Castle Rock
U.S. Hwy. 2, 3 miles north of the Mackinac Bridge, St. Ignace • (906) 643-8268

Long ago, Castle Rock was an important lookout for generations of Ojibwa who called the Straits area, or "Michinemackinong," home. Today, you can take advantage of the modern benefits of stairs and handrails to climb to the top of Castle Rock, which rises close to 200 feet above the neighboring landscape. From the top, you can see Mackinac Island and a panoramic sweep of the Straits. You won't miss Castle Rock; there are enormous statues of Paul Bunyan and his blue ox, Babe, sitting at the base. Castle Rock and its gift shop are open daily from mid-May through mid-October.

Deer Ranch
1510 W. U.S. Hwy. 2, St. Ignace • (906) 643-7760

Bambi lovers will love the Deer Ranch! Dozens of native Michigan white-tailed deer live in a natural wooded setting. Visitors can observe and photograph these gentle animals.

Fenced areas separate the deer from the rest of us, but you can easily see them graze, sleep and casually watch their visitors. Bags of feed are available for 25¢ and are sure to bring several deer to nuzzle into your hand for a snack. A gift shop features traditional souvenir fare and a large selection of deerskin products and moccasins. Admission is $2 for adults and teens, $1 for children 5 through 12, and free for children younger than 5.

Fort de Buade Indian Museum
334 State St., St. Ignace • (906) 643-6622

The original Fort de Buade was built by the French in 1681 and served as the first of the three forts to stand in the Straits area. The others were Colonial Michilimackinac in Mackinaw City and Fort Mackinac on Mackinac Island (see previous entries). This museum chronicles the region's early French period and its Native Americans through displays featuring the region's largest collection of authentic Straits-area artifacts. Fort de Buade Indian Museum is open daily from 9 AM to 9 PM between Memorial Day and October 1. Admission is $2.50 for adults and teens, and $1.50 for children 12 and younger.

Marquette Mission Park and Museum of Ojibwa Culture
500 N. State St., St. Ignace • (906) 643-9161

This city-owned museum is relatively small but packed with excellent, innovative displays that explore the earliest years of upper Great Lakes history. Much is devoted to Native American history — in particular, to the heritage of the Ojibwa, or Chippewa, and the Huron who made their homes here. The displays are fascinating interpretations of the cultures and help illustrate what the Native Americans and French explorers learned from each other. The Ojibwa Museum Gift Shop is at the back of the museum and features an array of locally made Native American works and a nice selection of books about the region's French and Native American history. You'll find quill jewelry, birch bark boxes, black ash baskets and other unique items. The museum and gift shop are housed in a 19th-century white church. Outdoors, a small memorial and pleasant courtyard commemorate Father Pierre Marquette and his role in establishing the early settlement of St. Ignace. This is the oldest documented archaeological site in Michigan and marks the spot where Father Marquette founded a mission among the Huron in 1671. The grounds next to the museum and park are transformed into hubs of colorful activity during the Festival of Native American Culture each August and the Michinemackinong Powwow each Labor Day weekend (see our Annual Events chapter for more on the powwow). The Museum of Ojibwa Culture is open daily from 10 AM to 8 PM between mid-May and late September, although hours are abbreviated on Sunday before Memorial Day and after Labor Day. Admission in $2 for adults and teens, $1 for children 12 and younger, and $5 for a family.

Mystery Spot
U.S. Hwy. 2, 5 miles west of Mackinac Bridge, St. Ignace • (906) 643-8322

The feature attraction here is a wooden shed built into a steep hill where visitors stand at 45-degree angles, balls roll uphill, chairs balance on two legs and optical contradictions are the norm. Tour guides walk you through these novelties and encourage photo taking along the way. The Mystery Spot has been attracting tourists for decades as a fun stop along the route of Straits-area attractions. Minigolf, a maze and arcade games are also available. The Mystery Spot is open daily from mid-May through late October. Admission is $5 for adults and kids 12 and older, $3.50 for children 5 through 11, and free for children younger than age 5.

Straits State Park and Father Marquette National Memorial and Museum
720 Church St., St. Ignace • (906) 643-9394

Stop here for a magnificent view of the Mackinac Bridge and the Straits of Mackinac as well as to visit an open-air memorial and museum that highlights the influence of missionary and explorer Jacques Marquette. The museum interprets the initial meeting of French and Native American cultures deep in this northern wilderness during the late 1600s. French Heritage Days are held twice during the summer — usually for a day or two in July and August — to commemorate local history. The park is open between late May and late September. Hours are 9:30 AM to 8 PM between June and late August. Call ahead for hours in late August and September. A state park motor vehicle permit is required. Permits are $4 a day or $20 a year and can be purchased at any state park entrance.

Totem Village
1230 U.S. Hwy. 2, St. Ignace
• (906) 643-8888

Totem Village bills itself as an authentic, historic Indian lore museum. Exhibits at the 1-acre museum display a historic sugar camp, Native American artifacts, handcarved totem poles, scale models of the Soo Locks and a lumber camp, and replicas of Fort Fond du Lac and a John Jacob Astor sailing ship. A live wildlife exhibit and gift shop are also on the grounds. Totem Village is open from mid-May to mid-September. Admission is $1 for adults, 50¢ for children ages 5 to 18 and free for children younger than 5.

Wineries of Grand Traverse

Tip a toast to the grapes of Grand Traverse with a tour and a taste of the region's fine wineries. There are currently nine excellent wineries operating full-tilt on the Old Mission and Leelanau peninsulas. We invite you to enjoy the fruit of their vines with us.

Why wine, and why Traverse, you ask? Although this doesn't look like the wine country of France or California, the region shares many of the unique characteristics needed to cultivate fine vineyards. All of these wineries are near the 45th parallel, which passes through the tip of the Old Mission Peninsula — and through the Bordeaux region of France. The peninsulas are surrounded by Grand Traverse Bay and Lake Michigan, which create a tempering microclimate that keeps springs a bit cooler (delaying early buds prone to freezing) and autumns a bit warmer (extending the season until the vines are harvested). Winter's snow provides an insulating blanket for the vines, while our magnificent summers bring the perfect cooler temperatures needed for a fruitful

growing season. This is the same natural phenomenon that makes our orchards so productive and has led the region to become the national cherry capital — but that's another story! The result is a flourishing industry that has matured over the past 20-plus years.

Our region's wine tradition began when a Northwestern Michigan College librarian planted the area's first grapes on his Leelanau County land. Today, that vineyard is home to Boskydel Vineyards (see the listing in this chapter).

We have reviewed the area's nine major wineries. All offer public tours and tastings in varying degrees of availability. It's always best to call ahead to determine the most current schedules as they often change with the season. Several also host tasting rooms in retail locations, and the fruits of their labor can easily be found on wine lists and market shelves throughout Northwest Michigan.

By the way, if you'd like to peruse the full lineup of regional wines, bottle by bottle, stop by and chat with the folks at Wine Country Market, the Village Wine Shop, Burritt's Meat Market or Maxbauer Market (all are listed in our Shopping chapter). These shops have extensive wine selections, and staff are happy to discuss the intricacies of the grape and help you make your choice.

Bowers Harbor Vineyards
2896 Bowers Harbor Rd., Traverse City
• (616) 223-7615

This small, family-run winery on the Old Mission peninsula specializes in Chardonnay, Riesling, Johannesburg Riesling, sparkling and cherry wines. Hours between June and October are 11 AM to 6 PM daily, and noon to 6 PM daily on Sunday. Between November and May the vineyards are open weekends only or by appointment.

Chateau Chantal
15900 Rue de Vin, Traverse City
• (616) 223-4110

Chateau Chantal combines a unique bed and breakfast with its winery on 65 acres on the Old Mission Peninsula overlooking both East and West Grand Traverse Bay. Vinifera wines are produced here: Chardonnay, Riesling, Pinot Noir, Gewurztraminer, Merlot and Pinot Menier. Hours are 11 AM to 5 PM Monday through Saturday between November and mid-June. Hours extend to 7 PM in September and October, and to 9 PM from mid-June to Labor Day. Hours on Sunday are always noon to 5 PM. The Chateau also hosts Jazz at Sunset performances (see our Nightlife chapter) during the summer and fall. An additional retail outlet is at the Grand Traverse Mall.

Chateau Grand Traverse
12239 Center Rd., Traverse City
• **(616) 223-7355**

Chateau Grand Traverse was the first Old Mission winery to produce vinifera wines and is one of the region's original vineyards. The large facility produces several award-winning estate-grown wines, including its Chardonnays, Rieslings and Ice Wines. It also produces a line of Traverse City fruit wines, such as Cherry Riesling. Hours are 10 AM to 5 PM Monday through Saturday, and noon to 5 PM on Sunday between November and April. Closing times extend to 6 PM in May and October, and to 7 PM between June and September. Additional tasting centers are at Peppercorn in downtown Traverse City, 226 E. Front Street, (616) 941-4146, and at the Chateau Shop in Williamsburg, 4176 Mich. Highway 72 E., (616) 938-2291.

Peninsula Cellars
18250 Mission Rd., Old Mission
• **(616) 223-4050 winery, (616) 223-4310 tasting room**

Peninsula Cellars is the area's newest local winery and specializes in wines made from the finest fruits representative of the area. These wines are produced with minimal handling and are estate bottled. Hours are 10 AM to 6 PM Monday through Saturday, and noon to 6 PM on Sunday. An additional tasting room is in Northport at 106 Waukazoo Street, (616) 386-7282.

Boskydel Vineyards
7501 E. Otto Rd., Lake Leelanau
• **(616) 256-7272**

Boskydel Vineyards is the one that started them all when NMC librarian Bernie Rink planted his first grapes two decades ago. Overlooking Lake Leelanau, this became the first vineyard and winery in the Grand Traverse region. It specializes in dry and semi-dry table wines, which are crafted in very small quantities. The now-retired Rink still entertains visitors in Boskydel's fascinating tasting room. Hours are 1 to 6 PM year round.

Good Harbor Vineyards
34 S. Manitour Tr., Lake Leelanau
• **(616) 256-7165**

Good Harbor Vineyards is known for Chardonnays, Rieslings and varieties often named with a local slant. Tall Ship Chardonnay, Trillium and Fishtown White are just a few that come to mind immediately. Hours are 11 AM to 5 PM Monday through Saturday, and noon to 5 PM on Sunday between mid-May and November.

Leelanau Wine Cellars
12683 E. Tatch Rd., Omena
• **(616) 386-5201**

Leelanau Wine Cellars produces a large selection of vinifera, hybrid and fruit wines. Hours are 11 AM to 5 PM Monday through Saturday, and noon to 5 PM Sunday year round. Additional tasting centers following the same hours are hosted in Leland at 102 Main Street, (616) 256-8858, and in Empire at the Country Shop, Mich. Highway 22, (616) 326-8858.

L. Mawby Vineyards
4519 S. Elm Valley Rd., Suttons Bay
• **(616) 271-3522**

The L. Mawby Vineyards are very close to Suttons Bay in "The Valley" area. It has produced award-winning wines that are estate grown and bottled with an emphasis on white table wines and sparkling wines. Hours are 1 to 6 PM Thursday through Sunday between early May and late October.

Shady Lane Cellars
9580 Shady Ln., Suttons Bay
• **(616) 947-8865**

Another new vineyard, this winery sits on the Leelanau peninsula between Suttons Bay and Traverse City. Shady Lane produces excellent bottle-fermented sparkling wines as well as Pinot Noir, Riesling and Chardonnay. Tastings are available by appointment.

In these parts, where
agriculture is a key
contributor to the
economy, life's truly
a bowl of cherries,
and fun does grow
on trees.

Kidstuff

If you wonder whether your northern experience will meet the expectations of the fast-paced younger generation, take heart. The word "bored" does not exist in the up north vacation vocabulary.

Peruse the listings in this chapter to discover some of the area's most unique and appealing attractions for kids. You'll find places to learn, places to create, and places of wonder and delight.

Before you map out a family itinerary, take the time to explore our other chapters. Northwest Michigan resorts, four-season recreational activities, festivals and attractions are very family oriented. Few events are planned without the younger set in mind.

Whether your children are toddlers or teens, get set for some great times. Scores of beautiful northern beaches offer one of the most popular ways to enjoy a sunny summer day. Parks and preserves offer an array of family hiking, biking and sightseeing opportunities. Museums, theaters, libraries, community festivals and country fairs often have activities just for children.

When it comes to dining, you'll find the region's restaurants cheerfully accommodate youngsters. Many provide coloring materials to occupy the waiting time and offer special menus. For desserts, visit one of our wonderful ice cream parlors, candy or cookie shops.

In these parts, where agriculture is a key contributor to the economy, life's truly a bowl of cherries, and fun does grow on trees. There are many luscious local fruit products to experience. For a country adventure, take the family out to one of the u-pick farms and pluck a bucket of cherries, apples, strawberries, blueberries or peaches. (See our Shopping chapter to learn more about local orchards or check the classifieds in local newspapers.) In the fall, there are pumpkin fields to visit. In November and December, Christmas tree plantations invite families to cut their own evergreens. Discover for yourself how the simple pleasures and great treasures of Northwest Michigan are the perfect formula for rewarding family adventure and play.

Grand Traverse

Clinch Park Zoo & Con Foster Museum
Grandview Pkwy. between Cass and Union Sts., Traverse City
• **(616) 922-4904 zoo, (616) 922-4905 museum**

This tiny zoo is packed with native feathered and four-legged residents. Clinch Park Zoo showcases animals that call Michigan home, including black bears, beaver, otter, bobcat, lynx, coyote, wolf, bison, elk and deer. You'll also find an aquarium filled with native fish, a turtle pond and a bird area with owls, eagles, hawks and a crow that likes to talk.

Our favorite stop is the otter display, where two river otters play, roll, swim, tease and dive tirelessly through the day. A miniature train pulled by an authentic steam engine circles the zoo and passes by the adjacent Open Space, marina and beach. The train departs near the entrance to the Con Foster Museum, a small but delightful facility that highlights the natural and social history of the Traverse City area with revolving themed displays.

A concession stand with ample outdoor tables is open between Memorial Day and Labor Day, or you can walk to downtown eateries just a short one-block walk away. Bring along your swimsuits for the beach and you can easily spend the day at Clinch Park. The zoo is open daily from 9:30 AM to 4:30 PM from mid-April to November 1, with summer hours extending to 7:30 PM. Admission is $2 for adults, $1.50 for children 5-12, and free for those younger than 5.

Zookeepers usually open the doors one

Sunday afternoon each month during December, January, February and March. The train runs from Memorial Day to Labor Day. Cost is $1 per ride for adults, 50¢ for children 5 to 12 and no charge for those younger than 5. Con Foster Museum is open 10 AM to 4:30 PM daily during the summer and on a reduced, primarily weekend, schedule during other times of the year. Call ahead for the most current hours. Admission at Con Foster is $1 for adults, 50¢ for children 5 to 12, and $3 for a family.

www.insiders.com

See this and many other Insiders' Guide® destinations online — in their entirety.

Visit us today!

Dennos Museum Center — Discovery Room
1705 E. Front St., Traverse City
• **(616) 922-1055, (800) 748-0566**

Little hands can explore to their heart's content in the Discovery Room at the Dennos Museum Center (see full museum listing in our Attractions chapter). Art, science and technology meld together through a variety of interactive exhibits ranging from traditional "hands-on" favorites to unique high tech wonders. Don't miss Recollections, an interactive video where your body's movement triggers psychedelic changes and images on an enormous screen. This is one of the few interactive video displays of this scale in the United States.

Another favorite is the Weisse Wall, a textured wall, which, when touched in any variety of patterns, acts as a huge instrument for making notes and sounds. Older children will enjoy the Inuit Gallery with its native sculptures, prints and historical notes as well as the changing displays in the museum galleries and sculpture court. The gift shop has a wonderful selection of hands-on craft kits, children's books, unique toys and other treasures in an affordable range of prices. Hours are usually 10 AM to 5 PM Monday through Saturday, and 1 to 5 PM Sunday. Hours are sometimes extended during the summer or when special events or performances are scheduled. Admission is $2 for adults and $1 for children.

F&M Park
Intersection of State, Railroad and Washington Sts., Traverse City

F&M Park takes up a full block near downtown Traverse City. Before Kids Kove (see below) was built, this city park was the best playground for young children. It is still a local favorite. Large wooden play structures resembling a train engine, car and caboose stretch along one side with countless opportunities for climbing, hiding, swinging and simply playing. Parents can lounge or picnic on blankets spread over the sprawling, grassy park property or join the kids at the swings or the ball field. F&M's central location makes it a popular destination.

Kids Kove, Grand Traverse County Civic Center
11125 W. Civic Center Dr., Traverse City
• **(616) 922-4818**

Kids Kove is a massive public play structure that was a labor of love for the hundreds of local volunteers who planned for months and then built it over a long spring weekend in 1995. This is play heaven! You'll find walking bridges, twisty slides, swinging bars, hiding spaces, tire swings and climbing bars. A toddler area is geared toward younger visitors. Kids Kove is located on the southeast corner of the Grand Traverse County Civic Center, near the Titus Street entrance. Traditional swings, slides and a picnic shelter at the original Civic Center playground are next to Kids Kove. Ball fields are nearby and a 1-mile multi-purpose track circles the center's perimeter, so bring along a soccer ball, or your favorite kind of wheels for an afternoon of play.

INSIDERS' TIP

The zany Scottville Clown Band consists of musicians from around the state. Kids and grownups alike enjoy their lively costumed performances at festivals and special events throughout the region.

Northwestern Michigan College — Extended Education
1705 E. Front St., Traverse City
- **(616) 922-1700**

Northwestern Michigan College has always offered a comprehensive array of lifelong learning courses for community residents through its Extended Education Department, including a wonderful selection of enrichment classes for children. These include weeklong Super Summer classes in art, science, computers and music as well as Super Saturday art classes during the school year. Each course's curriculum is geared toward lower elementary, upper elementary or junior high school students with age-appropriate activities. Grandparents special interest classes are also available with dual enrollment for an adult and a child. Course costs and materials fees range from $30-100 per class. You can register in person at the Extended Education office located at the College's University Center campus or by phone if paying with a major credit card. When signing up, make sure you have your student's social security number handy to complete the registration process.

Northwest Michigan Artists and Craftsmen — Creative Child Art Classes
720 S. Elmwood St., Traverse City
- **(616) 941-9488**

The Northwest Michigan Artists and Craftsmen (NMAC) sponsor Creative Child Art Classes on many Saturdays during the year. The instructors, who are professional artists, focus on a specific art area and guide children in creating during three-hour classes. Past classes have worked on watercolors, beads, acrylics, inks, collages, Eskimo Art, African culture, tie dye, pastels and wildlife art. The Saturday before Christmas has traditionally been set aside for a creative giftmaking workshop. The classes are especially appropriate for elementary age children. Classes usually run from 11 AM to 2 PM and cost $10. All materials are provided unless otherwise specified (for example, participants usually provide their own T-shirts for painting or tie dye). Children should bring a sack lunch and wear clothes that can get messy. Call the NMAC Art Center for a current schedule of classes and to preregister.

Old Town Playhouse — Traverse City Children's and Teen Theater
148 E. Eighth St., Traverse City
- **(616) 943-9198 Children's Theater, (616) 947-2210 Old Town Business Office, (616) 947-2243 Box Office**

Old Town Playhouse is the home of the Traverse City Civic Players (see full listing in Arts and Culture chapter). One subsidiary of Old Town is the Traverse City Children's Theater where aspiring young thespians can participate in workshops and often play key roles in children's and main stage performances. Past productions, held at various times throughout the year, involved large numbers of children and have included the *Wizard of Oz*, *Oliver* and *The Sound of Music*. Contact the Children's Theater for information and costs for upcoming workshops or contact the Old Town box office for its current slate of performances. Ticket prices are usually $8 for adults and $5 for children, although prices for major musicals can be higher.

Pebble Brook Golf
2072 U.S. Hwy. 31 N., Traverse City
- **(616) 938-2066**

You can play miniature golf across a covered bridge, over a babbling brook and along rolling courses at Pebble Brook. Mini-duffers can play on two different courses totaling 36 fun holes. The setting is pleasant and inviting. After golf, kids can test their road skills on Pebble Brook's Go Karts or try out the array of games located inside the Arcade and Snack Bar. There are games for all ages and everyone wins a prize, even toddlers. Top off the day with a hand-dipped ice cream cone, one of the Snack Bar's specialties. Costs average $5 per game. Pebble Brook is open from mid-May to mid-September, weather permitting. Summer hours are 10 AM to 10 PM.

Pirate's Cove Adventure Park
1710 U.S. Hwy. 31 N., Traverse City
- **(616) 938-9599**

Pirate's Cove has grown from a favorite adventure golf destination into a full family attraction. The minigolf courses alone are worth the visit. Two 18-hole courses challenge putting skill as players weave through pirates' caves, over footbridges and under waterfalls. The pirate

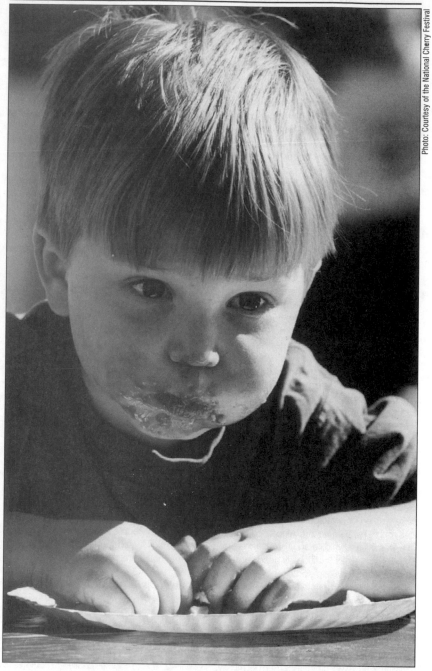

Photo: Courtesy of the National Cherry Festival

Kids enjoy participating in the annual Cherry Pie Eating
Contest, at the National Cherry Festival.

theme with little legends and related paraphernalia is well interpreted throughout the park. On a hot day, kids will love the Pirate's Plunge Watercoaster with the appropriate number of wet dips, drops and twisting curves. Skid cars let older children race on a slick track while little ones go behind the wheel on kiddie cars. Hoop shoot lets basketball fans compete against life-size robotic defense players. Pizza Hut, Little Caesar's and Dairy Queen all share parking lots with Pirate's Cove. The park is open from mid-May into October, weather permitting. Hours are 10 AM to 11 PM. Adventure golf fees average $5.50 per game, while value packs are sold for various combinations of golf, watercoaster and cars with prices ranging between $8.50 and $11 per person.

Pocket Change
Grand Traverse Mall, 3130 S. Airport Rd., Traverse City • (616) 946-2022

Pinball wizards may have given way to the high-tech pizzazz of video avengers but arcade games are always favorites. Pocket Change at the Grand Traverse Mall seems like a world unto itself with a massive supply of video games, pinball machines, simulators, kiddie games and arcade ball games. Children and teens can happily wile away the rainiest and snowiest days in this high-tech cocoon. Most games will cost the token equivalent of 50¢. While the older kids play, parents can grab a quick cup of coffee or a snack at the mall's adjacent food court or can take little ones for a ride on the mall's full-size antique reproduction carousel, also in the food court. Carousel rides are $1.

The Pottery Lodge
120 E. Front St., Traverse City • (616) 932-9007

Like its parent store in Petoskey, The Pottery Lodge offers a wonderful outlet for creative urges as children and adults paint their own pottery. See the full listing in the subsequent Little Traverse section of this chapter.

Ranch Rudolf
6841 Brown Bridge Rd., Traverse City • (616) 947-9529

Ranch Rudolf brings the fun of the West to life in the north woods. Nestled on 195 acres of wooded property along the Boardman River, the ranch is surrounded by the scenic Pere Marquette Forest. You'll find any number of activities from horseback riding and hiking in the woods to canoeing and rumpbumping (a.k.a. tubing) down the river as well as hay rides, sleigh rides, snowshoeing and cross-country skiing. Horseback rides take place daily between 10 AM and 4 PM between Memorial Day and Labor Day, and on weekends between May and October. All trail rides are led by guides. Children must be at least 8 years old and 4½ feet tall to ride. Younger children between 3 and 8 aren't forgotten. They also have the chance to ride their own horses as long as they are being led by a parent. After the playing is over, the entire family can relax at the ranch's rustically decorated restaurant or in front of the huge fireplace in the lounge.

Horses average $20 per hour. Parent-led children's horse rides are calculated at $5 for the first 15 minutes and $4 for each additional 15 minutes. Rumpbumping will run $7 to $10 per person while canoeing ranges from $17 to $26 per person. Hay rides and sleigh rides cost $5 per person with a $50 minimum per ride and should be scheduled one week in advance. For winter fun, complete cross-country ski packages for adults run $14.50 on weekends and $10.50 during the week, and for children $9.50 on weekends, $7.50 during the week. Snowshoes rent for $8 per half day. Finding Ranch Rudolf in the woods can be little tricky if you're unfamiliar with the area. Call ahead for the best directions from your location, then follow the RR signs to the ranch.

River Country Funland
1076 U.S. Hwy. 31 N., Traverse City • (616) 946-6663

Ideally situated right next to the Traverse City State Park and directly across from the State Park beach, River Country Funland offers a flurry of fun for all ages. An 18-hole miniature golf course lies along the park's west side while bumper cars and bumper boats add to the offerings. It's easy to find River Country by its telltale life-size riverboat ice cream stand docked in front. River Country is seasonal, operating at full tilt between Memorial Day and Labor Day with additional days added if the weather cooperates. Admission charges vary with activities, ranging from $5 to $8 per person.

Skate World
1669 S. Garfield St., Traverse City
• (616) 941-1400

Get ready to roll! Skate World is your roller skating connection in Traverse City. Skating times are held daily with varying schedules and activities. Traditional four-wheeled and in-line skates are available to rent or you can bring your own. Arcade games and concessions are on hand for those breaks from action on the rink. Admission prices are the same for adults and children and range from $3 to $4.25 based on day of the week and time of the day. Rental skates are $1.50 for conventional skates or $5 for in-line skates.

Traverse Area District Library
322 Sixth St., Traverse City
• (616) 922-4820

On summer Saturdays, the Traverse Area District Library hosts Songs and Stories in the Park. A rotating roster of guest performers entertain families outdoors on a grassy hill overlooking the Boardman River beginning at 11 AM. Bring along a blanket and enjoy the many talented storytellers and music makers that bring words to life. The library also sponsors a number of youth reading activities throughout the year, in particular during summer vacation times. Story times are held several times during the week, including the popular Wigglers Story Time especially for toddlers. Call the library for a current schedule. Many other libraries through our Insiders region also host story hours and reading clubs. A full listing of the many libraries serving our communities appears at the end of this chapter.

Saturday Symphony — Traverse City Symphony Orchestra
3055 Cass Rd., Traverse City
• (616) 947-7120

Family adventures in music await guests who attend any Saturday Symphony presented by the Traverse Symphony Orchestra. Each concert highlights a specific ensemble with an entertaining musical performance designed for families with children. Past Saturdays have showcased a brass quintet, a string quartet, a percussion ensemble, a woodwind quintet and a chamber orchestra. The programs, which last about 45 minutes, are timed for young attention spans and encourage interaction between audience and performers. An instrument "petting zoo" held before and after each performance gives children a hands-on chance to meet the music makers. Saturday Symphony concerts are usually held five times between September and April with performances beginning at 2 PM. Advance tickets are $2, or $3 at the door. There is a discount for season tickets. Saturday Symphony locations have shifted from year to year. Call the Symphony office for an up-to-date performance schedule and locations.

Wildwood Lanes
1705 S. Garfield St., Traverse City
• (616) 941-7400

There are no gutter balls with bumper bowling offered at Wildwood Lanes. Pint-sized bowling shoes, five-pound bowling balls and long tubes inserted along the lanes' gutters assure that players of any age can walk away as winners. This is a great family activity for a rainy afternoon. Call ahead to make sure no leagues are playing and that the bumper lanes are available. Costs average $2 to 2.50 per game with shoe rental averaging $1 for children and adults.

Amon's Orchards
8066 U.S. Hwy. 31 N., Williamsburg
• (616) 938-9160, (800) 937-1644

Amon's Orchard is a family-owned commercial orchard with the smallest, yet most well known, part of their property set aside for u-pick fruit, orchard tours, a family farm market and all sorts of seasonal activities. Drive by in the fall and you'll see pumpkins hanging from the "pumpkin" trees (okay, they're really cherry trees in Halloween garb!) while youngsters can visit the pumpki patch to pick their own or can frolic in the farm's corn-husk maze. At other times of the year, you can see the magnificent cherry blossoms, take an orchard tour or pick a pint of the latest harvest. The farm market features a "see-it-made" working kitchen used to produce Amon's line of cherry and other fruit products and baked goods. At

Photo: Kevin Poirier

Just ducky, thanks. Kids enjoy feeding the numerous Mallard ducks that inhabit northern Michigan waters.

various times, visitors have been entertained by a farm petting zoo, an apiary, an antique cider press, taste testings and the general comings and goings of a modern fruit farm. There is no charge to visit the market or special activities. Amon's is open daily between mid-June and October, and on weekends for the rest of the year.

Fun Country
9320 U.S. Hwy. 31 S., Interlochen
• (616) 276-6360

You can easily spend the day at Fun Country. This large park is filled with rides, games and fun for the entire family. Big Blue Betsie, a 330-foot water slide, stands out as a teen favorite while little ones can slide down Little Blue Betsie or splash away in the Little Beaver Pond. You will also find kiddie bumper boats, an antique carousel, motorized go-carts, an 18-hole minigolf course, an arcade game room and plenty of places to sit and relax. An authentic 24-gauge train engine chugs on a 1-mile journey through the park's adjacent woods. The FC Mercantile sells souvenirs while the snack bar assures that nobody will go hungry. Changing rooms, showers and lockers are available. Fun Country is open daily from Memorial Weekend through Labor Daily.

Sleeping Bear National Lakeshore — Dunes Climb
Mich. Hwy. 109 halfway between Glen Arbor and Empire • (616) 326-5134

Spend an afternoon playing in nature's sandbox! The Dune Climb at the Sleeping Bear Dunes National Lakeshore is one of the most enduringly popular activities for children of all ages. This huge wall of sand measures about 150 feet from top to base and stretches at least 2 miles to Lake Michigan. Kids love running to the top only to skip and tumble back down and do it over again. The initial walk up the face of the dune rewards hikers with beautiful views of Glen Lake and the Leelanau landscape. One word of caution: Lake Michigan looks deceptively close. Each rise and fall of rolling sand leads to another and then another. Walking several miles in the hot sand takes hours each way and can be exhausting, even for the physically fit. Take plenty of water and wear sunscreen. You'll be met with an incredible view of Lake Michigan. If you have young children, you might opt for a shorter trek closer to the beginning of the climb. There are picnic tables near the parking lot at the base of the dunes, along with a concession stand and gift shop. When you've shaken off the sand and headed back to the car, think about taking the 7-mile Pierce Stocking scenic drive. The entrance is 1 mile south of the Dunes Climb with several magnificent overlooks of the water and the dunes. Designated picnic spots can also be found along the drive. See our full National Lakeshore listing in the Parks chapter.

Glen Arbor Art Association
Art Classes
Lake Street Studios, 6023 Lake St., Glen Arbor • (616) 334-6112

Leelanau County is home to many northern Michigan artists. They share their talents and creative passions with future artists through weekly summer classes. Courses range from The Young at Art for preschoolers and lower elementary ages to Art Exploration Printmaking, Porcelain Jewelry and Paper Box Making for upper elementary and junior high ages. If your child is a performer, try the dance or theater classes. Each course varies but many run two hours, often 10 AM to noon or 1 to 3 PM on consecutive weekdays. Costs average $60 to $90.

Grand Traverse Lighthouse
Leelanau State Park, 15390 N. Lighthouse Pt. Rd., Northport • (616) 386-5422

Standing at the very tip of the Leelanau Peninsula, the Grand Traverse Lighthouse stands as a scenic vision of turn-of-the-century seafaring life. The actual lighthouse has been restored as a living museum with period furnishings and nautical memorabilia transporting visitors to another era. Learn about the rugged, isolated life of the keeper's family as well as the importance of Great Lakes shipping at the turn of the century by taking a tour. While there, you can climb to the top of the lighthouse or simply stroll the grounds and inspect the restored buildings and breathtaking shoreline. Of special interest is a fourth order Fresnel lens on display, and a number of unique pebble sculptures and birdhouses crafted by a past lighthouse keeper during the long winters. The son of that same keeper lives on the premises today and serves as

museum curator. A gift shop is located inside the fog signal building. State park picnic areas and a playground are nearby. A Michigan State Park motor vehicle permit is required for admission to the grounds. Fees are $4 per day or $20 per year. The lighthouse museum is open mid-May through October on weekends from noon to 5 PM, and admission is $1.

Grass River Natural Area
Alden Highway (4 miles south of Bellaire), Bellaire • (616) 533-8314

The Grass River Natural Area (see our Parks chapter for full listing) sponsors a number of environmental education classes and guided walks for children during the summer. Kids can learn about wildflowers, reptiles, bird identification and water ecology through hikes, crafts, stories and other special activities. The offerings change each season. The morning classes usually cost $3. Contact the office for a schedule and registration information.

Partee Time Miniature Golf and Sonny's Pizza
Mich. Hwy. 88, Bellaire • (616) 533-6568

Fun for all ages is promised at Partee Time Miniature Golf and Sonny's Pizza in Bellaire. This indoor 18-hole miniature course comes complete with fountain, ponds and streams. Round out your round of minigolf with homemade pizza, chicken wings, salad and bread sticks at Partee Time's restaurant. Hours can vary with each season. Please call ahead for the most current schedule. Partee Time is located right next to Prevo's grocery store on Mich. Highway 88 in Bellaire.

Call of the Wild
850 S. Wisconsin Ave., Gaylord • (517) 732-4336, (800) 835-4347

Dubbed a "wilderness adventure," Call of the Wild is a unique museum of North American Wildlife that is especially geared toward children. There are more than 60 displays of North American animals against a handpainted backdrop illustrating their natural environment. Displays

INSIDERS' TIP

When you come up north, pack the family suitcase for all kinds of weather. You can see 70-degree days in March or snow in May.

showcase whitetail deer, elk, black bear, timber wolves, coyotes and raccoons as well as Michigan history, the seasons and an observation beehive. The gift shop here is quite extensive and includes a large western apparel area that is popular with adults. Call of the Wild is open daily year round from 9:30 AM to 6 PM. Hours extend in the summer to 8:30 PM. In addition, the museum also operates Bavarian Falls Park outdoors between April and October. The park offers 18-hole adventure golf and a ¼-mile go-cart track with krazy kars for elementary age youth and tot rides for little ones. Fees are $4 to $5 for golf, $4 for go-carts, $3.50 for krazy kars and $1.50 for the tot rides. Children must be at least 9 to drive the go-carts. Bavarian Falls Park is open from 9:30 AM to 11 PM daily in season.

Imagination Station
Laurel and Court Sts., Kalkaska

Like Kids Kove in Traverse City, the Imagination Station is another massive wooden play structure with 10,000 feet of crawling, twisting, sliding play space waiting to delight children of all ages.

Lake Michigan Shoreline and Cadillac

Manistee Fire Hall
281 First St., Manistee • (616) 723-1549

At some point in their young lives, all kids dream of being courageous firefighters. At the Manistee Fire Hall, kids can get a firsthand look at what firefighting is all about. Built in 1888, the fire hall is the oldest continuously active fire station in Michigan. Local firefighters are proud of their tradition and will gladly take time out to show off the fire station to visitors. The hall is formally open for tours 10 AM to 2 PM on Saturdays during the summer, but as long as there's no emergency and it's not mealtime, feel free to drop in and say hello.

White Pine Village
1687 S. Lakeshore Dr., Ludington
• (616) 843-4808

If the kids misbehave, send them to the dunce's chair at White Pine Village's restored one-room schoolhouse. Here, youngsters can imagine what it was like to learn the ABCs on a slate. The historic village represents small-town Michigan life in the late 1800s and features 21 original and replica buildings. There's the town hall, post office, farmhouse, general store, doc's office and more. The Old Fashioned Ice Cream Parlor still scoops delicious hand-dipped treats. Sport fans will enjoy the Ludington Old Time Base Ball Club matches. Matches take place on the village grounds. Players wear uniforms of the 1912-1926 Ludington minor league team and follow 1860 rules. Throughout the season, special events are scheduled. Call the village office to learn what's on tap. White Pine Village is open from mid-April through mid-October. Spring and fall hours are from 11 AM to 4 PM, Tuesday through Saturday. Summer hours are from 11 AM to 4:30 PM, Tuesday through Sunday. Summer admission charges are $5 for adults, $15 for families and $4 for students younger than 18. Spring and fall rates are slightly less.

Adventure Island
5089 W. U.S. Hwy. 10, Ludington
• (616) 843-3159

Go-carts at Adventure Island provide an exciting simulated highway experience with both a track overpass and underpass. Family fun can last all day here. Bumper boats, batting cages, mountain golf, a game arcade and a golf driving range offer recreation for all age groups. Costs are $4 for mountain golf, $4.50 for go-carts, and $4 for bumper boats. Driving-range golf balls are $3 and $4, batting cages and arcade games are pay as you go. The park is open daily from June 20 to Labor Day. Hours are 10 AM to 11 PM.

Mac Wood's Dune Rides
629 N. 18th Ave., Mears • (616) 873-2817

This is one of a handful of commercial dune rides still operating in the nation. Mac Wood invented the Dune Scooter 69 years ago to offer his resort guests tours of the Silver Lake Sand Dunes. The dunes, preserved by the Michigan Department of Natural Resources, cover 1,800 acres between Silver Lake and Lake Michigan. Wood's 18-passenger vehicles offer a 40-minute tour of the open dunes. Drivers provide an informative narrative. It's worth the 30-minute drive from Ludington to experience this massive natural wonder. Fun for all ages, rides are available from mid-May through mid-October. From mid-June through August, hours are 9:30 AM to sunset. At other times, from 9:30 AM to 5 PM. Rates are $11 for adults, $7 for children younger than 12 and free for children younger than 3.

Johnny's Fish & Game Park
5465 E. 46½ Rd., Cadillac
• **(616) 775-3700**

For a real commune with nature's creatures, visit Johnny's Fish and Game Park. Deer, goats and lambs gather round your feet and feed from your hand. They'll follow you like puppies through the park as you visit buffalo, llamas, horses, cows, kittens, raccoons and rabbits. Kids can cuddle the tame creatures, big and small, to their hearts' content. Johnny's private fish pond guarantees young anglers a catch. They provide the bait and poles all the kids do is throw in the line. They'll even fillet and wrap your catch. Open from May to September, this is one place you don't want to forget to bring your camera.

Planet Playland
252 Bell Ave., Cadillac • (616) 779-5270

When rain cancels beach plans, take the kids to Planet Playland to work their sillies out. This is an indoor playground for 10-month-olds to 12 year-olds. They'll spend hours climbing the plastic tubes and jumping in the ball valley. A variety of arcade games keeps most restless kids entertained. A concession counter offers light meals and snacks. Admission is $3 per child. Hours are 3 to 7 PM Tuesday, 11 AM to 8 PM Wednesday through Friday, 10 AM to 9 PM Saturday and noon to 6 PM Sunday.

Skate On Roller Rink
2592 N. Lake Mitchell Dr., Cadillac
• **(616) 779-0055**

Roller skating is alive and well in Cadillac. The whole family will enjoy strapping on the wheels and playing group games like Hokey-Pokey and Shoot the Duck. The rink is open Friday and Saturday evenings from 6 to 10 PM, and weekends from 2 to 4 PM. Admission is $3 for the 6 to 8 PM skate and 8 to 10 PM skate on Friday and Saturday night, or $5 for the entire night. On Saturday and Sunday afternoons, admission is $2.75. Skate rentals are $1.25.

Adventure Island
6083 E. Mich. Hwy. 115, Cadillac
• **(616) 775-5665**

When the summer sun sizzles, it's a good time to try out the waterslides at Adventure Island. Not for the faint of heart, the park offers two exciting slides, one featuring an underground pass. Bumper boats, batting cages, go-carts, mountain golf and a game arcade provide fun for the entire family. Costs are $4 for 30-minute waterslide use or $12 per day, $4.50 for go-cart rides, $4 for bumper boat rides, $4.50 for 18 holes of minigolf and $1 for 16 pitches in the batting cage. The park is open daily from Memorial Day weekend through Labor Day. Hours are 10 AM to 11 PM.

Chittenden Education Center
1070 Nursery Rd., Wellston
• **(616) 848-4858**

A regional science, math and technology center, Chittenden provides programming for more than 40,000 students, teachers and business professionals each year. The facility serves Manistee, Wexford-Missaukee, Osceola, Lake and Grand Traverse school districts with a variety of sessions from one-day enhancement workshops to weeklong programs. There are also summer programs and distant learning advanced science courses. Nestled within a remote 80-acre wooded site, the facility features a conference and learning center, five classrooms, a group presentation area, dining room and dorm as well as an outdoor initiative-and-ropes course designed to push participants beyond their comfort zones. Outdoor education focuses primarily on environmental learning. During the summer months, the center is open to teacher groups, corporate groups and sports groups.

Little Traverse

Hunting Petoskey Stones

Rockhounds will enjoy combing Little Traverse Bay beaches for Petoskey stones. These fossils, Michigan's state stone, are found only along river and lake shores in this area. The unusual stones are used to make jewelry, paperweights and other mementoes. The stones are recognized by the unique hexagon pattern covering their surfaces. The best hunting periods are in early spring when winter thaws wash a new load of stones to shore, or after a storm. Roadside parks along U.S. 31 are great hunting grounds as are Fisherman's Island State Park and Charlevoix's Lake Michigan Beach, south of the pier near the city's downtown. (See our Close-up on Petoskey stones in the Recreation chapter.)

Raven Hill Discovery Center
04503 Fuller Rd., East Jordan
• (616) 536-3369

Hug a boa, pet a python or get friendly with a hedgehog and a variety of other exotic creatures at Raven Hill. The center brings science, technology, art and history together with hands-on experience. In the museum, you can try your hand weaving on an antique loom, experiment with a four-foot magnet and play with antique toys great-grandpa and great-grandma once treasured. The center's 150-acre outdoor education area features walking trails through woodlands, meadows, swamps, creeks and along a pond. Admission is $4 per person. Raven Hill is open daily June 10 through Labor Day. Summer hours are 10 AM to 4 PM Monday through Friday, noon to 4 PM Saturday and 2 to 4 PM Sunday. Other times of the year, it's open noon to 4 PM Saturday and 2 to 4 PM Sunday, or by appointment.

Stonehenge Petting Farm
2246 Pesek Rd., East Jordan
• (616) 536-2779

Meet Petunia the potbellied pig and 100 of her four-legged friends at Stonehenge Petting Farm. Still a working farm, Stonehenge was built in 1868 and the original barn and log home are part of the charming atmosphere. Established to promote learning, guided tours educate visitors on the history and use of domesticated animals. Many of the animals are ancient breeds, such as the Highland cattle. At the Woolly Wonders Craft Shed you'll find

original gift items created by Farmer Deb. Deb processes wool from the farm's sheep, spins and weaves and produces unique fiber items. There is no admission fee; however, donations are welcome.

SEE-North Regional Math-Science Center
Petoskey • (616) 348-9700

One of Michigan's 25 registered regional math/science centers, SEE-North's focus is on environmental learning for upper-elementary and middle-school students. The center provides programming for youth in 13 northern Michigan counties, offers educators curriculum support and serves as a resource clearinghouse. SEE-North works cooperatively with North Wings Birds of Prey Sanctuary, 526-7203, a licensed raptor-rehabilitation facility.

Pirate's Cove
1230 U.S. Hwy. 31 N., Petoskey
• (616) 347-1123

If your family enjoys adventure golf, you'll want to play this course. A pirate theme sets a mood of mystery. The 18-hole course is set off by two waterfalls and a cave. Open daily from May through mid-October. Hours are 9:30 AM to 11 PM. Rates are $5.50 for adults, $5 for children 12 and younger.

The Jungle
753 Spring St., Petoskey
• (616) 348-8787

You can't miss this attraction. Just look for the giant jungle animals greeting you from amidst the line of Spring Street businesses. The Jungle offers an 18-hole adventure golf course, simulated golf play and an arcade, all indoors. The adventure course features a cascading waterfall, tropical plants and an erupting volcano. At the smoke-free arcade, play basketball, hockey and pinball games for prizes or shoot some pool. From this same indoor facility serious golfers can play nine

---

INSIDERS' TIP

If you have younger children, you may prefer to select a beach on an inland lake. Usually the water temperature of inland lakes is warmer than Lake Michigan, and you won't have to worry about dangerous undertows.

famous courses such as Pebble Beach, Pinehurst and Spyglass. The simulated courses use real course pictures and real golf equipment. Bring your own equipment or use theirs. Walk-ins are welcome or you can reserve your tee time. Simulated play is $18 per hour. Adventure golf rates are $4.50 for adults, $3.50 for children 12 and younger, and $2 for children 5 and younger.

The Pottery Lodge
201 Howard St., Petoskey
• **(616) 348-7577**
120 E. Front St., Traverse City
• **(616) 932-9007**

Unleash imagination in a creative adventure at The Pottery Lodge in downtown Petoskey or the studio's Traverse City location (see the listing in this chapter). All ages, individuals, families and groups are welcome at northern Michigan's first alternative ceramic studios. No talent is necessary, just a willingness to have fun. You paint and design your own masterpiece from a tempting variety of functional pottery including bowls, mugs, plates, vases and more. All supplies and a work area are provided for you. Your work is glazed and fired in just a few days. If your visit to the area will be short, you can arrange to have your finished pieces shipped home. Unfinished pieces begin at $1. Rates for unlimited use of colors, glaze, firing and instruction are $6.50 per person, per hour. Summer hours at both locations are 10 AM to 8 PM Monday through Thursday, 10 AM to 10 PM Friday and Saturday, and noon to 6 PM Sunday. Off-season hours are 10 AM to 6 PM Monday through Thursday, 10 AM to 8 PM Friday and Saturday, and noon to 6 PM Sunday.

Boyer Glassworks
207 N. State St., Harbor Springs
• **(616) 526-6359**

The entire family will be fascinated watching artisans Kathleen and Harry Boyer practice the ancient art of glassblowing at their Harbor Springs studio. See hot, molten glass manipulated into functional vases and bowls and one-of-a-kind works of art. The Boyers' signature designs are acquired by collectors worldwide and their studio/gallery features a wonderful selection of their exquisite, hand-signed pieces.

Harbor Springs Municipal Skating Rink
740 E. Main St., Harbor Springs
• **(616) 526-5810**

In a day when indoor ice rinks are readily available, an old-fashioned skate beneath the starry sky can seem very special. Bring your own skates to the Harbor Springs public rink and enjoy a great outdoor experience. While the rink's opening date depends on weather conditions, it's usually ready for the Christmas holiday season and is maintained through the winter, until about March. You may want to call ahead to verify hours, but can generally expect the rink to open from 3 to 9 PM Tuesday through Friday, noon to 9 PM Saturday, and 1 to 7 PM Sunday.

Mackinac Straits

Butterfly House of Mackinac Island
Mission Hill behind Ste. Anne's Church, Mackinac Island • (906) 847-3972

Aptly named, the Butterfly House is a greenhouse filled with more than 400 butterflies flitting among the flowers. These beautiful butterflies hail from all corners of the globe, making their home in this intimate conservatory. Educational displays depict the life cycle of butterflies from egg to adult as well as their role in the world environment. Admission is $3 for adults and $2 for children 12 and younger. Don't forget to bring a camera!

Children's Discovery Room
Fort Mackinac, Mackinac Island
• **(906) 847-3328**

When visiting Fort Mackinac (see full listing in Attractions chapter), don't miss the Officers Stone Quarters where the Children's Discovery Rooms is housed. Hands-on displays help children learn the sights, sounds and symbols of turn-of-the-century island life. Youngsters love to try on uniforms, pose with blown-up photos, feel animal pelts and generally explore the various pieces of Fort trivia on hand in the Discovery Room. Before your trip winds down, make a trip through Sutler's Store Museum Shop where children will find reproductions of antique toys as well as books and crafts reminiscent of another era.

Haunted Theater
Huron St., Mackinac Island
- (906) 847-6545

Walk near the Haunted Theater and you can't help but hear teenage squeals of feigned terror. This is a haunted house and wax monster display that promises a visit filled with fun. According to the theater's claims, "it won't take long to see but will take a long time to forget!" Admission is $4.50 for adults, $4 for children 6 to 12, and free for children 5 and younger.

Animal Tracks Adventure Golf
220 S. Huron St., Mackinaw City
- (616) 436-5597

Challenging rounds of miniature golf await duffers at Animal Tracks Adventure Golf. This golfing fun park overlooks the ferry docks and the Mackinaw Bridge. This is highly popular with families staying at the many nearby hotels or daytrippers visiting nearby Courtyards of Mackinaw and the historic sites. Relax afterwards with an ice cream cone or let parents and teens sneak in a little shopping at the large Traverse Bay Woolen store next door.

Kid-Friendly Restaurants

Grand Traverse

Dill's Olde Towne Saloon
423 S. Union St., Traverse City
- (616) 947-7534

Within one of Traverse City's oldest eateries, Dill's is a great restaurant for all ages and for many reasons (see full listing in Restaurants chapter). Children enjoy it for the crayons, the train, the karaoke or all of the above. Wooden booths and tables are lined with brown paper, offering the perfect canvas for doodlers while a Lionel train and a long string of cars periodically rolls around a track mounted overhead. What makes Dill's especially fun, however, is karaoke with the restaurant's lively host, Princess Laura. Kids have fun watching as well as performing on a stage lined with larger-than-life props.

Don's Drive-In
2030 N. U.S. Hwy. 31 S., Traverse City
- (616) 938-1860

Don's Drive-In is a favorite for all ages (see our Restaurants chapter). Kids love to order from their cars with the help of old fashioned car hops. Those eating inside are fascinated by the restaurant's workings whether it's watching burgers and shakes made the old-fashioned way, sitting in '50s-style booths or hovering over a vintage jukebox that plays records — not CDs! — surrounded by Day-Glo lights. The children's menu features baskets of fries and hot dogs, burgers or chicken, which arrive in a colorful, foot-long rendition of a fifties Pink Cadillac or Red T-bird.

Gordie Howe's Tavern & Eatery
851 S. Garfield St., Traverse City
- (616) 929-4693

Hockey legend Gordie Howe makes his home in Traverse City. This is his family's restaurant, and it's definitely designed for families. The menu is affordable and varied. Pizzas in a unique assortment of varieties are a specialty along with burgers, sandwiches and accompaniments. Young sports fans, as well as the young at heart, will love to peruse the hundreds of skating mementoes, family photos and hockey paraphernalia that line the walls and pay tribute to Howe's incredible contribution to the sport. When you're there, remember to look for Gordie's special booth and try out the seat in the penalty box.

La Senorita
1245 S. Garfield, Traverse City
- (616) 947-8820
2455 U.S. Hwy. 31 S., Traverse City
- (616) 946-4545
737 W. Main St., Gaylord
- (616) 732-1771
1700 S. Mitchell St., Cadillac
- (616) 779-3636
1285 U.S. Hwy. 31 N., Petoskey
- (616) 347-7750

It's always a family fiesta at La Senorita. This local chain of Mexican restaurants is based in Traverse City with additional locations in Gaylord, Cadillac, Petoskey and several other Michigan cities (see full listing in our Restaurants chapter). This is a great place for families to gather. High chairs are plentiful, placemats and crayons supply the tools for an ever-changing art display and a barrel of tiny toys offer treasures to take home. The Little Amigos menu includes tacos, nachos, burgers and hot dogs. Tortilla chips on the table keep the hungries at bay until the food arrives. Prices are very reasonable, service is fast and friendly, and there's something on the menu for everybody. Sunday has traditionally been Little Amigos night with all children's meals discounted.

Pizzarama
807 S. Airport Rd., Traverse City
• **(616) 947-1577**
Family food and fun is the promise at Pizzarama. Pizza, sandwiches and similar fare are the specialty while kids can play arcade games to their hearts' content. Games fill half of the dining room promising many opportunities to try your skills. This is a favorite location for children's birthday parties.

Lake Michigan Shoreline and Cadillac

A&W Restaurant and Drive-In
Corner of Mich. Hwy. 115 and Mich. Hwy. 22, Frankfort • (616) 352-9021
Cruise into Frankfort's A&W for a nostalgic experience. Not only can you get a great root-beer float, you still get carhop service here. You can't get more casual than this and prices are family-friendly. Tuesday is Coney Day and every Friday there are fish specials. Full-service dining is available inside, or you can order your meal to go.

House of Flavors Restaurant
402 W. Ludington Ave., Ludington
• **(616) 845-5785**
Take your kids on a trip back in time to the 1950s. Period music, decor and waitresses uniformed in '50s style right down to their hairdos, creates a real *Happy Days* setting. This is more than an old-fashioned ice cream parlor serving 45 flavors and the best breakfast deal in town, it's a museum. There are four large display cases of memorabilia and an old Wurlitzer jukebox dating back to 1957. The wallpaper is custom-made from photos taken in the Ludington area during the 1930s through the 1950s. But the best treat for the kids is the view. The family-owned restaurant is adjacent to the factory, which produces 15 million gallons of ice cream annually. Operations are visible from the windows within the restaurant.

Kodiak's Internet Coffeehouse
112 N. Mitchell St., Cadillac
• **(616) 775-5282**
Kodiak's in downtown Cadillac is a stop older kids will enjoy. A relaxed homelike atmosphere features a large-screen TV and offers Internet access from a computer counter. Internet rates are $3 for a half hour or $5 for one hour. Made-to-order sandwiches and other light fare are available.

Little Traverse

Juilleret's
130 State St., Harbor Springs
• **(616) 526-2821**
This is Michigan's oldest family-run restaurant. The entire family will get a kick out of eating homemade ice cream at the old-fashioned soda fountain. Be sure to try some of their famous whitefish. The light and spacious restaurant is a comfortable, relaxing atmosphere for all ages. Open May through October for breakfast, lunch, dinner and treats.

Tell Me A Story . . . Read Me a Book

Public libraries have always been a magical haven for young readers to explore the wonders inside the covers of books. Northwest Michigan is filled with libraries — small and large — serving the communities dotting our map. A listing of libraries, locations and phone numbers follows. Many offer story times and special children's activities and displays. Libraries in smaller or seasonal communities may only be open for a limited number of days each week, or their hours may fluctuate with the season. Call ahead for current story times and hours.

For more storytelling stops, check at local bookstores for the next children's event or story time. They are held regularly at Borders, Horizon Books and other community book shops. See our Shopping chapter for a full listing of bookstores.

Grand Traverse

Traverse City Area

•Traverse Area District Library, Main Library, 322 Sixth Street, Traverse City, (616) 922-4820

•Traverse Area District Library, East Bay Branch, 1989 Three Mile Road, Traverse City, (616) 922-2085

•Peninsula Community Library, 2735 Island View Road, Traverse City, (616) 223-7700

•Fife Lake Public Library, 137 Merritt Street, Fife Lake, (616) 879-4101

•Interlochen Public Library, 9700 Riley Road, Interlochen, (616) 276-6767

•Kingsley Public Library, 104 S. Brownson Avenue, Kingsley, (616) 263-5484

Leelanau County

•Glen Lake Community Library, 10115 E. Front Street, Empire, (616) 326-5361

•Leland Township Library, 203 E. Cedar Street, Leland, (616) 256-9152

•Leelanau Township Library, 119 E. Naganoba Street, Northport, (616) 386-5131

•Suttons Bay Public Library, 416 Front Street, Suttons Bay, (616) 271-3512

Antrim-Kalkaska

•Bellaire Public Library, 111 S. Bridge Street, Bellaire, (616) 533-8814

•Elk Rapids District Library, 300 Noble Street, Elk Rapids, (616) 264-9979

•Kalkaska County Library, 247 S. Cedar Street, Kalkaska, (616) 258-9411

•Mancelona Public Library, 202 W. State Street, Mancelona, (616) 587-9451

•Otsego County Library, 700 S. Otsego Street, Gaylord, (517) 732-5841

Lake Michigan Shoreline and Cadillac

•Benzie Shores District Library, 630 Main Street, Frankfort, (616) 352-4671

•Benzonia Public Library, 891 Michigan Avenue, Benzonia, (616) 882-4111

•Beulah Public Library, 7228 Commercial Drive, Beulah, (616) 882-4037

•Elberta Public Library, 704 Frankfort Avenue, Elberta, (616) 352-4351

•Manistee County Library, 95 Maple Street, Manistee, (616) 723-2519

•Mason County Library, 204 E. State Street, Scottville, (616) 757-2588

•Ludington Public Library, 217 E. Ludington Avenue, Ludington, (616) 843-8465

•Betsie Valley District Library, 14731 Thompson Avenue, Thompsonville, (616) 378-2716

•Cadillac and Wexford County Public Library, 411 S. Lake Street, Cadillac, (616) 775-6541

•Falmouth Area Library, 219 E. Prosper Road, Falmouth, (616) 826-3738

•Manton Public Library, 404 W. Main Street, Manton, (616) 824-3584

•McBain Community Library, 107 E. Maple Street, McBain, (616) 825-2197

•Mesick Public Library, 117 N. Eugene Street, Mesick, (616) 885-1120

•Missaukee County Library, 103 Canal Street, Lake City, (616) 839-2166

Little Traverse

•Jordan Valley District Library, 1 Library Lane, East Jordan, (616) 536-7131

•Charlevoix Public Library, 109 Clinton Street, Charlevoix, (616) 547-2651

•Crooked Tree District Library, 2167 N. Shore Drive, Walloon Lake, (616) 535-2111

•Petoskey City Library, 451 E. Mitchell Street, Petoskey, (616) 347-4211

•Harbor Springs Library, 206 S. Spring Street, Harbor Springs, (616) 526-2531

Mackinac Straits

•Mackinac Island Public Library, Mackinac Island, (906) 847-3421

•Mackinaw City Public Library, Mackinaw City, (616) 436-5451

•St. Ignace Public Library, 6 Spring Street, St. Ignace, (906) 643-8318

There's no doubt
that Northwest Michigan
loves its foods, its music
and its festivals. We'd
like you to love
them, too!

Annual Events

Ready to celebrate? We are!

Northwest Michigan is always ready for a party. Summer, winter, spring or fall, we're sure to have an occasion to set your toes tapping and your spirits soaring.

Do you like great food? Try the Leland Food and Wine Festival or Northport's Famous Whitefish Boil or lick your fingers at Traverse City's Ribs, Bibs, Tall Ships and Kids.

Are you having an art attack? Time to find Petoskey's Art in the Park or the Suttons Bay Arts Festival or any number of community arts fairs.

Does music ring your bell? Head to Suttons Bay's JazzFest, Alden's Evening Strolls or Traverse City's Art Below Zero.

Looking for history? Visit Manistee for its Victorian Christmas or Colonial Michilimackinac's Memorial Day Pageant.

Love the water? Set sail for the Ludington Car Ferry Festival, Charlevoix's Venetian Festival, Elk Rapids' Harbor Days or the Mackinac Island regattas.

Feeling athletic? Join the North American Vasa or walk the Mackinac Bridge or even paddle a canoe in the Au Sable marathon.

Craving ethnic fun? Kick up your heels at the Cedar Polka Festival or Gaylord's Alpenfest. Or watch the traditional dances at the Native American Powwows.

And, don't forget the parades. We have a lot of them! The National Cherry Festival has three all by itself. The Lilac Festival uses horses to pull its floats while the Venetian Festival relies on lighted boats. Whether we're celebrating cherries or forests or harbors or fish, there's probably a related parade lining up.

There's no doubt that Northwest Michigan loves its foods, its music and its festivals. We'd like you to love them, too! Listed below is a sampling of annual fun held throughout Northwest Michigan. It's a month-by-month calendar listing that has been divided among our four major geographic areas. You'll see that we rarely list a date. That's because, with the exception of major holidays, the dates are rarely the same from year to year. Instead, we've tried to indicate each festival and the approximate time of the month that it's held. If you're planning a trip specifically for a particular event, call the contact listed for specific information or check with the closest visitors' bureau.

In many cases we've listed admission costs from the most recent season. Please remember that costs often fluctuate from season to season, and the prices listed here should serve as a guide only.

While you peruse the listings below, remember that these are highlights of the hundreds of events that take place throughout the year. A visit to any of Northwest Michigan's many towns and villages will illuminate any number of other community gatherings. Check local newspapers and community calendars when you arrive up north and join us for a little hometown hospitality.

A few things not listed are the countless Fourth of July festivities held throughout the region. Fireworks light up the sky in many communities while patriotic parades and village picnics are popular.

Other events not specifically noted are the holiday traditions that so many communities

INSIDERS' TIP

Our summers are short in Northwest Michigan, so we celebrate with gusto! You can find at least one community event taking place every weekend and most weekdays during the peak weeks between early June and late August.

host. Look for tree lightings, caroling, cookie sales, visits from Santa and holiday strolls when shopkeepers open their doors in old fashioned hospitality. In the fall, watch for Halloween haunted houses, scarecrow festivals and apple days at the cider mills. When the snow falls, winterfests brighten cold days across the map.

www.insiders.com
See this and many other
Insiders' Guide® destinations
online — in their entirety.
Visit us today!

Join us. Festival fun is yours for the taking. It's time to pick your party and celebrate!

January

Grand Traverse

Art Below Zero
Traverse Area Arts Council, Traverse City • (616) 947-2282
The synergy of creative forces brings Art Below Zero to warm our spirits. One weekend each winter, the area's many artists combine talents to share an evening filled with music, movement, words and images. Visual artists display their work while writers, dancers, musicians, singers and actors entertain the audience with a tightly choreographed performance. This is a fund-raiser for the Traverse Area Arts Council, and everyone is there for the love of the arts. It's also a tangible reminder of how our large arts community is richly talented and diverse. Formats vary year to year, but you can always expect wonderful entertainment, beautiful artwork and a fabulous audience. Tickets are $15 in advance and $18 at the door.

Lake Michigan Shoreline and Cadillac

Ludington Winter Fun Fest
Ludington • (616) 845-0324, (800) 542-4600
Whether you like keeping warm and comfy indoors or enjoy the invigorating cold and snow, the Ludington Winter Fun Fest can provide you with some pleasant distractions from

the long gray winter. Held the last weekend in January and the first weekend in February, area merchants join the celebration by offering indoor sidewalk sales. The Jaycees stir up fun sponsoring Las Vegas Night featuring games, food and beverages. Local restaurants strut their stuff and warm you up with a chili cook-off. Outdoor enthusiasts are invited to participate in the Four Mile Winter Lark Run or cross-country ski races at West Shore Community College. For young and old alike, the highlight of the event is the ice carving competition. This contest of creativity and skill draws people from throughout Michigan to demonstrate artistry in ice. You can see the array of imaginative sculptures at the Ludington City Park. There is no admission fee for general attendance.

Little Traverse

Twelfth Night Celebration
Camp Daggett, 03001 Church Rd., Petoskey • (616) 348-9700
Nub's Nob, 4021 Nub's Nob, Harbor Springs • (616) 348-9700
According to folk legend, during the days following the Christmas holiday animals have the gift of speech. SEE-North educational center in Petoskey marks the magical period with an annual candlelit trail walk through the forest. Staff and volunteers dress the part of animals and offer an enlightening presentation beneath the stars. Children will enjoy mask making and face painting. This evening event takes place on two dates in early January at two Boyne County locations, which are subject to change. Admission is $4 per person. Insiders suggest you bring sleds for toddlers and young children.

Mackinac Straits

Winterfest
Mackinaw City • (616) 436-5574, (800) 666-0160
The winters are long up north. And, so is

Photo: Kevin Poirier

The Blue Angels perform annually at the National Cherry Festival.

Winterfest, Mackinaw City's three-week cold weather celebration beginning in mid-January. Free weekend events lead up to the exciting Mackinaw Mush Sled Dog Races in early February. Highlights include the Big Mac Snowmobile Extravaganza and enormous displays of professional snow sculpting.

February

Grand Traverse

Winterfest
Gaylord • (517) 732-4000, (800) 345-8621

Gaylord puts an end to the January doldrums with its Winterfest celebration. For 10 days at the beginning of February, the streets are overtaken by ice and snow sculptures while cold weather activities abound. Try your hand at outdoor volleyball, winter golf, outdoor softball or the youth fishing derby, or warm up inside at the merchants' indoor sidewalk sales. Snowmobilers can race in the Radar Run, or join the Crunch and Munch 100-mile safari. Skiers can tour the trails, compete in slalom races or cheer on the Special Olympics Ski-a-thon. Events are free if you buy a $1 Winterfest button.

White Pine Stampede
Bellaire • (616) 587-8812

Slated for the first weekend in February, the White Pine Stampede is often held just a week or two before Traverse City's North American Vasa. The White Pine is also a major Midwest cross country ski race that attracts hundreds of racers to the starting line in 10-, 20- and 50K runs. The very hilly course travels through the wooded forests winding around the Shanty Creek resort properties. This Nordic race is an annual benefit for Children's Hospital of Michigan. Race fees average around $45.

North American Vasa
Traverse City • (616) 938-4400

Wax your skis and join the fun at the North American Vasa. Named after Sweden's internationally renowned Vasaloppet Nordic marathon, this is the second-largest cross country ski race in the United States (the Birkebeiner in Wisconsin is the largest) and is one of eight legs in the American Ski Marathon Series. Elite skiers join more than 1,000 amateurs at the starting line for a shotgun start on a mid-February Saturday morning. Competitions are held for 13-, 27- and 47K. Participants choose their method — skating or classic — that will take them through the rolling, forested Vasa trail. A family fun day with a children's loop and visit by the mascot Vasasaurus takes place on Sunday. Pre-race activities by ski shops, local Nordic centers, manufacturers and professional skiers build enthusiasm through the week. A special highlight is the Vasa sprints, usually held the night before. Tons of snow are hauled in to create a course through Traverse City's downtown Front Street. Race fees are $15 for the 13K and $35 to $50 for the 27- and 47K races depending on the date of registration.

Downtown Chili Cook-off
City Opera House, 112½ E. Front St., Traverse City • (616) 922-2050

Chase away those winter chills with a red-hot dose of Traverse City chili at the Annual Downtown Chili Cook-off. This favorite local food fest is always held on a Sunday afternoon in mid-February at the City Opera House. Local chefs from almost 30 of the area's favorite restaurants ladle up samples of their best chili recipes for more than 600 hungry patrons, who vote for their favorites. Categories include 1-, 2- and 3-alarm, vegetarian, white, no bean, ethnic, seafood and the people's choice. Chili lovers can purchase tickets for a sample size of eight chilis for $5, or, for heftier appetites, full bowls cost $3 per bowl.

Lake Michigan Shoreline and Cadillac

North American Snowmobile Festival
Wexford Civic Arena and Lake Cadillac, Cadillac • (616) 775-0657

The North American Snowmobile Festival (NASF) is a great cure for cabin fever. The whir of snow machines and the high excitement of the sport will stir you out of winter's doldrums. Considered the largest snowmobile festival in the United States, the event brings out more than 12,000 snowmobilers and spectators for exhilarating winter recreation on lakes Cadillac and Mitchell. The rumble of zooming sleds fills the air as novice and expert drivers compete in speed events and competitive course racing. Always held the first weekend in February, the full five-day slate features activities for winter enthusiasts of all ages. On the ice, festivalgoers try an older, gentler type of transportation than the snowmobile, a horse-drawn sleigh. Children's games, a brilliant display of fireworks and the annual nighttime snowmobile parade across Lake Cadillac makes for great memories. One of the most popular festival events is the Poker Run. A treasure hunt of sorts, participants travel by sled from business to business collecting a playing card at each stop. At the end of the route, the best poker hand wins. Other activities include a chili cook-off, grand parade and the Ms. NASF contest. The purchase of a $3 NASF button is required for participation in events.

Little Traverse

Petoskey Winter Carnival
Petoskey Winter Sports Park, Winter Ln., Petoskey • (616) 347-2500

The Carnival is Petoskey's tonic for winter doldrums. The one-day event is held mid-February and is sponsored by the Petoskey Department of Parks and Recreation. Competitions, for fun only, include bump jumping, a sport virtually established in Petoskey. In this race, daring bump jumpers make their way downhill on a short ski with a seat attached. You'll also see the cardboard sled competition, a local favorite. Sleds are homemade according to contest specifications prior to the carnival date. This is one event you must pre-register for in order to participate. You can also look forward to seeing ice skating demonstrations and competitions, and being warmed by the traditional Christmas tree bonfire. The good times are free for participants and spectators.

Mackinac Straits

The Mackinaw Mush
Mackinaw Wilderness Run
Mackinaw City • (616) 436-5243

Sled dogs hit the snow running during

The Mackinaw Mush and Mackinaw Wilderness Run races. The Mackinaw Mush is a two-day event held during the first weekend of February or the end of January. Sled dog teams compete for the best times in short distance speed races. Courses are 4, 6 and 10 miles long with categories for teams of four, six, eight or 10 dogs. Racers' fees range from $15 to $45.

A three-dog junior race for $5 and a free two-dog children's race are held for the younger set. Participants and public celebrate during the event's Musher Banquet on Friday and Saturday nights. Banquet tickets are $25 for adults and $10 for children age 12 and younger.

The following weekend, endurance is tested during the 25- and 50-mile Mackinaw Wilderness Run. Teams of six and 10 dogs run a mid-distance course from Mackinaw City to Wilderness State Park and back. To cheer their efforts, a public Musher Awards Breakfast is held at the Pancake Chef Restaurant. The breakfast costs $10. Racers' fees range from $25 to $65 and include one breakfast ticket.

March

Grand Traverse

Twin Bays Skating Club Annual Ice Show
Centre I.C.E. Arena, Traverse City
• (616) 947-2267

It's not the Olympics, but nationally ranked guest performers along with 200 local skaters bring the lights and lavishness of a big time show to an enthusiastic small town crowd. The guest skaters are wonderful — one of the latest demonstrated quad jumps and triple axles — but the real show stealers are the preschoolers whose brief appearance to many oohs and aahs always steal the show. The shimmering blades, great music and sheer production of it all help brighten up the last dregs of winter's gray days. The show usually runs on a mid-March Thursday through Saturday with four packed performances. Admission has been $6-10.

Lake Michigan Shoreline and Cadillac

St. Patrick's Day Parade
Downtown historic Manistee
• (616) 723-1031

Manistee's St. Patrick's Day Parade is billed as the shortest parade in the world, but its not short on spirit. Folks of all nationalities gather for the two-block procession, which draws to an end at a local pub. Here, folks gather for a bit of merriment and to play games benefiting local nonprofit organizations. The parade is sponsored by the First Street Merchants Association and is free to spectators.

Little Traverse

Fiddlers' Jamboree
210 S. Lake St., East Jordan
• (616) 547-1311

Fiddlers come from far and wide for this day-long hoedown held the first Saturday in March. Enjoy fiddle performances throughout the day at the host facility, the Jordan Valley Express, a dance hall featuring a 10,000-square-foot floor. Grab your partner when the sun goes down for an evening of old-fashioned square dancing. Novices and experienced dancers alike enjoy the true American-style celebration. There is no admission fee.

April

Grand Traverse

Rotary Show
Lars Hockstad Auditorium, 301 W. Seventh St., Traverse City
• (616) 941-5421

For a unique slice of small town life, attend the annual Rotary Show, which has been a community favorite for decades. The evening is filled with one-liners, ham acting, music and fun as the local Rotary Club takes a slightly skewed look at the past year's news and local celebrities. Nothing is sacred in this annual roast. Half the fun is watching Traverse City's normally staid professionals donning candy-striped vests and straw hats as they entertain their neighbors. The money raised by these erstwhile performers benefits many civic programs supported by the Rotary Club's Good Works Fund. Admission is $5.

National Trout Festival
Kalkaska County Fairgrounds, Kalkaska
• (616) 258-9103, (800) 4-TROUT-0

Fishing is wildly popular in Northwest Michigan, and Kalkaska tips its rod in salute to the sport at the National Trout Festival held in late April. Passing through Kalkaska, you can't miss this small town's obsession as shown by the enormous 20-foot painted trout standing on its tail in the middle of downtown. The festival celebrates the return of spring and the beginning of trout season with free fishing contests for children and adults, special activities, a parade and the year's new Trout King and Queen.

Celebration for Young Children
(616) 922-2050

Family fun fills the day during the Annual Celebration for Young Children held on the last Saturday of April. Festival events are scattered throughout Traverse City, with a full slate of activities for children of all ages, including storytelling, creative movement sessions, a young people's symphony performance, fire engine rides, museum exhibits, a zoo open house and countless hands-on activities with local merchants. This popular event attracts more than 3,000 children and their families each year, but there's always room for more! The fun is free, thanks to the support of several local organizations.

May

Grand Traverse

Blossom Days
Old Mission Peninsula, Traverse City
• (616) 223-4110

Reminiscent of the "Blessing of the Blossoms" held for local cherry growers during the early half of this century, Blossom Days welcomes spring and salutes the cherry industry with festivities at local orchards, wineries and eateries on Traverse City's Old Mission Peninsula. This weekend event is usually held during mid-May with barrel tastings at peninsula wineries, guided blossom walks through the cherry orchards, art exhibits at Bella Galleria and seasonal menus and specials at many Old Mission restaurants. The Blessing of the Blossoms, in hopes for a productive growing season, takes place on Sunday morning. Admission is $5. The best part of the weekend is driving through the half-million blossoming cherry trees that line the peninsula's rolling hills and roadways.

Northwestern Michigan College Buffalo Barbecue
1701 E. Front St., Traverse City
• (616) 922-1019

Rain or shine, Traverse City turns out to eat buffalo and salute the biggest little college in Michigan on the third Sunday in May. "The Barbecue" has been a local tradition since 1955 when Northwestern Michigan College became the state's first community college. More than 10,000 area residents join their neighbors for an enormous community picnic on the college grounds. The menu never changes — buffalo burgers and hot dogs, baked beans, salad and ice cream. It's all donated by the local Oleson family, longtime college patrons and owners of the Oleson's Food Stores and the "largest buffalo herd east of the Mississippi." Children's activities, live music, open air entertainment, clowns and, with luck, sunshine add a holiday-like atmosphere to the festivities. Barbecue hours run from 11 AM to 5 PM on the campus of Northwestern Michigan College. Tickets are $4 in advance at any Oleson's store and $5 on Barbecue day.

Mancelona Bass Festival
Palmer Park, Mancelona
• (616) 587-8700

Mancelona salutes its favorite fish at the Mancelona Bass Festival held the last weekend in May. Fishing contests, fireworks, a parade, a carnival, a flea market and a craft show fill the slate of free festival events.

Lake Michigan Shoreline and Cadillac

Ludington Carferry Festival
Ludington • (616) 845-0324, (800) 542-4600

The Carferry Festival launches a new season for the SS *Badger*, one of the last great steam-powered ships still sailing the Great Lakes and harbored in Ludington. For more than 100 years, Ludington has provided travelers with carferry service, something the community believes is worth celebrating in a big way. The two-day nautical-themed event held in mid-May draws about 10,000 participants and lots of free entertainment. You can enjoy a festival parade through downtown streets, an open class car show, a Venetian boat parade and fireworks. The weekend highlight for many is a shoreline cruise and celebration aboard the SS *Badger*. The two-hour party cruise features live entertainment, a food buffet and a cash bar. Expect to pay about $25 per person. A limited number of tickets are available for the Carferry Festival cruise. To secure reservations, you should call the Lake Michigan Carferry company at least three weeks in advance at (800) 239-7002. All major credit cards are accepted.

Little Traverse

National Morel Mushroom Hunting Championship and Festival
Boyne City • (616) 582-6222

When the snow melts and spring rains wash the winter-dreary landscape, it's mushroom-hunting time again in Northwest Michigan. Morel madness strikes in mid-May. Hundreds of people head to the woods to search for the wild delicacy. The National Morel Mushroom Hunting Championship and Festival heralds the natural event with guided morel mushroom hunts, seminars on wild edibles and a celebration of Michigan foods including wild leeks and asparagus. The festival highlight is the morel hunting championship, where you can compete for the title of best mushroom hunter. Winners are honored with cash prizes for their foraging skills.

Mackinac Straits

Memorial Day Weekend Pageant
Colonial Michilimackinac, Mackinaw City
- **(616) 436-5563**

In 1763, Michilimackinac was thriving as a French fur-trading village and military outpost until a surprise attack by Chief Pontiac left it in chaos. The historic events of 1763 are reenacted every Memorial Day weekend in what has become the longest-running free attraction in Michigan. The outdoor pageant, which runs several times during the weekend, is a labor of love by the local community and the Michigan State Historic Parks. A cast of 200 volunteers, playing the roles of traders, soldiers and Native Americans, will gather outside the palisades of Colonial Michilimackinac to reenact frontier life, play and the unexpected fall of the British fort to Chief Pontiac's Native American allies. Period music, colonial programs and special activities fill out the weekend.

June

Grand Traverse

Leland Food and Wine Festival
Marina Park, Fishtown, Leland
- **(616) 256-9895**

Lift your spirits sampling the spirits of the Leelanau Peninsula. The Leland Food and Wine Festival is held in mid-June where, rain or shine, more than 20 favorite wineries and peninsula eateries gather under an enormous tent to showcase their wares. Next to the Leland Yacht Harbor and Fishtown, the event also spotlights the area's many musicians and entertainers who perform in the adjacent park all day. The sample sizes are more than ample, with items ranging from crab cakes to truffles, fajitas to smoked fish pâté. Couple the food with a glass or two of the region's best wines and it's very easy to kick back, listen to the music and thoroughly enjoy the day in the park. The adult admission of $6 includes a souvenir wine glass and tickets good for two wine samples. Additional wine tickets can be purchased during the event. There is a nominal entry fee for children.

Ribs, Bibs, Tall Ships and Kids
Open Space, Traverse City
• **(616) 946-2723**

Bring your appetites and your cameras to this huge picnic by the bay. Ribs, ribs and ribs (with a few fixings) are on the menu as local restaurants vie for "best tasting" votes in an outdoor cook-off. Meal tickets are $10. Try three different, finger-licking specialties, then pass the "wet-ones" and relax in the early summer sun. The event is at the Open Space in downtown Traverse City, a piece of land that juts into West Grand Traverse Bay next to Clinch Park Marina. The former site of a cannery plant, it's a favorite site for walking, playing and hosting community events. You'll see families relaxing on blankets, kids flying kites, teens strolling and people reading under trees while the gentle bay waters lap against the breakwall. During Ribs and Bibs, Northwest Michigan's resident tall ships will join other watercraft on the bay. The *Malabar* and *Madeline* from Traverse City and the *Manitou* from Northport are usually in full sail for a picturesque parade. The event, a benefit for Big Brothers & Big Sisters, is always held on the second Sunday in June. One word of advice — if it's a beautiful day, arrive early while ribs and tickets are plentiful.

Strawberry Social
Munson Community Health Center Grounds, 550 Munson Ave., Traverse City • (616) 935-6631

Traverse City's annual Strawberry Social gathers thousands of residents and visitors onto the grounds of the Munson Community Health Center in this annual healthcare fundraiser held in mid-June. The all-day event is highlighted by fresh shortcake topped with strawberries and vanilla ice cream. Children's games, musical entertainment and an arts and crafts show add to the family festivities. The Strawberry Social has been a Traverse City tradition for decades. It was begun by the old Traverse City Osteopathic Hospital Auxiliary, who used to pick all of the strawberries and bake hundreds of shortcakes for the early summer event. The social is free. Shortcake tickets are $3.50.

Michigan Open Golf Tournament
Grand Traverse Resort, 100 Grand Traverse Village Blvd., Acme
• **(616) 938-2100**

Michigan's golf pros and top amateurs vie for top prizes at this prestigious event held in late June at the Grand Traverse Resort's Jack Nicklaus-designed course, The Bear. Competitors have earned their spots by placing in qualifying rounds earlier in the season at various Michigan courses. Approximately $110,000 is awarded during this four-day event. Spectators are admitted free. This is a chance to watch great golf on a great course with the best in the state.

Lake Michigan Shoreline and Cadillac

Cadillac Free Family Fishing Festival
Lakes Cadillac and Mitchell
• **(616) 775-9776**

You don't need a fishing license and there are no fees to participate in any of Cadillac's Free Family Fishing Festival events. Just bring your poles and be ready for relaxation and fun. The festival is held the first Saturday in June in conjunction with Michigan's Free Fishing Weekend, two days when all fishing license and trout/salmon stamp fees are waived for both Michigan and out-of-state anglers. While there are no charges or fares, the payoff for your fishing adventure in Cadillac can be big. Catching a tagged fish can bring you cash awards of up to $10,000. Prizes are presented in all age divi-

INSIDERS' TIP

Avoid traffic jams during the National Cherry Festival by riding a bike along the TART trail or through the Central and Boardman neighborhoods.

sions and men, women, boys and girls divisions. To be eligible for cash and other prizes, you must register at least one day prior to the event. You can sign-up at many local businesses, hotels, motels or the Cadillac Visitors Bureau. More than 1,500 anglers participate in the one-day fishing spree, which begins at dawn and lasts until late afternoon. Fishing takes place from shore and offshore. Rental boats are available from several of the lakeside motels. In addition to fishing, there are ongoing demonstrations by well-known anglers. Check out the action at festival headquarters at Cadillac's downtown lakefront pavilion.

Little Traverse

Little Traverse Bay Historical Festival
100 Depot St., Petoskey • (616) 347-2620

Experience firsthand the hard work and good times of yesteryear at this major fundraiser for the Little Traverse History Museum. The waterfront museum serves as a hub for the day's historically based activities. Here, on the green, you can stroll the Petoskey Midway, a re-creation of the community's turn-of-the-century. Along the Midway, an open-air shopping district, artisans and craftsmen demonstrate traditional lace making, quilting, weaving and pottery techniques, while local vendors market their modern goods in the old-fashioned manner. The younger set is entertained by historically authentic games. Also available is something that will never go out of style: pony rides and hay rides. Period dress and live entertainment add to the old-time ambiance. If all of this celebrating works up your appetite, experience a Taste of the North. About 20 Petoskey area restaurants bring their most popular dishes down to the green for visitors to sample. With the purchase of a $1 ticket per sampling, you can try anything from white fish pâté to strawberry soup. Later, you may want to work off your snack by joining one of the walking tours. Tours lead small groups through Petoskey's historic downtown and waterfront and along the Bear River where lumber mills once thrived. Held the first Saturday in June, a $1 donation allows you to participate in most activities.

Mackinac Straits

Lilac Festival
Mackinac Island • (906) 847-6418, (800) 4-LILACS

Spring comes late to tiny Mackinac Island but, when the lilacs bloom, it's cause for celebration! Marking the first sign of summer, the Lilac Festival celebrates the new season and the island's unique community with 10 days of theme activities during the first week of June. Events range from serious to silly with wine tastings, family hayrides, street dancing, historic open houses, kite flying, sunset cruises, kids day and a stuffed-animal pet show. A perennial favorite is the "Fudgie Fun Olympics," featuring suitcase toss, blindfold waiter games and tug of war. The festival closes with a horse-drawn Grand Parade. By the way, saluting the lilacs is very appropriate, the island is home to more than 60 varieties of lilac bushes that have grown to treelike proportions. When they bloom, the island is blanketed with their wonderful fragrance and countless blooms of deep violet, lilac, white and rose.

Straits Area Antique Auto Show
St. Ignace • (906) 643-8717, (800) 338-6660

More than 2,000 antique and custom collector vehicles take over the St. Ignace streets during the annual Straits Area Antique Auto

INSIDERS' TIP

Traverse City's Wayne Hill, on the west side of town, is a great place to watch Fourth of July fireworks. If the night is especially clear, you'll also get a glimpse of the fireworks display in Kalkaska. This is also a great spot to watch the Cherry Festival air show, especially if the headliners are the U.S. Navy's Blue Angels.

Show in late June. This has grown into one of the major collector-car festivals in the United States and often includes many auto world personalities. The free festivities kick off on Friday evening with the "Down Memory Lane" parade of participating autos followed by the weekend transformation of St. Ignace's main street into a mile-long exhibition of vintage vehicles.

July

Grand Traverse

Cedar Polka Festival
Junction of County Rds. 651 and 616, Cedar • (616) 228-3378

The Cedar Polka Festival is a Grand Traverse ethnic institution featuring a wealth of toe-tapping Polish bands, favorite foods, spirits and constant dancing. The party's on all day and much of the night inside a tent that seems like it's almost as large as the village of Cedar. This is a great time to get your fill of brats, sauerkraut and pierogies washed down with endlessly flowing beer and soft drinks. Games and a nearby playground help entertain the children, although they have just as much fun on the dance floor as their parents. To get into the true Polish spirit, wear red and white — the colors of Poland's national flag. One of the more unique aspects of the festival is the annual Polka Mass, a Catholic service held right on the stage on Sunday morning. When the service is finished, the bands take over and the festival continues. Admission ranges from $4 to $6 each day or $14 for a 3-day pass. Children age 12 and younger are admitted for free if accompanied by an adult.

Harbor Days
Haserot Park and G. Marsten Dame Marina, Northport • (616) 386-5806

Celebrate an old-fashioned Fourth of July at Harbor Days in the village of Northport. Small-town hospitality and community fun fill this two-day festival, usually held to coincide with the Fourth of July. The festivities are centered by the waterfront near downtown Northport at neighboring Haserot Park and G.

Marsten Dame Marina. Plan to play by joining in beach volleyball, the tug of war, running race or the kids' Popeye Boat Regatta. Food lovers must attend the "Famous Whitefish Boil," where the cooked fish reputedly tastes like lobster. Regardless, it's a great community picnic! Meal tickets are $9 for adults and $4 for children age 12 and younger. An art fair, waterfront entertainment and, of course, Fourth of July fireworks round out the holiday.

National Cherry Festival
Traverse City • (616) 947-4230

Life's a bowl of cherries for eight days each July when the National Cherry Festival takes over Traverse City. This is one of the biggest festivals in the Midwest with three large parades, headliner entertainment, air shows, band competitions, bike tours, ice cream socials, a Native American Powwow, fireworks and more cherry products than you can imagine. It's fun, it's frantic, it's crowded . . . it's festival week and the energy is contagious. More than 150 activities fill the calendar. Most are available at no charge thanks to an abundance of national and local sponsors. There are too many to list here (see the Close-up in this chapter) but keep your eyes open for a few local favorites: the milk carton regatta, where sailors who have spent the spring building a ship out of discarded milk cartons, try to actually sail their creations against other crazy milkboaters; the bed race, which pits crews of normally rational adults against each other as they race their full-size, fully-decorated beds replete with huge wheels and blankets along main street without losing their passengers or parts; or the children's pet show, where otherwise "petless" children have been known to dress up a pet human, a.k.a Dad! By the way, since it wouldn't be a festival without a queen, we do that too.

Alpenfest
Gaylord • (616) 732-4000, (800) 345-8621

The spirit of Switzerland descends upon Gaylord each July for Alpenfest. Usually held in mid-July during the week following Traverse City's National Cherry Festival, this five-day celebration salutes the heritage of the Alpine Village with ethnic traditions and newfangled fun. Neighbors and visitors don lederhosen

Photo: Kevin Poirier

Tribes from around the Great Lakes gather at annual powwows.

and dirndls to lead the revelry with parades, yodeling, Swiss stone spitting, contests and games. Main street is transformed into the Alpenstrasse, an open-air craft show, while entertainment continues through the week on the Alpenstage. Early in the week, shopkeepers, neighbors and visitors gather at tables along main street for the world's largest coffee break — "Die Groste Caffe Pause." All you need for admission is a $1 Alpenfest pin.

Alden Summer Stroll
Downtown Alden
Meander through the charming streets of Alden during the annual free summer strolls held on Thursday evenings in July and August. Shopkeepers, neighbors and visitors greet each other during these pleasant evenings highlighted by strolling musicians, street entertainers and buskers. The village of Alden is charming, the shops are unique and summer is high season for this lovely community near Torch Lake.

Traverse Bay Outdoor Art Fair
Northwestern Michigan College, 1701 E. Front St., Traverse City • (616) 941-9488
On the last weekend of July, Michigan artists come together on the pine-canopied campus at Northwestern Michigan College to display their work, toast the arts and share a summer Saturday. The peaceful, shaded setting along with the faint scent of pine makes the Traverse Bay Outdoor Art Fair an especially pleasant rendezvous. This juried art show is one of the oldest in the region. It is sponsored by the Northwest Michigan Artists and Craftsmen Association. Rain or shine, 120 fine artists will be in their booths sharing all genres of art. Outdoor entertainment and food vendors are on tap all day. Admission is free.

JazzFest
Marina Park, Suttons Bay
• **(616) 271-4444**
Northwest Michigan has become a haven for jazz musicians. During JazzFest, they gather and share great classic jazz under a huge tent in Suttons Bay's Marina Park. The bay waters provide a scenic backdrop as festivalgoers sit on the grassy grounds and listen

to the strains of Dixieland, swing and big band classics. Leelanau foods and wines are served throughout the day. The music starts at noon and continues until the stars come out. Plan to bring blankets or lawn chairs to lounge on and, if the weather is hot, bring a swimsuit for a quick dip in the bay. JazzFest is held on the fourth Saturday in July. Tickets are usually $10 with discounts for advance purchases at local music stores.

Au Sable River Canoe Marathon
Penrod's Canoe Livery, Grayling
• **(517) 348-4425, (800) YES-8837**
How fast can you paddle a canoe in the middle of the night? That's just one question that comes to mind during the Au Sable River Canoe Race held during the last weekend of July. Canoeists from across the United States and Canada compete in this grueling 120-mile race to Lake Huron. At least 40 teams compete in the race, beginning with sprints for starting position earlier in the week. The actual marathon begins with a LeMans start at 9 PM on Saturday night as the teams, with canoes in hand, race through Grayling's streets and plunge into the Au Sable to begin their trek. The paddling continues through the night and well into Sunday until they reach the finish line at Oscoda at least 14 hours later. The canoeists aren't the only ones up all night. Hundreds of spectators drive from one viewing spot to another through the entire length of the journey. An arts and crafts fair, antique auto show, fun run, ice cream social, parade and other festivities build up anticipation for the actual race.

Lake Michigan Shoreline and Cadillac

Manistee National Forest Festival
Douglas Park, Manistee
• **(616) 723-2575, (800) 288-2286**
To celebrate the lumbering industry, which served as the economic catalyst for the community, Manistee puts on one of Michigan's largest July 4th celebrations. U.S. Forest Service rangers offer guided forest hikes in the Manistee National Forest and canoeing expe-

riences along the Manistee River to commemorate the piney woods. The four-day July 4th weekend event will entertain you with three parades, a juried arts and crafts show, a 5K and 10K competitive run and bike, raft and bed races. Manistee was once a production site for the highly-acclaimed Century boat and several events highlight this heritage. You can see an array of Century boats from all across the country as owners display their prized crafts along the Manistee Riverwalk docks. All types of boat owners are welcome to join the Venetian Boat Parade. Held after dark, decorated lighted crafts cruise the Manistee River sending shimmering reflections into the waters as the procession winds through town. Boaters take the advantage when it comes to viewing the fireworks display following the Venetian parade. You can also find prime viewing along the shores of city beaches. General attendance is free.

Greatest Fourth in the North
Lake City • (616) 839-4969

Known as the Greatest Fourth in the North for almost 25 years, the community works hard to maintain its reputation. The festival agenda is packed with four full days of activities during the July 4th holiday week. A carnival and midway, nightly entertainment, a two-day arts and crafts show, a children's day with games and entertainment and a beach-volleyball tournament, promise something of interest to every member of the family. Other key festival activities are sponsored by local organizations and include Christian concerts, horseback riding and a 5K and 10K run. Each year the Greatest Fourth in the North swells the tiny town with thousands of visitors. On the day of the Grand Parade, be prepared to find your spot on main street an hour or more ahead of time for a good view of the procession. The parade features marching bands, floats, horses, fire trucks, tractors, clowns, Girl Scouts, Boy Scouts, Veterans and more. In a time-honored Lake City tradition, hot and deliciously sloppy ox roast sandwiches are served to the crowds following the parade. Don't leave town too early or you'll miss the festival finale, a grand fireworks display over Lake Missaukee and the raffle of a new car. General admission is free.

Gus Macker 3-on-3 Charity Basketball Tournament
Ludington City Beach, Ludington
• (616) 845-0324, (800) 542-4600

It's an entire weekend of heavy-duty street ball played for charity. Considered one of the most popular tourneys on the Gus Macker Michigan circuit, the event attracts 40,000 players and spectators each year. Held the third weekend in July, the Macker is a fund-raiser for Ludington area nonprofit groups. The roster includes 1,500 teams. Players shoot hoops on street courts backdropped by the town's magnificent Lake Michigan beach. For enthusiasts of the sport, it's basketball heaven. The pounding beat of the ball and the cheering of crowds is nonstop all weekend. Heated competitions include men's and women's divisions and age divisions ranging from 10 years old and younger to 40 and older. To register a team, contact the Ludington Chamber of Commerce in May. Playing fees run about $88 per team. There is no admission fee for spectators.

Cadillac Festival of the Arts
City Lakefront Park, Cadillac
• (616) 775-1872

A festival for art lovers of all ages, the Cadillac event offers a full plate of cultural activities. Taking place the third weekend in July, the festival kicks off Friday night with a food fair and live big band music at the city lakefront park and pavilion. A juried art show opens Saturday morning. The works of more than 100 artists and craftsman are displayed. Youngsters delight in the annual festival Create-In where they are offered supervised opportunities to paint, print, glitter and glue to their heart's content. The annual String Thing, presented by the Cadillac Symphony orchestra, gives youngsters a hands-on introduction to the violin, cello and viola. Live entertainment is available throughout the day, including performances by the local symphony, high-school musicians, barbershop groups and kitchen bands. Activities and entertainment are free.

Aux Bec Scies Rendezvous
Mineral Springs Park, Frankfort
• (616) 352-7251

The Aux Bec Scies Rendezvous is a historical reenactment of the area's French fur-

The Cherry Capital of the World

More than 2 million cherry trees blanket the rolling hills of Grand Traverse, Leelanau, Antrim and Benzie counties, earning the region the distinction of being the "Cherry Capital of the World." With a reputation like that, a festival is only appropriate. But we don't do things half way up north. This is *the* National Cherry Festival, and you'll be hard-pressed to match the frenzy of fun and fruity festivities that fill eight days each July.

This is one of the biggest festivals in the Midwest and earns increasing national attention each year as parades fill the streets and big-name entertainers perform. There's much to do, much to see, and much to eat.

Close-up

Traverse City's Open Space (Union Street at Grandview Parkway) is the hub of the action. The best way to get your bearings is to stop at the information booth near the streetside pedestrian walk. Free booklets have a comprehensive schedule of daily activities, entertainment and parades, while friendly volunteers assist with directions, information and maps.

Dubbed "Cherry Festival Ambassadors," volunteers host events, give directions, serve refreshments and herd floats and bands through the crowd. They are easily recognized by their cherry-red and white shirts, friendly smiles and ambassador name tags. If you need assistance, don't hesitate to tap the expertise of these pleasant Insiders.

At the Open Space, you'll find the food court, family oasis, entertainment stage, cherry farm market and souvenir tent. Area restaurants serve sandwiches, salads and specialties along with an endless assortment of cherry treats. The family oasis is a shaded area with tables and chairs where families can relax and care for little ones.

The entertainment stage showcases performers during most day and evening hours, while festivalgoers enjoy the music from blankets and seats scattered nearby. Headliners take center stage each evening for the night's free concert. (In addition to the Open Space performances, you can buy tickets to see top-name entertainers such as LeAnn Rimes and the Steve Miller Band at the Cherry Festival music stage at the Northwestern Michigan Fairgrounds. Or, if you prefer the lively music of marching bands, the Open Band competition takes place at Thirlby Field.)

The Open Space is also the focal point for many of the special activities associated with the festival, including a weekend air show. A festival favorite, the air show often showcases the spectacular high-flying precision of the U.S. Navy Blue Angels. The air show can also be seen most places along the West Bay shoreline, and many observers line the lawns and beaches near the TART trail with blankets and lawn chairs.

— continued on next page

Photo: National Cherry Festival

Youngsters create their own cherry treasures at the "Arts and Crafts for Kids" session.

In addition to the activities on the Open Space, you'll find the Hole-in-One golf contest at Bay Meadows Golf Course, the Big Wheel Race and Bike Rodeo at the Horizon Outlet Center parking lot, and the children's pet show at F&M. Actual locations may vary from festival to festival as new sponsors and activities are added, but all are listed with maps, times and descriptions in the official program book.

At almost every activity you're bound to bump into royalty. The National Cherry Queen presides over the celebration along with the five finalists who are vying to become the next queen. You'll see the court, dressed alike, in all of the parades and at activities throughout the week. The new queen is crowned on the final Saturday night and serves as the cherry industry's goodwill ambassador for the upcoming year.

Festival week is also highlighted by our favorite cherry royals — the many junior princes and princesses representing the elementary schools throughout the region. These delightful 2nd graders, who are chosen through school drawings, are decked out in their cherry finery at all of the children's events and ride along with their school floats in the Junior Royale and Cherry Royale parades.

Three parades — each with its own distinct personality — weave through the streets on Tuesday, Thursday and Saturday. Tuesday's Heritage Parade showcases the region's past with countless antique autos, horse-drawn carriages, local bands and related floats. The Junior Royale on Thursday evening is one of the nation's largest children's parades. You'll see whimsical entries, countless clowns, enormous balloons, school floats and hundreds of costumed children riding bikes, walking pets and marching with scout troops. Both lead up to the grand Cherry Royale Parade filled with extravagant floats, local personalities and marching bands from the Midwest and Canada. The parades start at the intersection of Front and Railroad streets near Grandview Parkway, then head west on Front Street turning south on Union Street. Plan to arrive at least an hour before the start, which is 7 PM on Tuesday, 6:30 PM on Thursday, and 10:45 AM on Saturday, and bring along a lawn chair to stay comfy. Until recently, locals would save prime space by leaving chairs along curbsides a day or two ahead of the parades, but new ordinances prohibit chairs until two hours before parade time. Families often bring along a small cooler with refreshments and snacks, but you can also purchase soft drinks from street vendors and school children pulling wagons filled with chilled cans of pop.

trading days of the 1700s. When you travel through Benzie County, you'll notice the name Betsie tagged to many natural landmarks such as Point Betsie, Betsie Lake, Betsie Bay and Betsie River. The English name Betsie is derived from Aux Bec Scies, the French version of the Native American word for the sawbilled duck. On the last weekend in July, the French once again appear to descend. Dressed as fur traders, festival participants pitch handmade skin tents. You'll see men, women and children cook on open fires, conduct trade, present period demonstrations and tell stories. Just watch, or step back into time with them. Historically based bead work and clothing is for sale so you can dress the part.

Though usually held in downtown Frankfort, in 1998 the festivities will take place on Mackinac Island for the filming of a documentary. General admission is free.

Gold Coast Festival Arts and Crafts Show
Ludington City Park, Ludington
• **(616) 845-0324, (800) 542-4600**

Year after year, art lovers return to the Gold Coast Festival two-day arts and craft show, which takes place beneath the umbrella of tall shady trees in Ludington's City Park. On the last weekend in July, more than 200 artisans and crafters from across the country bring their work to the non-juried show and sale. Stroll through the park and you'll enjoy a wide array of wood crafts, pottery, jewelry, painting, photography, candles and other creations. Admission is free.

Little Traverse

Venetian Festival
Charlevoix • (616) 547-2101

What began as just a boat parade many years ago is now a full-fledged four-day summer festival, but the highlight of the event remains the Venetian Grand Electric Boat Parade. You can catch the boat procession traveling along the waters of Round Lake in Charlevoix, beginning at 10 PM Saturday night. The parade is typically followed by a spectacular light display. Held the last weekend in July, other activities in the lineup include a carnival, live entertainment, demonstrations, the presentation of the new Miss Charlevoix, a 1-mile, 5K and 10K foot race, and the Venetian Street Parade. The street parade proceeds from Bridge Street to Clinton Street and features bands, floats, drill teams, color guards, antique vehicles, horses and more. General admission is free.

Art in the Park
Pennsylvania Park, Petoskey
• (616) 347-4150

Petoskey art lovers look forward to this annual fine art show with great anticipation. More than 100 artists and crafters come from around the country to exhibit works including everything from painting and jewelry to photography. A children's tent offers activities and reasonably priced artwork for kids to purchase. It's a free event held the third Saturday in July at Petoskey's historic Gaslight District in Pennsylvania Park. Come once and you'll be hooked.

The Petoskey Summer Antiques Festival
Emmet County Fairgrounds, Petoskey
• (810) 469-1706

An upscale show set in the old-time country atmosphere of the Emmet County Fairgrounds, the festival is ranked by many antique enthusiasts as the best show in the north.

The event features more than 100 national and regional dealers who exhibit a wide variety of goods. The reputation and knowledge of the dealers and the charming ambiance of the setting, likewise draws festivalgoers from across the United States. A two-day event held the first weekend in July and again during the first weekend in August, each show provides you with a fun-filled weekend of historical treasure hunting as well as live musical entertainment and delicious taste treats. You won't find hot dog concession at these shows. Instead, local chefs are on hand to prepare gourmet snacks and lunches. Admission is $4 for adults. Children 12 years old and younger are admitted free.

Mackinac Straits

Chicago to Mackinac Island Yacht Race
Mackinac Island • (906) 847-6418, (800) 4-LILACS

Serious sailing takes center stage on back-to-back weekends when the yacht races to Mackinac Island begin. The Chicago to Mackinac Island Yacht Race pits at least 2,500 sailors in 300 boats against each other in a 333-mile trek that spans the length of Lake Michigan. The trip usually takes three days to complete, as long as the winds are helpful. Always sponsored by the Chicago Yacht Club, the "Chicago to Mack" race celebrates its centennial year in 1998. Race weekends fill the island with a frenzy of activity as well as people! All of the slips at the harbor are reserved for racers with many of the additional boats docked along the Arnold Dock. The Pink Pony bar at the Chippewa Hotel is a favorite spot for sailors and spectators to watch the incoming sailboats. The viewing is free. Enjoy!

Port Huron to Mackinac Island Yacht Race
Mackinac Island • (906) 847-6418, (800) 4-LILACS

Remember the Chicago sailors that braved Lake Michigan in their quest to reach Mackinac? They do it all over again one week later! This time, the regatta leaves Port Huron for the 256 mile trek north across Lake Huron.

August

Grand Traverse

Friday Night Live
Downtown Traverse City
• (616) 922-2050

Whether you're on vacation or simply ending the work week, TGIF! Late summer marks the annual return of Traverse City's favorite block party, Friday Night Live, to downtown on August (and late July) Fridays from 5:30 to 9:30 PM. Every Friday, from the end of July through Labor Day, the downtown area is closed to cars as musicians, dancers, artists and food vendors take over the 100 and 200 blocks of East Front Street. The energy is contagious as neighbors, friends and fudgies (a term of endearment for tourists, often in search of fudge) fill the streets to enjoy an eclectic mix of outdoor food, fun and entertainment. Themes change each year and each Friday. Past nights have included chalk art, line dancing, strolling actors, watercolor artists, wall climbing, kite flying, clowns, magicians and mimes. It's best to expect the unexpected and join in the fun.

Suttons Bay Art Festival
Marina Park, Suttons Bay
• (616) 271-5077

Held the first weekend of August, the Suttons Bay Art Festival marries art with nature's beauty thanks to a beautiful setting on the scenic shores of West Grand Traverse Bay. More than 90 artists display their work for two days in canopied booths surrounding Marina Park. Many of these artists live at least part of the year in Leelanau County or the Grand Traverse area, which bears testament to the creative atmosphere that permeates this beautiful region. This free show has always been a personal favorite! By the way,

nobody will go hungry. A food tent sells specialties by local restaurants and civic groups, and a pancake breakfast is held on Sunday morning. The Suttons Bay Art Festival runs 10 AM to 6 PM on Saturday and 11 AM to 5 PM on Sunday.

Harbor Days Festival
Elk Rapids • (616) 264-8202

The village of Elk Rapids is alive with free activity during its annual Harbor Days Festival held for four days during early August. The festival fun includes a street dance, midway rides, carnival games, children's activities, contests, a parade and a spectacular fireworks display.

Leelanau Peninsula Wine Festival
Haserot Park, Northport • (616) 386-5806

Like the Leland Food and Wine Festival held earlier in the summer, the Leelanau Peninsula Wine Festival is a pleasant way to sample the peninsula's best wines and foods. The event is usually held on the second Saturday of August at Northport's lovely Haserot Park. At least 15 restaurants and wineries usually participate along with a host of musical performers. The fun begins at noon and continues to 6 PM, rain or shine. If it's a nice day, bring along a blanket to relax in the park. Admission is $10 for adults and includes a glass and three wine samples. Children accompanied by an adult are admitted free.

Buckley Old Engine Show
1 mi. W. of Buckley on Mich. Hwy. 37
• (616) 263-5096

The Northwest Michigan Engine and Thrasher Club's extraordinary collection of antique machines draws 50,000 people to its show grounds each summer. History chugs, huffs, puffs and really comes to life at exhibits throughout a 200-acre setting. The Old Engine Show features 300 antique tractors, 600 antique gas and oil engines, a

---

INSIDERS' TIP

Pack your swimsuit and a blanket when heading to the Suttons Bay Art Fair. You can take a break from art with a quick dip and an afternoon snooze at the beach next to Marina Park.

working sawmill dating back to the 1800s, a bowl mill and a turn-of-the-century cider press. Held the third weekend in August, your $5 entrance fee (children 15 and younger are admitted free) entitles you to a 1-mile train ride in a 1800s passenger car pulled by a steam-powered locomotive. Progress in wheat harvesting is demonstrated with working farm equipment ranging from the early thrashing machines to today's self-propelled combines. Amish furniture makers, spinners, weavers and quilters exhibit and explain their time-honored crafts. An antique car show, arts and crafts booths and a flea market provide plenty of good browsing opportunities. You can tour the grounds for an entire day and still not see all there is to see and experience at the Old Engine Show. To linger a day or two longer, take advantage of free camping on the grounds and enjoy nightly square dances. Throughout the four-day festival, old time fiddles, banjos and dulcimers help bring back the spirit of the good ol' days.

Renaissance Fair
Grand Traverse Commons, near Elmwood and 10th Sts., Traverse City
• (616) 947-4750

Lords, ladies, knights and knaves stride the grounds of the Grand Traverse Commons during the last Sunday of August to celebrate the annual Medieval Festival and benefit the Grand Traverse Medical Care Facility. The party runs from 11 AM to 6 PM. A king's banquet of barbecued chicken and royal fixings is served throughout the day as games are played and stories are told. Strolling minstrels play their tunes while knights joust, jesters prance and the lords and ladies of the court dance. Local actors, street performers and history buffs gear up for this annual step back in time as they take on roles from days of yore. A local fa-

vorite is Crazy Richard who swallows fire and juggles while eating apples! There are plenty of activities for children and entertainment for adults. Festival admission is $3. Banquet fare is à la carte.

Lake Michigan Shoreline and Cadillac

Betsie Bay Jazz Festival
Frankfort • (616) 352-4568

The Big Band era comes alive in Benzie County each second weekend in August. Professional and amateur jazz musicians from throughout the state gather for this four-day jam session. Thursday through Saturday, Big Band, Swing and Dixieland fill the air from the Frankfort park and shake the walls of local establishments including Hotel Frankfort and the Cabbage Shed in Elberta. Between 1 and 9 PM on Sunday, the Frankfort Eagles Club hosts the Bob Baker Open Jam Session where dozens of musicians cook up swing as food and beverages are prepared by volunteers for you to enjoy.

Little Traverse

Polish Festival
Boyne Falls • (616) 638-2755,
(800) 845-2828

Polka your heart out at the Polish Festival in downtown Boyne Falls. Taking place the first weekend in August you'll find Polish music, Polish food and a beer tent. The three-day festival is almost as much fun as a Polish wedding. In addition to theme tents, the event features a carnival and midway and an arts and crafts show. The 1998 celebration marks the festival's 24th anniversary. Put on your dancing shoes and come on down.

INSIDERS' TIP

The lilacs celebrated on Mackinac Island were first introduced there by French missionaries during the 1600s. At least 60 varieties thrive on the island today, often growing on former shrubs that have reached treelike proportions.

Mackinac Straits

International Ironworkers Festival
Corvette Crossroads Auto Show
Mackinaw City • (616) 436-5574, (800) 666-0160

Ironworkers played an enormous role in building the Mackinac Bridge. Mackinaw City's annual Ironworkers Festival, held in late August, commemorates this spectacular 1957 feat. Ironworkers from around the world test their skills in events like column climbing in pursuit of the top prize, the gold belt buckle award. If this festival whets your interest, stop by the Mackinac Bridge museum where the ironworkers contribution to the bridge is documented in photos, film and paraphernalia. (See the Attractions chapter for more on the museum.)

The Corvette Crossroads Auto Show is usually held simultaneously with the Ironworkers Festival, but is always held on the last weekend before Labor Day. More than 225 Corvette owners participate in this three-day event beginning with a 'Vette parade through town, across the Mackinac Bridge and back. Stop by and ogle the sports coupe of your dreams and add your vote to the People's Choice award.

There is no admission charge for either event.

September

Grand Traverse

Detroit Red Wings Training Camp
Centre I.C.E., Traverse City
• (616) 933-RINK

The 1997 Stanley Cup champions, the Detroit Red Wings, held their fall training camp here in September 1997. They had such a great time in Traverse City that they decided to return. Schedules vary by the day and the season, but at least one practice is usually held daily as well as a scrimmage or two at the end of the week. Viewing is open to the public but tickets are necessary and limited. They usually go on sale just a few weeks before camp begins. If your heart is set on watching, plan to get in line early. Expect to pay $5 for practices and $10 for scrimmages.

Lake Michigan Shoreline and Cadillac

Festival of the Pines
Lake City • (616) 839-4969

Cradled in the heart of Christmas tree country, each year Lake City celebrates the industry and the area's logging history. It may be the only place in Michigan where you can win a prize for having the most handsome beard or for your accurate aim with an ax. Taking place the third weekend in September, there are bucksaw, antique saw, chainsaw and other cutting contests in Saturday's Lumberjack Competitions where prizes are awarded in several divisions for men, women and youth. In the Christmas tree baling contest, three-person teams are pitted against one another in a race against time. Other favorite festival activities include the Festival of the Pines Parade featuring logging trucks and equipment, lumberjacks and the junior Prince and Princess of the Pines. Always popular is the beverage tent where the atmosphere for Saturday night's best-beard contest is a little rough and rowdy but the food, beer and wine go down pretty easy. Admission is free.

Victorian Port City Festival
Manistee Business District
• (616) 723-2575, (800) 288-2286

Manistee officials close River Street in the historic business district to bring the past to life during the town's Victorian Port City Festival held the first weekend in September. During the two-day event celebrating the community's rich heritage, you'll hear bands playing music in the streets and be treated to free trolley rides. Downtown merchants don period garb and get into the spirit. Victorians in Person, known as the VIPs, a group promoting Manistee's roots, present their annual Victorian Promenade during the lunch hour on Saturday. Dressed in vintage wear, group members show off fashions of yesteryear on one of two street stages set up for the weekend. From the second stage, magicians and puppeteers present low-tech entertainment for children. If you are a history buff, you'll appreciate the building tours presented by the Manistee Historical Museum. Once one of the leading ports along Lake Michigan, the town is home to numerous buildings designed by nationally known architects. For the artistic minded, working artisans demonstrate time-honored crafts such as loom weaving, while an arts and crafts show provides a bounty of browsing and buying opportunities. Ethnic foods and an antique auto show are other favorite events. Come Sunday morning, count your blessings in a new way by joining the community's lively outdoor Dixieland church service. Admission is free.

Little Traverse

Taste of Harbor Springs
Bay St. Waterfront, Harbor Springs
• (616) 526-7999
Gourmet foods and beverages are grilled, baked, steamed and brewed by some of the area's top chefs for this premier dining event held the third Saturday in September. From booths set up along the Harbor Springs waterfront, more than 20 restaurants offer samples of their best culinary creations for you to enjoy. Ticket holders enjoy unlimited sampling of appetizers, soups, entrees and desserts, as well as tastes of local wines and beers. Hot buffalo chili, melt-in-your-mouth pastries, Greek, Polish and Southwestern dishes have all appeared on the menu. Sampling is between noon and 3 PM. Tickets are $12 in advance, and $15 at the gate. A limited number are available, so you would be wise to purchase your tickets in August. Call (616) 526-7999. Major credit cards are accepted.

Mackinac Straits

Labor Day Bridge Walk
Mackinac Bridge
On completion of the Mackinac Bridge in 1957, then-Governor G. Mennon (Soapy) Williams walked across the bridge on Labor Day to celebrate. Forty years later, we are still celebrating Labor Day by walking across the 5-mile Mackinac Bridge along with the governor and his family. An estimated 60,000 people make the trek each fall from St. Ignace to Mackinaw City. Buses make a Herculean effort to shuttle participants between their cars on one side of the bridge, and the start and end points. A number of rules are in place — such as no running, in-line skating or playing tag — to help assure safety. Most are obvious, some are more subtle, but this attention to detail has resulted in an excellent safety record. Guidelines noting the rules as well as starting times, transportation and trivia are available at Mackinaw City and St. Ignace visitors centers. Participation is free.

Michinemackinong Powwow
Arts Dockside
St. Ignace • (906) 643-8717,
(800) 338-6660
A celebration of Native American traditions takes place during the annual Michinemackinong Powwow always held on the Saturday and Sunday of Labor Day weekend at Marquette Mission Park in St. Ignace. Sponsored by the Mackinac Band of Chippewa Indians and the Museum of Ojibwa Culture, the powwow is a traditional celebration of thanksgiving, prayer and gathering for family and friends. Activity centers around the dance arena, which represents the cycle of life, the moon, the sun and the earth. A shaded area in the center holds "The Drum," which actually includes the drummers and a large drum that together represent the heartbeat of the Native American people. Dancers in various traditional garb perform all day and evening with several grand entrances taking place during the weekend. In addition to the dancing, local artisans display traditional arts and crafts, native foods like fry bread and corn are served and the adjacent Museum of Ojibwa Culture is open to attendees. Recommended donation for weekend admission is $5 for adults, $2 for children younger than 14 and $15 for families.

Across the street, Arts Dockside is held during the same weekend. Over 100 exhibitors display an array of handmade arts and crafts items along the waterfront at Dock #2. Musicians, entertainment and concessions add to the festivities. Admission is free.

Photo: Grand Traverse Resort

The annual Northwood Festival of Lights is a holiday celebration you won't want to miss.

October

Grand Traverse

Norwegian Pumpkin Rolling Festival
Hitchpoint Cider Mill, 11274 Munro Rd., Williamsburg • (616) 264-8371

Grab your pumpkin and prepare to roll! The Norwegian Pumpkin Rolling Festival hearkens back to ethnic traditions with children rolling fresh pumpkins down a large hill at Hitchpoint Cider Mill. In modern times, it's actually a wonderful impetus to spend a sunny autumn Saturday at a picturesque cider mill. Hitchpoint is unique because it relies on large Norwegian work horses to power the antique cider press. A visit to Hitchpoint is well worth the short scenic drive from Traverse City on any autumn weekend. Fresh donuts, caramel apples, just-pressed cider and other goodies are available to purchase. During the Pumpkin Rolling Festival, many free children's activities take place like pony rides, corn cob tosses, pumpkin rolling, coloring and other games.

Lake Michigan Shoreline and Cadillac

Autumn Fest
Ludington • (616) 845-0324

When frost covers the pumpkin it signals celebration time for the Ludington Community. Retailers, nonprofit and business organizations present a variety of Autumn Fest treats during the second and third weeks of October. You won't want to miss seeing the fields of brilliantly colored pumpkins at Major Produce, 10 miles south of Scottville on U.S. Highway 31. Visitors to the Pumpkin Patch wander a cornfield maze, enjoy pumpkin carving, scenic wagon rides and sample fresh apple cider and hot doughnuts. Pumpkin Patch admission is about $4 per person. The Ludington Area Chamber of Commerce gets into the spirit with its annual Haunted Forest held at Cartier Park in Ludington. Tickets for a scary wagon trip through the forest are $4 per person. Merchants have Moonlight Madness sales and pumpkin decorating contests. Kiddie costume competitions, an annual Country Western Dance and a fall festival at White Pine Village also highlight Autumn Fest. (See our Kidstuff chapter to learn more about historic White Pine Village.)

Little Traverse

Charlevoix Apple Fest
East Park, Charlevoix • (616) 547-2101

When the leaves are flaming orange and red and the air is cool and crisp, celebrating the fall apple harvest is a wonderful way to enjoy the season's bounty. Charlevoix marks the harvest with its Apple Fest the second weekend of each October. East Park in downtown Charlevoix is the hub for festival activities and events. Friday through Sunday, growers set up stations around the park and offer 30 varieties of locally produced apples for sale. Crunchy, sweet, shiny red, yellow or green, you can buy them by the bushel or the peck. Food booths will tempt you with a wide selection of apple products, jams, jellies, cider, apple cake and donuts. You might even get a head start on your Christmas shopping at the Apple Fest Craft Show, which features more than 75 exhibitors from across the state. For the youngsters, the festival provides a petting farm and free pony rides. Free horse-drawn carriage rides add the perfect touch to the festival's country charm. Admission is free.

November

Grand Traverse

Iceman Cometh Challenge
Traverse City • (616) 938-5887

Mountain bikers make a last brisk race through the north woods at the Annual Iceman Cometh Challenge held the first weekend of November. The Challenge is a 27-mile, point-to-point mountain bike race sanctioned by the National Off-Road Bicycle Association (NORBA), and is NORBA's American Mountain Bike Challenge Eastern Regional Series Final. Almost 2,000 racers will battle rain, sleet, mud and even snow as they trek along paved and dirt roads, two tracks, abandoned railroad beds and the Vasa cross-country ski trails (see our Winter Recreation chapter) on a course stretching between Kalkaska and Traverse City. The winners share $20,000 in cash and prizes. The Iceman Cometh is open to amateur and professional mountain bike racers with registration averaging $30. Spectators are welcome to watch the fun for free.

Northwood Festival of Lights
Grand Traverse Resort, Acme
• (616) 938-2100

The holiday season kicks off with the flick of a switch when the lights go on for the Northwood Festival of Lights at the Grand Traverse Resort. The festive displays run from mid-November through the Christmas holidays. More than 250,000 white lights set the resort grounds ablaze with twinkling reindeer, trees and wreaths guiding your way. Elaborate decorations, animated characters and a freshly baked, life-size gingerbread house light up the lobby areas while traditional tunes fill the air. Added highlights like choral groups, dinner theater, Santa visits and gallery specials help make the season sparkle. There is no charge to visit and admire the lights.

Christmas Craft Show
Grand Traverse Resort, Acme
• (616) 941-9488

The Grand Ballroom at the Grand Traverse Resort is transformed into a showcase for holiday gifts and decorations during this huge, early-season art show. Local artisans of all genres display their work, demonstrate their skills and sell their wares during this two-day event in mid-November. Sponsored by the Northwest Michigan Artists and Craftsmen, the show begins on a Friday night and continues all day on Saturday. Refreshments and musical entertainment complete the slate of activities. A $1 donation is gladly accepted.

Festival of the Trees
Park Place Hotel Dome, 300 E. State St., Traverse City • (616) 947-1120

Tannenbaums dressed in glitter, lights and bows fill the Park Place Dome in a dazzling display of holiday spirit. More than 50 trees are on display as well as wreaths, garlands and countless seasonal accoutrements. Many of the trees have been professionally decorated using a variety of themes and creative garnishes while others have been trimmed by local school children. Seasonal music, children's activities and an opening night gala add to the holiday spirit. The Festival of Trees is usually held during mid- to late November, often including Thanksgiving weekend.

Lake Michigan Shoreline and Cadillac

Deer Hunter Open House
Carl T. Johnson Hunting and Fishing Center, Cadillac • (616) 779-1321

November is Buck Fever time at the Carl T. Johnson Hunting and Fishing Center on Mich. Highway 115 in Cadillac. Scheduled in

mid-November, prior to the opening of the state's firearm season, the Deer Hunter's Open House is an opportunity for hunters to clarify any concerns or questions regarding the rules and regulations for the year's hunting season with some of the state's top experts in the field. Representatives from the Michigan Department of Natural Resources and U.S. Forest Service are on hand to share their knowledge of the sport. All hunters are welcome to bring along their prize rack to display and to share their best hunting story. Educational videos, maps and other materials are available, as well as prizes and complimentary refreshments. Admission is free. See the Close-up in our Camping and RV Park chapter to learn more about the Carl T. Johnson Hunting and Fishing Center.

Little Traverse

Hospice of Little Traverse Bay Benefit Auction
Boyne Highlands Resort, 600 Highlands Dr., Harbor Springs • (616) 487-4422

This annual benefit auction is one of the highlights of the Boyne Country social calendar. The event is held the first Saturday in November at the world-class Boyne Highlands Resort. Guests relish the great buys, good food and good company. Coveted items auctioned at a recent fund-raiser included a 1947 Willy's Army Jeep, fine art, golf packages and celebrity outings. More than 25 local chefs and beverage vendors contribute their talents to a wonderful buffet. All proceeds support Hospice of Little Traverse Bay patient care programs. Tickets are $25 per person in advance and $30 at the door.

December

Grand Traverse

Twelve Days of Christmas
Shanty Creek, Bellaire • (616) 533-8621, (800) 678-4111

Holiday activities fill the slate beginning mid-November at Shanty Creek in Bellaire. This community-wide event includes an art and crafts show, storytelling, musical ensembles, caroling, a slopeside torchlight parade, dinner specials, children's activities and, of course, Santa! A festive dinner featuring a performance by the Traverse Symphony Orchestra is an annual favorite. The specifics change each year but the fun and warm holiday memories are always wonderful.

Santa Parade and Christmas Stroll
Gaylord • (517) 732-4000

Gaylord rings in its holiday season during the first weekend of December with the Santa Parade and Christmas Stroll. Jolly old St. Nick, Mrs. Claus and assorted elves arrive early evening in a lighted procession winding through the Alpine Village and arriving at the Courthouse lawn. The entourage then lights the Community Christmas Tree, leads a caroling session and invites every youngster to visit with Santa. The old-fashioned festivities, which are free, continue during the weekend as merchants host open houses, special sales, children's activities and holiday promotions. Supervised film matinees keep little ones entertained while parents shop.

Christmas for the Animals
Clinch Park Zoo, Traverse City
• (616) 922-4904

Children of all ages love to share the holidays with their furry friends at the Christmas for the Animals held in mid-December at the Clinch Park Zoo. Since the zoo is normally closed during the winter months, it's always fun to visit the animals as they start sporting their heavy new coats and frolicking in the snow. Our favorites are the river otters who love to dive, frolic and perform regardless of the snowflakes or chilly air. There is no admission fee to visit Christmas for the Animals, but everyone is encouraged to bring a little gift that the animals can use all winter long — carrots, apples, dog food and

zoo bread are favorites. Hot cider, children's activities, seasonal music and sleigh rides by the bay help warm the day.

Lake Michigan Shoreline and Cadillac

Victorian Christmas Sleighbell Parade and Old Christmas Weekend
Downtown Manistee • (616) 723-2575, (800) 288-2286

From the jingle of sleighbells to Santa in his Victorian suit, experience Christmas the way it used to be at the Old Christmas Weekend in the historic port city of Manistee. Held the first weekend in December, the holiday celebration kicks off Thursday with dining and musical events. Festivities continue through Sunday. Saturday's Victorian Sleighbell Parade features only non-motorized units. Horse-drawn buggies, marching bands playing favorite Christmas songs, school children and firemen in turn-of-the-century dress march through the downtown, which is listed in the National Register of Historic Places. The parade concludes as the community Christmas tree is pulled upright through Manistee streets by Belgian draft horses. A tree-lighting ceremony follows. In an attempt to bring the true meaning of Christmas to you, activities focus on noncommercial pleasures such as musical concerts, caroling and a holiday production at the Ramsdell Theater. Historic building tours offer a glimpse into the romance of life in the Victorian age. Vintage transportation, trolley and surrey rides are available and provide an enjoyable experience for the entire family. Holiday shopping along main street takes on an old-time flavor this weekend as merchants dress in period apparel while steamy roasted chestnuts are sold from street corners. General admission is free.

INSIDERS' TIP

Fireworks light the sky over the magnificent Mackinac Bridge in a picturesque Fourth of July salute that can be seen from shorelines on both sides of the bridge as well as from Mackinac Island.

Little Traverse

Trolley Tour of Lights
Downtown Boyne City • (616) 582-6222

Boyne City has a unique way of sharing the holiday spirit with visitors to their community. The free Trolley Tour of Lights takes guests on a one-hour trip through business and residential districts, showcasing the town's best Christmas decorations. The tours run from mid-December to December 29, with the exception of Christmas Eve and Christmas Day. Catch the trolley in downtown Boyne City in front of Boyne Country Books, 125 Water Street. Tours depart at 6 and 7 PM daily.

Fair Time!

Going to the fair . . . going to the fair . . . going to the Northwestern Michigan fair!" So goes the song of late summer in Traverse City. The fair song was written several years ago to promote attendance and awareness. It worked. Today, it only takes a few bars of this locally familiar melody to bring visions of intentionally corny commercials coupled with the down-home fun of the actual fair.

Fairs are held throughout Michigan during July and August (although a few sneak in early during June or wait until September). Reflecting the rural nature of so many communities in northern Michigan, fair weeks are times to celebrate the harvest and show off 4-H livestock projects, homebaked goodies and homegrown specialties. Cows, horses, pigs and chickens line the stalls while country music, midway rides, harness racing, demolition derbies and old-fashioned fun fill the days.

Here's a general list of county fairs and the approximate week they are held. Check with the local fair associations or visitors bureaus for exact dates and schedules:

July

Kalkaska County Fair, Kalkaska, (616) 258-9103, third week of July
Manistee County Fair, Onekama, (616) 889-5566, fourth week of July
Missaukee Falmouth Youth Show, Falmouth, (616) 825-2959, late July

August

Northwestern Michigan Fair, Traverse City, (616) 943-4150, first week of August
Otsego County Fair, Gaylord, (517) 732-4000, (800) 345-8621, first week of August
Antrim County Farm and Family Fair, Bellaire, (616) 533-6023, early August
Northern District Fair, Cadillac, (616) 775-6361, second week of August
Western Michigan Fair, Ludington, (616) 845-0710, third week of August
Emmet-Charlevoix County Fair, Petoskey, (616) 347-1010, third week of August

The region's natural beauty serves as inspiration to artists, musicians and writers.

The Arts

We are truly blessed with cultural riches in Northwest Michigan. Whether your tastes run from chamber music to avant garde jazz, live theater to modern dance, studio art to gallery work, you're sure to find something tantalizing in our area.

Few places in Michigan can match our abundance of resident professional artists. The region's natural beauty serves as inspiration to artists, musicians and writers.

We have listed a number of artistic venues below. You'll find listings of large galleries, intimate studios, theater stages, musical ensembles and frequent performers who make up the local arts scene. We invite you to meet them and absorb the creative ambiance that fills the region.

Before we begin our artistic sampler, we need to point out a few local quirks about shop hours and seasonality. As a rule of thumb, most of the galleries associated with shopping areas will have hours that reflect their communities' shopping styles. For example, the Traverse City and Petoskey-based galleries will likely be open daily year round except during the winter months when they will limit hours or close on Sunday. Galleries in the more seasonal communities welcome visitors daily from late May through Labor Day and on weekends in October and during the holidays. Many of the galleries listed are working studios. Their hours can vary with the season, the weather or simply by whim. The artists generally have expanded hours between Memorial Day and Labor Day and around holidays. It's always best to call ahead to verify hours and directions. In the listings below, assume that all of these galleries are open year round unless noted otherwise.

You can check on the region's performance schedules and upcoming exhibits by reading local entertainment guides, *Traverse* magazine, the *Northern Express* and the Friday edition of the *Traverse City Record-Eagle* for the latest slate of events. Finally, keep your eyes and ears open. You'll find local tunes playing in our shops and local paintings filling area restaurants. Everywhere you turn, you should find evidence that the arts are alive, well and thriving in this corner of Michigan.

Galleries

Grand Traverse

Traverse City Area

The Bella Galleria
17015 Center Rd., Traverse City
• (616) 223-4142

The Bella Galleria is a beautiful fine art gallery beside the Old Mission Tavern (see our Restaurants chapter) near the tip of the Old Mission Peninsula. It showcases the work of owner and sculptor Verna Bartnik along with more than 50 area artists. Bartnick is known for her bronze sculptures that stand in many northern Michigan churches and at Northwestern Michigan College. Her sculpture studio gallery is also here, and, periodically, guided tours of the workshop are offered. The Bella Galleria, as well as the Old Mission Tavern, display only original works of art. Both are open daily.

Belstone Gallery
321 E. Front St., Traverse City
• (616) 946-0610

This contemporary gallery is a wonderful art source. Inside this lovely space, you'll find handcrafted jewelry, pottery, watercolors, oils, prints, blown glass, wood and metal work and Soleri wind chimes. Many of the works showcase local talent. Belstone is open daily. (See our Shopping chapter for more information.)

Dennos Museum Center
1701 E. Front St., Traverse City
• (616) 922-1055

The Dennos Museum Center has become the cultural hub of the Grand Traverse region and certainly lives up to its slogan to "Come Alive Inside." It hosts the Dancing Bear Music series, Jazz at the Museum and countless guest performances on the stage of its Milliken Auditorium as well as top-quality rotating displays in the art galleries.

The museum features two permanent galleries: the Inuit Gallery, which displays the Museum's extensive collection of Inuit art; and the Discovery Gallery (see our Kidstuff chapter), where children can explore their five senses through art and science via a number of interactive displays. Three additional galleries and a sculpture court bring an always fascinating collection of revolving exhibits to Traverse City. One of the most recent exhibits, titled *Picasso to Warhol*, featured a retrospective of 20th-century modern art on loan from the Detroit Institute of Arts. The gift shop tailors its wares to complement current showings but always carries a nice selection of children's projects, art books and works by local artists.

www.insiders.com
See this and many other **Insiders' Guide®** destinations online — in their entirety.
Visit us today!

Evergreen Gallery
531 W. Front St., Traverse City
• (616) 929-9522

Several local artisans have collaborated to create the Evergreen Gallery. The charming storefront displays and sells an array of handpainted furniture, mirrors and porcelain as well as functional pottery, original dolls, wreaths, fine art cards and fun jewelry.

NMAC Art Center Exhibit Gallery
720 S. Elmwood St., Traverse City
• (616) 941-9488

This is the gallery for the Northwestern Michigan Artists and Craftsmen Association (NMAC) and showcases the works of its members with monthly showings. See the Classes and Support section of this chapter for more about NMAC.

Riecker's Outdoor Gallery
134 E. Front St., Traverse City
• (616) 946-0414

The work of wildlife artists is featured at this unique gallery appealing to sports enthusiasts. Sculptures, paintings and assorted gifts are showcased in a beautifully renovated, vintage shop in the heart of downtown Traverse City. You'll find the work of many local artists whose creations reflect the natural beauty and abundant wildlife that fills the Traverse Bay region. Riecker's is open daily.

State of the Art
430 W. 14th St., Traverse City
• (616) 947-5456

State of the Art is a high-quality framing shop that doubles as a showcase for top local artists. Passersby are treated to a peek at the art on busy 14th Street — several large canvases rotate on easels near the shop's large, windowed storefront. Works, which are also for sale, often feature several pieces by noted local watercolorist Charles Murphy, who also hosts a showing of new works most summers.

Traverse Area Arts Council Showcase Gallery
106½ E. Front St., Traverse City
• (616) 947-2282

This cozy second-floor gallery is nestled between the City Opera House and Dance Arts Academy in the heart of downtown Traverse City. It is hosted by the Traverse Area Arts Council and serves as the hub for its activities. Shows change each month. For more on the council, see the subsequent listing in the Classes and Support section.

Watermelon Sugar Gallery and Gifts
153 E. Front St., Traverse City
• (616) 929-7426

Watermelon Sugar is a newer downtown gallery and specialty shop that features a rotating assortment of works by local and regional artists. During a recent stop, we saw Forest Flowers — intricate, lifelike porcelain flowers with cop-

Photo: Kevin Poirier

Take time to see some of our region's outstanding fine art exhibits.

per and silver leaves created by Glen Arbor artist Ananda Bricker — as well as paintings and drawings by Ron Gianola and an array of other works.

Wooden Gallery
116 E. Front St., Traverse City
• (616) 941-0823

Delightful framed art without glass is showcased at the Wooden Gallery. This picture-filled showroom is nestled along a covered walkway leading off downtown's East Front Street in the center of the 100 block. All of the works here are limited productions of beautiful prints that have undergone the distinctive, trademarked Wooden Gallery Process, which involves saturating and mounting the prints with acrylic emulsion formula that results in enhanced color and protection. The final coats are hand-textured for additional detail and richness, before each print is finished in a rich wood frame, with complement-

ing border and brass title plate. The images reflect regional photos and paintings as well as images with universal appeal. Our favorites capture the quiet beauty of our Northwest Michigan waters at sunrise and sunset. The gallery displays an extensive collection of works. You'll also see a number of these distinctive Wooden Gallery pieces gracing the walls of offices, restaurants and shops throughout the region. The Wooden Gallery is open daily.

Petals and Pine
118 State St., Fife Lake • (616) 879-4714

Handcrafted furniture is the specialty at Petals and Pine. You'll find handmade shaker furniture and handpainted furniture along with a selection of dried florals, pottery, dolls, home signs, dipped candles, holiday ornaments and Santas. Petals and Pines is open on weekends only from May through December.

INSIDERS' TIP

Northwest Michigan Artists and Craftsmen publishes an annual guide to area art titled *Art Craft Trails*, which is available at local visitors centers, chambers of commerce and artists' studios. The publication features a listing of about 50 local artists and galleries that are open to the public as well as regional map and calendar of major art fairs. You can get a free copy of *Art Craft Trails* by sending a self-addressed, stamped business-size envelope to: Art Craft Trails, c/o NMAC, 720 S. Elmwood Street, Suite 3, Traverse City, MI 49684.

Brass Owl Gallery and Gifts
W. Silver Lake Rd., Grawn
• **(616) 943-8855**

This contemporary gallery is housed in a vintage redesigned inn. Sculpture is featured along with works in bronze, marble, onyx, alabaster and African Shona. You'll also find paintings, prints, ceramics, hand-blown glass and jewelry on display. The gallery is open seasonally between June and October.

Woody Hill Pottery
4303 County Rd. 633, Grawn
• **(616) 276-9816**

Woody Hill is an appropriate name for this artist's studio nestled in the woods along a hilly drive. Functional and decorative pottery is created and shown by Dorothy Biegler. You can see it between May and December on Thursday, Friday and Saturday afternoons.

Pipigwa Pottery and Gallery
Nessen City and Karlin Rds., Karlin
• **(616) 263-7141**

Stoneware pottery by Mary Ann Ettawageshik and traditional woodland pottery by Frank Ettawageshik are showcased at Pipigwa Pottery and Gallery, 4 miles south of Interlochen Center for the Arts off County Road 137. Works by other Michigan artists are also displayed. Pipigwa Pottery is open Thursdays through Saturdays or by appointment.

Interlochen Center for the Arts Gallery
Mich. Hwy. 137, Interlochen
• **(616) 276-7200**

This is the gallery for the Interlochen Center for the Arts. You'll find it in the campus' Visual Arts Building, providing rotating displays of student works in all genres of art. For more on Interlochen, see subsequent listing and this chapter's Close-up.

Leelanau County

Leelanau Trading Company
13030 S. Coleman Rd., Empire
• **(616) 228-6575**

This unique gallery features handcrafted wooden boats and canoes, leather backpacks and luggage and a distinctive line of leather journals and photo albums by Leelanau artisans Ted and Ruth Gilmer. The gallery also features an eclectic selection of art objects from all corners of the United States and Mexico.

The Secret Garden
Mich. Hwy. 72, Empire • **(616) 326-5428**

This contemporary seasonal gallery showcases an array of American handcrafts in the heart of downtown Empire. You'll find watercolors, pastels, photography, pottery, dolls, toys, quilts, jewelry and other forms of wearable art representing the work of more than 100 artists. The Secret Garden is open between Memorial Day weekend and Labor Day and on weekends during fall.

Becky Thatcher Designs
Lake St., Glen Arbor • **(616) 334-3826**
Harbor Square, Leland • **(616) 256-2229**

Jewelry artisan Becky Thatcher displays her beautiful and unique works at these two Leelanau peninsula locations. Thatcher's creations feature designs in gold and silver complementing native Michigan stones and unusual colored gemstones from the Orient. The Glen Arbor studio is open all year; the Leland location is limited to summer. Call ahead for current hours.

INSIDERS' TIP

Do you support your local art museum? The Dennos Museum Center participates in the Michigan Art Museums Reciprocal Membership, which waives admission fees to people who hold valid memberships at other participating Michigan art museums such as the Detroit Institute of Arts, Grand Rapids Art Museum, the University of Michigan Museum of Art and others. The Clinch Park Zoo has a similar reciprocity arrangement with other zoos.

Photo: Interlochen Center for the Arts

Enjoy some of our region's live theater.

Glen Lake Artists Gallery
Arbor Light Building, Lake St., Glen Arbor • (616) 334-4230

Local artists and craftspeople showcase their work in this co-op gallery in the heart of the artistic community of Glen Arbor. You'll find all types of media represented. The artists that created the works take turns working here, so you can always strike up delightful conversations about the many works and the creative process. The Glen Lake artists are highlighted daily from mid-June through August and on weekends in the spring and fall through Christmas.

Hepburn-Holt Designs
6640 Western Ave. (Mich. Hwy. 109), Glen Arbor • (616) 334-6470

This is a working jewelry studio and gallery in the heart of Glen Arbor. Susan Hepburn-Holt creates beautiful works with sterling silver, gold and niobium that take the form of unique jewelry, candle snuffers, baby spoons and other distinctive items. The gallery also showcases painted clothing by Leah Artwear, photographs by Ken Scott, pottery by Gwen Schaiberger and several other local artists. The gallery is open daily between May and December.

Lake Street Studios
6123 Lake St., Glen Arbor • (616) 334-6112

The Lake Street Studios are housed in a picturesque old barn in the center of this artistic town. These are the working studios for several local artists include Susan Stupka Wilson, known for her regionally inspired watercolors, Ben Bricker, who creates metal craft and jewelry, and Ananda Bricker, who recreates delicate regional wildflowers in porcelain and metal sculpture.

Ruth Conklin Gallery
Lake Isle Shops, Mich. Hwy. 109, Glen Arbor • (616) 334-3880

The Ruth Conklin Gallery spotlights the essence of the northern part of Michigan with a lovely selection of artwork. You'll find handprinted wood blocks and pastels, created by Conklin, that feature local landscapes and wildlife. There are also paintings by Molly Phinney and driftwood wildlife carvings by Al Rollings. Handcrafted jewelry, pottery and furniture are also on display. This seasonal gallery is open daily between May and October.

Synchronicity Gallery
Mich. Hwy. 109, Glen Arbor
• (616) 334-4732

Synchronicity displays original works by at least 50 contemporary Michigan artists. This is a newer gallery that has featured an array of media, styles and subjects in its showcased pieces. Synchronicity is seasonal, with daily hours between Memorial Day and Labor Day and weekend times during September and October.

Main Street Gallery
307 S. Main St., Leland • (616) 256-7787

The ambiance of the northern part of the state is carried through the many original artworks displayed at the Main Street Gallery. More than 25 artists are showcased at this charming gallery, including the noted Leelanau painter Nell Revel Smith. Custom picture framing can also be handled here.

The Beech Tree
202 Waukazoo St., Northport
• (616) 386-5200

The Beech Tree is a fun contemporary craft gallery with an eclectic collection on display. The fiber arts are highlighted with fine art quilts, weavings, handcrafted clothing and wearable accessories. You'll also find jewelry, pottery, wood furniture and a selection of whimsical birdhouses. The Beech Tree is open during summer and fall but is usually closed on Tuesdays. Each year, the shop hosts a summer quilt art show and a fall fiber show.

Joppich's Bay Street Gallery
109 N. Rose St., Northport
• (616) 386-7428

Michigan-made art is the order of the day at Joppich's Bay Street Gallery, which showcases the work of more than 50 professional artists from throughout the state. The collection is chosen by owner Edee Joppich, with a large selection of paintings, original prints, sculpture and fine art crafts. Joppich's Bay Street Gallery is open daily during July and August and on the weekends during June, September and October.

Tamarack Craftsmen Gallery
Mich. Hwy. 22, Omena • (616) 386-5529

Tamarack Craftsmen Gallery is one of the premier galleries in Northwest Michigan. Tucked into a lovely storefront in tiny, picturesque Omena, the Tamarack Gallery has been showing contemporary fine art for more than 25 years and has earned an outstanding reputation. More than 100 artists are showcased with a large array of works including contemporary folk art, hand-blown glass, paintings, ceramics, graphics, metalwork, jewelry, fiber works, sculpture and furniture.

Brightheart Gallery
Elm Valley Rd., Suttons Bay
• (616) 271-3052

The Valley lies between the rolling hills lining Leelanau County's interior. Several artists and unique businesses are situated in the Valley, off Shady Lane Road south of Suttons Bay and west of Mich. 22, including Brightheart Gallery. This is the gallery and studio where Sue Brightheart shows her distinctive sculptured porcelain and hand-built functional ware as well as her watercolors, pastels, oils and jewelry. Other works by Peg Core and Krys Lieffers include basketry, letter-press note and holiday cards, textile art and mixed fiber sculpture. Brightheart Gallery is usually open in the afternoons Wednesdays through Saturdays, but call ahead to check hours.

Brisling Pottery
Mich. Hwy. 204, Suttons Bay
• (616) 271-3892

Brisling Pottery, just 2 miles west of Suttons Bay in the rural Leelanau countryside, spotlights the handcrafted stoneware pottery created by artisans Karl and Beverly Sporck. Brisling Pottery is open daily between May and October and by appointment other times of the year.

Michigan Artists Gallery
309 St. Joseph Ave., Suttons Bay
• (616) 271-4922

The region's outdoor influence is reflected in the works at Michigan Artists Gallery. The shop is split into two sides with one showcasing wildlife artists and the other featuring landscapes, florals and still life. Works are by local artists in oils, acrylics and photography along with wood turning and furniture. The gallery is open daily during spring and summer, and weekends the rest of the year. Call ahead to verify hours.

Painted Bird
216 St. Joseph Ave., Suttons Bay
• (616) 271-3050

The Painted Bird is a favorite among locals and longtime visitors. It features fine art and contemporary crafts by more than 80 regional artists. The quality is high and the selection delightful. You'll find handcrafted clothing, jewelry, decorative and functional art, furniture, custom rug weaving and contemporary crafts for the home. The collection changes with each new creation, but this shop and gallery is always filled with a friendly mix of classic and whimsical designs. The Painted Bird is open daily year round.

Antrim-Kalkaska

North Bridge Gallery
404 N. Bridge St., Bellaire
• (616) 533-8039

The North Bridge Gallery showcases the work of artists Nancy Hunt and Amy Annoye, who specialize in landscape and floral paintings. This seasonal gallery is open Wednesdays through Saturdays between mid-June and Labor Day.

Torch Tip Ironworks
2530 E. Torch Lake Dr., Eastport
• (616) 544-8206

Metal artisan Art Brown creates and exhibits his art at Torch Tip Ironworks. Pieces include handcrafted metal furnishings and custom architectural details with motifs bearing Michigan wildlife and French and contemporary designs. Torch Tip Ironworks showroom hours may vary; call ahead for current times.

Bitter Melon
138 River St., Elk Rapids
• (616) 264-9106

Delightful works by local and national artisans are found at Bitter Melon. This charming and spacious downtown Elk Rapids gallery and gift shop displays handcrafted journals, glass works, jewelry, wearable art and unique home items. Many reflect an Oriental influence. Bitter Melon is open May through December.

Mullaly's 128 Studio and Gallery
128 River St., Elk Rapids
• (616) 264-6660

Mullaly's 128 bears the name of owner and multimedia artist William Mullaly, who uses it as his studio as well as a contemporary gallery. It showcases fine arts and crafts in a variety of genres by more than 300 artists from the United States and Canada.

Lake Michigan Shoreline and Cadillac

Presscraft Papers
5140 River Rd., Benzonia
• (616) 882-5505

Naturalist and artist Gwen Frostic has earned a national reputation for her original block prints. Frostic's working print shop and gift store is nestled along the Betsie River on a 250-acre personal wildlife preserve. See the presses roll out the 90-year-old artist's exquisite books, prints, napkins, notepapers and postcards. For more information, check our Attractions chapter.

Roland Roycraft Art Studio and Gallery
8479 Orchard Hill Rd., Beulah
• (616) 882-4627

Roland Roycraft is an internationally known watercolorist and author of *Fill Your Watercolors with Light and Color*. His paintings are available at his Beulah studio, which is open to visitors. Roycraft's award-winning works feature a variety of Michigan landscapes and florals. Students come from around the globe to study under Roycraft, one of the area's most distinguished paint-

Photo: Terry W. Phipps/Mackinac Island Chamber of Commerce

Jack-o'-lanterns add a seasonal touch to one of the region's many art galleries.

ers. His studio is open year round but call ahead for hours.

Michigan Legacy Art Park
12500 Crystal Mountain Resort, Thompsonville • (616) 378-2000

Michigan Legacy Art Park is an imaginative and enchanting collection of 19 permanent sculptures nestled along the Crystal Mountain Resort's trail system, which was carved out of some of the prettiest forest land in the north. To view this wild, wacky and exciting collection of works by Michigan artists, you must hike, cross-county ski or snowshoe the trail. It's an art adventure long remembered.

Black Bear Trading Company
13663 Caberfae Hwy., Wellston
• (616) 848-4655

A wonderful wildlife gallery, Black Bear Trading Company features the chain-saw folk carvings of co-owner Fred Campbell. Campbell's bears, cigar store Indians, fishermen and sea captains are sold in shops across the country. The trading post also offers the works of some of the nation's highest regarded decoy carvers such as Jim Nelson and Jim Pullen, and the works of master carver Bob Kurkewicz. Other pieces in the collection include photography by Bob Paetschow and paintings by Helen Van Wyk and David Knowlton III.

Lloyd Henry's Gallery of Fine Art
429 River St., Manistee • (616) 723-0003

Set amidst the elegant, historic Victorian buildings of downtown Manistee, Lloyd Henry's Gallery of Fine Art is the only gallery in this part of Michigan featuring the graceful, free-form wooden sculptures of Les Scruggs. The gallery also offers original paintings, glassware and three-dimensional works by a variety of regional artists. Hours are seasonal, so call ahead.

The Wooden Fish Gallery
8925 Norconk Rd., Bear Lake
• (616) 864-2754

The Wooden Fish Gallery is devoted entirely to the fishing enthusiast. The carving studio and fishing museum feature thousands of pieces — a real eyeful of decoys, lures, rods and reels. Owner Dave Kober, a fourth-generation carver, has been honored with the Michigan Heritage Award by the Traditional Arts Council at Michigan State University. His work is showcased in exhibits and wildlife shows throughout the Midwest. It's a great place to browse, reminisce and buy, sell or trade tackle and fishing gear.

Cadillac Art Gallery & Interiors
209 N. Mitchell St., Cadillac
• (616) 775-0753

Cadillac Art Gallery & Interiors is known by Insiders as a peaceful place to browse. The gallery features three floors of original art and prints by nationally known artists Thomas Kinkaid, Terry Redlin and Nita Engle. You'll also find Western and wildlife sculptures from the Legends collection, plus antique reproductions, home decor items, furnishings by Norwalk and British Traditions and a full interior design service.

Little Traverse

Bier Art Gallery & Pottery Studio
Corner of U.S. Hwy. 31 and Ferry Rd., Charlevoix • (616) 547-2288

The pottery studio of Ray and Tami Bier is housed in a historic school building overlooking Lake Michigan. Their selection of functional and decorative works includes nativity sets, wildlife creations and pieces with hand-applied designs. The work of noted potter Bonnie Staffel is also available as well as glass, batik and woodcuts from more than 40 Midwest artists. Bier Gallery is open daily through the summer. Winter hours vary, so call ahead.

Dhaseleer Ceramics & Gallery
15794 Paddock Rd., Charlevoix
• (616) 547-6945

A charming countryside gallery on an old family farm, Dhaseleer Ceramics features handmade tiles, creative tableware, original wildlife paintings, fur and leather pieces.

Otis Pottery
01691 Mich. Hwy. 66, East Jordan
• (616) 536-7856

Potters David and June Otis create functional and decorative pieces through hand-thrown and wood-fired techniques. Their time-honored methods lend pieces a truly distinctive look. The Otis showroom features a nice collection of teapots, dinnerware and platters as well as thought-provoking and whimsical two-dimensional framed works.

Arktos Fine Art Studio & Gallery
117 Howard St., Petoskey
• **(616) 347-5199**

In the heart of Petoskey's famed Gaslight Shopping District, Arktos Gallery features the bright and cheerful watercolors of Dana Constand. Arktos contemporary collection celebrates animal life and the joy of color with works created in all media by 40 artists from throughout the United States.

Perry Sherwood Gallery
200 Howard St., Petoskey
• **(616) 348-5079**

The Perry Sherwood Gallery showcases the works of prominent artists and designers from northern Michigan and across the United States. Their extensive fine art collection features original paintings, limited edition prints, sculptural glass, ceramics, chic gifts and jewelry. Custom framing is available.

Sturgeon River Pottery and Wild Bird Supply
3031 Charlevoix Ave., Petoskey
• **(616) 347-0590**

The working studio and showroom of potters Karen and Steve Andrews is located among green grass and ponds in an idyllic country setting. Their work includes functional and decorative pieces hand-formed and glazed with the original formulas. You'll also find a wide array of works produced by more than 150 crafters. The shop's wild bird supply section features seeds, feeders, baths and birding books and tapes.

Ward & Eis Gallery
315 Lake St., Petoskey • (616) 347-2750

Have you always coveted the boss's fine handmade leather briefcase, portfolio or planner? This might be where he or she bought it. Ward & Eis Gallery features the work of more than 190 artisans. More than 40 leather workers

create the gallery's selection of exquisite purses, and there's no larger selection anywhere. In addition to fine leather pieces, the gallery collection features Native-American pieces, Zuni jewelry and fetishes and sculpture.

By the Bay
172 E. Main St., Harbor Springs
• **(616) 526-3964**

By the Bay is the largest marine gallery in the Midwest. Its fine collection of work features originals and limited edition prints by noted artists John Stobart and Michael Blaser. The gallery spans three levels filled with nautical art, sculpture, jewelry, furniture and more than 2,000 marine books.

Coyote Woman Gallery
160 E. Main St., Harbor Springs
• **(616) 526-5889**

Coyote Woman Gallery is one of the reasons art lovers make a special trip to Harbor Springs when in the market for original or limited edition works. The gallery's wide selection of fine art features the work of Western artist David Devary and the nostalgic Victorian works of Richard Zolan. You'll enjoy the gallery's eclectic selection containing everything from contemporary to Southwest wall art, designer jewelry and sculpture.

Pierre Bittar Gallery
188 E. Main St., Harbor Springs
• **(616) 526-6750**

Pierre Bittar Gallery showcases the latest original oil paintings and limited edition prints of this world-renowned French Impressionist artist. Bittar's northern Michigan and French landscapes are displayed in an elegant setting appealing to the fine art connoisseur.

Tvedten Fine Art
284 E. Third St., Harbor Springs
• **(616) 526-2299**

Tvedten's fine art gallery features the pleasing pastels and watercolors of noted artist Margaret Tvedten as well as the works of more than 20 other Michigan artists. In addition to wall art, you'll discover a lovely collection of sculpture, ceramics, metalworks, wood and jewelry. Tvedten Gallery is open daily in the summer. Hours vary in the off-season, so call ahead.

Good Hart Glassworks Studio
212 W. Townline Rd., Good Hart
- **(616) 526-7283**

Good Hart Glassworks is a contemporary art glass studio featuring a wondrous range of colorful pieces. Full-time glassblowers Lynn Dinning and Chris Asbury produce vases, bowls, perfume bottles, marbles, sculptures and more. Call ahead for seasonal hours or to arrange tours.

Mackinac Straits

Market Street Gallery
Market St., Mackinac Island
- **(906) 847-3600**

The Market Street Gallery displays and sells prints, original artwork, posters and photographs by island photographer Robert Jerstrom. Our favorite pieces illustrate winter on Mackinac Island.

Paintings by Wolfgang
Market St., Mackinac Island
- **(906) 847-3771**

Noted naturalist painter Richard Wolfgang spends summers on Mackinac Island. This is the gallery and shop for his beautiful original watercolors, which often depict the soft beauty of the island life in full bloom. Wolfgang's work has been exhibited throughout Michigan and is in many private and corporate collections throughout the country. For several years, he has created the lovely Lilac Festival collector posters (see our Annual Events chapter), which are also used as covers for the Chamber of Commerce visitors' guide.

Teysen's Gift Shop
300 E. Central Ave., Mackinaw City
- **(616) 436-7011**

This gift shop also showcases traditional Native-American art created by local artists, including a nice selection of quill boxes. Teysen's is also listed under the specialty shop category in our Shopping chapter.

Views of the Past
148 S. Huron Ave., Mackinaw City
- **(616) 436-7793**

History buffs will love to visit Views of the Past. It houses the state's largest private photographic archive with vintage exposures on all geographic areas of Michigan and on virtually any subject. The storefront also has a 3-D stereo arcade, a museum of photography, copy and restoration services, antique replica frames and archival photo albums.

Calypso Pottery
99 Stockbridge St., St. Ignace
- **(906) 643-8196**

Calypso Pottery is the studio and showroom for St. Ignace artists John and Sally Herbon. You'll find beautiful works in high-fire stoneware and functional pottery. It is open by appointment during much of the year. Call ahead to discuss convenient hours to visit.

Mackinac Straits Photography Gallery
208 N. State St., St. Ignace
- **(906) 643-0250**

Award-winning photographic artist David M. Black exhibits his work at Mackinac Straits Photography Gallery. The essence of the Straits natural beauty is evoked in Black's colorful images of local wildlife, waterfalls, lighthouses, the Northern Lights, lightning strikes, Mackinac Island vistas and distinctive scenes of the Mackinac Bridge.

Performing Arts

Grand Traverse

Ballet Ensemble Etc.
705 Boon St., Traverse City
- **(616) 929-2787**

Ballet Ensemble Etc. is the youth performing troupe from local dance school Ballet Etc. The school's owner, Tom Morrell, is a popular Traverse-area performer who often collaborates with other artists in song and dance and choreographs in a variety of venues.

Company Dance Traverse
106½ E. Front St., Traverse City
- **(616) 941-4244**

Company Dance Traverse, often referred to as CDT, is Northwest Michigan's first professional modern dance company. The company brings innovative choreography and an array of modern dance styles to local stages with regional dancers and guest performers. The company presents several concerts each season and often collaborates in artistic endeavors with other regional performing troupes. CDT has sponsored workshops and master classes in collaboration with Dance Arts Academy and sponsors an active touring program for local schools.

Dancing Bear Music Series
Dennos Museum Center, 1701 E. Front St., Traverse City • (616) 922-1553

The Dancing Bear Music Series brings chamber music to the Grand Traverse region with a wonderful selection of concerts performed at the Milliken Auditorium at the Dennos Museum Center. Five or six concerts are presented by professional chamber ensembles between September and May each year. The series name and logo design were inspired by artist Pauta Saila's sculpture Dancing Bear, which stands on display in the Dennos' Inuit Gallery.

Encore Society of Music
821 Hastings St., Ste. 252, Traverse City • (616) 486-7200

Encore's mission is to present excellent music in entertaining formats and to provide a quality experience for the area's fine musicians to return their talents to the community. The society accomplishes its goals with aplomb. Approximately six major concerts are held each year featuring the Encore Winds, a regional wind orchestra of 50 musicians, and the Encore Voices, a 10-12 member vocal ensemble, usually performing at the Dennos Museum Center. The concert schedule always features a creative lineup of classical and popular fare. Encore often collaborates with regional dancers, musicians and performers to bring an added artistic facet to its concerts. Several small ensembles of Encore musicians participate in school concerts and additional performances in cozier venues.

Northern Michigan Jazz Society
Dennos Museum Center, 1701 E. Front St., Traverse City • (616) 922-1553

The Northern Michigan Jazz Society has been bringing wonderful music to local stages since the early 1990s. Founded by popular Traverse City musician Jeff Haas, the Jazz Society hosts Jazz at the Museum concerts at Milliken Auditorium in the Dennos Museum Center. Performances are usually held on a Saturday evening mid-month between November and May. Past performers have included jazz pianist Marian McPartland, flautist Alexander Zonjic, clarinetist Harry Goldson, trumpeter Marcus Belgrave and the local talents of the Jeff Haas Trio. Every concert and every season is unique, with six concerts usually on each year's docket.

Old Town Playhouse
148 E. Eighth St., Traverse City • (616) 947-2210

Civic theater is alive and well in Traverse City thanks to the thespians at Old Town Playhouse. Old Town is housed in a cozy, red brick building, which, was once a neighborhood church. Today, it is home to an ambitious community theater program with at least five main stage productions, three studio theater plays and two children's theater shows each year. The main stage performances usually include two major musicals with a live orchestra accompanying the entertainers. The studio theater periodically premiers an original script, often written by a local author. All Old Town endeavors showcase the incredible pool of local talent that resides in the region.

Traverse Symphony Orchestra
3055 Cass Rd., Ste. 204, Traverse City • (616) 947-7120

The Traverse Symphony Orchestra has been bringing wonderful classical concerts to Northwest Michigan since 1951. The symphony usually presents six major concerts each season with a mix of pops and symphonic performances. A local favorite is the annual Home for the Holidays concert usually held on a Friday and Saturday evening in early December. Concerts are often held at Lars Hockstad Auditorium inside Central Grade School, 301 W. Seventh Street, Traverse City, or in Corson Auditorium at Interlochen Center for the Arts. The symphony recently inaugurated a children's Saturday Symphony series, which presents musical programs for families on several Saturday mornings each season (see our Kidstuff chapter).

Traverse City Youth Ballet Company
1143 Woodmere St., Traverse City
• (616) 947-6820

This is the performing arm of the Dance Center, a longtime Traverse City school of dance for children and adults. The youth ballet company was begun recently to provide educational and performance opportunities to its advanced students.

Interlochen Center for the Arts
Mich. Hwy. 137, Interlochen
• (616) 276-7200

At the world-renowned Interlochen Center for the Arts, you can enjoy almost daily performances by the talented students, faculty and guests who create their art under the aura of Interlochen. The arts center is home to Interlochen Arts Camp, formerly known as the National Music Camp, which attracts hundreds of young people to train with nationally respected teachers during the summer. It is also home to Interlochen Arts Academy during the September to June academic year. The academy is an independent high school specializing in a strong academic curriculum with intense training in the creative writing, dance, music, theater and the visual arts. Student and faculty recitals, performances and gallery showings are featured on a weekly basis. In addition, nationally known performers are featured during the Summer Arts Festival and throughout the year.

Beach Bards
The Leelanau School, Mich. Hwy. 22,
Glen Arbor • (616) 332-4062

The Beach Bards delight beachfront audiences with poetry and stories in the oral tradition every summer Friday. These talented performers include local poet and writer Anne Marie Oomen. All perform an array of memo-

Nurturing Up-North Talent

Dance, music, words and art take flight from the magical, pine-filled campus at Interlochen Center for the Arts. The shore of Green Lake, south of Traverse City, is home to the nationally renowned Interlochen Arts Camp and Interlochen Arts Academy as well as the spectacular Interlochen Arts Festival and respected Interlochen Public Radio.

For more than 60 years, Interlochen has nurtured the creative talents of young students and inspired generations of new artists to share their gifts with the world. Its alumni list, which tops 67,000, includes famous names such as actors Meredith Baxter, Richard Brooks, Tom Hulce and Linda Hunt; dancers Peter Sparling and Janet Eilber; musicians Peter Yarrow, Jewel, Jessye Norman, Peter Erskine and Lorin Maazel; writers Pamela White Hadas and Cathy Guisewite; journalist Mike Wallace; and visual artists

Wendy Midener and Keane Paradiso. Interlochen alumni make up at least 10 percent of the nation's major symphony orchestras.

The Interlochen legacy dates back to 1928 when music educators Dr. Joseph E. Maddy and Thaddeus P. Gidding founded the first music-oriented summer program in the country, the National High School Orchestra Camp at Interlochen, and pursued Maddy's dream of offering a permanent training ground for young artists. The summer program officially became known as the National Music Camp in 1932, later evolving into today's multidisciplinary Interlochen Arts Camp, which offers a full spectrum of arts education. Dr. Maddy led Interlochen through the decades until his death in 1966.

Interlochen Arts Camp continues to be recognized as one of the leading summer

— continued on next page

arts camps in the world. More than 2,000 students from 8 through 18 attend two- to eight-week programs in music, dance, theater, visual arts and creative writing. These young people come from every state as well as 38 foreign countries. During the summer, they will participate in more than 500 exhibitions, concerts, and theatrical and dance productions along with Interlochen's many faculty, staff and guest artists. The World Youth Symphony Orchestra, comprised of 130 top high school-age musicians, highlights the summer roundup with performances throughout the season that often feature such notable guest artists and conductors as Itzhak Perlman, Yo-Yo Ma and Neeme Järvi.

Photo: Interlochen Center for the Arts

Musicians, dancers and artists train in the beauty of Northwest Michigan.

Interlochen Arts Academy combines arts training with academic excellence. It was established in 1962 as the nation's first independent high school dedicated to the arts. As a high school boarding school, the Arts Academy draws close to 450 students each year representing 46 states and 17 foreign countries. A strong college-preparatory curriculum complements the arts training with 95 percent of academy graduates continuing their education at the nation's top universities and conservatories.

Interlochen Arts Festival is the center's performance arm. Every year, more than 750 concerts, art exhibits, theatrical productions and dance performances are presented by the center's students, faculty, staff and guest artists. The most ambitious schedule is in the summer when the 4,000-seat outdoor Kresge Auditorium stage hosts artists such as James Taylor, Marvin Hamlisch, Natalie Cole, James Galway, the Canadian Brass, Chicago, the Beach Boys, Dolly Parton, k.d. lang, Bill Cosby, the Chieftains, Garrison Keillor, and Peter, Paul and Mary. Between mid-June and Labor Day, it's possible to see at least one Interlochen exhibition or performance every day. The fall/winter Arts Festival attracts similar high-profile talent, while also showcasing the artistic work of its students. As the public flocks to the major concerts, Interlochen students benefit from one-on-one exposure to these world-class performers. Guest artists often conduct workshops, master classes, private lessons, lectures and informal talks with Interlochen students, sometimes tapping a few to perform with them on stage.

Begun in 1963, Interlochen Public Radio has a loyal and large following throughout the region for its strong local news coverage, high-quality classical music and National Public Radio programming. Using the call letters WIAA, the station broadcasts at the 88.7 FM and 100.9 FM radio frequencies.

Interlochen's many facets are covered elsewhere in this Insider's guide. Please read listings in this Arts chapter under Galleries and Performing Arts as well as references in the Education and Media chapters.

Founder Joseph Maddy referred to Interlochen as ". . . the dream city of youth . . . where talented young people gather for inspiration, specialized training and self appraisal." Those words, spoken decades ago, continue to ring true as each new generation shares the wonderful legacy of Interlochen Center for the Arts.

rized works along the Lake Michigan shoreline at The Leelanau School in Glen Arbor. Children's literature are the words of choice between 8:30 and 9:30 PM before the focus shifts to adult work from 9:30 PM to midnight. The Bards gather between mid-June and Labor Day. To join them, go to The Leelanau School off Mich. Highway 22 just north of Glen Arbor. Park in the school lot and take the adjoining trail to the beach. There is no admission charge, but donations are gladly accepted.

Lake Michigan Shoreline and Cadillac

Benzie Area Symphonette
Benzie County • (616) 882-5477

What began as a small local string group in the late 1970s now draws a full complement of musicians from three counties. The Benzie Area Symphonette consists of 25 musicians hailing from Benzie, Manistee and Grand Traverse counties. The group presents outdoor concerts throughout the summer in area communities and is known for its annual Christmas program. This is a true community symphony with musicians ranging in age from teens to age 70 and including players of varying skill levels.

Benzie County Players
Benzie County • (616) 352-7549

This lively thespian group established in 1978 consists of 75 players ranging from teenagers to retirees. They produce three to four comedy shows annually and regularly perform dinner theater at the Sail Inn in Benzonia.

Ramsdell Theatre
101 Maple St., Manistee • (616) 723-9948

Well-known thespian James Earl Jones received his first taste of the acting life on the stage of the Ramsdell Theatre. Built in 1903, this historic Gothic theater is home to the Manistee Civic Players, who present nine productions each year and a variety of musical concerts from bluegrass to classical. Adult and children's drama workshops and adult painting classes are offered in spring and

summer. Original murals bedeck the lobby and dome of this historic theatrical treasure. The Ramsdell is an anchor for the Manistee arts community and features an exhibit hall for the visual arts, showcasing talents from the area and beyond. The Ramsdell ballroom has a capacity of 400 and serves as a rental hall for weddings, proms and community events. Tours of the theater complex are available year round by appointment.

Cadillac Area Symphony Orchestra
Cadillac • (616) 825-2642

The Cadillac Area Symphony Orchestra is a 50-piece orchestra offering local musicians opportunities to maintain and sharpen skills and to perform for their community. Three to four concerts, often featuring a guest artist, are presented each year at the Cadillac Community Auditorium. The orchestra rehearses weekly and welcomes new musicians.

Footliters Community Theatre
601 Selma St., Cadillac • (616) 775-7336

For 30 years the Footliters have been the theatrical hub of the greater Cadillac area. The group is a member of the Community Theater Association of Michigan, and performs musicals, dramas, comedy and children's productions with volunteer thespians and technical support staff.

Gopherwood Folk Society
Cadillac • (616) 775-7084

Gopherwood Folk Society promotes ethnic, eclectic and traditional music. The group sponsors monthly concerts, dances and workshops for adults, children and families. Check local publications to learn what's on tap from this lively, down-home group.

Jazz in the Park Series
Rotary Lakefront Pavilion, Cadillac • (800) 369-3836

What can beat an evening of great jazz accompanied by a brilliant sunset beside a quiet inland lake? The Cadillac Jazz in the park series presents an impressive lineup of world-class musicians hailing from throughout the Midwest. Performances are from 7 to 9 PM Thursday evenings from mid-June through August. Admission is free.

Sweet Adelines Timber Tones Chapter

Cadillac • (616) 775-4716

This dedicated women's group of amateur vocalists is a part of the national Sweet Adelines organization. Members sing four-part harmony, barbershop style. The group presents concerts for local audiences and participates in state vocal competitions. Weekly rehearsals are held at the Cadillac Middle School.

Little Traverse

Bay View Association

Petoskey • (616) 439-9240

Bay View has been a vigorous northern cultural pocket for more than 100 years. Established as a Methodist resort community in 1875, the association still carries out much of its original programming. Presentations and concerts take place at the John M. Hall Auditorium, which seats 1,500. Here, throughout the summer months, Bay View presents a series of free lectures by nationally known speakers. Sunday church services and evening vespers are as popular as they were 100 years ago. The Bay View Conservatory of Music draws an elite group of students from around the country. The Conservatory presents weekly concerts featuring local and regional talent. Bay View's Theater Arts Department offers dance and theater workshops and presents dance concerts, musicals and operas. Tickets for all events are available at the door. The public is invited to participate in Bay View's wide variety of classes and entertainment opportunities in the visual arts, literature, film, culinary arts and more. Contact the Bay View office for a schedule.

Little Traverse Choral Society

1511 Resort Pike, Petoskey
• (616) 526-6577

Little Traverse Choral Society is in its 11th season of performing classical works. The 50-member group consists of male and female vocalists from Emmet and Charlevoix counties. The group exists to offer vocalists opportunities to enrich their lives with performing experiences and presents three concerts each year. The group is open to all vocalists and rehearses weekly at Concord Academy in Petoskey.

Little Traverse Civic Theatre Group

461 E. Mitchell St., Petoskey
• (616) 348-1850

The Little Traverse Civic Theatre Group has more than 50 seasons of performances to its credit and is a cultural tradition in the Petoskey region. The 125-member group is the resident company for Petoskey's Virginia McCune Arts Center and presents three productions annually at the Center's Ross Stoakes Theatre. Productions run the gamut from musicals to dramas and comedy. You can always expect to see a well-produced show. Ticket prices are $10 for adults, $5 for children between 6 and 12, and free for children younger than 5. All seats for Thursday night previews are $5, and all seats for Sunday matinees are $6. Reservations are recommended.

Northern Michigan Chorale

461 E. Mitchell St., Petoskey
• (616) 347-4488

Northern Michigan Chorale performs Broadway hits, Big Band favorites and patriotic tunes. The 100 male and female vocalists present two well-attended concerts each year. Auditions are not required to join the group, which rehearses weekly at the Petoskey Middle School.

Music in the Park

Pennsylvania Park, Petoskey
• (616) 347-4150

Local and regional talent present free outdoor concerts throughout the summer months in historic Gaslight District's Pennsylvania Park in Petoskey. Concerts, featuring a variety of musical styles, take place at noon and 7 PM Tuesday, and at noon Friday in the summer.

Mackinac Straits

Mackinac Island Summer Music Society

Mackinac Island • (800) 4-LILACS

The Society is a wonderful outlet for Island songbirds. The group meets every Tuesday and Thursday evening from 8 to 9 PM at Trinity Church, and performs at least one public concert during the summer.

Music on the Marina Lawn
Municipal Marina, Mackinaw City
• (616) 436-5574

Musicians perform on the relaxed grounds of Mackinaw City's marina with the beauty and energy of the summer Straits acting as a scenic backdrop. Band concerts are held every Tuesday, Wednesday and Thursday evening in July and August beginning at 8 PM. Admission is free but donations are welcome. Complementing the concert series, strolling musicians perform along the city's charming streetscapes several evenings each week throughout the summer as part of the Music in Mackinaw series.

In Support of the Arts

Grand Traverse

Grand Traverse Writers
Horizon Books, 243 E. Front St.,
Traverse City • (616) 943-3765

The Grand Traverse Writers meet at 7 PM on the second and fourth Tuesday of each month in the cafe at Horizon Books to share their work and provide feedback and support. New writers are always welcome.

Northwestern Michigan Artists and Craftsmen (NMAC)
720 S. Elmwood St., Traverse City
• (616) 941-9488

The Northwestern Michigan Artists and Craftsmen is a nonprofit artists' organization that promotes awareness and growth of the arts in the Traverse Bay region. The nearly 200 members include beginning artists to seasoned professionals who work in all mediums. Housed at the Art Center in the former All Faiths Chapel near the Grand Traverse Commons, the group sponsors art classes, children's Super Saturday classes (see our Kidstuff chapter) and summer workshops with national artists as well as rotating gallery exhibits, local art fairs and support.

Northwestern Michigan College Extended Education
1701 E. Front St., Traverse City
• (616) 922-1700

Extended Education Services offers numerous classes each term in a variety of the artistic fields. Most are appropriate for adults of all ages and are flexible enough to accommodate a range of expertise in a friendly, noncompetitive environment. Classes usually meet once each week for one to four weeks, although some are as long as 12 weeks. Subjects have included creative writing, choral music, art history, pottery, poetry writing, painting, modern dance and piano. All are geared for the lifelong learner.

Traverse Area Arts Council
106½ E. Front St., Traverse City
• (616) 947-2282

The volunteer-driven Traverse Area Arts Council represents and promotes all facets of the arts in the Grand Traverse Area. In addition to its gallery space noted in the Galleries section of this chapter, it hosts a monthly film series, publishes the community publication *Art Borealis* six times per year, serves as a resource for area artists and acts as a regranting agency for local funding requests for the Michigan Council for the Arts.

Lake Michigan Shoreline and Cadillac

Crystal Lake Art Center
432 Sutter Rd., Frankfort
• (616) 352-4151

Crystal Lake Art Center has a 41-year tradition of promoting the arts in Benzie County. It offers a full slate of classes and workshops for youth and adults during summer months. Instruction is provided by local artists and artisans as well as national talent. Programming changes every year but always includes an excellent variety of fine art media and crafts.

Manistee Art Institute
Manistee • (616) 723-4050

The Manistee Art Institute boasts 100 members, all dedicated to preserving the region's rich visual arts legacy. The organization presents four major exhibits annually at the T. Walter Hardy Exhibit Hall in the historic Ramsdell Theatre, 101 Maple Street, Manistee. (To learn more about the Ramsdell Theatre see the listing in this chapter under Performing Arts.) Exhibits feature period collections and contemporary works. The Institute also presents lectures and demonstrations and operates an arts appreciation program in local schools.

West Shore Art League
Ludington • (616) 845-1738

West Shore Art League has been promoting the visual arts in the Mason County area for 31 years. The group has 100 members and meets the fourth Monday of each month at the Ludington Methodist Church. Guests are always welcome. The League sponsors the Ludington Fine Arts and Crafts Fair each July 4th weekend. The juried show features 200 exhibitors from across the country.

Photo: Kevin Poirier

Blues artist, Buddy Guy performs at the Interlochen Center for the Arts.

Cadillac Community Integrated Arts
601 Chestnut St., Cadillac
• **(616) 779-1254**

Cadillac Community Integrated Arts serves to involve young and old from all walks of life in a variety of culturally enriching activities. The group sponsors classes and workshops ranging from tap dancing to cartooning to tatting. It hosts a local jazz band and invites all sectors of the community to participate in special exhibits and creative events.

Cadillac Area Artists Association
Cadillac • (616) 775-7853

This 30-member group is dedicated to encouraging area visual artists by offering continuing education and exhibition opportunities and promoting visual arts in the Cadillac community. They sponsor an annual juried art fair in conjunction with the Cadillac summer arts festival.

Cadillac Area Council for the Arts
Cadillac • (616) 775-4438

The Cadillac Council for the Arts was established in 1968 to promote the community's cultural development. The council consists of representatives from performing and visual arts groups as well as members-at-large. The group meets the fourth Monday of each month at the Cadillac Municipal Complex at 200 N. Lake Street in Cadillac.

Little Traverse

Jordan River Arts Council
301 Main St., East Jordan
• **(616) 536-3385**

The Jordan River Arts Council consists of more than 200 members dedicated to expanding community opportunities for self-expression and enriching the lives of the young and old through the arts. The group's Art Reach Program takes fine art into the classrooms of eight local schools without regular arts curriculum. The all-volunteer organization sponsors member and student shows and hosts numerous fund-raising events throughout the year.

Virginia McCune Arts Center
461 E. Mitchell St., Petoskey
• **(616) 347-4337**

Housed in a historic church building, the McCune Arts Center is owned and operated by the Crooked Tree Arts Council. The Council's mission is to bring arts into the community through a wide variety of programming, and it provides support for the arts through its fund-raising efforts. The McCune Center theater seats 260 and is used by numerous local performing groups, including the Little Traverse Civic Theater, Northern Michigan Chorale, Little Traverse Chorale Society and the Petoskey Film Theater. Center programming offers concerts throughout the year by local artists as well as regional and national talent. The Center's main gallery presents 12 shows per year. Shows feature local artists and traveling exhibits. More than 800 students participate in the Center's school of the arts annually. Classes for adults and youth include dance, instrumental music, voice and the visual arts.

Northwest Michigan preserves provide an opportunity to experience some of the world's most unique natural communities.

Parks

Like the village square of yore, community parks in Northwest Michigan serve to draw townspeople together in celebration and to welcome visitors into the fold. Wherever you travel in the region, from quiet villages to booming cities, you'll find a green space inviting you to make yourself at home, to relax and restore yourself.

Beach parks are the pride of many of our hospitable communities. Along the Lake Michigan shoreline, from Ludington to Mackinaw City, you'll find dozens of gorgeous public beaches. Inland communities also offer outstanding swimming and boating parks and some maintain public skating rinks and sledding hills for winter recreation. You'll discover the region offers an unequaled array of natural parks, preserves and set-asides for low impact recreation such as hiking, birding and nature study. State parks, described in our Campgrounds and RV Parks chapter, provide additional outdoor recreational opportunities. Though Michigan has long been a leader in land preservation and conservation movements only 2 percent of Michigan remains the way Native Americans once knew it. About 47 species have been lost forever and there are 69 endangered and 257 threatened plant and animal species in the state. Some of these rare species can be observed at area preserves.

Northwest Michigan preserves provide an opportunity to experience some of the world's most unique natural communities. Because Michigan enjoys more Great Lakes coastline than any other state, it has some of the best examples of native plants and animals and natural communities. Rare communities include Great Lakes marsh, dune and swale, cobble beach, open dunes, calcareous fen wetland, oak savanna, and bedrock beach. Rare species include Mitchell's satyr butterfly, dwarf lake iris, pitcher's thistle, lynx, Kirtland warbler, piping plover, Houghton's goldenrod

and the bald eagle. The foresight and determined efforts of Michigan citizens ensures that the state's natural resource heritage will exist for future generations. Many organizations operate on various levels to achieve this shared goal. The Little Traverse Conservancy celebrated its 25th anniversary in 1997. A nonprofit organization and one of the oldest conservancies in Michigan, it works to protect the natural diversity and beauty of Northern Michigan in Emmet, Charlevoix, Chippewa, Mackinac and Cheboygan counties. Through land acquisition and conservation easement agreements, it has protected 10,000 acres of significant natural areas.

The Grand Traverse Regional Land Conservancy was founded in 1991. Working in Antrim, Grand Traverse, Kalkaska and Benzie counties, the organization aims to balance community growth with efforts to protect scenic and fragile natural lands. Since founded, it has established 16 nature preserves, protecting more than 3,400 acres of land and 15 miles of shoreline. The new kid on the block, the Cadillac Area Land Conservancy, was granted its nonprofit status in 1995. The fledgling organization works to protect natural areas in Wexford, Missaukee, Lake and Osceola counties. The Leelanau Conservancy, launched in 1988, has established major protection projects. State and national conservancy organizations are also involved in efforts to protect the flora, fauna and magnificent beauty of the northland.

While these groups serve tirelessly, a great responsibility for preservation of the resources falls on the shoulders of private property owners. At this grassroots level, ordinary citizens work to preserve the quality of our resources by forming neighborhood groups. There are many local lake associations consisting of waterfront property owners. These groups tackle fertilizer and sewage problems, shoreline erosion concerns and other issues involving environmental quality. In farm country, area agriculture producers have earned a reputation for going beyond what is legally required to protect the soil and water table from contamination. To this noble end, numerous organizations apply efforts to develop solutions to environmental problems and protection matters. Active area groups include the Tip of the Mitt Watershed, Grand Traverse Watershed Initiative, Northern Michigan Environmental Action Council, St. Clair Lake-Six Mile Lake Natural Area Committee, Manistee and Pine River Citizen Advisory groups, Mackinac Chapter of the Sierra Club, Grass River Natural Area volunteers and Friends of the Jordan River Watershed.

www.insiders.com

See this and many other **Insiders' Guide®** destinations online — in their entirety.

Visit us today!

To fully appreciate Michigan's great natural heritage, take time to visit a preserve. We've provided a full address for the preserves when possible. Or, when an address is not available, we provide driving directions from the nearest community. Pack your camera, binoculars and bug spray and prepare for an experience guaranteed to waken your finer sensibilities.

Parks

Grand Traverse

Traverse City Area

Bryant Park
Peninsula Dr. and Garfield Ave.,
Traverse City

Nestled at the base of the Old Mission Peninsula, Bryant Park is a cozy haven overlooking West Grand Traverse Bay. A large, sandy beach is great for splashing and swimming during the summer, but the shoreline is wonderful all year long. Park benches are scattered throughout the grounds. You can also bring along a blanket for relaxing on the sand or grass. Mature trees shade picnic tables and barbecue grills. Swings, including those with toddler seats, are strategically located near tables and shore. Bryant Park is one of

Traverse City's most popular family parks. Its central location makes it a great meeting or resting spot while its serene setting and magnificent sunsets can keep you here for hours.

Clinch Park
Grandview Pkwy. between Union and Park Sts., Traverse City

Clinch Park rests in the heart of Downtown Traverse City. Just a short block from the busy Front Street shops and eateries, Clinch Park stretches along the shoreline of West Grand Traverse Bay with a public beach, zoo and marina. The beach is sandy, shallow and highly popular. It's not unusual to see boaters moored in the adjacent waters spending the day on the bay. Larger boats and yachts are docked nearby at the Clinch Park Marina. The 102-slip marina hosts resident and transient craft as well as marauding sea gulls and the several families of ducks. Take a leisurely stroll along the docks and watch the park activity on land or the serenity of our beautiful bay vistas on the water side. Clinch Park Zoo is a favorite among children (see our Kidstuff chapter) who love to visit the resident animals — primarily Michigan natives — and ride the zoo's miniature train around the park. Con Foster Museum is adjacent to the zoo with rotating displays highlighting local history (see our Attractions chapter). Since Clinch Park lies along the popular TART recreational trail, you'll see a constant parade of bicyclists, walkers and in-line skaters passing by.

Grand Traverse County Civic Center
1125 W. Civic Center Dr., Traverse City
• (616) 922-4830 info/events hotline,
(616) 922-4818

The Civic Center sits on Traverse City's former fairgrounds with spacious grounds centrally located near Northwestern Michigan College and the Old Mission Peninsula. A large indoor facility houses Howe Ice Arena and Easling Pool at the north end of the property, but the remaining space of the 45-acre grounds is filled with playgrounds and areas for ball games, picnicking and walking. The Civic Center is home to Kids Kove, a massive wood play park filled with a seemingly endless maze of creative play spaces, as well as another traditional play area hosting the requisite slides, swings and merry-go-round. A sheltered picnic area sits alongside the older play area. A 1-mile paved multipurpose path surrounds the entire Civic Center property. The path is a favorite for all ages. You'll see senior citizens strolling while preschoolers maneuver their training-wheeled bikes. All share a friendly wave or smile along the way.

Medalie Park
South Airport Rd. at the Boardman River near Logan's Landing, Traverse City

This is a charming roadside park where children delight in watching the many swans, geese and ducks that also frequent the property. Medalie Park is situated behind the Logan's Landing shopping complex. Just drive past the parking lot and you'll see the paved walking paths leading along the Boardman Lake and River shorelines as well as the bevy of feathered residents splashing and squawking away. You'll also find a picnic pavilion, fishing platforms, a field sports area and benches for simply relaxing.

Old Mission Lighthouse Park
End of Mich. Hwy. 37 at Old Mission

Bring your camera, swimsuit and a picnic, and head north on the Old Mission Peninsula until it ends at the Old Mission Lighthouse. You are now at the 45th Parallel, exactly halfway between the Equator and the North Pole. The old 1870 lighthouse, today serves as a home for the park supervisor and family. A display near the park entrance discusses the 45th Parallel as well as the role of the lighthouse in Great Lakes navigation. The park's beach is narrow but memorable, stretching along the scenic shores of West Grand Traverse Bay. The land leading to the shoreline and lighthouse is heavily forested with trails weaving through. If you're looking for a playground, drive just a few miles back down the peninsula. Take the turnoff to the tiny berg of Old Mission and follow it straight to Haserot Park where you will find a playground, picnic tables and restrooms. One of the nicest ben-

efits of visiting Lighthouse Park is the drive through the Old Mission Peninsula with cherry orchards, sweeping shorelines and rolling hills, considered to be one of the prettiest drives in the region.

Open Space
Grandview Pkwy. at Union St., Traverse City

Appropriately named, this city landmark is, quite literally, an open green space jutting into West Grand Traverse Bay. The Open Space is close to the hearts and souls of Traverse Citians. This park encompasses property that had once been filled with a commercial cannery and its related manufacturing facilities. A grassroots effort several decades ago brought the property into public hands and traded smokestacks for grassy knolls and lapping waves. Today, the Open Space is the home for many community celebrations, most notably the National Cherry Festival. It is also in constant use by the countless residents and visitors who toss a Frisbee across the grounds, relax with a book under the trees or simply stroll along the paved perimeter while watching the water's many moods.

Traverse City State Park Beach
U.S. Hwy. 31 and Three Mile Rd., Traverse City • (616) 922-5270

You'll need a State Park motor vehicle permit to enter this popular park, but you will find yourself on a gorgeous stretch of sugar sand shoreline bordering East Grand Traverse Bay. The state park beach, which includes a nice picnic area, lies across busy U.S. Highway 31 from the park's campground. A pedestrian overpass links the two. Beach parking is ample. See the Campgrounds and RV Parks chapter for a full description. Vehicle permits are $4 daily or $20 for an annual pass and are available at the park entrance.

Interlochen State Park
Mich. Hwy. 137 across from Interlochen Center for the Arts, Interlochen
• (616) 276-9511

Interlochen State Park is nested in the pine trees that are especially predominant in this corner of Traverse. Like all state parks, Interlochen requires a motor vehicle permit for admission. The beach is large and the inland waters of Duck Lake are much warmer than those flowing through Grand Traverse Bay. The setting is relaxing, picnic areas are plentiful and the play area is fun. For a full description see our Campgrounds and RV Parks chapter. Vehicle permits are $4 per day or $20 for an annual pass, available at the park entrance.

Whitewater Township Park
Elk Lake Rd., Williamsburg
• **(616) 267-5091**

This 112-acre park sits along Elk Lake, approximately 15 miles northeast of Traverse City in rural Whitewater Township. You'll find pleasant picnic areas, a beach, a boat launch and 40 campsites. The park is open from mid-May through mid-September.

Leelanau County

Empire Village Park and South Bar Lake
End of Niagara St., Empire

These parks lie across the street from each other in the tiny village of Empire. Their proximity to Lake Michigan and the Sleeping Bear Dunes let you easily walk between the sandy shoreline and Empire Bluffs within the National Lakeshore. At South Bar, which you get to via the public access route, you'll find warmer inland waters, a small dock, a nice sandy beach and scads of lily pads. Be careful not to pick the water lilies because it's illegal! Across the street at Empire Beach, you'll find basketball and volleyball courts, picnic facilities and a great shoreline for skipping stones. Plan to stay until dusk when Mother Nature shares the most magnificent sunsets.

Leelanau State Park
15310 N. Lighthouse Rd. off Mich. Hwy. 201, Northport • (616) 386-5422

This is home to the Grand Traverse Lighthouse, a lovely playground and picnic area and one of the region's prettiest campgrounds. This is a lovely retreat any season of the year. See a full park listing in the Campgrounds and RV Parks chapter as well as information about the lighthouse in the Attractions and Kidstuff chapters.

Enjoying the fresh snow, kids play in one of the area's many parks.

Peterson Park
Peterson Park Rd. off Mich. Hwy. 201, Northport

Breathtaking views of Lake Michigan and the Manitou Islands await visitors to Peterson Park. Perched high on a western bluff near the tip of the Leelanau Peninsula, the park overlooks mesmerizing vistas of the Great Lake. This is a delightful place to picnic. You'll find plenty of tables and grills as well as a pavilion and swings for little ones. If you're feeling energetic, trek down the bluff to the rocky shoreline. This is a favorite spot for Petoskey stone hunting (see our Close-up in the Recreation chapter). Poke around and watch for the distinctive honeycomb-like markings. (A hint — you'll see them better when they're wet!)

Suttons Bay Municipal Park and Beach
Front St. between Grove and Adams Sts., Suttons Bay

Nestled behind the charming shops that comprise Suttons Bay's downtown, this municipal park and beach is a lovely place to relax and play. Shaded, grassy areas over-

Photo: Kevin Poirier/Courtesy of Traverse City Record-Eagle

look the scenic public beach and nearby marina and are wonderful for picnics. Swings and play structures entertain children. This park is a local favorite for its comfortable size, scenic setting and friendly ambiance. It also hosts several popular community gatherings including Jazzfest in July and the Suttons Bay Art Fair in August (see our Annual Events chapter).

Antrim-Kalkaska

Elk Rapids County Park
Bayshore Dr. off U.S. Hwy. 31, Elk Rapids

This is a lovely family park overlooking East Grand Traverse Bay and Traverse City's Old Mission Peninsula. The beach is large and sandy, perfect for sunbathing and sandcastle building. A playground entertains children. Trees shade picnic areas and create more secluded areas for families to gather. Several trails wind through the many evergreens and hardwoods covering this 13-acre park.

Otsego Lake County Park
W. Otsego Lake Dr., Gaylord

Picnics and play are popular local pastimes at Otsego Lake County Park. Situated on a quiet area of the lake, it's perfect for family fun with ample playground equipment, picnic tables and barbecue pits near the beach's edge. Pavilions are available for large gatherings or in case of unexpected rain.

Lake Michigan Shoreline and Cadillac

Lake Michigan Beach and Cannon Park
Frankfort

Surrounded by towering coastal bluffs, Frankfort's public beach offers a wide, sandy slice of Lake Michigan shoreline. Frequent whitecaps make swimming and body surfing a thrill here, but the spot is most popular at sunset when nature puts on a spectacular show. Anglers are often seen casting their lines from the pier. Other visitors simply enjoy walking the pier, watching waves crash at their feet. Across the parking lot from the beach, there are picnic facilities at Cannon Park. It's named for the mysterious Civil War cannon displayed on the green. Ironically, no one in town remembers the landmark's history or why it's there. The park and beach are located at the end of Main Street.

Beulah Village Park and Beach
Beulah

Situated along the sandy shores of Crystal Lake in the quiet village of Beulah, the park provides sunbathing, swimming and picnic opportunities. You'll find a beach house with a public boat launch nearby. Picnic tables, playground facilities and a pavilion are all available.

Douglas Park/First Street Beach
Manistee

Recreational headquarters for the City of Manistee, Douglas Park stretches along the white sandy shores of Lake Michigan. Lifeguards watch the beautiful public beach daily during the summer so the kids can enjoy the surf while you relax in the sun. Facilities include a kiddie playground featuring animal-shaped swings and a rocket slide, tennis and basketball courts, picnic tables and grills. It's a favorite park among anglers. Fish from the beach or city pier or set out on your own boat from the municipal launch. A fish-cleaning station is available. The park is located at the end of First Street.

Fifth Avenue Beach
Manistee

Manistee's North Pier Lighthouse and Catwalk make Fifth Avenue Beach a true landmark. The catwalk, one of four remaining catwalks on the west Michigan coast, is listed on

---

INSIDERS' TIP

Northwest Michigan is known as the Land of the Million-Dollar Sunset. Our parks are wonderful places for viewing the unforgettable nightly panorama on Lake Michigan.

the State Registry of Historic Sites and is worth seeing. The beach is also home to the Manistee U.S. Coast Guard Station. Recreational facilities include a picnic area, volleyball and tennis courts, a playground and swimming area. Lifeguards are posted daily during the summer. From U.S. 31, turn west on Monroe St. and follow until it ends at the park.

Lake Michigan Recreation Area
Southwest of Manistee • (616) 723-2211

Watch the big red sun sink into the horizon from the mile-long gorgeous Lake Michigan beach. Covering about 450 acres in the Manistee National Forest, it offers 3.5 miles of gravel hiking/biking trails, picnic, beach, family and group camping opportunities. (See our Campgrounds and RV chapter to learn more.) It's a great place to experience fresh Lake Michigan breezes, to listen to the pounding surf, explore open sand dunes or simply enjoy some incredible scenery from its two viewing decks. Technically, the area is open year round, but you won't want to enter if roads are snow-covered. There is no winter maintenance of these roads and even private tow trucks will not assist you if you get stuck. Call the Manistee Ranger Station at the above number during the winter months to find out if the park is accessible. To get to the park, go 9 miles south of Manistee on U.S. 31, then go west on Forest Trail and travel another 9 miles to the entrance.

Stearns Park
Ludington

Stearns Park offers 2,500 feet of fine white Lake Michigan beach, right in the heart of downtown Ludington. You'll find the swimming area marked and lifeguards on duty. Bring your picnic basket or grab something at the concession stand and enjoy the park's picnic facilities. When you're ready for action, make use of volleyball, shuffleboard, miniature golf

and boat-launch facilities. A pathway through the park provides a walking tour of Ludington's waterfront including the historic Ludington North Breakwater Light and Ludington U.S. Coast Guard Station. The park is at the end of Ludington Avenue.

Cadillac Lakefront Park
Cadillac

You'll find Cadillac's Lakefront area is the site of many community activities as well as the perfect place for a quiet afternoon stroll. Under the shade of towering oaks, the historic Shay Steam Locomotive is on permanent display. Just across the street, along the shores of Lake Cadillac, is a performing arts pavilion. A floating dock provides anglers a place to cast their lines, and a mile-long paved pathway, accented by gaslights and a wooded bridge over the Clam River, provides opportunities for scenic walks. Called the Keith McKellop Walkway, the walk connects to a 7.5-mile, paved path encircling the entire lake. The park is one block west of downtown Cadillac.

Kenwood Park
Cadillac

Lifeguards are on duty all summer and swimming areas are marked for safety at Kenwood Beach along Lake Cadillac. The sandy beach is beside a wooded oasis where you'll find picnic tables, grills, a pavilion, two playgrounds, hiking trails, volleyball, disc golf facilities and a boat ramp. It's a favorite spot for locals and visitors alike. The park is on North Boulevard, off Mich. Highway 115.

Missaukee County Park
Lake Missaukee • (616) 839-4945

Considered one of the nicest beaches in the greater Cadillac area, the swimming zone at Missaukee County Park is well marked by buoys. The shallow, sandy shoreline along Lake Missaukee provides good splashing and

![INSIDERS' TIP]

An autumn view of the Jordan Valley from Deadman's Hill near East Jordan will take your breath away. The spot is located a half mile west of the U.S. Highway 131 and Mich. Highway 32 intersection. The hill was named for Big Sam, a Polish lumberjack who lost his life here in 1910 while hauling a load of lumber.

swimming for youngsters. While 117 camp-sites are available, there are day-use facilities including a beach house, boat launch, play-ground, picnic tables, grills and pavilion. Open May through October, there is a $1 entry fee per vehicle.

Little Traverse

East Park
Charlevoix

A well-manicured greenbelt in the very center of downtown Charlevoix, East Park overlooks the Round Lake yacht basin. Generally a quiet place to relax and watch the boats drift by, the park comes to life during community festivals such as Venetian Weekend, Apple Fest and the Waterfront Art Fair. (See our Annual Events chapter to learn more about these celebrations.) During the summer months, you'll find a variety of live entertainment presented regularly at the Clarence A. Odmark Pavilion. East Park is on Bridge Street overlooking Round Lake.

Ferry Beach
Charlevoix

Ferry Park offers plenty of shady spots and plenty of full sun, so when you come, take your preference. On the shores of Lake Charlevoix at Ferry Beach you'll find good swimming for both little tikes and the experienced swimmer. Lifeguards are on duty and diving is permitted from the pier. Concessions, picnic tables, a covered pavilion, playground equipment and concessions are all available. The beach is at the corner of Ferry Avenue and Stover Road.

Mt. McSauba
Charlevoix

Mt. McSauba is the tallest dune north of Charlevoix and the centerpiece of the city's 50-acre recreational park complex. In the winter, rentals are available for downhill and cross-country skiing. During the summer, Mt. McSauba is the site for a city-operated day camp for boys and girls. To get to Mt. McSauba, take U.S. 31 through Charlevoix, turn left on Mercer Road, then turn right on Pleasant Road and you'll see the park.

Elm Pointe
East Jordan

Elm Pointe is a pleasant place to wile away a summer's day. It covers 11 acres with frontage along the south arm of Lake Charlevoix. You can swim and picnic here, and you can visit two museums, Portside Art and Historical Museum. The Historical Museum features a collection of local artifacts while the Cygred Riley Art Gallery displays works purchased from prize-winning participants of the Portside Arts Fair. During July and August, you can visit the museums between 1 and 4 PM, Thursday through Sunday. During June, September and October, the museums open only on weekends. Elm Pointe is along Mich. Highway 66 at the south arm of Lake Charlevoix.

Pennsylvania Park
Petoskey

A classic city park, this greenspace in downtown Petoskey is the site for many annual festivals and special events. Like many larger parks, you'll find a war memorial and an attractive gazebo, where musical entertainment is presented twice weekly during July and August. Benches and picnic tables make it a pleasant spot to enjoy some fresh air, an espresso or a break from exploring Petoskey's well-known Gaslight Shopping District. The park is between Mitchell and Lake streets.

Petoskey Waterfront Park
On Little Traverse Bay along U.S. Hwy. 31 in downtown Petoskey

Petoskey's Waterfront Park is a mile-long gem. The green space is along a beautiful stretch of Little Traverse Bay. It's great for strolling and viewing the brilliant bay sunsets. Facilities include a municipal marina, picnic area, public restrooms and an underground walkway leading to the Gaslight Shopping District. The park connects to local biking and walking trails and a scenic lookout at the adjacent Sunset Park where you can check out the magnificent scenery with public viewfinders.

Petoskey Winter Sports Park
Petoskey • (616) 347-1252

Come here for fun that won't drain your piggy bank. Petoskey Winter Sports Park offers a free rope tow for downhill ski enthusiasts. There's bump jumping, old-fashioned sledding and a skating rink for figure skating and hockey play. Skate rentals are available. Operated by Petoskey's Recreation Department, the park is open weekdays from 4 to 9 PM and on weekends from noon to 9 PM. The park is off U.S. Hwy 31 on Winter Park Lane.

Deer Park
Harbor Springs

The dozen or so deer who live in this fenced area next to the city police station are practically town mascots. They're so friendly, they eat right from your hand. You can buy pellets to feed them from on-site vending machines or bring down carrots and crackers to get acquainted with these gentle city ambassadors. You'll find plenty of available parking and an open grassy area with picnic facilities. Deer Park is just inside the east city limits on Zoll Street.

Zorn Park
Harbor Springs

The calm waters along Little Traverse Bay at Zorn Park make it a favorite family swimming beach. Lifeguards are posted from 9 AM to 5 PM daily during summer months. There are two swimming rafts, one in shallow waters for the younger set and one out deeper for diving. Facilities include a beach house and shady picnic area. Zorn Park is frequently the chosen site for community fairs, festivals and special events. The park is along W. Bay Street.

Mackinac Straits

Marquette Park
Huron St., Mackinac Island

Located at the base of Fort Mackinac, Marquette Park is named for the large bronze sculpture of Jesuit missionary Father Jacques Marquette, which stands within a sea of green grass beneath the bright white fort walls. Families gather here on blankets to share a picnic, relax from sightseeing or simply to give toddlers the chance to run, play and work off energy. This pleasant park is a great spot to watch the bustle of downtown and marina activity. One word of warning — the resident sea gulls also consider this park their own. When they aren't perched on Father Marquette's head, they are shamelessly begging for food.

Nature Preserves

Grand Traverse

Traverse City Area

Grand Traverse Natural Education Reserve
Cass and Keystone Rds., Traverse City
• (616) 922-4818

The Natural Education Reserve is a 370-acre property managed by the Grand Traverse County Parks and Recreation Department. Its boundaries encompass several miles of frontage on the Sabin and Boardman hydroponds and the Boardman River. You will find at least 7 miles of self-guided nature trails, picnic areas, canoe portage sites and areas for bird watching and trout fishing. Wildlife range from beavers to white-tailed deer.

Power Island
Bowers Harbor, West Grand Traverse Bay, Traverse City • (616) 922-4818

Formerly known as Marion Island but recently renamed for philanthropist Eugene Power of Ann Arbor, this is a 205-acre island nature preserve in West Grand Traverse Bay just off Bower's Harbor. This island is one of the last undeveloped Great Lakes islands in close proximity to an urban area. It is filled with a beautiful stand of northern hardwoods, including beech, sugar maple, basswood and red oak, as well as more than 250 plant species. Wildlife include red fox and bobcat who prey on such small mammals as the meadow vole, woodland deer mouse and short-tailed shrew. Bird-watchers will likely see the red-eyed vireo, American goldfinch, veery and bank and tree swallow. Approximately 11 miles of hiking trails weave through the island's interior. Due to Power Island's proximity to Traverse City, it is a popular boating and picnicking destination. A few rustic camping sites are available on nearby Bassett Island, which is connected to Power Island by an isthmus.

Pyatt Lake Natural Area
Pyatt Lake Rd., Old Mission Peninsula, Traverse City • (616) 929-7911

As the Old Mission Peninsula becomes increasingly developed, the Pyatt Lake Natural Area stands as one of its few remaining undisturbed natural areas. It is one of several regional preserves under the watch of the Grand Traverse Regional Land Conservancy. Classified as a "wooded dune and swale complex," it is considered to be one of the county's most botanically diverse areas with dune swales, cedar swamps, wet meadows and fens. Its wetlands protect the water quality of nearby Bowers Harbor as well as West Grand Traverse Bay by filtering and retaining nutrients and sediment. There are more than 250 plant species on the preserve with trees predominantly hemlock, maple and old growth big-toothed aspens. Wildlife include fox, muskrats, porcupines, barred owls, great blue herons, water snakes, raccoons and various species of birds.

Reffitt Nature Preserve
Three Mile Rd. near Parsons Rd., Traverse City • (616) 929-7911

The 52-acre Reffitt Nature Preserve is one of the closest nature preserves to the center of Traverse City. It was donated by Ronald G. Reffitt to the Grand Traverse Regional Land Conservancy in honor of his parents George and Ada Reffitt and to preserve the property's fragile ecosystem as well as that of the Mitchell Creek watershed. It offers residents and visitors the chance to appreciate the importance of protecting our watersheds, streams and lakes as this surrounding region continues to be urbanized. Trails weave through the property and connect with the TART trail to encourage public educational and recreational use.

Sand Lakes Quiet Area
Broomhead Rd. off Mich. Hwy. 72, Williamsburg • (616) 922-5280

Sand Lakes Quiet Area is a local favorite all year round. Its proximity to Traverse City, easy access and serene beauty have made it a popular destination for family hiking, cross-country skiing and communing with nature. The park stretches over 2,500 acres of the Pere Marquette State Forest. The gently rolling, sandy hills are filled with a mixed hardwood and conifer forest as well as 10 miles of trails and several small secluded lakes. Sand Lakes is a wonderful destination for recreational novices, while seasoned hikers like its longer treks and backcountry camping (see our Campgrounds and RV Parks chapter).

Sleeping Bear Dunes National Lakeshore
Philip A. Hart Visitors Center, 9922 Front St. (Mich. Hwy. 72), Empire • (616) 326-5134

Named a national lakeshore in order to preserve its unique ecological systems, Sleeping Bear Dunes National Lakeshore features 37 miles of coastal dunes, covering 71,000 acres in western Benzie and Leelanau counties. Hiking, camping, swimming, beachcombing, hunting, boating and cross-country ski opportunities are abundant throughout the park. Entrance fees are $7 per vehicle for a one- to seven-day pass. Annual passes and senior rates are available. (See our Close-Up on the park and the listing in our Parks and Preserves chapter.)

Solon Swamp, Pere Marquette State Forest
County Rd. 614, Cedar • (517) 373-1275

Managed by the Nature Conservancy and owned by the State of Michigan, Solon Swamp lies within the Pere Marquette State Forest near the southern end of Lake Leelanau. The swamp portion represents 40 acres of a 1,540 acre portion of state forest. It is an undeveloped wetland supporting bald eagles and osprey. A dense northern lowland forest consists of white cedar, balsam fir, white birch and black ash. Wildlife includes black bear, bobcat, beaver and otter. Two streams, Victory Creek and Cedar Run, flow through the swamp to Lake Leelanau. Access to this pre-

---

INSIDERS' TIP

Each year more than 5,000 children participate in environmental programs and field trips led by the Little Traverse Conservancy.

serve is found along an old logging trail where County Road 614 joins with the Pere Marquette State Forest. There are no developed trails and a compass is recommended.

Antrim-Kalkaska

Jordan River Pathway
Deadman's Hill Rd. off U.S. Hwy. 131, Alba • (517) 732-3541

Part of the Mackinaw State Forest, the Jordan River was designated as Michigan's first "wild and scenic river" with 1.2 miles protected by the state's Nature Conservancy. It is one of the state's top cold-water streams with fast moving, frigid waters that are especially hospitable to brook trout and brown trout. Tree growth is heavy along the river banks with lowland forests of white cedar, fir, birch, spruce and aspen along with many wild iris and orchids. Hiking trails wind through the Jordan River Valley with trailheads starting off Deadman's Hill Road, approximately 30 miles northeast of Traverse City.

Grass River Natural Area
Alden Hwy., Bellaire • (616) 533-8314

Stretching along Grass River, this preserve includes more than 1,000 acres of wetlands, a variety of natural habitats and a wealth of plant and wildlife. The Grass River connects Lake Bellaire and Clam Lake along Antrim County's Chain of Lakes. Close to one quarter of the property has been designated for education and passive recreation, and the volunteer organization overseeing the area offers an ambitious series of guided tours and environmental education classes for adults and children. The Grass River Natural Area Interpretive Center is open daily with environmental displays, trail guides, local information and related books. Boardwalks and bark trails crisscross the educational site's 225 acres. A trail for the handicapped can accommodate wheelchairs. Unique footbridges that incorporate bench seats stretch across Finch Creek while several observation platforms are strategically located. Naturalists have identified more than 400 species of flora and fauna including 49 species of mammals and 65 species of birds. Eagles, loons, osprey, beaver, deer and a sea of wildflowers are frequently sighted. The Grass River Natural Area access is off Alden Highway, approximately 2.5 miles east of Chapman Road and .5 mile west of Comfort Road.

Palmer-Wilcox-Gates
Bayshore Dr. off Ames St. at U.S. Hwy. 31 N., Elk Rapids • (616) 929-7911

The Palmer-Wilcox-Gates preserve protects 2,500 feet of undeveloped East Grand Traverse Bay shoreline north of Elk Rapids. Today's preserve combines an original 16 acres of dune lands with a newly acquired 18 acres of adjacent hardwood property. Trails are limited to those leading to the sandy, scenic shoreline just 30 yards from the Bayshore Drive access site. Trees edge the beach and fill the land with hemlock, white cedar, balsam fir, pine, juniper and northern hardwoods. Wildflowers fill the forest floor and dunes, include several rare varieties such as pitcher's thistle, Lake Huron Tansy and creeping juniper. Bird-watchers will find many shorebirds, waterfowl and warblers that thrive here, especially the red-breasted nuthatches and wood warblers that nest among the conifers.

St. Clair/Six Mile Lake
County Rd. 626, Ellsworth • (616) 929-7911

The St. Clair/Six Mile Lake nature area includes one of the longest stretches of undeveloped shoreline in the Elk River watershed. It is in the upper Chain of Lakes with a variety of habitats including marshlands, hardwoods/conifer swamps and shrub-dominated wetlands. Plant life is highlighted by wild roses, cardinal flowers, ferns and vivid marsh plants along the shores. Access is on the south side of County Road 626, approximately 1 mile east of Ellsworth.

Skegemog Lake Wildlife Area
Mich. Hwy. 72 between Williamsburg and Kalkaska • (616) 258-2711

Scenic pathways weave through this wildlife area on the east side of Skegemog Lake. Or, simply absorb nature and watch such Skegemog residents as blue herons, snakes, frogs, ducks and birds from one of the wildlife

Photo: Kevin Poirier

Several beach volleyball courts are available on the shores of West Bay.

observation areas. The most notable view of the area is the breathtaking vista showcased from the Skegemog Lake scenic stop along Mich. Highway 72 halfway between Williamsburg and Kalkaska.

Kewadin Wetlands
Elk Tip Rd., Kewadin • (616) 929-7911

The Kewadin Wetlands protect the water of Elk Lake from nearby urban and agricultural runoff. Visitors will find several natural habitats including a submerged aquatic bed, marshes, shrub-scrub swamps and forest wetlands. Viewing platforms and a boardwalk are under way for increased viewing of northern lakes wildlife. The Kewadin Wetlands can be accessed from the end of Elk Tip Road, located off Cherry Avenue on Elk Lakes northern tip.

Pigeon River Country State Forest
Sturgeon Valley Rd., Vanderbilt
• (517) 732-3541

This 95,000 acre area within the Mackinaw State Forest is home to the only elk herd east of the Mississippi River. More than 1,000 of these massive animals reside within a 600-mile area stretching through Otsego, Cheboygan, Presque Isle and Montmorency counties but the greatest concentration lies within the Pigeon River property. The adult elk are magnificent creatures, with bulls measuring eight feet from head to tail, weighing 700 to 900 pounds and often racked with massive antlers. Cows measure a foot smaller and one third less in weight but both sport beautiful, chocolate-colored manes and tawny hides and are quite tolerant, even bored, by humans. Other wildlife are also plentiful including bear, coyote, bobcat, beaver, otter, grouse, bald eagles, osprey, loons and blue herons. The forest is 13 miles east of Vanderbilt, which is east of Gaylord. From U.S. 27 in Vanderbilt, turn east onto Main Street, which turns into Sturgeon Valley Road and continue to Twin Lakes Road, go north for 1 mile and look for the log DNR headquarters building.

Lake Michigan Shoreline and Cadillac

Point Betsie Dunes Preserve
Frankfort

Covering 71 acres near Frankfort, this preserve provides examples of interdunal wetlands and open dunes. It is home to thriving populations of species found only on the Great Lakes shoreline such as pitcher's thistle and Lake Huron locust. The 1,100 feet of Lake Michigan frontage is considered potential nesting habitat for the globally endangered piping plover. You'll find pockets of fir forest scattered throughout the preserve. It is managed by the Nature Conservancy. To get to the preserve from Frankfort, take Mich. Highway 22 north for 4 miles to Point Betsie Road. Turn left and follow Point Betsie Road until it ends at Lake Michigan. Park at the U.S. Coast Guard Station and walk south for .25 mile. The preserve is signed.

Arcadia Marsh
Arcadia

While not officially designated a preserve or sanctuary, this wetland, also referred to as the Arcadia Bayou, attracts a multitude of migratory birds including Canada geese and ducks. It's home to a healthy population of graceful swans, coots, muskrats, mink, turtles, red fox, deer and coyote. Situated in a fragile valley carved by mighty glaciers, the wetlands are surrounded by beautiful hills. The system consists of Lake Michigan, Bar Lake, marshes and two creeks. It's along Mich. Highway 22 in south Arcadia.

Lake Bluff Audubon Center
2890 Lake Shore Rd., Manistee
• (616) 723-4042

More than 70 acres of meadows with one-quarter mile of Lake Michigan beach, the sanctuary provides habitat for a wonderful variety of species including woodpeckers, orioles, woodcocks and gulls. Trails lace the preserve

INSIDERS' TIP

Picking wildflowers in Michigan is against the law.

where you'll find exotic botanical specimens. It was originally established as a private sanctuary by a wealthy businessman and later donated to the Audubon Society. Built on a bluff overlooking Lake Michigan, the patron's home is now a nature center providing offices, conference space and meeting rooms.

Nordhouse Dunes Wilderness
(616) 723-2211

Nordhouse Dunes Wilderness is the only federally designated wilderness in Michigan's lower peninsula. Designated by the Michigan Wilderness Act of 1987, it covers 3,450 acres of National Forest. Many of the towering dunes within the preserve are more than 3,500 years old. Nordhouse Dunes features five distinct ecosystems. Unlike other dune systems, it features woody vegetation including juniper, jack pine and hemlock. Nordhouse and surrounding lands have the largest area of interdunal ponds in the world. Small water holes, marshes and dune grass are found scattered throughout. The ecosystem provides habitat for a wide variety of flora and fauna. The 3 miles of beach are treasured for natural scenic beauty and solitude. Although the area is minimally marked and limited, hikers enjoy 10 miles of Nordhouse Wilderness trails. Insiders strongly recommend adventurers bring a compass and detailed map. When planning a wilderness getaway, keep in mind that the summer months bring the most visitors to the dunes, especially holiday weekends. Opening day of deer firearm season in mid-November is also a time of heavy use. Like hunters, hikers should wear blaze-orange clothing during hunting seasons. Managed by the U.S. Forest Service, camping is permitted in the area. (See our Campgrounds and RV Parks chapter to learn more about camping at the dunes.) The preserve is 12 miles southwest of Manistee off Nurmberg Road.

Heritage Nature Trail/Carl T. Johnson Hunting & Fishing Center
6093 Mich. Hwy. 115, Cadillac
• **(616) 779-1321**

Adjacent to the Carl T. Johnson Center at Cadillac's William Mitchell State Park is Heritage Nature Trail, a 70-acre wetland preserve.

Well-maintained trails wind through the diverse ecosystem where you may catch sight of beaver, muskrats, turtles, snakes, mallards, heron or even a bald eagle. Guided tours are offered and maps are available for self-guided hikes. Year-round programming at the preserve includes night hikes, cross-country ski and snowshoe romps. (See our Close-up on the Carl T. Johnson Hunting & Fishing Center in the Campgrounds and RV Parks chapter .)

Waldeck Island
Cadillac

The first natural area placed under the protection of the Cadillac Area Land Conservancy, Waldeck Island is situated within one of Wexford County's smaller inland lakes, Stone Ledge Lake. You can explore the pristine 9-acre island, designated for educational and scientific use, from a 1-mile trail. The preserve features a full range of northern foliage including hemlock, pine, birch, maple, elm, ash and wild cherry. Island wildlife includes deer, partridge and heron. To get to Waldeck, take Mich. Highway 115 south of Cadillac, turn right on 43 Road, then turn left on Frederick Drive where you'll see the parking area. A marked walking path takes you over to the island.

Little Traverse

Charles A. Ransom Nature Preserve
Charlevoix

This 80-acre preserve offers one of the most breathtaking views in northern Michigan. Viewed from the preserve's high point, an elevation of 320 feet, the panoramic vista stretches from Leelanau Peninsula to Beaver Island. The preserve is part of the northern hardwood forest. You'll find large sugar maple, American beech, basswood and aspen. The thriving forest is home to a variety of wildlife, chipmunks, raccoons, deer, porcupine, turkey and many other birds. You'll find an abundance of wildflowers and many kinds of mushrooms blanketing the forest floor. Meadow land and shrub-thickets also cover the area. Brochures are available for a self-guided tour of the well-marked trail. To get to the preserve from Charlevoix, take U.S. 31 north to County

Sleeping Bear Dunes National Lakeshore

The legend of Sleeping Bear Dunes, passed down through the generations by Chippewa Indian story weavers, is a poignant tale explaining the origins of the landmark. By flickering campfires they told of a brave mother bear and her two cubs who swam across Lake Michigan from Wisconsin to escape a raging forest fire. When the mother bear reached the Michigan shore, she climbed to the top of a bluff to await her cubs. The young, weaker cubs, lagged behind. Too tired to go on, the cubs succumbed to a cold, watery death. The legend says the little bears became North and South Manitou Islands. Sleeping Bear, a solitary dune overlooking Lake Michigan, marks the place where the faithful mother bear waited.

Thousands come to visit Sleeping Bear Dunes National Lakeshore each year to experience the majestic beauty of the preserve's bluffs, lakes and forests. Its coastal dunes stretch for 37 miles along the Lake Michigan shoreline from Benzie County into the Leelanau Peninsula. Altogether, the park covers more than 71,000 acres and offers a variety of recreational opportunities. You'll find it's an exciting place to spend a day or an entire vacation.

You can reach the park from several roads including U.S. Highway 31, via Mich. Highway 22, traveling either south or north, or via Mich. Highway 72 from Traverse City. Begin your stay at the Philip A. Hart Visitor Center and park headquarters at 9922 Front Street in the village of Empire. Modern interactive exhibits and slide presentations offer a historical look at the preserve. Friendly rangers are on hand to answer your questions and provide directions. You can also pick up brochures, maps and books here to get you started on your adventure. Entrance fees are required park-wide. Passes for one to seven days are $7 per vehicle. Annual passes and senior passes are available at special rates.

— continued on next page

Photo: National Park Service

Sleeping Bear Dunes National Lakeshore is a unique
ecological area popular with vacationers.

Day visitors will want to head north to the Sleeping Bear Dune Climb. A climb to the top provides a truly breathtaking view of Glen Lake and the surrounding Leelanau countryside. These dunes cover 4 square miles and offer some rare hiking opportunities. Plenty of parking, restroom and picnic facilities, a concession stand and gift shop are at the base of the dune.

The Pierce Stocking Drive is another area you won't want to miss. The 7.4-mile driving tour offers unbelievably beautiful vistas of Sleeping Bear Dunes, Glen Lake and Lake Michigan. Open between May and mid-October to bicyclists, pedestrians and motor vehicles, the route marks 12 scenic and ecological spots of interest, including a picturesque covered wooden bridge. From the Sleeping Bear Dune Overlook you can view North and South Manitou Islands floating amidst the shimmering water. Today, these islands are considered among the best hiking and backpacking destinations in the Midwest. Both are accessed by ferry from the village of Leland.

North Manitou, offers 15,000 acres of wilderness to explore with backcountry camping, beachcombing, fishing and hunting. South Manitou adventurers enjoy hiking, backcountry camping and visiting the island's old-growth cedars, the lighthouse and other historic spots. Guided tours are available. In addition to the islands, two other camping facilities are available at the preserve, the Platte River and D.H. Day campgrounds. The Platte River campground offers modern facilities with kayak, canoe and inner tube rentals nearby. D.H. Day has only water and vault toilets, but puts you near the heart of the park's trail system. To learn more about camping at Sleeping Bear, see our Campground and RV Park chapter. Overnight accommodations are also available in Glen Lake, Beulah, Empire and Leland.

Another attraction is the Sleeping Bear Point Coast Guard Station Maritime Museum. The restored station offers a glimpse into the everyday life and rescue work of the men stationed at this key Lake Michigan post. The museum is open daily from 10 AM to 5 PM between Memorial Day and Labor Day. Admission is included in your park pass. Contact park headquarters at (616) 326-5134 for museum program schedules.

While summer is the most popular time for visits to Sleeping Bear, the winter months offer visitors great cross-country skiing opportunities. You'll find 50 miles of park trails blanketed in peace by the snow. To get around safely, pick up a map at the visitor center or at trailheads. More information about the park is available by writing Sleeping Bear Dunes National Lakeshore, 9922 Front Street, Mich. Highway 72, Empire, MI 49630, or call (616) 326-5134.

Road 56 and turn right to Quarterline Rd., then turn left on Maple Grove Road and travel for .75 mile.

North Point Preserve
Charlevoix

Adjacent to the Mt. McSauba recreation park, North Point Preserve offers 27 acres of tranquillity and diversity. Trails wander though the natural area, which provides habitat for deer, porcupine, squirrels, rabbits, ducks and other shore birds, loons, eagles and blue heron. Three threatened plant species are found here, pitcher's thistle, Lake Huron Tansy

and Pumpell's Bromegrass. The preserve includes 2,800 feet of Lake Michigan shoreline. To get there from Charlevoix, take Mercer Road north to Pleasant Street. Turn left onto Mt. McSauba Street. Turn right before the dirt road, and you'll find the preserve on your left.

Resort Township Parks
Bay Harbor

Two parks at Bay Harbor offer a variety of uses. East Park has 2,500 feet of Lake Michigan shoreline. From its non-motorized trail system you can access foot trails, scenic overlooks and a bridge, which cross a small coastal brook. There is access to Bay Harbor Lake, a local hot spot for steelhead fishing. A boat launch is available for small outboard crafts or canoes. At West Park, you'll find wood-chip trails, an observation deck overlooking wetland areas and interpretive information on the natural and cultural history of Little Traverse Bay. Trails are open to hiking, biking, snowshoeing and cross-country skiing. The park provides access to Lake Michigan and has 600 feet of frontage. From Petoskey, take U.S. 31 S. to Bay Harbor. East Park is off Quarry Road. West Park is accessible from County Line Road.

McCune Nature Preserve
Petoskey

Hardwood forest dominates this beautiful 168-acre preserve but you will also find scotch pine, white and red pine plantations, meadow, creek and floodplain. The spring-fed Minnehaha Creek flows through the preserve to Crooked Lake. The creek is an example of the many beautiful streams found in northern Michigan. A trail system loops through various habitats on the preserve. To get there from Petoskey, take Mitchell Road east to Maxwell Road. Turn right and travel about .75 mile. The preserve is on the right and is signed.

Spring Lake Park
Petoskey

Spring Lake Park is an Insiders' favorite fishing hole and a good place for picnicking and observing swans and other wildlife. Located near the southern end of Mich. Highway 119, it is the starting point for "the Gateway to Harbor Project." Sponsored by the Little Traverse Conservancy, the project aims to protect natural areas along Mich. Highway 119 between Petoskey and Harbor Springs. From Petoskey, take Mich. Highway 119 north about one-half mile. The park is on the right.

Round Lake Nature Preserve
Harbor Springs

Round Lake Preserve is the site for Little Traverse Conservancy offices. The natural area covers 60 acres featuring 2,500 feet of frontage on Round Lake. Here, you'll find the head of the inland water route that Native Ameri-

cans once used to canoe from Little Traverse Bay to Lake Huron. Lush and diverse vegetation provides excellent habitat for woodland wildlife. White pines tower above thick alder and wild roses along the lakeshore. Cedar, red maples and hemlocks support many bird species, and wildflowers bloom in abundance. To get to the preserve from Petoskey, take U.S. 31 N. to Mich. Highway 119, take Mich. Highway 119 and drive 2 miles north, turn right on Powell Road and drive until you come to Little Traverse Conservancy offices, where there is plenty of parking.

Thorne Swift Nature Preserve
6696 Lower Shore Dr., Harbor Springs
• (616) 526-6401

Established in 1982, Thorne Swift protects two significant types of natural areas, coastal dunes and cedar swamp. You can experience the preserve's natural wealth from boardwalk trails that wander through rich wetlands and from the Cedar Trail near the lakeshore use area. Thorne Swift includes a 300-foot slice of sandy Lake Michigan shoreline. Swimming is permitted; however, be aware that lifeguards are not posted. Before you head out to see the wildlife and scenery, put on insect repellent, then stop at the Elizabeth Kennedy Nature Center, near the parking area. A naturalist is on duty daily from 10 AM to dusk, Memorial Day through Labor Day and on weekends during May and September. At the nature center, you'll find maps and brochures and learn about the preserve's special programs and activities.

Headlands
Emmet County

Owned by Emmet County, the 600-acre preserve known as the Headlands features more than 2 miles of rocky frontage along the Straits of Mackinac. It is the largest and least-disturbed forest tract in the Mackinaw City area. The preserve is a significant resting stop and staging area for raptors and neotropical birds migrating across the Straits. It also supports endangered flora including Dwarf Lake Iris and the threatened Lake Huron Tansy and pitcher's thistle. Operated as a public park, it is open to cross-country skiing, hiking, bird-watching, nature study, mountain biking and picnicking.

From the headlands, you can travel to Wilderness State Park via public land. To get to the park from Mackinac City, take Central Avenue west to its end. Turn south and travel .25 mile to the entrance.

Mackinac Straits

Wilderness State Park
898 Wilderness Park Dr., Carp Lake
• (616) 436-5381

Wilderness State Park is profiled fully in our Camping and RV Parks chapter but this beautiful park's natural areas deserve a mention here as well. The Wilderness boundaries stretch over 8,000 acres of wild, low dunes, forested back country and limestone shores lining Lake Michigan with numerous trails crisscrossing the way. Bird watchers love Wilderness for the more than 100 species that nest or migrate through the park, including the rare Piping Plover that nests along the shoreline. As with all state parks, a motor vehicle permit is required. Cost is $4 per day or $20 per year, payable at the park entrance.

Horseshoe Bay Wilderness
Mackinac Trail at Foley Creek National Forest Campground, St. Ignace
• (906) 248-5231

Many consider Horseshoe Bay Wilderness to be among the Strait's best-kept secrets. This great wilderness area is situated within the Hiawatha National Forest but just 6 miles from the bustle of St. Ignace. Its boundaries include 7 miles of Lake Huron shoreline as well as thousands of acres of forest and swamp. Much of it looks as it might have during the days of the voyageurs and the early settlers. It seems as though very little has touched the area since the final lumbering days. Wildlife includes a large deer population along with bear, coyote, otter, mink, eagles, osprey, great blue herons, gulls and various ducks. You'll have to hike to get to the shoreline wilderness area. Trails lead from the Foley Creek Campground for about 1 mile to the beach area. To get to the wilderness from St. Ignace, travel on I-75 for approximately 6 miles to exit 352 at Mich. Highway 123. Travel just a short way to Mackinac Trail and travel south to Foley Creek Campground approximately 2 miles away.

From foraging the forest
floor to hiking dense
backcountry, there
are many ways to
explore our picturesque
countryside, coastal
dunes and sparkling
waterways.

Recreation

From the first breath of spring to winter's first icy grip, Northwest Michigan wonders unfold in a flow of color. The multitude of the region's recreational opportunities will impress any outdoor enthusiast. From foraging the forest floor to hiking dense backcountry to navigating our rivers, there are many ways to explore our picturesque countryside, coastal dunes and sparkling waterways.

Hundreds of lakes in Northwest Michigan provide excellent swimming. Public beaches are found in the center of small towns, tucked into secluded forests, along the magnificent Great Lakes coast. Many of the region's beaches are listed in our Parks and Campgrounds and RV Parks chapters, but we've included Insiders' favorites here. The swimming season in Northwest Michigan differs from year to year. Brave spirits may take the plunge in mid-May, or it might be mid-June before waters warm sufficiently for anyone but the polar bears. Swimming often continues to mid-September. Keep in mind that you can expect Lake Michigan water temperatures to be cooler than those of inland lakes.

Boating and canoeing are popular in Northwest Michigan. Wherever you are in the region, you are never more than 6 miles away from a lake or stream.

When you are boating, hiking or partaking in any number of outdoor recreational activities you should stay updated on local weather conditions by listening to commercial radio or television stations. Boaters on Lake Michigan should be aware that dangerous storm conditions occur most frequently over water when humidity and temperature ashore are high. Northwest Michigan is also subject to tornadoes, especially in early summer when thunderstorms roll across the area.

Remember, weather here is unpredictable. When packing for a north country journey, bring a little of everything. Hot, cold, sun and snow are always possible, especially in spring and fall.

Our well-developed recreational resources offer easy access to a broad range of opportunities. Multiuse trail systems weave through the region's outstanding parks, preserves and forests making biking and hiking very popular from spring through fall. The low-impact sports are a great way to experience the north's natural treasures.

The north woods are a prime spot to forage for the famous morel mushroom. You'll find all the tips you need below to get you started on the spring hunt. But don't stop there. Our woods and meadows will treat you to wild berries of all kinds, sun-ripened strawberries, blackberries and blueberries. Wildflowers, while protected by law and not for picking, decorate our landscape in delicate and brilliant ways beginning in early spring when white trillium blanket the woodland floor.

As autumn arrives and frost covers the pumpkins, the north woods are painted in unbelievable hues of gold, red and orange. Area chambers of commerce provide maps, either free or for a nominal fee, for self-guided auto tours. But it's not the only way to enjoy the show. Hit a trail on foot or by bike or enjoy lakeshore colors from a boat on one of the hundreds of inland lakes.

Come the frosty winter, our forests continue to put on a spectacular show. Contact the United States Forest Service office at 1755 S. Mitchell Street, Cadillac, (616) 775-2421, to learn about permits to cut firewood or a fresh evergreen for your Christmas tree on national land.

Remember, a vehicle permit is required to enter all state parks. Fees are $4 daily or $20 for an annual pass, payable at the park entrance. One permit will admit you to all parks.

Don't forget, we have Winter Recreation, Parks, Golf, and Fishing and Hunting chapters for other pursuits. You'll find Northwest

Michigan's abundant resources provide a world of treasures to enjoy any time of the year.

What does it cost?

If you came to town without your wheels or paddle, we can help! We've listed a number of locations to rent bicycles, in-line skates, canoes, kayaks and tubes. Each has its own policies and pricing, but most fall close to the following averages. These guidelines are based on weekend, adult rates for one day in the Grand Traverse region.

Bikes (usually includes helmet)	$15 per day
	$75 per week
Performance Bikes	$25 per day
(usually includes helmet)	
Tandem Bikes	$25-50 per day,
	$10 for 2 hours
Trailers or Trail-A-Bikes	$10
Child Seat	$5
Baby Joggers	$10
In-Line Skates	$10
(includes helmet and pads)	
Protective Gear	$2-5 per item
(i.e. helmet, pads)	
Car Racks	$7-10
Travel Boxes	$7
Kayaks	$35 per day
(includes paddle, PFD)	$55 per weekend
	$150 per week
Kayak Carriers	$10

Beaches

Great Lakes, inland lakes and hundreds of miles of shoreline fill Northwest Michigan so you're never too far from a friendly beach. Many locals keep their beach bags, folding chairs, sand toys and towels in their trunks all season just in case the urge to spend a few minutes (or hours!) at the shore strikes. Beaches — large and small — can be found in virtually every community up north. Many are part of larger state or community parks and include picnic areas, playgrounds, restrooms and other facilities. We discussed a number of these in depth in our Parks and Preserves chapter, but are briefly listing our favorites again below.

Grand Traverse

Traverse City Area

Bryant Park
Peninsula Dr. and Garfield Ave., Traverse City

Bryant Park is one of Traverse City's most popular family parks with a central location overlooking West Bay. Picnic tables, grills, play equipment and modern restrooms are on site.

Clinch Park Beach
Grandview Parkway between Union and Park Sts., Traverse City

Clinch Park Beach stretches along West Bay just to the east from Clinch Park Zoo and Marina. Since it runs parallel to downtown's busy Front Street, the beach is highly popular with visitors who split their time along the shore and in the stores. You'll find picnic tables, park benches, restrooms and a concession stand. Parking is available in the lots across Grandview Parkway. A pedestrian underpass takes you from side to side.

East Bay Beach
East End of Front St., Traverse City

This is a great beach for children, with much play equipment, a large sandy beach and shallow East Bay waters. Picnic tables and restrooms are also on site. To find the beach, continue to the left on Front Street after the main road forks to the right, curving into Munson Avenue. Follow it for several residential blocks until it ends at the beach. It is also accessible by turning north from Munson Avenue onto Eighth Street, and then west onto East Bay Boulevard.

Elmwood Township Park
Mich. Hwy. 22, Traverse City

Elmwood Township Park overlooking West Grand Traverse Bay is a pleasant spot to spend the day or a leisurely afternoon. Picnic pavilions are perfect for groups to gather, while little ones love the play equipment, beach and resident ducks. You'll find the park off Mich. Highway 22, approximately a mile north of the Mich. Highway 72 intersection. The park is next to the Elmwood Township Marina.

Gilbert Park
North Long Lake Rd., Traverse City

Gilbert Park is directly across from Long Lake Grocery Store (9374 N. Long Lake Road) approximately 8 miles west of Traverse City. It is a beautiful, large, sandy beach on the shores of Long Lake. This spot is a local favorite for its warmer inland waters, and because it is not as well-known among visitors as the city beaches along the bays. Picnic tables and restrooms are available.

Old Mission Lighthouse Park/ Hasserot Park
End of Mich. Hwy. 37 at Old Mission

This beach brings you to the tip of the Old Mission Peninsula and on the line of the 45th Parallel, exactly halfway between the Equator and the North Pole. The narrow beach stretches along the scenic shores of West Grand Traverse Bay. Families might prefer Hasserot Park, also off Mich. Highway 37, just a couple of miles before Lighthouse Park, where you'll find picnic tables, restrooms and a playground along with another beach.

Traverse City State Park Beach
U.S. Hwy. 31 N. and Three Mile Rd., Traverse City • (616) 922-5270

This popular beach stretches along 700 feet of beautiful East Bay shoreline across the street (U.S. Highway 31 N.) from the Traverse City State Park. Many locals buy a state park sticker each year just to use this wonderful beach and the one at Interlochen State Park (see subsequent listing). Picnic tables and restrooms are available. Parking is convenient and plentiful.

West End Beach
Grandview Pkwy. and Division St., Traverse City

West End Beach and surrounding public spaces epitomize the ambiance of Traverse City. The swimming area, restrooms and parking lot are just west of the busy intersection of Grandview Parkway and Division Street, but the sandy, public shoreline actually extends eastward for more than half a mile to the Open Space. The West Bay shore is buffered by grassy knolls that lie between it and the TART Trail and Grandview Parkway that run parallel. Friendly activity is constant and contagious!

Bayside Park
U.S. Hwy. 31 N., south of Mich. Hwy. 72, Acme

Bayside Park is a pleasant beach and roadside park on East Grand Traverse Bay. Picnic tables, restrooms and play equipment help make your stay pleasant.

Interlochen State Park
Mich. Hwy. 137, across from Interlochen Center for the Arts, Interlochen
• (616) 276-9511

Interlochen State Park's beach sits along the inland shores of Duck Lake. The beach area is quite large, with ample picnic facilities, a playground, restrooms and shaded areas. You can easily spend all day here.

Whitewater Township Park
Elk Lake Rd. off Mich. Hwy. 72, Williamsburg • (616) 267-5091

Rural Whitewater Township is home to this pleasant beach and picnic area. The park is open from mid-May through mid-September.

Leelanau County

Empire Village Park and South Bar Lake
End of Niagara St., Empire

These beaches lie across the street from each other in the tiny village of Empire. South Bar features a nice sandy beach on a warm inland lake, while Empire Beach stretches along the Lake Michigan shoreline with picnic tables, a playground and restrooms. Sleeping Bear Dunes National Lakeshore is just a stone's throw away.

Northport Beach
Naganoba St., Northport

Northport Beach is a pleasant beach right on the edge of the village's charming downtown. To find it, simply follow the main street,

Naganoba, until it ends at the park. Picnic tables, restrooms and play equipment are available.

Suttons Bay Municipal Park and Beach
Front St. between Grove and Adams Sts., Suttons Bay

This municipal beach is one of our favorite spots to spend a Saturday afternoon. The picnic area is shaded and the play equipment is right near the shore. Downtown is just a few steps away. To find the beach, drive (or walk!) down St. Joseph Street in the shopping area and turn east on either Grove or Adam St.; both are side streets that end at the park.

www.insiders.com

See this and many other **Insiders' Guide®** destinations online — in their entirety.

Visit us today!

Antrim-Kalkaska

Elk Rapids County Park
Bayshore Dr. off U.S. Hwy. 31, Elk Rapids

This great family park is tucked along the Elk Rapids shores of East Grand Traverse Bay with a large, sandy beach, playground, picnic areas and restrooms. Wooded trails offer a scenic respite from the sun.

Otsego Lake County Park
W. Otsego Lake Dr., Gaylord

Otsego Lake County Park is where Gaylord-area families gather for a day at the beach. Otsego Lake is a large inland lake, and this beach is tucked into a quieter corner with fewer boaters and jet-skiers passing by. Playground equipment, picnic tables, barbecue pits and restrooms stand near the beach's edge.

Lake Michigan Shoreline and Cadillac

Lake Michigan Beach
end of Main St., Frankfort

An expansive sandy beach surrounded by gorgeous rugged coastal dunes makes swimming here refreshing for the body and the soul. Park swings, a great historic lighthouse and pier, all within walking distance to Frankfort's marina, shops and restaurants make this beach a great place to enjoy an entire day.

Beulah Village Beach
Beulah

While northern Michigan can boast of numerous beautiful lakes, few compare to the clear waters of Crystal Lake. The Beulah Beach in downtown Beulah offers swimming, a beach house, picnic facilities and a nearby boat launch.

Douglas Park/First Street Beach
end of First St., Manistee

Manistee's beaches along Lake Michigan are among the best, yet least known, in the north. Douglas Park features wide, sandy strips of uncrowded beach offering picnic facilities, playground equipment and ball courts. Lifeguards are on duty daily during summer months.

Fifth Avenue Beach
Manistee

Manistee oozes history, even at its beaches.

INSIDERS' TIP

Biking between peninsulas? The Mackinac Bridge Authority will provide transportation for groups of up to 11 riders. When you arrive at the bridge, stop at the toll plaza on the north end or use the pay phone on the south end to notify the Authority. Groups of 11 riders or more require an advance permit and will be escorted across the bridge. Permit requests must be made in writing to: Executive Secretary, Mackinac Bridge Authority, P.O. Box 217, St. Ignace, MI 49781. The bike toll is $1 per bike and rider.

The Fifth Avenue beach features the North Pier Lighthouse and Catwalk, which is listed on the State Registry of Historic Sites. Lifeguards are posted daily during summer at this great swimming beach. You'll also find a playground, a picnic area, and tennis and volleyball courts. To find the beach, turn west on Monroe Street from U.S. Highway 31, and follow it to the end.

Lake Michigan Recreation Area
Manistee Ranger District
• **(616) 723-2211**

Enjoy a mile of uncrowded, uncluttered, natural Lake Michigan coastline. Bordering 450 acres of the Manistee National Forest, this beach offers good swimming with hiking trails, picnic facilities and camping in the adjacent area.

Stearns Park
end of Ludington Ave., Ludington

You just won't find beaches anywhere in the world more awesome than those in the Ludington area. Stearns Park offers 2,500 feet of fine white Lake Michigan beach in the heart of downtown Ludington. Swim areas are marked and lifeguards are posted. Playground equipment, picnic facilities and ball courts are all found at the park.

Kenwood Beach
North Blvd. off Mich. Hwy. 115, Cadillac

A good family swimming area along Lake Cadillac, Kenwood Beach posts lifeguards daily during summer months. There's shady beach for Mom and Dad and plenty of sandy shoreline for sun lovers. Picnic facilities, a boat launch and hiking trails are all here nestled in tall stands of northern hardwoods.

Missaukee County Park
Lake City • (616) 839-4945

An Insiders' favorite, Missaukee County Park Beach along Lake Missaukee offers nice inland swimming. The shallow shoreline is especially good for small children. Swim areas are well-marked and protected from boaters. The park offers playground equipment, picnic facilities and a boat launch. It is open May through October, and there is a $1 entry fee.

Little Traverse

Ferry Beach
corner of Ferry Ave. and Stover Rd., Charlevoix

Whether you prefer bathing in the sun or shade, Ferry Beach has it your way. On the shores of beautiful Lake Charlevoix, it's a good spot for young swimmers. Lifeguards are posted and diving is permitted from the pier. Playground equipment, picnic facilities and concessions area all available.

Elm Pointe
East Jordan

Elm Pointe Beach is along the south arm of Lake Charlevoix in an 11-acre park. In one of East Jordan's most lovely parks, this beach offers good swimming and picnic facilities, an art and a historic museum.

Magnus Park Beach
901 W. Lake St., Petoskey
• **(616) 347-1027**

Magnus Beach stretches along the incomparable Little Traverse Bay and is a part of the city's Magnus campground facility. Open to the public, it's a Insiders' favorite for strolling and hunting Petoskey stones.

Zorn Park Beach
151 W. Bay St., Harbor Springs
• **(616) 526-7999**

Zorn Park Beach is a sandy municipal beach on the harbor front. A lifeguard is posted daily during summer months and swimming is excellent. It offers picnic facilities and a brand new beach house.

Boat Rentals and Water Toys

Tall ships, yachts, row boats, power boats, paddle boats, rafts, jet skis (about anything that floats) can be found in Northwest Michigan waters providing endless water recreation opportunities. But you should know Michigan law requires all motorboats, sailboats and privately owned rowboats more than 16 feet in length be registered if Michigan is the state of principal use. Applications are available at any Secretary of State office, located in most communities. Check local phone books and call for hours. Depending on the craft, registration fees range from $9 to $448.

A complete guide to Michigan boating regulations can be obtained from Michigan Department of Natural Resources offices. District offices are in Cadillac, (616) 775-9727, and Gaylord, (616) 732-3541. If you choose to rent a watercraft, we've included a selection of boat rental sources and canoe liveries. These are staffed by friendly Insiders who are willing to help you make the most of your outdoor experience.

Grand Traverse

Traverse City Area

Aqua Dog Boat Rental
1941 U.S. Hwy. 31 N., Traverse City
• (616) 938-2826
Aqua Dog is right on the shore of East Grand Traverse Bay behind the Knights Inn. You can rent Sea-Doo Jet Skis, Sea-Doo Sportster Jet Boats and paddle boats on an hourly basis and pontoon boats for a minimum of two hours. Half-day rates are available. All rentals include safety equipment and one free tank of gas.

Brick Wheels
736 E. Eighth St., Traverse City
• (616) 947-4274
Brick Wheels rents wake boards for boats. The boards are used in lieu of water skis, functioning in the same way a snowboard does. The teen crowd made them highly popular.

Break 'N Waves
1265 U.S. Hwy. 31 N., Traverse City
• (616) 929-2539
You'll find Break 'N Waves right on the beach in front of the Bay Winds Restaurant and across the street from the Traverse City State Park. Whether your tastes run from a leisurely float to wave-making Jet Skis, you can rent your choice of watercraft here. Pontoon boats, jet boats, Hobie Cat sailboats, paddle boats and Sea-Doos are all available.

Jet Sport and Recreation
833 E. Front St., Traverse City
• (616) 947-2900
Relax on the beach at the Bayshore Resort, while you take turns playing with the water toys from Jet Sport and Recreation. You can rent Jet Skis, jet boats and paddle boats. Instruction is provided on site. Reservations are recommended, but walk-ins are welcome.

Ruby's Water Sports Rental
2061 U.S. Hwy. 31 N., Traverse City
• (616) 938-1100
You'll find Ruby's Water Sports Rentals at the Waterfront Inn on East Grand Traverse Bay. Rentals include Polaris 650 SL Watercraft for one or two riders, paddle boats for up to four passengers and paddle boards for one. Hourly and ½-hour rates are available. Paid reservations are accepted for the day of use.

Sail and Power Boat Rental
Coal Dock 8, 13255 W. Bayshore Dr., Traverse City • (616) 929-1717
This is your connection for boating on West Bay. You can rent Sea-Doo GTS jet skis, Sea-Doo Jet Boats, 20- to 24-foot pontoon boats, 12- to 19-foot power boats, 14- to 24-foot sail boats, sail boards and motors. Water skis, tubes, knee boards and wet suits are also available for an additional charge. Fees are calculated on an hourly, daily and weekly basis. Advance reservations are recommended. Delivery can be arranged for rentals lasting eight hours or more. If you're interested in boating lessons or a personal charter, a USCG-licensed captain is happy to accommodate. Sail and Power Boat Rental is directly across from Harbor Boat Shop on West Grand Traverse Bay.

Leelanau County

On the Narrows Marina
8137 S. Glen Lake Rd., Glen Arbor
• (616) 334-4891
Watercraft in all shapes and sizes are ready for renting at On the Narrows Marina. The marina serves Big and Little Glen Lakes with rentals, marine supplies, bait, tackle, picnic fare and clothing. You'll find 15- to 19-foot power boats, Sea-Doo personal watercraft, pontoon

Photo: Mackinac Island Chamber of Commerce

Mackinac Island's harbor is a bustling port.

boats, small sailboats, 12- to 16-foot fishing boats, Mistral sailboards, paddle boats, kayaks, canoes, motors and wet suits available by reservation by the day or week. Half-day and two-hour rentals are available on a first come, first served basis. Life jackets and safety equipment is provided. Security deposits are required.

Antrim-Kalkaska

Riverside Marina
115 Cayuga St., Bellaire
• **(616) 533-8559**

You'll find Riverside Marina on the river in downtown Bellaire, where you can rent power boats, pontoons, jet skis and other watercraft to help you explore the Antrim County's Chain of Lakes.

Torch River Marine
12906 Cherry Ave., Rapid City
• **(616) 322-4495**

Torch River Marine rents pontoons, ski boats, fishing boats, sailboats and jet skis from its boat shop on the south end of Torch Lake. Rentals are available on an hourly, daily, weekly or monthly basis. If you're in the market for your own watercraft, you'll also find sales and service for Chris Craft, Crownline, Sun Cruiser, Baja and Sea Nymph oats as well as Mercury, MerCruiser, OMC, Johnson, Force and Volvo engines.

Lake Michigan Shoreline and Cadillac

Crystal Lake Marina Inc.
7271 Crystal Dr., Beulah
• **(616) 882-9636**

Open seven days during the summer peak season, Crystal Lake Marina rents WaveRunners, pontoons, ski boats and butterfly-class sail boats. Rental options include hourly, daily and weekly rentals.

Portage Point Inn
8513 S. Portage Point Rd., Onekama
• **(800) 878-7248**

Nestled on the shores of Portage Lake and along a channel to Lake Michigan, Portage Point Inn watercraft rentals provide fun on both the inland lake and the Great Lake. Rentals are offered dawn to dusk, and you'll find a nice array of options including catamarans, WaveRunners, rowboats, speed boats and pontoons. Reservations are strongly encouraged.

North Bayou Resort
4849 N. Lakeshore Dr., Ludington
• **(616) 845-5820**

Hamlin Lake is known for its excellent fishing. The people of North Bayou Resort are happy to help you enjoy this little piece of angler's heaven. They rent fishing boats and motors, pontoons and jet skis from May through October. Options range from half-hour to weekly packages.

Waterside Resort and Marina
3298 N. Lakeshore Dr., Ludington
• **(616) 843-8481**

If you enjoy fishing with a party, rent one of Waterside Resort's large pontoons featuring an 18-person capacity. If you prefer solitude, they also offer fishing boat rentals, but for the more active crowd, reserve a 5-passenger jet boat. Rental options include hourly daily and weekly options and reservations are encouraged.

Pilgrim's Village
181 S. Lake Mitchell Dr., Cadillac
• **(616) 775-5412**

From Pilgrim's Village you can access two great fishing lakes, Lake Cadillac and Lake Mitchell. The Village offers fishing boat rentals, and their shop offers everything under the sun in bait and tackle. So, don't worry about bringing gear from home. Just hop in the car and come north. Rentals are available on a daily or weekly basis and are equipped with a 4- to 10- horsepower Mercury motor. Reservations are encouraged.

Track & Trail
6600 E. Mich. Hwy. 115, Cadillac
• **(616) 775-7880**

Rent a pontoon from Track & Trail for a party, a leisurely cruise or an easygoing fishing adventure. Rentals offer access to both lakes Cadillac and Mitchell for a double-good time. Pontoons feature a 12-person capacity and are available by the day or week.

Little Traverse

Jordan Valley Outfitters
311 N. Lake St., East Jordan
• **(616) 536-0006**

Jordan Valley Outfitters offers kayaks, tubes, canoes and rafts with a capacity for 6 adults. Options range from hourly to day-long rentals. The outfitter is across the street from the south arm of Lake Charlevoix. Guided lake tours are available.

Windjammer Marina and Sports Center
3654 Oden Rd., Oden • **(616) 347-6103**

Travel the 40-mile-long inland waterway from Crooked Lake to Lake Huron with rental craft from Windjammer Marina. The beautiful trip traverses three lakes and three rivers. Just 6 miles north of Petoskey, Windjammer offers you daily, weekly and monthly rentals of houseboats, pontoons, ski boats, personal watercraft and fishing boats. Reservations are strongly encouraged.

INSIDERS' TIP

During spring treks down the trails, keep your eyes open for Northwest Michigan's unique wildflower, the trillium. This gentle flower blankets our forest floors for just a few weeks in May before disappearing until the next spring. You'll know it for its distinctive three petaled, white bloom and sturdy, 8-inch-tall stem.

Swan Valley Marina
02474 Mich. Hwy. 66 S., East Jordan
• (616) 536-2672

Swan Valley Marina offers a good variety of boating options for Lake Charlevoix. It rents 24-foot pontoons, powerful ski boats, classic fishing boats and Sea-Doos. Sea-Doos rent by the hour and other crafts are rented by the half-day, day or week.

Mackinac Straits

Waterventures Watercraft Rentals
11476 U.S. Hwy. 23, Mackinaw City
• (616) 436-7144

You're bound to find the water toys to make your vacation take sail at Waterventures Watercraft Rentals. Yamaha Jet Boats, Yamaha WaveRunners, Hobie Cat Sailboats, a 30-foot Aqua Jump water trampoline and paddle boats are a sampling of the possibilities. Free sailing lessons help you learn the ropes before you hit the water.

Mackinac Adventure Company, Inc.
1141 N. State St., St. Ignace
• (906) 643-7840, (800) 446-8938, (800) I GOT WET

WaveRunner rentals are the specialty at Mackinac Adventure Company. Jump on board and enjoy the fun on Lake Huron. An instructional video and friendly staff help first timers. Wet suits are included with rentals. Mackinac Adventure Company also rents paddleboats for fun at a slower pace.

Canoes/Kayaks/Tubes

Northwest Michigan's lakes and rivers are a water playground for anglers, skiers, sailors, cruisers and canoeists. To ensure public safety and environmental integrity our world-class waterways are governed by various regulations. The beautiful Pere Marquette and the Pine river are both classified National Wild and Scenic rivers, and, as a result, are subject to certain rules. Persons entering these waterways between May 15 and September 15 with any type of floating device, whether inner tube, raft, canoe, kayak or any other type of craft, must have a permit. The permits are free and

can be obtained from the Baldwin Ranger District station at 650 N. Michigan Avenue in Baldwin, or the Cadillac district office at (616) 775-8539. River hours for the two waterways are from 9 AM to 6 PM. In 1997, more than 3,000 permits were issued for use of the Pine River alone. To avoid overuse and protect the natural resource for future generations, waterway traffic is limited on the two rivers. Rangers strongly suggest you call ahead to secure reservations for your adventure. There are no fees for use.

Grand Traverse

Several rivers weave and flow through the Grand Traverse area including the Upper and Lower Platte, Crystal, Boardman, Betsie and Jordan rivers. The most challenging is the narrow, fast-moving Upper Platte River, with many quick turns and overhanging branches. Plan to get wet on this one because half of the canoes that travel it tip over. Average depth is only 2 to 3 feet, but experience in maneuvering is a must. The Lower Platte is more family-friendly, with a gentle current that passes through Loon Lake and the Sleeping Bear Dunes National Lakeshore on its trek toward Lake Michigan.

The Crystal River is a lovely, shallow stream, with a gentle current that makes it ideal for families and novices. Its tree-lined course flows through the heart of the Sleeping Bear Dunes National Lakeshore. Nearer to Traverse City, the Boardman River is shallow with a moderate current that flows through the Pere Marquette State Forest south of town, past Logan's Landing and into Boardman Lake before continuing through the heart of town, emptying into West Grand Traverse Bay. Further south and west, the Betsie River winds through the wooded forests between Interlochen and Frankfort. Veterans recommend that beginners stay with routes along the river's upper portion. The Jordan River takes us to the eastern side of our Grand Traverse boundaries in scenic Antrim County. The waters stretch from the Jordan River Valley northward to Ellsworth.

Now that we've introduced you to our rivers, let's tell you more about them and the liveries that serve them. The major liveries are listed individually below.

Traverse City Area

Ranch Rudolf
6841 Brown Bridge Rd., Traverse City
• **(616) 947-9529**

Ranch Rudolf's many recreational activities (see listings above and in our Winter Recreation and Kidstuff chapters) include jaunts down the Boardman River in the Pere Marquette National Forest. Tubing at Ranch Rudolf has been dubbed "Rump Bumping" and takes riders on 2- and 4-mile trips lasting one to three hours. Canoeing runs measure 4 and 9 miles and last approximately 1½ to 3½ hours. Ranch Rudolf is open year round, but canoeing runs between May and October.

Alvina's Canoe and Boat Livery
6470 Betsie River Rd., Interlochen
• **(616) 276-9514**

Alvina's Canoes and Boats leads you to the Betsie River with trips appropriate for beginning and intermediate paddlers. Runs last from one to four hours with canoes, kayaks and boats available for rental. Alvina's is usually open from Memorial Day weekend until late September.

Leelanau County

Crystal River Canoe Livery
6052 Western Ave., Glen Arbor
• **(616) 334-3090**

Enjoy the sparkling water of the Crystal River with trips through the Sleeping Bear Dunes National Lake Shore via Crystal River Canoe Livery. These are great trips for beginning paddlers, with runs lasting 1½ to 2½ hours. Canoes, kayaks and tubes are available for family fun. Car spotting and bus service is available. Crystal River Canoe Livery opens in early May and runs through mid-October.

Riverside Canoe Trips
Mich. Hwy. 22, Honor • **(616) 325-5622**

Riverside Canoe Livery is the place to begin your fun on the Platte River in the Sleeping Bear Dunes National Lakeshore. River trips last two to four hours with beginner runs down the gentle Lower Platte and longer, advanced journeys down the fast-moving Upper Platte.

Tube trips that are great for families take place on the Lower Platte with a 50-minute "Loon and Walk" combining a fun float with a short walk through the woods, and "Weir to Lake Michigan," a two-hour float directly to Lake Michigan beach. Rentals are also available for canoes, kayaks, tubes, 2- to 6-person rafts, paddle boards, motorboats and row boats with placement and pickup service available for private canoes. Reservations are recommended, with cancellations due at least two days in advance for refunds. Group cancellations are due at least 10 days in advance. Riverside is open early May through mid-October.

Antrim-Kalkaska

Swiss Hideaway
Gray's Crossing Rd. east of Mich. Hwy. 66, Mancelona • **(616) 536-2341**

Swiss Hideaway serves the gentle, scenic Jordan River from its rural Mancelona area livery. River trips last one to three hours and can take place via canoe, kayak or tube. Car spotting and bus service is offered. Swiss Hideaway is open from the first of May through late October.

Lake Michigan Shoreline and Cadillac

Manistee River
Manistee Ranger District Station, 412 Red Apple Rd., Manistee
• **(616) 723-2211**

The Manistee River is a designated Wild and Scenic River flowing through the Huron-Manistee National Forest in southern Manistee County, through the western boundaries of Wexford County, through Manistee Lake and into Lake Michigan. Between Hodenpyl Dam, near Mesick and Tippy Dam near Brethren, the river is characterized by steep banks and numerous sharp bends. This segment of the river is ideal for novice canoeists and those who like to float wide, swift waters. Below Tippy Dam, there is a wider stream channel and slow, wide bends that are also excellent for novice canoeist. The river offers 46 canoeable miles with access and facilities such as restrooms, campsites and launches, at eight points, including Hodenpyl Dam Pond, Red Bridge, two points at Tippy dam, High Bridge, Blacksmith Bayou, Bear Creek and Rainbow Bend. From these points, float time ranges from 1½ to 4 hours. Boating season on the river is from May 1 to October 1. On weekends and holidays canoe traffic on this river is moderate, but during weekdays you'll find more seclusion. Check with the Manistee Ranger District for maps and seasonal information before launching.

Little Manistee River
Manistee Ranger Station, 412 Red Apple Rd., Manistee • (616) 723-2211

The Little Manistee River offers gorgeous scenery, good fishing and opportunities for viewing wildlife. The river flows through southern Manistee County and northern Lake and Mason counties, emptying into Manistee Lake. River banks are covered with lowland brush, conifers, pine and oaks. Canoeists should be aware that this river has many dangerous bends and water levels can be shallow during dry summer months. The beautiful Little Manistee River offers 85 canoeable miles with float time from access points ranging from 1 hour to 3½ hours. There are seven major access sites along the river, including Driftwood Valley Campground, Eighteen Mile Bridge, Bear Track Campground, Nine Mile Bridge, Six Mile Bridge, Old Stronach Bridge and Stronach Township Park. While the canoeing season ranges from May 1 to October 1, call the Manistee Ranger Station for seasonal updates.

Big Sauble River
Manistee Ranger District, 412 Red Apple Rd., Manistee • (616) 723-2211

The Big Sable River is known for offering good opportunities for viewing native wildlife. Along its 37 scenic miles you may catch sight of deer, raccoon, otter, beaver, woodchuck and a wonderful variety of songbirds. The Big Sable flows through western Lake County and northern Mason county emptying into Hamlin Lake and Lake Michigan. There are 10 road crossings where you can launch a canoe, but no developed access sites at theses cross-

ings. From the various launch points, float time ranges from 30 minutes to 3½ hours.

Pere Marquette River
Baldwin Ranger District, 650 N. Michigan Ave., Baldwin • (616) 745-4631

The Pere Marquette River was designated a National Scenic River in 1980. A fairly swift river with plenty of bends, it is a favorite with novice canoeists, kayakers and anglers. The river offers 66 miles of clean, sparkling water flowing through the Manistee National Forest in Lake and Mason counties. As you canoe this, you'll enjoy the unsurpassed beauty of stately hardwoods, sandy beaches and pine-scented banks. About 9 miles downstream from Baldwin, canoeists encounter Rainbow Rapids, 5 minutes of easy-to-navigate mini-rapids. There are 13 marked landings along the river, and restrooms, parking, picnic areas and campsites are available. Float time from access points ranges from 25 minutes to 6 hours. For maps, contact the Baldwin Ranger Station or the Ludington Convention and Visitors Bureau at (800) 542-4600.

Pine River
Baldwin Ranger Station, 650 N. Michigan Ave. • (616) 745-4631

A designated National Scenic River, the Pine has a national reputation as a premier canoeing waterway. Traveling for 60 miles through southern Wexford, southeastern Manistee and northern Lake counties, the river features many sharp bends, short choppy riffles, log and debris jams. A section from the Dobson launch south features Class 2 white-water rapids. Only advanced canoeists should consider experiencing the Pine River. The U.S. Forest Service has four access sites along the pine and the Michigan Department of Natural Resources has three landings. Like other designation National Scenic Rivers, a permit is required for enjoying water sports between May and October. Permits can be obtained by calling the Baldwin Ranger Station, (616) 745-4631, or by visiting a U.S. Forest Service station in Baldwin, Cadillac or Manistee. See the introduction to the this section for more information regarding use of this National Scenic River.

Wilderness Canoes
6052 Riverview Rd., Mesick
- **(616) 885-1485, (800) 873-6379**

Wilderness Canoes offers trips ranging from one hour to 10 days in length for beginners as well as experienced canoeists. Feature excursions include the Family, Waterfall and Island, Nature and High Roll-Away trips. The livery is along the Big Manistee River and is open from May 1 to October 31. Trips begin at 8 AM daily, or earlier by reservation. For those who own canoes, placement and pickup service is available. For other river adventures, Wilderness rents kayaks and tubes, and group rental rates are available.

Chippewa Landing
371 N. Turnerville Rd., Lake City
- **(616) 839-5511**

For 20 years Chippewa Landing has been providing outdoor enthusiasts with excellent canoeing adventures along the relatively unsettled Manistee River. Whether you want an easygoing afternoon trip or an exciting overnight campout, Chippewa Landing will help you plan, explore and enjoy the area's great natural resources. The livery is open from May 1 to mid-October, weekends only during the shoulder seasons, and daily from Memorial Day to Labor Day.

Sportsman's Port Canoe Campgrounds
Rural Rt. No. 1, W. Caberfae Hwy., Wellston • (616) 862-3571

A convenient livery and campground along the challenging Pine River, Sportsman's Port offers canoeing through federal, state and private land. Camping, fishing, swimming and hiking are also available. They accommodate special requests, offer good rates for two-day trips and spot for those owning their own canoes.

Baldwin Canoe Rental
3 miles south of Baldwin on Mich. Hwy. 37 • (616) 745-4669

Baldwin Canoe Rental offers water adventures along the Pere Marquette, a designated National Wild and Scenic River. It operates from April 1 through October during the regulated river hours of 9 AM to 6 PM. You can rent kayaks and rafts with a capacity of six. You'll find some good weekly group rates here and spotting service for those who own canoes.

Little Traverse

Bear River
Emmet County

Bear River has long been known for great trout fishing. It was a favorite fishing spot for one of Little Traverse's most famous Insiders, author Ernest Hemingway. The Bear begins at Walloon Lake in Emmet County and flows to Lake Michigan. A calm, gentle river, it's good for family canoeing experiences, but it's the great wildlife viewing opportunities that seem to bring people back. The river area abounds with deer, possum, mink, raccoon, turtles, owls as well as some unique bird species and rare flowers. Water depth averages from 2 to 6.5 feet as the river weaves and winds through lovely forests. For more information, call the Michigan Department of Natural Resources Gaylord office at (517) 732-3541.

Bear River Canoe Livery
2517 McDougal Rd., Petoskey
- **(616) 347-9038**

The only livery on the Bear River, Bear River Canoe Livery offers friendly service and very reasonable rates. You may be lucky enough to engage a special guide during your canoe trip from here. For the past 18 years, a resident blue heron has been following livery canoeists on their trips from journey's start to end. The graceful natural guide doesn't miss a day! Canoe rentals begin mid-April and are available through mid-November. Hours of operation are 8 AM to 8 PM, but owners will accommodate your schedule if you call ahead. For those who own canoes the livery offers spotting services for a nominal fee.

Mackinac Straits

Sturgeon River

Many consider the Sturgeon River to be the lower peninsula's fastest and most challenging river. Its fast current carries adventurous paddlers northward from the

Vanderbilt area north of Gaylord through Wolverine and continues until it flows into Burt Lake near Indian River. Experienced canoeists and kayakers will find the Sturgeon to be narrow and swift, but manageable with many undercut banks and deep bends. The Pigeon River offers a more relaxing float as it flows through the beautiful Pigeon River Country State Forest.

Sturgeon and Pigeon River Outfitters
4271 S. Straits Hwy., Indian River
• **(616) 238-8181**

Sturgeon and Pigeon River Outfitters is your one-stop shop for fun on the rivers it's named after. You can rent all the gear for canoe, kayak and tube trips, or participate in one arranged by the outfitters. One of the newest options is family rafting trips. You can find Sturgeon and Pigeon River Outfitters approximately 27 miles south of Mackinaw City just off the Indian River Exit 310 from I-75. It's open from the first of May to mid-October.

Color Tours

Grand Traverse

Traverse City/Northport/Frankfort

The colors near Traverse City begin to peak in late September and are in blazing glory through mid-October. We've outlined a colorful trip that will take you through Grand Traverse, Leelanau and Benzie counties with a route totaling close to 190 miles.

There are two distinct portions of the tour, which can be taken separately or together: First, a trip up and down Traverse City's Old Mission Peninsula; and second, a large westward loop linking all three counties.

The first leg starts in the heart of Traverse City. You will travel the full 27-mile length of the Old Mission Peninsula along Mich. Highway 37 to Old Mission Lighthouse, and then turn around and return along the same route.

For the second leg, let's begin again in the Traverse City limits at the base of the Old Mission Peninsula. Follow Mich. Highway 37 until it intersects with Mich. Highway 72 and U.S.

Highway 31 (East Front Street) where you should turn west; continue onto Grandview Parkway and then toward Suttons Bay via Mich. Highway 22. Go north on Mich. Highway 22 (West Bayshore Drive) and drive along the West Grand Traverse Bay shoreline through the charming villages of Suttons Bay, Omena and Northport. In Northport, Mich. Highway 22 meets County Road 201, which will take you to the end of the peninsula at Leelanau State Park.

Head back south to Mich. Highway 22 in Northport and go south on the western side of the Mich. 22 loop as it meanders along the Lake Michigan shoreline, through the villages of Leland, Glen Arbor and Empire. You'll pass the Sleeping Bear Dunes National Lakeshore and the well-marked entrance to the Pierce Stocking scenic drive. If you have time, take a lovely half-hour detour off this route and follow the Pierce Stocking Drive to see the National Lakeshore and its surrounding forests and hills bursting in full autumn splendor. (For more information on Stocking Drive, see the Sleeping Bear Dunes National Lakeshore listing in the Hiking and Biking section of this chapter.)

Back on Mich. Highway 22, another 20 miles south will lead you to the Pt. Betsie Lighthouse and into Frankfort where Mich. Highway 22 intersects with Mich. Highway 115. Take Mich. 115 east past the Crystal River to Benzonia and southeast to Copemish. In Copemish go northeast on Mich. Highway 137 past Karlin, the Interlochen State Park, Interlochen Center for the Arts and Grawn, where Mich. 137 intersects with U.S. 31. Follow U.S. 31 north back into Traverse City.

Grayling/Torch Lake/Lake City

This tour goes through Antrim and Kalkaska counties beginning at the eastern outskirts of Traverse City near Bunker Hill Rd. on U.S. 31 North. This trip will touch on destinations that are just on the opposite side of our Insiders' boundaries in Grayling and on the northern fringes of Missaukee and Wexford counties in the Lake Michigan Shoreline and Cadillac area. The entire loop stretches about 170 miles.

Let's begin near the Traverse City State Park, at the intersection of Three Mile Road and U.S. Highway 31 N. and Mich. Highway 72 (Munson Avenue). Driving northeast along U.S. 31, you'll pass the last of the retail shops, eateries and hotels as you curve along East Grand Traverse Bay, past the Grand Traverse Resort and northward to Elk Rapids and Eastport. In Eastport, go west on Mich. Highway 88, and then quickly turn south on County Road 593, which will take you along the Torch Lake shoreline past Alden and Rapid City, eventually merging with Mich. 72. Once on Mich. Highway 72, drive east through the peaceful, rural Kalkaska county countryside and the tree-lined land leading to Grayling at I-75. Take I-75 south from Grayling and get on U.S. 27 near Higgins Lake. Continue south on U.S. 27 through Houghton Lake to Mich. 55. Go west on Mich. 55 to Lake City. From Lake City, take Mich. Highway 42 to Manton and then turn north onto U.S. 131 heading toward Traverse City via Fife Lake.

Lake Michigan Shoreline and Cadillac

Benzie County

Benzie County Chamber of Commerce at 826 Michigan Avenue, (616) 882-5801, offers color tour maps of the hills and woodlands of this uncommonly beautiful countryside. The Insiders' pick in Benzie County begins in the village of Beulah. From here, head north on U.S. Highway 31 to Indian Hill Road, just past the Cherry Bowl Drive-in Theater. Turn left on Indian Hill Road and travel one block to Dead Stream Road. Follow Dead Stream Road to Mich. Highway 22 until you reach Sutters Road. Travel along Sutters Road back to Mich. 22 all the way to Frankfort. Along this 15-mile route you'll encounter brilliant hardwoods accented by evergreens and two-color canopy tunnels, one over Dead Stream Road and another along Sutters Road. Mapped Benzie County tours feature four connecting loops allowing you to plan your own course.

Manistee County

For a spectacular autumn palette accented by the brilliant blue waters of Lake Michigan, plan a color tour in Manistee County. You'll find the county's fertile soil produces a mix of glowing hardwoods and provides fantastic views. The Manistee Chamber of Commerce at 11 Cypress Street, (616) 723-2575, offers maps outlining several stunning routes through the county. The Insiders' pick is a Lake Michigan tour beginning at Manistee and following Mich. 22 north around Portage Lake, through the community of Onekama, into the hilly countryside of Arcadia. Leave Arcadia by continuing north on Mich. 22. Turn left on Norman Road. You may want to explore this area going north at the east end of Norman Road or head north on Gilbert and Taylor roads. To continue from Norman Road, turn right on St. Pierre Road then left on Glovers Lake Road and go east for about 1 mile. Head right on Gilbert Road and stay on the paved road for 4.5 miles. The road name changes to Lumley, then Iverson and Norconk Road. From this course, turn south onto Butwell Road and follow to Bear Lake along Lakeside Avenue, which intersects with U.S. Highway 31. Follow U.S. 31 south to Manistee.

For the more active outdoors enthusiasts, another great Manistee tour is a trek along the Manistee River Trail. The hiking trail provides 11.6 miles of breathtaking autumn views.

Mason County

Autumn blankets the Mason County countryside in orange and red, an irresistible invitation to explore the county's varied landscapes and wonderful vistas. The Ludington Area Convention and Visitors Bureau at 5827 W. U.S. Highway 10, (800) 542-4600, can provide maps to help you plot a course through the county's dense forests and scenic coastal region. For an unforgettable tour, we suggest you drive west on U.S. Highway 10 through Ludington, turn north on Lakeshore Drive past Hamlin Lake. Hamlin Lake stretches for a full colorful 12 miles and is bordered on the north by the Manistee National Forest. From the lake, follow Dewey Road west to Jebavy Drive and go north to Barnhart Road. Then circle back along Sherman Road and Shagway. Go south on Jebavy Drive back to U.S. Highway 10 to South Pere Marquette Highway. At Iris Road go north to Lakeshore Drive to the Butterfield Penin-

Leaving No Stone Unturned

Michigan's state rock — the Petoskey stone — is found throughout Northwest Michigan, particularly in its namesake community. Petoskeys are noted for their distinctive honeycomb-like appearance and are often sought as Northern Michigan mementos.

Officially known as *Hexagonaria Percarinata*, Petoskey stones are actually fragments of petrified coral reefs that lived 350 million years ago in the warm, shallow seas

that covered the land from what is now Charlevoix to Alpena and northward. According to the Michigan Department of Environmental Quality, this specific fossil coral is found only in the rock strata known as the Gravel Point Formation of the Traverse Group of Devonian Age and is a mixture of limestone and shales. The outcrops of these rocks, which are restricted to the Little Traverse Bay area, created much of the region's bedrock. Scientists believe that Pleistocene glaciers plucked many Petoskeys and other rocks from the bedrock approximately 2 million years ago and spread them throughout the state.

Petoskey stones are primarily calcite, although quartz, pyrite and other minerals might also be present. Since the corals are found in limestone, a great deal of clay may be present.

These stones were born from soft living tissue or polyps with long tentacles appearing almost flowerlike. They hardened after the polyps secreted a limey substance and created a corallite skeleton with concave depressions where the polyps once lived. When these corallite skeletons combined, they formed a colony of corals known as a coralla. Petoskey stones are made of large corallas, bearing testimony to our region's prehistoric marine life.

The stones are silvery gray with edges that were rounded by ancient glaciers and centuries of water action. A unique ringlike design appears when the stones are wet, making it much easier to find Petoskeys under water, several feet from shore.

You can hunt for the rocks year round, but the best season for spotting these spotted stones is in the spring when you can forage through the remains of winter debris along shorelines.

One of the best places to hunt for Petoskey stones is in Fisherman's Island State Park near Charlevoix. Rocky limestone alternates with sandy beach along the park's picturesque 6-mile Lake Michigan shoreline, also known as Bell's Bay. The state park has 90 rustic campsites and 3,400 acres of undeveloped forests, cedar swamps and scenic overlooks. Park rangers hand out maps of the shoreline, along with information on Petoskey stones. The main entrance is on Bell's Bay Road, off U.S. Highway 31, 2 miles south of

Photo: Mary Gillett

The unique Petoskey Stone is Michigan's state stone.

— continued on next page

Charlevoix. To enter the park you must have an annual state park sticker, which costs $20, or a $4 day pass, either of which can be purchased and used at any state park.

Other great spots for rock hunting are the shorelines rimming Petoskey, especially those at Magnus City Park near downtown and at the south end of the beach at Petoskey State Park, off U.S. Highway 131 and Mich. Highway 119, northwest of Petoskey. There is no admission charge to Magnus Park, but Petoskey State Park, like Fisherman's Island, requires an annual sticker or day pass for entry.

Once you have a stone in hand, take it home as an up-north souvenir, or try your hand at rock polishing to show off your Petoskey in all its glory. Several toy and specialty stores, such as Enerdyne in Suttons Bay (see our Shopping chapter), sell simple rock-polishing kits, which are appropriate for the whole family.

If your hunting efforts leave you stoneless, you don't have to leave town empty-handed. Many gift shops sell polished stones and jewelry made with especially nice specimens. Read the Specialty Shop section of our Shopping chapter for some ideas, but don't be surprised to find Petoskey stones near cash registers in all types of shops, especially in Petoskey and Charlevoix.

Two other options are Davidson's Rock Shop at 531 Randolph Street in Traverse City, (616) 946-4520, and The Petoskey Stone Shop at 26 Shopper's Lane in Petoskey, (616) 347-8090. Davidson's Rock Shop is an old-fashioned rock shop. The owner cuts and shapes rocks into assorted shapes. She often keeps Petoskey stones in buckets of water outside the door, and passersby are welcome to take a sample. Polished and perfected specimens are sold indoors. The Petoskey Stone Shop features beautiful carvings, jewelry and polished stones. You can often observe owner Ron Blanchard sculpting works of art out of Petoskey stones. Blanchard has been featured on CNN and in *USA Today,* and is often sought as a resource on Petoskey stones.

sula, where famous explorer Father Pere Marquette died. See our Attractions chapter for more information, and check out the monument dedicated to this famous Jesuit priest. From here, head south again on Lakeshore Drive along the Lake Michigan shoreline to Bass Lake.

Wexford/Missaukee Counties

The Manistee National Forest contains a blend of colorful hardwoods and towering pines, which provide a picture-perfect color tour. Routes range from 20 to 64 miles and are marked with red and white tour signs posted along the route by the U.S. Forest Service. Excellent maps are available from the Huron-Manistee National Forest District Headquarters at 1755 S. Mitchell Street in Cadillac, (616) 775-2421, and at the Cadillac Area Chamber of Commerce at 222 N. Lake Street, (616) 775-9776. Routes in the Wexford-Missaukee region cross sparkling inland lakes and the scenic Manistee and

Pine rivers, and feature a lookout perch within the Caberfae hill range.

Little Traverse

Charlevoix County

There are many wonderful mapped color tours throughout Charlevoix County. An Insiders' favorite encircles beautiful Lake Charlevoix. The Charlevoix Area Chamber of Commerce at 408 Bridge Street, (616) 547-2101, will provide you with maps for several routes but to begin the 45-mile lake route, start at the intersection of U.S. Highway 31 and Mich. Highway 66 in Charlevoix. Travel south to East Jordan then turn left on Advance Road. Follow Advance Road to Lake Shore Road and turn right, following it into Boyne City. Stay on Lake Shore Road until you come to the Charlevoix/Boyne City road marked C-56. It will take you back into Charlevoix. The route promises a wonderful panorama of color and classic autumn vistas.

Emmet County

Emmet County features an array of unique color routes, including the Jordan River Valley tour, Circle Lake Charlevoix, a Tri-County tour and Surf and Turf, which is a tour of area lakes and family farms. Maps of incredible autumn vista tours are available from the Harbor Springs Chamber of Commerce at 205 State Street, (616) 526-7999, and the Petoskey Chamber of Commerce at 401 E. Mitchell Street, (616) 347-4150. One of the most breathtaking Emmet County fall landscapes is the "Tunnel of Trees." The glowing gold, red and oranges of birch, maple and oaks canopy a narrow, winding stretch of Mich. 119. To enjoy this tour, begin in Harbor Springs and head north on Mich. 119 to Cross Village. You may want to stop in Cross Village at the historic Legs Inn for refreshments or a meal. (See our Restaurants to learn more about the historic attraction.) From Legs Inn go straight to the first stop sign, then take a left to Lake Shore Drive. Follow Lake Shore Drive to Lakeview Road at Sturgeon Bay, where you can explore dunes and beaches. Continue until Lakeview Road becomes Gill Road, and from this point you can either return to Harbor Springs or extend your tour to Mackinaw City.

Mackinac Straits

Since Mackinaw City is so close to Petoskey and Charlevoix, these color tours overlap with the ones noted in our previous Little Traverse listings. Please check there for directions for lower peninsula tours.

St. Ignace/Whitefish Point/ Engadine

This Straits area color tour takes you into Michigan's upper peninsula and, at times, a bit out of our Insiders' boundaries. These areas that go beyond the St. Ignace area of our boundaries are included in the Daytrips chapter of this book.

The upper peninsula is magnificent in autumn, with colors reaching their vivid climax in late September and early October. The peninsula's low population coupled with heavy forests and spectacular scenery make it a much-sought-after site.

Start on the north side of the Mackinac Bridge in St. Ignace and head north on I-75 to County Road 123, just north of the St. Ignace area. Follow County Road 123 northwest for approximately 60 miles, passing through the Hiawatha National Forest, and the villages of Trout Lake, Eckerman and Paradise, before ending at Whitefish Point, which juts into Lake Superior. From Whitefish Point, backtrack to Paradise, then continue the County Road 123 loop by heading southeast for almost 45 miles through Tahquamenon Falls State Park and Newberry. Just south of Newberry, you'll reach Mich. Highway 28, where you will turn west. Travel on Mich. 28 for 3 miles, then go south on County Road 117 through Engadine and on to intersect with U.S. Highway 2. Heading east on U.S. 2, you'll travel along the Lake Michigan shoreline, which was noted by *USA Today* as one of the nation's top color tour routes. Along the 50-mile trek between Engadine and St. Ignace, you'll pass by Top of the Lake Roadside Park not far from Naubinway, which stands at Lake Michigan's northernmost tip. This entire tour measures 170 miles.

Foraging

May is a great time to enjoy the woodlands as winter gives way to the spring awakening, and mushrooming only makes it better. People flock from all corners of the state to participate Northwest Michigan's annual rite of spring, the wild morel mushroom pursuit. During this time, aspen forests and old apple orchards become happy hunting grounds for hundreds of foragers. Local communities honor the mushroom with festivals and northern chefs feature the delicacies in spring menus. Follow these guidelines, and if you're lucky, you'll be adding tender morel tidbits to your next omelet.

May is the month of the mushroom, but the emergence of the fungi depends on Mother Nature. Morels pop out of the forest floor following sunny spring days and misty nights. They are most often found in mixed stands of aspen, maple and birch, old apple orchards and along roadsides or power lines. The mushrooms grow 2 to 4 inches high and feature long ridges on the head, which can range from tan to black. Pits on the cap are longer than wide, forming up and down ridges along a pointed head. This species is called the true morel. Foragers must be aware that the forest also produces an inedible false morel, and you need to be able to distinguish between the varieties. True morels have a hollow head connected at the base to the hollow neck. False morels have a cap attached to the top of the stalk, which may flare out at the bottom like a bell or puff out and roll in. False morels feature fewer ridges or wrinkles than the true morel. If you are in doubt about your find, locals will be happy to help you. Ask at mushroom country chambers and businesses in the towns surrounding the Huron-Manistee National Forest. You can also check with the U.S. Forest Service or Michigan Department of Natural Resources for identifying information. Many bookstores in the region stock field guides, which can also provide guidance. Mushrooming is a wonderful spring outdoor adventure. Be forewarned, once you taste these fresh delicacies, you'll be hooked for life.

The community of Mesick in northwestern Wexford County is otherwise known as the Mushroom Capital of the world. The town celebrates the morel each Mother's Day weekend with the Mesick Area Mushroom Festival, an old-fashioned country event. In addition to awarding prizes for the largest mushroom picked, the festival features a parade, live music, carnival, flea market, arts and crafts fair, community breakfast, chicken barbecue, rodeo, horseshoe competition, softball and bingo. The spring event draws 10,000 mushroomers to the area each year to participate in this springtime tradition. For more information, contact the Mesick Area Mushroom Festival Committee, P.O. Box 538, Mesick, MI 49668.

Hiking and Biking

Many of Northwest Michigan's numerous hiking areas double as hot spots for off-road biking. Those trails that do double duty are noted. You'll find separate listing for wonderful northern treks that are for hikers only.

Bicycles are permitted on all Michigan highways except for posted limited-access freeways and roads. Bikes are also allowed on all road systems including those in state forests, state parks and recreation areas and national forest trails, unless otherwise posted. You'll find all-terrain bikes best suited for most public north country trails. Remember all laws that pertain to automobile drivers pertain to bicyclists. Typically, you'll find rentals available wherever there are good trails. See the chart in the introduction to this chapter for rental price information. You'll also find in-line skate rentals available at many bike rental sources.

Grand Traverse

Traverse City Area

Cherry Capital Cycling Club
(616) 941-BIKE

Local biking enthusiasts gather under the umbrella of the Cherry Capital Cycling Club to promote participation and create cycling opportunities in the Traverse area. Various membership sections address bicycle touring, recreational mountain biking and racing on and off the road. The club sponsors invitational rides like Ride Around Torch (R.A.T.) from Elk Rapids every July, and the Leelanau Harvest Tour in Leelanau County every September. Nonmembers and visitors are welcome to join regularly scheduled rides and learn more about the cycling club. Newsletters with current schedules are carried in local bike shops or through the club's "rideline" listed above. The club also publishes a water-resistant bicycle map that is sold at local bike shops or by mail. This is a comprehensive map of biking routes in the Grand Traverse region north to Mackinaw City, with detailed information on 17 recommended routes as well as adequate mapping to design your own trek. Cycling resources for rentals, service, equipment, supplies and related needs are included. This is a publication created by the many local cyclers who are passionate about all aspects of their popular sport. If you plan to embark on a local biking adventure, we highly recommend that you purchase a copy to maximize your enjoyment.

Michigan Bicycle Touring
3512 Red School Rd., Kingsley
• **(616) 263-5885**

Michigan Bicycle Touring has been creating bicycling vacations since 1977. Based in the village of Kingsley, the company leads two- and five-day tours throughout the state for riders of all ages and fitness levels. Several trips offer the option to canoe, kayak or hike as well. All include meals and lodging along with a noncompetitive trip itinerary that lets bikers choose the length and pace they prefer. Tours are designed to take you off the beaten path with scenic routes, charming inns, distinctive meals and friendly staff. You can take a gentle jaunt near Crystal Lake or Saugatuck, a long sojourn through the upper peninsula, or an off-road adventure near the Au Sable River with plenty of extra time for exploring and relaxing. Trips take place between May and October with many scheduled over weekends. Rental equipment is available for an additional charge. Call Michigan Bicycle Touring for a color catalog and a current tour schedule.

Brown Bridge Pond Natural Area
Traverse City

Brown Bridge pond is tucked in a wooded southeast corner of Traverse City where the Boardman River dam created this pretty lake. Trails for both hiking and mountain biking parallel the river and weave through a hardwood forest. There are several viewing platforms that stretch out over high bluffs to share panoramic views while tall sets of steps provide access to the lake or river. Brown Bridge is a good choice for families and beginners.

Traverse Area Recreational Trail (TART)

Known locally simply as the TART, the Traverse Area Recreational Trail is an 8-foot-wide asphalt path for non-motorized recreational use that stretches from the Grand Traverse county line on the west to Bunker Hill Road in the village of Acme on the east. The first few miles on the west side parallel West Grand Traverse Bay before turning south on Barlow Street and then head east along Parsons Road and a woodsy corridor behind the Traverse City State Park and Munson Avenue. This is a much used and much loved crosstown route that has

been mentioned several other times in this Insiders' Guide (see our Getting Here, Getting Around chapter). At any time of the day, you're likely to see a host of children and adults who are busy biking, skating, walking and jogging. Jump on wherever you like!

Vasa Pathway
Traverse City

The Vasa Pathway, which earned its initial fame as a cross-country ski trail, is home to the nationally known North American Vasa Nordic race (see our Winter Recreation and Annual Events chapters). Mountain bikers love it for the same scenery and challenge that make it so popular with the skiers. Loops measure 5K, 13K and 27K with many hills. You'll find the main trailhead as well as parking, restrooms and the Vasa office in Acme Township Park, which is just off Bunker Hill Road on Bartlett Road. Pick up trail maps there and don't hesitate to ask questions of the friendly staff. Beginning cyclers or those with children might want to try the pathway's flatter trails on the south and east, which can be reached via Supply Road or Williamsburg Road.

The Grand Traverse Resort
100 Grand Traverse Village Blvd., Acme
• **(616) 938-2100**

The Grand Traverse Resort recently added 6 miles of trails that weave around the property. Trails include a short stretch that has been paved and works well with in-line skates. You can get to the Village Pathway off Dock Road. Maps are available at the health club desk with friendly staff on hand to assist. The health club is also your source for bicycle and in-line skate rentals.

Sand Lakes Quiet Area
Williamsburg

This trail system is popular with Nordic skiers and showshoers. After the snow melts, the Sand Lakes Quiet Area shifts focus to biking and hiking. All motorized vehicles are prohibited. You'll find almost 10 miles of connecting trails through an incredibly beautiful natural setting. The longest route is 8 miles, but loops can be shortened, modified and lengthened thanks to all of the interconnecting paths. There is sure to be trail perfectly suited to your interest and fitness level. To get to Sand Lakes from Traverse City, take Mich. Highway 72 east to Broomhead Road, just past Williamsburg, and continue south for about 4 miles.

Leelanau County

Sugar Loaf Resort
4500 Sugar Loaf Mountain Rd., Cedar
• **(616) 228-5461, (800) 968-0574**
This popular ski area transforms into a top mountain bike destination after the snow melts. All of the resort trails (see Winter Recreation) are open for biking and hiking. Bicycle rentals are available.

The Leelanau Trail
Greilickville to Suttons Bay
• **(616) 946-7650 Ext. 148**
The Leelanau Trail hosts a 15-mile trail from Traverse City to Suttons Bay. The Leelanau Trail extends along a former railway corridor and is a local example of the popular "rails to trails" movement in communities throughout the state. The relatively flat, groomed trail is a good choice for family mountain biking, hiking, jogging and cross-country skiing. You can hop on the trail from the former railroad depot in Suttons Bay and at the DNR launch site at the south side of Cedar Lake in Greilickville, next to Traverse City. Much of the trail is unpaved but quite firm, due to its former career with the railroad. In-line skating is permitted only along the short path near Suttons Bay that is paved.

Sleeping Bear Dunes National Lakeshore
Mich. Hwy. 109 between Glen Haven and Empire
Pierce Stocking Drive is one of the most beautiful motor routes in Northwest Michigan, sharing breathtaking views of Lake Michigan and the Manitou Islands. You can also bike this same 7-mile route. This is not a ride for novices or those who don't like hills. The drive weaves through majestic hardwoods and scenic views on its trek up to the showpiece Main Dune Overlook that rises 450 feet above Lake Michigan. The ride back down the hills is fast and rolling. Make sure your brakes are in good working order before your descent.

Hiking trails weave and wind throughout the National Lakeshore. We recommend that you stop by the park's visitor center in Empire at 9922 Front Street, (616) 326-5134, for comprehensive maps and advice from the experts on the best trails for you. Family favorites to look for include the famous Dunes Climb noted in our Attractions and Kidstuff chapters; the Cottonwood Trail, which begins halfway through the Pierce Stocking Drive and stretches across dune sands and beach grass leading to a shoreline overlook; and the Empire Bluffs Trail through former farm fields and woodlands leading to panoramic Lake Michigan views atop a 400-foot dune. Another trail favorite, which is for the more experienced hiker, is Pyramid Point with hilly climbs and longer loop through hardwood forests and meadows. The dune overlook at Pyramid Point shares a magnificent look at the Manitou Passage and the Manitou Islands.

Antrim-Kalkaska

Grass River Natural Area
County Rd. 618, Bellaire
• **(616) 533-8576, (616) 533-8314**
This 1,100-acre preserve has 3½ miles of footpaths and boardwalk through its forest lands and river shoreline. The trek is gentle and gorgeous, making it a popular choice for families and novice hikers. Two viewing platforms offer a nice break with lovely views overlooking the Grass River. Naturalist-led hikes are offered during the summer months as part of the preserve's ambitious educational program (see our Parks and Kidstuff chapters). You'll find the Grass River trailhead off County Road 618 approximately 4 miles north of Alden. (See more about the Grass River Natural Area in our Parks chapter.)

Pigeon River Country State Forest
Vanderbilt • (517) 732-3541 DNR, (517) 732-4000 Gaylord Information Center
The Pigeon River Country State Forest, which begins at the edge of our Insiders' Boundaries and stretches eastward, is home to the largest elk herd east of the Mississippi River. Hikers will enjoy the Shingles Mill Pathway, where you can choose loops of varying

length and intensity from a short three-quarter and 1.25 mile routes that are great for families to longer 6-, 10- and 11-mile treks. Viewing areas are sprinkled throughout, sharing beautiful views of the Pigeon River.

Shanty Creek
1 Shanty Creek Rd., Bellaire
- **(616) 533-8621, (800) 632-7118**

Shanty Creek is another major resort whose ski hills wear two hats. The busy Nordic trails of winter (see our Winter Recreation chapter) are equally busy during spring, summer and fall as riders weave their way between Summit and Schuss Villages. Shanty Creek is home to the Sleeping Bear Mountain Bike Race, a major national race held annually.

Lake Michigan Shoreline and Cadillac

Manistee Forest Hiking Trails
Huron-Manistee Forest Headquarters, 1755 S. Mitchell St., Cadillac
- **(616) 775-2421**

The national forests have more than 330 miles of hiking trails, cross-country and horse trails. One of the most unique is the Arboretum Trail in southern Manistee County, about 1 mile southwest of Wellston. It's a short, easy and pleasant trail walk, scenic and secluded. The trail passes through a variety of trees planted as an experiment in the 1940s and is signed for educational purposes. You'll see species from Europe, Asia and across the United States including Black Cherry, Austrian Pine and Table Mountain Pine. To reach the trailhead from Wellston, travel west on Mich. 55 for 1 mile to the Bosschem Road junction and travel 1 mile south to where it intersects with Pine Lake Road. Parking is available at this point.

The Manistee River Trail, another fantas-

tic hiking opportunity, is found in one of the more scenic areas of the Manistee National Forest. The marked foot trail features steep slopes, sharp turns and weaves through stately hardwoods and pines. Hikers experience spectacular views of the Manistee River Valley, an 8-foot waterfall, an arched timber bridge and boardwalks across low wetland areas. The 18-inch-wide, 12-mile-long trail begins at Seaton Creek campground on the backwaters of Hodenpyl Dam Pond on the Manistee River.

To reach the Seaton Creek trailhead, travel south on Mich. 37 for 6 miles from Mesick, or north 9 miles from the Mich. 55 junction. Turn west on 26 Road, travel 1.7 miles, then turn right on O'Rourke Drive and travel 1.3 miles, then right again on Forest Service Road 5993. Proceed for .4 miles to the Seaton Creek campground. Other access points are detailed in trail maps available from the Cadillac-Manistee Ranger Districts, 412 Red Apple Road, Manistee, or from the Huron-Manistee National Forests Headquarters, 1755 S. Mitchell Street, Cadillac. These offices provide maps for all trails in the Manistee National Forest.

For hiking, biking and cross-country skiing, the North Country trail is as good as it gets. The marked trail system weaves through Wexford, Manistee, Lake and Newaygo counties for more than 100 miles. Easily accessed, North Country trailheads are found in Marilla, Udell, Freesoil, Timber Creek, Bowmna Lake, Baldwin, Nichols Lake, near White Cloud and Newaygo. The trail covers a variety of terrain from flat lands to rolling hills and offers breathtaking views of clean rivers and sparkling streams. Water sources are limited so be sure to pack in plenty.

Nordhouse Dunes Wilderness Area is also in the National Forest and provides 14.5 miles of foot trails in a unique Great Lakes dune environment. See our Parks chapter for the complete listing.

INSIDERS' TIP

Look but don't touch! Northwest Michigan is blessed with beautiful flora and fauna near its many trails and pathways. Resist the urge to pick wildflowers as some — like northern Michigan's trillium — are protected species.

Orchard Beach State Park
2064 Lakeshore Rd., Manistee
• (616) 723-7422

Bicyclists will find Orchard Beach State Park an excellent point from which to enjoy a variety of north country tours. There are seven mapped routes extending from Manistee to the Peterson Bridge. Other mapped routes in the Manistee National Forest are available from the Manistee Area Chamber of Commerce, 11 Cypress Street, Manistee, (800) 288-2286. The Orchard Beach/Manistee 10-mile tour along the Manistee River channel provides close-ups of fishing docks and old buildings. The Orchard Beach/Arcadia Loop tour is 50 miles and traverses scenic rolling hills, picture-perfect resort country and maple syrup country. It takes you to Portage Lake, where you can dip in cool waters, and continues to Bear and Arcadia lakes.

Ludington State Park
Mich. Hwy. 116, Ludington
• (616) 843-8671

While Ludington State Park features some of the best fishing and beaches in the north, it also is a great site for biking. Five mapped bike tours are available from area chambers of commerce. Routes range from 30 to 78 miles in and take you through gorgeous forest land, historic waterways and rich farmland. The 30-mile Ludington/Indian Pete Bayou/ Memorial Park route traverses moderate hills and hugs the Hamlin Lake shore. Another great bike tour is the Ludington/Manistee Forest Loop. It's mostly a forest and river route and makes a good overnight trip if you camp at state forest sites along the Little Manistee River. You'll find great fishing along this route, but be sure to pack in whatever you may need, because few stores or service stations are along the route.

Lake Cadillac Bike Path/Keith McKellop Walkway
Cadillac • (616) 775-0657

Bikers, walkers and in-line skaters enjoy this pleasant 7.5-mile, paved pathway encircling Lake Cadillac and traveling through Cadillac West to the downtown area. See our Getting Here, Getting Around chapter for a complete description.

Little Traverse

Jordan River Pathway
At Deadman's Hill .5 miles west of U.S. Hwy. 131 and 1 mile south of the Mich. Hwy. 32 intersection • (616) 536-7351

The Jordan River Pathway provides hiking and backpacking opportunities showcasing the natural wonders and historical aspects of the uncommonly beautiful and peaceful Jordan River Valley. Highlights include northern hardwoods, beaver dams, glacier-carved hills and the Jordan River, Michigan's first designated scenic river. Backpacking the entire 18-mile pathway is a two-day adventure (rustic camping is available), but several loops offer a variety of hiking options. While this is not a strenuous trail, hikers should be in good physical condition. Maps are available form the East Jordan Chamber of Commerce, 118 N. Lake East Jordan.

Charlevoix Area Tours
Charlevoix Convention and Visitors Bureau, 408 Bridge St., Charlevoix • (616) 547-2101

Enjoy Charlevoix the Beautiful by bicycle. The Charlevoix Convention and Visitors Bureau will provide you with maps for four city tours ranging from 3.8 to 7.8 miles in length.

INSIDERS' TIP

The Michigan Department of Transportation and the League of Michigan Bicyclists jointly publish an annual poster calendar listing state bicycling events. It's available at no charge from the Michigan Department of Transportation, P.O. Box 30500, Lansing, MI 48909, (517) 373-9192. The Department of Transportation also publishes county maps with information on rural roads, traffic volume, designated bike facilities, paved shoulders and DNR recreational facilities.

Photo: Kevin Poirier

Hot air balloon rides are one of many enjoyable ways to see the Traverse Bay Region.

Routes showcase area attractions including Mt. McSauba Recreation Area, Depot beach, the yacht harbor and Fisherman's Island State Park. For longer adventures the bureau will provide you with information on cycling to East Jordan (14 miles), around Lake Charlevoix (42 miles) or to Petoskey (18 miles.)

Little Traverse Wheelway
Petoskey-Harbor Springs

The Little Traverse Wheelway is a state-designated bike trail running between Petoskey and Harbor Springs. It offers wonderful views of the bay and is especially beautiful in the fall. See our Getting Here, Getting Around chapter to learn more.

Tomahawk Trail
Emmet County

Insiders find the Tomahawk Trail a challenging stretch offering good mileage for the upper-intermediate cyclist. Check area bike shops (listed in this chapter) for more details.

Fitness Source and Cycle Tours
100 N. Division Rd., Petoskey
• (616) 347-6877

To tour the Little Traverse area with real Insiders, contact the Fitness Source and Cycle shop in Petoskey. They organize weekly rides throughout the spring, summer and fall seasons. Road bike rides are scheduled every Tuesday, and mountain bike rides every Thursday. Everyone is welcome to join the free rides. Call Fitness Source and Cycle for details.

Harbor Springs Cycling Club
Harbor Springs • (616) 526-7152

The Harbor Springs Cycling Club organizes weekly mountain bike and road rides in the Harbor Springs area throughout the biking season. The 100-member group cosponsors organized regional bike rides and sponsors weekly mountain and road rides throughout the cycling season. Weekly rides are free. Call for times, days and starting locations.

Warner Creek Pathway
Mackinaw State Forest • (616) 536-7351

A strictly non-motorized trail, Warner Creek Pathway takes hikers through wetlands and hardwood stands along a 3.8-mile loop within the Mackinaw State Forest. The pathway is marked, and parking is available at the trailhead off Mich. 32, about 11 miles south of East Jordan.

Mackinac Straits

Mackinac Island State Park
Mackinac Island

Mackinac Island is a hiker and biker playground. Since cars are prohibited, bicycles and horses are the primary mode of transportation in this picturesque land. More than 80 percent of the island's 1,800 acres belong to the State of Michigan and are maintained to preserve and showcase the island's unique, natural beauty. There are hike and bike routes for all ages, skill levels and endurance. You would need a solid weekend to explore all of the roads, trails and pathways that weave and wind around the island. You can travel around the 10-mile shoreline, cross through the center on British Landing Road or trek through the countless miles of interior roads, forests and hilly overlooks. The best way to get started is to pick up a detailed map at the chamber of commerce booth or the Mackinac State Historic Parks Visitors Center. The island bike rental shops, and even several fudge shops, share biking route tips and maps.

Wilderness State Park
Wilderness Park Dr., Carp Lake
• (616) 436-5381

Nature lovers will love Wilderness State Park, 11 miles west of Mackinaw City. Hiking trails stretch 16 miles along the Lake Michigan shoreline and through scenic hardwood forests. The park is open year round for hiking, snowmobiling and cross-country skiing, but its related campground is only open between April and December.

Bicycle Rental

Grand Traverse

Traverse City Area

Brick Wheels
736 E. Eighth St., Traverse City
• (616) 947-4274

As noted in our Winter Recreation chapter, Brick Wheels is a wonderful source for the various rental equipment needed for active recreation. Bicycles are available in a number of options including traditional, performance, elite demo and road styles for children and adults. Tandem bikes as well as children's seats, trailers and trail-a-bike attachments are also options. Bicycle helmets are always included with rentals. If you need to transport those bikes, you can rent a bike rack for your car or use Brick Wheels' delivery service to have your wheels delivered to a local motel. Or, since Brick Wheels is next to Traverse City's TART recreational trail, you can ride your rental from the door to the trail in less than a minute. In addition to your biking needs, Brick Wheels can also outfit you with in-line skates, roller skis and all of the needed protective gear. Rates are set in daily increments.

Ralston Cycle and Sales
750 E. Eighth St., Traverse City
• (616) 941-7161

Ralston Cycle rents wheeled equipment just steps from Traverse City's TART trail. You'll find a supply of bicycles for children and adults as well as tandem bikes, trailers, in-line skates, baby joggers and car racks. Helmets are supplied with all bikes, while skates come complete with pads and helmets. Fees are calculated in two-hour, daily, weekend and weekly increments. Daily rates are for a 24-hour period, while weekends are considered Friday through Sunday.

Leelanau County

Bear Bikes
11679 LaCore Rd., Empire
• (616) 326-6100

Bear Bikes, on the edge of Sleeping Bear Dunes National Lakeshore, provides mountain bike rentals, bicycle repair and supplies. Hourly, daily and weekly rates are available, and trail maps and tour routes are provided. You'll find Bear Bikes just off Mich. 22. It's open from May through October.

Geo Bikes
River and Grand Sts., Leland
• (616) 256-9696

Geo Bikes helps you see the sites of the western side of Leelanau County with its line of rental bicycles and repair services while you wait. Geo Bikes carries mountain bikes, autobikes and Infinity recumbants during warm weather, and cross-country ski equipment after the snow falls. You'll find it open during daylight hours in the heart of downtown Leland.

Lake Michigan Shoreline and Cadillac

Manistee Cyclery & Fitness
475 Water St., Manistee • (616) 723-3100

Rent a 3-person surrey from Manistee Cyclery to enjoy a unique tour of the historic port city of Manistee. They also rent 6-speed cruising bikes. Options include hourly, daily and weekly rentals. See our Shopping chapter for a complete listing.

Trailhead Bike Shop
216 W. Ludington Ave., Ludington
• (616) 845-0545

Road bikes, mountain bikes, kids' bikes or bicycles built for two, take your pick, Trailhead Bike Shop rents them all — and in-line skates too. Options include hourly, half-day and weekly rentals. The shop also offers bike sales and repair service.

Pilgrim's Village
181 S. Lake Mitchell Dr., Cadillac
• (616) 775-5412

Pilgrim's Village in Cadillac West provides access to the Cadillac Bike Path, a 7.5-mile paved trail winding around beautiful Lake Cadillac. Rental options for basic street bikes include hourly, five-hour and full-day options.

Little Traverse

Jordan Valley Outfitters
311 N. Lake St., East Jordan
• (616) 536-0006

For seeing the sights by wheel, stop at Jordan Valley Outfitters and rent one of their street bicycles. Options include hourly or daily rentals.

Adventure Sports
2286 Mich. Hwy. 119, Petoskey
• (616) 347-3041

Adventure Sports sells, services and rents bikes. Rentals are primarily mountain style. See our Shopping chapter for more information.

Touring Gear
114 E. Third St., Harbor Springs
• (616) 526-7152

Touring Gear rents kids' bikes, standard, mountain and hybrid bikes on an hourly, daily or weekly basis. You can get good recommendations for local road routes, and some maps are available. They also offer a complete line of mountain and road bike sales and service, featuring Trek, Cannondale and Klein bicycles, Pearl Izumi clothing and Burley trailers as well as helmets, shoes and accessories.

Mackinac Straits

Iroquois Bike Rental
Mackinac Island • (906) 847-3321
Next to the Shepler Dock, Iroquois Bike Rental has a fleet of 100 quality bikes.

Island Bicycle Rentals
Mackinac Island • (906) 847-6288
Island Bicycle Rentals calls itself the Schwinn rental ship. Visitors can rent single speed, tandem, 5-speed and 12-speed bicycles and 18-speed mountain bikes by the hour, day or week.

Lakeside/Streetside Bike Rentals
Mackinac Island • (906) 847-3351
Promising the best bike seats on the island, Lakeside/Streetside Bike Rentals offers a full range of bikes for children and adults as well as child carrier seats with helmets. The Lakeside rentals can be found at the end of the Arnold dock, while the Streetside rentals sit next to the Taxi Stand on Huron Street.

Orr Kids Bikes
Mackinac Island • (906) 847-3211
Orr Kids Bikes caters to families, with discounts and bikes to fit all ages. Strollers are available, and Burley carts may be rented or purchased here.

Ryba's Bicycle Rental
Mackinac Island • (906) 847-6261
Ryba's has three Huron Street rental locations with stands at the Island House Hotel, next to the Chippewa Hotel and across from the Lakeview Hotel. Electric mobility carts are available here as well as Burley carts, strollers and single, tandem, three-speed and mountain bikes.

Balsam Sports Outfitter
219 E. Central Ave., Mackinaw City
• (616) 436-6395
20 N. State St., St. Ignace
• (906) 643-6395
Bicycle rental, service and sales can be found on both sides of the Mackinaw Bridge at Balsam Sports Outfitter. Certified mechanics are on duty for fast repair of major or minor mechanical problems. The shop rents 21-speed Trek mountain bikes and sells Trek, Schwinn and Cannondale bikes along with camping equipment, backpacks and supplies. Nordic ski and snowshoe rentals are available during the winter.

Mackinaw Wheels
110 S. Huron St., Mackinaw City
• (616) 436-5199
You can rent all types of wheeled cycles at Mackinaw Wheels. This is one of the more unique rental spots in the region simply for the many unusual vehicle choices offered. You'll find a nice selection of road cruisers and mountain bikes along with Italian Surreys, Rollerbykes, Rascal Electric Scooters and trailers for little ones. Mackinaw Wheels is in Mackinaw Crossings.

Horseback Riding

Grand Traverse

Ranch Rudolf
6841 Brown Bridge Rd., Traverse City
• (616) 947-9529
Horseback riding is a perennial favorite at Ranch Rudolf. Trail guides from Circle H Stables lead daily one-hour rides through the adjacent Pere Marquette State Forest. Riders must be at least 8 years old and at least 54 inches tall. The rides are held on a first come, first served basis from 10 AM to 4 PM every day between Memorial Day and Labor Day, and on weekends during May, September and October. Cost is $20 per person. Short rides for children 3 to 8 (with parents leading the horse) are available for $5 per 15 minutes. Experienced riders who are at least 13 years old can arrange for three-hour morning or early evening rides Monday through Thursday. Three-hour rides require a minimum of four people, but no more than six, and require reservations at least two days in advance. Cost is $55 per person. Hay rides offer an alternative trot through the forest. Belgian horses haul hay wagons and passengers on 45-minute rides for groups of up to 20. Rates are $5 per person, but require a minimum $50 charge for groups less than 10. Hay-ride reservations should be made at least one week in advance.

Lake Michigan Shoreline and Cadillac

Ridge Runner Trail Rides
780 Claybank Rd., Manistee
• **(616) 398-0072**

Get on the Manistee River trail at Ridge Runner horse stables. Trails weave through breathtaking scenery. A free guide service is available for both beginners and advanced riders and buggies are available for non-riders. The stable offers overnight trips, furnishing tents and meals cooked over an open fire. Rent a horse at $15 an hour, or bring your own. Stalls are available for $10 a night. There are also camp sites for overnight guests. Reservations are encouraged.

Indian Ridge Riding Stables
1525 S. Poplar St., Custer
• **(616) 843-4955**

Take a scenic horseback tour through Manistee Forest country. Indian Ridge offers guided trail excursions for experienced riders. They prefer groups of at least five people. Rates are $15 per hour per person. Make your reservations at least one day in advance.

Mackinac Straits

Chambers Riding Stable
Market St., Mackinac Island
• **(906) 847-6231**

Explore Mackinac Island's wooded trails on horses that know them well. Chambers Riding Stables rents saddle horses by the hour from its corner at Market Street and Grand Avenue. Rentals run $22 for the first hour and $20 for each additional hour. Young riders should be at least 9 to rent horses, but little ones can take a turn in the saddle at Chambers' pony ride.

Cindy's Riding Stable
Market St., Mackinac Island
• **(906) 847-3572**

Another popular source for island horses, Cindy's rents saddle horses by the hour from its stable on Market Street directly behind the

The Leelanau Trail provides runners, bikers and cross-country skiers the opportunity to enjoy the countryside without motor traffic.

Lilac Tree Hotel. Horses are the family business; Cindy's Riding Stables is owned by the same family that operates Jack's Livery Stable (see subsequent listing). Rates are $22 for the first hour and $20 per hour for additional time. Cindy's recommends that children be at least 9 years old to ride.

Jack's Livery Stable
Mahoney St., Mackinac Island
• **(906) 847-3391**

Ride in the old-fashioned comfort of a horse and buggy with a rental from Jack's Livery Stable. Carriages come as cozy two-seaters or in four- and six-passenger styles. The horses are relaxed and well-behaved and have been taking visitors along these island routes for years. Carriage rates are based on the carriage size but average $34 to $50 per hour. Make sure to pick up a map to plan your trek across or around the island. The friendly staff is happy to assist. Allow adequate time for your travels, as the horses usually move at a leisurely pace.

Outdoor Adventures

Grand Traverse

**Grand Traverse Bay Area
Adventure School
11180 Cedar Run Rd., Traverse City**
• **(616) 275-7929**

Bay Area Adventure School hosts indoor and outdoor climbing walls that are available for public use. The indoor wall, which is open year round, is on the grounds of the Traverse City Commons at the New Campus school gymnasium. It is open on Wednesday and Friday evenings 6 to 10:30 PM, and Sundays 2 to 6 PM. An outdoor wall, on the Bay Area Adventure School grounds, is available from mid-June to August. Fees are $5 per person with additional nominal charges for harness rental and first-time instruction.

Organized Adventures
631 E. Orchard Dr., Traverse City
• **(616) 933-EASY, (616) 357-3703**

Organized Adventures takes the planning out of your vacation activities by arranging half-day, full-day or package adventures for a single traveler, a family or a group. Choose from one of the organization's standard activities like hiking, mountain biking, horseback riding, river tubing, treasure hunts, vineyard tours and tastings, and sightseeing and shopping, or let the staff plan a unique experience made to order. Excursion prices range from $10 to $55 per person and always include transportation, gear and refreshments. Several sports-oriented packages are also avail-

able. The price of these 3- to 6-day packages includes lodging, meals and activities. Call for a schedule of current activities.

Tennis

Grand Traverse

**Grand Traverse Tennis Camps
and Tournaments
1306 Peninsula Dr., Traverse City**
• **(616) 946-4557**

Every summer, a team of top local tennis coaches and players host the Grand Traverse Tennis Camps and Tournaments for youth and adult players. Beginner and intermediate camps are offered in two-week blocks for 90 minutes four mornings per week for just about anyone who wants to learn to play tennis. Teens can also take part in eight week Jr. Excellence or High School Team Camps, while adults can participate in weekly tennis mixers or evening instruction. Three major tournaments are held including the GTTC Summer Tennis Classic in mid-June, the Cherry Festival Open during Cherry Festival Week in July and the Governors Cup Mixed Doubles Tennis Tournament in early August. Novice tournament classes for youth are held on alternating Friday mornings. Private and semiprivate lessons can be arranged. The program runs from mid-June to early August at the Traverse City Central High School Courts on Eastern Avenue near Milliken Drive. Applications are available through the mail, but are often available by late May and during the season at the Camps' sponsoring businesses such as Pru-

INSIDERS' TIP

Watching for wildlife? Visit a state park and watch for signs with a binocular logo. These are the universal signs being used by the Michigan Department of Natural Resources to designate 120 "Wildlife Viewing Areas" and to help direct travelers to lesser known paths in the state parks' forests. State parks in our Insiders' boundaries with designated wildlife viewing areas include Wilderness State Park near Mackinaw City and Mitchell State Park in Cadillac. For a comprehensive list of all designated locations, pick up a copy of *The Michigan Wildlife View Guide* at a local bookstore.

dential Securities, Taco Bell, Traverse City Record Eagle and Varsity Golf and Tennis.

Traverse City Area Public Schools
Traverse City

Tennis courts that are used by the local schools for instruction and athletics are also available for public use. You'll find eight courts at Traverse City Central High School. The official address is 1150 Milliken Drive, but the courts are actually around the corner on Eastern Avenue right next to Eastern Elementary School. Traverse City West Junior High School at 3950 W. Silver Lake Road has eight courts. They are by the athletic fields with a separate driveway and parking lot just east of the main school entrance. Traverse City East Junior High School has six fairly new courts southeast of the school's main parking lot. An additional 12 new courts are on the campus of Traverse City West High School at 5376 N. Long Lake Road.

Traverse City Parks and Recreation
Traverse City

Several public tennis courts are tucked near neighborhood parks throughout the community. In many cases, the upkeep is adequate, but not always on par with competitive courts. Two of the most popular are at Veterans Park and the Traverse City Senior Center. Veterans Park has four courts not far from West End Beach and the TART trail. You'll find them at the corner of Bay and Wayne streets, just off Division and Grandview Parkway. A small parking lot is off Wayne Street. The three courts next to the Senior Center at 801 E. Front Street back up to the West Bay shoreline with a wonderful backdrop of blue bay waters. The driveway is easy to miss between Barlow Street on the Center's west side and the Bayshore Resort entrance on the east.

Grand Traverse Resort
100 Grand Traverse Village Blvd., Acme
• (616) 938-2100, (800) 748-0303

The Grand Traverse Resort operates the only year-round tennis program in the Grand Traverse region. Its Village Health Club features both indoor and outdoor DecoTurf II tennis courts. There are five indoor and four outdoor courts. Resident tennis pros offer private and group instruction with a busy schedule of leagues, adult and children's classes and hourly rentals. Classes are scheduled in 12-week blocks, but weekly sessions like "Stroke of the Day" are available on a daily basis. Schedules vary with the seasons, check for the current lineup of activities. Reservations are needed for courts or lessons, and can be made through the Health Club. In addition to the tennis courts, the Health Club also operates indoor racquetball courts, weight/fitness facilities, aerobic dance classes, swimming lessons, a lap pool and indoor and outdoor recreational pools.

Lake Michigan Shoreline and Cadillac

McGuire's Resort
7880 Mackinaw Tr., Cadillac
• (616) 775-9947

Guests and the public may enjoy the resort's two lighted outdoor courts. Court fees are $6 per hour. Call McGuire's pro shop to reserve time.

Manistee City Courts
• (616) 723-7132

The City of Manistee maintains free tennis courts at three locations. All operate on a first come, first served basis. There are four lighted courts at the First Street Beach, four unlighted courts at Sands Park and two at the Fifth Avenue Beach and park.

Ludington Public Schools
Corner of E. Tinkham Ave. and Washington St., Ludington
• (616) 845-7303

Operated by the school's athletic department, these outdoor courts are available to the general public when not in use by the schools. There are no fees, and they are not lighted.

Little Traverse

North Central Michigan College
1515 Howard St., Petoskey
• (616) 348-6605

Two lighted outdoor tennis courts at the college are available for use by the general public. Call the college for scheduling information.

Harbor Springs Municipal Tennis Courts
Municipal Marina, Harbor Springs
- **(616) 526-5355**

Probably the tennis courts with the best view you'll ever find, Harbor Springs offers four lighted courts along the city harbor on Little Traverse Bay. There are no fees for playing here or at the municipal courts on Fairview Street. The new Fairview facility features four lighted courts. No reservations are required.

Boyne Mountain Resort
Boyne Mountain Rd., Boyne Falls
- **(616) 549-6000**

Boyne Mountain Resort offers 12 lighted hard courts for use by guests and non-guests. Call ahead to check if courts are available and to inquire about current rates.

Mackinac Straits

Grand Hotel
Mackinac Island • (906) 847-3331

The four well-maintained, clay tennis courts at the Grand Hotel can be rented for private play. Fees average $15 per hour with advance reservations.

Mackinac Island Public Tennis Courts
Huron Rd., Mackinac Island

The island has three courts that are available for free, public use. They are in the woods behind Fort Mackinac, near Huron Road off the South Bicycle Trail.

Tours and Cruises

Grand Traverse

Cherry Capital Aviation
1190 Airport Access Rd., Traverse City
- **(616) 941-1740**

Cherry Capital Aviation will take you on a sunny sky tour of the Grand Traverse region any day of the week. The air service is at Traverse City's Cherry Capital Airport and provides airplane tours in 15-, 30- and 60-minute flights for up to three people. Passengers can determine the flight plan as long as the length and route fit into the designated air time.

Grand Traverse Balloon Rides
225 Cross Country Tr., Traverse City
- **(616) 947-7433**

Float over the Grand Traverse treetops and shorelines with Grand Traverse Balloons, Inc. Multicolored, hot-air balloons measuring seven stories tall lift passengers to the sky for a panoramic Northern Michigan adventure. Flights are usually launched to observe sunrise or sunset and last almost an hour. Afterwards passengers toast the trip with a champagne reception and receive a flight certificate, color photo and cloisonné balloon pin.

Manitou Island Transit
Fishtown, Leland • (616) 256-9061

Enjoy the Sleeping Bear Dunes National Lakeshore from the water's perspective when you take Manitou Island Transit's evening Shoreline Cruise. You'll follow the passage between the mainland and the Manitou Islands while relaxing on board. This is the same company that provides regular transportation to and from the North and South Manitou Islands between May and October (see our Getting Here, Getting Around chapter). The Shoreline Cruise lasts two hours and usually runs 6:30 to 8:30 PM from the Transit's dock at Fishtown. The ticket office is in the shop closest to Lake Michigan. Special charter trips for groups can be arranged.

Nauti-Cat Cruises
615 E. Front St., Traverse City
- **(616) 947-1730, (800) 743-1400**

You can skim along the bay in a 47-foot custom-designed Catamaran on board the *Nauti-Cat*. This modern sailboat was built for ocean faring so it promises a smooth ride as it tours the scenic waters of West Grand Traverse Bay. The *Nauti-Cat* can carry up to 41 passengers on each of its four daily cruises, including two-hour lunch and afternoon sails, a 90-minute morning "kids kruise," and a three-hour sunset dinner cruise. The *Nauti-Cat* sails from its home base at the Holiday Inn near downtown Traverse

City. Fares range from $15 to $48. All excursions include a meal or snack and assorted beverages. Reservations are accepted up to two weeks prior to your sail date. Limited tickets may be available the day of the sail.

The Schooner Manitou
13390 W. Bayshore Dr., Traverse City
• (616) 941-2000, (800) 968-8800

The *Manitou* is a tall ship sailing the Great Lakes much like large inland sea schooners did a century ago. This is a 114-foot traditional two-masted topsail schooner that carries passengers on three- to six-day windjammer cruises through the northern waters of Lake Michigan, Lake Huron and the North Channel. During the cruises, passengers are promised a Great Lakes adventure with great sailing, island beachcombing, swimming, home-cooked meals and lodging on board. The *Manitou* is operated by Traverse Tall Ships, that parent company for both *Manitou* and *Malabar*. Cruises depart from and return to the home dock in Northport.

Tall Ship Malabar
13390 W. Bayshore Dr., Traverse City
• (616) 941-2000, (800) 968-8800

Board the *Malabar* and ride the bay waters as the early settlers did. The *Malabar* is an authentic replica of an 18th-century topsail gaff-rigged sailing vessel measuring 105 feet long. Simply referred to as a "tall ship," the schooner is reminiscent of an era when the Great Lakes bustled with seafaring activity. Today, the *Malabar* in full sail is a familiar image floating across West Bay with the panorama of the water, peninsulas and Traverse City shoreline as backdrop. Cruises set out three times each day and can accommodate about 40 passengers, who can stroll along the schooner and sit and enjoy the magnificent scenery. The noon sail runs to 2 PM and includes a picnic lunch, the afternoon sail is from 3 to 5 PM, and — our favorite — the sunset sail departs at 7 PM with a picnic meal on deck and returns at 9:30 PM. During 1997, midweek sunset sails also share several Traverse-area talents. In past seasons, the Beach Bards entertained with song and verse in the oral tradition on Tuesdays, while the popular Song of the Lakes musical group performed unique tunes that evoke the heritage of the Great Lakes. The *Malabar* can be reserved for private parties and has become a delightful spot for small weddings. It sails from mid-May through mid-October from its dock along West Bayshore Drive, approximately a mile northwest of Traverse City. Parking, tickets and information are across the street at the end of the marked, gray building. Call for reservations and current sailing and entertainment schedules.

Lake Michigan Shoreline and Cadillac

Mac Wood's Dune
629 N. 18th Ave., Mears • (616) 873-2817

Mac Wood invented the dune scooter 69 years ago, and it's still providing thrilling tours of the Silver Lake Sand Dunes. The 18-passenger vehicles takes a 40-minute ride through one of the north's great natural wonders. (See our Kidstuff chapter to learn more.)

Orchard Beach Aviation
2323 Airport Rd., Manistee
• (616) 723-8095

Based at the Manistee County Airport, Orchard Beach Aviation provides aerial tours offering phenomenal views of the Lake Michigan coast, historic Manistee and Portage Lake. The company operates daily year round, weather permitting. Rates for the 12- to 15-minute tour are $15 for adults and $10 for children.

Mason County Aviation
5300 W. U.S. Hwy. 10, Ludington
• (616) 843-2049

Operating from the Mason County Airport, this flight service offers aerial tours of all of Ludington's great attractions. See the carferry, lighthouses, Hamlin Lake and Lake Michigan shoreline from the sky. Rates are a flat $40 for one to three persons. Reservations are encouraged.

Sandy Korners Jeep Rentals
1762 N. Hill Rd., Mears • (616) 873-5048

Get behind the wheel of a Jeep and explore the Silver Lake dunes on your own terms, or hit the two-tracks in the Manistee National Forest. Guides are provided and child car seats are available. The season runs from April through October. Reservations are a must.

Scenic Seaplanes
on Hamlin Lake • (616) 845-2877

Take off and land on the water from this company's Cessna 206 seaplane. The 6-person float plane will take you on a 20-minute tour of the beautiful Ludington area. There is a $40 minimum for two people. Bring your camera!

Mackinac Straits

Mackinac Island Carriage Tours
Huron St., Mackinac Island
• (906) 847-3325

Enjoy a horse-drawn tour of Mackinac Island. Mackinac Island Carriage Tours has been transporting visitors since 1948 with a fleet of 75 horse-drawn vehicles and over 300 horses. Drivers entertain their passengers with historical highlights and local trivia as they travel by the island's many historic and natural points of interest. You can hop on in the center of downtown's busy main street and then journey along the shore, past the Grand Hotel, near the fort, by the Victorian residences, through the island's interior, to the Arch Rock overlook and many sites in between. Tickets can be purchased at the outdoor ticket office on Huron Street right next to the Chamber of Commerce. Fares average $12.50 to $15 for adults and teen, and $6 for children 12 and younger.

Sunday Vesper Cruise
State Ferry Dock, S. Huron Ave.,
Mackinaw City • (616) 436-5574,
(800) 666-0160

The Straits Area Resort Ministry has conducted its nondenominational Sunday Vesper Cruise since 1969. A ferry sets off at 8 PM every Sunday evening from mid-June through Labor Day weekend for a 90-minute sunset sail under the Mackinac Bridge and through the Straits of Mackinac. A brief meditation and song service is conducted, but much of the time is spent in reflection as the boat

glides through the Straits. The ferry, which is operated by the Arnold Transit Company, departs from the State Ferry Dock off South Huron Avenue, across from the shopping district along Railroad and Wendell streets. Reservations are not needed, but seating is limited to the first 600 people. Passengers should be in line for boarding at the dock by 7:30 PM. There is no charge for the cruise, but an offering will be taken on board to help offset ferry costs.

Badger Helicopter, Inc.
251 S. State St., St. Ignace
• (906) 643-8151 summer,
(800) 439-4005

Get a bird's-eye view of the Mackinac Bridge from the seat of a whirlibird. Badger Helicopter, Inc. takes passengers on scenic tours around the Straits and St. Ignace area. You'll appreciate the majesty and breadth of architectural detailing that is the Mackinac Bridge from a completely unique perspective. Reservations are needed. Call Badger Helicopters for a current flight and rate schedule.

Watersports

Dive into a water adventure and learn of Northwest Michigan's inland sea legends and lore. The experience is yours for the taking at the Manitou Passage State Underwater Preserve. The preserve is under the jurisdiction of the Michigan Department of Natural Resources, but your local source of information is the Sleeping Bear Dunes National Lakeshore Visitor Center, 9922 Front Street, Empire (616) 326-5134. The first underwater preserve established in Michigan, it includes 282 square miles of fresh water containing 11 shipwreck sites, historic sites and unique geological features.

Encompassed by Sleeping Bear Dunes National Lakeshore, the Manitou Passage Preserve extends from the mouth of the Platte River to just south of Leland. You'll find it's one of the richest places for scuba or skin diving explorations in the north. Preserve visitors need to be aware that state and federal laws prohibit disturbing or removing property in, on or over the bottomland preserves. Maps are available from the Sleeping Bear

Dunes National Lakeshore Visitor Center, 9922 Front Street, Empire, (616) 326-5134, or Northwest Michigan Maritime Museum, 7067 Severence Street, Benzonia. Check the listings below to learn where you can rent gear for a dive and for other water sport recreation sources.

Grand Traverse

Grand Traverse Parasail
1265 U.S. Hwy. 31 N., Traverse City
• **(616) 929-7272**

According to the advertising, "if you can sit, you can fly" with Grand Traverse Parasail. The company gives you the wings to fly 500 feet above Grand Traverse Bay. A self-contained Para-Sail winch boat lets riders take off and land on board without getting wet. Standard line length is 600 feet with 800 feet available for an additional fee. All flyers, up to six, ride in the boat and take turns in the air. The boat ride lasts between 60 and 90 minutes. Air time averages 10 to 12 minutes per flyer. Tandem rides are available. Flyers must weigh at least 90 pounds, but no more than 250 pounds. No alcohol is allowed on board, and anyone who is the least bit intoxicated will not be allowed to fly. Costs average $45, group rates and private parties can be arranged. Rides usually begin at 11 AM and run through sunset. Early bird rides can be arranged by appointment.

Scuba North
13380 W. Bay Shore Dr., Traverse City
• **(616) 947-2520**

Scuba North can teach you to dive, outfit you with gear and take you to the dive site. The shop conducts beginning dive classes as well as advanced training in particular scuba techniques. It also rents and sells equipment, leads local dives and arranges group diving trips to destinations such as Cozumel and Grand Caymen. The staff is friendly, helpful and knowledgable. Call for a schedule of upcoming dives and classes, or to arrange a personalized dive trip for you and your group.

Lake Michigan Shoreline and Cadillac

T'Bones Dive Shop
Beulah • (616) 882-DIVE

T'Bones is a full-service dive shop with instructors on staff. They invite you to "take the plunge" with them or journey aboard their 24-foot pontoon. Daily tours of Crystal Lake are available. Call for tour times.

Rod's Reef
3134 W. Johnson Rd., Ludington
• **(616) 843-8688**

Rod's Reef is a complete scuba outfitter offering absolutely everything you need for your underwater journey, whether you're heading out into the Great Lakes, inland lakes or to southern waters. You can expect to pay about $40 per day for a full set of gear. Rod's also offers charter trips to shipwreck sites in the greater Ludington area. Reservations for holiday weekends are a must.

Mackinac Straits

Straits of Mackinac Underwater Preserve
St. Ignace Chamber of Commerce
560 N. State St., St. Ignace
• **(906) 643-8717**

The Straits of Mackinac are dotted with shipwrecks reflecting the waterway's key role in Great Lakes navigation. There are 41 known shipwrecks, with many dating back to the mid-1800s and early 1900s. Contact the St. Ignace Chamber and area scuba centers for maps and information.

Straits Scuba Center
897 N. State St., St. Ignace
• **(906) 643-7009, (810) 558-9922**

The Straits Scuba Center is your resource for scuba diving equipment, air fills and charters to Straits-area shipwrecks. The 42-foot dive boat is USCG-licensed for 38 passengers and can be reserved for private charters.

Thanks to lake-effect snows, the region is blessed with an average annual snowfall of up to 150 inches.

Winter Recreation

Hints of Jack Frost and northern winters can be felt as early as October when the first few snowflakes fall. And with the snow comes the promise of another memorable season of skiing, snowmobiling, ice fishing, skating, dog sledding and snowshoeing.

Thanks to lake-effect snows, the region is blessed with an average annual snowfall of about 150 inches. There is a blanket of snow by mid-November, and the array of cold weather recreation, which begins around Thanksgiving, generally lasts until Easter.

If skiing is your forte, you'll find our region is home to some of the Midwest's premier resorts. Boyne Country facilities alone offer 100 spectacular downhill runs, and nearly 30 lifts, accommodating the beginner or those who seek the black diamond challenge. Freewheeling snowboarders will find excellent terrain parks and professional instruction at the many topnotch ski areas. Nordic skiers and snowshoe enthusiasts are invited to experience hundreds of miles of groomed trails meandering through exquisite forests and along scenic lakes and streams.

In our neck of the woods, snowmobiling is one of the most popular cold-weather activities. Hundreds of miles of marked and groomed trails throughout the north penetrate deep into national and state forests, linking to cross-state connections. The Cadillac area has been ranked as one of the top snowmobiling destinations in the nation. Cadillac is also the host site of the North American Snowmobile Festival (see our Annual Events and Festivals chapter).

Anyone operating a snowmobile in Michigan on public property must have a valid snowmobile registration and snowmobile trail permit. Annual permits cost $10 and can be obtained through the Michigan Department of Natural Resources Cadillac District Office at (616) 775-9727, the Gaylord District Office at (517) 732-3541, or the Michigan Snowmobile Association at (616) 361-2285. To rent a machine, most rental firms require customers to be 18 years or older and possess a valid driver's license. Deposits between $300 and $500 can be expected, and snowmobile reservations are highly recommended, especially for holiday weekends.

The winter is long and the days are short in the north country, but we northerners know how to delight in the season's simple pleasures. Visitors are welcome to don their mittens and join the fun. Nearly every community from Ludington to St. Ignace maintains a public sledding hill and skating rink. Following zero-degree nights in late November, ice shanties pop up like mushrooms on the region's frozen lakes as anglers set their sights on great winter fishing. See our Fishing and Hunting chapter to find out where the fish are biting.

In Mackinaw City, hundreds of mushers harness their huskies to compete in one of the nation's largest and most exciting dog sled races. See our Close-up in this chapter to find out about the famed Mackinaw Mush.

Winter recreational equipment rentals are available at most resorts, but we've included additional rental sources here. See our chart below for area rental rates. You can also refer to the Sports Shops in our Shopping chapter.

Whether this is your first winter visit north or your hundredth, we know you'll agree that a vacation in Northwest Michigan is winter-perfect.

What does it cost?

Rental fees fluctuate slightly from location to location, but most are in the same range throughout the region. If you would like to rent equipment for some fun in the snow, here's a guideline on costs based on adult weekend usage.

Downhill Skis $28 per day
(includes bindings, boots, poles)
Cross-Country Skis $15 per day
(including bindings, boots, poles)
Snowboards $20-25 per 4-hour/half day
(includes bindings, boots) $30-40 per day
Snowblades $10 per partial day
Snowshoes $15 per day
Ice Skates $5 per partial day
Snowmobiles $150-200 per day
(plus damage deposit of $300 to $500)

Winter Recreational Adventures

Grand Traverse

Ranch Rudolf
6841 Brownbridge Rd., Traverse City
• (616) 947-9529

The same Belgian horses that create memorable hay rides during autumn return for a winter encore. Sleigh rides meander along the snow-laden, pine-lined, country roads winding around the Ranch Rudolf property (see our Hotels, Motels and Resorts chapter).

Rides last for approximately 45 minutes and can accommodate up to 20 people. Cost is usually $5 per person, but a $50 minimum is required for rides with two to 10 people on board. Reservations are recommended, and should be made one week in advance.

Lake Michigan Shoreline and Cadillac

Ridge Runner Trail Rides
780 Claybank Rd., Manistee
• (616) 398-0072

During the week prior to Christmas, Ridge Runner offers sleigh rides on scenic trails and along old logging trails near the picturesque Little Manistee River. See our Recreation chapter for more information on the stable.

White Pine Stables
9754 S. 33 Rd., Cadillac • (616) 775-5243

At White Pine Stables you can book an hour-long romantic sleigh ride through the piney woods or take along a party of up to 18. Building facilities accommodate gatherings of all kinds. Sleigh rides are by reservation only so call ahead. See our Recreation chapter to learn more of what this stable offers.

Little Traverse

Bliss Meadow Farms
450 Sturgeon Bay Tr., Bliss
• (616) 537-2406

Softly falling snow and the jingling of bells will remind you of a more peaceful era as you

---

INSIDERS' TIP

Like to race down those slopes? NASTAR (National Standard Race) programs are hosted by Boyne Mountain in Boyne City, Caberfae Ski Area in Cadillac, Crystal Mountain in Thompsonville, the Homestead in Empire, Mt. Holiday in Traverse City, Shanty Creek in Bellaire and Sugar Loaf in Cedar. Races are usually held each weekend and racers (youth and adult) sign up the same day. Skiers vie against times that were set by the fastest skiers on the U.S. Ski Team and then handicapped by the fastest local skiers. Gold, silver and bronze medals are awarded in many age categories.

enjoy a sleigh ride through the countryside at Bliss Meadow Farms. They will arrange bonfires and cookouts for you upon request. Call for an appointment.

On the Slopes

Grand Traverse

Hickory Hills
End of Randolph St., Traverse City
• **(616) 947-8566, (616) 922-4909**
Snow Line

Hickory Hills, a city-owned ski area on Traverse City's west side, is a favorite among families and school children who flock here after school. The 125-acre site has cross-country trails (see the On the Trail section of this chapter) and eight downhill runs serviced by five rope tows. Runs include one beginning, five intermediate and two advanced with a vertical drop of 300 feet. Night skiing is available on six of the runs. Snowmaking capabilities service four runs. Snowboards are allowed. A lodge, with a fireplace, concessions and ample seating for warm-ups, sits at the base of the runs. Hickory Hills is open, weather permitting, from mid-December to early March. Hours on weekdays are 4 PM to 9 PM, and weekend hours are 11 AM to 9 PM. Additional times are often added to accommodate days when school hours are reduced. Hickory Hills is also home to the Grand Traverse Ski Club, (616) 946-7525, which offers an ambitious recreation program with ski lessons and races for area youth. Rates range from $7 to $11.

Mt. Holiday Ski Area
3100 Holiday Rd., Traverse City
• **(616) 938-2500**

Mt. Holiday stands on Traverse City's east side with a 200-foot vertical drop. The 12 runs are divided between three beginner, three intermediate and six advanced, and are served by two chairlifts and two tow ropes. The ski area's proximity to the center of Traverse City makes it a favorite for after-school skiing and snowboarding. Snowboarders enjoy their own half-pipe area, while the youngest skiers can practice their skills in a terrain garden. There

is also a tube run for inflatable sled-like inner tubes. Grown-ups can take advantage of an adult lounge with a bar and fireplace overlooking the beginner runs. Night skiing, ski lessons and rentals are available. Day passes range from $12 to $22.

Sugar Loaf Resort
4500 Sugar Loaf Mountain Rd., Cedar
• **(616) 228-5461, (800) 952-6390**

From the top of the Sugar Loaf slopes, skiers look out on panoramic views of Lake Michigan and the sweeping Leelanau countryside. There are 26 runs served by six chairlifts, including 11 beginner, seven intermediate and eight advanced runs. Vertical drop is 500 feet, and the longest run measures 5,280 feet. Expert skiers will want to try Awful Awful, which is one of the steepest runs in the area. The younger set, between 5 and 12, can spend the day at the Kids Klub for supervised skiing and instruction, while preschoolers have fun at the Sugar Bear Kids Center. Snowboarding takes place in a designated terrain park, and snowboarding lessons and rentals are available. A new quarter-mile tubing run was added recently and comes equipped with a rope tow and lights for nighttime tubing. In addition to the slopes, Sugar Loaf is a full resort with an array of lodging options, restaurants, ski school, ski shop and equipment rentals. The hotel offers lodging and lift packages as well as early and late-season "Learn to Ski — Learn to Ski Better" specials.

Shanty Creek
1 Shanty Creek Rd., Bellaire
• **(616) 533-8621, (800) 678-4111**

This large resort offers downhill skiing on the Summit Slopes and nearby Schuss Mountain. Schuss Mountain has a 450-foot vertical drop and four quad chairlifts serving 29 runs. It has six advanced runs including the signature Goosebumps course. Vertical drop is 450 feet, with the longest run measuring 5,280 feet. The 11 Summit Slopes runs are gentler, with three ranked beginner and six intermediate. Snowboarders can shred the day away on the Schuss Mountain Dew Drop Zone Alpine Terrain Park or at the Summit's Dish the Dew snowboard half-pipe. Ski and snowboard equipment is available for rent at both sites.

You'll also find ski schools, snowboarding instruction, restaurants, lounges and child care. Preschoolers can take advantage of the Snow Stars ski and play program, while children ages 6 to 11 can participate in the Kids Academy instructional program. Night skiing is available on the Summit Slopes. Superticket passes, averaging $36 on weekends and holidays, allow skiers to use both Summit and Schuss ski areas with free shuttles conveniently linking the two.

The Homestead
Mich. Hwy. 22, Glen Arbor
• **(616) 334-5000**

The Homestead hosts a cozy ski area from its scenic site overlooking Lake Michigan. Skiing hours are geared toward long weekends and holidays. There are 14 runs nestled near the resort's ski village area, which also houses a child-care center, equipment rental, eateries and a lounge. The slopes are served by three chairlifts as well as a tow rope on the learners' hill. Vertical drop is 375 feet, and the longest run is 1,320 feet. Night skiing is available, and snowboarding is allowed.

Hidden Valley
Mich. Hwy. 32 E., Gaylord
• **(517) 732-5181, (800) 752-5510**

Hidden Valley is home to the Otsego Club, a private club for skiing and snowboarding that allows a maximum of 1,000 families per year. In addition to annual memberships, Hidden Valley allows nonmembers to purchase lift tickets, which cost $20 to $25, on designated weekends in December and March. Hidden Valley's 18 slopes overlook the scenic Sturgeon River Valley, and are served by five chairlifts and two rope tows. Snowboarders will enjoy the snowboard terrain park and licensed Pipe Dragon-groomed half-pipe. Youngsters have fun in the designated children's park, instructional ski program and child-care center.

Treetops Sylvan Resort
3962 Wilkinson Rd., Gaylord
• **(517) 732-6711, (888) TREETOPS**

Treetops stands near the center of the lower peninsula's northern tip in the midst of heavily wooded rolling hills. The ski slopes host 19 runs served by three triple chairlifts, one double chair and four rope tows. The slopes have a vertical drop of 225 feet, with the longest run stretching to 2,200 feet. Snowboarders have their own half-pipe area while youngsters age 4 to 10 can join the Sylvan Snow Puppies to learn and play games in the children's terrain park. For added fun, a separate snow tubing run, complete with tow, has become especially popular with families. A licensed child development center is nearby for indoor supervision. Treetops offers a comprehensive ski school, including specialty lessons in snowboarding, racing and adaptive skiing. Equipment rental, a ski shop, two eateries, a sports bar, ice skating, snowshoeing, Nordic trails (see the On the Trail section of this chapter) and night skiing are also available.

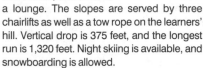

See this and many other **Insiders' Guide®** destinations online — in their entirety.

Lake Michigan Shoreline and Cadillac

Crystal Mountain Resort
12500 Crystal Mountain Dr.,
Thompsonville • **(616) 378-2000**

Majestic scenery, 25 slopes, a 375-foot vertical drop, beginner tows, quad, double and triple lifts are just some of the reasons Crystal

INSIDERS' TIP

Snowmobilers beware: Sledding on frozen lakes and rivers can be dangerous. If you are in an unfamiliar area, ask local authorities or residents about ice conditions, inlets, outlets, springs and other hazards.

is a great place to spend a winter's day (or night; 13 of the runs are lighted) or an entire vacation. Facilities include a 300-foot snowboard half-pipe and terrain park. There are ice skating, sleigh rides, good food and great lodging. Instructions, ski equipment, including telemark, and snowboard rentals are available. See our Accommodations and Restaurants chapters for more information.

Caberfae Peaks
6440 S. 11th Rd., Cadillac
• (616) 862-3300

Caberfae Peaks boasts one of the highest lift-served peaks in Michigan. A bustling big-league resort, it features 16 runs, six lifts and a 485-foot vertical drop. The resort is nestled among a range of hills in the beautiful Manistee National Forest, a natural snowbelt. Snowboarders enjoy a terrain park and are permitted in all areas. Ski equipment and snowboard rentals are available.

Little Traverse

Mt. McSauba Ski Hill
Charlevoix • (616) 547-3267

The community-operated Mt. McSauba Ski Hill features seven runs and a 120-foot vertical drop. Facilities include three tows. Enjoy night skiing or snowboarding. Instructions and ski rentals are available.

Boyne Mountain Resort
Boyne Mountain Rd. (U.S. Hwy. 31 at Boyne Falls), Boyne Falls
• (616) 549-6000

Boyne Mountain appeals to both the beginner and the advanced skier. A Bavarian motif sets a charming atmosphere amidst a pristine countryside. Slopes feature 41 runs and a 500-foot vertical drop, 10 lifts including America's first 6-person lift, and one tow. There's a 20-acre beginner area and a snowboard half-pipe and terrain park. The resort's Austrian-American ski school is ranked among the best in the nation. Professional snowboarding instruction is available, as are ski equipment and snowboard rentals. To learn about the resort's base facilities, see our Accommodations and Restaurants chapters.

Petoskey Winter Sports Park
Winter Park Ln., Petoskey
• (616) 347-1252

Petoskey Winter Sports Park is a beautiful community facility offering free skiing, bump jumping, sledding and skating. The facility features one run with a 100-foot vertical and a free tow rope. Snowboarders are welcome. Instruction is available.

Boyne Highlands Resort
600 Highlands Dr., Harbor Springs
• (616) 526-3000

Family-friendly Boyne Highlands is Midwest skiing at its best. Slopes offer views of gorgeous northern terrain. Facilities include 42 runs, a 550-foot vertical drop, two tows and eight lifts, including a high-speed quad chairlift. There's a beginner's area and a snowboard half-pipe and terrain park. Boyne sponsors a highly rated Austrian-American ski school. Mogul masters provide topnotch snowboarding instruction and clinics. See our Accommodations and Restaurants chapters to learn more about Boyne resorts.

Nub's Nob
500 Nub's Nob Rd., Harbor Springs
• (616) 526-2131

Fantastic snow, a variety of terrain and great programming make Nub's a popular winter destination. The resort is very snowboarder-friendly, offering outstanding race camps and training sessions for them. Slopes feature 38 runs, a 427-foot vertical drop, two snowboard half-pipes and a snowboard park, six chairlifts, two tows and night skiing. Ski and snowboarding instruction is available. The rental shop offers both ski and snowboarding equipment. Child care is also available.

Mackinac Straits

There is only one small, beginner's ski area within the Mackinac Straits area. Since this geographical area is relatively close to Gaylord (under the Grand Traverse listings) and Little Traverse resorts, local alpine skiers and snowboarders pursue their sport there. Other local favorites, outside our Insiders' boundaries, include Searchmont Ski Resort in Sault Ste. Marie, Ontario, Canada, (705) 781-2340, and Marquette Mountain in Marquette, (906) 225-1155, (800) 944-SNOW.

Silver Mountain Ski Area
West U.S. Hwy. 2, St. Ignace
• (906) 643-7578

Silver Mountain stands just 5 miles west of St. Ignace offering convenient, community skiing. There are three ski runs served by one rope tow. All are appropriate for beginner or intermediate skiers.

On the Trails

Grand Traverse

Traverse City Area

Hickory Hills
end of Randolph St., Traverse City
• (616) 947-8566, (616) 922-4909
Snow Line

Hickory Hills hosts 5K of groomed trails that loop around this city-owned ski area (see the On the Slope section of this chapter). A 1K trail is lighted for night skiing. Nordic rates are $2 per day or $25 for an annual pass. A central lodge serves concessions near a cozy fire pit.

Jellystone Park
4050 E. Hammond Rd., Traverse City
• (616) 947-2770

Jellystone Park uses lovable Yogi Bear as its mascot at this family campground and cross-country ski center. Jellystone has been a leader in promoting Nordic skiing in the Traverse area and often hosts weekly clinics for adults and children. You'll find 2K in groomed and tracked trails adjoining the 27K Vasa trail through the Pere Marquette State Forest. Cross-country skis, boots and showshoes are available for rent. Warm up afterwards in front the large fireplace in Jellystone's cozy lodge.

Ranch Rudolf
6841 Brownbridge Rd., Traverse City
• (616) 947-9529

Ranch Rudolf's trail system includes six groomed, marked trails measuring 25K, which connect with the groomed Muncie Lakes Pathway trails through the peaceful Boardman River Valley. Equipment rentals are available for full- or half-day cross-country packages, or separately for skis, boots and poles. Showshoes can be rented on a half-day basis.

Photo: Grand Traverse Resort

As the winter sets in, go dashing in a horse-drawn sleigh.

Grand Traverse Resort
6300 N. U.S. Hwy. 31, Acme
• **(616) 938-2100, (800) 748-0303**

The gently rolling knolls of the Grand Traverse Resort's golf courses transform into woven loops of cross-country trails each winter. Likewise, the pro shop takes on the persona of the Grand Traverse Resort Nordic Center, complete with equipment rental, instruction, a ski shop and restaurant. There are four beginner and intermediate trails measuring 8K. Rates average $4. An added benefit to the Resort trails is the proximity to the Vasa Pathway and Sand Lakes Quiet Area (see the listing below).

Vasa Pathway

The Vasa Pathway was created to be the course for the annual North American Vasa Nordic marathon held on the second Saturday of February (see our Annual Events chapter). The public enjoys the trail during the remaining 364 days each year. During the Vasa's early years, the competition course was temporary, utilizing a combination of public and private lands as volunteers worked toward establishing a permanent trail system. Today's trail through the Pere Marquette State Forest has been in place since the early '90s. It is a true labor of love by local Nordic enthusiasts, who not only built it, but help maintain its 35K of groomed classic and free-skating trails through the wooded hills east of Traverse City. You can get to the trailhead off Bunker Hill Road at Bartlett Road southeast of Acme. Loops are 3K, 10K and 25K. Snowshoeing is allowed. While you're on the trails, keep a lookout for the bald eagles that often soar near the headwaters of Acme Creek. There are no fees to use the Vasa trail, but donations to the nonprofit Vasa organization are used for trail upkeep, equipment and improvements.

Sand Lakes Quiet Area
Broomhead Rd., Acme

The Sand Lakes Quiet Area is a wonderful trail system tucked into a nonmotorized portion of the Pere Marquette State Forest. Locals love Sand Lakes and flock here on Nordic skis and snowshoes during the winter, and in hiking boots and on mountain bikes during warmer weather. The heavily wooded, ungroomed trails weave around several small inland lakes, the Sand Lakes, and measure close to 15K, with appropriate loops for all abilities. Don't be surprised to see an assortment of furry and feathered friends along the way. Fox, grouse and bobcat are just a sampling of the inhabitants of this peaceful wilderness area. You'll find the trailhead on Broomhead Road, about 4 miles south of Acme on Mich. Highway 72 East. There is no fee to use state forest pathways, but donations are used toward upkeep and improvements.

Lost Lake Ski Trail
Wildwood Rd., Interlochen

This is one of the area's most popular public trail systems, with 9K of marked trails winding through the scenic Lost Lake Natural Area near Lake Dubonnet and tiny Lost Lake. Gentle trails and proximity to Traverse City make it an ideal destination for a family cross-country outing. Lost Lake hosts two ungroomed trails measuring 9K. The trailhead is on Wildwood Road, just a mile north of U.S. Highway 31 and east of Interlochen Corners. Donations are accepted.

Leelanau County

Sugar Loaf Resort
4500 Sugar Loaf Mountain Rd., Cedar
• **(616) 228-5461**

Sugar Loaf's cross-country program stands alongside the resort's downhill skiing and snowboarding programs to offer top winter recreation. There are eight groomed trails, totaling 26K, weaving through the wooded Sugar Loaf property, including several lighted runs for night skiing. Rental equipment and instruction are available, and snowshoeing is allowed. See the listing in the On the Slopes section of this chapter for additional hospitality services at the resort.

Sleeping Bear Dunes National Lakeshore
Philip A. Hart Visitors Center, 9922 Front St. (Mich. Hwy. 72), Empire
• **(616) 326-5134**

The Sleeping Bear Dunes National Lakeshore has been discussed in several other chapters (see Parks, Attractions, Kidstuff and Recreation), but this 70,000-acre northern treasure is also home to seven trails that stretch 80K through some of the most magnificent scenery in Michigan. The most breathtaking overlooks of Lake Michigan, Glen Lake and the beautiful shoreline landscapes are along the Alligator Hill, Empire Bluffs and Scenic Drive Trails. Bay View Trail and Alligator Hill offer the most versatility with beginner, intermediate and advanced loops. Good Harbor Bay is a good beginner trail, while Windy Moraine is best left to advanced skiers. Access to the trailheads stretches the length of the park lands. You can access Alligator Hill and Scenic Drive Trail off Pierce Stocking Scenic Drive just off Mich. Highway 109 in Glen Arbor. Bay View Trail is almost 4 miles further north on the north end of Thoreson Road. Good Harbor Bay is 10 miles northeast of Glen Arbor on Lake Michigan Road off County Road 669. Windy Moraine is on Welch Road north of Empire on Mich. Highway 109. Empire Bluffs is off Wilco Road near Mich. Highway 22 south of Empire. Platte Plains is off Esch Road or south of Trails End Road on Mich. 22. Trail maps are available at the visitors center.

Snowshoeing is also popular on the Lakeshore property. Guided tours are periodically conducted by prearrangement.

The Homestead
Mich. Hwy. 22, Glen Arbor
• (616) 334-5000

Since The Homestead is nestled along the Sleeping Bear Dunes National Lakeshore, it is surrounded by many miles of Nordic trails stretching through the Lakeshore lands (see the previous Sleeping Bear listing). The resort operates six of its own trails measuring 18K. Several are lighted for night skiing. Rental equipment and instruction is available as are the same child-care services, restaurant and ski shop noted in the downhill listing above.

Antrim-Kalkaska

Shanty Creek
1 Shanty Creek Rd., Bellaire
• (616) 533-8621, (800) 632-7118

Shanty Creek is home to the White Pine Stampede, a major cross-country ski race held during the first weekend of February each year (see Annual Events chapter). The same trails that attract amateur and elite skiers to the Stampede are available for Nordic fun throughout the season. You'll find 12 groomed trails measuring 30K meandering and linking to the Schuss Mountain and Summit Village areas. The trails closest to the downhill base stretch along each area's respective golf course with gently rolling paths, while the hardwood-lined trails linking the two villages are more advanced. Rental equipment, a ski shop, restaurant and Nordic instruction are available (see also the Shanty Creek entry in the On the Slopes section of this chapter).

Marsh Ridge
4815 Old 27 S., Gaylord • (517) 732-6794

Marsh Ridge maintains 20K of groomed trails, including 4K that are lighted for night skiing. Ten loops gently meander through the gently rolling property and share many scenic vistas. Nordic instruction and rental equipment is available. After skiing, Marsh Ridge guests can relax in a steaming outdoor thermal pool or with a meal at Jac's Place Restaurant.

Michaywé Resort
1535 Opal Lake Rd., Gaylord
• (517) 939-8911, (800) 322-6636

Michaywé Resort offers approximately 20K of groomed trails including a 2K loop lighted for night skiing, and designated loops for skating and diagonal skiing. Instruction and rental equipment are available as are meals, snacks and lodging. The resort offers lodging and meal packages for cross-country skiers.

Treetops Sylvan Resort
3962 Wilkinson Rd., Gaylord
• (517) 732-6711, (888) TREETOPS

Treetops overlooks the scenic Pigeon River Valley with 20K of beautifully groomed cross-country trails and a full downhill skiing program. The 18 trail loops are appropriate for a variety of skill levels from beginner through advanced. A 5K trail is lighted for night skiing. Snowshoes are allowed. Rental equipment and instruction are available. Other amenities and information on downhill skiing are in the On the Slopes section in this chapter.

Wilderness Valley
7189 Mancelona Rd., Gaylord
• **(616) 585-7141**

Wilderness Valley has one of the most extensive Nordic trail systems in Northwest Michigan with 56K of groomed trails that wind through heavily wooded hills. You'll enjoy panoramic vistas while exploring the seven trails, including 30K of groomed diagonal trails and 25K of skating trails. There is no night skiing, and snowshoeing is not allowed. Ski instruction, rentals, meals, snacks, a lounge, day lodge and lodging are available.

Lake Michigan Shoreline and Cadillac

Crystal Mountain Resort
12500 Crystal Mountain Dr.,
Thompsonville • (616) 378-2000

Family owned and operated, Crystal Mountain features 35K of trackset groomed cross-country trails for the novice, intermediate and advanced skier. Trails cross a variety of terrain, are groomed daily and are well-marked. The system features 6K of lit night trails, making it one of the Midwest's longest lit cross-country trail systems. Ski and snowshoe rentals and instruction for all ability levels are available.

Big M
Manistee National Forest
• **(616) 723-6121**

Big M has some of the most beautiful trails in northern Michigan. It's a 30K trackset groomed trail system through the heart of the Manistee National Forest. The system is operated by the Manistee Cross Country Ski Council in cooperation with the U.S. Forest Service. Big M features trails for novices, intermediate and advanced skiers. Most trails are one-way and are not patrolled. It is recommended you ski Big M with at least one other individual. To access trails from Manistee take Mich. High-

way 55 14 miles east to Udell Hills Road. Take this road south 3.5 miles to Big M.

Ludington State Park
Mich. Hwy. 116, Ludington
• **(616) 843-8671**

The cross-country experience at Ludington State Park offers scenic views of a snow-dusted river, coastal dunes and quiet forest. Two marked trails with loops graduate from 1.5 to 6 miles in length providing opportunities for the beginner and more advanced skier. Mini cabins are available for overnight rentals. See our Camping and RV Parks chapter to learn more.

Cadillac Pathway
Wexford County

Cadillac Pathway has 11 miles of groomed, marked trails within the Pere Marquette State Forest. A rating system helps you plot a course according to your skill level. Access the Cadillac Pathway from Boon Road, 3.5 miles west of U.S. Highway 31. Maps are available from the Cadillac Area Chamber of Commerce at 222 N. Lake Street.

Cool's Cross Country Farm
16557 210th Ave., Leroy • (616) 768-4624

Cool's trails cross a pristine landscape among the lower peninsula's highest terrain. Just south of Cadillac the forest abounds with many kinds of wildlife. The Cool Ski Area features 40K of trails, some groomed, some untracked. Equipment rentals are available.

Mackenzie Trail
Wexford County

The Mackenzie Trail is an outstanding cross-country trail set in a beautiful hardwood forest near Caberfae Peaks, west of Cadillac. It is groomed by the Cadillac Winter Promotions group, and use is free. To reach the trail, follow Mich. Highway 55 west from Cadillac to Caberfae Road, then travel north 2 miles. Enter on 38 Road, 1 mile west of Caberfae Peaks.

INSIDERS' TIP

Michigan has 5,900 miles of state-funded groomed snowmobile trails.

Mushing in Mackinaw

It happens in the coldest month of winter, when daytime temperatures hover near the zero mark and bitter Great Lake winds assault the small northern town of Mackinaw City. Folks bundled in colorful down and fur crowd downtown streets in frigid anticipation. Ice hangs from the rough beards of men and fresh snow clings to their dogs' thick coats. Then you hear it, "Three, two, one!" and the Mackinaw Mush dog sled race begins.

With 200 participating teams, the Mackinaw Mush is the largest dog sled race in the United States. The competition was established nine years ago by Deane Cheadle, a  Siberian husky breeder and a founder of Alaska's famous Iditarod race. Since its inception, the Mackinaw Mush has become a premier North American dog sled event. It draws mushers and 2,000 spectators from throughout the Midwest and Canada.

For two weekends every February, dog sledding becomes the focus of activity at the Mackinaw Straits. The Mackinaw Mush takes place the first weekend of the month and the Mackinaw Wilderness Run is held the following weekend. While avid mushers seem to need little encouragement to race, $10,000 in purse money raises stakes and guarantees heated competition.

The Mush is an important winter event for the Mackinaw City community as well as for dog sledders. Townspeople kick things off Saturday morning with a Mushers' Pancake Breakfast. A snow-sculpture contest inspires the artistic spirit with sculpting competitions in two classes, professional and amateur. Typically the contest features a dozen or more ice designs.

Official Mackinaw Mush activities usually begin about 9 AM Saturday morning. Dog teams line up in for competition in a lot along Central Avenue and then are given the signal to begin the race, two at a time. The Mush features sprint competitions in three classes; the three-dog, 3-mile race; six-dog, 6-mile race; and eight-dog, 8-mile race. Runs are thrilling to watch as drivers lead their teams of highly-trained, powerful animals to the finish line.

The second race, the Mackinaw Wilderness Run, is another breed of competition, a mid-distance race. The 50-mile run begins in Mackinaw City. Mushers proceed to Wilderness State Park and return to the starting point. An Iditarod-style competition, The Wilderness Run features a six-dog and a 10-dog class.

The growing popularity of the Mackinaw races attests to increased interest in dog sledding in recent years. The sport's versatility may account for much of its appeal. It can be a challenging, disciplined individual sport or a family-oriented activ-

Photo: W.J. Platten

The six-dog class is one of several races in the Mackinaw Mush, the largest sled dog competition in the nation.

— continued on next page

ity. Intelligent running dogs can be trained to pull in-line skaters while some freewheeling individuals enjoy skijoring, a dog-powered cross-country skiing experience.

In Mackinaw City, Cheadle has turned his passion for the mushing sport into his business. Cheadle owns Tund-Dra Outfitters, 221 E. Central Avenue, Mackinaw City (See our Shopping chapter) and its sister store in Nunica, Michigan. Everything you need for dog sledding can be found at Cheadle's unassuming Straits-area store including harnesses, sleds, training books, clothing and friendly, knowledgeable advice from Cheadle's daughter/shop manager Cheryl Cheadle. Tun-Dra also offers tours to Alaska, Finland, Nova Scotia and Michigan wilderness areas. Visiting Tun-Dra Outfitters will give you a taste of this exciting sport and may entice you to revisit at Mush time.

McGuire's Resort
7880 S. Mackinaw Tr., Cadillac
• (616) 775-9947

Overlooking the beautiful Cadillac area, McGuire's features 320 acres of rolling terrain with 7K of groomed trails. Three are lighted for night skiing on Friday, Saturday and Sunday. Cross-country ski and snowshoe rentals are available.

Little Traverse

Fisherman's Island State Park
Bell's Bay Rd., Charlevoix
• (616) 547-6641

Located along the shores of Lake Michigan at Bell's Bay, the park offers a 3K scenic trail and plenty of open space for skiers to forge their own paths. The pristine scenery is memorable. See our Camping and RV Parks chapter to learn more about this park.

Mt. McSauba Park
Charlevoix • (616) 547-2101

Mt. McSauba is a city-operated facility featuring a 1- to 6K looped trail system suitable for the novice to advanced skier. Terrain ranges from flat ground to steep hills. Trails are groomed and marked, and maps are available.

Boyne Nordican
Boyne Mountain Resort, Boyne Falls
• (616) 549-6000

A premier Nordic ski area at the base of Boyne Mountain resort, the center offers a 60K trail system regarded as one of the finest cross country facilities in Michigan. System terrain accommodates skiers of all ability levels and includes 10K of flat terrain, 10K of rolling hills and 15K of world-class hill trails. Three kilometers of trails are lighted for night skiing. Ski lessons, workshops and nature tours are offered and equipment rentals, including snowshoes, are available. (For more information, see Boyne Mountain Resort in our Accommodations chapter.)

Petoskey State Park
2475 Mich. Hwy. 119, Petoskey
• (616) 347-2311

Petoskey State Park offers two loops featuring a total of 5.5K of ungroomed trails to explore amidst the park's 300 acres. While the park's campground is closed during winter months, access is maintained. See our Camping and RV Parks chapter to learn more about the park.

Boyne Highlands
600 Highlands Dr., Harbor Springs
• (616) 526-3000

A world-class resort, Boyne Highlands offers 25K of cross-country trails for novice and intermediate skiers. Trails are marked and groomed, maps are provided, and some night skiing is available. See Boyne Highlands in our Accommodations chapter to learn more about this outstanding facility.

Nub's Nob Ski Area
500 Nub's Nob Rd., Harbor Springs
• (616) 526-2131

Nub's Nob is known for its great variety of ski terrain. Trails offer 28K of cross-country skiing for novice, intermediate and advanced skiers. Featuring some of the best groomed trails in the Midwest, the system accommodates diagonal striders and skate skiers. Skiers are invited to use the locker room, which offers waxing benches and daily condition updates. Instructions, maps, snowshoe demonstrations and ski equipment rentals are available. Call for rental information.

Young State Park
02280 Boyne City Rd., Boyne City
• **(616) 582-7523**

Northwest Michigan's State Parks offer skiers great scenery, and Young State Park is no exception. The trail system features 64K with three loops winding along the northern shores of Lake Charlevoix. Trails are suitable for beginning and intermediate skiers. Only 2 miles north of Boyne City, accommodations, restaurants and shopping are a snowball's throw down the road. See our Camping and RV Parks chapter to learn more about the park.

Mackinac Straits

Mackinac Island
Mackinac Island, (800) 4-LILACS

Virtually the entire island is open for cross-country skiing during the winter, including the roadways and trails. In fact, if the ice bridge has formed across the Straits of Mackinac, you can even ski to Mackinac Island from St. Ignace. Winter transforms the island into a winter wonderland, blanketed in heavy snow barely touched by human traffic. Only 600 residents remain on Mackinac Island during the winter. The Chamber of Commerce can provide maps of designated cross-country trails, which double as hiking and biking paths in warmer weather.

Wilderness State Park
Wilderness Dr., Carp Lake
• **(616) 436-5381**

A winter wilderness experience awaits when you don skis and glide through Wilderness State Park. You'll find eight trails measuring 30K that weave through this serenely beautiful, heavily forested 8,300-acre state park. Don't be surprised to see resident wild-

life, as many parts of this large park have remained undeveloped.

Sand Dunes Cross Country Ski Trails
U.S. Hwy. 2 near County Rd. H-57, St. Ignace • **(906) 643-7900, (800) 338-6660**

The Sand Dunes Cross Country Ski Trails include seven loops measuring a total of 19K. These groomed and marked trails travel through the scenic Hiawatha National Forest 11 miles west of St. Ignace on U.S. Highway 2, approximately a half-mile north of County Road H-57. Trails are appropriate for beginners through advanced skiers with loops ranging from 2.4K to 10K.

In the Driver's Seat

Grand Traverse

Traverse City Area

Grand Traverse Area Snowmobile Council

The Grand Traverse area has more than 200 miles of interconnecting, marked, groomed trails with an additional 100 miles of secondary trails. They are groomed on a weekly basis by volunteers from the Grand Traverse Area Snowmobile Council. The council, which is also part of the Michigan Snowmobile Association, publishes an excellent trail map available through the Traverse City Convention and Visitors Bureau, local chambers of commerce and snowmobile suppliers. Additional trail maps are available through the Michigan Department of Natural Resources main offices in Lansing at (517) 373-1275, or through DNR regional offices in Gaylord at (517) 732-3541, or Cadillac at (616) 775-9727.

Boardman Valley Trail System

This 81-mile trail twists through the scenic landscape in Grand Traverse County and the Pere Marquette State Forest. Gently rolling hills combine with majestic hardwoods, snowy pine trees and lovely views. You can access the trail via staging areas in Kalkaska off U.S. Highway 131 at First Street, in Fife Lake off Mich.

Highway 186 at Pierce Road, and at Hoosier Valley off Vance Road east of Mich. Highway 37 and south of the U.S. Highway 31 junction.

Kalkaska Area Trails

The Kalkaska Area Trails connect with extensive trails in the Little Traverse and Grayling areas. Two of the most popular are the Blue Bear Trail and the Mis-Kal Line Trail. Blue Bear begins 11 miles east of Kalkaska on north side of Mich. Highway 72 East. It measures 45 miles, winding to Frederic and Grayling, with further connection northward to Gaylord. The Mis-Kal Line stretches between Higgins Lake just outside our Insiders' boundaries to the east and Manton, which is in the Lake Michigan Shoreline and Cadillac area. The bulk of the line's 48 miles of trails lie within our Grand Traverse area, weaving across the beautifully wooded forests of Kalkaska county and linking with others such as the Cranberry Lake Trail, which connects it with the Blue Bear Trail. You can access these trails from staging areas in Fife Lake, in Kalkaska off U.S. Highway 131 or between Kalkaska and Grayling on the Blue Bear Trail.

Lake Michigan Shoreline and Cadillac

Benzie/Manistee Trail System

Running from Manistee north to Leelanau County, the Benzie/Manistee Trail System features 130 miles of groomed and marked trails. Trails meander through some of the state's most gorgeous pine and hardwood forest lands. Highlights of the system include the Betsie River Trail, which crosses 36 miles through the Pere Marquette State Forest. The key access point is Turtle Lake, where restrooms are available. Other access points are in Benzonia, Beulah, Honor and Thompsonville. The Betsie River Trail connects to the Platte River section. Here, 22 miles of trails traverse beautiful Benzie County and 4 miles of Leelanau County along unplowed county roads and state forest.

The most scenic section of the system begins at Bear Lake in Manistee County and hooks into the Thompsonville trails, then the Luhtanen trail. The Luhtanen section covers 40 miles, with half of that winding along scenic Manistee river backwaters, through red pine stands and majestic hardwoods. The Benzie/Manistee trail system connects to the Wellston and Caberfae systems offering snowmobilers additional trail and travel options. Parking and restroom facilities are provided at designated points throughout the Benzie/Manistee system and locations are noted on trail maps. Maps can be obtained from the Benzie County Chamber of Commerce by calling (616) 882-5801, from the Manistee Chamber of Commerce at (616) 723-2575, and from many businesses in Benzie and Manistee counties.

Huron-Manistee National Forest Trails

Cadillac Ranger Station
• **(616) 775-8539**
Manistee Ranger Station
• **(616) 723-2211**
Baldwin Ranger Station
• **(616) 745-4631**

The rugged beauty of the Huron-Manistee National Forest makes for a thrilling snowmobile adventure. Three forest districts in Baldwin, Manistee and Cadillac include more than 350 miles of marked trails. Well-groomed pathways pass towering pines, stately hardwoods, swamps, lakes and the scenic Manistee and Pine rivers. Park rangers suggest snowmobilers always use a map. Maps are available at most lodging facilities in Cadillac, and the Cadillac Area Visitors Bureau at 222 Lake Street.

White Pine Trail State Park

Access on Mich. Hwy. 115 between U.S. Hwy. 131 and Cadillac • (517) 335-4824

Cadillac marks the northern boundary of the White Pine Trail, Michigan's finest linear State Park. The park is the longest trailway in the lower peninsula, extending along a converted railroad corridor for nearly 100 miles south to the Grand Rapids area. The White Pine is accessed wherever it crosses a public road, including access points in Cadillac at 44 Road, where parking and restrooms are available. Cross-country skiers, hikers and bikers are all welcome on the trail system. Contact the Cadillac Visitors Bureau, (616) 775-0657, for maps.

Miss-Kal Line
Michigan Department of Natural Resources Manton Field Office, 521 N. Michigan St., Manton • (616) 824-3591

The Miss-Kal trail features 48 miles of groomed trails along the Missaukee and Kalkaska county lines. Well-signed and groomed by the Department of Natural Resources, these trails have several access points. The key trailhead is found 4 miles north of Manton on U.S. Highway 131. Parking is directly off the highway. From this point, trail systems will take you to Fife Lake and Traverse City. Heading east you can connect to systems in the Houghton Lake area. Good sources for maps of this popular trail are the Manton DNR Field office or the Lake City Chamber of Commerce, 229 S. Main Street, (616) 839-4969.

Little Traverse

Chandler Hill-Wolverine Trail System

Enter snowmobiler's paradise. This trail system featuring 51 miles of trails set among Northwest Michigan's majestic winter wonderland. Access the system 5 miles west of Boyne Falls on County Road 626, 2 miles north of Slashing Road and a quarter-mile west on Chandler Road. The 34-mile Jordan River State Forest Trail begins east of Walloon Lake village, near the intersection of Howard and Chandler roads, and connects to the Jordan Valley Trail to the south and the Wolverine Trail to the north. Trail maps and conditions can be obtained from the Indian River Chamber of Commerce, (616) 238-9325.

Charlevoix Trail
Charlevoix Area Convention and Visitors Bureau, 408 Bridge St., Charlevoix • (616) 547-2101

The Charlevoix Trail is a 19-mile trail that runs between Charlevoix and East Jordan. The trailhead is found .5 miles south of Charlevoix along U.S. Highway 31. The East Jordan trailhead and snowmobile clubhouse are situated at Mich. Highway 32 and the Mt. Bill Road intersection, south of East Jordan. Maps are available from the Charlevoix Convention and Visitors Bureau,

(800) 367-8557, or the East Jordan Chamber of Commerce at (616) 536-7351.

Jordan Valley Trail
East Jordan Chamber of Commerce, 118 N. Lake St., East Jordan • (616) 536-7351

The Jordan Valley Trail features 48 miles of scenic groomed trails meandering through the uncommonly beautiful Jordan Valley. The system includes 19 miles of the East Jordan-Charlevoix trail and provides access to the extensive Gaylord area trail system.

Moose Jaw Trail
Harbor Springs • (616) 526-7999

Moose Jaw Trail is groomed and marked winding through 58 miles of Boyne Country, Alanson, Pellston and Mackinaw City. For maps contact the Harbor Springs Chamber of Commerce at (616) 526-7999.

Petoskey Snowmobile Club
(616) 348-1895

The Club grooms 51 miles of marked trails in Emmet County. For maps and trail conditions, contact the Petoskey Snowmobile Club at (616) 348-1895 or the Petoskey Chamber of Commerce at (616) 347-4150.

Mackinac Straits

Mackinac Island

The roar of snowmobiles brings motorized transportation to Mackinac Island during the snowy months of winter. Snowmobile traffic is restricted to residential and downtown areas as well as the adjoining roadways. There are snowmobile trails through the nonresidential areas that are overseen by the Mackinac State Historic Parks. Maps are available from the Chamber of Commerce or the parks' visitor center. However, snowmobiling on Mackinac Island takes some planning since there are no snowmobile rentals available on the island. The only ones that are on the island in winter belong to residents, were transported before the last ferry on January 2 or were driven across the Straits on the "ice bridge." (See our Getting Here, Getting Around chapter for more on the ice bridge).

Photo: Grand Traverse Resort

Everyone enjoys up-north winter recreation.

St. Ignace-Castle Rock

This upper peninsula trail stretches 32 miles through hardwood forests, high bluffs and the Lake Michigan shoreline west of St. Ignace. The trail can be accessed from staging areas 3 miles northeast of Brevort off Worth Road, 2 miles southwest of Trout Lake or 4 miles north of St. Ignace off I-75.

On the Ice

Grand Traverse

Centre ICE
Traverse City • (616) 933-RINK

Centre ICE is the newest indoor ice skating facility in Traverse City. Owned and operated by the nonprofit community group known as I.C.E., or Involved Citizens Enterprises, the facility opened in spring 1997. The arena houses two NHL-size ice surfaces along with 16 locker rooms, a pro shop, concessions and rental skates. Much of the activity revolves around youth hockey and figure skating programs as well as adult hockey and public skating. Operating throughout the year, it hosts several hockey camps during the summer. Public skating times vary with the season and availability but are usually offered at least once each weekend. Fees are $2 for adults, and $1 for children for public skating, $5 for drop-in hockey or drop-in figure skating, and $3 to rent skates.

Howe Arena
Traverse City • (616) 922-4893

Howe Arena, named after legendary hockey star and Traverse City resident Gordie Howe, is on the north side of the Grand Traverse County Civic Center in the same structure that houses the Easling community swimming pool. The arena was built during the late 1980s as a unique collaboration between county government and the volunteer organization I.C.E., which spearheaded recreational skating programs in the area. I.C.E., which also operates Centre I.C.E. (see our previous listing), leases the arena for skating programs approximately six months each year, from early September until mid-March. During the remaining months, the space — sans ice — is used for trade shows and large community events. Howe Arena sponsors most of the indoor public skating times available in Traverse City, including open skating on Fridays, Saturdays and Sundays, adult public skating and adult drop-in hockey during lunchtime, and drop-in figure skating, and parent-and-tot skating several times each week. A concession stand and rental skates are available. Fees are $2 for adults and $1 for children for public skating, $5 for drop-in hockey or drop-in figure skating, and $3 for rental skates.

14th Street Rink
Traverse City

The outdoor 14th Street Rink is always ready for open skating, as long as Mother Nature cooperates. This free, public rink is operated by the Traverse City Parks and Recreation Department in an open field area on 14th Street between Oak and Union Streets. This is a good-sized rink where neighbor children can gather for impromptu skating with their friends. A warming house stands near the rink's edge. With our chilly winters, you can usually count on the rink to be running from late December until early March.

Otsego County Sportsplex
1250 Gornick Ave., Gaylord
• (517) 731-3546 Sportsplex,
(517) 732-4447 Gaylord Grizzlies

The Otsego County Sportsplex brought indoor skating and swimming to the Gaylord area when it opened in 1996. Open skating is offered on Tuesday, Thursday and Saturday evenings, family skating on Sundays, breakfast skating on Monday, Tuesday and Thursday, and lunch skating every weekday. The Sportsplex is open year round. Fees

are $4 for families during family skate, and $2.50 for adults, $2 for children 3 to 17 and $1.25 for senior citizens older than 60 at all other times. Skate rental is $2.25. If you prefer to come to the rink as a spectator, check out the current playing schedule for the Gaylord Grizzlies, a Junior A hockey team, which is part of the North American Hockey League and features amateur players 16 to 20 years old. The Grizzlies play at the Sportsplex in scheduled home games from late September to early April.

Lake Michigan Shoreline and Cadillac

Sands Park
Corner of Eighth and Maple Sts.,
Manistee • (616) 723-1588

Sands Park's public outdoor ice rink opens for free skating in January and February. Hours are weekdays from 4 to 8:30 PM, and weekends from 1 to 8:30 PM. The rink is lighted for night skating and a limited number of skates are available for free use. Enjoy hot chocolate at the concession stand and warm up in the shelter. Instructional programming includes a five-week learn-to-skate course.

Mason County Ice Recreation Association
Western Michigan Fairgrounds
• (800) 542-4600

The Mason County Ice Recreation Association maintains an outdoor rink at the Western Michigan Fairgrounds in Ludington. The rink is open to the public. Call the Ludington Area Chamber of Commerce or Visitors Bureau for hours. The rink is home ice for local men's, women's and youth hockey leagues. Hockey learn-to-skate instruction is available.

Wexford County Ice Arena
Corner of U.S. Hwy. 131 and 13th St.,
Cadillac • (616) 779-9520

A new indoor facility opened in the winter of 1998, the ice arena is host to area hockey leagues and offers learn-to-skate programs. Skating runs from fall through spring. Public skate hours are Monday through Friday noon to 12:50 PM, Wednesday 3 to 4:50 PM, Friday 10 to 11:50 AM, Friday and Saturday 7 to 8:50 PM, Saturday and Sunday 2 to 3:50 PM. Admission is $1.50 for the noon skates, and $3 for other times. Skate rentals are $1.50. The ice can be rented for special events or parties, and skate rentals are available.

Little Traverse

Avalanche Preserve
1129 Wilson St., Boyne City
• **(616) 582-3641**
Avalanche Preserve offers outdoor ice skating (bring your own equipment) and sledding. The facility is open weekday evenings and weekend days and evenings. There's no charge for use.

Petoskey Winter Sports Park
Winter Park Ln., Petoskey
• **(616) 347-1252**
A community winter tradition, Petoskey Winter Park features two public outdoor ice rinks. Programming for adults and youth includes a five-week figure skating course beginning in January. The park also hosts area hockey leagues. Limited skate rentals are available. The park offers free skiing, bump jumping and sledding.

Harbor Springs Skating Rink
740 E. Main St., Harbor Springs
• **(616) 526-5810**
Enjoy free use of this outdoor ice arena. Facility hours are 3 to 9 PM Tuesday to Friday, noon to 3 PM on Saturday, and 1 to 6 PM Sunday.

Kiwanis Park
Arbor St., Harbor Springs
• **(616) 526-5847**
Kiwanis Park offers old-fashioned family

sledding fun. Hours are 3 to 8 PM Tuesday through Thursday, 3 to 9 PM Friday, noon to 9 PM Saturday, and 1 to 6 PM Sunday.

Equipment Rentals

Grand Traverse

Traverse City Area

Backcountry Outfitters
227 E. Front St., Traverse City
• **(616) 946-1339**
Backcountry rents snowshoes, and will help you with virtually any outfitting need. This downtown shop is a favorite stop for camping, canoeing and trekking gear. Snowshoe rentals are by the day or weekend.

Brick Wheels
736 E. Eighth St., Traverse City
• **(616) 947-4274**
Brick Wheels is your rental connection for a full array of outdoor recreational equipment. For winter sports, you can rent all of the gear for cross-country, telemark and downhill skiing and snowboarding, ice skating and snowshoeing. You have the option to rent a full package of boots, bindings, poles and skis or board. You can also rent the individual piece of equipment that you need. Cross-country, downhill, snowboard and ice skating equipment come in children's sizes (and prices!) as well as adult, but snowshoes and telemark boots and skis are restricted to the adult versions only. Cross-country gear comes in classic, skating and back-country versions. Rentals are available for one day or at reduced rates for multiple days. Brick Wheels does not take reservations. If you're trying a sport for the first time, don't hesitate to ask the staff for assistance. They are known for their expertise and friendly advice. Trail maps are available.

INSIDERS' TIP

Snow conditions are just a phone call away. Call (800) 72-SKI-TC for up-to-date snow conditions for downhill skiing, cross-country skiing and snowmobiling in the Grand Traverse region. The hotline is sponsored and updated by the Traverse City Area Convention and Visitors Bureau.

Harbor Sea Doo
13240 S. W. Bayshore Dr., Traverse City
• (616) 922-3020

Ski-Doo Touring LE snowmobiles are featured rentals at Harbor Sea Doo. Rentals include a full tank of fuel, free delivery and pickup to local trailheads, trail maps and full safety instructions. Custom, guided tours are available. All renters must be at least 21 years old and possess a valid driver's license. A $500 damage deposit is required per unit. Reservations are highly recommended.

McClain Cycle and Fitness
2786 Garfield Ave., Traverse City
• (616) 941-8855, (800) 972-9253

McClain rents traditional and lightweight aluminum snowshoes on a daily and weekend basis. Daily rates are $10 for a 24-hour rental; weekend fees run $20 for use from noon Friday until Monday morning. If you're thinking of purchasing snowshoes, McLain will apply your first rental fee toward the purchase of a new pair of snowshoes. Area trail maps are available.

Rentals Unlimited
3100 N. U.S. Hwy. 31 S., Traverse City
• (616) 941-0311

Rentals Unlimited can provide you with rental snowmobiles and trailers. Delivery and pickup is an option as are guided tours. Rates are based on 24-hour usage with reduced rates in effect during midweek. Reservations are recommended.

Sureway Guided Tours, Inc.
3892 Forest Lakes Dr., Traverse City
• (616) 946-9243

Sureway provides guided tours through the Grand Traverse area. The company rents snowmobiles on either an 8- or 24-hour basis. Weekend rates are also available. All snowmobiles used for tours or rentals accommodate two people. A valid driver's license is required for operation. Reservations are recommended.

Gaylord Motor Sports
2572 Old 27 S., Gaylord • (517) 732-4331

Ski-Doo snowmobiles are available at Gaylord Motor Sports by the day or the weekend.

J.D. Rental
1829 Old 27 S., Gaylord • (517) 732-6754

Daily or weekend rentals are available for Arctic Cat snowmobiles at J.D. Rental.

Northern Motor and Power Sports
2370 Old 27 S., Gaylord • (517) 731-4515

Northern Motor and Power Sports rents Polaris and Yamaha snowmobiles by the day or the weekend.

Lake Michigan Shoreline and Cadillac

Portage Point Inn
8513 S. Portage Point Dr., Onekama
• (616) 889-4222

Portage Point is the only snowmobile rental facility in Mason County. Sled rentals are available to guests and non-guests. The facility offers long track machines featuring electric start and thumb warmers. Helmet rentals are extra. Service includes free delivery to local trailheads. Rentals are popular and machines limited, so reservations are highly recommended. Rental options include one-, two-, three-day and weekly rates, which include your first tank of fuel.

Funtime Rentals, Inc.
Mich. Hwy. 115 at Mich. Hwy. 55,
Cadillac • (616) 775-2407

Funtime Rentals Inc. offers two-person Polaris 440 machines. Rental options include midweek and weekend rates. Helmets are included in fees. Reservations are recommended.

INSIDERS' TIP

Are you a golden skier? Skiers who are older than 55 can often take advantage of significant senior discounts on lift tickets and rentals at most Northwest Michigan ski areas. Several also host midweek Senior Days with added perks.

Rental One
3910 U.S. Hwy. 31 N., Cadillac
- **(616) 775-8562**

Rental One offers new-model Arctic Cat Pumas and Polaris Indy Sport Touring sleds. Options include weekend packages and 24-hour rentals during weekdays. Trailers and delivery are also available. Plan to reserve a sled at least six weeks in advance if you wish to secure weekend rentals.

Little Traverse

Fun-Be-Us
02474 S. Mich. Hwy., East Jordan
- **(616) 536-2672**

Fun-Be-Us rents two-person Ski-Doo sleds and trailers along the Jordan Valley Trail, considered one of the most beautiful systems in the state. Options include 4-hour, daily, weekend and weekly packages. Helmets and maps are available. Owners recommend you make weekend, holiday or group reservations at least three weeks in advance.

Galmore's Inc.
105 Second St., East Jordan
- **(616) 536-7582**

From Galmore's door you can hit the beautiful Jordan Valley Trail, and they'll provide the maps you need for a great adventure. Galmore's offers two-person Ski-Doo machines on a daily basis. Helmets cost extra. If you're planning a weekend or holiday excursion, be sure you reserve a sled well in advance.

County Wide Services
8535 Mich. Hwy. 119, Harbor Springs
- **(616) 347-8822**

County Wide begins taking reservations for sleds in August so be sure to secure sled reservations here as far in advance as possible. County Wide Services is conveniently located along the Moose Jaw Trail system for easy access. Rentals include two-person model Polaris Sport 440 machines. Options include 4-hour, 8-hour, 24-hour and two-day packages. Helmets rentals are extra.

The Traverse City
area is an angler's
heaven. There are more
than 250 miles of
shoreline, more than
300 inland lakes in
Grand Traverse County
alone, and miles upon
miles of fish-rich
brooks, rivers
and streams.

Fishing and Hunting

Fishing

The beauty of Northwest Michigan's waters and its bountiful fisheries draw anglers to the region year round. Hundreds of small lakes, miles upon miles of blue-ribbon streams and the freshwater sea provide many opportunities to enjoy the sport. Fishing also plays an important role in Michigan's economy. Anglers spend an estimated $1.4 billion annually in pursuit of sport fishing.

While there are about 146 kinds of fish existing in Michigan waters, sport fishing focuses on 25 species. In the cold waters of Lake Michigan, a variety of salmon and trout provide exciting, high-quality angling experiences. Trout abound in the region's rivers while panfish, pike and other species are abundant in the inland lakes.

The mighty fighting **salmon** are landed in the big lake from piers and in the near-shore surf. Chinook and coho salmon forage in open water within 10 miles of the shoreline. On the big lake, anglers hook the 20- to 30-pound fish by trolling with bait or artificial lures and using downriggers to adjust line depth. They also use a technique called mooching, slow trolling and drifting using a two-hook bait harness with a chunk of bait impaled. In streams, the salmon are taken on spawn or artificials. Spinners, spoons and plugs and fly-fishing with streamers or nymphs are successful.

Trout, weighing 30 pounds or more, are found in large inland lakes and Lake Michigan. The fish can be caught in lake-edge shallows casting or trolling with large spoons in early spring and fall. In summer or winter anglers have the most success still-fishing using dead or live bait. In the fall, when the fish spawn, lake trout move into stream mouths and casting with artificial bait is usually successful. Silvery rainbow trout, also known as steelhead, spawn and run in the spring and

fall, entering trout streams as early as June. These 10-pound fish can be found in the big lake, inland lakes and streams. In the spring, anglers use salmon eggs or the roe from a captured rainbow, placed in a small net sack and bumped along the river bottom. Spinners and various other forms of artificial baits also work well. For fly-fishing use streamer flies or nymphs. On the inland lakes, live bait fishing with minnows or trolling with small spoons or spinners gets you the best catch. Brook trout, often called brookies, can be snagged with a light spinning rod or fly rod, a little skill and a lot of patience. Another nice catch is the brown trout found in streams, inland lakes and the Great Lakes. You'll find they are best caught by casting artificial lures, still-fishing using night crawlers or by trolling. They're found along rocky piers and the shallow inshore waters of Lake Michigan. For the most success, fish streams after dark, drifting bait. Night crawlers, worms and minnows make good natural bait for these 10- to 20-pound relatives of the Atlantic salmon.

In quiet lakes and ponds, and sometimes streams, you'll find largemouth and smallmouth **bass**. The largemouth bass is a good fighter and can be taken by casting using crankbaits, spinners, jigs and rubber worms, or by fly-fishing with poppers or streamer flies and by still-fishing with night crawlers or minnows. They can be feisty and put on quite a jumping display. The smallmouth bass is distinguished from the largemouth by the extension of the upper lip that reaches to the rear of the eye. It can be taken with light tackle. Be alert. The smallmouth strikes artificial lures fast. Natural bait, minnows and crayfish may require more patience.

Another popular inland lake fish is the **walleye**. A bottom hugger, the school-running walleye is best caught on dark days or in the late afternoon and evening. Jigging, drifting or trolling are good methods for hooking one of these tasty fish. Preferred natural bait are minnows and night crawlers. Artificial bait used successfully to land walleye include Flatfish and Pikey Minnows.

The most frequently caught sport fish in Michigan is the yellow **perch**. There are no size limits or closed seasons on perch, but a good keeper averages 7 to 10 inches and jumbos, sometimes caught in the Great Lakes, will run up to 15 inches. Perch are school-runners, and they don't go for artificial lures or flies but prefer minnows and crayfish, worms, wigglers, night crawlers or crickets.

Living in the quiet shallows of inland lakes, northern **pike** strike at all kinds of artificial lures, either cast or trolled, but in summer, still-fishing deeper waters using large minnows or trolling past weed beds are the preferred methods. Pike fishing is best in early morning or after 4 PM.

While salmon will put up a good fight and impress you with their size, the common **sunfish** is easy to catch, tasty to eat and found prolifically in most lakes and streams. The varieties include bluegill, pumpkinseed and the green sunfish. Found in shallows and the weedy water's edge, the sunfish is best caught in early morning and evening but can be caught most anytime. Fly fishing with small popping bugs or rubber spiders is successful as is a simple cane pole with worms or crickets. During the hot summer months, the sunfish are found in deeper, cooler waters.

Whatever method of sport fishing you enjoy, whichever species you prefer to land, it's important to have a good understanding of state regulations regarding harvesting and possession of fish. Regulations vary from river to river and lake to lake. Information on seasons, size limitations, when and where fishing is allowed and how you can take the fish is all outlined in the *Michigan Fishing Guide*. Published by the state's Department of Natural Resources Fisheries Division, the booklets are available free of charge from all fish licensing dealers. Even if you've been fishing Michigan's waters for decades, it's wise to review the updated publication each year. Major regulation changes are highlighted, as well as new fees, programs and safety issues.

Northwest Michigan has a long, rich fishing heritage. Enjoy your role in it but also consider your responsibility in preserving opportunities for future anglers. You may wish to join the growing number of anglers who are practicing catch-and-release. Informal reports indicate on some streams, as many as 90 percent of the anglers release their catches. Some guide services require release of all but wounded fish. For those just beginning to practice catch-and-release, you'll find that trained guides and sporting dealers will teach handling methods that will increase the survival rate of the released fish and preserve the natural bounty.

Department of Natural Resources district offices can provide you with applications, licenses and all the information you need to fish, hunt or trap lawfully. In some instances, they may refer you to one of the many field offices located throughout Northwest Michigan. District offices are staffed from 9 AM to 5 PM Monday through Friday. The Cadillac District Headquarters is at 8015 Mackinaw Trail in Cadillac, (616) 775-9727. The Gaylord District Headquarters is at 1732 Mich. Highway 32 W., Gaylord, (517) 732-3541.

Fishing Licenses

All Michigan residents and nonresidents, 17 years of age or older, are required to purchase a license to fish Michigan waters. They are available from many sporting goods and bait shops as well as most Michigan Department of Natural Resource offices.

While Michigan fishing licenses are not required for children 16 and younger, kids 12 and older can become a part of the state's fishing legacy by joining the Young Angler Program. For a $2 voluntary license fee, kids receive a colorful patch and a quarterly newsletter from the Michigan Department of Natural Resources. Fees support youth hunting and fishing education outreaches. Sign up with any license dealer.

www.insiders.com

See this and many other **Insiders' Guide®** destinations online — in their entirety.

Visit us today!

Fishing Licenses

The following rates were valid for the 1997-98 season. At press time the 1998-99 fees had not been established.

24 hour license — All species
Resident/nonresident, age 17-64	$6.00
All Seniors, age 65+	$3.00

Restricted License — All species except trout and salmon
Resident, age 17-64	$13.00
Resident Senior, age 65+	$5.20
Nonresident, any age	$26.00

All Species License
Resident, age 17-64	$26.00
Resident Senior, age 65+	$10.40
Nonresident, any age	$39.00
Young Angler, age 12-16	$2.00

(Young Angler license is voluntary)

Fish Consumption Advisory

Before dishing out your Great Lakes catch, there are some things you need to know about fish caught in the region. Due to toxic chemicals found in Michigan lakes and streams and in the Great Lakes, the U.S. Environmental Protection Agency (EPA) and the Michigan Department of Community Health (MDCH) advises consumers to limit fish consumption from these waters. Since 1988, the MDCH has issued an advisory pertaining to all inland lakes and reservoirs in the state, due to mercury pollution. The level of chemicals found in these waters is not known to cause any immediate harm, but they can collect in the body and possibly affect your health or that of your children.

The MDCH advises that no one eat more than one meal per week of fish of the following kinds and sizes from any of Michigan's inland lakes: rock bass, yellow perch or crappie over 9 inches in length; bass, walleye, northern pike, muskellunge of any size.

Mothers who are breast-feeding, pregnant women, women who intend to have children and children younger than 15 should not eat more than one meal per month of the fish listed above.

The *Michigan Fishing Guide*, available free from fishing license dealers and the DNR, includes detailed advisory listings. You can also obtain a listing by calling (800) 648-6942 and requesting a Michigan Fish Advisory chart. Likewise, the EPA has set forth an advisory pertaining to Great Lakes waters and their watersheds. Some of the species included in this advisory are coho, chinook, lake trout, brown trout and walleye. To protect your health, it's important to follow the fish consumption advice set forth. A chart listing safe consumption levels is available from the EPA, (800) 621-8431. By understanding and following the guidelines, and by learning how to correctly filet and cook your fish, your catch can be a healthful, enjoyable addition to your diet.

Fishin' Holes

Grand Traverse

Traverse City Area

The Traverse City area is an angler's heaven. There are more than 250 miles of Lake Michigan shoreline, more than 300 inland lakes in Grand Traverse County alone, and miles upon miles of fish-rich brooks, rivers and streams, all offering opportunities for good sport fishing. Local bait shops will provide friendly advice and help you identify the area hot spots such as **Deepwater Point** in the East Arm of Grand Traverse Bay along Acme where you can hook brown trout weighing 10

INSIDERS' TIP

You can receive up-to-date reports on statewide angling conditions, learn where to launch your boat, or get licensing information and other pertinent sport-fishing information by calling (800) ASK-FISH.

to 15 pounds. In the West Arm of Grand Traverse Bay, near **Bowers Harbor**, the rocky areas have produced brown trout catches up to 20 pounds. The **Boardman River** produces excellent brown and rainbow trout catches at the upper reaches and at the lower reaches of the river, you can expect to hook salmon and steelhead during the spring and fall spawning runs. **Green Lake** and **Duck Lake** in Interlochen are known for their smallmouth bass, smelt, northern pike and lake trout. **Silver Lake** produces walleye, bluegill, smallmouth bass and largemouth bass, while at **Fife Lake** you can look forward to hooking some nice walleye and largemouth bass. Whatever the season, anglers fishing the waters near Traverse City aren't likely to go home disappointed.

Leelanau County

Long ago, Native Americans dubbed Leelanau County the "Land of Delights." They must have had fishing in mind! Nestled on a peninsula between Lake Michigan and Lake Leelanau at Leland harbor is historic **Fishtown**. From here, anglers can book charters trips to the bountiful fisheries near the **Manitou Islands**. For inland lake fishing, **Big Glen Lake** is known for its splake and lake trout while **South Lake Leelanau** rewards anglers with northern pike, smallmouth bass and walleye. If you want to fish in paradise, this is it.

Antrim-Kalkaska Area

Trout fishing in Kalkaska County is so good, locals honor the species each spring with its own festival called the National Trout Festival. (See our Annual Events and Festivals chapter to learn more.) Fishing along Kalkaska's 275 miles of trout streams is truly superior. The clear, pure waters of the **Rapid River** produce large brookies and brown trout. The many blue-ribbon streams meandering through the county are considered world-class angling waterways for rainbow, brook and brown trout. The county also boasts excellent inland lake fishing from its 86 lakes. **Skegemog Lake** is a widely recognized hot spot for smallmouth bass. **Torch Lake** is a topnotch inland fishery. A bit north, in Antrim County, you'll find 76 inland lakes and another magnificent river, the **Jordan River**,

along which you can travel for miles through untouched wild lands and hook brown, rainbow and brook trout.

Lake Michigan Shoreline and Cadillac

Benzie County

Anglers come from far and wide to experience Great Lakes fishing from the **Frankfort Harbor** in Benzie County. Here, sparkling waters, rugged dunes and old lighthouses provide a picturesque backdrop for excellent sport fishing. An equally rugged underwater landscape provides a habitat for a wide variety of species, including brown trout, lake trout, steelhead, king salmon, coho and chinook. Those 30-pound fighting salmon also bring anglers to Benzie County's **Platte and Betsie rivers** during spawning season. The clear, shallow Platte was one of the first Michigan streams planted with coho and the fall spawning run is said to produce some of the Midwest's best fishing. Nearby, the clean, rock-bottomed Betsie River draws its share of anglers to its waters for prize king salmon and coho catches.

Inland lake fishing in the county is also popular. Beautiful **Crystal Lake**, with a depth of 160 feet and a gravel bottom, produces rainbow and lake trout, bass and perch. Featuring nearly 10,000 acres of water, winter anglers enjoy hooking lake trout and perch on the ice.

Manistee

More trophy-sized fish have come out of the Manistee area than any other location in Michigan. The **Big Manistee** and **Little Manistee** river system see a good return of planted fish. This complements a healthy wild fish population. The result is true world-class fishing in waters untouched by modern industrialization. Numerous launching sites along the waterway make the river easily accessible to anglers. In Lake Michigan, off the Manistee coastline, anglers see a lot action and pull in large, feisty salmon, steelhead and brown trout. There's always a rich variety swimming the waters; however, the peak season is June through September. Inland, you'll find good bass and pan fishing at any of the county's numerous small lakes, including **Portage** and **Bear Lakes**. **Manistee Lake** is another good option.

Ludington

Four seasons of great fishing are launched in January in the Ludington area. The month marks northern pike spearing season. You can find plenty of action at **Hamlin**, **Pere Marquette** and **Lincoln** lakes. Tip-ups and ice shanties dot frozen lakes as winter anglers brave the cold in hopes of a good panfish catch. By March, steelhead swimming upstream to spawn in the Pere Marquette River, a designated National Wild and Scenic River, provide anglers with outstanding sport fishing. Cool spring nights in April bring smelt dippers to the shores of the many tributaries feeding into Lake Michigan in the area. After dark, smelters line the **Ludington Pier** and fill their buckets with the tiny silver fish. Walleye season opens at the end of April. In recent years, more than 400,000 walleyes have been planted in the river-fed **Hamlin Lake**. Northern pike, muskie and trout season also opens and anglers find brook, rainbow and brown trout abundant in the **Pere Marquette River** as well as along **Lake Michigan**'s coastline. During May and June, the brown trout cluster in the shallows of Lake Michigan and charter boats are in full gear. About mid-August, the Pacific salmon arrive. The 30-pound fighting fish makes more great sport fishing. Throughout the fall, the salmon and steelhead action is fast and furious, but in early fall, the mouth of the Pere Marquette River is considered one of the hot spots. It's not unusual for small boat anglers to hook a 30-pound chinook from the deep holes of the lower river. Come October, the river provides opportunities for catching a fighting steelhead on its journey to spawning grounds. Depending on weather conditions, steelhead can be caught through February. The **Big Sable River**, winding through Ludington State Park, is known for producing good fall steelhead and big salmon fishing. On area inland lakes, crappie, bluegill and smallmouth bass fishing is excellent during September. By mid-December, anglers have the tip-ups out on **Hamlin Lake** once again catching famous trophy-sized bluegill, black

crappies and yellow perch, and the cycle begins once more.

Cadillac Area and Missaukee County

A few miles inland from the coastline you'll find some of the best lake fishing in the state. Missaukee County boasts 25 inland lakes, popular for hooking bass, walleye, northern pike, rainbow trout and many species of panfish. The **Clam River**, spanning Missaukee and Wexford counties, is noted for producing large brookies. In Wexford County, anglers fish year round in lakes **Cadillac and Mitchell**. Linked by a canal, the lakes offer 3,700 acres of prime fish habitat, including walleye, northern pike, crappies, bluegill, perch, largemouth and smallmouth bass. Many Michigan anglers get their initial taste of ice fishing in the Cadillac area, where the lakes are known to be the first in the north to freeze each year. Five bait shops are situated nearby the lakes to provide tips on what's biting year round. River angling in the county is equally productive. The **Pine and Manistee rivers** are famed for producing walleye, pike, rainbow and brook trout. Downstream, below the Tippy Dam, the Manistee River banks are low and there are slow wide bends making for excellent steelhead and salmon fishing.

Little Traverse

One of the world's most famous fishing buffs, author Ernest Hemingway, grew up along the shores of **Walloon Lake** in the Little Traverse region. The great American writer enjoyed fishing these waters, especially the **Bear River**, and shared his northern outdoor experiences in his work.

Today, the region is still an angling paradise for devotees of the sport. An inland waterway system, popular with modern anglers, was once traveled by American Indians, French voyageurs and loggers. From Crooked Lake near Petoskey, boats up to 30 feet can travel this 38-mile long waterway across the northern end of the lower peninsula to Lake Huron. Because of the many species harbored in the network of rivers, streams, inland lakes to Lake Michigan and Lake Huron, there's an element of surprise to the Little Traverse fish-

Ing experience. Old timers claim you never know what's on your hook until you reel it in. However, you can be sure to encounter good fishing almost anywhere in the region. In the fall, salmon, steelhead and brown trout catches are good on **Lake Michigan**.

In the springtime anglers fish the rivers for brown, rainbow and brook trout. The inland lakes, including **Round**, **Crooked** and **Pick-erel**, are popular and productive year round with walleye, pike, perch and bass. In Charlevoix, anglers never need to cancel because of foul weather on Lake Michigan. From local docking stations, vessels can access the big lake, as well as **Lake Charlevoix** and **Round Lake**. So if conditions on one body of water are poor, anglers can head to the other.

While Lake Michigan provides king salmon, lake trout, brown trout and steelhead, angling Lake Charlevoix can produce lake trout, brown trout, smallmouth bass and panfish, and at times, steelhead and king salmon when they move into the waters from Lake Michigan. According to Insiders, Lake Charlevoix fishing is sometimes superior to angling on the big lake. Another great angling opportunity can be had on **Beaver Island**, 32 miles off the Charlevoix harbor, where you'll find good pan fishing at five of the island's seven inland lakes. The spring and fall perch runs at the island's St. James Bay is an event many anglers eagerly anticipate.

Mackinac Straits Area

Even though the season is shorter than in other coastal areas, lasting only from June through September, angler's find fishing the waters of the scenic Mackinac Straits exciting and rewarding. The deep water produces an abundance of large, feisty brown trout, lake trout, steelhead and king salmon. The best Great Lake fishing is in **Lake Huron**, east of the Mighty Mackinac Bridge that links Michigan's two peninsulas and Lakes Michigan and Huron. On the inland lakes, fishing is best in early summer and fall when bass, walleye and perch bite in **Paradise**, **Burt** and **Mullet** lakes.

Bait and Tackle Shops

With the spectacular network of waterways and lakes gracing Northwest Michigan, there's fishing going on about anywhere and anytime. Because of this abundance of angling opportunities, you'll find you never have to travel far to find a bait and tackle shop. Listed below are a few Insiders' favorites. Shop hours are year round unless otherwise noted.

Grand Traverse

Traverse City Area

MC Sports Outdoor Center and Traverse Bay Tackle
3450 S. Airport Rd., Traverse City
• (616) 933-6158

It might be the next best thing to fishing itself. MC Sports Outdoor Center features more than 25,000 square feet of fishing and hunting supplies, gear, bait, tackle and licenses. From fly-fishing to deepwater angling, they offer everything you might need for sport fishing and more. Popular brands stocked include St. Croix and Fenwick. The mega-sport store is open daily.

Orvis Streamside Shop
100 Grand Traverse Village Blvd., Grand Traverse Resort, Acme • (616) 938-5337

The only Orvis dealer in the Traverse City area, the shop boasts the largest fly selection in the region. Here, you'll also find outdoor clothing, classes and Orvis-endorsed guide services. The shop is open daily.

Tackle Town
13680 S.W. Bayshore Dr., Traverse City
• (616) 941-5420

Looking for a reel like Grandpa had? You

INSIDERS' TIP

Having been around for 400 million years, the lake sturgeon is one of the oldest fish inhabiting Michigan waters. They can weigh up to 200 pounds and are most often caught by spearing through the ice.

might find it at Tackle Town. They carry many hard-to-find items, including old lures, reels and rods. They also carry licenses, a full selection of seasonal live bait, marine supplies, archery equipment, muzzleloaders and more. The store is closed only on major holidays.

Leelanau County

John's Barber Shop
115 Madison St., Suttons Bay
• **(616) 271-3424**

Like in many of the small towns in Northwest Michigan, you'll find licenses and bait for sale in Suttons Bay where you might least expect it, the village barber shop. John will sell you wigglers, cut your hair and trim your beard! Whether you're heading out to the big lake, inland lakes or area streams, John has what you need in bait and tackle. In the summer the shop is open Monday through Saturday; off season, Tuesday through Saturday.

Antrim-Kalkaska Area

Jack's Sport Shop
212 S. Cedar St., Kalkaska
• **(616) 258-8892**

Featuring one of the largest tackle selections in northern Michigan, if Jack's Sport Shop doesn't have it in stock, they'll order it for you. They carry a full selection of live bait, including crawlers, wigglers, minnows and crickets. In addition to fishing supplies and licenses, you'll find archery equipment, guns and ammo, outdoor boots and Columbia clothing for men and women. The store is open daily.

Lake Michigan Shoreline and Cadillac

Backcast Fly Shop
1675 U.S. Hwy. 31, Benzonia
• **(800) 717-5222**

Backcast is more than a fly shop. The outfitter handles archery, camping and hunting equipment, in addition to fly-fishing and flytying supplies, rod building items, rods and reels, tackle, licenses and pet supplies. The shop is open daily except for Christmas, New Year's Day and Easter.

Frankfort Tackle Box
903 Main St., Frankfort • **(616) 352-7673**

Whether you fish the area's rivers, inland lakes or streams, you'll find tackle and bait to meet your needs at this downtown Frankfort shop. You'll also find rods, reels, downriggers, marine supplies and licenses. The shop is open daily from early March until early December.

Insta-Launch
20 Park Ave., Manistee • **(616) 723-3901**

Insta-Launch Campground store claims they stock the largest selection of fishing gear, bait and tackle within 50 miles of Manistee. Their motto is, "If we don't have it, you don't need it." Licenses are available. The store opens at 5 AM in the summer, but off-season hours vary.

Northwind Sports
400 Parkdale Ave., Manistee
• **(616) 723-2255**

Tackle, bait and licenses for fishing the big lake, inland lakes, area rivers and streams are all available at Northwind Sports. Live bait includes waxworms, crawlers, leeches, wigglers and leafworms. They carry Columbia clothing, hunting, camping, golf and water sport items. The store hours open daily with extended hours during Christmas and winter ski season.

North Bayou Resort Tackle Shop & Marina
4849 N. Lakeshore Dr., Ludington
• **(616) 845-5820, (800) 261-7415**

Situated on Lower Hamlin Lake, the shop specializes in tackle, bait and gear for inland lake fishing. They carry a wide variety of tackle as well as licenses, boating supplies, snacks and refreshments. The shop is open daily in spring, summer and fall.

Pere Marquette Sport Center
214 W. Ludington Ave., Ludington
• **(616) 843-8676**

The Pere Marquette Sport Center offers one of the best selections of fishing gear in

Tastes of the Traverse Bay Region

Dolfi's Secret Slow-Cooked Venison

2 to 3 pounds of venison
1 stick of butter
1 sliced onion
1 sliced green pepper
1 clove of garlic
29 oz. of tomato sauce
1 can of tomato paste
1/2 teaspoon baking soda
2 tablespoons Italian seasoning
1 tablespoon beef bouillon pepper, salt and season to taste

Trim fat from venison. Melt butter in skillet. Brown venison, onion and green pepper in skillet. Put half of the tomato sauce and remainder of ingredients in a crockpot and

— continued on next page

Photo: Courtesy of Chef Hermann

Master chef Hermann Suhs delights patrons with Michigan game dishes, authentic international cuisine and tempting pastries.

stir. Add venison, onions, green pepper and butter to crockpot. Fill crockpot to the top with the rest of the tomato sauce. Cook on high until it boils, turn to low and cook 5 to 7 hours. Serve with rice.

This recipe was originally published by the Wildlife Division of the Michigan Department of Natural Resources in How to Field Dress a White-Tailed Deer and is printed here with their permission.

Venison Medallions Austrian Style

8 ounces venison leg, sliced and de-sinewed
(De-sinewed means all skin and fat have been removed.)
2 ounces butter
1 tablespoon red wine
1 tablespoon brandy
salt, pepper, thyme, lingonberries
2 ounces brown sauce
Lightly flour meat and saute in butter for 3 minutes. Add the seasonings and red wine; cook for 2 more minutes. Turn over and add brown sauce and brandy.

This recipe appears courtesy of Master Chef Hermann Suhs of Cadillac. It originally appeared in the book Cooking With Chef Hermann, available at Hermann's European Cafe and all Horizon Bookstores.

the Ludington area. The shop also offers seasonal live bait, licenses and friendly advice. There is an on-site fish freezing facility, rod and reel repair service, and the shop is an authorized Coleman repair center. Hunting and camping gear is available as well as Lake Michigan and river-fishing charter trips. The store is open daylight to dusk, year round.

Laura Lee's Landing
1749 North Blvd., Cadillac
• **(616) 775-2648**
On the shores of Lake Cadillac, this bait, tackle and party store offers all the live bait you'll ever want or need, not to mention cold beverages and the town's best ice cream cones. Here, you'll find minnows, wigglers, crawlers, leeches, crickets, waxworms and spikes. The shop is open seven days a week, year round. Marine fuel, a boat launch, boat and dock rentals and licenses are available.

Schafer's Bait Shop
2722 Sunnyside Dr., Cadillac
• **(616) 775-7085**
Pay a visit to Schafer's Bait Shop for free fishing advice in the Cadillac area. In west

Cadillac near Mitchell State Park, they can supply you with information and live bait for both summer and winter fishing. They also carry licenses, archery equipment and firearm ammunition. The shop is open seven days a week.

Little Traverse

Holiday Gas Station
1408 Bridge St., Charlevoix
• **(616) 547-2821**
The Holiday Gas Station in Charlevoix never closes. You can get tackle and bait at 3 o'clock in the morning and even on Christmas Day. The station carries what you need for big lake, inland lake and river fishing, including a variety of live bait and a good selection of tackle and licenses.

Whippoorwill Orvis Shop
305 E. Lake St., Petoskey
• **(616) 348-7061**
Whippoorwill specializes in Orvis top-of-the-line fly-fishing equipment. They carry men's and women's outdoor clothing and a collection of cottage furniture. Professional Orvis-

endorsed guided fly-fishing expeditions can be planned for anywhere in northern Michigan. Call for reservations about one week in advance. The Whippoorwill is open daily, and closed only on major holidays

Young's Bait and Party Store
7339 Burr Ave., Alanson
• **(616) 548-5286**

If you need advice regarding fishing in the Little Traverse region, this is where Insiders will send you. Young's large inventory includes fishing supplies, bait, archery equipment, guns and licenses. This friendly, helpful and well-stocked shop on Crooked River is open daily, 364 days a year.

Mackinac Straits

Coffman Hardware and Camp Store
227 Central Ave., Mackinaw City
• **(616) 436-5650**

Coffman's offers the best selection of tackle and live bait in Mackinaw for salmon and inland lake fishing. They also carry rods, reels and licenses. They're open seven days a week from April to November, but hours vary depending on demand.

Guided River Fishing

The unparalleled beauty of Northwest Michigan's river country and an abundance of sport fish make angling these waters an out of this world experience. The popularity of one-day fly-fishing expeditions aboard guided river boats is growing wildly. Whether you're a novice or expert angler, guided trips along Michigan's blue-ribbon rivers promise to be rewarding fishing adventures. In addition to the guide services listed below, refer to charter boat and outfitter listings. Some charter services and outdoor suppliers also offer guided trips. Local visitors bureaus and chambers of commerce also keep lists of fishing

guides on hand (see listings in our Getting Here and Getting Around chapter).

Orvis Streamside Shop
Grand Traverse Resort, Acme
• **(616) 938-5337**

Professional guides offer one-day fly-fishing trips along the world-renowned Manistee and Pere Marquette Rivers. Strictly catch-and-release trips, the sporting expeditions focus on hooking trout, steelhead and salmon. All equipment is provided, as are meals. The cost is $250 per day for two anglers. Some dates book as far as one year in advance, so call well ahead of your trip to secure reservations.

The Troutsman
4386 U.S. Hwy. 31 N., Traverse City
• **(616) 938-3474, (800) 308-7688**

At The Troutsman a staff of five professional guides specialize in Northwest Michigan coldwater fisheries, including the Manistee, Pere Marquette, Muskegon and Au Sable rivers. However, the company will book trips for you as far north as Canada. The Troutsman fly-fishing expeditions practice catch-and-release from drift boats. While it's often possible to show up and go, it's best to make reservations. Peak dates book one year in advance. All equipment and meals are provided. The 8- to 12-hour trips cost $275 for two people.

Wild Bill's Guide Service
1525 E. Old State, East Jordan
• **(616) 536-2289**

Wild Bill is the only guide currently working the spring-fed Jordan River. Specializing in the purest form of fly-fishing and using all hand-tied flies, his clients catch brook, rainbow and brown trout from the pristine Jordan waters. All equipment and meals are provided. Rates for up to three anglers are $150 for a half day and $225 for a full day. Summer trips are booked one year in advance, while spring and fall trips book about one month in advance.

INSIDERS' TIP

The first weekend in June marks Michigan's annual Free Fishing Weekend. For two days, all fishing license and trout/salmon stamp fees are waived.

Lake Michigan Charters

Charter boats offer big-water fishing adventures that all but guarantee a safe, successful trip. Michigan charter boats must comply with some of the strictest regulations in the nation for licensing. All vessels with a capacity of six passengers or less are regularly state inspected. Those of greater capacity undergo regular inspection by the U.S. Coast Guard. Many charter boats are specially rigged for game fishing and you can count on the captains to know the ways of the big lakes — and the big fish. Charters are available for individuals or groups. Most services provide all the equipment you need for your adventure; however, state law requires you to obtain a Michigan fishing license. They are available from many sporting good shops and most Department of Natural Resources offices. Visitors bureaus and chambers of commerce provide information on charter services (see our Getting Here and Getting Around chapter for listings).

Grand Traverse

Traverse City Area

Reel Fun Fishing Charters
4630 U.S. Hwy. 31 N., Traverse City
• (616) 938-2382, (616) 938-2763

The oldest charter service in West Grand Traverse Bay, Reel Fun books trips from early May until October. For 15 years, its charter anglers have been hooking brown trout, steelhead, lake trout, chinook and coho. Cost for a four-hour trip is $50 per person with a $150 minimum. Equipment is provided and your catch will be cleaned and bagged at no extra charge. It's often possible to show up and go, however, your best bet is to secure reservations at least 48 hours in advance.

TC Charters
10244 San Remo Blvd., Traverse City
• (616) 947-6612

Catch the big ones aboard the north's premier fishing yacht. TC Charters' 47-foot yacht is the largest sport-fishing vessel cruising these waters. Running in West Bay, the company guarantees catches from May through July. From the company's two modern yachts anglers land lake trout, brown trout, steelhead, coho and chinook. Half-day rates range from $250 to $295, depending on the season and the number of passengers. It's sometimes possible to show up and go, but the captain suggests you secure reservations one week in advance. Diving and sailing charters are also available.

Leelanau County

Carlson's Charter Service
205 W. River St., Leland
• (616) 256-9801

Carlson's fleet of 11 boats provides excellent fishing opportunities in the cool waters between Leland and the scenic Manitou Islands. A healthy ecosystem for fish, local waters produce lake trout, brown trout, salmon and steelhead catches. Equipment and ice are provided and cleaning and smoking facilities are on-site at the dock area. In 1997, prices were $60 per person for half-day trips and $450 for full-days, with a maximum of six passengers. Carlson's can often book your trip with 24 hours notice; however, they prefer reservations at least one week in advance.

Fishtown Charter Service
1657 N. Manitou Tr., Leland
• (616) 256-9639

Captain James Munoz has fished the waters between Leland and the Manitou Islands for 25 years. Fishtown Charter Service was the first charter service established in the quaint village of Leland. Munoz says fish are attracted to the islands like magnets, so the catch is always good. In midsummer, offshore steelhead fishing is popular, and Fishtown Charter customers also land lake trout, brown trout, coho and chinook. Half-day (five-hour) rates are $60 per person with a $240 minimum, and full-day (nine-hour) trips are a flat $500 for up to six people. For July and August trips, it's advised that you secure a reservation by May. At other times, if you can be a little flexible, the captain will try to accommodate your schedule.

Lake Michigan Shoreline and Cadillac

Linda Marie Charter Service
East Shore Marina, Frankfort
- **(616) 775-6272**

Captains Buzz and Linda Smith, sharing 25 years of angling experience, operate the Linda Marie Charter Service on Betsie Bay between Frankfort and Elberta. The 31' Cherokee Chief hardtop is licensed to carry six passengers and all fishing equipment is furnished. Half-day rates are $70 per person with a $280 minimum. Full-day rates are $130 per person with a $520 minimum. Reservations are available on a first-come, first-served basis.

Decoy Charter Service
4204 University Pl., Manistee
- **(616) 723-4063**

Decoy Charters operates year round providing Lake Michigan and Manistee River fishing adventures. From the captain's 18-foot, enclosed riverboat, anglers hook salmon, steelhead, brown trout and lake trout throughout the summer and winter months. While it's sometimes possible to show up and go, reservations are recommended. In 1997, Lake Michigan charters were $475 for a full-day trip, and $350 for a half-day for up to six people. River runs for two people are $280 for a full day.

Fish Are Us Charters
290 Fourth St., Manistee
- **(616) 723-7910**

A Manistee native, Captain Dave Gramza has been fishing area waters his whole life and knows the fishing hot spots like the back of his hand. He operates a 24-foot vessel outfitted with the latest in big lake-fishing technology. In spring, charter anglers hook brown trout, lake trout, rainbow trout and steelhead. From June through August, chinook and coho give anglers a sporting fight. Equipment is provided and your catch is cleaned and bagged for you. Rates are $300 for half-day trips, and $400 for full-day trips with up to four people.

Big Jon Pro-Team Charters Inc.
800 S. Washington Ave., Ludington
- **(616) 843-3555, (800) 528-5898**

Big Jon Charters will take you to the best spots for catching chinook, coho, steelhead, lake trout and brown trout and provide you with a free video of your Lake Michigan adventure as a souvenir! Licensed since 1988, the charter company furnishes all equipment and cleans and bags your catch. To reserve a date during prime summer weekends, the captain suggests you contact their office in January. Full-day rates are $100 per person, and half-day rates are $75, with a minimum of four people and a maximum of six people.

Captain Chuck's GLT Co. Charters & Tackle Shop
900 S. Washington Ave., Ludington
- **(616) 843-4458, (888) 227-8248**

This is Ludington's largest charter fleet. It features seven vessels for Lake Michigan salmon and steelhead sport fishing. Captain Chuck welcomes children. In fact, he lets children younger than 16 fish for free. With a four-person minimum, half-day rates are $290, and full-day charters run $340. All equipment is provided. Captain Chuck's Tackle store is a complete tackle shop for salmon and steelhead fishing. The captain carries about everything you might need for fishing the big lake, including rods, reels, downriggers, spoons and plugs. Anglers are welcome to call the Captain Chuck for local fishing update reports. The shop is open daily, mid-April through September.

Little Traverse

Blue Fin Sportfishing Charters
14226 W. Garfield St., Charlevoix
- **(616) 547-6808**

Foul weather need not change your fishing plans with Blue Fin Charters. If conditions prohibit fishing on Lake Michigan, you can enter the waterway into Lake Charlevoix. On the big lake, charter anglers hook king salmon, lake trout, brown trout and steelhead. On the quieter waters of Lake Charlevoix, the catch is lake trout, brown trout, bass, walleye and panfish, or, if the timing is right, salmon and steelhead. Blue Fin updates onboard fishing technology every two years and provides all the equipment and bait you need for a successful expedition. Charters run from May 1 through the end of October. Five-hour trips cost $275 for one to six passengers. Longer trips are available upon request.

Ward Brothers Boats Inc.
106 E. Antrim St., Charlevoix
• **(616) 547-2371**

From May 1 through October, Ward Brothers Boats Inc. charters Lake Michigan fishing trips aboard its fleet of three 31-foot vessels. Captains know the hot spots for hooking lake trout, brown trout salmon and steelhead. Rates are $70 per person for 4½-hour trips, and $600

for eight hours with a four person minimum and six person maximum. The company's Ship Store offers "a little of everything," including fishing tackle and bait, charts, boat cleaning supplies, fuses and more. The store is open daily in summer, weekdays in the off-season. Boat rentals, storage and repairs are also available.

Ruddy Duck Charters
3175 Country Club Rd., Petoskey
• **(616) 347-3232**

Ruddy Duck is the only charter service operating in Little Traverse Bay, one of the better lake trout ports on the coast. The charter service runs from mid-May until October. Other species found in the bay include brown trout,

Rearing Sport Fish at
Northwest Michigan's State Hatcheries

For those who equate utopia with the experience of hauling in a 30-pound salmon, there's great news. Sportfishing in Northwest Michigan is getting better every year. From the Ludington coast to the waters surrounding Mighty Mac, anglers are increasing their catches. The healthy fish population is the result, in part, of intensive stocking efforts. About one-third of all recreational fishing in Michigan depends on stocked fish. The Michigan Department of Natural Resources (DNR) Fisheries Division annually plants about 30 million fish in 1,067 lakes, rivers and streams, enhancing quality angling opportunities.

See for yourself how the DNR rears stock fish at one of Northwest Michigan's public hatcheries. Altogether, the state operates six hatcheries in its fish production program. In Northwest Michigan they are near the villages of Harrietta and Honor. Visitors are welcome year round.

The Harrietta State Hatchery, originally built in 1901, is one of the earliest hatchery facilities in the state. It's in Wexford County, south of Mesick off Michigan Highway 37, along West 30 Mile Road. You can explore the facility daily between 8 AM and 4:30 PM.

Each year, this hatchery produces 1 to 2 million rainbow and brown trout. The process begins in incubation trays. Trays used at the facility have a capacity to hold 8 million trout eggs or 5 million salmon eggs. Once hatched, fish are placed into one of the facility's nine indoor tanks. Each tank holds 445 cubic feet of water and will produce up to 1,650 pounds of fish. When the fish reach 2.2 inches in length, they are transferred to outdoor raceways. Raceways contain 2,118 cubic feet of water and produce 13,200 pounds of fish. While at the facility, the trout are fed an artificial diet with the help of automatic feeders. Come spring, fish 16 months of age, or about 6 inches long, are pumped from the raceways to specially equipped trucks and are transported to planting sites.

In Benzie County, tour the $6 million Platte River Anadromous Hatchery. Built in

— continued on next page

Workers at the Harrietta State Fish Hatchery vacuum raceway waters
to maintain an optimal growing environment for young trout.

Photo: Harrietta State Fish Hatchery

1974, it is Michigan's largest hatchery, as well as one of the most modern and well-equipped. You'll find it 4 miles east of Honor along U.S. Highway 31. Buildings are open for self-guided tours between 8 AM and 4 PM daily and the grounds can be toured from dawn until dusk. Each fall, salmon spawning runs begin a new cycle of egg-taking, hatching and rearing. The facility raises 1.2-million coho and 4-million chinook annually. Between mid-September and mid-October, you can see large numbers of salmon returning to the Platte River at the Lower Platte River Weir. In September and early November, you can view the natural spectacle at the upper Weir, located at the hatchery. At the Platte River spawn-taking station, you can observe collection of coho eggs daily from mid-October through the end of the month.

During the same period, Chinook egg-taking operations are ongoing at a facility on the Little Manistee River. In the spring, when the steelhead spawning run occurs, eggs are also collected at the Little Manistee unit. After collection and fertilization of the eggs at the river spawn-taking sites, the delicate eggs are transported to the hatchery's incubation room at the north end of the main hatchery building. Up to 20 million salmon eggs can be incubated there at one time. Due to the fragile nature of the young eggs, this room is not open to public viewing. Hatching occurs in about eight weeks after eggs are brought to the facility. After hatching, the young coho and chinook remain in incubators for three to four weeks. In January, they are transferred to one of the 12 indoor starter tanks. There, they are fed an artificial diet. As these future sport fish grow, they are moved into additional tanks or ponds. Chinooks are reared in the hatchery for only six months before they are planted, while coho are reared for 18 months before planting. When the fish, known as fingerlings and yearlings, have matured, they are transported on trucks that can haul up to 5,000 pounds and are equipped with aeration and recirculation systems. Fish reared at the Platte River Hatchery are transported and planted throughout the state, from the Detroit River in southern Michigan to waterways in the western end of the Upper Peninsula. Once released, the fish migrate downstream to the Great Lakes. Coho spend two summers and chinook three summers in the Great Lakes before they return to streams to spawn. By then, they have grown to between five and 30 pounds, making a prize catch for lucky anglers.

chinook and steelhead. Ruddy Duck rates for four hours are $140 for two people, and additional passengers are $30 each. Full-day rates are double. It's recommended that you make reservations as far in advance as possible, but they try to accommodate same day or next day requests.

Mackinac Straits

Great Turtle Charters
(800) 206-2124

The only charter fishing service operating from Mackinac Island, Great Turtle offers Lake Huron fishing June through September. Charter service is also available from Mackinaw City. Great Turtle's vessel features a full cabin and state-of-the-art electronic fishing equipment. Gear is provided and fish are cleaned and bagged. The captain takes angling seriously and usually doesn't head back to shore empty handed. In addition to fishing expeditions, Great Turtle offers sightseeing tours, day and night cruises and water transportation. For fishing charters, call two weeks in advance to secure reservations.

Fishing Schools

Orvis Streamside Shop
Grand Traverse Resort, Acme
• (616) 938-5337

No prior experience is necessary to enroll for the one-day fly-fishing workshops at the Orvis Streamside Shop at the Grand Traverse Resort. While classes focus on casting, you'll also learn about flies, insects, knots and equipment. Workshops run from 9 AM until 5 PM at Ranch Rudolf along the Boardman River. Equipment is provided. Two schools are scheduled during June and two in the month of July. Expect to pay $90 per person for workshops. Call the store for reservations.

Fish Markets

Carlson's Fish Market
Fishtown, Leland • (616) 256-9801
511 W. Front St., Traverse City
• (616) 941-9392

Strolling through the historic Leland fishing village you may catch a fragrant whiff from Carlson's fisheries' daily smoking operation. Follow your nose to the retail shop in the harbor where you can purchase delectable fish sausage, whitefish pâté and all types of fresh and smoked fish. A commercial- and charter-fishing business, Carlson's also operates a market in Traverse City. Fishtown is open May through October, with extended hours in July and August. The Traverse City shop is open Monday through Saturday year round.

Bortell's Fisheries
5510 S. Lakeshore Dr., Ludington
• (616) 843-3337

In the fish business for 100 years, Bortell's specializes in smoked fish, using old-fashioned, all-natural wood smoke. Since local commercial fishing no longer exists, the fishery ships in a wide variety of ocean fish, including Alaskan salmon and ocean perch. A full line of fresh fish is available, including walleye, catfish, trout and whitefish. Bortell's is open daily from mid-May through Labor Day. Off-season hours vary.

Bell's Fishery
229 S. Huron St., Mackinaw City
• (616) 436-7821

Operated as a family business for three generations, Bell's offer fresh whitefish, perch, trout and salmon from local waters. Smoked varieties include whitefish, trout, herring, salmon and chubs. While the family retails its fish, it also ships the freshwater prizes to markets in New York and Boston. In July and August, the shop is open daily. Off-season hours vary, so call ahead.

INSIDERS' TIP

The first catch for most Michigan anglers is the sunfish. You don't need sophisticated gear to hook one, and they are plentiful in most of the state's lakes and streams. Land them from shore, docks, boats or through the ice — morning, noon or night.

Hunting

With three major national forests and more acres of dedicated state forest lands than any other state in the nation, Michigan offers some exceptional hunting opportunities. In Northwest Michigan, you'll find rewarding hunts from a wide scope of big game, upland game and waterfowl.

Opening day of the firearm deer season in northern Michigan is an eagerly awaited holiday. On this mid-November date, some schools close and many businesses operate with limited staff as workers take to the woods. Special events are planned just for non-hunting spouses.

As popular as it is, hunting is more than outdoor recreation. It's an important component of Michigan's economy, especially in northern communities that rely heavily on tourist dollars. Deer hunters alone are estimated to spend between $400 and $500 million annually on food, lodging, transportation, licenses and hunting equipment.

The number of men and women who head into the fields and forests of Northwest Michigan to hunt is increasing each year. Before you join them, there are things you need to know. Managing Michigan's diverse wild game population calls for some complex, game-specific rules and regulations. These are outlined in the *Michigan Hunting and Trapping Guide* published by the Michigan Department of Natural Resources, and available free from DNR offices (see listings at the beginning of this chapter) and license dealers. Between this guidebook and application guides for individual game animals, you'll find all the information you need to ensure that your hunt is in compliance with Michigan hunting regulations.

One safety rule you must be aware of is that Michigan, like many other states, requires hunters to wear blaze-orange clothing. It can be a cap, hat, vest, jacket or rain gear. Like most rules, there are exceptions. In this case, the law does not apply to those hunting waterfowl, crow and wild turkey, or to archers hunting bear and deer, except during the November firearm deer season. Michigan also has protected wildlife, including swans, eagles, hawks, owls, wolves, lynx, moose, martens, cougars, bear cubs, sows and all-white or albino deer. Also protected are all nongame birds, except starlings, English sparrows and feral pigeons.

Numerous wildlife research projects are in progress in Michigan. The DNR Wildlife Division has marked several species involved in the studies. Some bears are outfitted with radio collars and hunters are asked not to take these research animals. If you harvest game with bands, collars or tags, follow the attached directions for reporting the specimen. If reporting directions are not provided, you can call any DNR office. Finally, consider your opportunity as a sportsperson to make a difference. You can donate your wild game meat to needy families. Several hunting and charitable organizations participate in programs utilizing the game harvest. Michigan Sportsmen Against Hunger operates an information hotline. Give them a call to locate the drop-off station nearest you, (313) 278-FOOD. See hunting license information at the beginning of this chapter.

Report all poaching to the Michigan Department of Natural Resources, (800) 292-7800.

Hunting Licenses

The types of hunting licenses are too numerous to list, but be aware that early deadlines apply for obtaining many game licenses. For example, the deadline to apply for bear permits is generally mid-June, even though the season is in the fall. Check with any DNR office for license information regarding specific species (see listings at the beginning of this chapter).

Deer

The quality of deer hunting in the state is legendary. Deer are by far the most-hunted game and are hunted in all Northwest Michigan counties. During the 1996 firearm season, an estimated 103,000 deer were harvested in the northern Lower Peninsula. Throughout Michigan, nearly 300,000 deer were harvested in that period. In Michigan deer hunters spend an estimated 12 million days afield, more than in any other state. This suc-

Photo: Greg Wright

Benzie County is an outstanding area for hunting ruffed grouse.

cess is explained, in part, by the many types of deer licenses available to hunters, and to Michigan's extended deer season.

Deer licenses are available to residents and, at a higher rate, to nonresidents. Antlerless licenses are available to residents only. While the DNR manages wildlife numbers by bag limits and the number of days in a season, they attempt to offer hunters as much consistency year to year as possible. Most recently, the archery hunting season was set to begin about October 1 and continue until mid-November when firearm season opened. Almost 50 percent of the year's harvest was taken during the first two days of firearm season, which continued through the end of November. Archery deer season resumed on the beginning of December, lasting until January. Other special dates are designated for muzzleloading. Check the current guidebook or call the DNR for specific hunt dates for the region where you are hunting.

Insiders say your best luck in landing a Michigan white-tailed deer is by using modern firearms, however Michigan leads the nation in deer-hunting opportunities for archers. It's estimated that there are about 400,000 bow hunters, 750,000 firearm deer hunters and 200,000 muzzleloading hunters in the fields each year. It's no wonder because Michigan's deer herd is one of the largest in the United States — exceeding one million. An extremely adaptable species, they are hunted in wetlands or upland in the brushy, forested lands. Your DNR guidebook outlines rules regarding the use of blinds, baiting and specific firearm regulations, the use of kill tags, hunting on private lands and youth hunting. For those of you who come down with a case of "Buck Fever" each fall, you might as well dream of landing a big one. The largest deer shot in Michigan was a 12-point buck weighing 354 pounds. That's a lot of venison!

Black Bear

Emmet County in the Little Traverse region is considered one of the prime bear-hunting locations in the north. An estimated 1,000 black bears roam the lands of northern Michigan. The bear is considered a prized-game species with permit applications increasing about 10 percent each year. Permits are quite limited and you must have a little luck to get one. Once the DNR sets a harvest quota for the subsequent season, Michigan hunters are awarded harvest tags through a lottery. Two percent of the total tags are set aside for out-of-state residents. In 1997, 5,592 permits were issued with expectations of a harvest of about 1,400 bears.

Dates for fall hunting seasons and harvest quotas vary among the state's ten Bear Management Units. The zones were established in 1990 for better managing the bear population. Northwest Michigan counties typically open for bear hunting include Benzie, Grand Traverse, Manistee, Missaukee, Kalkaska, Charlevoix, Emmet and Antrim. You'll find the black bear in different types of habitat, but they're most commonly found near wetland areas. The traditional method of hunting with dogs is still popular with most Michigan bear hunters. You need to check your DNR application guide for dog rules. Baiting is permitted, but once again, check the application guide for the complete rules. Most recently, the bag limit was one per year. Successful hunters are required to take their bear to a DNR check station within 72 hours of the kill. Information provided by hunters is considered a valuable research tool.

Elk

Landing a Michigan elk may be the easiest part of the hunting adventure. Getting the 700-pound animal out of the woods is the bigger challenge. Michigan's native elk disappeared around the late 1800, but were reintroduced in 1918. Today, the herd of 1,000, located in central northern Michigan, is managed for recreational hunting and viewing. About 200 elk licenses are issued annually to Michigan residents only via a lottery. In 1996, 42,000 applications were received for elk and antlerless-only elk licenses. Those awarded permits are required to attend a half-day training session near the elk hunt area the day prior to their scheduled hunt. If you're one of the lucky ones, you'll learn everything from hunter safety and carcass handling to elk behavior and recommended hunting locations.

Small Game

Rabbits, bobcats, coyote, raccoon, fox and squirrels are some of the small game hunted in Northwest Michigan's bountiful woodlands. About one million rabbits are harvested by Michigan hunters annually. You'll find snowshoe hares inhabit swamp edges, some pine plantations and brush land adjacent to swamps. Cottontails are abundant throughout the region. They rank second to the white-tailed deer as the most popular game animal in the state. The recent season on rabbits was September through March. In Northwest Michigan, bobcat are hunted in Antrim, Charlevoix, Emmet, Otsego, Kalkaska, Missaukee and Wexford counties. Bobcat season varies in the different zoned management areas, so check your DNR guidebook for season dates in the desired area. If you land a bobcat, you are required to take it to a DNR check station within five days of the kill for research purposes. Information on hunting and trapping other small game can be found in your DNR guidebook.

Birds

With the ruffed grouse and woodcock, as with other game, hunting season can vary. Northwest Michigan counties offer some of the state's best grouse and woodcock territories, thanks, in part, to the lumber industry. Where you find active timber harvesting operations, you'll find good grouse hunting in the cut-over areas. You'll find concentrations of woodcock in soft-soiled areas. Benzie County is considered outstanding for grouse hunting while Kalkaska's wild lands are considered one of the hot spots for woodcock. Don't be surprised to find flocks of wild turkey strolling across roads in Northwest Michigan. To motorists, they're an annoyance but to the turkey hunter, they're the essence of a great sport. Wild turkeys are found in the upland hardwood forests. There's a healthy population, but permits are limited and awarded through the lottery system, similar to bear and elk permits. Hunts take place in spring and fall. Turkey hunters are a special breed. Insiders say there's an ascetic element to this hunt.

INSIDERS' TIP

The graceful trumpeter swan is being reintroduced to wetlands in Michigan and is a protected species. These lovely birds weigh up to 30 pounds and have wing spans measuring 7 feet.

Hunters call birds using various techniques rather than stalking their target, taking turkeys with bows, modern firearms or muzzleloaders. Emmet, Charlevoix and Otsego counties are some of the top locations in Michigan for successful turkey hunts.

Waterfowl

Although Northwest Michigan is not located on the migratory flyway, hunters find some fairly good opportunities in the region. Among the hundreds of inland lakes, you'll find good local concentrations of mallards, wood ducks and Canada geese. However, there are some areas in Michigan posted closed to waterfowl hunting. In Grand Traverse County, Boardman Lake and those waters of the Boardman River lying north of Airport Road and south of the 8th Street Bridge are closed.

Hunters also need to be aware that a federal migratory bird-hunting stamp, a Michigan waterfowl hunting license and a Michigan small game license are all required for hunting migratory waterfowl in the state. Federal stamps are available at post offices and some retail licenses agents. All of the state and federal regulations are made clear in the Michigan Waterfowl Hunting Guide available from DNR offices. Use of decoys and blinds, seasons and bag limits on individual species are also outlined in the guide.

Taxidermy Services

If you decide you want to mount your wild game, remember, after the kill, time is of the essence. Taxidermists recommend freezing your game if you cannot get it to them within one to two days of capture.

Taxidermists are required to be licensed by the state. In addition, they may also hold federal licenses that permit handling of migratory birds. Prices for mounts are based on material and labor costs. While there are numerous skilled taxidermists in the region, the ones we've included have distinguished themselves as topnotch professionals. Operating full-time services, they are available for consultation during regular business hours.

Grand Traverse

Traverse City Area

Bay West Taxidermists
9980 Carter Rd., Traverse City
• **(616) 947-3886**

A specialist in white tail deer shoulder mounts, taxidermist Jim Dreves has taken first place in both national and international competitions. Rather than using commercial mannequins, Dreves sculpts his own. He is state and federally licensed and a full-service game and fish taxidermist. His shop is open weekdays.

Guntzviller Taxidermy
11060 U.S. Hwy. 31 S., Elk Rapids
• **(616) 264-5597**

Established in 1928, Guntzviller prepares top-quality mounts and has produced work for several of the area's wildlife museums. The company operates a wildlife museum called Spirit of the Woods, where more than 1,000 mounts are displayed. Guntzviller has experience preserving everything from small birds to big game. They are state and federally licensed and have been members of the National Association of Taxidermists for more than 60 years.

Arrowhead Taxidermy
15782 Hooker Rd., Lake Ann
• **(616) 275-5900**

Although he can handle anything from birds to big game, trout and steelhead mounts are owner Ken Howe's specialty. Howe has practiced his craft for 18 years, distinguishing himself as a topnotch taxidermist among statewide hunting organizations. His shop is open Tuesday through Saturday, and by appointment.

INSIDERS' TIP

Call the wildlife newsline at (517) 373-WILD for reports on hunting conditions.

Antrim-Kalkaska Area

Tony's Taxidermy
Mich. Hwy. 72 W., Grayling
• (517) 348-4789

Buffalo, moose, bear, Tony Rusiecki has preserved them all. The world-champion taxidermist specializes in head mounts and North American game. In his showroom you can see his award-winning white tail deer and bear. He offers pedestal mounts, custom and habitat work. Federally and state licensed, Rusiecki is a member of the Michigan Taxidermy Association, National Taxidermy Association and the International Guild of Taxidermists. His shop open Monday through Saturday. He will open on Sunday by appointment.

Lake Michigan Shoreline and Cadillac

Legends Taxidermy
6690 Virnetta Dr., Ludington
• (616) 843-6330

Award-wining taxidermists Brian Hendrickson and Jamie Flewelling have an excellent reputation for producing quality game and fish mounts. Their shop is open Monday through Saturday. Hours are extended during deer, turkey and bear seasons.

Wild Game Processing

Wild game can be healthful and tasty. Venison is lower in fat per serving than beef, pork or lamb, and higher in protein. Caribou, elk and bear taste very much like beef, bear being higher in fat content than the other big game and elk delivering the sweetest taste. We have listed area meat processors who will cut, wrap and freeze your wild game. All facilities listed uphold strict government standards for their industry. Prices are given only for deer processing because big game prices and individual product prices are variable and fair comparisons are difficult to present. We suggest you give the markets a call for these additional services. They'll be glad to quote you a price.

Grand Traverse

Traverse City Area

Burritt's Meat Market
535 W. Front St., Traverse City
• (616) 941-3474

Burritt's processes 400 deer during rifle season and another 200 during bow season. The processor is known for quick service and reasonable prices. The cost of skinning, cutting, wrapping and freezing is $45. They pro-

Photo: Courtesy of Greg Wright

Michigan offers exceptional hunting opportunities.

duce a full line of smoked and fresh sausages and jerky. Processing for any type of large game is available. The shop is closed Sunday.

Deering's Meat Market
827 S. Union St., Traverse City
• (616) 947-6165

Deering's Meat Market offers a full line of venison sausage and jerky, brats, hot dogs, summer sausage, hickory sticks, bologna and six flavors of jerky. For an additional charge, they can mix your venison with beef or pork. Prices for cutting, wrapping and freezing one deer is $70. It is open daily.

Antrim-Kalkaska Area

Kayner's Meats Inc.
4135 Schoolcraft Rd., Bellaire
• (616) 533-6056

Kayner's will turn your wild game into steaks, roasts, burgers and stew meat. They can add beef or pork to your ground meats or season it to your preference. The cost for cutting, wrapping and freezing one deer is $60. The shop is open Monday through Saturday.

Tri*County Meats
3885 Old Hwy. 27 S., Gaylord
• (517) 732-1234

Tri*County Meats extends their business hours during deer-hunting season to accommodate the demand for venison. Here, cutting, wrapping and freezing one deer costs $45. Products produced from your wild game include jerky and sausage. The shop is open daily.

Lake Michigan Shoreline and Cadillac

Joseph Sanders Inc.
237 S. Main St., Custer • (800) 968-5035

Sanders can produce any number of products from your game, including polish sausage, brats, hot dogs and hot or mild-stick salami. During turkey hunting season, they will smoke your wild bird for you. The price for cutting, wrapping and freezing one deer is $60.

Ebels Family Center
420 Prosper Rd., Falmouth
• (616) 826-3333

Tucked into the heart of Missaukee County's farm country, Ebels may be a bit out of your way, but their prices can make the drive worthwhile. The cost for cutting, wrapping and freezing one deer is $47. At the family-owned general store and market, the meat department can turn your game into several types of products, including summer and smoked sausage, brats, hot dogs, club franks, venison sticks and three kinds of jerky — regular, hot or honey barbecue. The store is closed Sunday.

Mackinac Straits

Krueger's Fish Market
230 W. Etherington St., Mackinaw City
• (616) 436-5946

Beer sausage, summer and pepper sausage, salami, and brats are some of the products Krueger's can produce from your wild game. Here, all boneless cuts, wrapped and frozen from one deer cost $55. It is open daily April through January.

Firearm and Archery Dealers

When shopping for hunting gear, check our listings of bait and tackle shops. Many retailers carry a complete line of outdoor supplies. In addition to locally owned shops, Kmart and Wal-Mart are reliable sources for outdoor equipment and supplies. You can find these chain stores in most of the larger communities in Northwest Michigan.

Grand Traverse

Dunham's Discount Sports
736 Munson Ave., Traverse City
• (616) 935-1414
910 Spring St., Petoskey
• (616) 347-9779
1905 N. Mitchell St., Cadillac
• (616) 775-0700

A mega-chain store, Dunham's promises

the best prices on your sporting-good purchases. They carry a wide selection of firearms, archery equipment and all the accessories at each Northwest Michigan location. Some of the brand names in firearms they feature include Marlin, Mossberg and Remington. You can find black-powder guns and accessories here too. In the archery department, Dunham's features Darton, Winchester and Bear compound bows and accessories. In addition to the hunting and fishing gear, you will find licenses, outdoor clothing and equipment for water fun, skiing, golf, tennis, hockey, bowling and other recreational sports. The stores are open daily.

Gauthier's Archery
1788 Mich. Hwy. 37, Traverse City
• **(616) 943-4432**

A full-time archery pro shop, Gauthier's claim they carry every brand of bow made, including Hoyt, Martin and Matthews. For practice shooting, try their 20-yard indoor air-conditioned range or their advanced interactive video target system. In the archery business for more than 20 years, they've earned their reputation as experts. The store also services all brands of bows and sells licenses. The shop is open daily.

Hampel's
710 Randolf St., Traverse City
• **(616) 946-5485**

Hampel's carries rifles, handguns and shotguns manufactured by nearly all of the leading firearm companies. They claim they have the largest reloading selection in northern Michigan. Along with their stock of more than 3,000 new and used guns, you'll find ammunition and accessories. The expertise offered by the shop's gunsmithing department is what sets Hampel's apart from other retailers. Hampel's lead gunsmith has 30 years of experience. The department draws customers from throughout Michigan and surrounding

states. The shop is open weekdays with limited hours on Sunday.

Antrim-Kalkaska Area

The Alphorn Shop
137 W. Main St., Gaylord
• **(616) 732-5616**

You'll get friendly advice along with your purchase at The Alphorn Shop. They know the hot spots for hunting and fishing in the area and know what you'll need for a successful outdoor adventure. The Alphorn sells rifles, hand guns, shotguns and ammo by Browning. They offer licenses, a good selection of archery equipment, binoculars, scopes, fly-fishing gear and outdoor clothing by Woolrich and Columbia. The shop is open daily except during the month of September when hours vary.

Lake Michigan Shoreline and Cadillac

Dewey's Gun Shop
321 Main St., Frankfort • (616) 352-7470

In business since 1963, Dewey's Gun Shop offers "a little bit of everything." You'll find Browning, Winchester and Ruger guns and ammunition, archery supplies, licenses, boots and outdoor clothing. A few hard-to-find items are also in stock, including the Winchester model 12 shotgun. Dewey's is open Monday through Saturday.

Riley Tackle & Gun
289 River St., Manistee • (616) 723-3354

Open 365 days a year, Riley's offers a good selection of archery equipment. While they sell mostly used guns, they'll order anything for you. You can get your Remington and Winchester ammunition here, as well as licenses.

INSIDERS' TIP

When you head to the fields, be prepared for field-dressing your game. Make sure you have these items with you: flashlight, sharp knife, your kill tag, rope, hunter-orange fabric to hang above the field-dressing site, a plastic bag and small pieces of string.

FPS Archery
7545 E. 34 Mile Rd., Cadillac
- **(616) 779-3772**

A full-service archery shop, FPS carries equipment by Hoyt, PSE, Darton and Matthews, Easton aluminum arrows and Beman carbon arrows. For practice shooting, try their Dart interactive video shooting system or standard 20-yard paper-target range. A limited selection of black powder guns is available, but they carry all the accessories and outdoor clothing. Store hours vary according to season.

Little Traverse

Triple T Archery
1100 Boyne Ave., Boyne City
- **(616) 582-4235**

While Triple T Archery carries leading brands and has hundreds of bows in stock, it's their outstanding customer service that sets them apart from others. They offer a 10-lane indoor practice range and six interactive video system lanes. They make custom arrows and sell a variety of hunting accessories, including camo clothes, boots, scents and bait. The store is open daily except in winter when they close on Sundays.

Mackinac Straits

Ace Hardware and Sporting Goods
7 South State St., St. Ignace
- **(906) 643-7721**

You'll find the most complete selection of hunting and fishing gear in the St. Ignace area at Ace. They stock compound bows, arrows and accessories, as well as rifles, shot guns, ammunition and gun cases. Leading brands they sell include Remington, Savage and Winchester. You can also find outdoor jackets and camo outfits for your hunting adventure here. Other items available include licenses, fishing gear, bait and tackle. The store is open daily except in January, February and March when they close Sunday.

Sport and Conservation Clubs

Ducks Unlimited Inc.

A national nonprofit volunteer organization, Ducks Unlimited Inc. works to restore wetlands and to promote wetland conservation. The organization has active chapters throughout Northwest Michigan. To locate a club near you, write to P.O. Box 213, Cheboygan, MI 49721.

The Ruffed Grouse Society
(412) 262-4044

Many local chapters of the Ruffed Grouse Society exist in Northwest Michigan, including Traverse City, Petoskey, Gaylord and Manistee. Volunteers raise funds and work to protect and develop habitat for grouse, woodcock and other upland species. For information about the chapter nearest you, call the number above, or write the national office 451 McCormick Street, Coraopolis, PA 15108.

Michigan Conservation Foundation
107 N. Mitchell St., Ste. 3A, Cadillac
- **(616) 775-5035**

The Michigan Conservation Foundation exists to generate private funds for habitat improvement on public lands. It is the parent organization of Michigan Whitetails. Michigan Whitetail members work to improve deer and grouse habitats in their local regions. There are six active chapters in Northwest Michigan. Call or write for more information.

Michigan United Conservation Clubs
(517) 371-1041

Michigan United Conservation Clubs (MUCC) acts as an umbrella for 480 affiliate clubs in Michigan. The nonprofit organization is devoted to protecting and enhancing Michigan's natural resources and promoting quality outdoor recreation. There are dozens of active affiliate groups throughout Northwest Michigan. To learn how to become involved, call the number above or write MUCC's state office at P.O. Box 30235, Lansing, MI 48909.

Spring and autumn are ideal times to take advantage of low off-season rates, less-crowded fairways and magnificent seasonal scenery.

Golf

Don't visit Northwest Michigan without your golf clubs! Known as Michigan's Golf Coast, the region is synonymous with the sport. Top-ranked courses dot the map, complemented by an equal number of par 3 courses and public links. Whether you're a skilled player or an enthusiastic novice, we've got the courses for you.

By the way, if you do leave your clubs home, we can help. Countless pro shops and sports stores specialize in catering to visiting golfers. Rentals, a new set of clubs or, perhaps, a custom-made putter are yours for the asking. Check with course pro shops and see the Sports Shops section of our Shopping chapter for ideas.

Cadillac serves as the southern gateway to great northern golf. Almost 100 courses fan out from here, sweeping along the entire Lake Michigan shoreline through the state's rural center and all points in between. Mother Nature helped nurture this golfing mecca. Glaciers carved the many rolling hills that are so heavily covered with northern pine and hardwoods, and helped dot the map with inland lakes and streams. Our cooler climate is excellent for bentgrass fairways and late evening sunshine keeps courses busy as late as 10 PM in the summer.

More than 50 regional courses are listed below. All are open to the public and reflect an enormous range of availability, quality and difficulty. To help you plan your play, we've included rate guidelines based on a full round of play with a cart during peak summer times for the 1997 season. Please remember that this is only a guide and that fees can change at any time. Call for the most current rates and more information.

Remember that Northwest Michigan rolls with the seasons. Spring and autumn are ideal times to take advantage of low off-season rates as well as less-crowded fairways and magnificent seasonal scenery. Several visitors bureaus coordinate a variety of golf and lodging packages for additional savings. Twilight golfing, which often begins mid-afternoon, is another avenue for great golf at great savings. Since Northwest Michigan is on the very western edge of the eastern time zone, it's easy to play for many hours on a summer evening without worrying about having adequate light. As an added bonus during twilight golf, you'll get treated to the magnificent sunsets that sweep across the region.

The courses we've listed in this chapter reflect the broad choices that are available. Top golfers can fashion their own pro tours by traveling among the celebrity-designed links. Novices will appreciate the more relaxing courses that challenge without frustration or pressure. All may benefit from a lesson with the course's pro or by attending one of the golf schools that many of the resorts sponsor.

Grand Traverse

Traverse City Area

Bay Meadows Golf Course
5220 Barney Rd., Traverse City
• (616) 946-7927

Families will love this friendly course only minutes from downtown Traverse City. Bay Meadows was designed with a range of ages and skills in mind. Sunday family specials are $30 with a cart. A three-hole practice course, putting and chipping greens, driving range and learning center offer ample opportunity to practice new strokes. Opened in 1996, it is one of the area's newest courses. Its nine-hole course is a mix of par 3 and par 4 holes.

Cedar Hills Golf Course
7525 Cedar Run Rd., Traverse City
• (616) 947-8237

Cedar Hills is one of the few par 3 courses

in the Grand Traverse area. A local favorite, the 18-hole course features large greens and wooded, rolling hills. The course measures 2981 yards and is a par 58. Cedar Hills is 4 miles west of Traverse City. Greens fees are $29.

The Crown
2411 W. Silver Lake Rd., Traverse City
• (616) 946-2975

The Crown is a pleasant 18-hole residential golf course featuring rolling hills and bentgrass fairways. This was formerly the Green Hills Golf Course, which was reworked and upgraded into the new for 1997 Crown course. Fees average $36. A driving range and restaurant are available.

Elmbrook Golf Course
420 E. Hammond Rd., Traverse City
• (616) 946-9180

Nature had a great hand in the rolling design and panoramic vistas that greet golfers at Elmbrook Golf Course. Gorgeous views of Traverse City, East and West Bays and the Leelanau Peninsula provide a scenic backdrop to holes that flow over and around the course's many high, rolling hills. Couple this with a friendly atmosphere, and you know why Elmbrook has been popular since it opened in 1966. Look for a couple of unique bunkers on holes three and six. The first are sand traps shaped like the Great Lakes. The upper peninsula gets attention on hole six where its image is reflected in another trap. The sixth hole is also known for having the most magnificent views. A mature, challenging course, Elmbrook's 18-hole layout plays to 6397 yards with a par 72. Rates are $30.

Mitchell Creek Golf Course
2846 Three Mile Rd., Traverse City
• (616) 941-5200

This affordable course is popular with families and local golf leagues. On the east side of Traverse City, it is convenient to Munson Avenue and the Traverse City State Park. The nine-hole Mitchell Creek course plays to 3200 yards with a par 36. Rates are a bargain at only $14.50 per round.

Grand Traverse Resort
4263 E. Mich. Hwy. 72, Acme
• (616) 938-1620, (616) 938-2100, (800) 748-0303

The Grand Traverse Resort has a well-deserved reputation for championship golf. Its signature course, The Bear, was designed by golf legend Jack Nicklaus, also known as The Bear. This is one of the toughest courses in the state with terraced greens, deep roughs, grass-edged bunkers, liberal mounding and many water hazards. Nicklaus credits the influence of Scottish courses for many of his design features. The course showcases northern Michigan's natural beauty as it winds through orchards and rolling hills. Home of the Michigan Open Pro Am, The Bear measures 7065 yards with a par 72. Rates run $130 for a round. Reservations should be made early for this popular course.

The resort's other course, Spruce Run, is also championship quality. It was designed by William Newcomb and served as former host to the Michigan Open. Many local enthusiasts consider Spruce Run to be the best-kept public course in Northwest Michigan. Sparkling bay views accompany a design that features water on 11 holes. The par 71 links measure 6579 yards. Greens fees are $95.

Watch for more top-flight courses to enter the lineup soon. Gary Player has designed the Resort's third course, the Northern Knight. Currently under construction, this will be his first course in Michigan, and is slated to open in mid-1998. In addition, a Lee Trevino signature course and new 17,000-foot clubhouse are in the works.

Interlochen Golf Club
10586 U.S. Hwy. 31 S., Interlochen
• (616) 275-7311

The scent of Michigan pine trees wafts over the Interlochen Golf Club, a popular walking course 13 miles southwest of Traverse City. This mature course was built in 1965 with a great balance of water, traps, trees and rolling terrain. At first glance, it appears easier than it is. Greens fees are $32. The course plays 6357 yards with a par 72. A driving range is also available.

www.insiders.com

See this and many other **Insiders' Guide®** destinations online — in their entirety.

Visit us today!

Photo: Mackinac Island Chamber of Commerce

The natural beauty of the region makes golfing enjoyable.

High Pointe Golf Club
5555 Arnold Rd., Williamsburg
• (616) 267-9900, (800) 753-PUTT

High Pointe Golf Club has been getting rave reviews since it was dubbed a top new course when it opened in 1989. This Tom Doak-designed course is unique for its utter contrast between the front and back nine. Scottish features identify the front nine's open links with heather roughs surrounding wide fairways. The back nine cuts through forested hills for a classic up-north feel. Reasonable greens fees at $44 and a design that works for all levels of golfer have made High Pointe one of the area's best golfing buys. This par 71 course plays to 6849 yards.

Leelanau County

King's Challenge
4555 S. Lime Lake Rd., Cedar
• (888) 228-0121

King's Challenge, an 18-hole championship course designed by Arnold Palmer, opened in 1997 to rave reviews. This is Palmer's second course in northern Michigan

INSIDERS' TIP

Visitors to the Grand Traverse region can take advantage of a centralized reservation system offered by the Traverse City Area Convention and Visitors Bureau. The bureau will arrange an itinerary of reserved tee times at any of its member courses. It will also place reservations for lodging and provide information on seasonal golf packages, upcoming tournaments and area golf schools. Sixteen top courses in Benzie, Leelanau, Grand Traverse and Antrim counties are included. Call (800) TRAVERS.

(the first is The Legend at Shanty Creek). The 6695 course sits in the heart of beautiful Leelanau county, with breathtaking views of Lake Michigan and the Manitou Islands. Players will find water, native grasses and woods, sloping greens and deep bunkers along the links. Greens fees are $85.

Sugar Loaf Resort
4500 Sugar Loaf Mountain Rd., Cedar
• (616) 228-5461

Views of Lake Michigan and the Manitou Islands complement play at the Resort Course at Sugar Loaf Resort. The layout winds through cherry orchards on the front nine and pine and hardwood forests on the back nine. Greens fees at Sugar Loaf are $60.

Dunes Golf Club
6464 W. Empire Hwy. (Mich. Hwy. 72), Empire • (616) 326-5390

The Dunes Golf Club offers challenging play for average golfers. This is an easy walking course that is quite nice for families. Its design reflects the familiar characteristics of the Leelanau Peninsula countryside. Consider hole six, at 469 yards, to be the most difficult. Greens fees are reasonable at $25.

Matheson Greens Golf Course
6701 N. Matheson Rd., Northport
• (616) 386-5171, (800) 443-6883

Located near the tip of the Leelanau Peninsula, Matheson Greens is on scenic rolling hills surrounded by panoramic views. Course layout moves in and out of the woods, demanding precise shots. This is another nice walking course that gives players the chance to absorb the picturesque scenery around them while perfecting their game. Matheson Greens plays to 6009 yards at 72 par. Greens fees are $45 with a cart, or $35 to walk. Carts are mandatory on weekends and holidays before 3 PM.

Veronica Valley Golf Course
4341 Lake Leelanau Dr., Lake Leelanau
• (616) 256-9449

Veronica Valley is probably one of the most unique courses in Michigan. Smithsonian-registered folk art and large handcrafted metal sculptures and woodcarvings decorate the fairways and add a quirky twist to each hole. You'll see gigantic metal sunflowers, handcarved totem poles, a replica of the Mackinac Bridge, extravagant birdhouses and a larger-than-life carved Kodiak bear that growls. It sounds crazy, but local golfers love it! The scenery is lovely, the objets d'art are fun and the holes offer a better-than-average challenge. Veronica Valley sits in the center of Leelanau County, 5 miles south of Lake Leelanau. Its nine hole course is a par 35 and measures 3203 yards. Affordable greens fees at $17 add to Veronica Valley's appeal.

Antrim-Kalkaska

Antrim Dells
12352 Antrim Dells Dr., Atwood
• (616) 599-2679, (800) 872-8561

The serenity of the northern Michigan countryside accompanies golfers along this quiet course overlooking Grand Traverse Bay north of Eastport, 35 miles north of Traverse City. Antrim Dells offers fun and challenge at all skill levels. Its layout features a fairly open front nine, which contrasts with the more wooded, narrow back nine. Several of the back holes have been cut through the trees for added difficulty. This 18-hole, par 72 course plays to 6670 yards with greens fees averaging $40.

Shanty Creek
One Shanty Creek Rd., Bellaire
• (800) 678-4111

Shanty Creek's signature course, The Legend, was created by none other than the legendary Arnold Palmer. Its unique semicircular design combines challenge with scenic beauty as it winds around rolling hills, ravines and woods. Added difficulty comes from long, narrow fairways coupled with a number of tree-lined sharp doglegs. The Legend earns its championship designation. The course plays to 6764 yards with a par 72. Legend greens fees run $95.

Two other courses stand alongside The Legend as part of the Shanty Creek golf family. The original Shanty Creek course was one of the first championship-caliber courses built in northern Michigan. Today, it continues to test golfing skills at all levels with its hilly terrain and well-bunkered, fast greens. This sce-

Photo: Grand Traverse Resort

Whether you're a skilled player or a novice, you'll find
a course to play in Northwest Michigan.

nic course plays to 6276 yards with a 71 par. Greens fees on the Shanty Creek course are $50.

The Schuss Mountain Golf Club is just a short shuttle ride away from the Shanty grounds. This course is noted for fast greens, rolling hills and tree-lined fairways. Water hazards and sand traps riddle it with difficulty. Brace yourself for the final four holes. They are tough! The Schuss course is a par 72 that plays to 6922 yards. Rates at the Schuss course are $65. A driving range is also on site.

More championship golf is coming to the Shanty. Tom Weiskopf is working on a new course that will weave around the Cedar River. The course, slated to open in 1999, marks Weiskopf's entry into the roster of Michigan course designers.

Twin Birch Golf Course
1030 Hwy. 612 N.E., Kalkaska
• **(616) 258-9691, (800) 968-9699**

Twin Birch Golf Course bills itself as your link to affordable golf. A driving range, sand practice pit and putting green help sharpen skills for this nicely groomed 18-hole course in Kalkaska. You'll find a friendly, relaxed atmosphere as you play along wooded fairways defined by red pine, birch and the winding Boardman River. Twin Birch plays to 6400 yards with a par 72. Rates are $39 but, if you

purchase a 20-play discount card, you can save up to $10 per round.

A-Ga-Ming Golf Course
735 E. West Torch Lake Dr., Kewadin
• **(616) 264-5081, (800) 678-0122**

Scenic A-Ga-Ming sits high on a bluff overlooking beautiful Torch Lake, halfway between Traverse City and Charlevoix. This challenging course stretches along rolling hills, through stately pines and mature hardwoods, and across several swiftly flowing creeks. Veteran golfers warn that the first three holes are quite a challenge, and advise bringing extra balls for the many water hazards. A-Ga-Ming is a par 72 course playing to 6700 yards. Greens fees average $41.

Lakes of the North
5950 Skytrails Ct., Mancelona
• **(616) 585-6800, (800) 851-4653**

The Deer Run golf course at Lakes of the North combines the original nine-hole course with a back nine designed by William Newcomb. The back layout winds past the headwaters of the Manistee River for a unique challenge in a scenic setting. The front nine is known for large greens and beautiful fairways. Greens fees are only $23. Lakes of the North is 10 minutes west of Old 27 South, near rural Mancelona.

Wilderness Valley
7519 Mancelona Rd., Gaylord
• (616) 585-7090

The Black Forest course at Wilderness Valley is one of the longest in the region, playing to 7044 yards. It is adjacent to the Black Forest south of Gaylord. The layout, designed by Tom Doak, has expansive green contouring, unique bunkers and knee-deep natural areas. This is a fairly new course that has been met with great reviews. Black Forest fees are $60 during the week and $65 on weekends.

The Valley Course was Gaylord's original signature course when it debuted in 1969 designed by Senior PGA national champion Al Watrous. It was designed for resort play with gently rolling hills, wide fairways, huge greens and minimal rough. This is a relaxing par 71 course with a friendly atmosphere. It plays to 6519 yards. Greens fees are $39.

Gaylord Country Club
Mich. Hwy. 32 W., Gaylord
• (616) 546-3376

The Gaylord Country Club offers a pleasant, scenic setting for its well-maintained course. The layout is a classic up and back design with open, rolling fairways and large greens. This course plays to 6477 yards with a par 72. It is 5 miles west of Gaylord. Weekend greens fees are $30 while midweek fees are $26.

Hidden Valley
Mich. Hwy. 32 E., Gaylord
• (517) 732-5181, (800) 752-5510

Hidden Valley resort operates three courses in the Gaylord area which, combined, offer 54 holes of championship golf. The original resort course is The Classic, designed by William H. Diddle. Its design features a good mix of open and wooded fairways along with some of the area's nicest greens. This par 71 course plays to 6386 yards. The Lake course combines three distinctive design styles for a shotmaker's challenge. The layout features six alpine holes that travel up and down ski hills, six holes with Scottish elements, and six water holes near Lake Michaywe. This scenic course plays to 6508 yards with a par 71. The Loon is the newest of the three courses. Since opening in 1994, it has become popular for its gently rolling fairways, strategically placed bunkers and user-friendly design. This par 71 course plays to 6670 yards. Hidden Valley's weekday rates are $15 at each course while weekend fees are $30 at The Classic and The Lake and $35 at The Loon.

Marsh Ridge
4815 Old 27 S., Gaylord
• (517) 732-6794, (800) 968-2633

Marsh Ridge is a beautiful resort course 5 miles south of Gaylord. Considered challenging but enjoyable, the layout stretches over an elevated ridge and through wetlands. Water hazards comes into play on 12 holes. This is a par 71 course that plays to 6100 yards. Fees at Marsh Ridge run $50 on weekdays and $60 on weekends.

Michaywe Hills Resort
1535 Opal Lake Rd., Gaylord
• (517) 939-8911

Northern Michigan is known for its white pine and birch trees. You can't miss them on The Pines course at Michaywe Hills Resort, 5 miles south of Gaylord. Secluded fairways carve through the forests along the beautiful Au Sable River. Strategic bunkering and water on seven holes add to the course's character. The Pines plays to 6835 yards with a par 72. Michaywe fees are $30 on weekdays and $40 on weekends.

The Natural
5004 W. Otsego Lake Dr., Gaylord
• (517) 732-1785

Watch out for local wildlife at The Natural, 5 miles south of Gaylord on Otsego Lake. The setting, which was originally part of a 1920s-era ski resort, is surrounded by nature. It includes some of the region's most scenic wetlands, which are also home to many furry and feathered friends. All add to the charm of this highly regarded course. Designer Jerry Mathew strove to create a challenging layout that still retained much of the natural environment. Veteran players warn that hole 18, at 440 yards, is the toughest on the course. The Natural plays to 6350 yards with a par 71. Fees are $45 on weekdays and $55 on weekends.

Treetops Sylvan Resort
3962 Wilkinson Rd., Gaylord
• **(517) 732-6711, (888) TREETOPS**

Golfing enthusiasts can swing to their hearts' content on the 81 holes of topnotch golf available among Treetops' four major courses. The Robert Trent Jones Sr. Masterpiece course features breathtaking views of the Pigeon River Valley coupled with a diverse design and dramatic elevation changes. Jones coined the name Treetops when taking in the panoramic, 30-mile valley view from hole 6. The Masterpiece is known for its challenging layout with heavy woods, many hills, elevated tees and four water holes. It plays to 7060 yards with a par 71. Greens fees at Treetops Jones are $74.

The Tom Fazio Premier course bears the name of its internationally acclaimed creator and is the only Fazio-designed course in Michigan. Considered to be a user-friendly course, it features rolling, bowl-shaped fairways designed to bring the ball back into play even for a less-than-perfect shot. The Fazio course shares the same magnificent natural setting as the other Treetops- and Gaylord-based courses. It's located at Treetops North, the resort's extension property 4 miles north of the main resort. The course plays to 6832 yards with a 72 par. Treetops Fazio's fees are $84.

The Rick Smith Signature course is also at Treetops North and displays the design work of resident pro Rick Smith. Pine, birch and various hardwoods paint a scenic backdrop to a demanding course known for its extremely large greens. Hole 3, known as "Hunters Heaven," is nestled between abundant trees, with a sprawling fairway and a huge green that measures 160 feet in diameter. The par 70 Smith course plays to 6653 yards. Treetops Smith fees average $74.

The Rick Smith Tradition is the newest course in the Treetops lineup. Strictly a walking course, Smith designed it to National Audubon Society specifications. The Tradition is reminiscent of classic courses of an earlier generation, and is noted for its gentle terrain and short distances between tee and green. Caddies, available but not required, add to the traditional ambience. This par 70 course plays to 6394 yards. Fees for Treetops Tradition are $52.

Try Threetops for a change of pace or a fun family afternoon. Also designed by Smith, it is Treetops' new par 3 course. Fees are just $21. Holes range from 96 to 216 yards on this 1178 yard course, so you can easily squeeze in a quick round in 90 minutes.

Black Bear Golf Resort
1500 W. Alexander Rd., Vanderbilt
• **(517) 983-4505, (800) 923-2711**

Why stop at 18 holes when you can play 19? The Black Bear Golf Resort in Vanderbilt, 8 miles north of Gaylord, has introduced the region's first 19-hole course. The first hole on this course is actually a par 3 practice hole, designed for players who arrive to play with little practice time before tee-off. The natural setting is classic northern Michigan with lovely views and trees. An unnatural but distinctive landmark to watch for is the 300-foot wall of water that buffers the links from adjacent I-75. Black Bear is a par 72 course that plays to 6504 yards.

Lake Michigan Shoreline and Cadillac

Crystal Lake Golf Club
8493 Fairway Dr., Beulah
• **(616) 882-4061**

Crystal Lake Golf Club lies in the midst of Beulah's beautiful, natural landscape and over-

---

INSIDERS' TIP

The weather up north can be unpredictable. But when Mother Nature throws us a curve ball, the hospitality industry just gets creative. When the last remnants of 1996's unduly long winter's snow refused to budge, several resorts ran ski and golf specials. Spring golfers broke in their season, while diehard skiers could be seen taking their runs on nearby slopes.

Photo: Grand Traverse Resort

Don't visit our region without your clubs!

looks picturesque Crystal Lake. This 18-hole course is noted for its apple orchard-lined fairways. The back nine holes are newer than the front links. Together, they play to 6535 yards. Greens fees average $35.

Pinecroft Golf Plantation
8260 Henry Rd., Beulah • (616) 882-9100

Gorgeous views of Crystal Lake can be enjoyed from each of Pinecroft Golf Plantation's 18 holes. This is a nice walking course with lush bluegrass fairways that opened just a few years ago. Fees are a reasonable $32. A second 18-hole course, Champion Hill, is under construction. Pinecroft plays to 6447 yards with 72 par.

Frankfort Golf Club
1857 Golf Ln., Frankfort • (616) 352-4101

The nine-hole course at the Frankfort Golf Club is a perfect practice ground for getting your golf game back in order. Filled with mature trees, it features a hilly, challenging lay-out that requires precision. There are no par 5s on this par 34 course that plays to 2552 yards. Greens fees run $15.

Mistwood Golf Course
7568 Sweet Lake Rd., Lake Ann
• (616) 275-5500

Mistwood Golf Course joined the Northwest Michigan golf roster in 1993 and has earned its reputation as a top public course. It was named after the location's characteristic misty mornings. Located 15 minutes west of Traverse City near the village of Lake Ann, Mistwood's 27-hole lay-out offers three distinctly different nine-hole courses. The White Course features rolling fairways with a series of shorter holes with quick elevation change. The Blue Course has the longest fairways, which are edged by woods and deep rough and water on five of the nine holes. The Red Course is the newest and places a premium on shot placement. Greens are well protected with many bunkers. Blue Number 8 is the architect's signature hole. Golfers have to

INSIDERS' TIP

The Wawashkamo Golf Links on Mackinac Island is the oldest continuously played course in Michigan. It is also one of the few true Scottish links clubs still in existence in the United States.

navigate 177 yards through a valley of natural wetlands to the hole's long, three-tiered green. Reservations can be made for any combination of courses with fees for 18 holes averaging $35. When you're through playing, check out the restaurant at Mistwood. The menu is admirable and sunsets from the deck are wonderful!

Crystal Mountain Resort
12500 Crystal Mountain Dr., Thompsonville • (616) 378-2000, (800) 968-7686

Three nine-hole courses weave through the wooded grounds at Crystal Mountain Resort. Eighteen of the 27 holes were designed by William Newcomb. The original front nine are on the Mountain Meadows course, noted for rolling meadows and birch-lined fairways. Water hazards dot the Mountain Creek course, with water in play at six of nine holes. Mountain Ridge is the newest of the three courses, with spectacular views of the Betsie River Valley. Sand and grass bunkers and large greens add to the challenge. No two fairways parallel each other. A fourth nine-hole course is in the works. When playing two of the three courses in tandem, pars are 71 or 72 while yardage fluctuates between 6215 for the Mountain Meadows/Mountain Ridge combination to 6689 for Mountain Meadows/Mountain Creek. Rates for any combination of 18 holes are $55. A Frequent Fairways discount program was launched in 1997 and offers discounts on daily greens fees and use of the resort's 10-acre practice center.

County Highlands Golf Club
U.S. Hwy. 31 S., Bear Lake
• (616) 864-3817

County Highlands Golf Club is a sleeper. Though not as well known as many of the other Northwest courses, it is well-maintained and considered by those who play here often to be one of the best public courses in the region. Watch for water on eight holes. County Highlands plays to 6132 yards. Greens fees are $34.

Manistee Golf and Country Club
500 Cherry St., Manistee
• (616) 723-2500

The Manistee Golf and Country Club is an older, semiprivate course that allows public play. Right along the shoreline, views of Lake

Michigan accompany golfers as they play on rolling fairways and small greens. This course plays to 5614 yards. Fees are $40. A driving range is available.

Caberfae Peaks Ski & Golf Resort
Caberfae Rd., Cadillac • (616) 862-3300

Best known as one of Michigan's oldest ski areas, Caberfae Peaks has begun developing what will become a 36-hole championship course. The first nine holes opened in 1995 as The Peaks Course. The second nine is under way. The layout carves through the majestic Manistee National Forest and alongside undisturbed heather, wetlands, creeks and waterways. The Peaks plays to 3248 yards with a par of 36. Fees for the nine-hole course are $21, or you can play two rounds for $38.

Cadillac Country Club
5428 Mich. Hwy. 55, Cadillac
• (616) 775-9442

The Cadillac Country Club has been hosting Cadillac area golfers since 1910. A private club that allows public play, this classic course is known for its mature trees, small greens and peaceful setting. It plays to 6107 yards with a par 70. Rates on weekends are $40 and midweek are $35.

Eldorado
7839 E. 46½ Rd., Cadillac
• (616) 779-9977, (888) DRIVE 18

The Eldorado opened in 1996 to much acclaim from local and visiting golfers. On the outskirts of Cadillac near the U.S. 131 and Mich. 115 interchange, this new course features well-maintained bentgrass tees, greens and fairways. The course plays to 7070 yards. Weekday rates are $40 and weekends are $45. You don't have to play to enjoy the Eldorado. The Cadillac Grill Restaurant provides a magnificent setting with high ceilings and countless windows overlooking the course's panoramic views.

Lakewood on the Green
128 Lakewood Dr., Cadillac
• (616) 775-4763

Plan to bring plenty of golf balls when you play at Lakewood on the Green. Play is deceptively challenging. The nine-hole layout features tight fairways and rolling greens as well as water on at least five holes of this scenic course. Lakewood on the Green plays to 2975 yards. The nine hole fees run $21 or you can play two rounds for $40.

McGuire's Resort
7880 S. Mackinaw Tr., Cadillac
• (616) 775-9947, (800) 632-7302

A longtime local favorite, McGuire's sits high on rolling hills that overlook Lake Cadillac, the town itself and the northwoods countryside. The view provides a panoramic backdrop for the 18-hole Spruce and 9-hole Norway courses. The championship Spruce plays to 6443 yards. Its wide fairways weave through pine forests and glacier-sculpted hills with a balanced blend of bunkers, berms and water hazards. The greens are well-kept and fast. Fees for the Spruce are $52 on weekends and $48 midweek. The easier Norway course shares the same beautiful setting but is an easier alternative for a fun afternoon on the links. It plays to 2792 yards. Rates for a nine-hole Norway round run $18.

The Rose Golf Course
16264 18 Mile Rd., LeRoy
• (616) 768-5060, (888) ROSEGOLF

The Rose Golf Course is south of Cadillac between the rural villages of LeRoy and Tustin. This secluded new course features a tight layout that cuts through forests filled with white pine, maple and birch trees. The Rose is a good place to fine tune your shotmaking. The par 71 course plays to 6000 yards. Greens fees at The Rose are $35.

Briar Downs
5441 E. Mich. Hwy. 115, Mesick
• (616) 885-1220

Experience the flavor of English-style golf at Briar Downs, 15 minutes northwest of Cadillac and 30 minutes southwest of Traverse City. The friendly atmosphere complements the course's well-maintained rolling terrain filled with woods, streams and ponds. The shorter front nine play along rolling fairways lined with hardwoods and ponds. The back nine are more open but abundant pine trees and streams add to the challenge. Briar Downs is a par 71 course that plays to 5876 yards. Rates run $31 during the week and $37 on weekends and holidays.

Little Traverse

Bay Harbor
850 Vista Dr., Bay Harbor
• (616) 439-4028

Bay Harbor is continually likened to Pebble Beach. With its many long fairways stretching along the Lake Michigan shoreline, the comparison is well deserved. The Bay Harbor courses are part of a massive, upscale development taking place along Bay Harbor between Petoskey and Charlevoix. This property lies on one of the most magnificent settings in a region already renowned for its stunning natural beauty. Three nine-hole courses opened in 1997 and are part of the Boyne group. They are spikeless, requiring polyurethane cleats as opposed to traditional metal spikes. The pro shop at Bay Harbor, as well as Boyne Highlands, will convert spikes at no charge.

The Links was the first to open with fairways built along bluffs and sand dunes. Eight of its holes play along Lake Michigan, sharing breathtaking views of Harbor Springs and Beaver Island. The Preserve cuts through heavily wooded areas where deer and other wildlife are commonly seen along with stunning vistas of Lake Michigan. The Quarry weaves

INSIDERS' TIP

Want to practice your golf swing while the snow is falling? Visit Varsity Golf and Tennis Centre, 6450 Secor Road in Traverse City, for a bucket of balls and time in their indoor practice facility. This is Northwest Michigan's only indoor range. It is open year round and sells custom clubs, attire and equipment, offers repair service and operates an outdoor practice range. Call (616) 947-1185 for more information.

through a magnificent shale quarry leading up to its bayside final hole. Fees for 18 holes are $140. One word of advice: If you're a golf connoisseur, play these courses while you can. After Bay Harbor is fully developed, the golfing portion will likely become private.

Boyne Mountain
Boyne Mountain Rd. (U.S. Hwy. 31 at Boyne Falls), Boyne Falls
• **(616) 549-6000, (800) GO-BOYNE**

Just say the word Boyne and thoughts go to golf in the summer and skiing in the winter. The prestigious Boyne family of resorts — including Boyne Mountain in Boyne Falls and Boyne Highlands in Harbor Springs — were pioneers in Northwest Michigan's fledgling tourism industry and continue to be a leading force today. Two championship golf courses are at Boyne Mountain, The Monument and the Alpine. Play at The Monument begins with an 1100-foot golf-cart ride to the top of Boyne Mountain. The course is, quite literally, down from here. Along the way, golfers will play along wooded, hilly fairways with large, quick greens. Gear up for hole 18. The green is on an island at the end of the course. The Alpine also starts at the summit. Watch for fairway bunkers and fast greens. Water is in play for six holes but there are no islands to contend with! Course yardage runs to 7086 at The Monument, and 7017 yards at The Alpine. Both are par 72. Fees average $80 for a round on either course. Boyne Mountain also offers The Hemlock, a nine-hole, par 3 course. It plays to 1774 yards with par at 28. Fees are only $10 without a cart.

Belvedere Golf Club
05731 Marion Center Rd., Charlevoix
• **(616) 547-2611**

The Belvedere course is a Charlevoix tradition. Known for its challenging layout, the course features rolling fairways, strategic bunkers and small greens. It is well-maintained. Belvedere plays to 6715 yards. Par is 72 and fees total $66.

Charlevoix Country Club
9600 Clubhouse Dr., Charlevoix
• **(616) 547-9796, (800) 618-9796**

An elegant addition to Little Traverse area golf, the Charlevoix Country Club course was recently designed by Jerry Mathews. Grooming is meticulous with hand-mown greens and approaches. The course plays to 6520 yards with a par 72. Greens fees are $72. A driving range is available.

Charlevoix Municipal Golf Course
Charlevoix Ave., Charlevoix
• **(616) 547-3268**

The Charlevoix Municipal Golf Course is a nine-hole public course. The layout is unique for requiring two trips across U.S. 31 during a round. This par 36 walking course plays to 3001 yards. Greens fees are $12 for one round or $18 for two.

Dunmaglas
09031 Boyne City Rd., Charlevoix
• **(616) 547-4653, (888) VIP-0909**

Stunning views coupled with a challenging layout make Dunmaglas in Charlevoix one of the region's favorite courses. The links cut through heavily wooded hills overlooking Lake Michigan and Lake Charlevoix. The first hole is spectacular with an elevated tee, hillside trees, nine pot bunkers, a two-tiered green and panoramic backdrop. Dunmaglas plays to 6898 yards with a par 72. Fees average $75 on weekdays and $85 on weekends.

Boyne Highlands
600 Highlands Dr., Harbor Springs
• **(616) 526-3000, (800) GO-BOYNE**

Three 18-hole, par 72 courses are at Boyne Highlands with a fourth under construction. This is the home of the Michigan PGA Championship. The top-rated Heather course was designed by Robert Trent Jones Sr. with tree-lined fairways, sculpted bunkers and several water hazards. Steep hills, thick woods and wetlands add to the difficulty of this challenging course,

INSIDERS' TIP

The Boyne courses — Boyne Mountain, Boyne Highlands, Crooked Tree and the new Bay Harbor — boast a combined total of 162 holes, more than any other in the state.

which ends with a dramatic, water-edged hole 18. The Heather plays to 7218 yards. This is a spikeless course with fees set at $110.

Doglegs, marshes and water holes add to the challenge on the Moor course. Large undulating greens are fronted by huge bunkers. Several holes are riddled with water hazards. The course plays 7179 yards. Fees at the Moor are $70.

The Donald Ross Memorial course re-creates 18 of the famous designer's most noted holes. They draw from famous courses from around the world like Inverness, Oakland Hills, Scioto, Seminole and Royal Dornoch. This is a spectacular course to play on. Yardage is 6840. The Ross course, like the Heather and the Bay Harbor courses, is spikeless. Fees are $99.

Nine holes of the new Arthur Hills course are open. The design shows distinctive detailing on each hole with huge sand traps and intimidating water holes throughout. The nine-hole course plays to 3500 yards. Watch for the second nine to debut soon. Rates for Hills nine holes in tandem with nine on the Moor course run $90.

Chestnut Valley
1875 Clubhouse Dr., Harbor Springs
• (616) 526-9100

Chestnut Valley is set in rolling wooded hills north of Harbor Springs at the corner of North Conway and Valley Roads. This is a championship course with five par 5 holes. It plays to 6700 yards with a 72 par. A driving range is available. Fees are $62 on weekends and $55 on weekdays.

Crooked Tree Golf Club
600 Crooked Tree Dr., Petoskey
• (616) 348-7000

Crooked Tree Golf Club recently joined the Boyne golf family. Reminiscent of seaside courses in the British Isles, the Crooked Tree course is set along high bluffs that overlook Little Traverse Bay and the new Bay Harbor development. It's an enjoyably playable design with stunning views. This par 71 course plays to 6584 yards. Greens fees are $75.

Little Traverse Bay Golf Club
995 Hideaway Valley Rd., Harbor Springs
• (616) 526-6200

Gorgeous views with sweeping vistas and spectacular scenery have made Little Traverse Bay Golf Club a longtime local favorite. As one golfer said, "This is what golf is all about!" The 18-hole design is an enjoyable challenge for golfers at all levels. Located in Harbor Springs, the Little Traverse Bay course plays to 6881 yards with a par of 72. Fees are $68 during the week and $78 on weekends.

Mackinac Straits

Wilderness Golf Course
10500 Cecil Bay Rd., Carp Lake
• (616) 537-4973

Wilderness Golf Course is an enjoyable nine-hole course just 10 minutes southwest of Mackinaw City. No tee times are needed for this pleasant, affordable, walking course. Greens fees are only $10. Wilderness plays to 2670 yards with a par of 35.

The Grand Hotel
Mackinac Island • (906) 847-3331

The Grand hosts two of Mackinac Island's three golf courses. All are nine holes although the hotel has linked its two distinctly different courses into a single 18-hole round known as

INSIDERS' TIP

The golf opportunities keep growing! Construction of new courses and additions to existing ones have become a continuing process in Northwest Michigan. Courses to debut soon are: Northern Knight, a Gary Player-designed course, at the Grand Traverse Resort in Acme; Champion Hill at Pinecroft Golf Plantation in Beulah; a fourth nine-hole course at Crystal Mountain in Thompsonville; a new 18-hole, Tom Weiskopf-designed course at Shanty Creek in Bellaire; and the Bay Harbor courses near Petoskey.

The Jewel. The front nine, which are also the original nine, comprise the Grand Nine course. It is adjacent to the historic Grand Hotel and overlooks the Straits of Mackinac. The course recently underwent a major redesign to upgrade the links and increase their level of difficulty. Plan to take a short break between front and back nine. The back nine, known as the Woods course, is surrounded by trees in the heart of the island's interior. A much newer course than the Grand Nine, it opened in 1994 near the island's airport and the hotel's Woods Restaurant. Horse-drawn carriages, specially equipped with bag racks, transport golfers from the Grand Nine to the Woods. Rates for The Jewel's combined courses are $75.

Wawashkamo Golf Links
British Landing Rd., Mackinac Island
• **(906) 847-3871**

Built in 1898 on the site of an 1814 conflict between American and British soldiers, Wawashkamo is one of the oldest continuously played courses in Michigan. It also stands as one of the few remaining links courses in the United States. Following Scottish tradition, the links layout relies only on the course's natural terrain. A few modest sand traps stand as the only modifications allowed. Wawashkamo plays to 3003 yards. Fees run $42.

The day traveler in
Michigan can find
pleasant diversions and
new adventures around
every corner.

Daytrips

You're ready for free-spirited adventure. Nothing compares to the sense of anticipation you feel. You have a full tank of gas, your luggage is tucked into the trunk and the kids are buckled securely in the back seat. As a day traveler in Michigan you can find pleasant diversions and new adventures around every corner. Insiders will tell you that you can live in the north all of your life and never run out of new places to see or wonderful things to experience.

Trekking just beyond the borders of Northwest Michigan opens vast new territories to the traveler and countless combinations for recreation. And a place is never quite the same in fall, winter, spring and summer.

Our daytrip listings include places Insiders share with their own visiting friends and relatives. Some listings are pure tradition, such as the Soo Locks, Tahquamenon Falls and Hartwick Pines. Few Michigan children grow up without learning about or seeing these three legendary sites. Others, for example, Beaver and Drummond islands, set out an irresistible call to the outdoor explorer.

Let this chapter be your inspiration for building travel memories. Depending on your personal interests, you may wish to visit a shipwreck, tour a lighthouse or see the dozens of waterfalls in the upper peninsula. You may be interested in seeking out the region's rare flora and fauna, creating your own art gallery tour, following the lengthy trail of antique shops or visiting Native-American points of interests.

If it sounds like old hat, do it in an all-new way, by horse, by snowmobile, by mountain bike. In Northwest Michigan, your traveling fulfillment is limited only by your imagination and sense of adventure. We guarantee you'll find up-north hospitality and good times whichever road you follow.

Beaver Island

While Beaver Island is a great daytrip destination, be forewarned: you may never want to leave. Residents describe Beaver Island, also known as America's Emerald Isle, as unspoiled, unhurried and unmatched in natural beauty. The largest island in Lake Michigan, the remote getaway offers peace, quiet, an abundance of wildlife and plenty of creature comforts.

Beaver Island sits 32 miles off Charlevoix's coastline. It's one of seven islands making up the Beaver Archipelago and the only isle in the chain with commercial development. You can reach the island either by ferry or air service. Ferry service is provided by **Beaver Island Boat Company**, 103 Bridge Park Drive, Charlevoix, (616) 547-2311. Operating from the downtown Charlevoix harbor, ferries make several two-hour runs to and from Beaver Island's St. James Harbor daily throughout the summer. Ferries operate from April through December with fewer runs in non-summer months.

INSIDERS' TIP

Is it Sault or Soo? Like the confusion over Mackinac and Mackinaw, both are correct. Both are pronounced sue. Sault Ste. Marie is the name for both cities, U.S. and Canadian, on either side of the International Bridge linking the two countries. The locks connecting Lake Superior and Lake Huron via the St. Mary's River are the Soo Locks. The Soo is also a nickname for the region and is often used interchangeably with the full Sault Ste. Marie name.

Two island airports accommodate private planes and charters. **Island Airways**, (616) 547-2141, transports you from the Charlevoix Airport to the island in just 15 minutes. The company offers year-round, daily flights by reservation. Round-trip tickets are $62 per person. Private planes can land either at **Beaver Island's Welke Airport** or the municipal airport. Welke features a 3,000-foot, well-maintained airstrip and is situated just 2.5 miles from the village of St. James. Overnight parking, taxi service and car rentals are available at Welke. Beaver Island Municipal Airport is in the center of the island. It is not staffed and facilities are limited. (See our Getting Here and Getting Around chapter for more transportation details.)

www.insiders.com

See this and many other **Insiders' Guide®** destinations online — in their entirety.

Visit us today!

St. James Harbor is on the northeast corner of the island and is one of the most protected natural harbors in the Great Lakes. Two marinas accommodate boat travelers: the **Beaver Island Municipal Boat Dock**, (616) 448-2252, and **Beaver Island Marine**, (616) 448-2500. Both offer transient and seasonal slips, restrooms and showers. A harbor master is on duty at the Municipal Dock, May through October.

Once on the 53-square-mile island, you'll find charm, solitude and natural wonders to fill a day, weekend or a week. Stop by the **Beaver Island Chamber of Commerce** (contact information at the end of this section), near the boat docks, for maps, guides and a copy of the *Beaver Island Explorer*. This guide will provide you with an understanding of island history and information on island attractions, shops, services and events.

The village of **St. James**, the island's hub, has 350 year-round residents. Several types of charter services are available. **Runway Charters**, (616) 448-2092, will take you to the outer islands to enjoy backpacking, camping and picnics. **Island Hopper Charter Service**, (616) 448-2309, and **Bonadeo Boat Charters**, (616) 448-2489, also provide transportation to the outer islands. **Van Arkel Fishing Charters**, (616) 448-2407, takes anglers to the hot spots for smallmouth bass and other catches.

For self-guided adventures, contact **Lakesports**, (616) 448-2166, along the harbor, south of the ferry dock. It's open year round and rents canoes, mountain bikes, kayaks, sailboats, pedal boats, windsurfers and camping gear.

Landlubbers can rent a variety of vehicles for exploring the 13-mile-long island via 100 miles of roads. You can rent Geo Trackers by the day or the week from two Beaver Island marine rentals locations, St. James Harbor docks and Welke Airport. Suburbans and mini-vans are available year-round from **Gordon's Auto Clinic**, (616) 448-2438. If you prefer leaving the driving to someone else, contact **Beaver Island Classic Tours**, (616) 590-9767, for dinner, sunset and outback tours.

Mountain biking and hiking are two of the most popular island pastimes. A state forest and two wildlife sanctuaries provide visitors with opportunities for beachcombing, wildlife observations, wild berry picking and outdoor photography. (Pick up extra film at **McDonough's Market**, 37900 Michigan Avenue, (616) 448-2733.) **Barney's Lake Nature Preserve**, owned by Little Traverse Conservancy, (616) 347-0991, is 3 miles southwest of St. James. It includes 120 acres of open bog, sedge meadows and cedar swamps where you'll find loons, great blue herons, deer, beaver and snowshoe hare. There are walking trails throughout the sanctuary. **Little Sand Bay Preserve**, also owned by Little Traverse Conservancy, is a few hundred feet south of Welke Airport. It features 60 acres of conifer forest, cedar swamp and sand dune habitats. The rare **Michigan Monkey Flower**, found growing in only 20 locations on earth, grows here. Little Sand Bay is stunning when the crystal-clear water turns a shimmering turquoise under a summer sun.

While Beaver Island draws many nature lovers, it also offers some fun shopping and distinctive museums. When you step off the docks you'll see a large island directory and map that provides directions to all island shops and destinations. **Livingstone Studio**, 26250 Main Street, (616) 448-2975, features local and ethnic art, fine crafts, collectibles and antiques. **Propeller Place**, 26215 Beaver Harbor Drive, is the place to stop for island souvenirs. You'll find shipwreck clothing items, shipwreck furniture, lighthouses, brass and nautical items. At **The Sommer Place**, 26455 Donnegal Bay Road, (616) 448-2250, you'll discover an array of hand-thrown pottery, jewelry, stained glass, clocks, clothing and more.

History buffs will want to visit the **Marine Museum**, 38105 Michigan Avenue, and the **Mormon Print Shop**, 26275 Main Street, for a look into the island's rich past. Both are operated by the Beaver Island Historical Society and open June through Labor Day. Museum admission is $3. At the **Antique Toy Museum**, (616) 448-2480, you'll find a good collection of antique toy trucks and small toys, outdoor garden ornaments, beads, handmade cards and island crafts.

Travelers from around the globe have enjoyed visits to the island's lighthouses. **Beaver Island Harbor Light** leads boats safely into St. James Harbor. Public tours of the **Whiskey Point Lighthouse** are not available but tourists are welcome to explore **Beaver Head Lighthouse**, found at the south tip of the island. This lighthouse is unique for its use of the original beacon lens. If these lighthouses, which have stood guard for many years, could speak, they would tell of the numerous shipwrecks off Beaver and the outer islands. Sport divers come each summer to explore the wrecks. If this is your interest, bring along your own equipment. Scuba gear rentals are not available locally.

When the sightseeing is over, indulge your taste buds at one of the island's restaurants. For a light meal, try **Daddy Franks**, 26320 Forest Avenue, (616) 448-2570. They serve legendary burgers, hot franks, Polish franks, fries, onion rings and ice cream in homemade waffle cones. The **Old Rectory Restaurant and Pub**, 26300 Old Church Crest Road, (616) 448-2318, serves breakfast, lunch and dinner. You'll enjoy dining on the deck overlooking Paradise Bay.

Overnighters can select from among many places to lodge. Insiders recommend you make reservations for your accommodations in advance or plan to bring your tent. A comfortable places to stay is the **Harbor View**

Motel, 26246 Back Highway, (616) 448-9901, a 6-unit motel perched on a bluff overlooking Lake Michigan. All the newly decorated rooms face an inner courtyard and pool and offer a great view of the big lake. Harbor View is open between May first and the end of November with off-season rates in May and October. **Laurain Lodge**, 38085 Beaver Lodge Drive, (616) 448-2099, is a quiet, new lodge offering one- and two-bedroom, furnished housekeeping units accommodating up to six people. Rates include free shuttle service to and from the ferry dock or airport and use of fishing boats on four of the island's seven lakes. A smoke-free, family-oriented facility, amenities include cable televisions and VCRs, a picnic area, grills, campfire pit and playground area. Laurain Lodge is open from May first until mid-November and has off-season package deals.

Two rustic campgrounds are available to the hearty overnight visitor. A municipal campground featuring 10 sites is 1 mile west of St. James. The **Bill Wagner Memorial Campground** is 8 miles south of the village and has 20 camp sites. Both campgrounds offer only pumped water and pit toilets. Rates are $5 per night at each park.

While the island is primarily a summer destination, limited lodging, restaurants and services are available year-round. Contact the **Beaver Island Chamber of Commerce**, 26250 Main Street, (616) 448-2505, for additional and seasonal information.

Sault Ste. Marie and the Tahquamenon Falls

The Michigan motto states, "if you seek a pleasant peninsula, look around you." In Northwest Michigan, this is illustrated with each shoreline shaping our tip of the mitt. In the Upper Peninsula, the lands are buffeted by Lake Superior to the north, Lake Michigan to the south and Lake Huron to the east. Its only connection with land lies far to the west on the Wisconsin border. Only the Mackinac Bridge links the state's two peninsulas together. Likewise, the International Bridge is the state's only link with its closest northern neighbor, Sault Ste. Marie, Ontario.

Photo: Balthazar Korab

Drummond Island offers gorgeous views, rare plants and abundant wildlife, making it a nature-lover's paradise.

This daytrip introduces you to our beautiful Upper Peninsula with a sampling of sights and excursions between Sault Ste. Marie and the Tahquamenon Falls. Both are within a 90-minute drive of our Insiders' northern boundaries near St. Ignace.

To begin, head north from St. Ignace on I-75. The 50-mile trip to Sault Ste. Marie will take you to the northern end of the interstate highway. Along the way, you'll pass through the **Hiawatha National Forest** and miles of vast rural lands.

Sault Ste. Marie is the oldest city in Michigan. It was already home to the Chippewa Indians when the first European voyageurs and Jesuit missionaries arrived during the mid-1600s. The first mission was established in 1668 and led to French priests naming the settlement in honor of the Virgin Mary. British and French fur traders often frequented the area as they traveled from port to port during the next 150 years. The Michigan Territory, including this region of the Upper Peninsula, was established as part of America and was given statehood in 1937.

The **Soo Locks** are one of the area's key attractions. The first lock was built in 1850 to allow shipping between Lake Huron, the connecting St. Mary's River and Lake Superior. Rapids from the St. Mary's River drop 21 feet from Lake Superior's water level to Lake Huron's. Today, there are four locks in place, representing the largest locking system in the world and facilitating the shipping of at least 95 million tons of freight through the Soo annually. They operate from March through December, depending on weather conditions.

To get to the locks from I-75, take the Ashmun Street exit to downtown Sault Ste. Marie and head to Portage Street. You can park your car for much of your stay since most of the attractions are nearby. The locks are fascinating to watch. There are several observation platforms in the adjacent Soo Locks Park overlooking the great ships and their rise and fall inside the gated locks. The U.S. Army Corps of Engineers, which operates the locks, maintains a great information center within the park area, sharing data and lore about the locks' construction, operation and history. The center is open from mid-May until mid-November.

You can experience the locking action with a ride on the **Soo Locks Boat Tours**, 515 and 1157 E. Portage Avenue, (906) 632-6301, (800) 432-6301, where guests enjoy a two-hour narrated ride including the 21-foot rise to the level of Lake Superior. Tours depart several times daily between mid-May and mid-October. Departures times fluctuate with the season, ranging from three per day in May and October to 20 per day in July and much of August. Fares are $13 for adults, $11 for teens between 13 and 18, $6 for children between 5 and 12, and free for children younger than 5. Three-hour sunset dinner cruises tour the St. Mary's River and the Old North Channel between Sugar Island and Canada. Cost for the dinner cruise is $33 for adults and $25 for children 3 to 12. The sunset tours are quite popular during the summer peak so it's always a good idea to call ahead for reservations.

Soo Locks Tour Trains, 315 W. Portage Avenue, (906) 635-5241, (800) 387-6200, take riders through Sault Ste. Marie and over the International Bridge for a panoramic view of the locking system. The train tours, which are actually conducted via trolley and double-decker buses, last one or two hours with fascinating tidbits about the two cities and the locks. Tours run daily between Memorial Day weekend and mid-October with departures every half hour between 9 AM and 7:30 PM during the summer peak. One-hour tickets are $5.25 for adults and $3.50 for children between 6 and 18, while prices for the two-hour Twin Sault Tour are $9.75 for adults and $6 for children between 6 and 18. If you would like to explore the Canadian Soo, which is four times larger than the U.S. side, take the Twin Sault Tour, or hop in your car and take nearby I-75 on the 3-mile trek across the International Bridge into Canada.

Back on land, **The Tower of History**, 501 E. Water Street, (906) 632-3658, takes visitors to the top of its 21-story structure for a birds-eye view of the locks and shipping traffic as well as a fabulous, panoramic look at 1,200 square miles of Michigan and Canadian landscape. The tower also houses local historical exhibits and a multimedia program. Admission is $3 for adults and $1.75 for children between 6 and 16. Children 5 and younger are admitted free. It is open daily between May 15 and October 15.

Another historical stop is the **Museum Ship**, *Valley Camp*, 501 E. Water Street, (906) 632-3658, a 1917 steam-powered Great Lakes freighter which houses a large Great Lakes maritime museum, an aquarium and a widely acclaimed *Edmund Fitzgerald* memo-

rial and exhibit. You can explore a replica of this entire freighter through captain's quarters, pilot house, steam engine, crew's quarters and dining room. The museum, which is in the large cargo hold, chronicles the region's rich maritime heritage. Two lifeboats from the doomed *Edmund Fitzgerald* are on display as well as a multimedia presentation on the tragic 1975 shipwreck. The museum is open daily between May 15 and October 15. Admission is $6 for adults and $3.50 for children between 6 and 16. Children 5 and younger are admitted free.

If you'd like to plan a longer stay, we suggest traveling to Sault Ste. Marie, Ontario, and booking a ride on the **Agawa Canyon Train Tour**. The train winds through 114 miles of Canadian wilderness to the beautiful Agawa Canyon where you will stop for two hours of hiking, exploring and enjoying this scenic area. The train is operated by **Algoma Central Railway**, 129 Bay Street, Sault Ste. Marie, Ontario P6A 6Y2, (705) 946-7300 or (800) 242-9287. The train runs from the beginning of June through the color season in mid-October. Runs normally depart the Soo at 8 AM, arrive in the Agawa Canyon at 11:30 AM for a two-hour stay before returning to Sault Ste Marie at 5 PM. Summer fares are $49 for adults, $40 for senior citizens, and $15 for children 5 to 18. Color season rates in September and October rise to $59 for all adults, and $34 for children 5 to 18. Rates for children younger than 5 are $10 at all times while babes in arms ride for free.

The train returns to the rails as the **Snow Train** between late December and early March with departures at 8 AM and returns at 4 PM. Due to heavy snow accumulation and low temperatures, there are no stops in the canyon. Winter fares are $41 for adults, $21 for children from 5 to 18, $9 for children younger than 5 and free for babes in arms. Dining-car service is available on all excursions for meals, snacks and beverages. Advance reservations are highly recommended and can be made by phone with a major credit card.

You can also try your luck around the clock at the gaming tables at the **Kewadin Casino**, 2186 Shunk Road, (906) 632-0530 or (800) KEWADIN, in Sault Ste. Marie or at the **Bay Mills Casinos**, 11386 W. Lakeshore Drive, (888) 4-BAY MILLS, in Brimley, 20 miles west of Sault Ste. Marie. The Kewadin Casino is one of several in northern lower Michigan and the Upper Peninsula (see our Nightlife and Casinos chapter). The Bay Mills Casinos is actually two facilities including the Bay Mills Casino and Resort in Brimley and the Kings Club Casino 2 miles away at 12140 W. Lakeshore Drive, Brimley, (906) 248-3227. The Kings Club Casino was the first tribal-run casino in the United States. Both Bay Mills and Kewadin have their own hotels.

Leaving Sault Ste. Marie, let's travel into the essence of the region's natural wonders. A visit to the Upper Peninsula is a journey through nature. Nowhere is this more beautifully illustrated than at **Tahquamenon Falls**, in Tahquamenon Falls State Park, Route 48, Paradise, (906) 492-3415. Over 150 waterfalls can be found in the Upper Peninsula but the most magnificent are Tahquamenon's near the tiny village of Paradise on the shores of Lake Superior's Whitefish Bay. The falls are approximately 75 miles from Sault Ste. Marie driving along I-75, Mich. Highway 28 and Mich. Highway 123 through the beautiful Hiawatha National Forest and the wooded Upper Peninsula countryside. You can also get to Tahquamenon Falls from St. Ignace by traveling along the scenic U.S. 2 shoreline route along Lake Michigan to Mich. Highway 117 and Mich. Highway 123. The Tahquamenon Falls State Park stretches across more than 60 square miles of untouched wilderness. Wildlife is everywhere with 1,000-pound moose and large black bears comfortably at home among tall pines, vintage hardwoods and the waters of the Tahquamenon River. This is one of Michigan's largest state parks. Its 40,000 acres include a 2,000-acre stand of old-growth hardwood forest as well as miles of hiking trails weaving through the wilderness and to the Upper and Lower Falls.

The less energetic can drive to the falls or stroll along several short, interpretive nature trails. Park rangers present an ambitious selection of summer nature programs every day for visitors. Refreshments and restaurants are available near the Upper Falls while picnic areas are scattered through the park.

The crown jewels are **Tahquamenon's Upper and Lower Falls**. Longfellow noted their beauty in the "Song of Hiawatha." Often referred to as Little Niagara, the Upper Falls is one of the largest waterfalls east of the Mississippi River, stretching 200 feet across and dropping 50 feet. The Lower Falls, 4 miles downstream, are actually a series of smaller waterfalls that cascade around an island. A footpath connects the two falls sharing stunning overlooks and a lovely hike.

If you plan to camp, you must enter through the Tahquamenon Falls State Park River Unit, which is off Mich. Highway 123, 5 miles south of Paradise. The park is open all year. A Michigan State Park motor vehicle permit is required for admission. Fees are $4 per day or $20 per year payable at the park entrance.

You can easily spend much of a day hiking and enjoying the state park but several nearby sites are also worth noting. **The Great Lakes Shipwreck Museum,** 110 Whitefish Point Road, (906) 635-1742, is on Whitefish Point, 11 miles north of Paradise and 20 miles northeast of the falls area. Exhibits chronicle the 300 shipping accidents and 320 deaths that have occurred since 1816 along Michigan's Lake Superior coastline. The most notable was the wreck of the *Edmund Fitzgerald*, 17 miles northwest of Whitefish Point on November 10, 1975. The doomed ship's bell is on display along with a video presentation, many artifacts and related lore. The museum is open daily between May 15 and October 15. Admission is $6 for adults and $3.50 for children between 6 and 16. Children 5 and younger are admitted free.

Also on site is the fully restored **Whitefish Point Light Station,** which was built in 1861 as Lake Superior's first lighthouse. The interior reflects turn-of-the-century life for the lightkeepers and their families. Next door is **Whitefish Point Bird Observatory**, 110 Whitefish Point Road, (906) 492-3596, whose 30-acre grounds are a bird watcher's paradise. There is no admission charge although donations to the Michigan Audubon Society, which operates the observatory, are welcome. This is one of the leading observatories in the country offering rare peeks at the migration of 300 species including hawks, loons, eagles, peregrine falcons, boreal, saw-whet, creal gray owls and many songbirds. An estimated 35,000 to 50,000 fly by on their annual treks, which peak in mid-April through May. Remember to bring binoculars.

If you plan to stay in the Upper Peninsula overnight, check with the various visitors centers for a comprehensive listing of accommodations. Due to the rural nature of the region, they aren't as plentiful as you would find in more densely populated tourist areas. One recommendation is the historic **Ojibway Hotel**, 240 West Portage Avenue, (906) 632-4100 or (800) 654-2929, overlooking the locks in Sault Ste. Marie. This historic hotel has been a mainstay of the Sault Ste. Marie waterfront since it opened in 1928. There are 71 guest rooms and deluxe suites available. Room rates average $124 per night from mid-June to mid-October and $98 per night during the rest of the year.

The casinos have affiliated hotels and several hotel chains offer local accommodations.

For more information on the area, call the **Sault Convention and Visitors Bureau**, (906) 632-3301. Call or drop by **Sault Ste. Marie Welcome Center**, 943 Portage Avenue, W., (906) 632-8242.

You can also get assistance from **Paradise Area Tourism Council**, P.O. Box 64, Paradise, MI 49768, (906) 492-3927, and **Michigan's Upper Peninsula Travel and Recreation Association**, P.O. Box 400, Iron Mountain, MI 49801, (906) 774-5480 or (800) 562-7134.

Drummond Island

If you're seeking a genuine northwoods wilderness experience but aren't the type who enjoys roughing it, schedule at least two days for a trip to Drummond Island. The isle is in the upper peninsula, about an hour's drive east of the Mighty Mac bridge along Mich. Highway 134. This pristine treasure has more than 40,000 acres of state forest. Visitors journey to the island to enjoy hunting, fishing, biking and snowmobiling opportunities as well as the island's abundant wildlife.

Access to Drummond Island is primarily by carferry. **Eastern U.P. Transportation Authority**, (906) 297-8851, operates the year-round carferry service. Ferries depart from De Tour city docks hourly between January 2 and March 31 and more frequently the rest of the

year. The 1-mile, 15-minute ride costs $8 for a car and driver, $2 for additional adults and 80¢ for students. Children younger than 12 are charged on a discretionary basis — sometimes they're charged, sometimes they're not. While regular air service to the island does not currently exist, the **Drummond Island Airport**, on Townline Road, provides a 4,000-foot lighted runway with an instrument approach for private planes. Facilities include a hanger, maintenance service, jet fuel and 100-octane fuel for smaller craft. The airport manager can be contacted at **Bailey's Services**, 223 Townline Road, (906) 493-5411. Bailey's Services also gives aerial tours of the island. Tour rates for up to four passengers are $100 for one-hour trips and $60 for 30-minute trips.

Those coming to the island via water will have no trouble finding docking facilities. Much of the island's activity takes place in what is called the "settlement." It stretches along Potagannissing Bay on the northwest section of the island. Nearly all of the island's resorts are here and most provide docking facilities. In addition, **H&H Marina**, (906) 493-5288, offers 50 seasonal and transient slips, also, a launch ramp, boat repair, canvas repair and boat rentals. Yacht owners often choose to moor at Harbor Island, which sits sheltered in the beautiful bay.

A popular destination for Canadian tourists, Drummond Island is called the "Gem of the Huron." At 87,000 square acres, it is the largest U.S.-owned island in the Great Lakes. The year-round population of 750 swells with summer residents and guests — primarily because the fishing is great. Anglers come here for spring and fall perch runs, the spring smelt run, and for pike, bass, walleye, salmon fishing and the phenomenal lake herring run in July.

Many island resorts offer boat rentals. Others to check out include **Fort Drummond Marine**, 491 Whitney Bay Road, (906) 493-5359, where pontoon boats rent for $75 per day and fishing boats rent for $95 per week. The marine store has groceries, ice, gas, tackle, marine supplies and repairs. Canoes and sea kayaks are available for rent from **Drummond Island Outfitters**, Channel Road, (906) 483-6410. From June through mid-September, Waverunners are available at

Watersport Rentals, 23594 E. Zeerip Drive, (906) 493-6366. Rates are $55 for one hour, $100 for two hours, and $150 for four hours. Wet suits are provided.

If you're looking for bait and tackle, the many full-service resorts sell angling supplies you need on-site. Other sources include **L&M Sports Shop,** 304 E. Johnswood Road, (906) 493-5507, the most complete outfitter on the island. They carry one of the largest selections of bait and tackle in the eastern upper peninsula. In addition, you can get hunting and fishing licenses, black-powder guns and ammo, archery equipment and knives. They're open seven days, year-round from 6 AM to 9 PM Monday through Saturday and 7 AM to 7 PM Sunday.

Many resorts book charters too. **Lucky Strike Charters and Guide Service**, (906) 493-5455, offers fishing trips from Memorial Day to Labor Day for $80 per person, with a $180 minimum for a five-hour trip. They provide island cruises and casino overnight cruises to Sault Ste. Marie for $250 per couple with a $500 minimum charge including lodging. Other options are **Fort Drummond Marine**, 491 Whitney Bay, (906) 493-5359, and **Nate's Marina** on Sturgeon Bay Road, (906) 493-5352.

While water sports are a favorite Drummond pastime, 100 miles of island roads make mountain biking a popular island sport. Bike rentals are available for $1.50 per hour from **Drummond Island Yacht Haven**, (800) 543-4743, located along Potagannissing Bay. An island trail system provides a challenging diversion for advanced riders. The narrow trail is characterized by rough terrain, rocks and steep grades. Off-road vehicle enthusiasts also enjoy these trails.

When cool summer breezes give way to chilling winter winds, snowmobiling becomes a major draw for island visitors. Lucky Strike Charters and Guide Service offers island snowmobile tours. Group rates are $50 per day. They also specialize in guided Canadian trips. Expeditions to places as far north as Hudson Bay are $100 per day for four riders. Each winter, routes across the frozen waters to Canada are marked by the **Drummond Island Snowmobile Club**, (906) 493-5045, and several Canadian clubs. If you're an experi-

enced rider and don't feel the need for guide service, you can enjoy the 100 miles of groomed island snowmobile trails or choose to access the 160,000 kilometer Canadian trail system. Bring your own sled (the Insiders' reference to snowmobiles), as snowmobile rentals are not available on the island. You'll find groomed cross-country ski trails at Woodmoor Resort (more information subsequently in this section).

Nature observers, botanists and photographers will appreciate the rare plants, birds and butterflies living on Drummond Island. Wild pussy willows, trillium, orchids and marsh marigolds color the lush landscape. **Maxton Plains** on the northern tip of the island is owned by the Nature Conservancy, (517) 332-1741. It is a unique protected area where arctic and subtropical plants coexist in a tundra-like landscape. Native island wildlife includes deer, bear, fox, coyote and rabbits. Eagles and osprey and more than 200 varieties of songbirds nest here.

The island's historical treasure is the **Drummond Island Museum,** (906) 493-5746, in the settlement area near Potagannissing Bay. Fort Drummond was the last British holding in the United States and items from the fort are among the museum's collection. The museum also features other local artifacts, including Native-American items and various homestead pieces tracing island development. Built from Drummond Island logs, the museum is open Memorial Day to October.

If you choose to stay overnight on the isle, you'll find everything here in lodging from campsites to rustic two-person cabins to a premier full-service resort. The island's newest facility, **Woodmoor Resort**, 33494 Maxton Road, (906) 493-1000, is on 2,000 acres and in true northern style, is a 40-room log hotel. Peak season weekend rates for two people are $99. The resort features an 18-hole championship golf course, a sport clay course, fine dining, boat rentals, dockage, tennis courts, an indoor gym, and walking and cross-country ski trails. Woodmoor also rents 12 charming cottages. Open year round, **Drummond Island Yacht Haven**, a resort and marina, (906) 493-5232, features 20 first-class cottages overlooking Potagannissing Bay. The three- and four-bedroom cottages are graced with limestone fireplaces and plenty of wood. They rent for $370 to $620 per week in the summer. The resort offers dockage, a launch ramp, fishing supplies, boat and motor rentals, a sand beach and laundry facilities. Other resorts along Potagannissing Bay to check out are **Vechell's Cedarview Resort**, (906) 493-5381, open spring through fall, with nine cabins with fireplaces, boats, picnic and fish cleaning facilities. **Sparzak's Misty Harbor Resort,** (906) 493-5280, has nine two-bedroom cabins along the shore of the bay. Cabins feature fully equipped kitchens, linens, towels, aluminum boats, motors and dock space. If you're the bed-and-breakfast type, check out **Annie's Attic Bed & Breakfast**, (906) 493-5378, nestled along Whitney Bay off the St. Mary's River and offering a view of Great Lakes freighter traffic. Stay year round in the charming carriage house or log cabin. **Captain's Cove Resort,** (906) 493-5344, also provides year-round lodging. One- and two-bedroom cottages feature fully equipped kitchens, boat launch, boats, motors, pontoons, gas, bait, freezer, picnic tables, grills and campfire pits. If you pack a tent, stay at the **Drummond Island Township Park** along Channel Road in the Potagannissing Bay area. It offers a combination of 50 rustic campsites and sites with electrical hookups. It provides pump water only and pit toilets. Camping fees are $6 per night for rustic sites and $7.50 per night for sites with electricity, all on a first-come, first-served basis.

Several restaurants are situated around the bays offering everything from hot dogs to ribs. The **Gourmet Galley**, 30420 E. Johnswood Road, (906) 493-5507, serves eight kinds of pizza, a variety of sandwiches, fresh and smoked fish, imported and domestic cheese, Ben & Jerry's ice cream and Mackinac Island fudge. Enjoy their cozy seating area or take the goodies with you. The **Northwood** on Johnswood Road, (906) 493-5282, is famous for its fresh whitefish. Open only in summer, they serve breakfast, lunch and dinner and in the evening the Northwood's bar becomes an island gathering spot. Carry-outs are available. For fine dining on the waterfront, try **Bayside Dining** at Woodmoor, 33494 Maxton Road, (906) 493-1014. Open from mid-May through mid-October, it's operated by the New England Culinary Institute of Vermont and has great early-bird specials.

Shopping on the island is pretty much limited to basic supplies. In addition to the outfitters several general stores around the island are stocked to meet your needs. In the bay settlement, you'll find **H&H General Store** and **Hometown IGA,** (906) 493-5288. They offer a full grocery line, deli meats and cheeses, ice, greeting cards, cameras and film. About 8 miles east of the bay settlement, at the Townline Road and Channel Road junction, you'll find **Sune's**, (906) 493-5250, in the One Stop Shopping Corner. Sune's includes grocery, hardware, dry goods, ice cream and souvenir shops. Fresh deli sandwiches and bakery items, produce and meats are available in the grocery shop. Sportswear, swimwear, souvenirs and T-shirts, magazines, film and housewares are sold in the dry goods building. Some operations are seasonal. Many services are also available on the island including a post office, dentist and pharmacy. So settle into island life, and enjoy your commune with nature.

For more information regarding island opportunities, contact the **Drummond Island Chamber of Commerce** at (906) 493-5245 or (800) 737-8666; or the **Drummond Island Tourism Association**, Box 200, Drummond Island, MI 49726, (800) 737-8666.

Hartwick Pines State Park

Just a short jaunt from our regional boundaries, Hartwick Pines stands as a majestic reminder of our lumbering past. This unique state park is just 9 miles northeast of Grayling and is home to one of the few remaining tracts of virgin pines in the Midwest. With 9,672 rolling, wooded acres, **Hartwick Pines State Park**, (517) 348-7068, is the largest state park in the Lower Peninsula. It overlooks the east branch of the Au Sable River and includes four small lakes, unique timber lands, miles of nature trails, a campground and a day visitors' picnic and play area. Park hours are 8 AM to 10 PM year round. You'll also find the Michigan Forests Visitors Center and Hartwick Pines Lumbering Museum. A Michigan State Park motor vehicle permit is required for admission to the park. Fees are $4 per day or $20 per year, which are available at the park entrance.

Visitors commune with nature on a grand scale while hiking within the park's 49-acre grove of virgin white pine. The forest provides a rare glimpse of what much of northern Michigan looked like before the onset of the lumbering era. White pine thrive in our region's poor, sandy soil. They grew up to 200 feet tall and lived for 500 years before the influx of white settlers during the 1800s. The pines covered almost one-third of our state land, more than 13 million of Michigan's 38 million acres. Unfortunately, the tall straight trunks that made them so grand also made them an ideal resource for building lumber.

By the time the lumbering era began to wane at the turn of the century, most of these magnificent pine forests were nothing more than cutover fields. This famous stand of old growth pine was originally passed over by lumber crews who felt it wasn't large enough for production. That land and its thousands of surrounding acres were purchased and donated to the state in 1927 by Mrs. Karen Hartwick of Detroit as a memorial to her husband, Major Edward E. Hartwick, who died during World War I. Mrs. Hartwick, who was the daughter and wife of lumbermen, had originally planned to buy the property as a gift for her husband. Both had grown up in Grayling and had been childhood sweethearts before marrying in 1898. After his death, she purchased and donated the land with three requests: that the land be protected from logging and fire by the Department of Conservation (later the Department of Natural Resources); that a structural memorial in honor of her late husband be constructed; and, that a highway linking U.S. 27 to the property be constructed. The park opened to the public in May 1928.

Today, visitors can easily spot the Hartwick Pines entrance, which is marked by a bright red "big wheel" that had originally been used to drag logs from the woods to the river. A park ranger will direct you to campsites, picnic areas or the popular visitors center. We suggest beginning at the **Michigan Forests Visitors Center**, (517) 348-2537, which is open daily between Memorial Day and Labor Day, and Tuesday through Sunday the rest of the year with the exception of Thanksgiving, Christmas and New Year's Day. You'll find ample parking outside the spacious center. Inside, you'll immediately notice the glass wall reaching from floor to vaulted ceiling that overlooks the forest and countless bird feeders. Glass displays showcase a full-size female bobcat, a black bear cub, forestry tools and the geology of the glaciers. A nearby door leads visitors past hands-on exhibits about trees and forest management. An audiovisual presentation, classroom and gift shop are also on site as is a wealth of informational material and trail maps about Hartwick Pines, Michigan forests and regional wildlife.

Several nature trails lead from the visitors center through the park lands. Guided tours are available with varying schedules. If you're interested, check directly with the park for the week's schedule or request availability of off-season walks. The Old Growth Forest Foot Trail is a very accessible, paved path leading through the virgin white pines, the log-cabin-style Chapel in the Woods and the Logging Museum. It stretches in a circular route between the Visitors Center and the day parking and picnic area. The Memorial Building, dedicated to Major Hartwick, stands next to the day parking lot. It was the park's first public structure and served as its visitor center for more than 60 years.

The logging museum at Hartwick Pines was built by the Civilian Conservation Corps in 1934-35. Exhibits include re-creations of a

INSIDERS' TIP

The most famous Hartwick pine was the magnificent Monarch. The tree, estimated to be at least 300 years old, stood 155 feet high and soared above its peers in this primeval forest. Unfortunately, the Monarch bowed to nature during a tremendous storm in 1996 that severely damaged its tallest branches. The tree still stands today, but is a shadow of its former grandeur.

19th-century logging camp bunkhouse, mess hall, company store and blacksmith shop along with many photographic displays documenting the heyday of Northern Michigan logging. Always fascinating, the museum and nearby outdoor steam-powered sawmill take on new life during special summer weekends. Period music fills the air while artisans demonstrate whittling, blacksmithing, spinning and other vintage crafts. The museum is open daily between Memorial Day and Labor Day, and with abbreviated hours September, October and May. It is closed November through April.

Several free events and educational activities are scheduled each season. Two of the most popular are in the summer. **Sawdust Days**, formerly known as Wood Shaving Days, are held the third weekend of July while **Black Iron Days** are usually slated for the fourth weekend of August.

Three trail loops designated for mountain biking and cross-country skiing can be accessed from the campground or the trail head near the Visitors Center parking lot. These range from the 3-mile Aspen trail to the 5-mile Deer Run trail and 7-mile Weary Legs trail. Mountain biking is restricted to these trails, park roads and parking areas. The Au Sable River foot trail leads through three wooded miles and crosses the Au Sable's East Branch in two locations. The Mertz Grade Foot Trail is an easier 2-mile trail weaving through forest lands and fields near the Visitors Center. Hikers are cautioned to leave no trace of their visits behind, and to note that hunting is permitted along portions of these trails during designated seasons.

Families will enjoy the half-mile Bright and Glory Lakes Nature Trail, which begins between sites 15 and 16 in the campground, meanders past several interesting forest sites and leads to the pretty Bright and Glory Lakes which are filled with native trout, bass, bluegill and perch. Interpretive maps for all trails are available at the Visitors Center. The Bright and Glory brochure is especially geared toward points of interest for the younger set.

Driving to and from Grayling is part of the pleasure of this scenic Hartwick Pines daytrip. It is in the heart of rural northern Michigan where you'll experience the wooded privacy that the local residents cherish. Make the trip

during late September or early October and you'll also enjoy the majesty of this wooded region in raging color.

To get to Hartwick Pines, take the nearest highway leading to I-75 and head toward Exit 259 once you're on the Interstate. Regardless of the direction, you'll likely pass vast farmlands, rolling hills and heavily wooded lands. From Traverse City, head east on Mich. Highway 72 past Lake Skegemog to Kalkaska about 20 miles away. After a quick southern jog through town and past Kalkaska's gigantic trout sculpture, turn onto the continuation of Mich. Highway 72 and drive straight to Grayling. Arriving in Grayling, you glimpse the many canoe liveries that line the adjacent Au Sable and Manistee Rivers, and play such a role in the famous Au Sable River Marathon each July (see our Annual Events chapter). Directions to Hartwick Pines are well marked and will easily guide you to the main entrance just northeast of town. The next 25 miles make a relaxing trip along heavily pine-lined roadways. Every so often, small signs warn of deer crossings or point the way to canoe rentals and fishing bait shops.

After your visit, consider continuing your auto tour to the north or the south — or both. Elk country lies to the north, just east of Gaylord and our Insiders' boundaries. From Hartwick Pines, head north on I-75 to Vanderbilt, then east on Sturgeon Valley Road. You'll be in the heart of the 96,000 acre **Pigeon River Country State Forest**, which is home to the largest elk herd east of the Mississippi River. Today's elk herd, estimated at close to 1,200, is descended from seven Rocky Mountain Elk that were released into Cheboygan county in 1918 to replace the region's native Eastern Elk, which had become extinct in Michigan by 1877. Today's herd roves over a 600-mile range between Cheboygan, Presque Isle, Montmorency and Otsego counties in the state's central to northeastern tip. The greatest concentration live in the wilderness areas of the Pigeon River property. The adult elk are magnificent creatures, with bulls measuring eight feet from head to tail, weighing 700 to 900 pounds and racked with massive antlers. Cows measure a foot smaller and one third less in weight. Both sport beautiful chocolate-colored manes and tawny hides, and are quite tolerant of humans.

A great daytrip in itself is to hike, snow-

Woodmoor resort's piney woods, cool water and log cottages reflect Drummond Island's easy-going northern lifestyle.

shoe or cross-country ski along the numerous trails winding through the forest. It's not unusual to glide past a group of resting elk who observe their visitors with quiet interest. By the way, there's much more than elk in this forest. Other wildlife include deer, bear, coyote, grouse, bobcat, woodcock, beaver, otter, muskrat, snowshoe hare and the rare pine marten. Add the scenic beauty of the Pigeon and Sturgeon Rivers, which flow through the forest, and you're guaranteed a wonderful outdoor experience.

After spending time in the historic forest at Hartwick Pines, your curiosity may be whetted for more information about our Michigan forests or our logging history. The **Civilian Conservation Corps Museum** in Roscommon, North Higgins Lake State Park, Roscommon Road, (517) 821-6125, salutes the work of the Depression-era Civilian Conservation Corp (CCC) and its tremendous impact on today's park lands. The CCC was created to help put

Americans back to work during the Great Depression. Between 1933 and 1942, 100,000 men were enrolled in the Michigan division where they planted 484 million trees and built 7,000 miles of truck trails, 504 bridges and 222 buildings in our state parks and national forests. The Hartwick Pines camp was the longest running in the state, a fact commemorated by the construction of the Memorial Building and Logging Camp Museum. The CCC ended with U.S. entry into World War II, but its impact on reforestation and conservation is experienced every day. The museum chronicles the members' work, daily lives and accomplishments through photographs and artifacts donated by CCC alumni. It takes about one hour to tour the museum and nearby structures such as the FDR Memorial, Pump Exhibit, Tree Nursery Packing House, Cone Barn, Ice House and Fire Tower. The CCC Museum is in North Higgins Lake State Park, 15 miles south of Grayling along Roscommon Road. Exits are off I-75 and U.S. 27. The museum is open from the beginning of June through Labor Day. A Michigan State Park motor vehicle permit is required for admission. Fees are $4 per day or $20 per year, payable at the park entrance. If you purchased a pass earlier in the day at Hartwick Pines, you can use the same one here and vice versa.

The Michigan Forest Resource Alliance, P.O. Box 388, Crystal Falls, MI 49920, (800) 474-1718, compiled a 67-mile auto tour of Michigan forest that stretches along U.S. 27 and I-75 between Harrison and Hartwick Pines. Brochures with directions are available in the Hartwick Pines Visitors Center as well as directly through the Alliance. There are 10 sites, each noted by a sign stating "The Living Forest" and correlating to the highway's mile markers noted in the brochure. The stops include a young Aspen forest, mature northern hardwoods, the Muskegon River Fishery and Wetland Habitat, a northern White Cedar swamp, an oak/pine forest and Hartwick Pines.

Bird lovers should plan to visit Mio, 30 miles east of Grayling on Mich. Highway 72, for spring sightings of the rare **Kirtland Warbler**. The U.S. Forest Service, (517) 826-3252 (Mio) or (517) 351-2555 (Grayling), leads free guided tours to the birds' nesting areas between mid-May and the beginning of July. The Jack Pine forest land near Mio is the only known area in the world in which the endangered Kirtland Warbler will breed today. They are highly protected and their breeding grounds are strictly off limits except during these guided walks. The free tours depart from both Grayling and Mio. In the past, tours have met at the Forest Service office in Mio, which is at the corner of Mich. Highway 33 and Court Street, or in Grayling at the Holiday Inn parking lot off the I-75 Business Loop.

Houghton Lake

If visiting the state's largest inland lake is not enough incentive for you, plan your visit to Houghton Lake in January during Tip-Up Town USA, Michigan's largest winter festival. You'll find Houghton Lake in the middle of the lower peninsula, about an hour southeast of Traverse City off Interstate 75.

The sparkling Houghton Lake features 72 miles of shoreline, covers 22,000 acres and is renowned for offering outstanding water recreation. Shallow and sandy near shorelines, the lake provides swimming enjoyment for both experienced and inexperienced swimmers.

For anglers, it's a year-round delight. Northern pike, walleye, largemouth and smallmouth bass, bluegill and crappies make good sport fishing. Some boaters enjoy the fact that Houghton Lake doesn't have any motor size restrictions and features many convenient launch sites.

From early spring through fall, boat rentals are available at numerous resorts and marinas. **Edgewater Beach Marina**, 8320 W. Houghton Lake Drive, (517) 422-4221, has three sizes of pontoon boats, which rent for $90 to $120 per day. Their 14-foot fishing boats with motors rent for $40 per day. **L&G Boat Rentals**, 6560 W. Houghton Lake Drive, (517) 422-3231, also rents 14-foot fishing boats with motors for $40 per day. Pontoon rentals range from $85 to $120 per day. Most companies require a deposit on watercraft rentals.

While summer has long been the peak season for this popular tourist destination, **Tip-Up Town USA**, (800) 248-LAKE, is breaking tradition. The United States Chamber of Commerce ranks Tip-Up Town the seventh-largest January festival in the nation. From the first Tip-Up Town event, held in 1953, to the present, the festival has grown to attract 50,000 visitors from across the Midwest. Held every third and fourth weekend in January, most festivities take place on the great expanse of ice. Tip-ups are the red signaling flags attached to ice-fishing rigs anglers use on the frozen water. Anglers hover over small, slushy openings and hundreds of ice shanties appear — some simple homemade shelters and some expensive, folding high-tech tents — creating an ice village or Tip-Up Town.

The festival features a Grand Parade, substantial prizes such as snowmobiles and vacations, fishing contests, spectacular fireworks over the ice, games, demonstrations and aerial performances. During the festival, thousands of snowmobiles can be seen racing across Houghton Lake. There are no entrance fees. To participate in some events, however, you are required to purchase a $3 Tip-Up Town badge, available from local merchants.

Snowmobile rentals are available from **Hacker's Yamaha & Honda**, 3901 W. Houghton Lake Drive, (517) 366-7015. You must be 25 to rent a sled and advance reservations are recommended. Daily rental fees are $125 and weekend rentals are $335. Helmets are included.

Houghton Lake fall color-tours and hunting are popular. About 175,000 acres of state land surrounds the community of Houghton Lake. The forests are filled with white-tailed deer, partridge, coons, rabbit and bear. In the spring, wild-mushroom hunters are drawn to the area. Come May, outdoor enthusiasts launch another season of canoeing, camping, hiking and golfing. Car-racing fans will enjoy spending an evening at **Merritt Speedway**, 15 miles west of Houghton Lake on Mich. Highway 55, (616) 328-4351. From mid-May to Labor Day, fast-paced stock car action draws drivers and spectators from around the state. The Saturday-only entertainment begins with time trials at 6 PM. Races begin at 7:30 PM. Admission is $9. Shows are canceled in inclement weather.

Other attractions in Houghton Lake include **Funland Amusement Park**, 6329 W. Houghton Lake Drive, (517) 422-5204. Strictly a summer operation, the mini-amusement park for the young and young at heart has kiddie rides, a game arcade, batting cages and a water slide. Movie fans won't want to miss Houghton Lake's one-of-a-kind **Pines Theater**, 4673 W. Houghton Lake Drive, (517) 366-9226. Here, the young Charleston Heston, a regular summer visitor to the area, spent many hours soaking up cinema tales. The old Pines movie house looks much the same as it did in the world-famous actor's youth. It's constructed of logs, and features a stone fireplace and wild game mounts, creating a real up-north atmosphere. **Zubler's** gift shop, 3282 W. Houghton Lake Drive, (517) 366-5691, is another attraction generations of tourists have enjoyed. Zubler's has hosted weekly Indian powwows for 52 years at its adjacent Indian village. The village features eight colorful tepees and several totem poles. Every Thursday from the end of June to the third week of July, Chippewa tribe members from mid-Michigan perform traditional Native-American dances. Performances are on the hour from 1 to 4 PM. Children in the audience are always invited to join the simpler dances. You'll hear Indian folk lore from the elders of the tribe and have the opportunity to purchase hot Indian fried bread, made on-site. Performances are free but donations are welcome. Zubler's shop, open year-round, specializes in Indian-made turquoise jewelry, with a nice selection of leather moccasins, T-shirts and souvenirs. The **Rockin' Chair Gift Shop**, 3881 W. Houghton Lake Drive, (517) 366-5223, is the most-photographed gift and souvenir shop in northern Michigan because there's a 10-foot rocking chair, a variety of animal statuary and an antique hearse in the front yard. They carry T-shirts, moccasins, jewelry, fudge and souvenir items.

You'll find dozens of shops, motels and restaurants lining Houghton Lake's 15-mile-long main street. The road follows the lake shoreline traversing Houghton Lake Heights, Houghton Lake and Prudenville. There's an array of familiar fast-food eateries and several family-owned restaurants along the strip. An Insiders' favorite is **Coyles Restaurant**, 9074 Old U.S. 27, (517) 422-3812, featuring popular buffets. Friday and Saturday night seafood buffets feature shrimp and frog legs. Relaxed and family-friendly, they also serve breakfast, lunch and dinner from a full menu and offer a full bar. **The Limberlost**, 4168 W. Houghton Lake Drive, (517) 366-7242, caters to young adults. The fun and lively shoreside restaurant and lounge brings in rock 'n' roll bands every weekend and is renowned for Friday and Saturday night summer beach parties. You can easily access The Limberlost by boat or snowmobile. They serve lunch and dinner featuring popular Mexican dishes.

Overnighters will find chain motels, bed and breakfast inns, mom and pop motels, full-service resorts, cabins and cottages from which to choose. The **Spring Brook Inn,** 565 West Branch Road, (517) 366-6347, nestled among 30 acres, has 8 units, each with a balcony overlooking the beautiful forest, gas-log fireplace and Polynesian spa. They have a heated pool and the Houghton Lake public access and boat launch is less than a mile away. The convenient **Inn Restaurant** serves breakfast and dinner and is known for their prime rib. Peak season rates for double occupancy range from $145 to $175 per night. For a good deal, ask about their packages, which include meals.

Houghton Lake's history as a northern Michigan tourist destination dates back to the 1940s. To feel a part of the history you may want to stay at one of the traditional resorts featuring mini-cottages. One is **Morris's Northernaire Resort**, 11544 W. Shore Drive, (517) 422-6644, with six two-bedroom lakefront cottages, all with charming knotty-pine interiors. The year-round resort provides cable TV, campfire pits, swings, shuffleboard and horseshoe pits. Cottages are rented on a weekly basis only during the summer when rates range from $450 to $550. Other lodging choices are **Lagoon Resort & Motel**, 6578 W. Houghton Lake Drive, (517) 422-5761. They feature large two- and three-bedroom shoreside cottages and motel units. **Val Halla Motel**, 9869 W. Shore Drive, (517) 422-5137, offers clean rooms with scenic views, patios and in-room coffee. **Way North Motel and Cabins**, 9052 W. Houghton Lake Drive, (517) 422-5523, has air-conditioned rooms, boat docking and a heated pool. Contact the **Houghton Lake Chamber of Commerce**, 1625 W. Houghton Lake Drive, (800) 248-LAKE, for a complete list of area lodging facilities, activities and events.

Frankenmuth

Known as Michigan's Little Bavaria, Frankenmuth combines Old World ambiance with modern-day tourism for a unique mix of shopping glitz and German hospitality. It's the home of famous chicken dinners, regional artisans and the largest Christmas store in the world. This tiny town, 150 miles southwest of Traverse City off I-75 near Saginaw, attracts 3 million visitors each year and has earned the reputation as one of Michigan's top tourist destinations.

The commercial district is decked in Bavarian attire. A stroll through town finds gingerbread architecture complete with balconies and stylized trim everywhere. Ethnic roots extend back to Lutheran settlers who left their native Franconia in Germany for a new life in the New World. They named their community Frankenmuth, meaning "courage of the Franconians." Today, German heritage remains strong although Bavarian and Alpen motifs have overtaken the sterner ways of the Franconian forebears.

Tourism in Frankenmuth was the child of circumstance. During the mid-1950s, American road systems were being transformed by the advent of interstate highways. Michigan's new stretch of I-75 diverted travelers away from Frankenmuth by seven miles. The Zehnder family, longtime town restaurateurs and innkeepers, responded by transforming their Fisher Hotel into the picturesque Bavarian Inn, laying the foundation for attracting travelers to Frankenmuth.

The **Bavarian Inn**, 713 S. Main Street, (517) 652-9941 or (800) BAVARIA, and the original **Zehnder's Restaurant**, 730 S. Main Street, (517) 652-0400 or (800) 863-7999, anchor the downtown district as two of the state's most popular restaurants. They are across the street from each other in the center of town. Both specialize in all-you-can-eat family-style chicken dinners as well as their individual specialties — German fare at the Bavarian Inn and popular American dishes at Zehnder's. The prices are reasonable, the food is great and the restaurants are huge. Plan to have a meal at the restaurants that have brought visitors to Frankenmuth for generations.

Outdoors, the Bavarian Inn's clock tower rings its 35-bell carillon several times daily while large carved characters depicting the story of the Pied Piper pop out of doors near the tower's top. After driving through Frankenmuth, park your car at one of the large parking lots behind the Bavarian Inn or Zehnder's and use the bell tower for your landmark as you peruse downtown's 100 unique specialty shops.

A visitors center next to the Bavarian Inn provides maps, advertising guides and ample advice for a pleasant stay. Stroll along Main Street and peruse the many Alpen shops lining the streets. There are over 100 stores in the Frankenmuth area with colorful names like Aunt Hattie's Corner, Books N Stuff, Chocolates Von Rittmueller, the Covered Bridge and Leather Shop, the Frankenmuth Mill, Kite Kraft, Frankenmuth Cheese Haus, Goin' Nuts, The Frankenmuth Clock Company, Gramma's House, Salmagundi, Zak's Candy Haus and Raus Country Store and Dollhouse Miniatures.

Many are unique, small specialty establishments. There are too many to list individually. Instead, we recommend you discover your favorites at your leisure.

While on your tour through Frankenmuth, though, we would like to point out a few notable stops and shops along the way. Most are open year round although it's not unusual for hours to be reduced during the winter months.

On Main Street, plan to stop at the **Frankenmuth Historical Museum,** 613 S. Main Street, (517) 652-9701. Exhibits explore Frankenmuth's past with explorations of its founding immigrants, logging, local brewing and even chicken dinners. Admission prices in 1997 were $1 for adults and 50¢ for children.

The **Frankenmuth Woodcarving Studio,** 976 S. Main Street, (517) 652-2975, showcases the work of internationally known wood sculptor Georg J. Keilhofer. This is a working studio and classroom where visitors are welcome to observe woodcarving classes in progress. The studio's gift shop carries an excellent selection of woodcarving tools and supplies.

The **Zeesenagel Alpine Village,** 780 Mill Street, (517) 652-2591, is behind Zehnder's and houses a treasure of handcrafted miniatures. More than 550 one-sixth scale figurines are displayed in 10 creative scenes depicting a northern Italian village celebrating Epiphany 200 years ago. Each miniature as well as the entire layout is a work of art by the Zeesenagel owners, nationally acclaimed artists Dave Zeese and Don Nagel. Tours are conducted several times each day with guides telling the Christmas story alongside the dioramas. Tour fees are $2 for adults and $1 for children younger than 12. The gift shop is unique with excellent international items and a very knowledgeable staff.

Moving beyond the center of town, stop by **Bronner's CHRISTmas Wonderland,** 25 Christmas Lane, (517) 652-9931 or (800) ALL-YEAR. This enormous store, 1 mile south of Frankenmuth off Main Street, is the size of four football fields and displays more than 50,000 holiday ornaments, lights and decorations. You'll find nativity scenes ranging from life-size down to tiny miniatures. Animated figures are on display at every turn,

creating a Disney-like feel of cheerful nonreality. A spectacular lighted display along "Christmas Tree Lane" shines outdoors every night, all year long. Bronner emphasizes the international and religious aspects of Christmas with Bibles, ornaments, banners and children's books in dozens of languages. Hanukkah and Kwanza items are also available. Allot adequate time to see this store. We would recommend planning on two hours although some super shoppers have been known to do it in less than 90 minutes. If you would like to relax while you're inside, make a stop at the refreshment area or watch an 18-minute audiovisual presentation about Bronner's that is shown on the hour. Nearby, the **Silent Night Memorial Chapel** is open daily for visits and meditation.

Near Bronner's is the **Zeilinger Wool Company,** 1130 Weiss Street, (517) 652-2920, which has processed raw wool for more than 80 years. Self-guided tours demonstrate the entire process from raw materials to final product. Handstitched wool quilts, batting and mattress pads are sold here, as well as spinning and quilting supplies and fabrics. Also nearby is the unique **Michigan's Own Military and Space Museum,** 1250 Weiss Street, (517) 652-8005, highlighting the contributions of the state's distinguished military veterans and astronauts with uniforms, memorabilia and rotating displays. Admission prices in 1997 were $2.50 for adults, $2 for senior citizens and $1 for children 6 to 18. Children younger than 5 are admitted free.

St. Lorenz Lutheran Church, 10165 Tuscola Street at Mayer Street, (517) 652-6141, 1 mile west of town, is classic Gothic architecture complemented by a series of intricate, beautiful stained-glass windows illustrating the story of the original Franconian missionaries who founded Frankenmuth. Take a self-guided tour of the sanctuary or make advance arrangements to tour the congregation's original log church, its 1800s-era brick church and the town's first cemetery. A German-language service is still held Sunday mornings.

Take a pleasant excursion aboard the **Frankenmuth Riverboat Tours,** 445 S. Main Street, (517) 652-8844, where lively narrators will entertain guests with local tales and trivia as the *Riverview Queen* paddles past sights along the Cass River. The riverboat usually makes four trips each day between May and October. If you'd like to ride during the busier summer months, it's wise to purchase your tickets early. Fares in 1997 were $6 for adults and $3 for children between 3 and 12.

Keep your appetite — and thirst — at bay at the **Black Forest Brewing Company,** 781 Heinlein Street, (517) 652-6060, close to Bronner's. This restaurant claims it is North America's largest brew pub. Its menu features American favorites complemented by an extensive line of homemade beers. Diners enjoy live entertainment featuring a variety of talented performers.

If your shopping urges haven't been filled yet, it may be time to trek to Birch Run to visit the largest outlet shopping center in Michigan, the **Outlets at Birch Run,** 12240 S. Beyer Road, Birch Run, (517) 624-SHOP or (800) 866-5900. You name it, it's probably sold here at a discount. There are at least 200 shops including J. Crew, Calvin Klein, Polo, Evan-Picone, Eddie Bauer, Sony, Guess, Woolrich, Lenox, Mikasa and American Tourister. This place is enormous. Wear comfortable shoes since you could easily spend an entire day here. The outlet center is 7 miles north of Frankenmuth just off I-75 at the Birch Run exit (136).

If you're planning your visit during mid-June, you can join the celebration at the annual Bavarian Festival, usually held during the second week of the month. It's a week filled with arts and crafts, special activities and endless German foods, music and dancing. Enjoy!

A daytrip to Frankenmuth can easily stretch to several days. If you need accommodations, contact the **Frankenmuth Convention and Visitors Bureau**, 635 S. Main Street, (517) 652-6106 or (800) 386-8696, for a full listing of available hotels, campgrounds and bed and breakfasts as well as answers to all of your travel questions.

We have a few suggestions:

The **Bavarian Inn Lodge**, One Covered Bridge Lane, (517) 652-2651 or (888) 77-LODGE, is a large lodge in downtown Frankenmuth that bills itself as North America's largest Bavarian-themed family resort. With the equivalent of 7 acres under its roof, it houses 354 guest rooms, three indoor pools, three whirlpools, an 18-hole indoor minigolf course, a family fun center, two lounges, two gift shops, four tennis courts and the family-friendly Oma's restaurant. Rates average $115-195 per night all year.

Frankenmuth Motel, 1218 Weiss Street, (517) 652-6171, is known as the town's most affordable lodging. There are 70 ground-floor rooms. The motel is within walking distance of Bronner's. Room rates average $50-75 per night between April and December, and $39-49 during the winter.

Another option is **Zehnder's Bavarian Haus**, 1365 S. Main Street, (517) 652-6144, which features 137 deluxe guest rooms in a two-story structure on spacious, landscaped grounds. The lodge houses indoor and outdoor pools, a game room, sauna and whirlpool. An 18-hole golf course is nearby. All rooms offer free movies, and some have refrigerators and coffee makers. Room rates range from $79 to $205 from mid-June through October, $55-175 from December to March, and $60-175 during November, April, May and early June.

Our diverse geography provides home settings along scenic coastlines, in thick piney woods and within charming historic towns.

Real Estate

Go ahead, indulge yourself in the Great Northern Dream — the fantasy of owning a luxury condo on the lake, a hunting cabin in a hardwood forest or an upscale natural log home. Then make your dream reality. You can fill your fondest housing fantasy in Northwest Michigan, whether it is residential, vacation or rental property. Real estate here is geared to complement every lifestyle from active to reclusive. Our diverse geography provides home settings along scenic coastlines, in thick piney woods and within charming historic towns. We have a variety of developments: world-class lakeshores; golf or ski communities; friendly family neighborhoods; streets lined with stately Victorian mansions; and green acres graced with old farmhouses, rolling hills and cherry blossoms.

In Northwest Michigan, as in other sections of the nation, the migration of baby boomers to lake and resort communities is rapidly changing the character of the real estate market. Boomers are flocking in unprecedented numbers from Detroit, Chicago and northern Indiana metropolises to enjoy our sweet air, clean waters and easy northern living. The region's Realtors report that for many agencies, relocating urbanites, and those investing in property for future moves, account for as much as 50 percent of transactions in recent years. The clamor for prime northern property has dramatically affected property prices. In 1997, the Traverse City area was noted by industry experts for one of the biggest property value increases in the United States. In a single year, values increased more than 30 percent. The impact of activity in the Traverse City market ripples out to other northern counties. In the same year, Benzie County Realtors also reported property value increases of about 30 percent. In Wexford County, the price of acreage quadrupled in two years. Because of high demand, in some counties there is an extremely limited waterfront or acreage market, while in others, opportunities remain plentiful.

Some of the priciest year-round homes are found in Emmet and Charlevoix counties. You can spend $1.4 million for a Bay Harbor lot in Petoskey, or $2 million for a Belvedere Avenue address in Charlevoix. The best housing values may be found in Manistee, where it's possible for a savvy buyer to pick up a Victorian beauty in need of TLC for as little as $75,000.

The 11 counties we've included have a broad spectrum of communities and varying real estate availability. Some market areas cross county lines, while others are clearly defined by county borders. Despite the wide diversity of property types, we've tried to offer an accurate overview of the current real estate picture in each geographic area by providing average housing prices for each region. Keep in mind the real estate industry determines existing home values by the square foot, while coveted water property values are often determined by the shoreline foot, and large parcels of land are calculated by the acre.

If your northern stay is temporary, you may be seeking a cabin, cottage or condo to rent. In that case, check our Real Estate Resources for rental management offices. Daily, weekly or monthly rentals are available in most communities. But if it's finally time to make your Great Northern Dream come true, write or call area Realtor boards. They will provide a list of reputable real estate agencies. In either case, our Real Estate Resources listings can help you get started.

We're confident you'll find what you dream of in our corner of Michigan.

Welcome home.

Grand Traverse

The Grand Traverse area real estate market is traditionally defined by our local Realtors as covering Grand Traverse, Leelanau, Benzie, Antrim and Kalkaska counties. With the exception of Benzie county, which is being included with our subsequent Lake Michigan Shoreline section, the boundaries are the same for this Insiders' Guide.

If you're in the market for real estate, your best resource is the Traverse Area Association of Realtors at 852 S. Garfield Avenue, Traverse City, (616) 947-2050. More than 800 real estate practitioners and professionals in related fields are on the roster with members from each of the five counties. The members represent more than 90 real estate firms. The association links Realtors, related professionals, homebuyers, homeowners and communities. It does so through newsletters, training and industry-related activities for the Realtors. For homebuyers, sellers and the communities it provides information, referrals and advocacy. The Realtors' association maintains a computerized Multiple Listing System with photographs of all area properties on the market.

If you would prefer to build a home, contact the Home Builders Association of the Grand Traverse Area at 3040 Sunset Lane, Traverse City, (616) 946-2305. Much like the Realtors' Association, the Homebuilders Association is a link between the many professional builders and potential consumers.

Additional resources include the Traverse City Area Chamber of Commerce, which maintains an up-to-date list of area real estate firms, appraisers, developers, apartment buildings, condominiums, property management companies, subsidized housing, senior citizen housing and companies specializing in commercial and industrial properties.

The Grand Traverse area has high-quality, affordable housing comparable to other states and Michigan regions. To illustrate this, let's use a typical home with three bedrooms, two baths, a family room and a two-car garage to compare prices. Average local cost would be $126,060. In Ann Arbor the same home would cost $135,333, or in Detroit's Wayne County, $128,667. In Grand Rapids the home would cost $103,333, and in Lansing, $87,833. The region fares well compared to communities around the United States and Canada, such

as Baltimore at $183,333; the Chicago suburbs at $296,000; Dallas at $133,700; Denver, $140,333; Montreal, $130,030; Toronto, $218,566; Miami, $130,030; or New York City's Suffolk County at $226,416.

It's important to note that Grand Traverse area property values are significantly impacted by the overwhelming beauty of our scenic waterfronts and natural settings. The quality of life here is also extremely attractive, with excellent schools, low crime rates, competitive services, environmental quality and a wholesome, small-town ambiance. As a result our population has been growing at significant rates. This is a marvelous place to live and our housing prices are somewhat higher because of it.

An important issue in considering local real estate is whether property is on the water. The Multiple Listing System divides all listings between the categories of waterfront and non-waterfront. The term "waterfront" encompasses a range of further options, including direct waterfront, shared waterfront, bay frontage, Lake Michigan shoreline, inland lakes frontage, river frontage and view lots. As you might expect, direct waterfront along Grand Traverse Bay and the Lake Michigan shoreline are among the most expensive properties. Recent properties like these have sold for at least $2,500 per foot of shoreline. A prime lot on Lake Michigan can easily run $500,000. Properties in these areas with existing homes often run $350,000 to $750,000, with a few peaking over $1 million.

Water frontage can be found on the smaller inland lakes for as low as $500 per shoreline foot although this will depend on various desirability factors, such as whether it is an all-sports lake (i.e. appropriate for a variety of recreational pursuits); if it has a summer vs. a year-round population; what the nearest town is; the quality of the school district, the view and the natural setting. The most expensive lake properties are those on Long, Torch and Glen lakes, followed by Elk Lake and Lake Leelanau. Other lakes, such as Green, Duck and Arbutus, are geared toward summer residents, but have been attracting an increasing number of year-round homeowners.

www.insiders.com

See this and many other **Insiders' Guide®** destinations online — in their entirety.

Visit us today!

CHUCK KALCHIK
BROKER

Specializing in resort, commercial, orchard, waterfront properties and homes in Leelanau country.

**301 MILL STREET • P.O. BOX 417
NORTHPORT, MI 49670**

**BUSINESS (616) 386-5161
HOME (616) 386-5381**

NORTHPORT | PROPERTIES LTD

The major issue in considering water frontage isn't cost so much as availability. Demand for direct water frontage exceeds the supply. According to one local real estate professional, many times during the year there are no water properties on the market. When such a property appears on the market, as many as 500 agents may be watching for it, causing competitive bidding and sales within a very short time. It's not uncommon for waterfront property to be on the market for only one week. As a result, waterfront property values have doubled during the past 10 years.

An alternative to direct frontage is shared frontage. It is common for a subdivision or development in close proximity to the water to own a stretch of adjacent or nearby water frontage that is used as a common beach, boat dock and picnic area for resident use. The neighborhood association assesses fees for upkeep and sets rules for use. Shared frontage is becoming increasingly popular as development continues to spread through the Old Mission Peninsula, the Leelanau Peninsula and other land near our many waterways in the Grand Traverse area. Recent prices showed that a typical subdivision lot on Old Mission Peninsula with shared frontage averaged $60,000. An existing three bedroom home in the same subdivision would run $250,000.

Moving off the water and into our towns, the first thing to note is that non-waterfront doesn't mean inferior. Non-waterfront may be 20 acres in the Pere Marquette forest, a former lumber baron's mansion in town or a spacious contemporary with bay views. To use a specific example, a home on top of a hill overlooking Traverse City has a view of the bay, city lights and the panoramic landscape. The public beach is less than a mile away, schools are close, and downtown shopping is within 5 miles.

Properties within the city limits are characteristically at least 50 years old. An average three-bedroom home on a small city lot costs $100,000 to $150,000 either in town or in a subdivision very close to the city limits. In one of the rural townships 5 to 10 miles from downtown, that same house on 3 to 5 acres of land will cost the same amount of money. In the Traverse City area, if the property were even farther away, perhaps near Kingsley or Buckley, the cost would drop.

Former urbanites moving to the Grand Traverse area look for properties with acreage and find the best selection south of Traverse City or in the more rural areas near Kalkaska and the eastern side of Antrim county. For example, East Bay township, just east of the Traverse City city limits and stretching south toward Wexford county, has had a significant growth in residential development because of its affordability and availability.

There are also growing subdivisions on the west side of Traverse City in relative proximity to a new high school that opened in Long Lake township during 1998. Lot prices are running between $25,000 and $37,000, including water and sewer, while houses average $180,000.

Unfortunately, supply again has not kept up with demand. This is especially true of affordable housing. The Grand Traverse area population has increased by approximately 20 percent in the past 10 years. In 1997, the area's commercial and residential property sales exceeded $260 million, including the sale of more than 2,000 homes. Half were on the market for less than two months. This represented a 30 percent increase in sales over the past year. The early months of 1998 indicate growth continuing on a similar rise. New home construction and major renovation is also bustling. In Grand Traverse county alone, close to 300 residential building permits were awarded in 1997.

As a result of this growth, the limits of what we once considered to be Traverse City continue to be stretched and molded to fit our burgeoning needs. Similarly, the land surrounding the smaller communities of Leelanau, Antrim and Kalkaska counties are also expanding. Areas that one time were considered too far away, are now common bedroom communities for the Traverse City area. It's not unusual for people to commute into Traverse City from Kingsley and Fife Lake to the south, Kalkaska to the east, Elk Lake and much of Antrim county to the northeast, and Suttons Bay and much of Leelanau county to the northwest. While each community retains its individual personality, we are meshing together more often as the entire region thrives and grows.

The Leelanau communities of Northport and Leland and the Antrim communities near Torch Lake remain primarily seasonal, but both counties are seeing an increasing number of summer homes converted into year-round residences as retirees make the region their permanent home.

Condominiums, manufactured housing and apartments are somewhat limited. Most apartment complexes are in, or close to, Traverse City. Monthly rentals of unfurnished, one and two bedroom units range from $550 to $675 per month. Townhouses, often managed by the same companies, average $600 to $750 per month. Apartments in older homes are available in most communities, with rent ranging from $375 to $575 per month in the rural areas, and $425 to $650 per month for prime locations. Rental homes are also available in most communities with prices averaging $600 to $850 per month. To investigate rental opportunities, contact the local chambers of commerce for a list of management companies and individuals who rent properties (see our Getting Here and Getting Around chapter for chamber of commerce listings). Also, check the classified ads in the *Traverse City Record-Eagle* and the *Preview Community Weekly*. Although rental opportunities have increased significantly over the past 10 years, availability of rental property is limited. If you plan to rely on rental housing when you relocate, plan ahead.

Condominium prices parallel local housing trends with prices ranging in the $125,000 to $160,000 for an in-town, two-bedroom, two-bath unit, while larger, upscale condos along the waterfront or on heavily wooded peninsula lots may command $350,000. Manufactured housing is available through a number of developments, with a wide variation in prices from a $7,000 older used mobile home to a newer, large $60,000 unit. The local chambers and the Realtors association, as well as newspaper advertising, can help locate these.

If you think you might like to try life up north before purchasing property or signing a

INSIDERS' TIP

The exclusive Bay Harbor community near Petoskey was designed to be environmentally sensitive to the coastal lands it inhabits. The success of careful planning efforts earned it the Michigan Chamber of Commerce Environmental Excellence Award.

Photo: Kevin Poirier

Lake Michigan provides many beautiful vistas in the Traverse Bay Region.

lease, consider renting a local cottage or vacation property. These properties are usually leased by the week during the summer and holidays. These are often properties that are owned by part-time residents living elsewhere or additional holdings by area homeowners. The local chambers of commerce have lists of companies that specialize in vacation property management as well as individuals that rent their own property.

Lake Michigan Shoreline and Cadillac

Benzie County

The most coveted properties in Benzie County are found in the old logging town of Frankfort, and along the shores of beautiful Crystal Lake. Lake frontage beside the deep, clean Crystal Lake costs about $2,500 per foot. While frontage along Platte Lake, farther north, runs $2,000, and the smaller Long Lake from $1,500 to $1,700. Water frontage availability for these lakes is fair.

Just a 30-minute drive from Traverse City, the rolling hills of Benzie County are appealing, and the demand for vacant acreage is skyrocketing. However, little is available. When land here does hit the market, it sells for about $2,000 per acre.

The friendly Lake Michigan coastal community of Frankfort is home to many graceful Victorian homes. The market price for these beauties ranges from $300,000 to $400,000.

Another prime housing area in the county is at the very exclusive Crystal Downs golf course. The course is ranked as one of the best in the United States. The 100 homes surrounding the course are so popular that you almost have to be an Insider, or know one, to land one of these $400,000-plus treasures. Most sell before they hit the open market. Many less pricey housing options are available, and overall, the average existing home in Benzie County sells for $75,000. Whenever you add water frontage, the formula changes. The average price for a home in Benzie County with water frontage is $160,000. Availability of apartments, condos and rentals is quite slim, so count on purchasing a home if you intend to settle in this lovely corner of Northwest Michigan.

Manistee

Manistee County is one of the north's undiscovered gems, but it's destined not to remain that way for long. The wide, sandy beaches along the Lake Michigan coast, scenic rivers and fine inland lakes provide a wonderful environment for vacation and year-round living. Beautiful Lake Michigan and inland lake frontage is still available for a reasonable $1,000 to $3,000 per foot. Acreage is in high demand, especially if it is adjacent to the Manistee National Forest. It lists for about $1,000 per acre and up. The pride and joy of this community lies in its Victorian heritage, and many of Manistee's vintage homes have been lovingly restored, and occasionally hit the open market. Called "Painted Ladies," the homes are scattered in what is considered the most desirable location in town: the friendly family neighborhoods west of Maple Street. You can grab a great deal here if your timing is right. Victorian fixer-uppers can be purchased for as little as $75,000, the average existing home sale price. However, skillfully restored beauties sell for as much as $400,000. If you're more the condo type, check out Harbor Village, a newer 55-acre condo and home development along the Lake Michigan shoreline. The complex's small studio units sell for about $76,000, while the largest units are available for $400,000. Some include a boat slip. Several new family-oriented subdivisions are under construction where homes will range from $150,000 to $250,000. If apartment dwelling is your style, plan to look elsewhere. Apartments are limited and virtually impossible to land in the Manistee area.

Mason County

If lake living is your dream, you'll be pleased with the availability of water frontage properties in Mason County. The most desirable properties lie along the 4,990 acre Hamlin Lake. The lake offers great recreational opportunities including swimming, boating, fishing and snowmobiling. Frontage here is reasonably priced at about $1,000 per foot. Along the county's Lake Michigan shoreline, you can snatch up frontage for under $2,000 per foot. There's a good selection of reasonably priced townhouses and condos in the area too. Condos at the beautiful Crosswinds complex begin at $115,000. Another popular complex, the Starboard Tack, offers water frontage, car and boat parking, with unit prices ranging from $249,000 to $299,000. Apartment availability in the winter is good in the area, however, when summer residents enter the market, availability tightens.

New construction, like the rest of the real estate industry is booming in the Ludington area. The first golf course housing commu-

nity, Apple Wood Greens, is under development at Lakeside Links. One-acre lots, and those slightly smaller, are available for between $24,000 and $50,000 each. A $6 million harbor-front project is also under development in the region. The Waterside Plaza will offer upscale condo living at a range of $200,000 to $300,000 per unit. While buyers find the Mason County market offers good luxury and recreational lifestyle choices, families also find a selection of comfortable, affordable homes. In 1997, the average listing price for a single family residence in Mason County was a little more than $104,000.

Wexford and Missaukee Counties

Wexford County is blessed with prime hunting land, two large inland lakes and a myriad of lovely, smaller lakes. It's no surprise the demand for acreage has soared in this area in recent years with prices more than quadrupling in two years. Buyers will be hard-pressed to find land available and if they do, it will run more than $1,000 per acre. This is a family-oriented area where people tend to stay away from apartment and condo life, so rental units are very limited. The average home sale price, excluding water frontage, is $75,000. Surprisingly, small ranch homes have seen good appreciation rates in the past two years, due to demand at this level of the market. At the same time, the market for homes in the $200,000-and-up range has been fairly stagnant, and good values await the smart buyer.

If you're investing in a home with resale on your mind, Cadillac West is the best place to look. Here, executive homes range from $100,000 to $200,000, and move quickly when you need to sell. You may also want to consider investing in a home at Cadillac's premier address: Holly Road. Here, lakefront city homes sell for up to $300,000. Another elite neighborhood, Lakewood on the Green, is a newer golf course community with family homes ranging from $200,000 to $300,000. In Missaukee County, vacation property is a big mover. Here too, hunting land is in demand and sells for about $1,000 per acre. Cottages, cabins and lake frontage are available, although somewhat limited. Water frontage along beautiful Lake Missaukee sells for about

Photo: Kevin Poirier

Don't miss cherry blossom time in Northwest Michigan.

$1,000 per foot. Housing is generally less costly in the more rural Missaukee County than in Wexford County, and the county has seen an influx of working families from their neighbor to the west. As a result, new home construction has boomed in the past two years. Apartment units are extremely limited in Missaukee County.

Little Traverse

Charlevoix County

Charlevoix offers a perfect boating environment, so its no surprise water properties are in high demand throughout the county. Both the year-round residential and vacation markets are strong, and you'll find no shortage of high-priced luxury homes. Lakefront lots along Lake Michigan and beautiful Lake Charlevoix sell for about $2,000 per foot. The most prestigious addresses in the county are found along Belvedere Avenue. This is one of the more exclusive neighborhoods in the north,

and homes here go for $350,000 up to $2 million. However, the average home sale price in the county is a comfortable $130,000. Golf community housing available at Pine Lake Club and Charlevoix Country Club is becoming increasingly popular. In 1997 the influx of urbanites was a key factor leading to property value increases of 20 percent. Unlike some areas in the region, Charlevoix has a nice selection of condos in beautiful natural settings along lakes Charlevoix and Michigan and Round Lake. Units run from $150,000 to $600,000. But since there are only two apartment complexes in the area, those planning a move to the county should have another housing option in mind.

Emmet County

Emmet County's premier lakes feature some of the hottest properties in the north. Beautiful Lake Charlevoix, Burt and Mullet lakes offer great boating and, in addition, serve as waterways to the Great Lakes. Property values here have steadily increased in past years, and today, vacant waterfront lots sell for between $1,000 and $2,500 per foot, depending on the lake. Acreage is extremely limited and considered too valuable to be sold as hunting land. Immediately snatched up when it does come on the market, open land sells for between $2,500 and $3,500 per acre. The jewel of Emmet County's real estate scene, and indeed, the jewel of the entire northern market, is Bay Harbor, Petoskey's $100-million-plus development on 1,200 acres along Lake Michigan. Two miles south of Petoskey off U.S. Highway 31, the resort community features a golf course with the longest coastline of any course in America; yachting facilities; luxury custom homes, townhouses and condominiums; equestrian facilities; and an international hotel. The exclusive 5-mile-long development is unequaled anywhere in the world and lots here run from $99,000 to $1.4 million.

Emmet County is historically an elite resort area and features a variety of upscale housing opportunities. Housing near its world-class golf and ski communities is in high demand. This includes the Boyne resorts, Crooked Tree, and a newer development, Chestnut Valley golf course, which is expected to be popular. Condos are in high demand throughout the area, but availability is limited. There are several apartment complexes that appeal to the empty-nesters including Tannery Creek, Spring Lake and Pine Bluff. Vacationers will find a fair selection of temporary rentals, including private residences and condos. The most coveted addresses in Emmet County are Country Club Hills, Vantage View II in Petoskey and Walden Woods and Hardwoods of Harbor in Harbor Springs. Homes in these family neighborhoods run from $150,000 to $225,000. New construction is most active in Bear Creek and Resort Townships, where homes range from $150,000 to $280,000. Buyers should note that homes in both the lower and upper prices ranges are in short supply, and should be prepared to pay top dollar.

Mackinac Straits

The communities of St. Ignace and Mackinaw City are faced with the same waterfront vs. non-waterfront property value swings that affect the entire region. The prime waterfront properties are those edging Lake Michigan and Lake Huron, with priceless views of the Mackinaw Bridge commanding top dollar.

A recent Mackinaw City area property, advertised as one of the last large parcels on Lake Michigan, offered 14 acres on 400 feet of shoreline with panoramic views for close to $1 million. Another property near St. Ignace boasted a two-bedroom home on 482 acres with frontage on two small lakes for $750,000.

Although property values are impacted by location and frontage, costs don't reach the extreme highs experienced in some of the very upscale Little Traverse and Grand Traverse developments. If you're willing to forgo a home on a Great Lake shoreline, you can find a number of reasonably priced alternatives. Properties along the St. Ignace area's small inland lakes can range from $79,000 for a two-bedroom, one bath cottage, to $115,000 for a three-bedroom, one bath home to $195,000 for a five-bedroom, two-bath home with garage, deck and boat dock. Higher-priced properties would include a five-bedroom, cedar log home with a stone fireplace, hot tub, gazebo and extras on 13 acres of land, which would sell for $275,000. Near Mackinaw City, a small waterfront lot near Wilderness State Park was priced at $25,000, while starter homes were priced near $60,000.

Mackinac Island doesn't really fit into these same categories since the State of Michigan owns at least 80 percent of the land. Those gorgeous old Victorian homes that you see rising from the bluffs are traditionally passed through the generations to family members. Periodically, some of the older homes in the Annex area and near town range from $300,000 to $800,000. Availability is extremely limited. Condominium complexes have been increasing on the island, offering an attractive housing option. The largest complex in the Stonecliffe area is in the Island interior with units running $200,000 to $300,000.

There are a limited number of home sites available each year for construction with prices varying widely, but averaging near $100,000. Any new construction must follow strict architectural guidelines and must be approved in advance. Also, remember that construction on an island requires that all materials must be shipped, which escalates building costs.

Real Estate Resources

Grand Traverse Area

Traverse Area Association of Realtors
852 S. Garfield Ave., Traverse City
• (616) 947-2050

The Traverse Area Association of Realtors can provide referrals and information about its more than 90 member agencies in Grand Traverse, Leelanau, Benzie, Antrim and Kalkaska. It can also assist with general real estate information, legal issues, relocation information and referrals to overall support services.

Home Builders Association of the Grand Traverse Area
3040 Sunset Ln., Traverse City
• (616) 946-2305

The Home Builders Association can provide information about construction issues and requirements, and can provide referrals to its members. Membership includes construction firms, suppliers, financial institutions and attorneys specializing in real estate and construction.

Traverse City Area Chamber of Commerce
202 E. Grandview Pkwy., Traverse City
• (616) 947-5075

The Traverse City Area Chamber of Commerce provides relocation information and assistance, and maintains referral listings of real estate firms and individual Realtors, appraisers, developers, commercial and industrial real estate professionals, apartment buildings and condominiums, property management companies, subsidized housing and senior citizen housing.

Lake Michigan Shoreline and Cadillac

Benzie County Board of Realtors
P.O. Box 35, Beulah, MI 49617
• (616) 352-9870

The Benzie County Board of Realtors provides services for agencies in Benzie, north Manistee, and south Leelanau counties. Multiple Listing books are available.

Sleeping Bear Rentals
57 N. Michigan Ave., Beulah
• (616) 882-9681

Sleeping Bear Rentals offers vacation rentals within the Sleeping Bear National Lakeshore Park. Accommodations are along Crystal and Platte Lakes, the Betsie River and near Crystal Mountain Resort in Thompsonville.

Mason, Oceana, Manistee Board of Realtors
239 N. Jebavy Dr., Manistee
• (616) 845-1896

The Mason, Oceana, Manistee Board of Realtors has 350 members representing 36 agencies, plus affiliate trade members. Multiple Listing books are available.

Key Property Management
932 E. Ludington Ave., Ludington
• (616) 845-7368

Key Property Management handles vacation rentals in the Ludington area. Property listings are available at Carriage House Better Homes & Gardens real estate office, 932 E. Ludington Avenue in Ludington, (616) 845-5141.

Paul Bunyan Board of Realtors
2604 Sunnyside Dr., Ste. 7, Cadillac
• (616) 775-2660

The Paul Bunyan Board of Realtors provides services for Realtors primarily in Wexford, Missaukee and Roscommon counties. There are 250 Realtor members, plus 27 trade affiliates. Member agents have access to listings within nine other northern Michigan Board of Realtor coverage areas. Multiple Listing books are available.

Little Traverse

Antrim, Charlevoix and Kalkaska Board of Realtors
106 S. Lake St., Boyne City
• (616) 582-6394

This board provides its members with Mul-

Photo: Kevin Poirier

One of Traverse City's most picturesque streets, Sixth Street in the Central Neighborhood has a wide variety of charming turn-of-the-century homes.

tiple Listing Service and computer networking to national listing services.

Emmet Association Board of Realtors
616 Petoskey St., Ste. 310, Petoskey
• (616) 347-0700

The Emmet Association of Realtors consists of 170 Realtors representing 43 agencies. Multiple Listing books are available.

Holiday Accommodations Inc.
2310 Mich. Hwy. 119, Petoskey
• (616) 348-2765

Holiday Accommodations offers rentals for homes and cottages near Boyne Highlands, Lake Michigan, area inland lakes, Birchwood Farms Golf & Country Club and several area condo resorts.

Resort Property Management Co.
8430 Mich. Hwy. 119, Ste. 1, Harbor Springs • (616) 348-2500

Resort Property Management Co. handles homes and chalets near the world-class Boyne Highlands and Nub's Nob ski and golf resorts,

cottages on Round Lake, Lake Michigan, Douglas and Burt lakes.

Graham Management
163 E. Main St., Harbor Springs
• (616) 526-6001

Graham Management handles short-term rentals year round in Harbor Springs. They offer Harbor Springs area homes, cottages and condominium rentals by the week, month or season.

Accommodations North
111 S. Lake St., Boyne City
• (616) 582-3200

Accommodations North handles reservations for the Antrium Inn, The Landings Condominiums and specializes in Walloon Lake and Lake Charlevoix home and cottage rentals.

Mackinac Straits

Since the Straits area is small and quite rural, there are only a few real estate agencies, rather than a full Board of Realtors, serving the three communities. All are listed below.

Mackinac Island Realty
Market St., Mackinac Island
• **(906) 847-6483**

Mackinac Island Realty specializes in the sales of island properties including Victorian cottages, homes, condominiums, businesses and building lots. The office can also assist with weekly rentals on the island. Mackinac Island Realty gives you a peek at available properties with a large photo board displayed at the office's central Market Street storefront.

Coldwell Banker Northern Lakes
115 N. Huron Ave., Mackinaw City
• **(616) 436-4151**

This is the local office for the large Coldwell Banker real estate family. It is also the only resident real estate office serving Mackinaw City and is affiliated with the main Coldwell Banker Northern Lakes offices in Cheboygan. The firm specializes in waterfront property on Lake Huron and the area's inland lakes.

Mackinac Real Estate
U.S. Hwy. 2, Naubinway • (906) 477-6221

Mackinac Real Estate is based west of St. Ignace in Naubinway. It handles waterfront, vacation, residential and commercial properties as well as vacant acreage and vacation rentals for St. Ignace and the surrounding area.

Real Estate One
626 N. State St., St. Ignace
• **(906) 643-9800**

Real Estate One serves the eastern upper peninsula from its base in St. Ignace. The company handles residential and commercial real estate.

State Wide Real Estate
436 N. State St., St. Ignace
• **(906) 643-8525**

State Wide Real Estate has been St. Ignace's real estate resource for more than 40 years. The company primarily serves the Straits area and Mackinac county with properties listed throughout the eastern upper peninsula. The company can assist in all real estate needs, including vacation rentals.

Rental Management Firms

You'll find rental management brokers and firms throughout Northwest Michigan, who can arrange just the vacation accommodations you have in mind, whether it's a cozy lakeside cottage or luxury condo. Please refer to our Real Estate Resources listings in this chapter for assistance. Also, since many rentals are handled by owners or through small local firms, we suggest you also contact local chambers of commerce and visitors centers for help and referrals. See our Getting Here and Getting Around chapter for addresses and phone numbers of these organizations. If you prefer to make your own arrangements, take an aggressive approach, and check classified ads in local papers.

Public, private, vocational or collegiate, our schools specifically meet the educational needs and personalities of our hometowns.

Child Care
and Education

Life is centered around home and family in Northwest Michigan. With that commitment comes the equally high value that we place on education. Whether schooling our youth or the even greater number of lifelong learners, education is No. 1.

Our schools are as unique as our communities — as they should be. Public, private, vocational or collegiate, our schools specifically meet the educational needs and personalities of our hometowns. In the Traverse City area, that means operating a very large system with broad offerings and highly specialized services, while on Mackinac Island teachers focus on the challenge of conducting classes in a small, remote locale. We are fortunate that, large or small, there are no bad educational choices.

Child-care options in Northwest Michigan vary with each community. Unfortunately, the region lags behind its urban counterparts in offering comprehensive services. Finding the care that is right for you usually requires a search. The best place to start is with the Northwest Michigan 4 C council, which can assist with referrals to day-care homes, child-care centers, community programs and other resources. The local council is based in Traverse City but serves a 12-county region, which coincides with our Insiders boundaries. (See the subsequent listing under Referral Services.)

You'll find that group day-care homes are the primary resources in many areas, especially in the more rural communities. Homes usually offer care for one to six children, although larger homes with more than one provider can care for more children. Care may be full-time, part-time or drop-in based on each caregiver's rules, which vary greatly between communities and homes. Check in with the 4 C for local referrals. Also, check the classified ads or place your own ad in the local newspaper, check in with local schools, chambers of commerce or newcomers groups, and chat with neighbors, coworkers and local residents for ideas. Remember to proceed with caution. While most caregivers are very professional, there is no mandatory licensing of day-care homes in Michigan.

Large child-care centers are also options. Most are in or near Traverse City. As a rule of thumb, these larger centers are for children between 2½ and 6 who will be attending full-time. Several of these centers offer summer care for school-age children and reduced schedules for kindergarten students. Latchkey programs are offered in many elementary schools throughout the region.

Child Care
Newcomers Clubs

Most communities host newcomers clubs or similar organizations that welcome you to the community. If you're relocating, call your town's chamber of commerce for the most current local contact or watch for notices and ads in area newspapers. You will find information on local chambers of commerce in our Getting Here, Getting Around chapter. Many of these groups sponsor play groups, babysitting pools and related activities for parents and children to mingle with others in a fun, supportive atmosphere.

We have listed several child-care resources below including the referral services, large child-care centers and resort and hotel services.

Referral Services

Northwest Michigan 4 C Child Care Council
720 S. Elmwood St., Ste. 4, Traverse City
• **(616) 941-7767, (800) 968-4228**

Known simply as the 4Cs, this resource council has been serving children, families, businesses and early childhood professionals in Northwest Michigan since 1979. The 4Cs is a tremendous resource with a gold mine of information about all aspects of child care, providers, public issues and community programs. It is one of 15 regional 4Cs serving the state of Michigan. The council maintains a referral database with more than 1,200 state-approved child-care providers in its 12-county service area. All child-care providers that are referred to parents have already met the licensing and registration requirements of the State of Michigan and been approved by Michigan Child Care Licensing. Besides referrals, the 4Cs coordinates with other community agencies to address issues affecting children and families, and provides information and consultation on child-care issues to parents, providers and employers. A toy-lending library and mentoring program is available to parents and child-care providers. Resource libraries are available for public perusing during office hours Monday through Friday, 8:30 AM to 5:30 PM.

www.insiders.com

See this and many other **Insiders' Guide®** destinations online — in their entirety.

Visit us today!

Childcare Seekers Directory
917 Baldwin St., Traverse City
• **(616) 941-4933**

Childcare Seekers Directory is a compilation of Northwest Michigan child-care providers, day-care centers, preschools and educational programs and resources appropriate for toddlers and preschoolers. Published by a former day-care provider, it is a geographical listing of caregivers with their hours, state license numbers, ages accepted and related information. The directory is distributed free throughout Northwest Michigan, in particular at local libraries, bookstores, human services agencies and grocery stores.

Child-Care Centers

Grand Traverse

Alphabet Soup Pre-School & Child Care Center
222 E. 14th St., Traverse City
• **(616) 941-1330**

Alphabet Soup provides child care and preschool care to children older than 2½ years. The facility features a strong computer program as well as a nice playground and cheerful rooms. During the summer, Alphabet Soup runs computer camps for elementary-age children. The center is open Monday through Friday from 7 AM to 6 PM.

Bright Beginnings Child Care Center
121 S. Garfield Ave., Traverse City
• **(616) 941-7853**

Bright Beginnings places a Christian emphasis on its programs for children between the ages of 2½ to 10 years. Its goal is to provide a loving, learning and nurturing environment. Bright Beginnings uses the nearby Grand Traverse County Civic Center for its swimming pool, playground and other recreation facilities. Bright Beginnings is open Monday through Friday, 6:30 AM to 6 PM.

Central Day Care Center
222 Cass St., Traverse City
• **(616) 947-6131**

Central Day Care has been taking care of Traverse City's youngsters for 30 years. In the large Central Methodist Church building, it is steps away from downtown, the Traverse City library, Clinch Park Zoo and several public parks. It's not surprising to see the Central Day Care kids on the go, either holding a rope or holding hands, as they window-shop or head to play on their frequent excursions in the neighborhoods. The center offers full-time daily care for preschoolers and alternate kindergarten day care, complementing many of the local schools' alternate-day kindergarten classes. Central Day Care accepts children 2½ to 6 years. The center is open Mondays through Fridays between 6:30 AM and 6 PM.

Traverse Learning Center
601 E. Eighth St., Traverse City
• **(616) 946-4141**

The Traverse Learning Center specializes in quality care for the preschool years, ages 2½ to 6 years old. Before- and after-school programs are also available. The center is open weekdays from 6 AM to 6 PM.

Before- and After-School Care

The need for child care doesn't end when youngsters enter school. There are several options available to parents requiring before-and after-school care. As with younger children, day-care homes often offer the most flexibility and availability, especially in the rural areas. The referral resources noted above can assist in identifying these providers.

Several school districts and large child-care centers offer latchkey programs. Please refer back to the individual listings for schools and child-care centers for more information. Also, ask for specific referrals from your child's school. Local school offices have the most up-to-date information about their district's programs as well as informal listings of resources near the school. Some schools will allow you to place an ad for care in their newsletter.

Grand Traverse Bay YMCA
3000 Racquet Club Dr., Traverse City
• **(616) 947-5880**

The local Y oversees before- and after-school child-care programs in more than 20 Traverse City area public and private elementary schools. It also provides all-day care at the YMCA building during school vacation days, teacher in-service days, snow days and other times when schools are closed during the educational year. During the summer, elementary-age children can take part in its summer recreational camp by the week or for the entire summer. Slots can fill quickly for the Y latchkey programs, so it's always best to sign up early.

Resort and Hotel Programs

Babysitting services are available through many hotels, and some of the large resorts in the region offer full child-care programs to their guests. If you need child care while visiting, check with the concierge or front desk for assistance. Many keep lists of local sitters who will come to your hotel. If care services are mandatory to your stay, check with your hotel when making reservations.

The large resorts often offer full children's programs during peak periods like summer, Christmas and spring-break weeks as well as weekend activities through much of the year. All of the ski resorts have some type of child-care program near the slopes as well as various levels of supervised instruction for kids. A quick list of the resorts offering children's programs follows. For full information about each of the resorts, please refer to the Hotels, Motels and Resorts chapter.

INSIDERS' TIP

Traverse City's first public school was on the schooner *Madeline*. Classes were conducted below deck on this Great Lakes vessel during a late 1800s winter while the ship took refuge in Bowers Harbor until spring. A replica of the *Madeline*, built by local volunteers and sailing enthusiasts, is docked at Clinch Park during warm weather months.

Grand Traverse

• Grand Traverse Resort, 100 Grand Traverse Village Boulevard, Acme, (616) 938-2100, (800) 748-0303
• Shanty Creek, One Shanty Creek Road, Bellaire, (616) 533-8621, (800) 678-4111
• Homestead Resort, Wood Ridge Road, Glen Arbor, (616) 334-5000
• Sugar Loaf Resort, 4500 Sugar Loaf Mountain Road, Cedar, (616) 228-5461, (800) 952-6390
• Treetops Sylvan Resort, 3962 Wilkinson Road, Gaylord, (517) 732-6711, (800) 444-6711

Lake Michigan Shoreline and Cadillac

• Crystal Mountain Resort, 12500 Crystal Mountain Drive, Thompsonville, (616) 378-2000, (800) 968-7686

Little Traverse

• Boyne Mountain, Boyne Mountain Road, (U.S. Highway 31 at Boyne Falls), Boyne Falls, (616) 549-6000, (800) GO BOYNE
• Boyne Highlands, 600 Boyne Highlands Road, Harbor Springs, (616) 526-3000, (800) GO BOYNE

Mackinac Straits

• Grand Hotel, Cadotte Avenue, Mackinac Island, (906) 847-3331, (800) 33-GRAND
• Mission Point Resort, One Lakeshore Drive, Mackinac Island, (906) 847-3312, (800) 833-7711

Education

Our education choices in Northwest Michigan are numerous. Many times, they are also confusing and a tad overwhelming. That's where this chapter can help. We have compiled a snapshot of the many school districts in Northwest Michigan along with a few profiles to help illustrate the many faces of local education.

There are close to 50 public school districts serving Northwest Michigan as well as almost 40 private schools, six intermediate school districts and 12 colleges. Combined, there are more than 65,000 students enrolled in Northwest Michigan schools. More than 20 percent are in Traverse City, alone, while close to half are in the Grand Traverse region. Space limits the number of schools that we can list, so a few examples for each of our geographic areas have been noted along with a full listing of schools within the region with addresses and telephone numbers.

The listings are in three categories — Public, Private and Higher Education. Please remember that the private designation includes all nonpublic schools, both parochial and independent.

Public schools have been organized under the umbrellas of the intermediate school districts. Often referred to as ISDs, the intermediate districts are public and serve as central resources for collaborative programming, educational technology, media services, professional development and general education. They also provide all special education within their district boundaries, and often spearhead vocational training as well. Since all of our public and private schools, despite size, are served by a broader reaching ISD, we will use them as our section leaders.

The higher education listings offer a broad-brush look at the colleges and universities that serve the region.

Public Schools

Grand Traverse

Traverse Bay Area Intermediate School District
1101 Red Dr., Traverse City
• **(616) 922-6200 Administration**
880 Parsons Rd., Traverse City
• **(616) 922-6273 Career Tech Center**

The Traverse Bay Area Intermediate School District is among the largest in the state. Covering a geographic territory of 2,138 square miles, it serves almost 25,000 students at 16 school districts within five counties — Antrim, Benzie, Grand Traverse, Leelanau and Kalkaska. Participating districts range in size from more than 11,200 at the Traverse City Area Public Schools to just 190 at the tiny Alba system. The ISD is a key component in providing area teachers and students with access to a wide variety of programs and resources in the most cost-effective way. It also serves as a critical link between the various districts and educators for communication, professional development, educational resources and specialty programs as well as special education and vocational training.

Special education is provided for 1,300 children of all ages with all ranges of physical and mental handicaps. General education programs oversee gifted and talented, alternative and adult education and various enrichment programs that could enrich a total school program. Vocational programs offered at the TBA Career Tech Center train students for the bulk of U.S. jobs that require training below the baccalaureate level. One thousand daytime and 500 evening students attend 2½-hour classes at the Career Tech Center to study applied economics, business-office technology, computer-aided drafting and design, construction trades, electronics and many more. TBA oversees the Bay Area Adventure School, offering challenge ropes courses, and the REMCII Materials and Technical Center, which acts as a media clearinghouse and resource for the 14 counties in Northwest Michigan. TBA is also leading the Project Interconnect initiative, which will electronically link area high schools via an interactive television network for two-way audio, video and data communications.

Traverse City Area Public Schools
412 Webster St., Traverse City
• (616) 933-1700

In Northwest Michigan, where it's not unusual for district-wide enrollments to run into the hundreds, the Traverse City Area Public Schools is enormous! Eighteen elementary schools, two junior high schools and two high schools serve approximately 11,200 students residing in a 285-square-mile district. The district stretches across Grand Traverse county from Acme to Elmwood Township, south to Interlochen and north to the tip of the Old Mission peninsula.

Curriculum development is ongoing among the 1,300 certified teachers on staff resulting in programs like interdisciplinary core studies, service learning, classrooms of the future, advanced placement, dual enrollment, advanced music and partners in education. A magnet school is available for academically gifted upper-elementary students. Strong athletic and academic extracurricular activities open up student involvement in model United Nations, the debate team and numerous musical ensembles. In athletics, Traverse City schools are often leaders at the state and regional level for varsity and intramural sports.

Gaylord Community Schools
615 S. Elm St., Gaylord • (517) 732-6402

Gaylord Community Schools fall under the jurisdiction of the Cheboygan-Otsego-Presque Isle Intermediate School District, which primarily oversees districts not covered in this Insiders' Guide. Therefore, since Gaylord Community Schools are the only district within our Insiders' boundaries from the Cheboygan-Otsego-Presque Isle ISD, we focus specifically on the Gaylord system. There are approximately 3,500 students enrolled in the Gaylord Community Schools with attendance distributed between one high school for 9th through 12th grades, one middle school for 7th and 8th grades, one intermediate school for 4th through 6th grades, three elementary schools for kindergarten through 3rd grades, and one multi-age primary school. The Peak Academy is available for alternative education. The Gaylord Community Schools also offers a number of community education programs through the year.

Other Public Schools within the Traverse Bay Area Intermediate District

•Alba Public Schools, 5935 Elm Street, Alba, (616) 584-2000
•Bellaire Public Schools, 204 W. Forest Home Avenue, Bellaire, (616) 533-8141
•Benzie County Central Schools, 9222 Homestead Road, Benzonia, (616) 882-9653
•Buckley Community School District, 305 S. First Street, Buckley, (616) 269-3325
•Crawford School — Excelsior District #1, 5521 Mich. 72 N.E., Kalkaska, (616) 258-2934

• Elk Rapids Public Schools, 707 E. Third Street, Elk Rapids, (616) 264-8692

• Forest Area Community Schools, 7741 Shippy Road S.W., Fife Lake, (616) 369-4191

• Frankfort Elberta Area Schools, 613 Leelanau Avenue, Frankfort, (616) 352-4641

• Glen Lake Community Schools, 3375 W. Burdickville Road, Maple City, (616) 334-3061

• Kalkaska Public Schools, 315 S. Coral Street, Kalkaska, (616) 258-9109

• Kingsley Area Schools, Box 580, Kingsley, MI 49649, (616) 263-5262

• Leland Public Schools, 200 N. Grand Avenue, Leland, (616) 256-9857

• Mancelona Public Schools, 112 St. John Street, Mancelona, (616) 587-9764

• Northport Public Schools, 104 Wing Street, Northport, (616) 386-5153

• Suttons Bay Public Schools, 310 Elm Street, Suttons Bay, (616) 271-3846

Lake Michigan Shoreline and Cadillac

Manistee Intermediate School District
772 E. Parkdale Ave., Manistee
• (616) 723-6205

Coverage area for the Manistee Intermediate School District generally follows Manistee county lines. It serves four school districts and two public charter schools, which are all interlinked via computer for communications, instructional support, informational technology and general access to resources in this rural area. The district oversees special education services as well as specialized general education programs and professional development for all schools within its boundaries. Vocational programming is not emphasized due to availability of this type of technical training through nearby West Shore Community College located in Scottville.

Manistee Intermediate School District is noted for its consortium with the Wexford-Missuakee Intermediate School District in operating the Chittenden Education Center. Chittenden is a designated Regional Math/Science Access Center within the Manistee National Forest in former U.S. Forest Service facilities. Math, science and technology education is enhanced through on-site ecological studies. Meeting facilities combined with the beautiful natural setting make this an ideal destination for class field trips, community education and professional development. A challenge ropes course is also available.

Manistee Area Public Schools
550 Maple St., Manistee • (616) 723-3521

The Manistee Area Public Schools strive to provide all students with an appropriate educational environment and curricular program to achieve to the best of their ability. District enrollment totals 1,850 students attending four elementary schools, one middle school and one high school. Manistee High School is a Class B school with full academic and extracurricular programs for 9th through 12th grades. Manistee Middle School teaches 7th- and 8th-grade students. It is a secondary school extension of the unified approach followed at the elementary level. Under a unified system, all students within the district are grouped with just one other grade level within their school as opposed to the traditional neighborhood-based schools with multiple grades. All kindergartners attend Washington Elementary Center while 1st and 2nd grades attend Thomas Jefferson Elementary School, 3rd and 4th grades attend James Madison Elementary, and 5th and 6th grades attend John F. Kennedy Elementary. Art, music, Spanish and physical education teachers travel among the buildings.

Other Public Schools Within the Manistee Intermediate District:

• Bear Lake School District, 7748 Cody Street, Bear Lake, (616) 864-3133

• CASMAM Alternative Academy (Charter School), 225 Ninth Street, Manistee, (616) 723-4981

• Kaleva Norman Dickson School District, 4400 N. High Bridge Road, Brethren, (616) 477-5353

• Lake Bluff Academy (Charter School), 3031 Domres Road, Manistee, (616) 723-9158

• Onekama Consolidated School District, 5016 Main Street, Onekama, (616) 889-4251

Photo: Grand Traverse Resort

Every parent wants a safe and pleasant environment for their children.

Mason-Lake Intermediate School District
2130 W. U.S. Hwy. 10, Ludington
• **(616) 757-3716**

The Mason-Lake Intermediate School District covers the most southwestern edges of the Northwestern Michigan region that we've defined for this guide. It serves the public and private schools in Ludington, Scottville and rural communities to the south, and administers special education and general education programs to their rural communities.

Mason County Central Schools
300 W. Broadway St., Scottville
• **(616) 757-3713**

This is one of three public school systems within the Northwest Michigan Insiders' region as well as the Mason-Lake Intermediate School District. Three elementary schools, one middle school for 5th through

8th grades and one high school for 9th through 12th grades serve the youth of Scottville and Ludington. The high school curriculum is taught within a block scheduling system, which allows longer class times and more intense teaching. A number of vocational education classes are taught within the high school as well as in collaboration with Westshore Community College. The Mason district is known for its excellent enrichment and adult education programming.

Other Schools Within the Mason-Lake Intermediate District:

• Baldwin Community Schools, 525 W. Fourth Street, Baldwin, (616) 745-4791

• Ludington Area School District, 809 Tinkham Avenue, Ludington, (616) 845-7303

• Mason County Eastern Schools, 18 S. Main Street, Custer, (616) 757-3733

Wexford-Missaukee Intermediate School District

9905 E. 13th St., Cadillac
• (616) 775-5651 Administration
9901 E. 13th St., Cadillac
• (616) 876-2200 Career Center

The Wexford-Missaukee Intermediate School District serves seven kindergarten through 12th-grade districts and one kindergarten through 8th grade district. Special education addresses a full spectrum of services for handicapped students. General education covers programming for alternative education, substance abuse, school-age parents, the gifted and talented, technology and media services. The Wexford-Missaukee Career Technical Center is adjacent to the ISD administrative offices and provides vocational training for 650 students from the region. Programs focus on occupational areas like hospitality, building trades, clerical, healthcare technology, machine trades, cosmetology and food service.

Cadillac Area Public Schools

421 S. Mitchell St., Cadillac
• (616) 779-9300

Almost 4,000 students attend the Cadillac Area Public Schools. Known for offering a wide array of community and curricular activities, it provides a small-town atmosphere with the choices of a bigger city. This district is one of the larger ones in Northwest Michigan, spanning 284 square miles and overseeing eight schools.

The Cadillac public schools' mission statement emphasizes its belief that education is a continuous process in which all students can learn through shared responsibility of student, staff, parents and community. This has been implemented through academic programming that prepares students for further education and work as well as a future of lifelong learning. Five elementary schools teach students from kindergarten through 5th grade while two middle schools are designated for 6th and 7th grades or 8th and 9th grades while the Cadillac High School has 10th through 12th grades. A community auditorium links the high school and older middle school.

The school district hosts a number of community education and recreation programs, overseeing a teen center, senior citizens center, a public beach, recreational classes and a weekly summer camp, Camp Torenta.

Other Schools Within the Wexford-Missaukee Intermediate District:

• Lake City Area Schools, Russell Street, Lake City, (616) 839-4333
• Manton Consolidated Schools, 105 Fifth Street, Manton, (616) 824-6411
• Marion Public School, 510 W. Main Street, Marion, (616) 743-2486
• McBain Public School, 107 E. Maple Street, McBain, (616) 825-2165
• Mesick School, 210 Mesick Avenue, Mesick, (616) 885-1200
• Pine River Area Schools, 6375 Pine River School Road, Leroy, (616) 829-3141

Little Traverse

Char-Em Intermediate School District

08568 Mercer Blvd., Charlevoix
• (616) 547-9947 Administration

As with the other intermediate school districts in Northwest Michigan, the Char-Em ISD is devoted to augmenting education in its district schools through supplemental programming and resources as well as strong special education services for a full range of student impairments and special needs. The Char-Em ISD serves public, private and charter schools within Charlevoix and Emmet counties.

Public Schools of Petoskey

1130 Howard St., Petoskey
• (616) 348-0150

According to its slogan, the Public Schools of Petoskey is a special place for everyone. A broad range of academic and extracurricular programming assures that educational needs are met at all levels of ability and interest. Besides the college preparatory curriculum, technical career training and occupational classes are offered at a vocational center in the high school. Numerous extracurricular sports and enrichment programs allow many opportunities for student participation. Close to 3,000 youth are enrolled in the Petoskey system with classes conducted at four elementary schools, one middle school for 6th through 8th grades and one high school for 9th through 12th grades. The district covers 180 square miles encompassing Petoskey and the rural townships surrounding the city.

Charlevoix Public Schools
208 Clinton St., Charlevoix
• **(616) 547-3200**
The Charlevoix Public Schools offers a wide variety of curricular choices for students as well as the community. A strong emphasis on academics as well as athletic and extracurricular opportunities is evidenced by the district's consistently high ratings in statewide proficiency testing. Computer technology is incorporated across the curriculum from kindergarten through 12th grade. The elementary school uses a unique "star" program where various community members are brought into the classroom to help teach reading. The Charlevoix Public Schools include one elementary school for kindergarten through 5th grades, one middle school for 6th through 8th grades and one high school for 9th through 12th grades. Approximately 1,350 students are enrolled.

Other Schools Within the Char-Em Intermediate District:
• Beaver Island Community School, 37895 Kings Highway, St. James, (616) 448-2744
• Boyne City Public Schools, 1025 Boyne Avenue, Boyne City, (616) 582-6503
• Boyne Falls Public School, 2329 Center Street, Boyne Falls, (616) 549-2211
• Central Lake Public Schools, Central Lake (616) 544-3141
• Concord Academy — Boyne (Charter School), 00401 Dietz Road, Boyne City, (616) 582-0914
• Concord Academy (Charter School), 2240 E. Mitchell Street, Petoskey, (616) 347-1600
• East Jordan Public School, 304 E. Fourth Street, East Jordan, (616) 536-3131
• Ellsworth Community Schools, 9439 Main Street, Ellsworth, (616) 588-6148
• Harbor Springs Public Schools, 327 E. Bluff Drive, Harbor Springs, (616) 526-2801
• Littlefield Public School, 7400 North Street, Alanson, (616) 548-2261
• Northwest Academy (Charter School), 105 W. Hurlbert Street, Charlevoix, (616) 547-9000
• Pellston Public Schools, 172 N. Park Street, Pellston, (616) 539-8682

Mackinac Straits

Mackinac Island Public Schools
(906) 847-3377
There are less than 700 year-round residents on Mackinac Island, with close to 100 between 5 and 18 years old. These children attend the Mackinac Island Public School, a kindergarten through 12th grade building on the west edge of town. Students learn and play overlooking the water and in sight of the looming Mackinac Bridge.

Mackinaw City Public Schools
609 W. Central Ave., Mackinaw City
• **(616) 436-8211, (616) 436-5587**
Serving the youth in Mackinaw City and its surrounding rural townships, there is one high school and one elementary school in Mackinaw Public Schools system. There were 236 students enrolled in this kindergarten through 12th grade district in 1997.

St. Ignace Public Schools
850 Portage St., St. Ignace
• **(906) 643-8800**
The St. Ignace Public Schools are primarily comprised of LaSalle High School, St. Ignace Middle School and St. Ignace Elementary School, all in a shared building on the west side of town.

Private Schools

Grand Traverse

Grand Traverse Area Catholic Schools
123 E. 11th St., Traverse City
• **(616) 946-8100**
The Grand Traverse Area Catholic Schools is a consolidated, nonpublic school system, and is the largest Catholic school system in

Northwest Michigan. Almost 1,100 students are enrolled in four schools including a kindergarten through 2nd grade lower elementary school, a 3rd through 5th grade upper elementary school, a 6th through 8th grade middle school and a 9th through 12th grade high school. A large preschool also operates at the lower elementary school concurrently with the regular schedule. The curriculum at all levels stresses a Christ-centered, values-oriented education with an emphasis on solid academics and high expectations. Many extracurricular activities are available with over 90 percent of all students participating in at least one additional sport or club. Five Traverse City area parishes help support the consolidated Grand Traverse Area Catholic Schools.

Living God Christian School
1514 Birmley Rd., Traverse City
• **(616) 946-5276**
The school sees itself as an extension of church and family in reinforcing Christian values and principles, teaching subjects from a Christian perspective. Founded in 1979, Living God Christian School offers classes from kindergarten through 6th grade as well as a pre-K class. The 145 students enrolled come from a variety of area churches.

Pathfinder School
11930 S. West Bayshore Dr., Traverse City • **(616) 946-7820**
The Pathfinder School is an independent system nestled within 22 wooded acres on the western outskirts of Traverse City. Approximately 130 students from Grand Traverse, Leelanau and Benzie counties are enrolled in kindergarten through 8th grade. The setting at Pathfinder is magnificent. Cedar Lake laps along a hidden shoreline while mature trees, pines and wildflowers surround the rustic cottage classrooms. The curriculum emphasizes the academic areas of writing, math, creative thinking and problem solving while subjects like French, art, music, computers, science and physical education enhance the basics. Nature studies are conducted often. One of Pathfinders great strengths is its very personal, family-like atmosphere, aided by a nurturing staff and a very low teacher-to-student ratio of 1-to-14.

Trinity Lutheran
1003 S. Maple St., Traverse City
• **(616) 946-2720**
The teachings of the Lutheran Church comprise the academic foundation for Trinity Lutheran. One school building houses classrooms for approximately 175 students in kindergarten through 8th grade. Trinity emphasizes its curriculum as very Christ-centered. The school strives to maintain a small class size and present a strong, traditional curriculum. The local Trinity Lutheran Church is adjacent to the school in the center of Traverse City.

The Leelanau School
1 Old Homestead Rd., Glen Arbor
• **(616) 334-5820**
The Leelanau School is a nondenominational, private boarding school offering a college preparatory curriculum to students in grades 8 to 12. Day students residing in the Grand Traverse area are also enrolled. Founded in 1929, the school strives to develop in students the knowledge and discipline for successful college study, improve leadership skills, nurture a love of nature and environmental stewardship and uphold moral and spiritual standards grounded in traditional Judeo-Christian concepts. The 50-acre campus is nestled along the Sleeping Bear Dunes National Lakeshore. It is certified by the State of Michigan and accredited by the National Association of Independent Schools, and several other accrediting boards. Approximately 70 students are enrolled.

St. Mary's School
310 St. Mary St., Lake Leelanau
• **(616) 256-9636**
Often referred to as Leelanau St. Mary's, this tiny Catholic school has been teaching Leelanau county students for generations. Nestled in the rural center of Leelanau County, St. Mary's draws students from Cedar, Traverse City, Northport, Suttons Bay and other Leelanau county towns. Classes are held for more than 200 students enrolled in kindergarten through grade 12 with an emphasis on college preparatory at the upper levels.

St. Mary's Cathedral Schools
321 N. Otsego Ave., Gaylord
• **(517) 732-5801 Elementary**
310 N. Mitchell St., Gaylord
• **(517) 732-5303 Secondary**

St. Mary's Cathedral Schools offer a strong academic, values-oriented curriculum to students in kindergarten through 12th grade. The Catholic schools are divided between the elementary school for kindergarten through 6th grade, and the junior high/high school for 7th through 12th grades. St. Mary's is known for its family-oriented atmosphere with superb parental support and involvement. Both schools are housed in the same large building although each has its own principal. Approximately 500 students are enrolled. At the elementary level, the core curriculum is complemented by a strong music program, drama program and a well-equipped computer lab. The kindergarten classes follows a four-day format. The secondary school's college-prep curriculum has shared-time classes with the Gaylord Public Schools allowing St. Mary's students to take vocational classes, languages, and other academic offerings at the nearby public high school. Extracurricular activities are offered for all ages with a strong sports program in the secondary grades.

Interlochen Arts Academy
Interlochen • **(616) 276-7200**

Interlochen Center for the Arts, on a lovely 1,200 acre-campus 16 miles southwest of Traverse City, is home to the world-famous Interlochen Arts Academy and summer Interlochen Arts Camp. Established in 1962, the Academy was the nation's first independent high school dedicated to the arts. Today, student enrollment is close to 430 youth in 9th through 12th grades, representing 39 states and 18 foreign countries. Course work follows a strong college-preparatory curriculum, with several hours of added arts training each day in fields like music, theater arts, dance, creative writing and visual arts. Master classes are conducted throughout the year by visiting faculty and renowned artists who are slated to perform at the arts center (see our Arts chapter). Faculty strive to expand students' minds by teaching them how to think rather than what to think. Students may enroll as day or boarding students.

Lake Michigan Shoreline and Cadillac

Manistee Catholic Central Schools
1200 U.S. Hwy. 31 S., Manistee
• **(616) 723-2529**

One building houses 260 students enrolled in preschool through 12th grade classes at Manistee Catholic Central School. The parochial system opened in 1964 after consolidating several parish-based schools in the area. The curriculum stresses Christ-centered excellence in education with daily religious instruction and emphasis on Christian service projects. The high school has begun class scheduling using a block system with longer class periods. Many extracurricular activities offer opportunities for student participation. Five Catholic parishes support the system including Guardian Angels, St. Joseph and St. Mary of Mt. Carmel Shrine in Manistee, St. Joseph in Onekama and St. Bernard's in Irons.

Trinity Lutheran
420 Oak St., Manistee • **(616) 723-8700**

Trinity Lutheran offers a quality, Christian education for children in pre-K through 8th grade. Like the Trinity Lutheran school in Traverse City, it is affiliated with the Lutheran Church Missouri Synod. The curriculum has a computer lab and innovative outdoor education projects. Teachers take advantage of the school's proximity to the Lake Michigan shoreline and the Manistee National Forest with a variety of science projects and learning activities. The school enrolls almost 90 students in kindergarten through 8th grade. An additional 80 students participate in pre-kindergarten classes.

Ludington Area Catholic
700 E. Bryant Rd., Ludington
• **(616) 843-3188**

There are close to 180 students enrolled at Ludington Area Catholic in pre-K through 6th grade. The school is affiliated with St. Simon Catholic Church next door. The Christ-centered curriculum features a hands-on science program and a computer lab.

Heritage Christian School
1706 Wright St., Cadillac
• **(616) 775-4272**

Heritage Christian School has been offering a Christ-centered curriculum to students in the Cadillac area for 15 years. Close to 150 students attend classes from preschool through 12th grade. This parochial school is nondenominational and students represent at least 20 area churches. The elementary curriculum in complemented by an active music program and parent-teacher fellowship. At the secondary level students follow a college-preparatory curriculum with active sports and drama programs. Secondary students also have the opportunity to attend vocational classes through the Wexford-Missaukee Intermediate School District's Career Tech Center.

St. Ann's School
800 W. 13th St., Cadillac
• **(616) 775-1301**

St. Ann's School is a modern elementary complex with approximately 135 students in 1st through 5th grades. It is associated with St. Ann's Catholic Church, which shares the same property and often serves as a site for related curricular activities. Under the leadership of the pastors and Sisters of Mercy, St. Ann's School and Church have served the community since the early days of the century. Many of today's students are the second and third generation in their families to attend St. Ann's.

Northern Michigan Christian School
128 S. Martin St., McBain
• **(616) 825-2492**

Rooted in the teachings of the Christian Reformed Church, Northern Michigan Christian School serves students from Wexford, Missaukee and Osceola counties. This is one of the largest private schools outside Traverse City with almost 400 students in kindergarten through 12th grade. A preschool is also operated at the school, which is in rural McBain, west of Cadillac. A strong academic curriculum stresses Christian values and college preparation. Many graduates pursue higher education. The school also maintains a strong athletic tradition.

Little Traverse

Harbor Light Christian School
8333 Clayton Rd., Harbor Springs
• **(616) 347-7859**

Harbor Light Christian School brings a Christ-centered education with all curriculum based on the Bible to the Little Traverse area. More than 200 students are enrolled in this kindergarten through 12th grade system. A pre-kindergarten program is also provided.

St. Francis Xavier
412 Michigan St., Petoskey
• **(616) 347-3651**

A traditional Catholic curriculum is taught at St. Xavier Catholic school in Petoskey. Approximately 250 local students attend kindergarten through 8th grade in this parochial school in the city.

St. Mary's School
1005 Bridge St., Charlevoix
• **(616) 547-9441**

Students at St. Mary's School enjoy small

INSIDERS' TIP

Is it a snow day or delay? When winter weather conditions are looking bad, school officials start testing road conditions in the wee hours of the morning and make a decision about school closings around 5:30 AM. Since snow days must be made up, it's more common for them to delay the start of school by an hour or two until the sun comes up, and road crews have cleared the roads. All school delays and cancellations are broadcast on radio and television beginning at 6 AM. The best places to check for region-wide cancellations are television stations WPBN-TV (NBC) and WWTV (CBS).

class sizes in this longtime community school founded in 1906. There are approximately 95 students enrolled in pre-kindergarten through 5th grade. Kindergarten is offered in a half-day morning format, with pre-K offered half-days in the afternoon.

Higher Education

Grand Traverse

Great Lakes Maritime Academy
1701 E. Front St., Traverse City
• (616) 922-1200, (800) 748-0566
Ext. 1200

The Great Lakes Maritime Academy prepares students for a shipping career on the inland seas. The Maritime Academy is one of only seven such training schools in the United States and admits only 50 students each year. Training focuses on the deck program, which trains future pilots and mates to navigate Great Lakes freighters while the engine program trains students to become power plant engineers for these mighty vessels. Course work includes more than 200 days of sea time and academic studies through Northwestern Michigan College. After graduating from the three-year program, cadets are qualified to write the Coast Guard examinations.

Northwestern Michigan College
1701 E. Front St., Traverse City
• (616) 922-0650, (800) 748-0566

Northwest Michigan College (NMC) pioneered post-secondary education in northern Michigan when it was established as Michigan's first community college in 1951. NMC offers associate and certification programs in such areas as nursing, vocational and technical training, law enforcement, business administration, commercial art and liberal studies in arts and sciences as well as dual enrollment credit for high-school students. It is accredited by the North Central Association of Colleges and Schools.

Approximately 4,000 students enroll at NMC each semester on a full- and part-time basis. The average student age is 27 with many enrolled part-time to accommodate busy work and family schedules. In addition, thousands of adults and youth participate in noncredit community enrichment programs offered through the college's Extended Education Services and Senior Academy. Northwestern Michigan College is home to the Dennos Museum Center, Milliken Auditorium and the Oleson Center for Continuing Education, which are often used as sites for community programs and performances.

Northwestern Michigan College University Center
2200 Dendrinos Dr., Traverse City
• (616) 922-1777, (888) NMC-UCTC, (888) 662-8282

Northwestern Michigan College University Center is a partnership between NMC as a community college and nine Michigan colleges and universities to offer bachelor degree completion programs, graduate degrees, certificates and courses to residents of Northwest Michigan. Most classes take place on the University Center campus located off Cass Road on the south side of Traverse City although some are at the NMC main campus or in area schools.

Support services at the University Center campus include a computer lab, bookstore, interactive television, an electronic library and on-site administrative staff for each institution. Students interested in enrolling at the University Center should contact the college or university directly for admission and program information. Participating institutions include: Central Michigan University, (616) 922-1756; Davenport College, (616) 922-1740; Ferris State University, (616) 922-1734; Grand

INSIDERS' TIP

Interlochen Center for the Arts is world-renowned for its outstanding education and training of young artists, musicians, writers, dancers and actors. Interlochen alums include Meredith Baxter, David Brooks, Peter Yarrow and Jewel.

Photo: Interlochen Center for the Arts

Interlochen Center for the Arts combines outstanding arts training with strong academics at its scenic campus along the tree-lined shores of Green Lake.

Valley State University, (616) 922-1785; Lake Superior State University, (616) 922-1795; Michigan State University, (616) 929-3902; Oakland University, (616) 922-1770; Spring Arbor College, (616) 922-1760, (800) 648-5843; Western Michigan University, (616) 922-1788.

Lake Michigan Shoreline and Cadillac

West Shore Community College
300 N. Stiles Rd., Scottville
• (616) 845-6211, (800) 848-9722
West Shore Community College has served the communities areas of Scottville, Ludington and Manistee since opening in 1969. Accredited by the North Central Association of Colleges and Schools, it offers two-year liberal studies programs, which are transferable to four-year institutions, two-year career programs and one-year certification pro-

grams. Approximately 1,500 students attend class at West Shore, which is on a beautiful, wooded campus. Community members, as well as students, take advantage of the recreation center with an indoor pool, courts, weights and related facilities as well as the many cultural and performing arts events hosted on campus.

Baker College
9600 E. 13th St., Cadillac
• (616) 775-8458
A branch of the business-oriented Baker College of Flint, this school opened in 1986 as one of eight Baker College campuses serving a total of 12,000 Michigan students. Academic course work leads to four-year bachelor degrees, two-year associate degrees and certification and diplomas in 23 career training programs. Baker College has an open-door admission policy requiring only completion of a high-school degree. It is accredited by the North Central Association of Schools and Colleges.

INSIDERS' TIP

Northwestern Michigan College was the first community college in Michigan when it was formed in 1951. The first classes took place in a vacant airport building.

Northwestern Michigan College — Cadillac Campus
601 Chestnut St., Cadillac
• **(616) 775-8611**

This is an extension of Northwestern Michigan College located 50 miles north in Traverse City. Local college credit and community education classes are held in the evenings at Cadillac Senior High School. Please refer to the Traverse City listing for more on NMC.

Little Traverse

North Central Michigan College
1515 Howard St., Petoskey
• **(616) 348-6600**

North Central Community College offers two years of liberal arts curriculum, occupational programs in technical and vocational fields and general education classes.

Accredited by the North Central Association of Schools and Colleges, it was established in 1958 and currently operates day, evening and weekend classes from a hilltop campus on the northeast side of Petoskey. The campus includes a student center, library, dormitory and classroom buildings. Approximately 625 full-time and 1,500 part-time students attend class here with a faculty to student ration of 1-to-22. Lake Superior State University, based in Sault Ste. Marie, conducts additional educational programs on the North Central campus.

Northwest Michigan's magnificent natural beauty and wholesome lifestyle attract health professionals with the highest level of expertise.

Healthcare

Nobody plans to get sick. But illness and accidents can happen when we least expect them. It's comforting to know that, whether you need to soothe a sore throat or undergo open-heart surgery, necessary facilities and expertise abound in Northwest Michigan.

We are served by two major regional referral centers, Munson Medical Center in Traverse City and Northern Michigan Hospital in Petoskey. These centers offer a full range of adult medical and surgical services and all but the most specialized pediatric services. Between them, Munson Medical Center and Northern Michigan Hospital provide needed tertiary care services to the entire northern half of the lower peninsula and the eastern side of the upper peninsula.

These highly specialized tertiary services are complemented by the many local hospitals in the region and provide community-based primary care and emergency services. Due to the constant changes in healthcare and the continuing push for cost containment and managed care, many smaller hospitals and health services across the country are affiliating with major centers. Northwest Michigan is no different. The major systems reflect the regional referral centers that serve as their flagships — Munson Healthcare led by Munson Medical Center in Traverse City and The HealthShare Group led by Northern Michigan Hospital in Petoskey. Munson Healthcare is also the umbrella for several rural community hospitals in the region, including Leelanau Memorial in Northport, Paul Oliver Memorial in Frankfort and Kalkaska Memorial. The third largest system, Mercy Health Services North, represents hospitals in Cadillac and Grayling.

Physicians, nurses, medical technicians and a full array of healthcare professionals are the vital links that keep our hospitals, clinics and services strong. Northwest Michigan's magnificent natural beauty and wholesome lifestyle attract professionals with the highest level of expertise. These specialists have chosen to live, work and raise families here, bringing with them high standards of caregiving and a commitment to excellence that is infectious. Traverse City, Petoskey and Mackinac Island are common destinations for continuing medical education classes and advanced training programs, with local providers intensely involved as leaders as well as life long-learners.

Be assured that the best of care awaits if you need it. We've listed each of the region's hospitals and their phone numbers. You will also find a rundown of the major walk-in medical clinics, ambulance services and emergency numbers. If you have a question about where to go or need help locating a doctor, any of the referral lines listed will help connect you with the care you need.

Hospitals

Grand Traverse

Munson Medical Center
1105 Sixth St., Traverse City
• (616) 935-5000, (616) 935-6333
emergency

Munson Medical Center is the largest hospital in northern Michigan with 368 licensed beds, more than 200 physicians on the active medical staff and a solid system of primary- and tertiary-care services. The medical campus covers the entire 1100 block of Traverse City's Sixth Street and many of the buildings in the surrounding neighborhood. Doctors represent 35 different specialty areas, including heart surgery, neurosurgery, orthopedic surgery, neonatology and comprehensive cancer treatment. Nearly 27,000 patients are treated in the Munson emergency department each year by 11 physicians who are board certified in emergency medicine. The emergency team also works closely with NorthFlight EMS (see listing in this chapter) and the staff of trauma specialists.

Other services include open heart surgery, non-invasive cardiology, sophisticated radiological testing and intervention, mobile lithotripsy for kidney stones, extensive physical medicine and rehabilitation, neonatal intensive care, Munson is designated as a comprehensive community cancer center for its intensive multidisciplinary approach to treatment. Community-based programs range from the Carls Speech and Hearing Clinic's Ear Lab, Munson Home Service, Grand Traverse Area Hospice and Vital Choice Health and Fitness. Munson recently joined with Michigan State University's College of Human Medicine to provide clinical training for medical students and resident training in family practice for newly graduated physicians. Munson Medical Center is the flagship for Munson Healthcare.

www.insiders.com

See this and many other **Insiders' Guide®** destinations online — in their entirety.

Visit us today!

Leelanau Memorial Health Center
215 S. High St., Northport
• (616) 386-0000

Northport's Leelanau Memorial Health Center offers a range of acute-care and general nursing services in the 27-bed hospital. Emergency coverage is available, and many Munson Medical Center physicians travel here to offer specialty clinics and confer with patients. Surgery is limited to minor procedures that can be performed under local anesthesia. In addition to the hospital, a 72-bed long-term care facility is operated in an attached wing and the David H. Warm Memorial Pool and Fitness Center is available for community use. A walk-in clinic is housed through the emergency room for after-hours treatment and hospital-sponsored outreach clinics are offered in Suttons Bay and Lake Leelanau.

Otsego Memorial Hospital
825 N. Center St., Gaylord
• (517) 731-2100, (517) 731-2140 emergency

Otsego Memorial Hospital is a 53-bed full-service community hospital serving the Gaylord area. The hospital provides full acute, outpatient and 24-hour emergency services and operates an adjacent long-term care facility with 34 licensed beds. Thirty physicians are on the medical staff. Otsego Memorial recently partnered with Gratiot Renal Network to open an off-site renal dialysis service.

Grayling Mercy Hospital
1100 Michigan Ave., Grayling
• (517) 348-5461

Part of the Mercy North system, Grayling Mercy Hospital is licensed for 130 beds. Forty of these are designated for long-term care while the remaining 130 are used for acute care. The hospital provides 24-hour emergency services and, combined with Cadillac Mercy Hospital, has more than 100 doctors on its shared medical staff.

Kalkaska Memorial Health Center
419 S. Coral St., Kalkaska
• (616) 258-9142

Kalkaska Memorial Health Center offers a broad range of acute-care and general nursing services in a rural setting. Affiliated with Munson Healthcare, it includes acute care for six beds and a 67- bed care center for extended care. An in-house rural health clinic provides services to Medicare and Medicaid patients, while a walk-in clinic is available for after-hours medical needs. Five physicians are on staff.

Lake Michigan Shoreline and Cadillac

Paul Oliver Memorial Hospital
224 Park Ave., Frankfort
• (616) 352-9621

Part of the Munson Healthcare system, Paul Oliver Memorial Hospital is a full-service community hospital with comprehensive 24-hour emergency services and surgery, acute-care and specialty clinics. The atmosphere at

Sleeping Bear Dunes National Lakeshore is one of the country's well-known dune formations.

Photo: National Park Service

this 48-bed facility reflects the small-town friendliness of Frankfort. CT scanning, mammography and X-ray services are available on site as well as full physical therapy, pulmonary and cardiac rehabilitation, respite care and a laboratory. Munson specialists often travel to Paul Oliver to conduct specialty clinics, patient consultations and testing.

Westshore Community Hospital
1465 E. Parkdale Ave., Manistee
• (616) 723-3501

Westshore Community Hospital is a full-service community hospital providing comprehensive acute care and 24-hour ambulance and emergency services. Renal dialysis and

cardiac rehabilitation are available. There are 30 physicians on the medical staff at this 54-bed facility.

Memorial Medical Center of West Michigan
1 Atkinson Dr., Ludington
• (616) 843-2591, (800) 343-9566, (616) 845-2390 emergency

Memorial Medical Center of West Michigan promises excellence through caring and technology in providing services to the Ludington community. The hospital is licensed for 94 beds and provides full community hospital services, including acute and outpatient care and 24-hour, physician-staffed emergency services.

INSIDERS' TIP

Did you know that northern Michigan lies in a "kidney-stone belt"? High humidity and hot temps during the summer months lead to a higher-than-average occurrence of kidney stones in the upper Midwest. Prevent an unwelcome attack by drinking plenty of water to avoid dehydration.

Cadillac Mercy Hospital
400 Hobart St., Cadillac • (616) 876-7200

Cadillac Mercy Hospital has been caring for the Cadillac community since 1908 when the Sisters of Mercy first opened their doors in rural northern Michigan. Today, the hospital is part of Mercy Health Services North and one of 10 Mercy hospitals operating in Michigan. Mercy North has a combined medical staff of more than 100 physicians, with half being primary care practitioners. Cadillac Mercy has 174 beds and provides emergency coverage, comprehensive primary care and many specialty care services. This is the main center for Mercy Renal Dialysis Clinics.

Little Traverse

Charlevoix Area Hospital
14700 Lake Shore Dr., Charlevoix
• (616) 547-4024

Charlevoix Area Hospital has served Charlevoix and its nearby rural communities for almost 80 years. The hospital has 27 physicians on staff and provides a range of acute-care and outpatient services. It is a full-service community hospital with 24-hour emergency service and an after hours walk-in clinic.

Northern Michigan Hospital
416 Connable Ave., Petoskey
• (616) 487-4000, (616) 487-4520 emergency

As one of Northwest Michigan's designated regional referral centers, Northern Michigan Hospital services reach much of northern Michigan and well into the upper peninsula. It delivers care to 350,000 residents in 24 counties and serves as the flagship for the HealthShare Group, which also includes Boulder Park Terrace skilled nursing, Health Wares home medical equipment, Hospice of Little Traverse Bay, LifeLink EMS, Northern Michigan Hospital-Burns Clinic Foundation and Traverse Bay Regional Dialysis Center. More than 135 physicians are on the medical staff representing such specialties as cardiology, open heart surgery, general surgery, oncology, neurosurgery, neonatology, obstetrics, vascular surgery, behavioral medicine and emergency services. Northern Michigan Hospital has been a leader in heart services and was the first center in the region to provide open-heart surgery and balloon angioplasty. The hospital's radiology department recently underwent an enormous renovation bringing in the latest imaging and diagnostic technology. Behavioral services offer substance abuse and mental health services, addressing both inpatient and outpatient services, while cancer services emphasize comprehensive, integrated care. The emergency department works closely with LifeLink EMS and is able to provide rapid diagnosis and treatment in any medical situation around the clock.

Mackinac Straits

Mackinac Straits Hospital and Health Center
220 Burdette St., St. Ignace
• (906) 643-8585

The Mackinac Straits Hospital and Health Center provides 24-hour emergency service as well as inpatient and outpatient care. Staffed by two physicians, the 15-bed facility has an on-site lab, X-ray, physical and occupational therapy and respite care. A 99-bed long-term care facility is also housed within the facility.

Outpatient Services and Walk-In Clinics

Grand Traverse

Munson Community Health Center MedCare Walk-in Medical Services
550 Munson Ave. (U.S. Hwy. 31 N.),
Traverse City • (616) 935-8686

Munson Community Health Center stands on the site of the former Traverse City Osteopathic Hospital, later known as Traverse City Community Hospital, on the east side of town. Part of the Munson Healthcare System, this modern facility houses Munson MedCare Walk-in Medical Services for minor injuries and illnesses as well as a pharmacy, lab, radiology services, cardiac rehabilitation, physical rehabilitation services, occupational health and medicine services and a comprehensive pain management program. MedCare Walk-in is the perfect healthcare alternative for unexpected ear infections, colds and fevers, childhood diseases and cuts, sprains or strains. Board certified emergency and primary care physicians are on staff the clinic, which is open 7 AM to 10 PM daily.

Urgent Care
844 E. Front St., Traverse City
• **(616) 929-1234**
3074 N. U.S. Hwy. 31 S., Traverse City
• **(616) 933-5661**

Known as Traverse City's first walk-in clinic, Urgent Care is the answer to an unexpected bout with the flu or a mishap on the tennis court. The clinics provide treatment for those minor illnesses and injuries that might not warrant an emergency room visit but do require urgent medical attention. The original clinic is located on East Front Street near downtown Traverse City, while a newly opened second clinic sits south of town near the Grand Traverse Mall. Both are owned by the Burns Clinic in Petoskey. Seven board-certified primary-care physicians and three certified physician assistants rotate between the two locations. Both clinics are open daily, 9 AM to 9 PM.

Leelanau Memorial Hospital Clinic
211 S. High St., Northport
• **(616) 386-0000**

Leelanau Memorial Hospital provides daily walk-in medical services from 9 AM to 7 PM as well as specialty clinics by appointment. The specialists usually travel to the clinics from Munson Medical Center and represent general surgery, neurology, urology, cardiology, podiatry, gastroenterology and ophthalmology.

Suttons Bay Weekend Walk-in Clinic
508 St. Joseph Ave., Suttons Bay
• **(616) 271-6511**

General and pediatric medicine are the specialty at the Suttons Bay Weekend Walk-in Clinic. Located just a few block north of Suttons Bay's downtown, the clinic is operated by long-time resident, Dr. Fred Lamb. It's open on Wednesdays, Saturdays and Sundays from 9 AM to 5 PM.

Kalkaska Memorial Health Center Rural Health Clinic
419 S. Coral St., Kalkaska
• **(616) 258-9142**

This clinic is part of Kalkaska Memorial Health Center. Walk-in clinic services are available for urgent medical needs 24 hours per day, year-round.

Otsego Memorial Hospital MedCare Clinic
1507 Old 27 S., Gaylord • (517) 731-4111

Daily walk-in hours are 9 AM to 8 PM at the MedCare Clinic operated by Otsego Memorial Hospital. Physicians and physician assistants treat patients in a pleasant urgent-care setting.

Lake Michigan Shoreline and Cadillac

Paul Oliver Memorial Hospital Convenience Care
224 Park Ave., Frankfort
• **(616) 352-9621, (616) 352-2260 appointments**

The Convenience Care Clinic is open daily from 8 AM to 11 PM for urgent medical care and specialty clinics. A number of Munson Medical Center physicians also travel to Paul Oliver to conduct specialty clinics by appointment.

Little Traverse

Charlevoix Area Hospital After Hours Clinic
14700 Lake Shore Dr., Charlevoix
• **(616) 547-4024**

This after hours clinic provides urgent care after local doctors' offices are closed. Located within Charlevoix Area Hospital, the hours are 5 PM to 9 PM on weekdays and 9 AM to 9 PM on weekends and holidays.

Burns Clinic
560 W. Mitchell St., Petoskey
• **(616) 487-7000**

The Burns Clinic operates the largest multispecialty physician clinic in northern Michigan as well as a network of small primary-care clinics in rural communities throughout the region. Specialty services include audiology, general surgery, internal medicine, pediatrics, obstetrics, gynecology, neurology, dermatology, ophthalmology, orthopedic surgery, urology, endocrinology, nutrition counseling and family practice. Call "the Burns" for scheduling and individual clinic information.

Burns Clinic — Urgent Care
510 W. Mitchell St., Petoskey
• (616) 487-2140

Burns Clinic operates an independent Urgent Care department for walk-in medical services. Located on the ground floor of the Burns Clinic building, Urgent Care is staffed by three physicians and one physician assistant. Hours are 8 AM to 6 PM Monday through Thursday, 8 AM to 4 PM Friday and 9 AM to noon on Saturday and Sunday.

Mackinac Straits

Mackinac Straits Hospital and Health Center Walk-in Clinic
220 Burdette St., St. Ignace
• (906) 643-0400

Specializing in pediatrics and internal medicine, the Mackinac Straits Hospital and Health Center offers a daily walk-in clinic and an appointment-based family practice clinic. Hours are 8 AM to 7:30 PM Monday through Friday and 9 AM to 12:30 PM on Saturday.

Referral Services

Physicians Referral Service
Traverse City • (616) 935-6507,
(800) 533-5520

The Munson Healthcare Physicians Referral Service offers one-stop shopping for anyone seeking a local healthcare provider. Centralized information is maintained on more than 250 physicians and 35 different specialties. Callers can confidentially request doctors' names, office hours, location, types of service, insurance practices and educational background. The Physicians Referral Service represents physicians from Munson Medical Center, Kalkaska Memorial Health Center,

Photo: Grand Traverse Resort

The best defense is a good offense when it comes to your health.

Leelanau Memorial Hospital, West Shore Hospital and Paul Oliver Memorial Hospital. Hours are 8 AM to 5 PM Monday through Friday. A 24-hour voice-mail system is in place for response during the next business day.

Mercy Healthline
Cadillac • (800) 33-MERCY,
(800) 336-3729

The Mercy Healthline is provided by Mercy Health Services North, representing the Mercy Hospitals in Cadillac and Grayling and affiliated rural clinics. A registered nurse is on call from 8 AM to 6 PM to answer health questions or direct you to an appropriate provider. The Healthline nurse can answer general health questions, discuss symptoms or immediate health problems, outline available health services and programs and assist in physician referral. This is also the resource for local community health education programs.

Health Access
Petoskey • (800) 248-6777

A service of Northern Michigan Hospital, HealthAccess offers advice on healthcare and can assist in making a referral to a physician or other appropriate provider. Registered nurses answer the HealthAccess phones daily from 8 AM to 8 PM and are trained to help answer a variety of questions on a myriad of healthcare concerns. Callers are referred to an appropriate physician, clinic or service as needed. HealthAccess also handles registration for the hospital's community health education classes.

Crisis Assistance

Third Level Crisis Intervention Center
(800) 442-7315
1022 E. Front St., Traverse City
• (616) 922-4800
438 E. Lake St., Petoskey
• (616) 347-8933

Third Level provides 24-hour crisis services to 15 counties, including our Northwest Michigan region. More than 30,000 requests for crisis intervention, information or referrals are handled each year through offices in Traverse City and Petoskey. Crisis services provide 24-hour access to Community Mental Health emergency services staff, as well as crisis counseling services, on-site interventions and information about and referral to other community sources of assistance. Personal visits from people seeking crisis intervention are accepted, although most contact is initially made via the telephone. The agency's toll-free telephone line and TDD line for the hearing impaired extend access to those in need anywhere in Northwest Michigan.

Emergency Numbers

911 emergency response is available in the Traverse Bay Region except for:

Mackinac Island	(906) 847-3344
Mackinaw City	(616) 627-9911
St. Ignace	(906) 643-1911
Alcoholics Anonymous	(800) 297-2065
Traverse City	(616) 946-8823
Manistee	(616) 723-3515
Petoskey	(616) 348-5005
Mackinac County	(906) 495-7220
Cadillac Area Oasis/	
Family Resource Center	(616) 775-7299, (616) 779-0019, (800) 775-4646
Hearing and Speech Impaired	
Michigan Relay Center	(800) 849-3777
Narcotics Anonymous of Northwest Michigan	
Traverse City	(616) 941-9062
Gaylord	(616) 732-6761
Petoskey	(616) 348-1866
National Runaway Switchboard	(800) 621-4000
Poison Center, Western Michigan	(800) 764-7661
Women's Resource Center	(800) 554-4972
Traverse City	(616) 941-1210
Petoskey	(616) 347-0067

The Traverse Bay region is home to major television affiliates, many radio stations, a regional daily newspaper, a regional magazine, several community weekly papers and a number of specialty publications.

Media

We may live among Michigan's north woods, but Northwest Michigan's media services are far from remote. The Grand Traverse area is a hub for news and information services for the rest of the region. Traverse City and its neighbors are home to major television affiliates, numerous radio stations, a regional daily newspaper, a regional magazine, several community weekly newspapers and a number of weekly and monthly specialty publications. Additional print and electronic communications dot the Northwest Michigan map to offer comprehensive media coverage to the northern half of Michigan's Lower Peninsula and the eastern Upper Peninsula.

The *Traverse City Record-Eagle* is the region's major newspaper, complemented by dailies in Petoskey, Cadillac and Manistee. Weekly newspapers bring local information to most communities while a variety of specialty publications, including *Traverse* magazine, provide feature coverage on local and regional issues, entertainment and activities. You can find them at local newsstands grocery stores and distribution boxes as well as by subscription. Many urban publications are easily available up north. The *Grand Rapids Press*, *Detroit News* and *Detroit Free Press* commonly cover Northwest Michigan and are distributed daily via boxes, shops and home delivery. The *Chicago Tribune* is available in several areas as well, especially during the summer months. By the way, if you are hooked on the *New York Times* or the *Wall Street Journal*, you won't have to do without them during vacation. Bookstores in Traverse City, in particular Horizon Books and Borders, carry many U.S. and foreign newspapers. Check bookstores in Petoskey too.

Nearly 20 major radio and television stations are based in Northwest Michigan, with many in the Grand Traverse area. In light of our rural geography, all broadcast to an immense geographic area via modern technology. We introduce you to our local radio fa-

vorites below, with a sampling of stations. You will see that all of the major networks have local television affiliates here. Broadcasts originate from Traverse City or Cadillac and are then transmitted through a network of substations throughout the region. It's not unusual for a station to have several different call letters and channels, correlating to the various geographic substations.

Daily Newspapers

Grand Traverse

Traverse City Record-Eagle
120 W. Front St., Traverse City
• (616) 946-2000, (800) 968-8273

The *Traverse City Record-Eagle* sets the pace for print news throughout the region. Its coverage area is broader than the boundaries of this book with 13 counties extending across the northern half of Michigan's Lower Peninsula. Daily circulation reaches 29,500 during the week and 41,000 on Sundays. The *Record-Eagle*, a morning publication, covers the news and views of northern Michigan with a balance of political voices. The publication regularly wins top honors in competitions sponsored by the Michigan Press Association and other journalism organizations.

While some reporters use their stint here as a stepping stone to larger markets, many have chosen to make the region home, bringing blue-chip writing credentials and seasoned local insight into their coverage. Weekly sections focus on Food (Mondays), Education and Agriculture (Tuesday), Health (Wednesday), Business (Wednesday and Sunday), Home (Thursday) and Entertainment (Friday). *Northern Living* leads the feature section on Thursdays and Sundays with in-depth stories about the places, faces and interests that contribute to life up north. Friday's arts and entertainment section spotlights local talent, current shows and issues affecting the continually expanding local arts scene. Wednesday's full color *React* tabloid is strictly for teen readers. The Sunday edition includes a recap of local news highlights for the region with individual listings of news briefs for each county.

The *Record-Eagle* publishes a number of specialty sections throughout the year. These focus on fashion, home building, holiday highlights, health and wellness, recreation, auto care and many other topics. The best-known sections are regular publications in their own right. These include the monthly *Active Years* magazine which highlights issues and activities affecting our older residents, and the weekly *Northern Seasons* magazine which is published Fridays between Memorial Day and Labor Day with articles and upcoming activities especially geared for visitors. *Northern Seasons* Magazine transforms into a monthly publication during the remainder of the year. Also housed at the *Record-Eagle* is the local Associated Press reporter and the *Grand Traverse Herald*, a separate weekly newspaper for the Grand Traverse community (see the subsequent listing in this chapter). The Traverse City *Record-Eagle* is part of the Ottaway Newspapers Inc., a wholly owned subsidiary of Dow Jones Publishing Company which also publishes the *Wall Street Journal*.

www.insiders.com

See this and many other **Insiders' Guide®** destinations online — in their entirety.

Visit us today!

Lake Michigan Shoreline and Cadillac

Manistee News-Advocate
75 Maple St., Manistee • (616) 723-3592

The *Manistee News-Advocate* brings daily news and information to 6,000 residents of Manistee and part of Mason Counties. This independent paper, which is a Pioneer Group affiliate of J. B. Publications, also publishes community newspapers in Benzie and Manistee counties, Big Rapids and other locales on the west side of the state. The *News-Advocate* prints a mix of local, state and national news, with special emphasis on community news impacting Manistee area residents.

Ludington Daily News
202 N. Rath Ave., Ludington
• **(616) 845-5181**

The *Ludington Daily News* brings the latest in local issues and events to the residents of Mason, Oceana and Lake counties. The paper is published in the afternoon on Mondays through Saturdays. With a circulation of 8,400, it is distributed through local newsstands and home delivery.

Cadillac Evening News
130 N. Mitchell St., Cadillac
• **(616) 775-6565**

Local, state and national news is covered Monday through Saturday in the family-owned *Cadillac Evening News*. Published each morning with a circulation of 10,000, area news and events are emphasized. The primary communities served are Cadillac, Manton, Mesick, Tustin, Lake City, Marion and other communities lying in or near Wexford, Osceola and Missaukee counties. Distribution is via mail subscriptions and local newsstands.

Little Traverse

Petoskey News Review
319 State St., Petoskey • (616) 347-2544

The *Petoskey News Review* is published Monday through Friday afternoons. News coverage is a balanced mix of local, state and national coverage with a strong editorial commitment to community news of the Little Traverse area. This is the major newspaper for the residents of Petoskey, Charlevoix, Harbor Springs, Boyne City, Alanson, Boyne Falls and neighboring villages with a circulation of 12,000 available through subscription or local newsstands. Each summer, the *News Review* also publishes *Graphic* magazine with articles and events of interest to seasonal residents and visitors.

Other Newspapers

Grand Traverse

The Bay Area Times
(616) 929-7889

The Bay Area Times is a monthly publication with feature articles and business news about the Grand Traverse area. Monthly features include Cybernews, News Briefs, Biz Changes, the Happenings events calendar and Northern Nights entertainment calendar. The Bay Area Times is distributed free throughout the Grand Traverse area or by annual subscription.

The Business News
800 Hastings St., Traverse City
• (616) 929-7919

A monthly newspaper, The Business News takes an in-depth look at various regional industries and economic issues with each publication. Past issues have looked at healthcare, banking, hospitality, manufacturing and the media, to name just a few. A chart listing comparative data for all related local businesses is usually included. The Business News also keeps tabs on new or changing businesses, upcoming events and issues or legislation impacting the area's economy and business climate. Many featured columnists are business, legal or financial professionals. The Business News is sold in community bookstores, newsstands, shopping centers or by subscription and is distributed to 12,000 businesses in our ten Northwest Michigan counties.

Grand Traverse Herald
120 W. Front St., Traverse City
• (616) 946-2187, (616) 933-1412

Housed within the Traverse City Record-Eagle, the Grand Traverse Herald is operated as a completely separate publication with its own editorial and advertising staffs. The Herald is a large community newspaper with local news and ample features and photos about the residents of Grand Traverse County. This paper was begun several years ago as the Record-Eagle took on an increasing regional emphasis. The Herald, published on Wednesdays, is inserted into the same day's Record-Eagle circulation.

Northern Express
530 E. Eighth St., Traverse City
• (616) 947-8787

The Northern Express has a well-deserved following of loyal readers for its weekly publication. It covers art, entertainment, news and views for all of Northern Michigan. The Express originally began as a monthly newspaper focusing on sports and fitness. The emphasis shifted as the entertainment coverage became broader and increasingly more popular. This is a great place to check for local performances, upcoming events, alternative features, personal ads and liberal commentaries. There are 16,500 copies distributed weekly at more than 400 locations. You can find the Express at shops, restaurants and in red distribution boxes throughout the region.

Preview Community Weekly
3054 Cass Rd., Traverse City
• (616) 946-7650

The Preview is a free community weekly for the residents of Grand Traverse county and part of Leelanau county. Circulation reaches 28,000 during its peak periods. Editorial coverage is strictly focused on local news. Leading the paper each week are two in-depth feature stories, usually tied to an upcoming event or major issue. The Preview is distributed via home delivery on Thursdays. Several special interest supplements or independent publications are also produced throughout the year. This includes the free biweekly Entertainment Guide which highlights local attractions and upcoming performances with a combination of calendar listings and short articles. It is available in local hotels, restaurants, visitors centers and public locations. The Preview and Entertainment Guide are part of Noverr Publishing which publishes the NPI community phone guides throughout much of our Insiders region and has recently entered into digital communications through NPI Wireless.

Prime Time News & Observer
800 Hastings St., Ste. E, Traverse City
• (616) 929-7919

The Prime Time News is published monthly

for the senior citizens of Grand Traverse, Leelanau, Benzie, Antrim and Kalkaska Counties. Approximately 12,000 residents receive the magazine, which includes features profiling local seniors as well as news briefs, essays, book reviews and a travel log. The *Prime Time News and Observer* is distributed free in shops, restaurants and public lobbies throughout the region.

Leelanau Enterprise & Tribune
112 Chandler St., Leland
• **(616) 256-9827**

The Leelanau Enterprise and Tribune has chronicled life and news in the county since 1877. This tabloid-size paper highlights community events, local news and countywide issues for the residents of Suttons Bay, Northport, Leland, Glen Arbor, Cedar, Empire and other Leelanau communities. Its circulation is 7,800 distributed via mail and Leelanau newsstands on Wednesday.

Antrim County News
206 N. Bridge St., Bellaire
• **(616) 533-8523**

Antrim County News is published by Up North Publication headquartered in Bellaire. This weekly full-size newspaper is published on Wednesdays. Coverage focuses on local news and upcoming events of Antrim county communities like Bellaire, Mancelona, Alden, Elk Rapids and Ellsworth. Circulation is 5,700.

Elk Rapids Town Meeting
204 River St., Elk Rapids
• **(616) 264-9711**

The Elk Rapids Town Meeting is the community news source for the townspeople of Elk Rapids and Kewadin. This weekly tabloid newspaper is published on Wednesday by Up North Publications. Its circulation is 2,000 via subscription and local newsstands.

The Lake Country Gazette
102 Dexter St., Elk Rapids
• **(616) 264-6800**

The unique *Lake Country Gazette* is published 20 times each year by Fen's Rim Publications in Elk Rapids. Billing itself as a community news magazine, the *Gazette* takes a thoughtful, in-depth look at regional and environmental issues with each edition. Articles are well written, and are often accompanied by interesting photography. Upcoming events are posted on a simulated bulletin board of Best Bets. The *Lake Country Gazette* distributes 17,000 copies free throughout the Grand Traverse region. Look for its distinctive full photo cover at shops, bookstores, restaurants, hotels, recreational facilities and libraries throughout the region. Fen's Rim also publishes an excellent series of local maps for many of the Northwest Michigan communities included in this book. Maps are primarily available through Chambers of Commerce and Visitors Centers.

Leader & Kalkaskian
318 N. Cedar St., Kalkaska
• **(616) 258-4600**

Another Up North Publication product, the *Leader & Kalkaskian* is published Wednesdays in Kalkaska. It covers local news and features of interest to residents of rural Kalkaska county. The *Leader & Kalkaskian* is printed in a full-size broad sheet format for a circulation of 3,900.

Gaylord Herald Times
2066 Old 27 S., Gaylord • (517) 732-1111

Describing itself simply as a local paper publishing local news, the *Gaylord Herald Times* is published Thursdays. Community news primarily features Gaylord and other Otsego county towns as well as parts of nearby Crawford and Montmorency counties. The *Herald Times* has been cited by the Michigan

INSIDERS' TIP

Will Fido be visiting in October? Join radio station WKHQ for the hilarious "Dog-o-ween" pet costume contest held each year shortly before Halloween at the Grand Traverse Mall. Dogs and owners dress in their finest creations to vie for prizes and share laughs with the crowd.

Press Association for the past five years, and was recently named best weekly in the Midwest in the 5,000-10,000 circulation category by the American Press Association. A visitor's publication, *Northern Lights Magazine*, is added during the summer.

Lake Michigan Shoreline and Cadillac

Benzie Advisor
254 S. Benzie Blvd., Beulah
• **(616) 882-9613**

The *Benzie Advisor* brings community news to the residents of Benzie County. Published by Noverr Publishing which also produces the *Preview* and *Entertainment Guide* in Traverse City, the Benzie Advisor is delivered free to homes on Sunday mornings. Its circulation is 8,600.

Benzie County Record Patriot
417 Main St., Frankfort • (616) 352-9659

The *Benzie County Record Patriot* has served as the Frankfort community newspaper since 1888. Its coverage area stretches between the villages of Arcadia, Frankfort, Beulah and Benzonia with weekly circulation at 4,500. Due to the strong resort nature of this community, a *Summer Scene* magazine with visitor information and local activities is added during the summer months. The *Benzie County Record Patriot* is published Thursdays.

Pioneer Press
7714 Lake St., Bear Lake
• **(616) 864-3311**

The *Pioneer Press* is a weekly paper published on Wednesdays. It serves all of Manistee County with a circulation of 1,300. It is strictly a community news publication with timely information and local activities affecting the villages of Bear Lake, Onekama, Wellston, Kaleva and neighboring bergs. *Pioneer Press* was created after five tiny newspapers combined forces to publish a single weekly edition. Its parent company, J. B. Publications, also publishes the *Benzie County Record Patriot* and *Manistee News-Advocate* (see previous listings).

Missaukee Sentinel
130 N. Main St., Lake City
• **(616) 839-5400**

The *Missaukee Sentinel* is the hometown paper for Lake City and its neighbors in rural Missaukee County. Published each Wednesday, its editorial emphasis is on local community news and events. Its circulation is 2,200.

Little Traverse

Charlevoix Courier
112 Mason St., Charlevoix
• **(616) 547-6558**

This weekly Wednesday newspaper is published by the Petoskey News Review for the residents of the Charlevoix area. This is strictly a community newspaper with local news only and a circulation of 2,300.

Harbor Light
211 E. Third St., Harbor Springs
• **(616) 526-2191**

Harbor Light is the weekly newspaper serving the Harbor Springs community. It highlights local news and community events with a circulation of 2,000. *Harbor Light* is published by North Country Publishing, which also produces several supplements geared toward visitors and seasonal residents. These include *Northern Michigan Summer Life*, *Northern Michigan Winter Life* and *Northern Michigan Golf*.

Mackinac Straits

Mackinac Island Town Crier
34 Market St., Mackinac Island
• **(906) 847-3788**

Tiny Mackinac Island has been well-served by its community newspaper, the *Mackinac Island Town Crier*. The paper is published weekly on Fridays between May and September and once each month in October, December and April. Circulation is 3,500. The masthead still bears the name of publisher-editor emeritus Wesley H. Maurer, Sr. (1897-1995) who took over the newspaper as a retired University of Michigan professor and then used it for decades as a training ground for journalism interns from the University. Maurer was still writing at the time of his death at age 98. The Maurer family continues to publish the *Mackinac Island Town Crier* along with the *St. Ignace News* (see subsequent listing).

Mackinaw Marquee
Mackinaw City • (616) 436-5458

This tabloid summer weekly tracks the events and news of Mackinaw City. Published on Wednesdays, it includes a fair amount of visitor information as well as community news.

The St. Ignace News
359 Reagan St., St. Ignace
• (906) 643-9150

The *St. Ignace News* is a weekly newspaper published on Thursday. Filled with community news, activities and upcoming events, it serves St. Ignace and the tiny Eastern Upper Peninsula towns scattered nearby. Like the *Mackinac Island Town Crier*, it is owned and operated by the Maurer family whose patriarch created both publications. Circulation for the *News* is 6,500.

Straits Area Star
222 N. Main St., Cheboygan
• (616) 627-3151, (800) STAR-ADS

The *Straits Area Star* is a community-news weekly published on Sunday. It celebrates the Straits area, including St. Ignace, Mackinaw City and Mackinac Island, through coverage of weekly happenings and events along with display and classified advertising. Circulation is 15,300 via subscription and newsstands in St. Ignace and Mackinaw City (newsstands only), as well as Cheboygan. Although Cheboygan is not technically in our Insiders geographical boundaries, it lies just 15 miles east of Mackinaw City and often serves as a news and information center for the Straits area.

Magazines

Traverse, Northern Michigan's Magazine
148 E. Front St., Traverse City
• (616) 941-8174, (800) 678-3416

This beautifully designed, colorful publication is a well-written award-winning monthly magazine that celebrates Northern Michigan. Articles explore environmental topics, regional issues, northern lifestyles, entertainment, personalities and unique destinations. The photography is outstanding. Favorite monthly features include Word of Mouth, with news and notes from the north country, Table Talk, highlighting local products; restaurants or other epicurean discoveries; and the eclectic Great Northern Discoveries. A comprehensive dining guide appears in each issue as does an excellent monthly calendar of community events. Editorial content focuses primarily on the communities and issues of the northern half of the Lower Peninsula, but circulation of 20,000 stretches across the state, the Midwest and much of the country. Traverse is sold at newsstands nationwide or via subscription.

Traverse City, Your Guide to a Great Lakes Paradise
101 W. Grandview Pkwy., Traverse City
• (616) 947-1120

Published by the Traverse City Convention and Visitors Bureau, this full-color magazine awaits visitors in almost every hotel room in the Grand Traverse area. It is published twice annually with summer and winter editions. Feature stories are filled with beautiful photos and highlight recreational, cultural and seasonal topics. The editorial emphasis is definitely directed to visitors but each season's articles are fresh takes on familiar topics. Look for a wealth of quick community facts, prices, services, events and destinations. The magazine is also available at the Visitors Bureau in downtown Traverse City at the above address.

Jenkins Group, Inc.
121 E. Front St., 4th Floor, Traverse City
• (616) 933-0445

The Jenkins Group is an information services agency which publishes two magazines, *Independent Publisher* and *Publishing for Entrepreneurs*. It also presents nationally recognized conferences for publishers and, through its publishing arm Rhodes and Easton, publishes books on Michigan life and self-help books for self publishers. Rhodes and Easton also provides services like graphic design and marketing to authors who publish their own books. Based in

Traverse City, the Jenkins Group has earned a national reputation in the independent publishing field.

Independent Publisher, formerly known as *Small Press*, is a trade journal with news, information and reviews directed to independent and university presses. The bimonthly magazine has been in publication for 15 years and is filled with how-to articles, book reviews and industry issues and highlights. It has a circulation of 12,000 nationwide and in Canada and the United Kingdom.

Publishing for Entrepreneurs is a bimonthly how-to magazine for independent and self publishers. Editorial coverage explores ways to use technology to make the most of intellectual content. Past articles have ranged from 900 numbers to audio books to websites. Its circulation is 6,000 nationwide.

Both publications are available through subscription or on national and local newsstands.

Television

WGTU & WGTQ-TV 29 & 8
201 E. Front St., Traverse City
• **(616) 946-2900**

This ABC affiliate broadcasts from its studios in downtown Traverse City. Local programming features community information with an early morning talk and information show. There is no local news programming at noon or in the evening. Due to its prime location along East Front Street, the station often spearheads broadcasts of the National Cherry Festival parades and highlights.

WPBN-TV & WTOM-TV 7 & 4
8518 Mich. Hwy. 72 W., Traverse City
• **(616) 947-7770**

NBC's local affiliate has been a Traverse City institution for decades. It was established during television's earlier days as the Paul Bunyan broadcasting network, hence call letters WPBN. Its coverage area stretches

throughout our Insiders' region. Regional news and information has always been stressed with a number of locally produced programs including an early morning news show preceding NBC's *Today Show*, a noon news show, two evening news programs and a late-night news show that broadcasts "11 at 11," eleven minutes of coverage without commercial interruption. WPBN-TV periodically broadcasts special community events and Interlochen Arts Center performances. Look for WPBN-TV on channel 7 and WTOM-TV on channel 4.

WWTV & WWUP-TV 9 & 10
22320 N. 130th Ave., Cadillac
• **(616) 775-3478**
3920 N. U.S. Hwy. 31 S., Traverse City
• **(616) 947-7533**

WWTV has the broadest coverage area of the regional television stations with signals carrying as far south as Mount Pleasant and north into the eastern part of the Upper Peninsula. This CBS affiliate has its main studio south of Cadillac with an additional bureau in Traverse City. Local news programming is produced in both locations although the majority is headquartered in Cadillac. Local news is covered around-the-clock with local reporters on tap throughout the region. WWTV produces its own morning news and information show, which runs opposite competing network programs as well as strong noon, evening and late-night-news shows. WWTV is on channel 9 while substation WWUP-TV broadcasts on channel 10.

WGKI FOX-TV 33, 40 and 45
7400 S. 45 Rd., Cadillac • **(616) 775-9813**

Based in Cadillac, WGKI is the local Fox Broadcasting affiliate. The station is owned by a former local broadcaster who built the station into a regional media source. It features the Fox television lineup and broadcasts around the clock. You will find WGKI on channel 33 in Cadillac, channel 40 in Traverse City and channel 45 in Gaylord and Petoskey.

INSIDERS' TIP

The *Gaylord Herald Times* was cited as the best weekly newspaper in the Midwest by the American Press Association.

Newspaper stands in the heart of downtown Traverse City show just some of the local and statewide papers available in the area.

Radio

The following stations fill Northwestern Michigan's airwaves with music, talk and other entertainment. Many are listed in the Traverse City area, yet most are heard throughout the region with the help of simulcast signals to a host of transmitters. We've listed the stations by their points of origination or designated the primary local outlet within our Insiders' boundaries. Radio frequencies are noted next to the stations' call letters. Don't be surprised to find two listed due to simulcasting.

Grand Traverse

WBRW 98.1, 105.1, 107.1 FM (classic rock)
WCCW 107.5 FM (oldies)
WIAA 88.7 FM (public radio)
WKLT 97.5, 98.9 FM (rock)
WKPK 106.7 FM (top 40)
WLDR 101.9 FM (community news, adult contemporary)
WLJN 1400 AM, 89.9 FM (Christian)
WLXT 96.7, 96.3 FM (light, adult contemporary)
WNMC 90.7 FM (alternative and jazz) Northwestern Michigan College student station.
WOZN 95.5, 94.5, 93.9 (rock)
WTCM 103.5 FM, 580 AM (AM local news and syndicated news talk show; FM country music)

Lake Michigan Shoreline and Cadillac

WATT 1240 AM (news and talk)

Little Traverse

WAIR 92.5 FM (oldies)
WBCM 94.3 FM (country)
WKHQ 106 FM (light rock and top 40)
WLXT 96.7, 96.3 FM (light, adult contemporary)

Mackinac Straits

WKBG 102.9 FM (country)

Cable

Cable television is often a necessity in our rural region. Most of our households have been wired for cable since the mid-1960s, although those early cable days simply meant clear reception from Grand Rapids and the choice of eight channels. Few could have envisioned today's cable services with extensive movie channels, pay per view and dozens of channels. A fair number of households, especially those in extremely rural areas, use home satellite receivers, but most rely on their trusty cable service. Two cable companies serve Northwest Michigan. Cable Michigan, (800) 545-0994, is the largest with local offices serving residents in or near Traverse City, Leelanau County, Antrim County, Kalkaska, Cadillac, Benzie County, Manistee and Indian River. T. C. I. Cable Vision of Greater Michigan, (800) 968-4352, brings viewing to the residents of Petoskey, Charlevoix, Gaylord and the Straits area.

Meeting Your Present Interests and Future Needs

ORCHARD CREEK
ASSISTED LIVING APARTMENTS

All the elements come together at Orchard Creek to create an environment where life is **vibrant, secure,** and as **independent** as possible. Food and housekeeping services make living at Orchard Creek more like **life at a great hotel.** The staff creates a home-like **family environment.**

A **medically trained administrator,** and a staff dedicated to creating a **safe and friendly place** in which to live, gives Orchard Creek the security it takes to **feel at ease.**

Private Studio, One and Two Bedroom Apartments available.

616-932-9060

9715 East Cherrybend Road, 3½ miles from Traverse City

Retirement

An unhurried country pace, a rich array of natural resources, top-quality healthcare and an unending feast of recreational opportunities make Northwest Michigan a haven for today's active retirees. Enjoying the best of all worlds, the region's golden agers — 60,000 strong — are shedding the concept of growing old gracefully. Instead, they're getting out of their rockers and seizing the good life. These vivacious seniors study computer technology and the works of William Shakespeare. They jog, hike, play tennis and frequent the area's many superior golf courses. They contribute to the economy by staffing seasonal businesses, and they are the volunteer backbone of many local charities. Northwest Michigan seniors live, work and play as an integral part of the growing regional community.

However, when it comes to senior services, there are some areas in which the region is still coming of age. The need for affordable senior housing far exceeds current demand. It is not unusual for seniors to wait one to two years to secure an independent-living apartment. As a result, area senior service providers focus on delivering programs to help golden agers remain in their family home for as long as possible. Widely available in-home support programs include household maintenance, medication management, personal care, companionship, health monitoring, meal delivery and respite service for caregivers.

Overall, there is a strong network of senior-service agencies dedicated to providing quality care, fun and inspiration to the older generation. This chapter reviews some of the resources available to the active senior.

Senior Agencies and Services

Area Agencies on Aging

Area Agencies on Aging fund, develop and coordinate systems of service for older adults. Supported by federal and state money, the organizations contract access and information services, in-home care programs and other community-based services. The three agencies serving Northwest Michigan seniors are:

•Area Agency on Aging of Western Michigan, 1279 Cedar Street, N.E., Grand Rapids, (616) 456-5664 (Mason County residents);

•Area Agency on Aging Northeast Michigan Community Services Agency, 2373 Gordon Road, Alpena, (517) 356-3474 (Otsego County residents);

•Area Agency on Aging of Northwest Michigan, 1609 Park Drive, Traverse City, (616) 947-8920 (All other Northwest Michigan residents).

Councils and Commissions on Aging

Councils on aging act as local agents for state and federally funded senior programs. If you're older than 60, you will find a variety of services available to you, including information and referrals, housekeeping and home maintenance assistance, medical transportation, tax

INSIDERS' TIP

Is your new car a lemon? Have those social security checks stopped coming? If you need legal advice of any kind, call the Legal Hotline for Older Michiganians at (800) 347-5297. Someone is available to counsel you weekdays from 9 AM until 5 PM — and it's free!

assistance and more. If you need information or referral services, one of the best places to call is your county's council or commission on aging. In Northwest Michigan these are:

• Antrim County Commission on Aging, 4700 Scenic Highway, Bellaire, (616) 533-8703;

• Benzie County Commission on Aging, 448 Covert Place, Beulah, (616) 882-4851;

• Charlevoix Commission on Aging, 1505 Brockway Street, Boyne City, (616) 582-7301;

• Friendship Center of Emmet County, 453 E. Lake St., Petoskey, (616) 347-3211;

• Grand Traverse County Commission on Aging, 400 Boardman Avenue, Traverse City, (616) 922-4688;

• Kalkaska County Commission on Aging, 303 S. Coral Street, Kalkaska, (616) 258-5030;

• Leelanau County Commission on Aging, 209 St. Mary's Street, Lake Leelanau, (616) 256-7590;

• Manistee County Council on Aging, 457 River Street, Manistee, (616) 723-6477;

• Missaukee County Senior Citizens, 3728 S. Morey Road, Lake City, (616) 839-7554;

• Otsego County Commission on Aging, 120 Grandview Boulevard, Gaylord, (517) 732-1122;

• Wexford County Commission on Aging, 117 W. Cass Street, Cadillac, (616) 775-0133.

Senior Employment
1609 Park Dr., Traverse City
• (616) 947-8920

Many older northerners, by choice or necessity, remain active members of the labor force. Part-time positions in the clerical field, and the hospitality and retail industries are available and suited to the needs of the region's senior workers. A high percentage of these jobs are seasonal, allowing the golden-age worker to head to warmer climates during winter months. Operated through the Area Agency on Aging of Northwest Michigan, the Senior Employment Program offers skills training to help residents 55 or older enter or ad-

vance in today's job market. With on-the-job training, classroom skills training, resume writing and job interview counseling, seniors get the preparation necessary to meet the demands of the modern work world. For detailed information on Senior Employment Programs available in your community, contact your county's council or commission on aging listed at the beginning of this chapter.

Nutrition

There's nothing like a good hot meal to warm the spirit. Combine that with a friendly smile and you have the Elder Nutrition Program. Funded under Titles III and VI of the Older Americans Act, the program is a comprehensive nutrition service that includes meals, screening, education and counseling. The Area Agency on Aging of Northwest Michigan works with seven local contractors who prepare and serve meals to seniors in congregate settings and deliver them to private homes. In Northwest Michigan, the Meals on Wheels home delivery service provided 249,217 meals to homebound seniors in 1996, and 165,230 meals to seniors at group locations.

Congregate meals are served to those older than 60 at dozens of sites throughout the region. In most cases, meals are served each weekday during the lunch hour, although some sites offer service on a more limited basis. A suggested donation of $1.50 per meal is expected. Meals on Wheels, the nutrition program serving homebound seniors, offers several meal options. Seniors who qualify may receive hot meals, a snack and a light luncheon delivered by a friendly volunteer each weekday. Frozen meals may be provided for Saturday and Sunday. In some cases, meals are also available to spouses. Suggested donations for home-delivered meals range from $1.50 to $1.75, depending on the county where service is received. Your county council or commission on aging can help you qualify for Meals on Wheels or provide you with a list of

INSIDERS' TIP

Many restaurants, stores and commercial services offer unadvertised senior discounts. Before digging into your wallet, ask what senior benefits might apply to your purchase. You may be pleasantly surprised.

Private, Assisted Living for Seniors

- Enjoy a gracious home and tranquil wooded surroundings with friends of compatible interests.
- Private rooms each with half-baths, carpeting.
- A family-style dining room offers home-prepared meals and serves as a center for activities and companionship.

Rosegate

Licensed by State

Private Residential Care
(616) 941-7433
3090 LaFranier Rd.
Traverse City

congregate meal sites. Telephone numbers for these organizations are at the beginning of this chapter.

American Association of Retired Persons (AARP)

AARP is a national nonprofit association providing advocacy, information and benefit services for people older than 50. Local chapters serve as information clearinghouses and promote senior issues at the grassroots level. There are three active chapters in Northwest Michigan that meet monthly. The Traverse City chapter meets at 5 PM on the first Wednesday of each month at the Traverse City Senior Center, 901 East Front Street, 947-4846. Manistee's chapter meets the fourth Monday of each month at 1:30 PM at 457 River Street in Manistee. Call AARP at 723-3814 for information in Mason County. The Benzie Area chapter meets the second Monday of the month at 2 PM at the First Congregational Church, 900 Barber Street, Benzonia, (616) 882-9452.

Giving Something Back

Retired and Senior Volunteer Program (RSVP)

Through RSVP more than 1,000 Northwest Michigan seniors are making a difference in the lives of others. RSVP connects people 55 and older to volunteer opportunities among the region's dozens of nonprofit organizations. RSVP seniors meet the need for volunteers in a variety of settings ranging from county offices and museums to libraries and nursing homes. There are three RSVP offices in the region: Grand Traverse United Way, 521 South Street, Traverse City, (616) 929-2854; RSVP, P.O. Box 1025, Gaylord, MI 49734 (517) 732-6232; Friendship Centers of Emmet County, 1324 Anderson Road, Petoskey, (616) 347-5877.

Helping Hands
(800) STAR-910 Ext. 3154

Seniors are the backbone of many volunteer organizations. Their wisdom and skills are highly valued and much needed in various settings. You'll find northern seniors volunteering at animal shelters, schools, libraries, hospitals, local fairs and festivals, homeless shelters, for environmental groups and for many other worthy organizations. The Helping Hands hotline, sponsored by WWTV-WWUP TV 9&10 News, will help connect you to volunteer opportunities in any community in the region.

Senior Companion Program, Catholic Human Services

3210-B Racquet Club Dr., Traverse City
• (616) 929-7070

The Senior Companion Program offers financial assistance to seniors in exchange for providing companionship to other seniors. Helpers who are older than 60 and in a low-income bracket receive an hourly stipend, transportation fees and a meal allotment. Established 20 years ago, the program operates in Antrim, Benzie, Grand Traverse, Kalkaska and Leelanau counties.

www.insiders.com

See this and many other **Insiders' Guide®** destinations online — in their entirety.

Visit us today!

Service Corps of Retired Executives (SCORE)

SCORE is a nonprofit corporation and national network of volunteer business executives providing small business managerial counseling and training. About 30 volunteers are active with the Traverse City group. In Cadillac, a dozen volunteers conduct counseling sessions and periodically offer seminars. Petoskey's chapter pools the expertise of 16 retired executives. Northwest Michigan SCORE groups operate from local chambers of commerce. Offices are in Cadillac, 222 N. Lake Street, (616) 775-9776; in Petoskey, 401 E. Mitchell Street, (616) 347-4150; and in Traverse City, 202 E. Grandview Parkway, (616) 947-5075.

Foster Grandparent Program of Northwest Michigan

3210-B Racquet Club Dr., Traverse City
• (616) 929-7070

The Foster Grandparent Program specializes in building mutually beneficial intergenerational relationships. Volunteers offer emotional support to an assigned child on a weekly basis. Duties may include playing games, reading or tutoring. Older adults with limited incomes are eligible to serve as volunteers. Foster grandparents devote about 20 hours per week to the program and receive a nontaxable stipend for their services.

Exercising Mind and Body

Senior Academy

Northwestern Michigan College, 1701 E. Front St., Traverse City • (616) 922-1700

Whether you long to take up photography, astronomy, genealogy or Shakespearean study, the Senior Academy at Northwestern Michigan College can help. A division of the college's Extended Educational Services, the academy offers low cost, noncredit courses to anyone 55 or older. Classes vary from one-day workshops to 10-week sessions and are taught by retired educators, current college faculty and local experts. For a more social and informal learning format, seniors are invited to join a Brown Bag Forum, held monthly at the college's University Center at the Boardman Lake campus on the south side of Traverse City. Call for a Brown Bag Forum schedule and a current class listing.

Silver Streak Ski Days

You'll be surprised to see the number of golden agers out on the slopes in Northwest Michigan. Special rates and programs are offered to seniors at many area ski facilities, including some of the Midwest's premier resorts. Age qualifications for senior discounts vary. Some resorts feature a weekly senior day, others offer discounts daily. Check out the available options and perks by calling individual resorts. (For a list of ski facilities, see our Recreation chapter.)

Photo: Kevin Poirier

Fishing opportunities are never far away in our region.

Northwest Michigan Senior Games
• (616) 947-8920, (800) 442-1713

Every September more than 200 adults older than 55, from throughout the region, participate in competitive and noncompetitive events. Games range from relaxing to physically challenging, and some require accuracy rather than strength and stamina. Competitors can sign up for shuffleboard, horseshoes, bowling, pool, euchre, pinochle games, minigolf, table tennis or Frisbee toss. Hard-core senior athletes can test their fitness at a 17.5 mile bike race, a 5K or 1 mile run/walk. The one-day competition wraps up with an awards banquet and dance at the Traverse City Senior Center. Senior registration materials are available in early August from the Area Agency on Aging of Northwest Michigan. A nominal registration fee is required for some events.

Grand Traverse Bay YMCA
3000 Racquet Club Dr., Traverse City
• (616) 947-5880

The Traverse City YMCA offers aerobics, tennis, racquetball and a fitness center featuring treadmills, stair-steppers, rowing machine, Keiser strengthening equipment, free weights and hand weights. The YMCA is open weekdays from 6 AM until 9 PM in the summer. Fall, winter and spring hours are 6 AM until 10 PM

weekdays, 8 AM until 7 PM on Saturdays and 1 until 9 PM on Sundays. An annual membership costs $158 for an individual 60 or older and $255 for couples.

Practical Advice

Legal Services of Northern Michigan
207 Grandview Pkwy., Traverse City
• (616) 941-0658
446 E. Mitchell St., Petoskey
• (616) 347-8115

If you are 60 or older you can receive free legal services through Michigan senior citizen legal assistance programs. Two service locations in Northwest Michigan provide help in civil cases, problems pertaining to public benefits, housing issues, consumer problems, wills and other senior citizen issues.

Citizens for Better Care
346 E. State St., Traverse City
• (616) 938-0341

Citizens for Better Care, Michigan's long-term care ombudsman program, can help you plan long-term care for yourself or a family member. The ombudsman answers questions regarding nursing homes, homes for the aged and adult foster care. Local offices provide information, advocacy and referrals. The Traverse City office serves most of Northwest Michigan. Its hours are 9 AM to 5 PM Monday through Friday. There is no fee for services, but donations are accepted.

Social Security Administration
117 W. Cass St., Cadillac
• (616) 775-0721
525 Munson Ave., Traverse City
• (616) 946-8361
5710 W. U.S. Hwy. 10, Ludington
• (616) 843-3377
911 Spring St., Petoskey
• (616) 347-0692

Social Security offices administer Social Security retirement, survivor and disability benefits, Supplemental Security Income payments and Medicare health insurance entitlements. The Cadillac office is open Monday through Thursday from 9 AM until noon and from 1 until 4 PM. Traverse City, Ludington and Petoskey offices are open weekdays between 9 AM and 4 PM.

Senior Citizen Centers

At senior centers you can make a friend, learn a skill and receive important health care services. They are a great source for nutritious meals in exchange for a nominal donation. You will find at least two senior centers located in even the smallest Northwest Michigan county. Each has a group of golden agers with a character all its own. Hot meals are provided at all but one of the centers included in the listings below. The balanced meals are prepared at nine sites and delivered to individual centers. In addition to the key centers listed, congregate meals are served at numerous locations in each county. Senior centers are popular gathering sites because they provide food for the body, mind and the spirit. You'll find

caring staff, amicable peers, inspiration and recreation at any of these centers.

Grand Traverse

Traverse City Senior Center
801 E. Front St., Traverse City
• (616) 922-4911

This is one of the best senior centers in Michigan with a wide range of activities, classes, and opportunities for community involvement for those 50 and older. You can join a monthly hobby or exercise group, take computer classes or learn tap dancing. Sports enthusiasts can join a center tennis league, shuffleboard league or golf league. Tennis and shuffleboard courts are on-site. The group hosts an annual senior picnic and pig roast which draws more than 200 golden agers. Members also volunteer at a number of non-profit organizations. The center is one of three congregate meal sites in Grand Traverse County. Health services include foot clinics, immunizations, blood pressure checks and vision screenings. Experts appear regularly to keep seniors informed on the latest developments in senior health issues. The Traverse City Senior Center is open weekdays from 9 AM until 4 PM.

Friendship Community Center
201 Broadway St., Suttons Bay
• (616) 271-4630

This is a group of seniors willing to change with the times. Finding it too costly to maintain a facility on their own, they have merged with other groups in the village to become a community center. In this manner, they maximize the community's financial and human resources. To help fund renovation of their 100-year-old structure, the group conducts rummage sales, raffles and bake sales. Congregate meals are served on Wednesdays and

---

INSIDERS' TIP

You're not too old to learn to surf — the Internet that is. Get on the information highway at the Senior Academy in Traverse City. The Academy offers two levels of Internet training and other high-tech courses. Keep pace with today's computer science, call (616) 922-1700.

Fridays. Flu shots, foot clinics and health screenings are available on-site.

Bellaire Senior Center
308 Cayuga St., Bellaire
- **(616) 533-8703**

This seniors group loves the social life. Every month they take bus trips to Turtle Creek and Leelanau Sands casinos and Traverse City malls. On-site the seniors enjoy card games, potlucks and monthly dances. Bellaire is one of six congregate meal sites in Antrim County. Flu shots, blood pressure clinics, general health screenings and foot clinics are offered at the center. The seniors share the facility with the Benzie County Council on Aging and the Bellaire Area Seniors, a nonprofit group dedicated to community action and involvement. The center is open daily from 8:30 AM until 4:30 PM.

Kalkaska Senior Center
303 S. Coral St., Kalkaska
- **(616) 258-5030**

Kalkaska seniors gather in a spacious new facility for fitness and fellowship. Center veterans make a special effort to welcome and encourage newcomers to the group. Open weekdays from 8 AM until 4:30 PM, Kalkaska Senior Center is one of five congregate meal sites in Kalkaska County. Exercise classes are offered each Tuesday morning from 9 to 11 AM. On Mondays, Wednesdays and Fridays, fitness equipment is provided for a complete physical workout. Hearing and foot clinics, health screenings and flu shots are regularly provided. Seniors enjoy weekly craft and rug-hooking classes or spontaneous games of pool and table tennis. Once a month, the members take a bus trip to nearby Leelanau Sands and Turtle Creek casinos.

Gaylord Meal Site
120 Grandview Blvd., Gaylord
- **(517) 732-1122**

Gaylord seniors participate in a variety of outings organized by their center. Known as the Gaylord Meal Site, the site provides much more than nutritious food. Seniors can go on monthly bus trips to area casinos and popular attractions or attend a weekly movie matinee at a local theater. Potlucks, parties, dances and card games make for a full social schedule for the Gaylord golden agers. One of four congregate meal sites in the county, the site provides health services as well. Flu shot and foot clinics, glucose, blood pressure and vision testing and eyeglass cleaning are all available. The center is open weekdays from 8 AM until 4 PM.

Lake Michigan Shoreline and Cadillac

Harborview Senior Center
832 Main St., Frankfort • **(616) 352-4280**

Harborview seniors appreciate the opportunity for fellowship their center provides. The center offers flu shot clinics, foot clinics, meals for the homebound and help with home chores. These golden agers have birthday and holiday parties, barbecues in the summer and congregate breakfasts three times a month. The center is one of five congregate meal sites in Benzie County and is open weekdays from 8 AM until 3:30 PM.

Manistee County Senior Center
457 River St., Manistee • **(616) 723-6477**

The Manistee County Senior Center bridges the generation gap by bringing in local grade school students to share lunch, present concerts or decorate the facility. To reciprocate the kindness of the young people, the senior center hosts an annual Easter Bunny Breakfast for children and grandparents. Open weekdays from 8 AM until 4 PM, the Manistee County Senior Center is one of seven congregate meal sites in Manistee County. Other services provided at the center include blood pressure, vision and glaucoma screening. The 20-member walking club walks 1.5 miles along the Manistee Riverwalk every Thursday morning, beginning at 9 AM. Going beyond local borders, center seniors participate in color tours, Lake Michigan ferry trips to the Green Bay, Wisconsin casino and mall shopping excursions.

Ludington Senior Center
308 S. Rowe St., Ludington
- **(616) 845-6841**

There's little time for boredom if you attend the Ludington Senior Center. It offers adult-education courses, craft classes, traveling pool leagues, low-impact aerobics and yoga sessions. The center's Recreation for the Physically Limited group offers organized activities and outings for stroke survivors, the vision impaired and others with physical handicaps. This senior group volunteers for numerous local nonprofit organizations such as United Way, the American Cancer Society and the local Family Independence Agency. Open weekdays from 9 AM until 4:30 PM, the center is one of three congregate meal sites in Mason County. It also provides information and referrals, flu shot and foot clinics and blood sugar and blood pressure screening. Medicare and Medicaid counseling is available on-site, as well as access to the Michigan Emergency Pharmaceutical Program for Seniors.

Cadillac Senior Center
115 South St., Cadillac • (616) 779-9420

It may not be the fountain of youth, but music and dancing create a lively atmosphere that keeps Cadillac retirees feeling young. Cadillac Senior Center offers line-dance instruction, keyboard classes and senior dances with live music by the Little Accordion Band. The center sponsors a 25-member senior kitchen band which performs at various area functions. In the summer, senior groups regularly travel to Interlochen Center for the Arts to attend concerts. When the seniors aren't enjoying music, they're involved with arts and crafts classes, aqua-aerobics, aerobics, bowling and card games. Once a month, the Mature Minglers take to the road to dine at an out-of-town restaurant. Breakfast Buddies gather each Friday for a morning out in the Cadillac area. Health services include flu shots, foot clinics, blood pressure checks and hearing screenings. Tax preparation assistance is also available around tax time. Open weekdays from 10:30 AM until 3:30 PM, the center is one of seven congregate meal sites in Wexford County. Meals are served on Monday and Wednesday.

Lake City Area Senior Center
120 E. John St., Lake City
• (616) 839-4351

While services at the Lake City Senior Center are limited to information and referrals, this group of golden agers works hard to make a difference in their community. They collect food for the hungry and raise funds to send impoverished children to summer camp and to support student musicians. At Christmas, they donate knitted mittens, hats and scarves to protect the children in the community from the biting cold. Seniors call also sell their handmade crafts at the center's downtown storefront. A drop-in site, Lake City Area Senior Center is open from 10:30 until 3:30 Tuesdays through Fridays. Congregate meals are available at two other Missaukee County sites.

Little Traverse

Charlevoix County Senior Center
116 Main St., East Jordan
• (616) 536-7831

This group of seniors raises money for their center by providing quilting services to others in the community and serving a public luncheon. Center hours are from 7 AM to 1 PM Monday through Friday. It is one of three congregate meal sites in Charlevoix County. The center provides flu shot and foot clinics and blood pressure screenings.

Friendship Center of Emmet County
453 E. Lake St., Petoskey
• (616) 347-3211

The Friendship Center of Emmet County offers hiking, walking and swimming programs and hosts monthly support groups for Alzheimer and Parkinson's disease sufferers and their families. Year round, between 8:30 and 11:30 AM on Monday and Wednesday, seniors gather to exercise at Northern Michigan Hospital's fitness room and follow a one-mile walking course through the medical facility. Aqua-aerobics classes are held from 8:30 until 11:30 AM on Monday and Wednesday at a nearby pool. The center is one of four congregate meal sites in Emmet County and is open from 8:30 AM to 5 PM Monday through Friday, and 1 PM until the dishes are done on Sundays. Other services offered at the center include flu shot and foot clinics, manicures, vision, hearing, glaucoma and blood cholesterol screening.

Senior Housing

Affluent seniors will have no trouble locating an apartment or condo among the region's wide selection of modern housing complexes. Some attractive options are those that face the waterfront or golf courses. See our Real Estate chapter for more information on purchasing property in Northwest Michigan.

For seniors of limited means, a housing transition is likely to be more difficult and take longer; affordable housing is not easy to come by. Yet, good things come to those who wait, including safe, attractive and comfortable senior housing. Most area seniors take advantage of government-subsidized apartments that are available in all Northwest Michigan counties. Most of the apartment buildings noted in this chapter are available to the handicapped and disabled in addition to senior citizens. You will find a still broader selection of subsidized apartments to choose from if you don't mind living in buildings shared by young couples and families. To receive housing subsidies, applicants must be 62 or older. For those meeting income qualifications, rental rates are figured on a sliding scale. Income guidelines differ by county and are subject to change.

Your local council or commission on aging can help you with housing decisions and provide you with a list of options in your community. If your need for housing is pressing, it's worthwhile to apply at several different buildings to shorten the waiting period. All subsidized apartment buildings report long waiting lists. You may be lucky and find your wait is short, but it may take up to two years.

In selecting an apartment where you will spend your golden years, spend some time in the halls. Meet the staff and your future neighbors. Ask plenty of questions to get a clear picture of what life is like at the facility. If it doesn't meet your expectations, keep looking. There may be greener pastures on the other side of town.

Grand Traverse

Hillview Terrace
601 Fitzhugh Dr., Traverse City
• **(616) 946-6540**

Like other subsidized independent senior housing in Northwest Michigan, there is at least a one-year wait to obtain an apartment at Hillview Terrace. Perched on a hilltop on the edge of town, the three-story, 120-unit apartment building places malls, supermarkets and healthcare services almost at your door. The annual income ceiling for renters is $29,750 for one person and $33,200 for two people. Congregate meals are not available on-site, but other amenities include a craft and pool room and a community room with a big-screen television, kitchen and patio. Laundry facilities are available on each floor and a key-entry system provides tight security. An active resident council provides ongoing activities including bingo, card games, birthday and holiday parties. If you're a musician, or always wanted to be, you can join the resident kitchen band. The 20-member band meets regularly and performs at various local functions.

Riverview Terrace
150 Pine St., Traverse City
• **(616) 922-4915**

Situated along the gently flowing Boardman River in downtown Traverse City, Riverside Terrace features 116 government-subsidized apartments. Most of the apartments face either the river side or Grand Traverse Bay. Shopping, the post office, the Traverse City zoo and waterfront park are all just a stone's throw away. A newly renovated entry

INSIDERS' TIP

Eldercare Locator can connect you to senior resources anywhere in the country. By calling (800) 677-1116, you can receive information on housing, elder abuse, transportation, home-delivered meals and much more. This free service is sponsored by the National Association of Area Agencies on Aging. The Eldercare Locator line is open between 9 AM and 5 PM EST.

and lobby welcomes seniors and their guests to Riverside. Tenants are protected by a card-entry security system and each apartment has a 24-hour emergency call button. Riverside seniors enjoy on-site congregate meals on weekdays. They have access to a community room and library, shuffleboard, bingo and non-denominational church services. Organized events give seniors something look forward to year round, including fall color tours, Christmas tree light tours and other seasonal events. The annual income ceiling for one person is $24,250, and $27,700 for couples. Qualified seniors are placed on a waiting list.

Meadow View Apartments
4541 Mich. Hwy. 88 S., Bellaire
• **(616) 533-6440**

Friendly faces and a safe atmosphere make living at this senior apartment building a pleasant experience. Connected to the Meadow Brook Medical Care Facility, the independent-living complex consists of 21 apartments. The three-story building is situated in a wooded area on well-manicured grounds, accented by a fish pond. While there are no organized activities at Meadow View, there are coffee klatches and occasional luncheons for tenants to socialize. Amenities offered at the building include on-site laundry facilities, a community room, lending library, individual parking spaces and storage lockers. There is a six- to nine-month wait for one-bedroom apartments, which rent for between $365 and $425 per month.

Level Acres
504 S. Orange St., Kalkaska
• **(616) 258-9107**

These senior apartments built in a residential area feel like more like houses than apartments. Close to the Kalkaska commercial district, the federally subsidized one-story,

36-unit apartment building features a community room and beauty shop.

Lake Michigan Shoreline and Cadillac

Michigan Shores Cooperative
641 Michigan Ave., Frankfort
• **(616) 352-7217**

Michigan Shores offers affordable waterfront living, and is Michigan's only senior apartment cooperative. Share prices for 1998 range from $14,000 to $33,000, with monthly fees ranging from $600 to $1,150. This three-story, 54-unit co-op located on 19 acres, is perched on a bluff overlooking Lake Michigan. To qualify for co-op eligibility rules you must be 62 or older and monthly fees can't exceed 47 percent of your monthly income. Roomy and barrier-free, apartments range from 676-square-foot one bedroom units to 1,500-square-foot two-bedroom units, all featuring balconies or patios. Amenities include a library, indoor mail delivery, a phone-based security system, in-room 24-hour emergency call buttons and a great room with a grand piano. This active family of tenants regularly uses the community van for group trips. There is a waiting list of 100 people for these independent living units, but waiting time varies widely.

Century Terrace Apartments
237 Sixth Ave., Manistee
• **(616) 723-6201**

From your apartment at Century Terrace you can watch boats drift by in the Manistee Harbor. The building features 119 government-subsidized units. Annual income ceilings for Century Terrace apartments are $19,000 for one person and $22,900 for couples. The complex has on-site laundry facilities, a beauty

---

INSIDERS' TIP

Growing older doesn't have to mean you must give up driving. You may just need to learn some new tricks. Area senior organizations, in cooperation with local law enforcement agencies, provide defensive-driving programs for seniors. Refresher courses include classroom instruction, skill assessment and personal counseling. To register, call (616) 922-4911.

shop, a key-entry security system, two lounge rooms, a dining room and a sun porch with a sweeping view of the harbor. Many senior services are provided at the Manistee Senior Center, which is located within walking distance of Century Terrace. There is about a six-month wait for apartments.

Longfellow Towers
301 E. Court St., Ludington
• (616) 845-7900

If you like to live near shopping, the community library, post office, courthouse and pharmacies, you'll like the convenience of life at Longfellow Towers. Surrounded by tall trees, this government-subsidized 149-unit building offers many amenities. Each of the seven floors features a sitting room. There are on-site laundry facilities, a community room and solarium. Organized activities include potlucks, birthday parties, bingo, fall color tours and other seasonal celebrations and events. Church services and Bible studies are also held regularly at the building. Annual income ceilings are $18,950 for one person and $21,650 for two people. The waiting list averages between six and nine months.

Harbor View
329 South St., Cadillac • (616) 775-0831

You can watch sunsets, Jet Skiing, parades and fireworks from your Harbor View apartment overlooking Lake Cadillac. The government-subsidized 131-unit building is in the heart of the community within walking distance of lakefront parks, the public library, shopping and restaurants. If you can't get out, you will find many local stores and restaurants make deliveries to your door. At Harbor View, the annual income ceiling for one person is $18,950 and $21,650 for couples. There is a key-entry security system, a full-time security guard on site and each apartment has a 24-hour emergency call button. Other building amenities include on-site laundry facilities, a community room, a solarium, pool table, beauty shop and a big-screen television in the main lobby. Congregate meals are served weekdays. Harbor View's active resident council involves seniors in a variety of activities including picnics, potlucks, bingo, birthday parties and day trips. Visiting pastors offer regular church services. To secure an apartment here, there is an 18- to 24-month wait.

Little Traverse

Pine River Place
210 W. Garfield Ave., Charlevoix
• (616) 547-5451

This nicely landscaped, three-story apartment building offers seniors a central location in a neighborhood setting. Pine River Place features 62 government-subsidized apartments in the beautiful community of Charlevoix. Annual income ceiling at Pine River place is $19,000 for one person and $25,000 for two people. While apartments offer tenants independent living, a congregate meal is provided each weekday. A key-entry security system provide a safe environment. During the balmy northern summers, tenants can participate in shuffleboard games, lounge on the community patio or enjoy the private patios and balconies, which accompany each apartment.

Harbor Village
1501 Crestview Dr., Petoskey
• (616) 348-9730
1401 Crestview Dr., Petoskey
• (616) 348-3370

A pair of two-story buildings make up this senior-oriented complex set in a residential neighborhood one block from Petoskey's shopping district. The site, graced with trees and native wildflowers, has 46 government-subsidized apartments for independent living. The annual income ceiling is $16,320 for one person and $18,600 for two people. Buildings provide a key-entry security system, laundry facilities, a combined craft room and library and a community room.

The rich natural
resources and
unparalleled beauty of
Northwest Michigan
have historically been
the calling card for the
region's commercial
and religious
development.

Worship

Traveling through Northwest Michigan, you'll find the pastoral beauty of the countryside accented by tall, white church steeples among rolling hills and cornfields. These steadfast towers scattered across the landscape convey the values, traditions and the stability that religion has afforded generations of the region's people.

Native Americans, who first called the northern woodlands home, worshiped a Great Spirit and spirits that they believed inhabited the natural world, but it was French Jesuits who brought the Christian faith to the region. The two chief goals of the French in the late 1600s were to convert the region's natives to Christianity, and to develop a profitable fur trade. A young Jesuit priest named Father Jacques Marquette, was successful in both endeavors. In 1668, he established a small mission in the upper peninsula at Sault Ste. Marie. Marquette's mission became the first permanent settlement in Michigan.

In 1671, Marquette established a second mission in the state in the Mackinac Straits area. It is still debated whether this mission was originally on Mackinac Island or on the mainland, but it is a fact that the skilled woodsman and devout priest built a chapel at Moran Bay, founding the city of St. Ignace. From his headquarters in St. Ignace, Father Marquette set out on dangerous explorations, which opened the Great Lakes basin for development. Marquette and explorer Louis Joliet are remembered in history books as the first Europeans to map the Mississippi River.

Father Marquette died in 1675 while returning from a mission trip (for more information on Father Marquette, see our History chapter). Other French Jesuits followed Marquette to Northwest Michigan. In about 1700, Jesuits planted a mission among the L'Arbre Croche villages, an area stretching from Cross Village to Harbor Springs in Emmet County. More than a hundred years later, in 1852, a Presbyterian

missionary named Andrew Porter settled Petoskey. However, it was the arrival of the railroad and a group of Methodists that changed Petoskey from a primitive settlement to one of the country's most popular summer resort cities.

Encouraged by railroad companies who were looking to increase business for their passenger lines, Methodists established a summer retreat in Petoskey in 1875. They were attracted by the beautiful surroundings and proximity to rail and steamer lines, so they established a charming Victorian resort called Bay View. The resort drew thousands of visitors to the Little Traverse region. They came in droves to participate in religious programs and to hear sermons and lectures by such world-famous individuals as Helen Keller, William Jennings Bryan and Booker T. Washington. Today, the community of 440 cottages is one of 17 Michigan sites classified as a National Historic Landmark.

Over the years, Bay View programming has broadened to interest a wider range of people and remains hugely popular. The nation's leading Methodist preachers continue to present lectures and Sunday vespers throughout the summer. The services are open to the public and draw 1,000 people to the John Hall Auditorium each week. Bay View is a true cultural pocket in the Little Traverse region and offers a variety of concerts, plays and enrichment opportunities in visual arts, literature and film. For a current program schedule, call the Bay View office at (616) 439-9240.

The rich natural resources and unparalleled beauty of Northwest Michigan have historically been the calling card for the region's commercial and religious development. Plentiful game, an abundance of fishing, trapping and logging opportunities and a network of waterways gave settlers a new way of life.

In 1848, a group of Mormons settled on

Beaver Island, the largest island in Lake Michigan, 32 miles off the Charlevoix coast. By 1850, there more than 300 Mormons were living on the island. Colony founder James Strang crowned himself king, declaring the islands of the Great Lakes as his own. Strang was shot by disgruntled followers in 1856, and the remaining members of the religious colony were driven off the island by mainlanders.

Despite these unfortunate beginnings, Mormons remained in the north country and today, congregations exist in Traverse City, Cadillac, Gaylord, Sault Ste. Marie and Cheboygan.

Economics and religion go hand and hand in area history. Following the Great Chicago Fire in the summer of 1871, the same period wildfires ravaged the entire Midwest, the need to rebuild cities sent lumber demands skyrocketing. As a result, northern Michigan's logging industry flourished, bringing big money to the region and common men in search of an honest livelihood.

It was lumber money that built the port town of Manistee and its churches. The city's millionaire lumber barons displayed their wealth by building great Victorian mansions and grand churches. Today, four Manistee churches are on state and national historic registers. Built in the late 1800s, these churches reflect the opulence of the era.

The First Congregational United Church of Christ, 412 Fourth Street, features 36 stained-glass windows, including two from the famed Tiffany studios. In the clock tower hangs a prized Nels Johnson Century clock. At the time the church was built, Johnson's clocks were known for their accuracy and were in demand throughout the world. The church clock is still in working order, and suspended beneath it is a 3,200-pound bell installed in

www.insiders.com

See this and many other **Insiders' Guide®** destinations online — in their entirety.

Visit us today!

1905. In addition to its status as an excellent example of Romanesque architecture, the church is considered a significant historical treasure, because it is the only known church in Michigan designed by the father of the skyscraper, William LeBaron Jenny.

Another of Manistee's historic churches, Guardian Angels, a Roman Catholic church at 371 Fifth Street, opened its doors in 1891 to meet the spiritual needs of German and Irish immigrants. While the immigrants may have confessed their faith side by side, their cultural differences were clear. These differences are preserved in the building's stained-glass artwork. The windows on one side of the church depict the congregation's French Catholic heritage, and, on the other side, the windows illustrate Irish religious heritage.

St. Joseph's Roman Catholic Church, 254 Sixth Street, was built in 1885 and has since undergone several renovations. A 1960 addition was constructed over parts of the original structure, saving many of the mini-cathedral's historic features. St. Joseph's today has one of the largest congregations in the northern Roman Catholic Diocese.

Dating back to 1888, Holy Trinity Episcopal Church, 410 Second Street, differs from Manistee's other historical buildings in its simplicity. Built of hewn stone, it was designed to replicate the Church of England's small country churches. Our Savior Historical Church Museum, at 300 Walnut Street, is no longer in general use, but it is open for occasional services and public viewing. The building, looking just as it did a century ago, has an octagonal spire, a finial weather vane and a handcarved pulpit. It is the oldest Danish Evangelical Lutheran church in the United States.

Buses bring hundreds of tourists to

INSIDERS' TIP

You can see a rare stained-glass portrait at the First Congregational United Church in Manistee. The image is that of Lottie Billings, niece of a wealthy lumber baron. Lottie died of typhoid fever at the age of 11 and was commemorated in this unusual way by her uncle.

Photo: Terry W. Phipps/Mackinac Island Chamber of Commerce

The beauty of the Traverse Bay region is accented by church steeples.

Manistee each year to tour the historic churches. You can visit the buildings in the summer months between 1 and 4 PM Wednesday and Saturday. At other times of the year, call ahead for an appointment. For more information, contact the Manistee Area Chamber of Commerce at (616) 723-2575 or (800) 288-2286.

Between 1871 and 1874, logging jobs and cheap northern farmland attracted Dutch immigrants from the southeastern section of the state. These immigrants were members of the Christian Reformed Church and can be traced

from a group of 101 common folk who fled their native Netherlands in 1845 to escape religious persecution, poverty and starvation. After first settling in southeastern Michigan, members of the group migrated to Missaukee County. Some worked in logging camps and others bought farmland. From this humble beginning, 16 Christian Reformed churches have developed in Northwest Michigan, making it a one of the denomination's most significant nucleus sites in Michigan.

Prior to the arrival of the Christian Reformed group in Missaukee County, members of the

INSIDERS' TIP

Retired Roman Catholic priest Edwin Frederick, known simply as Father Fred, operates the Father Fred Foundation in Traverse City. The foundation is a nondenominational charitable organization funded by private donations. It offers the basic necessities of life, personal encouragement and assistance to those in need in the Grand Traverse Region.

Jewish faith settled in the Traverse City area. About 1840, sawmills and farms were beginning to thrive in the Grand Traverse Bay Region. A number of Jewish pack peddlers moved north to become part of it. Peddlers walked door-to-door with heavy packs on their backs, selling farm implements and household goods. These merchants later became proprietors of general stores. By 1885, there were 10 Jewish men living in the Traverse City area, the minimum required by Jewish doctrine to conduct services. When their numbers increased they constructed a synagogue at 311 Park Street forming congregation Beth El. The Reformed Jewish congregation's temple is the oldest synagogue in continuous use in Michigan and is on the National Register of Historic Places. The Jewish faith is still growing in the north, and there are now Jewish congregations in Traverse City and Petoskey.

In 1867, a small log church was built by Catholic settlers of present-day Empire in Leelanau County. The small drafty church was constructed along what was called the Benzonia Trail, the only road through the area at that time. Catholics in Traverse City, Glen Haven, Suttons Bay, Frankfort, Northport, Maple City, Fife Lake, Cadillac and other burgeoning settlements were served by traveling priests.

By 1870 there were about 20 Catholic families living in the Traverse City area, and they laid the foundation for St. Francis of Assisi Church, the first Catholic church in the community. The first Mass was held in December at a little parish built on Tenth Street between Union and Cass streets.

Today Roman Catholicism is the predominant religion in the region, with 82,000 members in 82 parishes in the Diocese of Gaylord.

You will find a United Methodist congregation in nearly every burg from Ludington to the Mackinac Straits. For a relaxed worship program, join the congregation of the Central United Methodist Church of Traverse City for an outdoor service along Grand Traverse Bay. Services are held 9 AM each Sunday between Father's Day and Labor Day at Sunset Park along Front Street, just east of the Holiday Inn.

We often take for granted how extensively religious groups have contributed to the economic, social, educational and cultural development of our communities and how much they still quietly and humbly offer to us on a daily basis. The region's many parochial schools (see our Education chapter), church-affiliated hospitals (see our Healthcare chapter), relief organizations and charitable groups, untiringly weave compassion, faith and hope into the fabric of Northwest Michigan's large and small communities, just as they have since Father Marquette's day.

While much has changed since the French explorers arrived in the northern woodlands, people of the north still turn to their faith for guidance, comfort and strength. It is estimated 40 percent of Northwest Michigan's residents attend church.

The region's churches welcome vacationers with open arms, and area clergy attempt to accommodate visitors' needs. Many churches offer early morning services throughout the summer months, so your days can be free for recreational activities. At most churches, the dress is casual.

The various denominations in Northwest Michigan are growing in membership through efforts to provide contemporary religious programming. As a rule, these congregations are involved in charitable work in their communities, offer youth activities and work cooperatively to achieve mutual goals.

In addition to the religious groups mentioned above, there are various groups in Grand Traverse, Benzie, Emmet and Leelanau counties practicing earth-centered spirituality. Earth-centered religions are non-hierarchical

INSIDERS' TIP

The Cross in the Woods Catholic Shrine is the world's largest crucifix. The shrine is 20 miles northeast of Petoskey in Indian River along Michigan Highway 68. Outdoor Mass is held at the site every Saturday and Sunday in the summer. For more information, see our Attractions chapter.

and based on the belief that there is interconnection between all things in the universe. These spiritualists practice Celtic, Native American or Inca traditions. They tend to meet in small groups. Others in the region practice Buddhism and Hinduism. Organization of these spiritual persuasions is loose and individuals tend to commute to the more populated downstate cities to join larger followings.

The best way to get in touch with those sharing these beliefs is to visit an alternative store such as Higher Self Book Store, 328 E. Front Street, Traverse City, (616) 941-5805. They may be able to provide you with local contacts.

Most chambers of commerce and visitor bureaus keep a current worship service schedule for local churches. Give them a call for worship times and directions. You'll find telephone numbers for many of the area chambers and visitor centers listed in our Getting Here and Getting Around chapter.

Index of Advertisers

Index

FALCON GUIDES ® leading the way

Travel the great outdoors with

A FALCON GUIDE ®

- Comprehensive information on essential outdoor skills, trails, trips, and the best places to go in each state.

- Detailed descriptions, maps, access information, photos, and safety tips.

- Easy-to-use, written by expert, and regularly updated and revised.

To locate your nearest bookseller or to order call

1-800-582-2665.

Ask for a FREE catalog featuring books on nature, outdoor recreation, travel, and the legendary American West.

FALCON®

Going Somewhere?

Insiders' Publishing presents 48 current and upcoming titles to popular destinations all over the country (including the titles below) — and we're planning on adding many more. To order a title, go to your local bookstore or call (800) 582-2665 and we'll direct you to one.

Adirondacks	Minneapolis/St. Paul, MN
Atlanta, GA	Mississippi
Bermuda	Myrtle Beach, SC
Boca Raton and the Palm Beaches, FL	Nashville, TN
Boulder, CO, and Rocky Mountain National Park	New Hampshire
Bradenton/Sarasota, FL	North Carolina's Central Coast and New Bern
Branson, MO, and the Ozark Mountains	North Carolina's Mountains
California's Wine Country	Outer Banks of North Carolina
Cape Cod, Nantucket and Martha's Vineyard, MA	The Pocono Mountains
Charleston, SC	Relocation
Cincinnati, OH	Richmond, VA
Civil War Sites in the Eastern Theater	Salt Lake City
Colorado's Mountains	Santa Fe
Denver, CO	Savannah
Florida Keys and Key West	Southwestern Utah
Florida's Great Northwest	Tampa/St. Petersburg, FL
Golf in the Carolinas	Tucson
Indianapolis, IN	Virginia's Blue Ridge
The Lake Superior Region	Virginia's Chesapeake Bay
Las Vegas	Washington, D.C.
Lexington, KY	Wichita, KS
Louisville, KY	Williamsburg, VA
Madison, WI	Wilmington, NC
Maine's Mid-Coast	Yellowstone

THE INSIDERS'® GUIDE

Insiders' Publishing · P.O. Box 2057 · Manteo, NC 27954
Phone (252) 473-6100 · Fax (252) 473-5869 · *www.insiders.com*